The Works of John Owen

THE

WORKS

OF

JOHN OWEN, D.D.

EDITED

BY THOMAS RUSSELL, M.A.

WITH

MEMOIRS OF HIS LIFE AND WRITINGS,
BY WILLIAM ORME.

VOL. VI.

CONTAINING

THE DOCTRINE OF THE SAINTS' PERSEVERANCE
EXPLAINED AND CONFIRMED.

LONDON:

PRINTED FOR RICHARD BAYNES, 28, PATERNOSTER ROW;

And sold by J. Parker, Oxford; Deighton and Sons, Cambridge; D. Brown,
Waugh and Innes, and H. S. Baynes and Co. Edinburgh; Chalmers and
Collins, and M. Ogle, Glasgow; M. Keene, and R. M. Tims, Dublin.

1826.

CONTENTS

OF

THE SIXTH VOLUME.

CHAP. I.

The various thoughts of men concerning the doctrine proposed to consideration. The great concernment of it (however stated) on all hands confessed Some special causes pressing to the present handling of it. The fearful backslid- ing of many in these days The great offence given, and taken thereby: with the provision made for its removal. The nature of that offence and temptation thence arising considered. Answer to some arguings of Mr. G. c. 9. from thence against the truth proposed. The use of trials and shakings grounds of believers' assurance that they are so. The same farther argued and debated Of the testimony of a man's own conscience concerning his uprightness, and what is required thereunto. 1 John iii 7 considered. Of the rule of self-judging, with principles of settlement for true believers, not- withstanding the apostacies of eminent professors. Corrupt teachings ren- dering the handling of this doctrine necessary · its enemies of old and of late. The particular undertaking of Mr. G. proposed to consideration. An en- trance into the stating of the question. The terms of the question explained of holiness in its several acceptations. Created holiness, original or adven- titious. Complete or inchoate. Typical by dedications, real by purifica- tion. Holiness evangelical, either so indeed, or by estimation. Real holi- ness, partial or universal. The partakers of the first, or temporary believers, not true believers maintained against Mr. G Ground of judging professors to be true believers Matt. vii. 20. considered, what is the rule of judging men therein given. What knowledge of the faith of others is to be obtained. What is meant by perseverance how in Scripture it is expressed. The grounds of it pointed at. What is intended by falling away ; whether it be possible the Spirit of grace may be lost, the habit of it, and how. The state of the controversy as laid down by Mr. G. The vanity thereof disco- vered. His judgment about believers' falling away examined , what princi- ples and means of perseverance he grants to them. The enemies of our per- severance. Indwelling sin in particular considered. No possibility of pro-

CHAP. II.

CHAP. III.

CHAP. IV.

CHAP V.

CHAP. VI.

CHAP. VII

The consideration of the oath of God deferred. The method first proposed somewhat waved. The influence of the mediation of Christ into God's free and unchangeable acceptance of believers proposed. Reasons of that proposal. Of the oblation of Christ Its influence into the saints' perseverance. All causes of separation between God and believers, taken away thereby. Moral and efficient causes thereby removed. The guilt of sin, how taken away by the death of Christ. Of the nature of redemption. Conscience of sin; how abolished by the sacrifice of Christ; Heb. x. 3, 4. 14. Dan ix. 24 opened, Rom. ii 34 Deliverance from all sin; how by the death of Christ. The law innovated in respect of the elect. The vindictive justice of God satisfied by the death of Christ; how that is done. Wherein satisfaction doth consist. Absolute, not conditional. The law; how fulfilled in the death of Christ. The truth of God thereby accomplished, his distributive justice engaged. Observations for the clearing of the former assertions. Whether any one, for whom Christ died, may die in sin The necessity of faith and obedience. The reasons thereof. The end of faith and holiness. The first argument for the proof of the former assertions concerning the fruit and efficacy of the death of Christ, Heb. ix. 14 The second The third. The compact between the Father and Son about the work of mediation. The

CHAP. VIII

CHAP. IX.

CHAP. X.

THE DOCTRINE

OF THE

SAINTS' PERSEVERANCE

EXPLAINED AND CONFIRMED:

OR

THE CERTAIN PERMANENCY OF THEIR ACCEPTATION
WITH GOD, AND SANCTIFICATION FROM GOD, MANIFESTED
AND PROVED,

FROM

THE ETERNAL PRINCIPLES, EFFECTUAL CAUSES, AND
EXTERNAL MEANS THERFOF; IN THE IMMUTABILITY OF THE NATURE,
DECREES, COVENANT, AND PROMISES OF GOD,
THE OBLATION AND INTERCESSION OF JESUS CHRIST,
THE PROMISES, EXHORTATIONS, AND THREATS OF THE GOSPEL,
IMPROVED IN ITS GENUINE TENDENCY TO OBEDIENCE
AND CONSOLATION, AND VINDICATED IN A FULL ANSWER
TO THE DISCOURSE OF MR. JOHN GOODWIN
AGAINST IT, IN HIS BOOK ENTITLED
REDEMPTION REDEEMED

WITH

SOME DIGRESSIONS CONCERNING THE IMMEDIATE EFFECTS OF
THE DEATH OF CHRIST, PERSONAL INDWELLING OF
THE SPIRIT, UNION WITH CHRIST, NATURE
OF GOSPEL PROMISES, &c.

ALSO

A PREFACE MANIFESTING THE JUDGMENT OF THE ANCIENTS CONCERNING
THE TRUTH CONTENDED FOR, WITH A DISCOURSE TOUCHING
THE EPISTLES OF IGNATIUS, THE EPISCOPACY IN THEM ASSERTED, AND SOME
ANIMADVERSIONS ON DR. H. H.'s DISSERTATIONS
ON THAT SUBJECT.

TO

HIS HIGHNESS,

OLIVER,

LORD-PROTECTOR OF THE COMMONWEALTH

OF

ENGLAND, SCOTLAND, AND IRELAND,

WITH THE DOMINIONS THEREOF

Sir,

The wise man tells us, that no man knoweth love or hatred, by all that is before him. The great va riety wherein God dispenseth outward things in the world, with the many changes and alterations, which according to the counsel of his will, he continually works in the dispensations of them, will not allow them nakedly in themselves, to be evidences of the fountain from whence they flow. Seeing also, that the want or abundance of them, may equally, by the goodness and wisdom of God, be ordered and cast into a useful subserviency to a good infinitely transcending what is, or may be, contained in them; there is no necessity, that in the distribution of them, God should walk according to any constant uniform law of procedure; all the various alterations about them, answering one eternal purpose for a de- terminate end. Of spiritual good things, there is another reason and condition; for as they are in themselves fruits, evidences, and pledges of an eter- nal unchangeable love; so the want of them in their whole kind, being not capable of a tendency to a

B 2

greater good than they are, the dispensation of them doth so far answer the eternal spring and fountain from whence it floweth, as in respect of its substance and being, not to be obnoxious to any alteration. This is that which in the ensuing treatise is contended for. In the midst of all the changes and mutations, which the infinitely wise providence of God doth daily effect in the greater and lesser things of this world, as to the communication of his love in Jesus Christ, and the merciful gracious distributions of the unsearchable riches of grace, and the hid treasures thereof purchased by his blood, he knows no repentance. Of both these you have had full experience. And though your concernment in the former, hath been as eminent as that of any person whatever in these latter ages of the world, yet your interest in, and acquaintance with, the latter, is, as of incomparable more importance in itself, so answerably of more value and esteem unto you. A sense of the excellency and sweetness of unchangeable love, emptying itself in the golden oil of distinguishing spiritual mercies, is one letter of that new name, which none can read, but he that hath it. The series and chain of eminent providences, whereby you have been carried on, and protected in all the hazardous work of your generation, which your God hath called you unto, is evident to all. Of your preservation by the power of God through faith, in a course of gospel obedience, upon the account of the immutability of the love, and infallibility of the promises of God, which are yea and amen in Jesus Christ, your own soul is only possessed with the experience. Therein is that abiding joy, that secret refreshment, which the world cannot give. That you and all the saints of God, may yet enjoy that peace and consolation which is in believing, that the eternal love of God is immutable, that he is faithful in his promises, that his covenant ratified in the death of his Son is unchangeable, that the fruits of the purchase of Christ, shall be certainly bestowed on all thém for whom he died, and that every one, who is really interested in these things, shall be kept unto salvation, is the aim of my present plea and contest. That I have taken upon me to present my weak endeavours in this cause of God to your Highness, is so far forth from my persuasion of your interest in the truth contended for (and than which, you have none so excellent or worthy), that without it, no other considerations whatever, either of that dignity and power whereunto of God you are called, nor of your peculiar regard to that society of men, whereof I am an unworthy member, nor any other personal respects whatever, could have prevailed with, or imboldened me thereunto. 'Sancta sanctis.' The things I treat of are such, as sometimes none of the princes of this world knew, and as yet few of them are acquainted with. Blessed are they who have their portion in them. When the urgency of your high and important affairs, wherein so many nations are concerned, will lend you so much leisure, as to take a view of what is here tendered, the knowledge which you have of me, will deliver you from a temptation of charging any weakness you may meet withal upon the doctrine which I assert and maintain. And so that may run and be glorified, whatever become of the nothing that 1 have done, in the defence thereof, I shall be abundantly satisfied. That is the shield which being safe, I can with contentment see these papers die. Unto your Highness, I have not any thing more to add; nor for you greater thing to pray, than that you may be established in the assurance and sense of that unchangeable love, and free acceptance in Christ which I contend for; and that therein you may be preserved, to the glory of God, the advancement of the gospel, and the real advantage of these nations.

Your Highness's most humble,

and most faithful servant,

JOHN OWEN.

TO THE RIGHT WORSHIPFUL,

HIS

REVEREND, LEARNED, AND WORTHY FRIENDS AND BRETHREN,

THE

HEADS AND GOVERNORS

OF THE

COLLEGES AND HALLS IN THE UNIVERSITY OF OXFORD.

SIRS,

THE dedication of books, to the names of men worthy
and of esteem in their generation, takes sanctuary in
so catholic and ancient prescription, that to use any
defensative about my walking in the same path, cannot but forfeit the loss of somewhat more than the
pains that would be spent therein. Now although
in addresses of this kind, men usually avail themselves of the occasion, to deliver their thoughts as to
particulars, in great variety, according as their concernments may be ; - yet the reasons which are generally pleaded as directions for the choice of them, to
whom with their labours and writings they so address themselves, are for the most part uniform ; and
in their various course, transgress not the rules of
certain heads, from whence they flow. To express
a gratitude for respects and favours received, by returning things in their kind eternal, for those which
are but temporal ; to obtain countenance and approbation unto their endeavours in their breaking forth
into the world, from names of more esteem, or at
least more known, than their own ; to advance in repute by a correspondency in judgment, with men of
such esteem, intimated thereby ; are the more ingenuous aims of men in the dedications of their writings.
Though these, and sundry other pretences of the
same kind, might justly be drawn into my plea, for
this address unto you ; yet your peculiar designation
and appointment, through the good hand of the pro-

vidence of God, to the defence of the gospel; and
your eminent furnishment with abilities from the
same hand, for the performance of that glorious duty,
is that alone, upon the account whereof I have satisfied myself, and hope that I may not dissatisfy others,
as to this present application. What there is of my
own peculiar concernment, wherein I am like to obtain a more favourable condescension in judgment,
as to my present undertaking, from you, than from
other men, will in the close of my address, crave leave
to have mention made thereof. Brethren! the outward obligations that are upon you from the God of
truth, with the advantages which he hath intrusted
you withal, for the defence of his truth, above the
most of men in the world, are evident, even to them
that walk by the way, and turn little aside to the
consideration of things of this nature, importance, and
condition. And it is to me an evidence of no small
encouragement, that God will yet graciously employ
you in the work and labour of his gospel, by his
constant giving a miscarrying womb to all them who
have attempted to defraud the nation, and the
churches of God therein, of those helps and furtherances of piety and literature, with whose management
for their service, you are at present intrusted. Of
the jewels of silver and gold, whereof by the Lord's
appointment, the children of Israel, coming out from
amongst them, spoiled the Egyptians, did they de-
dicate to the tabernacle in the wilderness; when the
'Lord planted the heavens, and laid the foundations
of the earth, and said to Sion, Thou art my people.'
Though some outward provisions, and furnitures of
literature, now, through the good hand of God, made
serviceable to you in your attendance upon the great
work and employment committed to you, were first
deposited, when thick darkness was over the land:
yet that they may be made eminently subservient to

the will of God, in raising up again the tabernacle of
David, that was fallen down, the experience of a few
years, I no way doubt, will abundantly reveal and
manifest. That in the vicissitude of all things, given
them by the mysterious and dreadful wheels of providence, your good things also (as every thing else
that is pleasant and desirable, or given of God unto
the sons of men hath done), have fallen into the possession and disposal of men, some enemies, others
utterly useless and unfruitful to the Lord in their
generations, cannot be denied. But what is there in
his ways or worship, in his works or word, that God
hath not, at some season or other, delivered into the
power of the men of the world, though they have
abused and perverted them to their own destruction?
Neither is there any other use of this consideration,
but only to inform them of the obligation they lie
under, to a due and zealous improvement of them, to
whose trust and care the Lord commits any of his
mercies, when he rescues them from the captivity
under which they have been detained, by ungodly
men. This is now your lot and condition, in reference to many who for sundry generations, possessed
those places, and advantages of eminent service for
the house of our God, which you now enjoy. What
may justly be the expectation of God from you, under
this signal dispensation of his goodness, what is the
hope, prayer, and expectation, of very many that
fear him, concerning you, in this nation; what are
the designs, desires, aims, and endeavours of all sorts
of them, who bear ill-will at whatsoever is comely,
or praiseworthy amongst us, you are not ignorant.
Whatever consideration at any time or season, may
seem to have had an efficacy upon the minds and
wills of men, under the like sacrament, and designment to the service of truth with yourselves, to incite

and provoke them to a singularly industrious and
faithful discharge of their duty, is eminently pressing
upon you also; and you are made a spectacle to men
and angels, as to the acquitment of yourselves. The
whole of your employment, I confess, both in the
general intendment of it, for the promoting and dif-
fusing of light, knowledge, and truth, in every kind
whatever, and in the more special design thereof, for
the defence, furtherance, and propagation of the ancient, inviolable, unchangeable truth of the gospel of
God, is in the days wherein we live, exposed to a
contention with as much opposition, contempt, scorn,
hatred, and reproach, as ever any such undertaking
was, in any place in the world, wherein men pretended
to love light more than darkness.

It is a hellish darkness, which the light of the sun
cannot expel. There is no ignorance so full of pride,
folly, and stubbornness, as that which maintains itself in the midst of plentiful means of light and knowledge. He that is in the dark, when the light of the
sun is as seven days, hath darkness in his eye; and
how great is that darkness? Such is the ignorance
you have to contend withal; stubborn, affected, prejudicate beyond expression; maintaining its darkness
at noon-day, expressly refusing to attend to the reason of things, as being that alone, in the thoughts of
those men (if they may be so called), who are possessed with it, wherewith the world is disturbed.
From those who being under the power of this en-
thralment, do seem to repine at God, that they are
not beasts, and clamorously traduce the more noble
part of that kind and offspring, whereof themselves
are; which attempts do heighten and improve the
difference between creatures of an intellectual race,
and them to whom their perishing composition gives
the utmost advancement; whose eternal seeds and

principles are laid by the hand of God in their respective beings, you will not, I am sure, think it much
if you meet with oppositions.   Those who are in any
measure acquainted with the secret, triumphing ex-
altations of wisdom and knowledge, against folly and
ignorance; with the principles and conditions, wherewith they advance themselves in their gloryings, even
then, when the precedency of (that which is bestial
in this world) force and violence outwardly bears
them down with insultation and contempt, will rather envy than pity you in any contest that on this
foot of account, you can be engaged in.   You are not
the first that have fought with men after the manner
of beasts; nor will be the last, who shall need to pray
to be delivered from absurd and unreasonable men,
seeing all men have not faith.

Men of profane and atheistical spirits, who are
ready to say, Who is the Lord? What is the Almighty that we should fear him? Or his truth that
we should regard it? Whose generation is of late
multiplied on the face of the earth, crying a confede-
racy with them, who professing better things, are
yet filled with grievous indignations at the sacrifice
that hath been made of their abominations before
their eyes, by that reformation of this place, wherein
you have been instrumental, are a continual goad on
the other side, and would quickly be a sword in your
very bowels, were not He, that is higher than the
highest, your dwelling-place, and refuge in your generation.   These are they upon whom God having
poured contempt, and stained their glory, who instead of accepting of his dispensations, are filled with
wrath, and labour to make others drink of the cup,
which hath been offered to themselves.   With their
reproaches, slightings, undervaluations, slanders, do
your worth, diligence, integrity, labours, contend

from one end of this earth to the other. He that
hath delivered doth deliver, and in him we trust
that he will deliver.

What other oppositions you do meet, or in your
progress may meet withal, I shall not mention; but
wait with patience on him, who gives men repentance, and change of heart to the acknowledgment
of the things that are of him. This in the midst of
all hath hitherto been a cause of great rejoicing, that
God hath graciously kept off ravenous wolves from
entering into your flocks, where are so many tender
lambs, and hath not suffered men to arise from
amongst yourselves speaking perverse things, and
drawing away disciples after them; but as he hath
given you, to obey from your heart that form of doctrine, which hath been delivered unto you, so he
hath preserved that faith amongst you, which was
once delivered to the saints.

Your peculiar designation to the service of the
gospel, and defence of the truth thereof, your abilities for that work, your abiding in it, notwithstanding the opposition you meet withal, in the midst of
a crooked and perverse generation, are as I said before, my encouragements in this address unto you;
wherein I shall crave leave a little farther to communicate my thoughts unto you as to the matter in
hand. Next to the Son of his love, who is the truth,
the greatest and most eminent gift, that God hath
bestowed on the sons of men, and communicated to
them, is his truth revealed in his word. The knowledge of him, his mind and will, according to the
discovery which he hath made of himself, from his
own bosom, having magnified his word, above all
his name. The importance hereof, as to the eternal
concernments of the sons of men, either in ignorance
refusing and resisting, or accepting and embracing

of it, is that which is owned, and lies as the bottom
and foundation of all that we any way engage ourselves into in this world; wherein we differ from
them, whose hope perisheth with them. Unto an
inquiry after, and entertainment of, this divine and
sacred *depositum*, hath God designed the fruit and
labour of that, wherein we retain the resemblance of
him, which whilst we have our being nothing can
abolish. The mind of man, and divine truth, are the
two most eminent excellencies, wherewith the Lord
hath adorned this lower part of his creation, which,
when they correspond, and are brought into conformity with each other, the mind being changed
into the image of truth, there is glory added to glory,
and the whole rendered exceeding glorious. By
what suitableness and proportion in the things themselves (that is, between truth and the mind of man),
as we are men; by what almighty, secret, and irresistible power, as we are corrupted men, our minds being full of darkness and folly, this is wrought, is not
my business now to discuss. This is on all hands
confessed; that, setting aside the consideration of
the eternal issues of things, every mistake of divine
truth, every opposition to it, or rejection of it, or any
part of it, is so far, a chaining up of the mind, under
the power of darkness, from a progress towards that
perfection which it is capable of. It is truth alone
that capacitates any soul to give glory to God, or to
be truly useful to them who are partakers of flesh
and blood with him: without being some way serviceable to which end, there is nothing short of the
fulness of wrath, that can be judged so miserable as
the life of a man. Easily so much might be delivered
on this account, as to evince the dread of that judgment, whereto some men in the infallibly wise counsel of God are doomed, even to the laying out of the

labour and travail of their minds, to spend their days
and strength in sore labour, in making opposition to
this truth of God.   Especially is the sadness of this
consideration increased, in reference to them, who
upon any account whatever, do bear forth themselves, and are looked upon by others, as guides of
the blind, as lights to them that sit in darkness, as
the instructors of the foolish, and teachers of babes.
For a man to set himself, or to be set by others, in
a way wherein are many turnings and cross paths,
some of them leading and tending to places of innumerable troubles, and perhaps death and slaughter;
undertaking to be a guide to direct them that travel
towards the place of their intendments, where they
would be, and where they shall meet with rest ; for
such a one, I say, to take hold of every one that passeth by, and pretending himself to be exceeding skilful, in all the windings and turnings of those ways
and paths, and to stand there on purpose to give direction, if he shall, with all his skill and rhetoric,
divert them out of the path wherein they have perhaps safely set out, and to guide them into those by-
ways, which will certainly lead them into snares and
troubles, if not to death itself; can he spend his time,
labour, and strength, in an employment more to be
abhorred ? or can he design any thing more desperately mischievous to them, whose good and welfare
he is bound and promiseth to seek and promote ? Is
any man's condition under heaven more to be la-
mented, or is any man's employment more perilous
than such a one's, who being not only endowed with
a mind and understanding capable of the truth, and
receiving impressions of the will of God, but also with
distinguishing abilities and enlargements for the receiving of greater measures of truth, than others,
and the more effectual improvement of what he doth

so receive, shall labour night and day, dispending
the richest treasure and furnishment of his soul, for
the rooting out, defacing, and destruction of the
truth, for the turning men out of the way, and paths
that lead to rest and peace? I never think of the uncomfortable drudgery which men give up themselves unto, in laying the hay and stubble of their
vain and false conceptions upon the foundation, and
heaping up the fruit of their souls, to make the fire
that consumes them the more fierce and severe, but
it forces compassionate thoughts of that sad condition, whereto mankind hath cast itself, by its apostacy from God. And yet there is not any thing in
the world, that men more willingly, with more delight and greediness, consecrate the flower of their
strength and abilities unto, than this of promoting
the delusions of their own minds, in opposition to
the truth and ways of God. It is a thing of obvious
observation and daily experience, that if by any
means whatever, any one closeth with some new,
and by-opinion, off from the faith delivered to, and
received by, the generality of the saints, that be it a
thing of never so small concernment in our walking
with God, in gospel obedience, and in love without
dissimulation one towards another, yet, instantly
more weight is laid upon it, more pains laid out
about it, and zeal dispended for its supportment
and propagation, than about all other most necessary
points of Christian religion. Have we not a deplor-
able cloud of examples, of men contending about
some circumstance or other in the administration
of an ordinance, biting and devouring all that stand
in their way, roving up and down to gain proselytes
unto their persuasion, and in the mean time, utterly
ignorant or negligent of the great doctrines and commands of the gospel of Jesus Christ, which are as in

him, the head and life of souls? How many a man
seems to have no manner of religion at all, but some
one error.   That is his God, his Christ, his worship,
that he preaches, that he discourseth of, that he labours to propagate; until by the righteous judgment of God it comes to pass that such men in all
other things wither and die away; all the sap and
vigour of their spirits, feeding that one monstrous
excrescency, which they grow up daily into. Desire
of emerging and being notable in the world, esteem
and respect in the hearts and mouths of them, whom
peculiarly they draw after them, with the like unworthy aims of self-advancement, may, without evil
surmising (when such attempts are, as in too many,
accompanied with irregularity in conversation), be
supposed to be advantages given into the hands of
the envious man, to make use of them for the sowing
of his tares, in the field of the poor seduced world.

That this procedure is also farthered by the bur-
densomeness of sound doctrine unto the generality
of men, who having itching ears, as far as they care
for these things do spend their time in religion, in
nothing else, but either to tell or to hear some new
thing, cannot be denied. Besides to defend, improve, give and add new light, unto old truths (a
work which hath so abundantly and excellently been
laboured in, by so many worthies of Christ, especially since the Reformation), in any eminent manner,
' so as to bring praise and repute unto the undertakers
(which whether men will confess or no, it is evident
that too many are enslaved unto) is no easy task.
And for the most part of what is done that way, you
may say, 'Quis leget hæc?' The world (says every
one) is burdened with discourses of this nature.
How many have we in our days, who might have
gone to the grave in silence among the residue of

their brethren, and their names have remained for a season in the voisinage, where they might have done God the service required of them in their generation, would they have kept themselves in the form of wholesome words and sound doctrine, that have now delivered their names into the mouths of all men, by engaging into some singular opinions, though perhaps raked out of the ashes of Popery, Socinianism, or some such fruitful heap of error, and false notions of the things of God?

I desire not to judge before the time; the day will manifest all things, and the hidden secrets of the hearts of men, shall by it be laid open; when all the ways, causes, and occasions of their deceiving, and being deceived, shall be brought to light, and every man according to his work shall have praise of God. Only, I say, as to the present state of things, this is evident (not to speak of those locusts from the bottomless pit, that professedly oppose their strength, to all that is of God, his name, word, worship, or truth, will, and commands, rasing the foundation of all hopes of eternity; nor of him, and his associates, who exalteth himself above all that is called God, being full of names of blasphemy, sealed up to destruction), very many amongst ourselves, of whom we hoped better things, do, some in greater, some in lesser matters, give up themselves to that unhappy labour we before mentioned, of opposing the truths of God, and exalting their own darkness, in the room of his glorious light.

> Ut jugulent homines, surgunt de nocte latrones
> Ut teipsum serves, non expergisceris?[a]

Reverend brethren, if other men can rise early, go to bed late, and eat the bread of carefulness, spend their lives and strength to do their own work, and

---

[a] Hor. Epis lib. 1. 2.

propagate their own conceptions, under a pretence
of doing the work of God; if the envious man
watcheth all night and waits all advantages to sow
his tares, how will you be able to lift up your heads
with joy, and behold your Master's face with boldness at his coming, if having received such eminent
abilities, endowments, and furnishments from him,
for his service, and the service of his sheep and lambs,
as you have done, you gird not up the loins of your
minds, and lay not out your strength to the uttermost, for the weeding out of the field and vineyard
of the Lord every plant which our heavenly Father
hath not planted, and for feeding the flock of Christ
with sincere milk. and strong meat, according as
they are able to bear ? What you have received, more
than others, is of free grace, which is God's way of
dealing with them, on whom he lays the most unconquerable and indispensable obligation unto service.   Flesh and blood hath not revealed unto you
the truth of God, which you do profess, but our Father which is in heaven; you do not upon any endeavour of your own, differ from them who are given
up to the sore judgment, and ever to be bewailed
condition, before-mentioned.   It hath not been from
your own endeavours or watchfulness, that you have
been hitherto preserved under the hour of temptation, which is come to try the men that live upon the
face of the earth.   It is not of yourselves, that you
are not industriously disturbing your own souls and
others, with this or that intrenchment upon the
doctrine of the gospel, and the free grace of God in
Jesus Christ, which not a few pride themselves in,
with the contempt of all otherwise minded.   And
doth not the present state of things, require the full
disbursing of all, that you have freely received for
the glory of him, from whom you have received it?

You are persons who, not only as doctors and teachers in a university, have a large, distinct disciplinary
knowledge of divinity; but also such as to whom
the Son of God is come, 'and hath given an understanding to know him that is true;' into whose hearts
God hath 'shined, to give the light of the knowledge
of his glory in the face of Jesus Christ;' and therefore
may say, 'What shall we render the Lord?' How
shall we serve him in any way answerable to the
grace we have received? I speak not this (the
Lord knows it, before whom I stand) with reflection
on any, as though I judged them neglecters of the
duty incumbent on them. 'Every one of us must
give an account of himself to the Lord.' The daily
pains, labour, and travail of many of you, in the work
of the gospel, the diligence and endeavours of others
in promoting other useful literature, is known unto
all. Only the consideration of my own present undertaking, joined with a sense of mine own insufficiency for this, or any other labour of this kind, and
of your larger furnishments with abilities of all sorts,
press me to this stirring up of your remembrance to
contend for the faith so much opposed and perverted: not that I would press, for the needless multiplying of books (whose plenty is the general customary complaint of all men versed in them), unless
necessity call thereto; 'Scribimus indocti, docti-
que.'—But that serious thoughts may be continually
dwelling in you, to lay out yourselves to obviate the
spreading of any error whatever, or the destruction
of any already propagated; by such ways and means
as the providence of God, and the circumstances of
the matter itself shall call you out unto, is in the desire of my soul.

Something you will find in this kind attempted,
by the weakest of your number, in this ensuing

treatise.   The matter of it, I know will have your
approbation, and that because it hath his, whom you
serve.   For the manner of handling it, it is humbly
given up to his grace and mercy, and freely left to
your Christian judgments :   the general concernments of this business are so known to all, that I
shall by no means burden you with a repetition of
them.   The attempt made by Mr. Goodwin against
the truth here asserted, was by all men judged so
considerable (especially the truth opposed, having a
more practical influence into the walking of the
saints with God, than any other by him assaulted,
and the defending of it, giving more advantage into
an inquiry after the mind of God, as delivered in innumerable places of Scripture, than any of the rest
opposed), as that a removal of his exceptions to our arguments, and an answer to his objections, was judged
necessary by all.   Other reasons manifesting this endeavour to be in order and in season, I have farther
communicated in the entrance of the treatise itself.
In my addresses to the work, I could by no means
content myself, with a mere discussing of what was
produced by my adversary.   For he having kept
himself, for the most part, within the compass of the
synodal writings of the remonstrants, which are already most clearly and solidly answered (by one especially, renowned Amesius), to have tied myself
unto a contest with him, had been merely *actum
agere*, without promoting the cause I had undertaken
in the least.   As I account it by no means an ingenuous proceeding, for men to bear up their own names,
by standing upon the shoulders of others, to deport
themselves authors, when indeed they are but col-
lectors and translators; so I am very remote from
being so far in love with this way of handling controversies in divinity, as to think it necessary to

multiply books of the same matter, without some
considerable addition of light and strength to the
cause, whose protection and promotion is undertaken. On this consideration, besides incident discourses, which I hope through the grace of him
that supplied seed to the sower, may be of use and
have an increase amongst the saints of God; I have
made it my aim (and what therein I have attained,
is with all submission of mind and judgment cast
before the thoughts of men, whose senses are exercised to discern good and evil) to place each argument insisted on, upon its own proper basis and
foundation: to resolve every reason and medium
whereby I have proceeded, into its own principles:
discovering the fountain and well-head of all the
streams that run in the field of this contest, as also to
give some clearings and evidence, to our conclusions
from the several texts of Scripture discussed, by discovering the reason of them, and intent of God in
them. Some arguments there are, and sundry texts
of Scripture, that are usually produced, and urged
in the defence of the cause under consideration, that
I have not insisted on: nor vindicated from the exceptions of the adversaries. Not that I judge them
indefensible against their most cunning, or most fu-
rious assaults, and so slighted what I could not hold;
for indeed I know not any one text of Scripture
commonly used for this end, nor any argument by
any sober man framed to the same purpose, that is
not capable of an easy and fair vindication: but
merely because they fell not in regularly in the method I had proposed to myself, nor would so do,
unless I had gone forth to the issue of my first intendment, and had handled the abode of believers with
God at large, from its principles and causes, as I
had done, that part of our doctrine which concerns

the continuance of the love of God with and unto
them; which the growth of the treatise under my
hand, would not give me leave to do. What hath
been or may yet farther be done, by others who
have made or shall make it their business to draw
the saw of this controversy, to and fro with Mr.
Goodwin, I hope will give satisfaction, as in other
things, so in the particulars by me omitted. As to
what I have to speak, or at least think it convenient to
speak, concerning him, with whom in this discourse
I have much to do, and the manner of my dealing
with him being a thing of personal concernment, not
having any influencing aspect on the merit of the
cause, I shall in not many words, absolve you of
your trouble in the consideration thereof. My adversary is a person whom his worth, pains, diligence,
and opinions, and the contests, wherein on their account he hath publicly engaged, have delivered from
being the object of any ordinary thoughts or expressions. Nothing not great, not considerable, not
some way eminent, is by any spoken of him, either
consenting with him or dissenting from him. To
interpose my judgment in the crowd, on the one
side or the other, I know neither warrant or sufficient
cause: we all stand or fall to our own masters;
and the fire will try all our works. This only I shall
crave liberty to say; that whether from his own genius and acrimony of spirit, or from the provocations of others, with whom he hath had to do, many
of his polemical treatises have been sprinkled with
satirical sarcasms, and contemptuous rebukes of the
persons with whom he hath had to do. So that were
I not relieved in my thoughts, by the consideration
of those exacerbations and exasperations of spirit,
which upon other accounts, besides bare difference
of opinion in religious things, have fallen out in the

days.and seasons which have passed over us, all of
them labouring to exert something of themselves, in
every undertaking of the persons brought under their
power, I should have been utterly discouraged from
any contests of this nature. Much indeed of his
irregularity in this kind, I cannot but ascribe to that
prompt facility he hath, in putting abroad every passion of his mind and all his conceptions, not only
decently clothed, with language of a full and choice
significancy, but also trimmed and adorned with all
manner of signal improvements, that may render it
keen or pleasant according to his intendment or desire. What the Latin lyric said of the Grecian poets
may be applied to him :

Monte decurrens velut amnis, imbres
Quem super notas aluere ripas,
Fervet, immensusque ruit profundo
Pindarus ore.[b]

And he is thereby plainly possessed of not a few
advantages. It is true that when the proof of his
opinion by argument, and the orderly pursuit of it
is incumbent on him (a course of all other wherein
he soonest faileth), the medium he useth and insist-
eth on, receiveth not the least contribution of real
strength from any dress of words, and expressions
wherewith it is adorned and accompanied : yet it
cannot be denied, but that his allegorical amplifications, illustrations, and exaggerations, of the things
he would insinuate, take great impressions upon the
minds of them, who are in any measure entangled
with the seeming probabilities, which are painted
over his arguments, by their sophistry and pretence
of truth. The apostle giving that caution to the
Colossians that they should heed, μή τις αὐτοὺς παρα-
λογίζηται ἐν πιθανολογίᾳ, manifesteth the prevalency of

b Hor. Od. lib. iv. 2.

false reasonings when in conjunction with rhetorical persuasions. The great store also of words and expressions, which for all occasions he hath lying by him, are of no little use to him, when being pressed with any arguments or testimonies of Scripture, and being not able to evade, he is forced to raise a cloud of them, wherewith after he hath a while darkened the wisdom and counsel of that wherewith he hath to do, he insensibly slips out of the cord, wherewith he appeared to have been detained, and triumphs as in a perfect conquest, when only an unarticulate sound hath been given by his trumpet, but the charge of his adversaries not once received or repelled. But not any where, doth he more industriously hoist up, and spread the sails of his luxuriant eloquence, than when he aims to render the opinion of his adversaries to be, 'monstrum horendum, informe ingens, cui lumen ademptum,' a dark, dismal, uncomfortable, fruitless, death-procuring doctrine; such as it is marvellous that ever any poor soul should embrace or choose for a companion or guide in its pilgrimage towards heaven. Rolling through this field, his expressions swell over all bounds and limits; metaphors, similitudes, parables, all help on the current: though the streams of it being shallow and wide, a little opposition easily turns it for the most part aside; a noise it makes indeed, with a goodly show and appearance.

> Herculeâ non mole minor—— Agylleus
> Sed non ille rigor, patriumque, in corpore robur.
> Luxuriant artus, effusaque sanguine laxo
> Membra natant——

This, as I said, prompts, I fear, the learned person of whom we speak, to deal so harshly with some of them with whom he hath to do. And it is still feared, that,

——parata tollit cornua ,
Qualis Lycambæ spretus infido gener,
Aut acer hostis Bupalo.[c]

It might indeed be the more excusable, if evident provocation were always ready at hand to be charged with the blame of this procedure, if he said only

An si quis atro dente me petiverit,
Inultus ut flebo puer ?[d]

But for a man to warm himself, by casting about his own pen, until it be so filled with indignation and scorn, as to blur every page and almost every line, is a course that will never promote the praise, nor adorn the truth of God.   For what remains concerning him,·' Do illi ingenium, do eloquentiam, et industriam ; fidem, et veritatem utinam coluisset.'

The course and condition of my procedure with him, whether it be such as becometh Christian modesty and sobriety, with an allowance of those ingredients of zeal, in contending for the truth, which in such cases the Holy Ghost gives a command for, is referred to the judgment of all, who are concerned, and account themselves so, in the things of God. As to any bitterness of expression, personal reflections by application of satirical invectives, I know nothing by myself, and yet I dare not account, that I am hereby justified.   The calm and indifferent reader, not sensible of those commotions, which the discovery of sophistical evasions, pressing of inconsequent consequences, bold assertions, &c. will sometimes raise in the most candid and ingenuous mind, may (and especially if he be an observer of failings in that kind) espy once and again, some signs and appearances of such exasperations as ought to have been allayed with a spirit of meekness, before the thoughts that stirred them up, had been turned out of doors, in the expressions observed.   Although

[c] Hor. Od. lib. v. 6.   [d] Ibid.

the weapons of it keener in their own soft breathings
than when sharpened in the forge of Aristotle. There
is a way of persuasion and conviction in the Scriptures that is more divine and sublime, than to be reduced to any rules of art that men can reach unto.
God in his word, instructs men to make them wise
unto salvation. Syllogisms are not, doubtless, the
only way of making men wise with human wisdom,
much less divine. Some testimonies, on this account
are left at their own liberty, improved only by explanation, that they might lose nothing of their own
strength, seeing no other can be added to them.
Where the corrupt philosophy, or sophistical arguings, or indeed regular syllogistical proceedings of
the adversaries, have rendered a more close logical
way of proceeding necessary, I hope your favourable
judgments, will not find cause to complain of the
want thereof. Whatever is amiss, whatever is defec-
tive, whatever upon any account, cometh short of
desire or expectation; as I know none in the world
more able to discern, and find out than yourselves,
so there are none from whom I can expect, and justly
promise myself, a more easy and candid censure, a
more free and general pardon, a more favourable acceptation of this endeavour for the service of the
truth, than from you. Besides that personal amity
and respect, which God by his providence hath given
me (one altogether unworthy of such an allay of common perplexities in his pilgrimage) with you, and
amongst you, besides that readiness and ingenuous
promptness of mind, unto condescension, and candid
reception of labours in this kind, which your own
great worth and abilities furnish you withal, exempting you, and lifting you above that pedantic severity
and humour of censure, which possesseth Sciolists
and men corrupted with a desire of emerging in the

repute of others. You know full well, in what
straits, under what diversions, employments, business of sundry natures incumbent on me, from the
relations wherein I stand, in the university, and on
sundry other accounts, this work hath been carried
on. The truth is, no small portion of it, owes its
rise to journeys, and such like avocations from my
ordinary course of studies and employments, with
some spare hours, for the most part in time of absence, from all books and assistances of that nature
whatever. Not longer to be burdensome unto you,
with things of no greater concernment, than what
may have respect to one every way so unworthy as
myself, what is of the seed which God graciously
supplied, I am sure will find acceptance with you;
and what is of its worthless author, or that I have
added, I am fully content may be consumed by the
fire, that tries our works of what sort they are.

My daily prayer, honoured brethren, shall be on
your behalf, that in the days wherein we see so
many fall from the truth, and oppose it, on the one
hand; a great indifference as to the things of God,
leading captive so many on the other; so few remaining, made useful to God in their generations by a conjunction of zeal for the truth, and ability unto its defence, and those for the most part so closely engaged
in, and their hands so filled, with the work of public
beseeching men to be reconciled to God in Christ,
and building up of them, who are called, in their most
holy faith; you may receive help from above, and
encouragement to engage you by all means possible
to spread abroad a savour of the gospel of Jesus
Christ, and to labour continually that the truths of
God (for whose defence you are particularly appointed) may not be cast down, nor trampled on under the feet of men of corrupt minds, lying in wait to

deceive, alluring and beguiling unstable souls, with enticing words of human wisdom, or any glorious show and pretence whatever, turning them from the simplicity of the gospel, and the truth as it is in Jesus : that you may not faint, nor wax weary, notwithstanding all the opposition, contempt, scorn, you do or may meet withal: nor even be turned aside to corrupt dalliances with error and falsehood, as is the manner of some, who yet would be accounted sound in the faith; but keeping close to the form of wholesome words, and answering the mould of gospel doctrine, whereunto you have been cast, may shine as lights, in the midst of a crooked and perverse generation; knowing that it is but yet a little while, and he that shall come, will come, and will not tarry ; yea, come, Lord Jesus, come, &c.

So prays

Your unworthy fellow-labourer and brother

in our dear Lord Jesus,

JOHN OWEN.

A PREFACE

THE READER.

Reader,

If thy inquiry be only after the substance of the truth in the ensuing treatise contended for, I desire thee not to stay at all upon this preliminary discourse, but to proceed thither, where it is expressly handled from the Scriptures, without the intermixture of any human testimonies, or other less necessary circumstances, wherein perhaps many of them may not be concerned, whose interest yet lies in the truth itself, and it is precious to their souls. That which now I intend and aim at, is to give an account to the learned reader, of some things nearly relating to the doctrine, whose protection, in the strength of him, who gives to his, suitable helps for the works and employments he calls them to, I have undertaken, and what entertainment it hath formerly found, and received in the church, and among the saints of God. For the accomplishment of this intendment, a brief mention of the doctrine itself will make way. Whom in this controversy we intend by the name of saints and believers, the treatise following will abundantly manifest. The word *perseverantia* is of most known use in ecclesiastical writers: Austin hath a book with the inscription of it in its forehead. The word in the New Testament signifying the same thing is, ἐπιμονὴ. Of them that followed Paul it is said that he persuaded them, ἐπιμένειν τῇ χάριτι τοῦ Θεοῦ ; Acts xiii. 43. that is, 'to persevere.' Ὑπομονὴ is of the same import. Ὁ δὲ ὑπομείνας εἰς τέλος οὗτος σωθήσεται, Matt. x. 22. ' He that persevereth to the end ;' the Vulgar Latin renders that word almost constantly by *persevero.* Καρτερία is a word also of the same signification, and which the Scripture useth to express the same thing: Κράτος is, sometimes by a metathesis expressed Κάρτος; thence is Κάρτα, *valde;* and Καρτερέω, spoken of him who is of a valiant resolved mind. ' By faith Moses left Egypt, not fearing the wrath of the king,' τὸν γὰρ ἀόρατον ὡς ὁρῶν ἐκαρτέρησε, Heb. xi. 27. ' As eyeing the invisible he endured (his trial) with a constant valiant mind.'

Προσκαρτερέω from thence is most frequently to persevere; Acts i. 14. and ἦσαν δὲ προσκαρτεροῦντες τῇ διδαχῇ τῶν Ἀποστόλων, Acts ii. 42. 'They persevered in the doctrine of the apostles.' Προσκαρτέρησις, once used in the New Testament, is rendered by our translators, 'perséverance;' Eph. vi. 18. In what variety of expression the thing is revealed in the Scripture, is in the treatise itself abundantly declared. The Latin word is classical, *persevero*, is *constanter sum severus ;* in that sense as Seneca says, 'Res severa est verum gaudium.' Its éxtreme in excess is, pertinacy; if these are not rather distinguished from their objects, than in themselves. Varro lib. 4. de ling. Lat. tells us that *pertinacia* is a continuance or going on, in that, wherein one ought not to continue, or proceed. *Perseverantia* is that, whereby any one continues in that wherein he ought so to do. Hence is that definition of it commonly given by the schoolmen from Austin; lib. 83. qu. 31. who took it from Cicero (one they little acquainted themselves withal), lib. 2. de Invent: it is say they, 'In ratione bene fundata stabilis et perpetua per mansio.' And this at present may pass for a general description of it, that is used in an ethical and evangelical sense. Perseverance was accounted a commendable thing among philosophers. Morally, perseverance is that part of fortitude whereby the mind is established in the performance of any good and necessary work, notwithstanding the assaults and opposition it meets withal, with that tediousness and wearisomeness, which the protraction of time, in the pursuit of any affairs, is attended withal. Aristotle informs us that it is exercised about things troublesome; lib. 7. Eth. Nicom. giving a difference between continence with its opposite vice, and forbearance, or perseverance, τούτων δ' ὁ μὲν περὶ ἡδονὰς, ἀκρατὴς, ὁ δὲ ἐγκρατής. Ὁ δὲ περὶ λύπας μαλακὸς, ὁ δὲ καρτερικός. He that abides in his undertaken work, so it be good and honest, notwithstanding that trouble and perplexity he may meet withal is Καρτερικός. Hence he tells us that Καρτερικῶς ζῆν as well as σωφρόνως is not pleasant to many; lib. 10. cap. 9. And that because so to live, implies difficulty and opposition. And he also, as Varro in the place above mentioned, distinguishes it from pertinacy; and of men infected with that depraved habit of mind, he says there are three sorts, ἰδιαγνώμονες, ἀμαθεῖς and ἀγροικοι : all these are in his judgment ἰσχυρογνώμονες. Nicom. lib. 7. cap. 9. Which perverse disposition of spirit he there clearly manifests to be sufficiently differenced from a stable resolved frame of mind, whatever it may resemble it in. Now though there is no question, but that of two persons continuing in the same work, or opinion, one may do it out of pertinacy, the other out of perseverance, yet amongst men who judge of the minds of others, by their fruits, and of the acts of their minds, by their objects, these two dispositions or habits are universally distinguished, as before, by Varro. Hence the terms of pertinacy and obstinacy being thrust into the definition of heresy, by them who renouncing any infallible living judge and determiner in matters of faith, to make way for the inflicting of punishment on the entertainers and maintainers thereof, they take no thought of proving it such, but only because it is found in persons embracing such errors; the same affection of mind, with the same fruits and demonstrations of it, in persons embracing the truth, would by the same men be termed perseverance. But this is not that whereof I treat.

Evangelical perseverance, is from the Scripture at large explained in the book itself. As it relates to our acceptation with God, and the immutability of justification (which is the chief and most eminent part of the doctrine contended for), as it hath no conformity in any thing with the moral perseverance before described, so indeed, it is not comprehended in that strict notion and signification of the word itself, which denotes the continuation of some act or acts in us, and not the uninterruptibleness of any act of God. This then is the cause of perseverance, rather than perseverance itself; yet such a cause, as being established, the effect will certainly and uncontrollably ensue. They who go about to assert a perseverance of saints, cut off from the absolute unchangeableness of the decree, purpose, and love of God, attended with a possibility of a contrary event, and that not only in respect of the free manner of its carrying on, whereby he that wills to persevere, may not will so to do, but also in respect of the issue and end itself, will, I doubt not, if they are serious in what they pretend, find themselves entangled in their undertaking. As perseverance is a grace in the subject on whom it is bestowed, so it relates either to the spi-

ritual habit of faith, or the principle of new life they have
received from God, or to the actual performance of those
duties wherein they ought to abide. In the first sense it
consists in the point of being, or not being. Whilst the
habit of faith remains, there is in respect thereof an uninterrupted perseverance in him in whom it is; and this we
contend for. As it respects actions flowing from that habit
and principle; so it expatiates itself in a large field. For as
it imports not at all a perpetual performance of such acts
without intermission (which were naturally as well as spiritually impossible, whilst we carry about us a body of death),
so neither doth it necessarily imply a constant tenor of proceeding in the performance of them, but is consistent with a
change in degrees of performance, and in other respects also,
not now to be insisted on. Perseverance in this sense being
the uninterrupted continuance of habitual grace, in the hearts
of believers without intercision, with such a walking in obedience, as God, according to the tenor of the new covenant
will accept, upon the whole of the matter, it is in its own
nature (as every thing also is that hath not its being from
itself), liable and obnoxious to alteration; and, therefore,
must be built and reposed on that which is in itself immutable, that it may be rendered on that supposition, immutable
also. Therefore is perseverance in this sense resolved into
that cause of it before mentioned, which to do is the chief
endeavour of the following treatise. Of the groundlessness
of their opinion, who granting final perseverance, do yet
plead for the possibility of a final apostacy, and an intercision of faith, no more need be spoken, but what upon the
account last mentioned hath been argued already. Some
discourses have passed both of old, and of late, concerning
the nature of this perseverance, and wherein it doth properly
consist. Many affirm it not really to differ from the habit
of faith and love itself, for which Bradwardine earnestly contends; Lib. 2. de Cau. Dei. cap. 7. Concluding his disputation, that ' Perseverantia habitualis, est justitia habituali-
ter perseverantia'; perseverantia actualis, est justitiæ perseverantia actualis, ipsum vero perseverare, est justitiam præ-
servare.' Whereupon ('suo more') he infers this corollary.
' Quod nomen perseverantiæ nullam rem absolutam essentialiter significat, sed accidentaliter, et relative, charitatem vi-

delicet, sive justitiam, cum respectu futuræ permansionis continue usque in finem; et quod non improbabiliter posset dici perseverantiam esse ipsam relationem hujus:' and therefore in the next chapter, to that objection, if perseverance be no more but charity, or righteousness, then every one that hath once obtained these, or true grace, must also persevere; he returns no answer at all: plainly insinuating his judgment to be so; of which afterward. And therefore he spends his thirteenth chapter of the same book to prove, that the Holy Spirit is that 'auxilium,' as he called it, whereby any persevere.

And chap. 1. he resolves all preservation from not being overcome by temptation, or not being tempted to a prevalency (the same for substance with perseverance), into the will and purpose of God. 'Quicunque,' saith he, 'non tentatur, hoc necessario est a deo, quod non tentatur. Sicut 11ª pars 13ª primi probat: et per 22ᵘᵐ primi, Deus necessario habet aliquem actum voluntatis circa talem non tentationem, et non nolitionem, quia tunc per decimum primi non tentaretur, ergo volitionem, quæ per idem decimum ipsum tentari non sinit,' &c. Others render it as a gift superadded to faith and love, of which judgment Austin seems to have been, who is followed by sundry of the schoolmen, with many of the divines of the reformed churches. Hence is that conclusion of Alvarez; de Auxil. lib. 10. disp. 103. 'Secundum fidem catholicam asserendum est, præter gratiam habitualem et virtutes infusas esse necessarium, ad perseverandum in bono usque in finem, auxilium speciale, supernaturale scilicet donum perseverantiæ.' And of this proposition he says, 'In hac omnes catholici conveniunt.' Of the same judgment was his master Thomas; lib. 3. con. Gen. cap. 155. Where also he gives this reason of his opinion; 'Illud quod natura sua est variabile, ad hoc quod figatur in uno, indiget auxilio alicujus moventis immobilis; sed liberum arbitrium, etiam existens in gratia habituali, ad huc manet variabile, et flexibile a bono in malum; ergo ad hoc quod figatur in bono, et perseveret in illo usque ad finem, indiget speciali Dei auxilio.' The same argument having been used before him by Bradwardine, though to another purpose, viz. not to prove perseverance to be a superadded gift to saving grace, which (as before was observed) he denied, but to manifest that it

was immediately and wholly from God. His words are, lib.
2. cap. cap. 8. Corol. ' Sicut secundum primi docet, omne
quod est naturale, et non est per se tale, sed est mutabile in
non tale, si manere debeat immutatum, oportet quod imita-
tur continue alicui per se fixo ; quare et continue quilibit
justus Deo.' The same school men also (a generation of men
exceeding ready to speak of any thing, though they know
not what they speak, nor whereof they affirm), go yet farther,
some of them, and will distinguish between the gift of perseverance and the gift confirmation in grace. He before mentioned, after a long dispute (viz. 104.) concludes, ' Ex his
sequitur differentiam inter donum perseverantiæ, et con-
firmationis in gratia (he means that which is granted in via)
in hoc consistere, quod donum perseverantiæ nullam perfectionem intrinsecam constituit in ipsa gratia habituali,
quam tamen perfectionem intrinsecam illi tribuit confirmatio
in gratia.' What this intrinsical perfection of habitual grace,
given it by confirmation, is, he cannot tell: for, in those who
are so confirmed in grace, he asserts only in impeccability
upon supposition, and that not alone from their intrinsical
principle, as it is with the blessed in heaven, but from help
and assistance also daily communicated from without. Du-
randus, in 3. d. 3. q. 4. assigns the deliverance from sin which
those who are confirmed in grace do obtain unto the Holy
Ghost: so far well: but he kicks down his milk by his addition, that he doth it only by the removal of all occasion of
sin.   But of these persons and their judgment in the point
under debate, more afterward.

For the thing itself last proposed, on what foot of account it is placed, and on what foundation asserted, the
treatise itself will discover. That the thing aimed at, is not
to be straitened or restrained to any one peculiar act of
grace, will easily appear. The main foundation of that
which we plead for, is, the eternal purpose of God, which
his own nature requireth to be absolutely immutable and
irreversible. The eternal act of the will of God designing
some to salvation by Christ, infallibly to be obtained, for
' the praise of the glory of his grace,' is the bottom of the
whole; even that foundation which standeth for ever, having
this seal, ' The Lord knoweth who are his.' For the accomplishment of this eternal purpose, and for the procurement of

all the good things, that lie within the compass of its intendment, are the oblation and intercession (the whole mediatory
undertaking of Christ), taking away sin, bringing in life and
immortality, interposed, giving farther casual influence into
the truth contended for.   In him and for his sake, as God
graciously, powerfully, and freely gives his Holy Spirit, faith,
with all the things that accompany salvation unto all them,
whom he accepts and pardons by his being made ' sin for
them,' and ' righteousness unto them,' so he takes them
thereby into an everlasting covenant that shall not be broken,
and hath therein given them innumerable promises that he
will continue to be their God for ever, and preserve them to
be, and in being, his people : to this end, because the principle of grace, and living to him, as in them inherent, is a
thing in its own nature changeable and liable to failing, he
doth, according to his promise, and for the accomplishment
of his purpose, daily make out to them, by his Holy Spirit,
from the great treasury and storehouse thereof, the Lord
Jesus Christ, helps and supplies, increasing of faith, love,
and holiness, recovering them from falls, healing their backslidings, strengthening them with all might according to his
glorious power, unto all patience and long-suffering with
joyfulness, so preserving them by his power through faith
unto salvation. And in this way of delivering the doctrine
contended about, it is clearly made out that the disputes
mentioned are as needless as groundless, so that we shall
not need to take them into the state of the controversy in
hand, though I shall have occasion once more to reflect
upon them, when I come to the consideration of the doctrine of the schoolmen, in reference to the opinion proposed
to debate.   The main of our inquiry, is after the purpose,
covenant, and promises of God, the undertaking of Christ,
the supplies of grace promised and bestowed in him : on
which accounts, we do assert and maintain ; that all true
believers who are in being so, interested in all those causes
of preservation, shall infallibly be preserved unto the end,
in the favour of God, and such a course of gospel obedience
as he will accept in Jesus Christ.

   That (as was formerly said), which at present I aim at in
reference to this truth is, to declare its rise and progress, its
course and opposition, which it hath found in several ages

of the church, with its state and condition at this day, in
respect of acceptance with the people of God.

Its rise, with all other divine truths, it owes only to revelation from God, manifested in the Scriptures of the Old
and New Testament; some of the most eminent places
wherein it is delivered in the Old Testament, are ; Gen in.
17. xvii. 1. Deut. xxxiii. 3. Josh. i. 5. 1 Sam. xii. 22. Psal.
i. 3. xxiii. 4. 6. xxxvii. 39, 40. lii. 8, 9. lxxxix. 31—35.
xxxiii. 9—11. xcii. 13, &c. Isa. xxvii. 3, 4. xlvi. 4. lix.
21. liv. 9, 10. iv. 4, 5. xl. 27—30. xliii. 1—8 Jer. iii. 3.
31—34. xxxii. 38—40. Ezek. xxxvi. 25—27. Hos. ii. 19, 20.
Zech. x. 12. Mal. iii. 6. with innumerable other places.   In
the New Testament God hath not left this truth and work
of his grace without witness; as in sundry other places, so it
is testified unto, Matt. vi. 13. vii. 24, 25. xii. 20. xvi. 18. xxiv.
24. Luke i. 70—75. viii. 5. 8. xxii. 32. John iii. 36. iv. 13, 14.
16. v. 24. vi. 35—39. 57. vii. 38. viii. 35. x. 27—30. xiii. 1.
xiv. 15—17. xvi. 27. xvii. throughout, Acts ii. 47. xiii. 48.
Rom. vi. 14. viii. 1. 16, 17. 28—34, &c. 1 Cor. i. 8, 9. x. 13,
14. xv. 49. 58. 2 Cor. i. 21. Eph. i. 13, 14. iii. 17. iv. 30.
v. 23. Gal. ii. 20. Phil. i. 6. ii. 13. 1 Thess. v. 24. 2 Tim. iv.
17, 18. Tit. i. 1. Heb. vi. 19. x. 38, 39. xii. ix. 14. xiii. 5.
21. 1 Pet. i. 2—5. 1 John ii. 19. 24. iii. 9. 19. v. 14. 18.
Jude 1. Rev. xx. 6.   So plentifully hath the Lord secured
this sacred truth, wherein he hath inwrapped so much (if not
as in the means of conveyance the whole) of that peace,
consolation, and joy, which he is willing the heirs of promise
should receive.   Whether the faith hereof thus plentifully
delivered to the saints, found acceptance with the primitive
Christians, to the most of whom it was given not 'only to believe, but also to suffer for Christ,' to me is unquestionable.
And I know no better proof of what those first churches did
believe, than by shewing what they ought to believe, which
I shall unquestionably be persuaded they did believe, unless
most pregnant testimony be given of their apostacy.   That
Paul believed it for himself and concerning others is evident;
Rom. viii. 38, 39. 1 Cor. i. 8, 9. Phil. i. 6. Heb. vi. 9, 10. are
sufficient proof of his faith herein.   That he built up others in
the same persuasion, to the enjoyment of the same peace and
assurance with himself is undeniable.   And if there be any
demonstration to be made of the belief of the first Christians,

of any evidence comparable unto this, I shall not deny but that it ought to be attended unto. But that we may not seem willing to decline the consideration of what those who went before us in the several ages and generations past, apprehended, and have by any means communicated unto us, of their thoughts about the business of our contest (having no reason so to be), I shall after a little preparation made to that work, present the reader with something of my observations to that end and purpose.

  Of the authority of the ancients in matters of religion and worship of God, of the right use and improvement of their writings, of the several considerations that are to be had and exercised by them who would read them with profit and advantage, after many disputes and contests between the Papists and divines of the reformed churches, the whole concernment of that controversy, is so clearly stated, managed, and resolved by Monsieur Daillé in his book of the Right Use of the Fathers, that I suppose all farther labour in that kind may be well spared. Those who intend to weigh their testimony to any head of Christian doctrine, do commonly distinguish them into three greater periods of time. The first of these is comprehensive of them, who lived and wrote before the doctrine, concerning which they are called out to give in their thoughts and verdict, had received any signal opposition, and eminent discussion in the church on that account. Such are the writers of the first three hundred years, before the Nicene council, in reference to the doctrine of the Trinity : and so the succeeding writers, before the stating of the Macedonian, Eutychian, and Nestorian heresies. In the next are they ranked who bare the burden and heat of the opposition made to any truth, and on that occasion wrote expressly and at large on the controverted doctrines. Which is the condition of Athanasius, Basil, Gregory, and some others in that Arian controversy. And in the last place succeed those who lived after such concussions, which are of less or more esteem, according as the doctrines inquired after were less or more corrupted in the general apostacy of the latter days. According to this order our first period of time will be with the rise of the Pelagian heresy, which gave occasion to the thorough, full, and clear discussion of the whole doctrine concerning the grace of God ; whereof that in whose defence we are engaged is no small portion. The next of those whom God raised up to make head against that subtle opposer of his grace with his followers, during the space of a hundred years and somewhat onwards, ensuing the promulgation of that heresy. What have been the thoughts of men in the latter ages until the Reformation, and of the Romanists since to this day, manifested in a few pregnant instances, will take up the third part of this design. Of the judgment of the reformed churches, as they are commonly called, I shall speak particularly in the close of this discourse. For the first of these: not to insist on the paucity of writers in the first three hundred years, sundry single persons in the following ages, having severally written three times as much as we have left and remaining of all the others (the names of many who are said to have written, being preserved by Eusebius Eccles. Hist. and Hierome lib. de Script. their writings being perished in their days), nor in general of that corruption, whereunto they have almost every one of them been unquestionably exposed, I must be forced to preface the nomination of them with some considerations. The first in that known passage of Hegesipus, in Euseb. Hist. Eccles. lib. 3. 26. Ὡς ἄρα μέχρι τῶν τότε χρόνων, παρθένος καθαρὰ καὶ ἀδιάφθορος ἔμεινεν ἡ ἐκκλησία εἰς δ᾽ ὁ ἱερὸς τῶν Ἀποστόλων χορὸς διάφορον εἴληφε τοῦ βίου τέλος, παρεληλύθει τὲ ἡ γενεὰ ἐκείνη τῶν αὐταῖς ἀκοαῖς τῆς ἔνθεν σοφίας ἐπακοῦσαι κατηξιωμένων, τῆς ἐνθέου ἀθεοῦ πλάνης τὴν ἀρχὴν ἐλάμβανεν ἡ σύστασις, διὰ τῆς τῶν ἑτεροδιδασκάλων ἀπάτης, οἳ καὶ ἅτε μηδένος ἔτι τῶν Ἀποστόλων λειπομένου, γυμνῇ λοιπὸν ἤδη τῇ κεφαλῇ τῷ τῆς ἀληθείας κηρύγματι τὴν ψευδώνυμον γνῶσιν ἀντικηρύττειν ἐπεχείρουν. So far he: setting out the corruption of the church even as to doctrine, immediately after the apostles fell asleep: whereof whosoever will impartially, and with disengaged judgments, search into the writings, that of those days do remain, will perhaps find more cause than is commonly imagined, with him to complain.

2. The main work of the writers of the first ages, being to contend with heathenish idolaters, to convince them of their madness and folly, to write apologies for the worship of God in Christ in general, so to dissuade their rulers from persecution, or in contesting with heretics, for the most part appearing to be men either corrupt in their lives, or mad and brainsick (as we say) as to their imaginations, or deny-

ing the truth of the person of Christ, what can we expect
from them, as delivered directly and on set purpose to the
matter of our present contest? Some principles may in
them possibly be discovered, from whence, by a regular deduction, some light may be obtained into their thoughts
concerning the points in difference. Thus Junius thinks,
and not without cause, that the whole business of predestination, may be stated upon this one principle, that faith is
the free gift of God flowing from his predestination and
mercy; and concerning this, saith he, 'Hoc autem omnes
patres uno consensu ex Christo et Paulo agnoverunt; ipse
Justinus Martyr in Apolog. 2. et gravissime vero Clemens
Alexandrinus, in hac alioquin palestra non ita exercitatus
ut sequentia secula,' Hom. lib. 2. 'Basilii et Valentini dog-
ma esse dicit, quod fides a natura sit;' Consid. Senten. Pet.
Baroni. Without this what advantage can be taken, or what
use can be made for the discovery of the mind of any of
the ancients by cropping off some occasional expressions,
from their occasions and aims, I know not. Especially, would
I more peremptorily affirm this could I imagine any of them
wrote as Jerome affirms of himself, that he sometimes did.
Epist. ad August. which is among his 89 Epist. T. 2. 'Itaque,'
saith he, 'ut simpliciter fateor, legi hæc omnia, et in mente
mea plurima coacervans, accito notario vel mea, vel aliena
dictavi, nec ordinis, nec verborum interdum nec sensuum
memor.' Should any one say so of himself in these
days, he would be accounted little better than a madman;
much then on this account (or at least not 'much to the
purpose) is not to be expected from the fathers of the
first ages.

3. Another observation to our purpose, lies well expressed in the beginning of the fourteenth chapter of Bellarmine's
second book de Grat. et lib. Arb. 'Præter Scripturas adfe-
runt alia testimonia patrum;' saith he, speaking of those
who opposed God's free predestination : to which he sub-
joins ; 'Neque est hoc novum argumentum, sed antiquissi-
mum. Scribit enim S. Prosper in Epistola ad S. Augustinum, Gallos qui sententiam ejusdem Augustini de predestinatione calumniabantur, illud potissimum objicere solitos
quod ea sententia doctrinæ veterum videbatur esse con-
traria. Sed respondet idem Augustinus in lib. de bono perse-

verantiæ, veteres patres, quí ante Pelagium floruerunt, quæs-
tionem istam nunquam accurate tractasse sed incidenter solum, et quasi per transitum illam attigisse.   Addit vero in
fundamento hujus sententiæ quod est gratiam dei non præ-
venire ab ullo opere nostro sed contra, ab illa omnia opera
nostra præveniri, ita ut nihil omnino boni, quod attinet ad
salutem sit in nobis, quod non est nobis ex deo, convenire
Catholicos omnes; et ibidem citat Cyprianum Ambrosium,
et Nazianzenum, quibus addere possumus Basilium et Cry-
sostomum.' To the same purpose with application to a particular person doth that great and holy doctor discourse, de
doctrin. Christiana, lib. 3. cap. 33. saith he, ' Non erat exper-
tus hanc hæresin Tychonius, quæ nostro tempore exorta,
multum nos ut gratiam dei quæ per dominum nostrum Jesum
Christum est adversus eam defenderemus exercuit, et secundum id quod ait Apostolus, oportet hæreses esse, ut probati
manifesti fiunt in nobis, multo vigilantiores, diligentioresque
reddidit, ut adverteremus in Scripturis Sanctis, quod istum
Tychonium minus attentum minusque sine hoste solicitum
fugit.' That also of Jerome in his second apology against
Ruffinus, in reference to a most weighty article of Christian
religion, is known to all; ' Fieri potest,' saith he, ' ut vel
simpliciter erraverint, vel alio sensu scripserint, vel a libra-
riis imperitis eorum paulatim scripta corrupta sint; vel
certe antequam in Alexandria quasi Dæmonium meridianum
Arius nasceretur, innocenter quædam, et minus cante locuti
sunt, et quæ non possunt perversorum hominum calumniam
declinare.' And what he spake of the writers before Arius, in
reference to the person of Christ, we may [say] of them before
Pelagius, in reference to his grace. Hence Pererius, in Rom.
c. 8. disput. 22. tells us (how truly *ipse viderit*, I am not altogether of his mind), that for those authors that lived before Austin's time, that all the Greek fathers, and a considerable part of the Latin, were of opinion, that the cause of
predestination, was the foresight which God had, either of
man's good works, or of their faith, either of which opinions,
he assures us is manifestly contrary, both to the authority
of the Scriptures, and particularly to the doctrine of St.
Paul.   I am not (as I said), wholly of his mind, partly upon
the account of the observations made by his fellow Jesuit
out of Austin, before-mentioned, partly upon other accounts

·also. Upon these and the like considerations, much I presume to the business in hand, will not be produced on either side, from the fathers that wrote before the rise of the Pelagian heresy. And if any one of the parties at this day litigant about the doctrines of the grace of God, should give that advice, that Sisinnius and Agellius the Novatians sometimes gave, as Zozomen reports of them (Hist. Eccles. lib. 7. cap. 12.), to Nectarius, by him communicated to the emperor Theodosius, to have the quarrel decided by those that wrote before the rise of the controversy, as it would be unreasonable in itself, so I persuade myself neither party would accept of the conditions, neither had the Catholics of those days got any thing, if they had attended to the advice of those Novatians. But these few observations premised, something as to particular testimonies, may be attended unto.

That we may proceed in some order, not leaving those we have nothing to say to, nor are willing to examine, whilst they are but thin, and come not in troops, unsaluted; the first writings that are imposed on us after the canonical Scriptures, are the eight books of Clement, commonly called the Apostles' Constitutions, being pretended to be written by him at their appointment, with the canons ascribed to the same persons. These we shall but salute, for besides that they are faintly defended by any of the Papists, disavowed and disclaimed as Apocryphal, by the most learned of them, as Bellarmine de script. Eccles. in Clem. who approves only of fifty canons, of eighty-five; Baronius, An. Dom. 102. 14. who adds thirty more, and Binius with a little enlargement of canons, in Tit. Can. T. 1. Con. pag. 17. and have been thoroughly disproved and decried by all Protestant writers, that have had any occasion to deal with them, their folly and falsity, their impostures and triflings, have of late been so fully manifested by Dallæus, de Pseudepigrapis Apostol. that nothing need be added thereunto. Of him may doctor H. H. learn the truth of that insinuation of his, Dissert. de Episcop. 2. cap. 6. sect. 3. 'Canone Apostolico secundo (semper inter genuinos habito),' but of the confidence of this author in his assertions afterward; this indeed (insisted on by Dallæus, and the learned Usher in his notes upon Ignatius) is childishly ridiculous in them, that whereas it is pretended that these constitutions were made at a convention of the

apostles, as l. 6. c. 14. they are brought in discoursing ἡμεῖς
οὖν ἐπὶ τὸ αὐτὸ γενόμενοι, πέτρος καὶ Ἀνδρέας Ἰάκωβος καὶ
Ἰωάννης υἱοὶ Ζεβαδαίου, &c.   They are made to inform us,
lib. 2. cap. 57. that the Acts written by Luke, and read in
the churches are theirs, and the four books of the gospel.
Whereas the story of the death of James (here said to be
together with the apostles), is related Acts xii. and John, by
the consent of all, wrote not his gospel until after the dissolution of his associates.   Also they make Stephen and
Paul to be together, at the making of those constitutions;
Const. lib. 8. cap. 4. (whereas the martyrdom of Stephen
was before the conversion of Paul) and yet also mentions
the stoning of Stephen; lib. 8. 46. They tell us whom they
appointed bishops of Jerusalem after the death of James,
and yet James is one of them, who is met together with
them, l. 7. c. 48. Nay mention is made of Cerinthus, and that
Mark the heretic, Menander, Basilides, and Saturninus,
were known and taken notice of by the apostles, who all
lived in the second century, about the reign of Hadrian, as
Eusebius manifesteth, and Clem. Alex. Strom. lib. 7.

But to leave such husks as these unto them who loath
manna, and will not feed on the bread that our heavenly Father hath so plentifully provided for all that live in his family, or any way belong to his house, let us look onward to
them that follow, of whose truth and honesty we have more
assurance.

The first genuine piece that presents itself unto us, on
the roll of antiquity, is that epistle of Clemens, which in the
name of the church of Rome, he wrote to the divided church
of Corinth, which being abundantly testified to of old, to the
great contentment of the Christian world, was published
here at Oxford some few years since; a writing full of ancient simplicity, humility, and zeal.   As to our present business much I confess cannot be pleaded from hence, beyond
a negative impeachment, of that great and false clamour
which our adversaries have raised, of the consent of the primitive Christians with them in their by-paths, and ways of
error.   It is true, treating of a subject diverse from any of
those heads of religion about which our contests are, it is not
to be expected that he should any where plainly, directly,
and evidently, deliver his judgment unto them.   This there-

fore I shall only say, that in that whole epistle, there is not
one word, iota, or syllable that gives countenance to the te-
net of our adversaries, in the matter of the saints' perseverance; but that on the contrary, there are sundry expres·
sions, asserting such a foundation of the doctrine we maintain, as will with good strength infer the truth of it. Page 4.
setting forth the virtues of the Corinthians before they fell
into the schism that occasioned his epistle, he minds them
that, ἀγών ἦν ὑμῖν ἡμήρας τε καὶ νυκτὸς ὑπερπάσης τῆς ἀδελ-
φότητος, εἰς τὸ σώζεσθαι μετ' ἐλέους καὶ συνειδήσεως τὸν ἀριθμὸν
τῶν ἐκλεκτῶν αὐτοῦ. That God hath a certain number of elect
to be saved, and for whose salvation by his mercy the church
is to contend with him, is a principle wholly inconsistent
with those, on which the doctrine of the saints' apostacy is
bottomed. Corresponding hereunto is that passage of his
concerning the will of God, p 12. πάντας οὖν τοὺς ἀγαπητοὺς
αὐτοῦ βουλόμενος μετανοίας μετασχεῖν, ἐστήριξεν τῷ παντοκρα-
τορικῷ βουλήματι αὐτοῦ. A mere consideration of this passage
causeth me to recall what but now was spoken, as though the
testimony given to the truth in this epistle was not so clear
as might be desired. The words now repeated, contain the
very thesis contended for. It is the beloved of God (or his
chosen), whom he will have made partakers of saving repentance; and hereunto he establisheth them (for with that word
is the defect in the sentence to be supplied), by, or with the
almighty will: because he will have his beloved partakers
of saving repentance, and the benefits thereof, he confirms
and establishes them in it, with his omnipotent or sovereign
will. The inconsistency and irreconcilableness of this assertion, with the doctrine of these saints' apostacy, the
learned reader needs not any assistance to manifest to him.
Answerably hereunto he saith of God, ἐκλογῆς μέρος ἡμᾶς
ἐποίησεν ἑαυτῷ, p. 38. and p. 66. mentioning the blessedness
of the forgiveness of sins, out of Psal. xxxii. he adds, Οὗτος
ὁ μακαρισμὸς ἐγένετο ἐπὶ τοὺς ἐκλελεγμένους ὑπὸ τοῦ θεοῦ διὰ
ἰησοῦ χριστοῦ τοῦ κυρίου ἡμῶν. The elect of whom he speaks,
are those on whom, through and for Christ, God bestows
the blessedness of justification; elect they are of God antecedently to the obtaining of that blessedness, and through
that they do obtain it: so that in that short sentence of this
author, the great pillar of the saints' perseverance, which is

their free election, the root of all the blessedness which afterward they enjoy, is established : other passages like to
these, there are in that epistle, which plainly deliver the primitive Christians of the church of Rome, from any communion in the doctrine of the saints' apostacy, and manifest
their perseverance in the doctrine of the saints' perseverance,
wherein they had been so plentifully instructed not long before, by the epistle of Paul unto them.

He who upon the roll of antiquity presents himself in
the next place to our consideration, is the renowned Ignatius, concerning whom I desire to beg so much favour of the
learned reader, as to allow me a diversion unto some thoughts
and observations, that belong to another subject, than that
which I have now peculiarly in hand, before I come to give
him a taste of his judgment in the doctrine under debate.

As this Ignatius bishop of the church at Antioch, was in
himself a man of an excellent spirit, eminent in holiness, and
to whom on the behalf of Christ it was given not only to believe on him, but also suffer for him, and on that account of
very great and high esteem among the Christians of that
age wherein he lived, and sundry others following, so no
great question can be made but that he wrote towards the
end of his pilgrimage, when he was on his way to be offered
up through the Holy Spirit by the mouths of wild beasts
to Jesus Christ, that he wrote sundry epistles to sundry
churches that were of chiefest note and name in the countries about.   The concurrent testimony of the ancients in
this matter of fact, will give as good assurance as in this
kind we are capable of: Eusebius reckons them up in order,
so doth Jerome.

After them frequent mention is made of them by others,
and special sayings in them are transcribed : and whereas it
is urged by some, that there is no mention of those epistles
before the Nicene council, before which time, it is as evident
as if it were written with the beams of the sun, that many
false and supposititious writings had been imposed on, and
were received by many in the church (as the story of Paul
and Tecla is mentioned and rejected by Tertull. de Baptis.
Hermæ Pastor by others), it is answered that they were mentioned by Irenæus some good while before; lib. 5. cap. 28.
saith he, 'Quemadmodum quidam de nostris dixit, propter

martyrium in Deum adjudicatus ad bestias; quoniam frumentum sum Christi et per dentes bestiarum molor ut mundus panis Dei inveniar.' Which words to the substance of them are found in these epistles: though some say nothing is here intimated of any epistles or writings, but of a speech that might pass among the Christians by tradition, such as they had many among themselves, even of our Saviour's; some whereof are mentioned by Grotius on these words of Paul, ' Remember that word of Christ, that it is more blessed to give than to receive.' What probability or ground for conviction there is in these or the like observations and answers, is left to the judgment of all. This is certain that the first mentioning of them in antiquities, is to be clearly received (and that perhaps with more than the bare word of him that recites and approves of the epistles of Jesus Christ to Agbarus the king of the Edessens, or of him that reckons Seneca among the ecclesiastical writers, upon the account of his epistles to Paul), or the following testimonies, which are heaped up in abundance by some who think (but falsely) that they have a peculiar interest inwrapped in the epistles, now extant, will be of very small weight or value.

For my part I am persuaded with that kind of persuasion wherein in things of no greater moment I am content to acquiesce, that he did write seven epistles, and that much of what he so wrote is preserved in those that are now extant, concerning which, the contests of learned men, have drawn deep and run high in these latter days, though little to the advantage of the most that have laboured in that cause, as shall be manifested in the process of our discourse.

A late[a] learned doctor in his dissertations about episcopacy, or dispute for it against Salmasius and Blondellus, tells us, that we may take a taste of his confidence in asserting, Dissert. 2. cap. 23. 1. that Salmasius and Blondellus 'mortalium omnium primi,' thought these epistles to be feigned, or counterfeit. And with more words, cap. 24. 1. he would make us believe that these epistles of Ignatius were always of the same esteem with that of Clemens from Rome to the Corinthians of which he treats at large in his fourth dissertation, or that of Polycarpus to the Philippians which we

---

[a] Unicum D. Blondellum aut alterum fortasse inter omnes mortales Walonem Messalinum, cap. 25 s. 3

have in Eusebius, and then he adds in the judgment of Salmasius and Blondellus, 'Solus Ignatius οἴχεται cujus tamen Epistolæ pari semper cum illis per universam ab omni ævo patrum nostrorum memoriam reverentia excipiebantur; nec prius a mortalium quovis in judicium vocabantur (multo minus ut in re certa et extra dubium posita inter plane ἀδό-κιμα et Κίβδηλα rejiciebantur), quam Presbyteri Anglicani patribus suis contumeliam facere cœpissent iisque aut suppetias ferre, aut rem gratam facere (quibus illecebris adducti nescio), hi duo non ignobiles Presbyteranæ causæ hyperaspistæ in seipsos recepissent.' Of his two learned antagonists, one is dead, and the other almost blind, or probably they would have dealt not much more gently with the doctor for his parenthesis ('quibus illecebris adducti nescio'), than one of them formerly did (Salmas. de subscribendis et signandis testamentis seu specimen Consula. Animad. Heraldi. cap. 1. p. 19. 'Nuper quidem etiam nebulo in Anglia, Capellanus ut audio regis, Hammondus nomine, libro quem edidit de potestate clavium Salmasio iratus quod aliam quam ipse sententiam probet ac defendat, haud potuit majus convicium, quod ei diceret, invenire, quam si Grammaticum appellaret') for his terming him a grammarian; yet indeed of him (such was the hard entertainment he found on all hands), it is by many supposed that he was 'illecebris adductus' (and they stick not to name the bait he was caught withal), wrought over in a manner to destroy the faith of that which he had before set up and established.

For the thing itself affirmed by the doctor, I cannot enough admire with what oscitancy or contempt, he considers his readers (of which manner of proceeding this is very far from being the only instance), that he should confidently impose such things upon them. He that hath written so much about Ignatius, and doth so triumph in his authority, ought doubtless to have considered those concernments of his author which are obvious to every ordinary inquirer; Vedelius's edition of Ignatius at Geneva came forth with his notes in the year 1623. long before either Salmasius or Blondellus had written any thing about the supposititiousness of these epistles, in the apology for Ignatius, whereto prefixed, he is forced to labour and sweat in the answer of one, whom he deservedly styles *Virum doctissimum;* arguing (not contemptibly) that Ignatius never wrote any such epistles, and that all those which were carried about in his name were false and counterfeit.

But perhaps the doctor had taken caution of one of the fathers of his church, that 'a Genevensibus istis Typographis præter fraudes, et fucos, et præstigias non est quod quicquam expectemus;' (Montacu. Appar. 1. lib. 5. sect. 47. p. 19.) and so thought not fit to look into any thing that comes from them.

Especially may this be supposed to have some influence upon him, considering the gentle censure added in the next words by that reverend father of his church concerning the endeavour of Vedelius in his notes on that edition. 'Neque audax ille et importunus Ignatii censor, quicquam attulit ad paginas suas implendas præter inscitiam, et incuriam, et impudentiam singularem (nec sævi magne sacerdos) dum ad suum Genevatismum antiquitatem detorquet invitissimam, non autem quod oportuit, Calvinismum amussitat ad antiquitatem.' And what, I pray, is the reason of his episcopal censure? That he should deal with poor Vedelius in that language wherewith men of his order and authority were wont to deal with preaching ministers at their visitations? Why this poor man, in that passage which you have in the Epistle to the Magnesians, (in that edition, p. 56.) where treating of the ancient fathers' expectations of the coming of Christ, retains the common reading of εἰς κενότητα ἐλπίδος ἦλθον referring the word to their expectation of seeing him come in the flesh; which upon the testimony of our Saviour himself, they desired to see, and saw it not, not correcting it by a change of κενότητα into κοινότητα ἐλπίδος, so referring it to their faith in Christ and salvation by him as in his judgment, he ought to have done:

'Ιδοὺ ὀλίγον πῦρ, ἡλίκην ἥλην ἀνάπτει

A little thing would provoke the indignation of a prelate against any thing that came from Geneva.

I say, I would suppose, that this might divert our doctor from casting his eye upon Vedelius, whose defensative would have informed him that these epistles had been opposed as false and counterfeit, before ever Salmasius or Blondellus had taken them into consideration; but that I find him sometimes insisting on that Geneva edition.

For whereas, Diss. 2. cap. 2. sect. 11. he tells you, that he intends to abide only upon the edition of Isaac Vossius, in Greek, published from the archives of the library of Lawrence de Medicis, and the Latin edition published by Bishop Usher, out of our library here at Oxford; yet, cap. 8. being pressed with the testimony of the writers of the Epistle to the Magnesians, in that edition calling episcopacy νεωτερικὴν τάξιν, plainly intimating a comparative novelty, in that order to others in the churches, and fearing (as well he might) that his translation of νεωτερικὴ τάξις into, 'the ordination of a young man,' would scarce be received by the men of his own prejudice (for surely he never supposed, that he should impose on any other, by such gross figments), he prefers the Vedelian edition (where these words are not so used) before it; and informs us that ' sic legendum (as it is in the Geneva edition) suadet tota epistolæ series.'   Now this truly is marvellous to me (if the doctor consulteth authors any farther than merely to serve his present turn), how he could ever advise with that edition of Vedelius, and yet so confidently affirm that Salmasius and Blondellus were the first that rejected these Epistles, as feigned and counterfeited.

But yet, a little farther, the first edition of these epistles in Latin was Augustæ Vindelicorum, An. 1529 ; in Greek, at Basil, 1566. Before which time I suppose the doctor expects not, that any opposition should be made to them, considering the heaps of filth and dung, that until about that time, were owned for the offspring of the ancient fathers.

Upon their first appearing in the world what is the entertainment they receive ? One who was dead before either the doctor, or either of his antagonists were born, and whose renown among the people of God, will live when they are all dead, gives them this welcome into the world ; ' Ignatium quod obtendunt, si velint quicquam habere momenti ; probent apostolos legem tulisse de quadragesima, et similibus corruptelis.   Nihil næniis istis quæ sub Ignatii nomine editæ sunt putidius.   Quo minus tolerabilis est eorum impudentia qui talibus larvis ad fallendum se instruunt ;' Cal. Instit. lib. 1. cap. 13. sect. 29.

Whatever be the judgment of our doctor concerning this man (as some there are of whom a learned bishop in this nation long ago complained, that they are still opening their mouths against Calvin, who helped them to mouths to speak with; Abbot. ad Thom.) he will in the judgment of some, be so far accounted somebody, as to take off from the confident assertion that Salmasius and Blondellus, were 'mortalium primi,' that rejected these epistles.

The Centuriators of Magdenburg were esteemed to be somebodies in their days; and yet they make bold to call these epistles into question: and to tender sundry arguments to the impairing of their credit and authority. This then they, Cent. 2. cap. 10. De Episcop. Antioch. ac primum de Ignatio.

'Lectori pio et attento considerandum relinquimus quantum sit illis epistolis tribuendum. Non enim dubitamus quin in lectione earum cuilibet ista in mentem veniant; primum quod fere in omnibus epistolis, licet satis copiosis, occasio scribendi praetermittitur, nec vel divinare licet, quare potissimum ad hanc vel illam ecclesiam literas voluerit mittere. Deinde ipsius peregrinationis ratio non parvum injicit scrupulum considerantibus, quod multo rectiore et breviori itinere, Romam potuerit navigare, ut testatur vel ipsius Pauli exemplum.—Expende quam longum sit iter, Antiochia ad littus Ægæi pelagi se recipere, ibique recta sursum versus Septentrionem ascendere, et præcipuas civitates in littore sitas usque ad Troadem perlustrare, cum tamen Romanum iter sit destinatum versus occasum. Tertio res ejusmodi in istas literas inspersæ sunt ut ad eas propemodum obstupescat lector, &c.—Hæc cum alias non somnolento lectori incidant, non existimaverimus,' &c.

Thus they at the world's first awaking, as to the consideration of things of this kind.

To them add the learned Whitaker, Cont. prima, de perfect. script. quæst. sexta, c. 12. where after he hath disputed against the credit of these epistles, jointly and severally, with sundry arguments, at length he concludes, 'Sed de his Epistolis satis multa, et de hoc Ignatio quid judicandum sit, satis ex iis constare potest quæ diximus. Ista Papistæ non audent tueri,' &c. To whom sundry others might be added, convincing Salmasius and Blondellus, not to have been 'mortalium primi,' that called them into question.

I have not insisted on what hath been spoken, as though

E 2

I were wholly of the mind of them, who utterly condemn
those epistles as false and counterfeit; though I know no
possibility of standing before the arguments levied against
them, notwithstanding the fore-mentioned doctor's attempt
to that purpose, without acknowledging so much corruption
in them, additions and detractions from what they were
when first written, as will render them not so clearly serviceable to any end or purpose, whereunto their testimony
may be required, as other unquestionable writings of their
antiquity are justly esteemed to be. That these epistles
have fallen into the hands of such unworthy impostors as
have filled the latter ages with labour and travail to discover
their deceits, the doctor himself granteth, dissert. 2. cap. 2.
sect. 6. 'Nulla,' saith he, ' quidem nobis incumbit necessi-
tas, ut in tanta exemplarium et editionum varietate et in-
constantia, nihil uspiam Ignatio interpolatum aut adsutum
affirmemus.'

And indeed the foisted passages in many places are so
evident, yea shameful, that no man who is not resolved to
say any thing, without care of proof or truth, can once appear in any defensative about them. Of this sort are the
shreds and pieces out of that branded counterfeit piece of
Clemens, or the Apostles' Constitutions, which are almost in
every epistle packed in, in a bungling manner, oftentimes
disturbing the sense and coherence of the place; yea sometimes such things are thence transcribed, as in them are
considerable arguments of their corruption and falsehood;
so is that period in the Epistle to the Magnesians taken from
Clemens. Constitut. lib. 6. cap. 2. Ἀβιδδαδὰν ὡσαύτως τῆς
κεφαλῆς ἀφαιρεῖται δι' ὁμοίαν αἰτίαν. This Abeddadan being
mentioned next after Absalom's dying by the loss of his
head, is therefore, supposed to be Sheba the son of Bickri,
but whence that counterfeit Clemens had that name is not
known. That the counterfeit Clemens by Abeddadan intended Sheba is evident from the words he assigns unto him
in the place mentioned. Abeddadan said, οὐκ ἐστὶ μοὶ μέρος
ἐν Δαβὶδ, οὐδὲ κληρονομία ἐν υἱῷ Ἰεσσάι. And joins him
with Absalom in his rebellion; such passages as these they
are supposed to have received from that vain and foolish
impostor; but if it be true, which some have observed, that
there is not the least mention made of any of those ficti-

tious Constitutions in the three first ages after Christ, and that the διδαχὴ 'Αποστόλων mentioned by Eusebius, and Athanasius, as also that διατάξις in Epiphanius, are quite other things, then those eight books of Constitutions we now have, it may rather be supposed, that that sottish deceiver rather raked up some of his filth from the corruption of these epistles, than that any thing out of him is crept into them. Other instances might be given of stuffing these epistles with the very garbage of that beast. Into what hands also these epistles have fallen by the way, in their journeying down towards these ends of the world, is evident from these citations made out of them, by them of old, which now appear not in them. Theodoret. Dial. 3. adv. Hære. gives us this sentence from Ignatius; Εὐχαριστίας καὶ προσφορὰς οὐκ ἀποδέχονται διὰ τὸ μὴ ὁμολογεῖν τὴν εὐχαριστίαν σάρκα εἶναι τοῦ σωτῆρος ἡμῶν ἰησοῦ χριστοῦ τὴν ὑπὲρ τῶν ἁμαρτιῶν ἡμῶν παθοῦσαν ἣν χρηστοτητι ὁ Πατὴρ ἤγειρεν. Which words you will scarcely find in that epistle to the church of Smyrna, from whence they were taken; Jerome also, Dial. 3. Con. Pelag. hath this passage of him, and from him. 'Ignatius vir apostolicus et martyr scribit audacter, elegit Dominus apostolos qui super omnes homines peccatores erant:' which words as they are not now in these epistles, so, as one observes, if ever he wrote them as is pretended, he did it *audacter* indeed. But of these things our doctor takes no notice.

The style of these epistles doth not a little weaken the credit of them, being turgent, swelling with uncouth words and phrases, affected manner and ways of expression, new compositions of words, multiplying titles of honour to men, exceedingly remote and distant from the plainness and simplicity of the first writers among the Christians, as is evident by comparing these with the epistles of Clemens before mentioned, that of Polycarpus in Eusebius, the churches of Vienna and Lyons in that same author, and others. Instances for the confirmation of this observation are multiplied by Blondellus: my designed work will not allow me to insist on particulars. In many good words this charge is waved, by affirming that the author of these epistles was an Assyrian, and near to martyrdom, and that in the Scriptures there are sundry words of as hard a composition, as these used by him; Ham.

disser. 2. cap. 3. And as he says, from this kind of writing an argument of sufficient validity may be drawn to evince him to be the author of these epistles. Jerome was of another mind speaking of Didymus. ' Imperitus,' saith he, ' sermone est, et non scientia, Apostolicum virum ex ipso sermone exprimens, tam sensuum nomine, quam simplicitate verborum.' But seeing Ignatius was a Syrian, and near to martyrdom (though he writes his epistles from Troas and Smyrna, which without doubt were not in his way to Rome from Antioch ; and yet every where he saith he is going to Rome : ad Eph. τὰ δεσμὰ ἀπὸ Συρίας μεχρὶ 'Ρώμης περιφέρω· which in the close he affirms he wrote from Smyrna, whither he was had to his martyrdom), what is it to any man what style he used in his writings, what swelling titles he gave to any, or words he made use of. Who shall call those writings (especially Ignatius being a Syrian) into question.

But perhaps some farther question may here arise (and which hath by sundry been already started), about the use of divers Latin words in those epistles, which doubtless cannot be handsomely laid on the same account of their author being a Syrian, and nigh to martyrdom ; ἀκκέπτα, δεπόσιτα δεσερτωρ, ἐξεμπλάριον, are usually instanced in words to whose use no Roman customs, observations, orders, nor rules of government, do administer the least occasion. Of these the doctor tells you, he wonders only that in so many epistles, there are no more of this kind. And why so ? The epistles are not so large a volume ; a very few hours will serve to read them over ; and yet I am persuaded that in all that compass of reading, in the Greek fathers, which our doctor owns, he cannot give so many instances of words barbarous to their language, no way occasioned by the means before mentioned, as have been given in these epistles. But he wonders there are no more, and some wonder that all are not of his mind. But he farther informs us that a diligent reader of the Scripture, may observe many more Latin words in the New Testament than are used in these epistles ; and for a proof of his diligence and observation, reckons up out of the end of Pasor's Lexicon sundry words of that kind, made use of by the sacred writers. I fear, unto some men, this will scarce be an apology prevalent to the dismission of these epistles, from under the censure of being at least

foully corrupted. Of the whole collection of words of that
sort made by Pasor, among which are those especially culled
out by our doctor to confirm his observations, there is
scarce one, but either it is expressive of some Roman office,
custom, money, order, or the like; words of which nature pass
as proper names (as one of those mentioned by the doctor is,
and no otherwise used in the New Testament), from one
country and language to another, or are indeed of a pure
Greek original, or at least were in common use in that age;
neither of which can be spoken of the words above mentioned, used in the epistles; which were never used by any
before or after them, nor is there any occasion imaginable
why they should : ' Parvas habent spes epistolæ, si tales habent :' I would indeed gladly see a fair, candid, and ingeni-
ous defensative of the style and manner of writing used in
·those epistles, departing so eminently from any thing that
was customary in the writings of the men of those days, or
is regular for men of any generation, in repetitions, affected
compositions, barbarisms, rhyming expressions, and the like;
for truly notwithstanding any thing that hitherto I have been
able to obtain for help in this kind, I am enforced to incline
to Vedelius's answers, to all the particular instances given
of this nature; this and that place is corrupted, this is
from Clemens's Constitutions, this from this or that tradition;
which also would much better free those epistles from the
word σιγῆς, used in the sense whereunto it was applied by
the Valentinians long after the death of Ignatius, than any
other apology, I have as yet seen, for the securing of its
abode in them.

It is not a little burdensome to the thoughts of sober
and learned men, to consider how frequently, causelessly,
absurdly, in the midst of discourses quite of another nature
and tendency, the author of those epistles (or somebody for
him) breaks in upon the commendation of church officers,
bishops, and presbyters, exalting them with titles of honour to
the greatest potentates on earth, and comparing them to God
the Father and Son; whereas none of the sacred writers
that went before him, nor any of those good and holy men
who (as is supposed) followed after him, do hold the least
communion or society with him. 'Αναγκαῖον οὖν ἐστιν, ὅσα-
περ ποιεῖτε, ἄνευ τοῦ Ἐπισκόπου μηδὲν πράττειν ὑμᾶς· Epist.

ad Tral. whereunto is immediately subjoined that doctrine concerning deacons which will scarcely be thought to be exegetical of Acts vi. Δεῖ δὲ καὶ τοὺς διακόνους ὄντας μυστερῖων χριστοῦ Ἰησοῦ κατὰ πάντα τρόπον ἀρεσκειν, οὐ γὰρ βρωτῶν καὶ ποτῶν εἰσι διάκονοι, ἀλλὰ, &c. And Τὶ γὰρ ἔστιν ἐπίσκοπος· ἀλλ᾽ ἤ πάσης ἀρχῆς καὶ ἐξουσίας ἐπέκεινα πάντων κρατῶν. What the writer of this passage intended to make of a bishop well I know not: but thus he speaks of him, Epist. ad Magnes. Πρέπον οὖν ἐστὶ καὶ ὑμᾶς ὑπακούειν τῷ Ἐπισκόπῳ ὑμῶν· καὶ κατὰ μηδὲν αὐτῷ ἀντιλέγειν. Φοβερὸν γάρ ἐστι (as the apostle speaks concerning God, Heb. vi. 10.) τοιούτῳ ἀντιλέγειν. Thus indeed some would have it, who to help the matter, have farther framed such an episcopacy, as was never thought on by any in the days of Ignatius, as shall afterward be made evident. And in the same epistle this is somewhat uncouth and strange. Ἑνώθητε τῷ ἐπισκόπῳ, ὑποτασσόμενοι τῷ Θεῷ δι᾽ αὐτοῦ ἐν Χριστῷ ὥσπερ οὖν ὁ Κύριος ἄνευ τοῦ πατρὸς οὐδὲν ποιεῖ, οὐ δύναμαι γὰρ, φησὶ, ποιεῖν ἀπ᾽ ἐμαυτοῦ οὐδὲν. Οὕτω καὶ ὑμεῖς ἄνευ τοῦ Ἐπισκόπου μηδὲ πρεσβύτερος, μὴ διάκονος, μὴ Λαικὸς μηδέ τι φαινέσθω ὑμῖν εὔλογον παρὰ τὴν ἐκείνου γνώμην. Whether the Lord Christ hath bound any such burden upon the shoulders of the saints, I much question ; nor can I tell what to make of the comparison, between God the Father and the bishop, Christ and the rest of the church ; the whole sentence in word and matter, being most remote from the least countenance from the sacred writings. Epist. ad Philadel. οἱ πρεσβύτεροι καὶ οἱ Διάκονοι καὶ ὁ λοιπὸς κλῆρος, ἅμα παντὶ τῷ λαῷ καὶ τοῖς στρατιώταις, καὶ τοῖς ἄρχουσι καὶ τῷ Καίσαρι (well aimed however), τῷ ἐπισκόπῳ πειθαρχείτωσαν. The epistle to the church at Smyrna is full of such stuff, inserted without any occasion, order, coherence, or any colour to induce us to believe that it is part of the epistle as first written. One passage I may not omit. Τίμα φησὶν (υἱὲ) τὸν Θεὸν, καὶ βασιλέα· ἐγὼ δὲ φημὶ (in the language of our Saviour repudiating the Pharisees' corrupted glosses on the law), τίμα μέν τὸν Θεὸν ὡς αἴτιον τῶν ὅλων καὶ κύριον, ἐπίσκοπον δὲ ὡς ἀρχιερέα Θεοῦ εἰκόνα φοροῦντα, κατὰ μὲν τὸ ἄρχειν Θεοῦ κατὰ δὲ τὸ ἱεροτεύειν Χριστοῦ καὶ μετὰ τούτων τιμᾶν χρὴ καὶ βασιλέα. So Peter's mistake is corrected : his reasons follow, οὔτε γὰρ τὶς κρείττων, Θεοῦ, ἤ παραπλήσιος ἐν πᾶσι ταῖς οὐσιν· οὔτε δὲ ἐν ἐκκλησίᾳ ἐπισκόπου τὶ μεῖζον ἱερωμένου Θεῷ· ὑπὲρ τῆς τοῦ κόσμου παντὸς

σωτηρίας (as was Jesus Christ); and it is added, εἰ ὁ βασιλεύ-
σιν ἐπεγειρόμενος κολάσεως ἄξιος δικαίως γενήσεται, ὡς γε παρα-
λύων τὴν κοινὴν εὐνομίαν, πόσῳ δοκεῖτε χείρονος ἀξιωθήσεται
τιμωρίας ὁ ἄνευ ἐπισκόπου τὶ ποιεῖν προαιρούμενος, &c. ἱερωσύνη
γάρ ἐστι τὸ πάντων ἀγαθῶν ἐν ἀνθρώποις ἀναβεβηκὸς. How
well this suits the doctrine of Peter and Paul, the reader
will easily discern. Cæsar or the king is upon all accounts
thrust behind the bishop, who is said to be consecrated to
.God for the salvation of the world : him he is exhoited to
obey; and in express opposition to the Holy Ghost, the
bishop's name is thrust in between God and the king, as in
a way of pre-eminence above the latter. and to do any thing
without the bishop is made a far greater crime than to rise
up against the king. As this seems scaice to be the language of one, going upon an accusation to appear before the
emperor, so I am certain, it is most remote from the likeness
of any thing, that in this affair we are instructed in from the
Scripture. Plainly this language is the same with that of
the false impostor, Pseudo-Clemens, in his pretended apostolical constitutions. At this rate, or somewhat beyond it,
have you him ranting. Lib. 2. cap. 2. Ἐπίσκοπον Θεοῦ τύπον
ἔχειν ἐν ἀνθρώποις, τῶν πάντων ἄρχειν ἀνθρώπων, ἱερέων, βα-
σιλέων, ἀρχόντων, πατέρων, υἱῶν, διδασκάλων καὶ πάντων ὁμοῦ
τῶν ὑπηκόων. 'All popes, all sorts of persons whatever, priests,
kings, and princes, fathers and children, all under the feet
of this exemplar of God, and ruler over men.' A passage
which doubtless eminently interprets and illustrates that
place of Peter, 1 Epistle, ch. 5. 1—3. ' The elders that are
among you I exhort, who also am an elder, and a witness of
the sufferings of Christ, and also a partaker of the glory that
shall be revealed; feed the flock of God, which is among you;
taking the oversight thereof not by constraint, but willingly,
not for filthy lucre, but of a ready mind, neither as being
lords over God's heritage, but being examples to the flock.'.
But yet as if the man were stark mad, with worldly pride and
pomp, he afterward in the name of the holy apostles of
Jesus Christ, commands all the laity (forsooth) to honour,
love, and fear the bishop, ὡς Κύριον, ὡς δεσπότην, ὡς Ἀρχιερέα
Θεοῦ. Lib. 2. cap. 20. And that you may see whether the
.man drives, and what he aims at, after he hath set out his
bishop like an emperor, or an eastern king, in all pomp and

glory; he adds, τοὺς ἐπισκόπους ἄρχοντας ὑμῶν καὶ βασιλέας ἡγεῖσθαι, νομίζετε καὶ δασμοὺς ὡς βασιλεῦσι προσφέρετε. The paying of tribute to them as kings is the issue of these descriptions, that they may have wherewithal to maintain their pomp and greatness, according to the institution of our Lord Jesus Christ and his blessed apostles. But I shall not rake farther into this dunghill, nor shall I add any more instances of this kind out of Ignatius, but close in one insisted on by our doctor, for the proof of his episcopacy. Dissert. 2. cap. 25. 7. Saith he, Quartò, Τῷ ἐπισκόπῳ προσέχετε, ἵνα καὶ ὁ Θεὸς ὑμῖν. 'Αντίψυχος ἐγὼ τῶν ὑποτασσομένων τῷ ἐπισκόπῳ, πρεσβυτέροις καὶ διακόνοις. 'Episcopo attendite, ut et vobis Deus attendat. Ego animam meam libenter eorum loco substitui cuperem quod Anglice optime dicimus' (my soul for theirs), 'qui episcopo, presbyteris, et diaconis obsequuntur.' I hope I may without great difficulty obtain the doctor's pardon, that I dare not be so bold with my soul as to jeopard it in that manner, especially being not mine own to dispose of.

Upon these and many more the like accounts do the epistles seem to me, to be like the children that the Jews had by their strange wives; Neh. xiii. 'Who spake part the language of Ashdod, and part the language of the Jews.' That there are in them many footsteps of a gracious spirit, every way worthy of, and becoming the great and holy personage, whose they are esteemed, so there is evidently a mixture of the working of that worldly and carnal spirit, which in his days was not so let loose as in after-times. For what is there in the Scripture, what is in the genuine epistle of Clemens, that gives countenance to those descriptions of episcopacy, bishops, and the subjection to them, that are in those epistles (as now we have them) so insisted on? What titles are given to bishops? What sovereignty, power, rule, dominion, is ascribed to them? Is there any thing of the like nature in the writings of the apostles? In Clemens, the epistle of Polycarpus, &c. Or any unquestionable legitimate offspring of any of the first worthies of Christianity? Whence have they their three orders of bishops, presbyters, and deacons, upon the distinct observation of which so much weight is laid? Is there any one word, iota, tittle, or syllable, in the whole book of God giving countenance to any such

distinctions? Eph. iv. 8. We have pastors and teachers.
Rom. xii. 7, 8. 'Him that teacheth, him that exhorteth, him
that ruleth, and him that sheweth mercy;' Phil. i. 1. We
have bishops and deacons, and their institutions with the
order of it, we have at large expressed, 1 Tim. iii. 1, 2. 'Bishops and deacons,' without the interposition of any other
order whatever. Deacons we have appointed, Acts vii. and
elders, Acts xiv. 23. Those who are bishops we find called
presbyters, Tit. i. 5. 7. And those who are presbyters, we
find termed bishops, Acts xx. 28. So that deacons we know,
and bishops who are presbyters, or presbyters who are bishops we know; but bishops, presbyters, and deacons, as
three distinct orders in the church, from the Scripture we
know not. Neither did Clemens, in his epistle to the Corinthians, know of any more than we do, which a few instances will manifest: saith he, speaking of the apostles,
Κατὰ χώρας οὖν καὶ πόλεις κηρύσσοντες καθίστανον τὰς ἀπαρ-
χὰς αὐτῶν δοκιμάσαντες τῷ πνεύματι εἰς ἐπισκόπους καὶ διακόνους τῶν μελλόντων πιστεύειν· καὶ τοῦτο οὐ καινῶς ἐκ γὰρ δὴ
πολλῶν χρόνων ἐγέγραπτο περὶ ἐπισκόπων καὶ διακόνων, &c.
Bishops and deacons (as in the church at Philippi) this man
knows: but the third order he is utterly unacquainted withal.
And that the difference of this man's expressions, concerning church rulers, from those in the epistle under consideration, may the better appear; and his asserting of bishops
and presbyters to be one and the same, may the more clearly
be evidenced, I shall transcribe one other passage from him,
whose length I hope will be excused, from the usefulness of
it to the purpose in hand. Page 57, 58. Καὶ οἱ Ἀπόστολοί
ἡμῶν ἔγνωσαν διὰ τοῦ κυρίου ἡμῶν Ἰησοῦ Χριστοῦ, ὅτι ἔρις ἔσται
ἐπὶ τοῦ ὀνόματος τῆς ἐπισκοπῆς, διὰ ταύτην οὖν αἰτίαν, πρόγνωσιν εἰληφότες τελείαν κατέστασαν τοὺς προειρημένους, καὶ μεταξὺ
ἐπινομὴν δεδώκασιν ὅπως ἐὰν κοιμηθῶσιν διαδέξωνται ἕτεροι δε-
δοκιμασμένοι ἄνδρες τὴν λειτουργίαν αὐτῶν τοὺς οὖν κατασταθέν-
τας ὑπ' ἐκείνων, ἢ μεταξὺ ὑφ' ἑτέρων ἐλλογίμων ἀνδρῶν συνευ-
δοκησάσης τῆς ἐκκλησίας πάσης (for so it seems was the manner of the church in his days, that their officers were appointed
by the consent of the whole church), καὶ λειτουργήσαντας
ἀμέμπτως τῷ ποιμνίῳ τοῦ Χριστοῦ μετὰ ταπεινοφροσύνης, ἡσύχως,
καὶ ἀβαναύσως μεμαρτυρημένους τεπολλοῖς χρόνοις, ὑπὸ πάντων
τούτους οὐ δικαίως νομίζομεν ἀποβάλλεσθαι τῆς λειτουργίας, ἁμαρτία

γὰρ οὐ μικρὰ ἡμῖν ἔσται, ἔαν τοὺς ἀμέμπτως καὶ ὁσίως προσενέγ·
κύντας τὰ δῶρα τῆς ἐπισκοπῆς ἀποβάλωμεν. Μακάριοι οἱ προο-
δοιπορήσαντες πρεσβύτεροι (or the bishops of whom he was
speaking), οἵτινες ἔγκαρπον καὶ τελείαν ἔσχον τὴν ἀνάλυσιν, &c.
And sundry other discoveries are there, in that epistle, of the
like nature. It is not my design, nor purpose, to insist upon
the parity of bishops and presbyters, or rather the identity
of office denoted, by sundry appellations from these and the
like places: this work is done to the full by Blondellus,
that our labour in this kind (were that the purpose in hand)
is prevented. He that thinks the arguments of that learned
man to this purpose are indeed answered thoroughly, and removed by D. H. in his fourth dissertation, where he proposes them to consideration, may one day think it needful
to be able to distinguish between words and things.   That
Clemens owns in a church but two sorts of officers, the first
whereof he calls sometimes bishops sometimes presbyters,
the other deacons, the doctor himself doth not deny.

That in the judgment of Clemens no more were instituted in the church is no less evident. And this carries the
conviction of its truth so clearly with it, that Lombard himself confesseth, ' Hoc solos ministrorum duos ordines ecclesiam primitivam habuisse, et de his solis præceptum apostoli
nos habere;' lib. 4. Sen. D. 24. It seems, moreover, that
those bishops and deacons in those days (as was observed)
were appointed to the office, by and with the consent of the
people, or whole body of the church : no less do those words
import, συνευδοκούσης τῆς ἐκκλησίας πάσης. Our doctor indeed
renders these words, ' Applaudente aut congratulante ecclesia tota;' and adds ('satis pro imperio) nihil hic de acceptatione totius ecclesiæ, sine qua episcopos et diaconos ab apostolis et apostolicis viris constitutos non esse, ex hoc loco
concludit Blondellus, quasi qui ex Dei jussu et approbatione
constituebantur populi etiam acceptatione indigere putandi
essent;' Dissert, 4. cap. 7, 8. 10. And who dares take that
confidence upon him, as to affirm any more, what so great a
doctor hath denied? Though the scope of the place, the nature of the thing, and first most common sense of the word
here used, being willingly to consent (as it is also used in
the Scripture for the most part; Acts viii. 1. 1 Cor. vii. 12.)
to a thing to be done, or to the doing of it, yet here it must

be taken to applaud or congratulate, or what else our doctor
pleases, because he will have it so. Ἐλλόγιμοι ἄνδρες also,
must be ' Viri apostolici,' men with apostolical or extraordinary power, when they are only the choice men of the church,
where such a constitution of officers is had, that are intended,
because it is our doctor's purpose to have the words so rendered. ' Ex jussu Dei et approbatione,' is added, as though
any particular command or approbation of God were intimated, for the constitution of the bishops and deacons mentioned, beyond the institution of the Lord Jesus Christ, that
elders should be ordained in every church, because this is
(it seems) to be exclusive wholly of the consent of the people, as any way needful or required to their constitution:
which yet as it is practically false, no such thing being·
mentioned by Clemens, who recounteth the ways and means,
whereby officers were continued in the church even after the
decease of the apostles, and those first ordained by them to
that holy employment, so also is it argumentatively weak
and unconcluding. God appointed, designed Saul to be
king, approving of his so being, and yet he would have the
people come together to choose him. So also was it in the
case of David. Though the apostles in the name and the
authority of God, appointed the deacons of the church at
Jerusalem, yet they would have the whole church ' look out
among themselves the men to be appointed.' And that the
ordaining of the elders was with the people's election, Acts
xiv. 23. it will ere long be manifested, that neither our doctor nor any of his associates have as yet disproved. This poor
thing the people, being the peculiar people of Christ, the
heritage of God and holy temple unto him, &c. will one
day be found to be another manner of thing, than many of
our great doctors have supposed. But he informs us, cap. 4.
sect. 3. from that testimony which we cited before, that the
apostles in the appointment of bishops and deacons (for so
the words expressly are) are said τῷ πνεύματι δοκιμάσαι, i. e.
saith he, ' Revelationibus edoctos esse, quibus demum hæc
dignitas communicanda esset;' that is, that they appointed
those, whom God revealed to them in extraordinary manner to be so ordained, and this is the meaning of τῷ πνεύματι
δοκιμάζοντες, and why so? The Holy Ghost orders concerning the appointment of deacons δοκιμαζέσθωσαν πρῶτον,

1 Tim. iii. 10. That those who are to be taken into office and power in the church had need first to be tried and approved, is granted. And this work the apostles give to the multitude of the church; Acts vi. Where yet after the people's election, and the apostles' approbation, and the trial of both, one that was chosen is supposed to have proved none of the best. And yet of him and them, are the apostles said by Clemens that they did, τῷ πνεύματι δοκιμάσαι. But how shall it be made to appear that *Spiritu probantes*, trying or proving by the Spirit, or spiritually proving them to try whether they were able ministers of the New Testament, not of the letter, but of the Spirit, proving them by that Spirit which was promised unto ' them, to lead them into all truth,' must needs signify they were taught whom they should appoint by immediate revelation. To prove by the Spirit, or spiritually, the persons that are to be made ministers, or bishops, is to have their names revealed to us. Stephen is said to speak, ἐν τῷ πνεύματι; Acts vi. 10. And Paul purposed ἐν τῷ πνεύματι; Acts xix. 21. And we are said to serve God, ἐν τῷ πνεύματι; Gal. v. 5. And to make supplication ἐν τῷ πνεύματι; Eph. vi. 18. With many more expressions of the like nature. Does all this relate to immediate revelation, and are all things done thereby which we are said to do in the Spirit? Before we were instructed in this mystery, and were informed that δοκιμάσαντες τῷ πνεύματι, did signify to be ' taught by revelation;' we had thought that the expression of doing any thing τῷ πνεύματι had manifested the assistance, guidance, and direction, which for the doing of it we receive, by the holy and blessed Spirit of God, promised unto us, and bestowed on, in, and through the Lord Jesus Christ. Yea, but he adds, that it is also spoken of the apostles. πρόγνωσιν *praecognitionem* (i. e.) *revelationem* εἰληφότες τελείαν, they appointed them bishops and deacons, by the helps and presence of the Spirit with them, the apostles examined, tried those who were to be appointed bishops, so obtaining and receiving a perfect foreknowledge or knowledge of them before their admission into office. This also expresses revelation (πρόγνωσιν εἰληφότες), upon trial it was revealed unto them, and so must any thing else be allowed to be, that our doctor will have to be so, now he is asserting to that purpose. But had the Ἑλλόγιμοι ἄνδρες, who ap-

pointed bishops and deacons after the apostles' time, had they also this special revelation? Or may they not be said, δοκιμάσαι τῷ πνεύματι. If not, how will you look upon them under the notion of ἐλλογίμων ανδρῶν, who neglected so great a duty: if they did, let us know when this way of constituting church officers by immediate revelation ceased; and what was afterward took up in the room thereof; and who they were that first proceeded on another account, and on what authority they did? There are a generation of men in the world, will thank the doctor for this insinuation, and will tie knots upon it, that will trouble him to loose.

Before we return, let us look but a little farther, and we shall have a little more light given us, into what was the condition and power of the people in the church in the days of Clemens, speaking of them who occasioned the division and schism in the church of Corinth, or them about whose exaltation into office, or dejection from it, that sad difference fell out; he gives them this advice: Τίς οὖν ἐν ὑμίν γενναῖος; τίς εὐσπλαγχνος; τὶς πεπληρωμένος ἀγάπης, εἰπάτω, εἰ δι' ἐμὲ στάσις καὶ ἔρις καὶ σχίσματα ἐκχωρῶ ἄπειμι οὗ ἐαν βούληϑε καὶ ποιῶ τὰ προστασσόμενα ὑπὸ τοῦ πλήθους, μόνον τὸ ποίμνιον τοῦ Χριστοῦ εἰρηνευέτω μετὰ τῶν καϑεσταμένων πρεσβυτέρων. It seems the πλῆϑος, the multitude, or the people, were not such poor inconsiderable things as they are reported to be, when he advises them to stop and stay the sedition, by yielding obedience to the things by them appointed and commanded. If it were in itself evil, disorderly, and not according to the mind of Christ, that the people should order and appoint things in the church, it had been simply evil for Clemens, to have advised any to yield obedience unto things by them so appointed. Where is now Ignatius's ὑποτάσσεσθε τῷ ἐπισκόπῳ et χωρὶς, &c. Even those who are contending about rule and government in the church, are advised to stand to the determination of the people, and to cry, τὰ προστασσόμενα ἀπὸ τοῦ πλήθους ποιῶμεν. This is also insisted on by Blondellus, who thence argues 'potestatem plebis Circa Sacra.' Disser. 5. cap. 8. sect. 4. 'Ad verba hæc;' saith our doctor, 'prodigii instar est quod notandum duxit Dav. Blondellus (potestatem Plebis Circa Sacra) (de qua tandem integram dissertationem elucubravit) artificiis quibuscunque asserturus. Hic (inquit) nos monet Clemens fideles etiam de episcopatu aut presbyterio contendentes, non ab episcopi singulari καὶ ὑπερέχοντος nutu, sed a multitudinis præceptis pependisse.' But let not our doctor be angry, nor cry out so fast of prodigies; a little time will manifest, that many things may not be prodigious, which yet are contrary to sundry of his conceptions and apprehensions. I cannot but acknowledge him to be provoked; but withal must say, that I have found very commonly, that reasons ushered in by such loud clamours, have in examination proved to have stood in need of some such noises, as might fright men from the consideration of them. What is in the next sections set up to shield the children of episcopacy from being affrighted with this prodigy, may perhaps be of more efficacy thereunto, than the exclamations before mentioned; he therefore proceeds, sect. 5. ' Certe,' saith he, ' si serio rem ageret Da. Blondellus de presbyteris suis (non de episcopis nostris) actum plane et triumphatum erit, nec enim ab universo aliquo presbyterorum collegio, quod ille tam afflictim ardet, sed a multitudinis solius Arbitrio, tum contendentes de episcopo, tum fideles omnes Corinthios pependisse æque concludendum erit.' If any man in the world hath manifested more desperate affection towards presbytery, than this doctor hath done towards episcopacy, for my part solus habeto. But though neither Clemens nor Blondellus speak any one word about the ordering of things, ' multitudinis solius arbitrio,' yet here is that said by them both, as is sufficiently destructive, not only to the episcopacy the doctor contends for, as a thing wholly inconsistent with the power and liberty here granted the people, but of any such presbytery also, as shall undertake the ordering and disposing of things in the church of God, without the consent and concurrent suffrage of the people. Such a presbytery it seems Blondellus does not defend. But yet neither the doctor's outcry as at a prodigy, nor this retortion upon presbytery, is any answer to the testimony of Clemens, nor indeed is there the least possible reflection upon an orderly gospel presbytery in any church, and over it, by what Clemens here professeth to be the power of the people, all the appearance of any such things is from the term ' solius,' foisted into the discourse of Blondellus by the doctor, in his taking of it up to retort at. Clemens in the very next words secures us from any thought, that all things depended 'a multitudinis solius arbitrio.' His very next words are, μόνον τὸ ποίμνιον τοῦ Χριστοῦ εἰρη-νευέτω μετὰ τῶν καθεσταμένων πρεσβυτέρων. Our doctors and masters having stuffed their imaginations with the shape and lineament of that hierarchical fabric, which the craft, policy, subtilty, avarice, pride, and ambition, of many ages successively, had formed and framed according to the pattern they saw in the mount of the world, and the governments therein, upon the first hearing of a church, a flock of Christ, walking in orderly subjection to their own elders, concurring with them, and consenting to them, in their rule and government, instantly as men amazed, cry out a prodigy. It is not imaginable into what ridiculous, contemptible miscarriages, pride, prejudice, and selfulness do oftentimes betray men, otherwise of good abilities in their ways, and very commendable industry.

But section the sixth; the doctor comes closer, and gives his reason why this testimony of Clemens is not of any efficacy to the purpose in hand: saith he, 'At quis (sodes) a fidelibus de Episcopatu (ut vis) contra ipsos ab apostolis constitutos episcopos contendentibus; quis a populo contra principem suum tumultus ciente; quis verbis ad retundendum seditionem ad plebem factis, argumenta ad authoritatem populo adjudicandum principi derogandum duci posse existimavit?' Though many words follow in the next section, yet this is all of answer that is given to this signal testimony of Clemens. I know the doctor, for the most part, meets not only with favourable readers, but also partial admirers; or else certainly his exclamation would scarce pass for an invincible argument, nor such rhetorical diversions as this, be esteemed solid answers. There is not by Blondellus any argument taken from the faithful's tumultuating against the bishops (that ' if appointed by the apostles,' which is thrust in, taken for the persons of those bishops, is against the express testimony of Clemens in this epistle), nor from the people's seditiously rebelling against their prince, nor from any word spoken to the people to repress their sedition; neither was any thing of this nature urged in the least by Blondellus; nor is there any colour given to such a collection from any thing in the words cited from the epistle, or the context of them. It is the advice of the church of Rome to the persons (whether already in office, or aspiring thereunto) about whom the contention and division was in the church of Corinth, that is insisted on. It is not the words nor plea of them who were in disorder; there is not any reprehension given to the body of the church, the multitude, or people, who are supposed to tumultuate, to quiet them, but a direction given (as was said) by the church of Rome to the persons that occasioned the difference, how to behave themselves so, that a timely issue might be put to the division of the church. To this end are they advised to observe the προστάγματα, the orders, precepts,. decrees, or appointments of the multitude, as (from Acts xv.) the body of the church is called. It is not, that they should yield to their tumultuating, but to yield obedience to their orderly precepts. Τὰ προστασσό-μενα ὑπὸ τοῦ πλήθους, are by him approved; and had it not been lawful for them, with the presbyters προστάττειν in the affairs of the church, Clemens writing this epistle to the whole church, could not possibly have led them into a greater snare.

It is a sad thing to consider the pitiful entanglements and snares that some men run into, who will undertake to make good what they have once engaged for, let what will come against them.

To return then; it is evident, that in the time of Clemens, there were but two sorts of officers in the church, bishops and deacons; whereas the epistles of Ignatius do precisely in every place where any mention is made of them, as there is upon occasions, and upon none at all, insist on three orders distinct, in name and things. With Clemens it is not so. Those whom he calls bishops in one place, the very same persons he immediately calls presbyters (after the example of Paul; Acts xx. 28. and Tit. i. 5. 7.) And plainly asserts episcopacy to be the office of presbyters. ἁμαρτία, saith he, οὐ μικρὰ ἡμῖν ἔσται ἐὰν τοὺς ἀμέμπτους, καὶ προσενεγκόντας τὰ δῶρα τῆς ἐπισκοπῆς ἀποβάλωμεν, μακάριοι οἱ προοδοιπερήσαντες πρεσβύτεροι, viz. Because they were in no danger to be cast from their episcopacy. And whereas the fault which he reproves in the church of Corinth, is their division, and want of due subjection to their spiritual governors, according to the order which Christ hath appointed in all the churches of the saints, he affirms plainly that those governors were the presbyters of the church: αἰσχρὰ, saith he, καὶ λίαν αἰσχρὰ, καὶ ἀνάξια τῆς ἐν Χρῖστῳ ἀγωγῆς ἀκούεσθαι τὴν βεβαιοτάτην ἀρχαίαν Κορινθίων ἐκκλησίαν, δι᾽ ἐν ἦ δυὸ πρόσωπα στασιάζειν πρὸς τοὺς πρεσβυτέρους. And in all places throughout the whole epistle, writing (ἐκκλησία τοῦ Θεοῦ παροικούσῃ κύρινθον) to that particular church of Corinth, the saints dwelling there, walking in the order and fellowship of the gospel, where he treats of those things, he still intimates a plurality of presbyters in the church (as there may, nay there ought to be in every single congregation; Acts xx. 28.) without the least intimation of any singular person, promoted upon any account whatever above his fellows. So in the advice given to the persons who occasioned the division before mentioned; μόνον τὸ ποίμνιον τοῦ Χριστοῦ εἰρηνευέτω, μετὰ τῶν καθισταμένων πρεσβυτέρων. Had there been a singular bishop at Corinth, much more a metropolitan, such as our doctor speaks him to have been, it had been impossible that he should be thus passed by in silence.

But the doctor gives you a double answer to this observation, with the several parts whereof, I doubt not but that he makes himself merry, if he can suppose that any men are so wedded to his dictates, as to give them entertainment: for indeed they are plainly jocular. But learned men must have leave sometimes to exercise their fancies, and to sport themselves with their own imaginations.

1. Then, for the mention that is made of many presbyters in the church of Corinth, to whom Clemens, in the name of the church of Rome, exhorts to give all due respect, honour, obedience. He tells you that by the church of Corinth, all the churches of Achaia are meant and intended. The epistle is directed only τῇ ἐκκλησία Θεοῦ παροικούσῃ Κόρινθον, without the least intimation of any other church or churches. The difference it is written about, was occasioned by one or two persons in that church only: it is that church alone that is exhorted to order, and due subjection to their elders. From the beginning to the end of the epistle, there is not one word, apex, or tittle, to intimate the designation of it, to any church or churches beyond the single church of Corinth: or that they had any concernment in the difference

spoken to. The fabric of after-ages lies so close to the doctor's imagination, that there is no entrance for the true frame of the primitive church of Christ; and therefore every thing must be wrested, and apportioned to the conceit of such an episcopacy as he hath entertained. Whereas he ought to crop off both head and heels of his own imagination, and the episcopacy of the latter days, which he too dearly affects; he chooseth rather to stretch and torture the ancient government of the church, that it may seem to answer the frame presently contended for. But let us a little attend to the doctor's learned arguments; whereby he endeavours to make good his assertion.

1. He tells you that Corinth was the chief city of Achaia: the metropolis (in a political sense and acceptation of the word) of Greece, where the proconsul had his residence: Diss. 5. cap. 2. sect. 3. Let us grant this to our learned doctor, least we should find nothing to gratify him withal; what then will follow? Hence, saith he, it will follow, sect. 4. that this epistle which was sent, 'Ecclesiæ παροικούσῃ Κόρινϑον, non ad unius civitatis ecclesiam, sed ad omnes totius Achaiæ Christianos, per singulas civitates et regiones, sub episcopis aut præfectis suis ubique collocatas missa existimetur.' But pray doctor why so? We poor creatures who are not so sharp-sighted, as to discern a metropolitan archbishop at Corinth, of whom all the bishops in Greece were dependant, nor can find any instituted church in the Scripture, or in Clemens, of one denomination, beyond a single congregation, cannot but think, that all the strength of this consectary, from the insinuation of such a state of things, in the church of God, is nothing but a pure begging of the thing in question, which will never be granted upon such terms.

Yea, but he adds, sect. 5. That 'Paul wrote his epistle not only to the church of Corinth, but also to all the churches of Achaia, therefore Clemens did so also.' At first view this argument seems not very conclusive, yea appears indeed very ridiculous: the enforcement of it, which ensues, may perhaps give new life and vigour to it. How then is it proved that Paul wrote not only to the church of Corinth, but to all them in Achaia also? Why saith he in the 2 Epistle, 1 chap. 1. verse, it is so expressed; he writes, τῇ ἐκκλησίᾳ τοῦ ϑεοῦ τῇ

ὄυση ἐν Κορίνϑῳ, σὺν τοῖς ἁγίοις πᾶσιτοῖς οὖσιν ἐν ὅλη τῇ Αχαίᾳ.
Very good ! It is indisputably evident that Paul wrote his
second epistle to the church at Corinth, and all the rest of
Achaia, for he expressly affirms himself so to do, and for the
first epistle, it is directed not only to the church of Corinth,
1. chap. 2. verse; but also πᾶσι τοῖς ἐπικαλουμένοις τὸ ὄνομα τοῦ
κυρίου ἡμῶν Ἰησοῦ χριστοῦ ἐν παντὶ τόπῳ; that is, saith our
doctor, in the whole region of Achaia. So indeed says the
doctor's great friend Grotius, to whom he is beholden for
more than one rare notion. I say it not in any way of any
reproach to the doctor, only I cannot but think, his careful
warding of himself against the thoughts of men that he
should be beholden to Grotius, doth exceedingly unbecome
the doctor's gravity and self-denial. This is complained of
by some who have tried it in reference to his late comment
on the Revelation. And in this dissertation, he is put by his
own thoughts (I will not say guilty), to an apology, cap. 1.
sect. 24. 'Qua in re suffragium suum tulisse Hugonem
Grotium τὸν πάνυ ex annotationibus posthumis, nuper editis,
et postquam hæc omnia Typographo transcripta essent, cur-
sim perlectis edoctum gratulor.' Let not the reader think
that Doctor Ham. had transmitted his papers full of rare conjectures to the printer, before Grotius's Annotations upon the
Revelations were published, but only before he had read them.
The doctor little thinks what a fly this is in his pot of oint-
ment, nor how indecent with all impartial men, such apologies,
subservient to a frame of spirit in bondage to a man's own
esteem and reputation, appear to be; but let this pass: and
let the saints that call upon the name of Jesus Christ in
every place, be the saints in every part of Achaia, though
the epistle itself (written indeed upon occasion taken from
the church of Corinth, yet) was given by inspiration from
God, for the use not only of all the saints in the whole world,
at that time wherein it was written, but of all those who
were to believe in any part or place of the world to the end
thereof; although the assertion of it be not built on any tolerable conjecture, but may be rejected with the same facility
wherewith it is tendered; what now will hence ensue? Why
hence it follows that Clemens also wrote his epistle to all
the churches in Achaia. Very good? Paul writing an epistle entitled chiefly to the Corinthians, expressly and ῥητῶς

directs it to the saints or churches of Achaia, yea to all that
call upon the name of God in every place, so that his epistle
being of catholic concernment, is not to be confined to the
church of Corinth only, although most of the particular
things mentioned in that epistle related only to that particular church; therefore, Clemens directing his epistle to the
church of Corinth only, not once mentioning nor insinuating
an intention of extending it to any other, handling in it only
the peculiar concernment of that church, and a difference
about one or two persons therein, must be supposed to have
written to all the churches of Achaia. And if such arguments as these, will not prove episcopacy to be of apostolical
constitution, what will prevail with men so to esteem it?
' Si Pergama dextra defendi possent, etiam hac defensa fuissent.' And this is the cause of naming many elders, or
presbyters in one church. For my part I suppose the doctor might more probably have adhered to a former conjecture
of his, Dissert. 4. cap. 10. sect. 9. Concerning two sundry
different churches, where were distinct officers in the same
city : ' Primo,' saith he, ' respondeo non usque quaque verum
est, quod pro concesso sumitur, quamvis enim in una ecclesia aut cœtu plures simul episcopi nunquam fuerint' (pray
except them mentioned, Acts xx. 28. and those, Acts xiv. 23.)
' nihil tamen obstare quin in eadem civitate duó aliquando
cœtus disterminati fuerint.' He might, I say, with more
show of probability have abode by this observation, than to
have rambled over all Greece, to relieve himself against his
adversaries. But yet neither would this suffice. What use
may, or will be, made of this concession shall elsewhere be
manifested. But the doctor hath yet another answer to this
multiplication of elders, and the mention of them with deacons, with the eminent identity that is between them and
bishops through the whole epistle, the same persons being
unquestionably intended in respect of the same office, by
both these appellations. Now this second answer is founded
upon the supposition of the former; (a goodly foundation!)
namely, that the epistle under consideration was written and
sent not to the church of Corinth only, but to all the churches
of Achaia, of which Corinth was the metropolitan.

Now this second answer is, that the elders or presbyters
here mentioned, were properly those whom he calls bishops,

diocesans: men of a third rank and order above deacons
and presbyters in the church-administrations and government. And for those who are properly called presbyters,
there were then none in the church, to give colour to this
miserable evasion, Dissert. 4. chap. 10, 11. He discourseth
about the government and ordering of church affairs .by bishops and deacons. In some churches that were small, not
yet formed or completed, nor come to perfection at the first
planting of them: how well this is accommodated to the
church of Corinth which Clemens calls, βεβαιοτάτην καὶ
ἀρχαίαν: and which himself would have to be a metropolitical
church, being confessedly great, numerous; furnished with
great and large gifts, and abilities seen with half an eye.
How ill also this shift is accommodated to help in the case
for whose service it was first invented, is no less evident.
It was to save the sword of Phil. i. 1. from the throat of
the episcopacy he contendeth for; that epistle is directed
to the saints or church at Philippi, with the bishops and
deacons. Two things do here trouble our doctor: 1. The
mention of more bishops than one at Philippi. 2. The knitting together of bishops and deacons, as the only two orders
in the church, bringing down episcopacy one degree at least
from that height whereto he would exalt it. For the first of
these, he tells you that Philippi was the metropolitan church
of the province of Macedonia, that the rest of the churches,
which had every one their several bishops (diocesan we
must suppose) were all comprised in the mentioning of Philippi: so that though the epistle be precisely directed τοῖς
ἁγίοις τοῖς οὖσιν ἐν Φιλίπποις, yet the bishops that were with
them, must be supposed to be bishops of the whole province
of Macedonia; because the church of Philippi was the metropolitan: the whole country must have been supposed to
be converted (and who that knows any thing of antiquity
will dispute that), and so divided with diocesans, as England of late was; the archbishop's see being at Philippi: but
how came it then to pass, that here is mention made of bishops and deacons only, without any one word of a third
order, or rank of men distinct from them called presbyters
or elders? To this he answers, 2dly, That when the church
was first planted, before any great number was converted,
or any fit to be made presbyters, there was only those two

orders instituted, bishops and deacons; so that this church at Philippi seems to have been a metropolitical infant. The truth is, if ever the doctor be put upon reconciling the contradictions of his answers one to another, not only in this but almost in every particular he deals withal (an entanglement which he is thrown into, by his bold and groundless conjectures), he will find it to be as endless as fruitless: but it is not my present business to interpose in his quarrels, either with himself or presbytery. As to the matter under consideration, I desire only to be resolved in these few queries.

1. If there were in the times of Clemens no presbyters in the churches, not in so great and flourishing a church as that of Corinth; and if all the places in the Scripture, where there is mention of elders, do precisely intend bishops, in a distinction from them who are only deacons and not bishops also, as he asserts, when, by whom, by what authority were elders, who are only so inferior to bishops, peculiarly so termed, instituted, and appointed in the churches? And how it comes to pass that there is such express mention made of the office of deacons, and the continuance of it, none at all of elders, who are acknowledged to be superior to them, and on whose shoulders in all their own churches, lies the great weight and burden of all ecclesiastical administration. As we say of their bishops, so shall we of any presbyter, not instituted and appointed by the authority of Jesus Christ in the church, let them 'go to the place from whence they came.'

2. I desire the doctor to inform me, in what sense he would have me to understand him: Disser. 2. cap. 29. 21, 22. where he disputes that those words of Jerome, ' Antequam studia in religione fierent, et diceretur in populis, ego sum Pauli, ego Cephæ, communi presbyterorum consensu ecclesiæ gubernabantur,' are to be understood of the times of the apostles, when the first schism was in the church of Corinth, when it seems that neither then nor a good while after, there was any such thing as presbyters in the church of Corinth, nor in any other church as we can hear of. As also to tell us whether all those presbyters, were bishops properly so called, distinct from elders who are only so, out of whom one man is chosen to be a bishop properly so called. To these inquiries I shall only add,

3. That whereas in the Scripture, we find clearly but

of two sorts of church-officers mentioned, as also in this epistle of Clemens; the third that was afterward introduced, be it what it will, or fall on whom it will, that we oppose. This (saith the doctor) is that of presbytery. Give us churches instituted according to the word of Christ, give us in every church, bishops and deacons (rather than we will quarrel give us a bishop and deacons), let those bishops attend the particular flock, over which they are appointed, preaching the word and administering the holy ordinances of the gospel, in and to their own flock; and I dare undertake for all the contenders for presbytery in this nation, and much more for the independents, that there shall be an end of this quarrel; that they will not strive with the doctor, nor any living, for the introduction of any third sort of persons (though they should be called presbyters) into church office and government.   Only this I must add, that the Scripture more frequently terms this second sort of men elders and presbyters, than it doth bishops; and that word having been appropriated to a third sort peculiarly, we desire leave of the doctor and his associates, if we also most frequently call them so, no ways declining the other appellation of bishops, so that it may be applied to signify the second, and not third rank of men.   But of this whole business, with the nature, constitution, and frame of the first churches; and the sad mistakes, that men have by their own prejudices been engaged into, in this delineation of them, a fuller opportunity (if God will) may ere long be afforded.

To return then to our Ignatius? Even upon this consideration of the difference, that is between the epistles ascribed to him, and the writings of one of the same time with him, or not long before him, as to their language and expression about church order and officers, it is evident that there hath been ill-favoured tampering with them, by them who thought to avail themselves of his authority, for the asserting of that which never came into his mind.

As I intimated before, I have not insisted on any of those things, nor do on them altogether, with the like that may be added, as a sufficient foundation for the total rejection of those epistles which go under the name of Ignatius.   There is in some of them a sweet and gracious spirit of faith, love, holiness, zeal for God, becoming so excellent and holy a

witness of Christ as he was, evidently breathing and working.   Neither is there any need at all, that for the defence
of our hypothesis concerning the non-institution of any
church-officer whatever, relating to more churches in his
office, or any other church, than a single particular congregation, that we should so reject them.   For although many
passages, usually insisted on, and carefully collected by D.
H. for the proof of such an episcopacy, to have been received by them of old as is now contended for, are exceedingly remote from the way and manner of the expressions of
those things, used by the divine writers, with them also that
followed after, both before, as hath been manifested, and
some while after, the days of Ignatius, as might be farther
clearly evinced, and are thrust into the series of the discourse with such an incoherent impertinency, as proclaims
an interpolation; being some of them, also, very ridiculous,
and so foolishly hyperbolical, that they fall very little short
of blasphemies, yet there are expressions in all, or most of
them, that will abundantly manifest, that he who was their
author (whoever he was) never dreamt of any such fabric
of church-order as in after-ages was insensibly received.
Men who are full of their own apprehensions, begotten in
them by such representations of things, as either their desirable presence hath exhibited to their mind, or any after-
prejudicate presumption hath possessed them with, are apt,
upon the least appearance of any likeness unto that church
they fancy, to imagine that they see the face and all the
lineaments thereof, when upon due examination it will be
easily discovered, that there is not indeed the least resemblance, between what they find in, and what they bring to,
the authors, in and of whom they make their inquiry; the
Papists having hatched and owned by several degrees, that
monstrous figment of transubstantiation (to instance among
many in that abomination), a folly, destructive to whatever
is in us, as being living creatures, men or Christians, or
whatever by sense, reason, or religion, we are furnished withal, offering violence to us in what we hear, in what we see
with our eyes, and look upon, in what our hands do handle,
and our palates taste, breaking in upon our understandings
with vagrant flying forms, self-subsisting accidents, with as
many express contradictions on sundry accounts, as the

nature of things is capable of relation unto, attended with
more gross idolatry than that of the poor naked Indians, who
fall down and worship a piece of red cloth; or of those who
first adore their gods, and then correct them; do yet upon
the discovery of any expressions among the ancients, which
they now make use of, quite to another end and purpose,
than they did who first ventured upon them, having minds
filled with their own abominations, presently cry out, and
triumph, as if they had found the whole fardle of the mass,
in its perfect dress, and their breaden god in the midst
of it.   It is no otherwise in the case of episcopacy: men of
these latter generations, from what they saw in present
being, and that usefulness of it to all their desires and interests, having entertained thoughts of love to it, and delight in it, searching antiquity, not to instruct them in the
truth, but to establish their prejudicate opinion received by
tradition from their fathers, and to consult them with whom
they have to do, whatever expressions they find, or can hear
of, that fall in, as to the sound of words, with what is now
insisted upon, instantly they cry out, *Vicimus Io Pæan!*
What a simple generation of presbyters and independents
have we, that are ignorant of all antiquity, or do not understand what they read and look upon.   Hence if we will not
believe that in Ignatius's days there were many parish
churches with their single priests, in subordination to a diocesan bishop, either immediately or by the interposed power
of a *chore-episcopus*, and the like; and those diocesans again
in the precincts of provinces, laid in a due subjection to their
metropolitans, who took care of them, as they of their parish
priests, every individual church having no officer but a presbyter, every diocesan church having no presbyter but a bishop, and every metropolitan church having neither presbyter nor bishop properly related unto it, as such, but an archbishop, we are worse than infidels; truly I cannot but wonder
whether it doth not sometimes enter into these men's thoughts
to apprehend, how contemptible they are in their proofs, for
the fathering of such an ecclesiastical distribution of governors and government, as undeniably lackeyed after the
civil divisions and constitutions of the times and places,
wherein it was introduced, upon those holy persons whose
souls never once entered into the secrets thereof.

Thus fares it with our doctor, and his Ignatius; οὐκ εἶδεν, ἀλλ᾽ ἐδόκησεν ἰδεῖν διὰ νύκτα σελήνην; I shall only crave leave to say to him as Augustus of Quintilius Varus, upon the loss of his legions in Germany under his command; ' Quintili Vare redde legiones : Domine doctor redde ecclesias.' Give us the churches of Christ such as they were in the days of the apostles, and down to Ignatius, though before that time (if Hegesippus may be believed) somewhat deflowered; and our contest about church-officers and government will be nearer at an end than perhaps you will readily imagine. Give us a church, all whose members are holy, called, sanctified, justified, living stones, temples for the Holy Ghost, saints, believers, united to Christ the head by the Spirit that is given to them and dwelleth in them, a church whose πλῆθος, is ὅπου ἂν φανῇ ὁ ἐπίσκοπος, that doth nothing by its members apart, that appertains to church-order, but when it is gathered ἐπὶ τὸ αὐτο; a church that being so gathered together, in one place, σπουδάζει πάντα πράσσειν ἐν ὁμονοίᾳ θεοῦ, προκαθημένου τοῦ ἐπισκόπου, acting in church things, in its whole body under the rule and presidence of its officers. A church walking in order, and not as some who ἐπίσκοπον μὲν καλοῦσιν, χῶρις δὲ αὐτοῦ πάντα πράσσουσιν (of whom saith Ignatius ὅι τοιοῦτοι οὐκ εὐσυνείδητοι μὲν εἶναι φαίνονται, Διὰ μὲν τὸ μὴ βεβαίως κατ᾽ ἐντολὴν συναθροίζεσθαι, such as calling the bishops to the assemblies, yet do all things without him (the manner of some in our days), he supposeth not to keep the assemblies according to the command of Christ); give us, I say, such a church; and let us come to them when they are πάντες ἐπὶ τὸ αὐτὸ, ἐν τῇ προσευχῇ ἅμα συναχθέντες, such as the churches in the days of Ignatius appear to have been, and are so rendered in the quotations taken from his epistles by the learned doctor, for the confirmation of episcopacy; and, as I said before, the contest of this present digression, will quickly draw to an issue. Being unwilling to go too far out of my way, I shall not,

1. Consider the severals instanced in, for the proof of episcopacy by the doctor. Seeing undeniably the interpretation must follow, and be proportioned by the general issue of that state of the church, in the days wherein those epistles were writ, or are pretended so to be; if that appear to

be such as I have mentioned, I presume the doctor himself
will confess, that his witnesses speak not one word to his
business, for whose confirmation he doth produce them.
Nor,

2. Shall I insist upon the degeneration of the institutions and appointments of Jesus Christ, concerning
church administrations in the management of the succeeding churches, as principled and spirited by the operative
and efficacious mystery of iniquity, occasioned and advantaged by the accommodation of ecclesiastical affairs to the
civil distributions and allotments of the political state of
things in those days; nor,

3. Insist much farther on the exceeding dissimilitude,
and unconformity that is between the expressions concerning church-officers and affairs in these epistles (whence-
ever they come), and those in the writings of unquestionable credit, immediately before and after them, as also the
utter silence of the Scripture in those things, wherewith they
so abound. The epistle of Clemens, of which mention was
made before, was written for the composing and quieting of
a division and distemper that was fallen out in the church
of Corinth. Of the cause of that dissension that then mi-
serably rent that congregation, he informs us in that complaint, that some (οὐ δικαίως ἀποβάλεσθαι τῆς λειτουργίας) were
wrongfully cast from the ministry, by the multitude; and he
tells you, that these were good honest men, and faithful in
the discharge of their duty; for, saith he, ὁρῶμεν ὅτι ἐνίους
ὑμεῖς μετηγάγετε, καλῶς πολιτευομένους, ἐκ τῆς ἀμέμπτως αὐτοῖς
τετιμημένης λειτουργίας: though they were unblamable both
in their conversation and ministry, yet they removed them
from their office. To reprove this evil, to convince them of
the sinfulness of it, to reduce them to a right understanding
of their duty and order, walking in the fellowship of the
gospel, what course doth he proceed in? what arguments
doth he use? He minds them of one God, one Christ, one
body, one faith, tells them that wicked men alone use such
ways and practices, bids them read the epistle of Paul
formerly written to them, upon occasion of another division,
and to be subject to their own elders; and all of them leave
off contending, quietly doing the things which the people,
or the body of the church, delivered and commanded. Now

had this person, writing on this occasion, using all sorts of arguments, artificial, or inartificial for his purpose, been baptized into the opinion and esteem of a single episcopal superintendent, whose exaltation seems to be the design of much which is said in the epistles of Ignatius, in the sense wherein his words are usually taken, would yet never once so much as bid them be subject to the bishop, that resemblance of God the Father, supplying of the place of Christ; nor told them how terrible a thing it was, to disobey him; nor pawned his soul for theirs, that should submit to him; that all that obeyed him were safe, all that disobeyed him, were rebellious, cursed, and separated from God. What apology can be made for the weakness and ignorance of that holy martyr, if we shall suppose him to have had apprehensions like those in these epistles of that sacred order, for omitting those all-conquering reasons, which they would have supplied him withal, to his purpose in hand, and pitching on arguments every way less cogent and useful. But, I say, I shall not insist on any such things as these, but only;

4. I say that there is not in any of the doctor's *excerpta* from those epistles, nor in any passage in them, any mention, or the least intimation, of any church whereunto any bishop was related, but such a one, as whose members met altogether in one place, and with their bishop disposed and ordered the affairs of the church. Such was that whereunto the holy martyr was related; such were those neighbouring churches, that sent bishops and elders to that church; and when the doctor proves the contrary, 'erit mihi magnus Apollo;' from the churches and their state and constitution, is the state and condition of their officers, and their relation to them to be taken. Let that be manifested to be such from the appointment of Jesus Christ by his apostles, or *de facto* in the days of Ignatius, or before the contemperation of ecclesiastical affairs occasionally, or by choice, to the civil constitution of cities and provinces in those days, as would, or possibly could, bear a rural diocesan metropolitical hierarchy, and this controversy will be at an end; when this is by any attempted to be demonstrated, I desire it may not be with such sentences as that urged by our doctor, from Epist. ad Eph. Ἰησοῦς Χριστὸς τοῦ πατρὸς ἡ γνώμη,

ὡς καὶ οἱ ἐπίσκοποι οἱ κατὰ τὰ πέρατα ὁρισθέντες Ἰησοῦ Χριστοῦ γνώμῃ εἰσὶν. The expression in it concerning Christ being unsound, unscriptural, concerning bishops unintelligible, or ridiculous ; but it may be said, what need we any more writing, what need we any truer proof or testimony? The learned doctor in his Dissertations, Diss. 4. cap. 5. hath abundantly discharged this work, and proved the seven bishops of the seven churches mentioned, Rev. ii. 3. to have been metropolitans, or archbishops, so that no just cause remains, why we should farther contend.

Let then the reader pardon this my utmost excursion in this digression, to whose compass I had not the least thoughts of going forth, at the entrance thereof, and I shall return thither whence I have turned aside.

Diss. 4. cap. 5. the doctor tells us, that, 'Septem ecclesiarum angeli, non tantum episcopi sed et metropolitæ ; i. e. archi-episcopi statuendi sunt; i. e. principalium urbium ἔξαρχοι ad quos provinciæ integræ et in iis multarum inferiorum urbium ecclesiæ, earumque episcopi tanquam ad archiepiscopum aut metropolitanum pertinebant.'

The doctor in this chapter commences *per saltum*, and taking it for granted that he hath proved diocesan bishops sufficiently before, though he hath scarce spoken any one word to that purpose in his whole book (for to prove one superintending in a church by the name of bishop, others acting in some kind of subordination to him, by the name of elders and presbyters, upon the account of what hath been offered concerning the state of the churches in those days, will no way reach to the maintenance of this presumption), he sacrifices his pains to the metropolitical archiepiscopal dignity, which, as we must suppose, is so clearly founded in Scripture and antiquity, that they are as blind as bats and moles, who cannot see the ground and foundation of it.

But, first, be it taken for granted, that the angels of the seven churches, are taken for the governors of those churches, then that each angel be an individual bishop of the church to which he did belong. 2. Be it also granted that they were bishops of the most eminent church or churches in that province, or Roman political distribution of those countries, in the management of the government of them, I

say, bishops of such churches, not *urbium* ἔξαρχοι (as the
doctor terms them), what advance is made by all this to the
assertion of a metropolitical archiepiscopacy, I cannot as
yet discover. That they were ordinary officers of Christ's
institution, relating in their office, and ordinary discharge
of it, not only to the particular churches wherein they were
placed, but to many churches also, no less committed to their
charge than these wherein they did reside; the officers,
rulers, governors of which churches, depended on them, not
only as to their advice and counsel, but as to their power
and jurisdiction, holding their place and employment from
them, is some part of that which in this undertaking is incumbent on our doctor to make good, if he will not be supposed to prevaricate in the cause in hand; to this end he
informs us, sect. secunda, that in the New Testament there
is, in sundry places, mention made of churches in the plural
number; as Gal. i. 21. 1 Thess. ii. 14. Acts ix. 31. xv. 41.
1 Cor. xvi. 1. Gal. i. 2. Rev. i. 11. sometimes of church only
in the singular number; as Acts viii. 1. xv. 4. 22. xi. 26.
Rom. xvi. 1. 1 Cor. i. 2. 2 Cor. i. 1. 1 Thess. i. 1. Rev. ii. 1.
8. 12. 18. Now this is an observation, which as we are not
at all beholden to the doctor for it, no more I suppose will
there be found to be to it, when the reason of it shall be a
little weighed and considered. The sum is, that the name
church, in the singular number, is never used, but when it
relates to the single congregation, in or of one city or town.
That of churches respecting the several churches, or congregations, that were gathered in any country or province;
manifest then is it from hence, that there is in the New Testament, no church of one denomination beyond a single congregation; and where there are more, they are always called
churches; how evidently this is destructive to any diocesan
or metropolitical officer, who hath no church left him thereby of Christ's institution to be related to, another opportunity will manifest. For the present let us see what use
our doctor makes of this observation.

Sect. 3. Says he, 'Judea and the rest of the places where
churches are mentioned, are the names of provinces, ἐπαρχιῶν,
quætenus eæ παροικίαις et διοικήσεσι, contradistinguntur.' But
if the doctor takes these words in an ecclesiastical sense,
he begs that which will, upon such unworthy terms, never

be granted him. If no more be intended, but that Judea,
Galatia, and the like names of countries, were provinces
wherein were many churches; Smyrna, Ephesus, of towns
and cities, wherein there was but one; we grant it with him.

And how much that concession of ours is to his advantage hath been intimated. And this seems to be his intendment by his following words, ' Provinciarum inquam in quibus plurimæ civitates singulæ singularum ecclesiarum sedes,
comprehendebantur, ideoque ecclesiæ in plurali istius sive
istius provinciæ, dicendæ.' Well, what then ? ' Cum tamen
unaquæque, civitas, cum territorio sibi adjuncto (λῆρος !)
ab episcopo suo administrata, singularis ecclesia dicenda sit:
ideoque quod κατ' ἐκκλησίαν, factum dicitur; Acts xiv. 25.
κατὰ πόλιν, fieri jubetur;' Tit. i. 5. That in every city there
was a singular church in those provinces (I speak of those
where any number were converted to the faith), I grant, for
the annexed territories let the doctor take care : there being
one church at Corinth, and another at Cenchrea. So that
every single city, had its own single church, with its bishops
in it, as at Philippi. The passage mentioned by the doctor,
concerning the epistle of Dionysius to the church at Goryna
in Crete, is very little to his purpose : neither doth he call
Philip the bishop of that church, the bishop of all the other
churches in Crete, as the doctor intimates : but the bishop
of them to whom especially and eminently he wrote.

Sect. 4. Application is made of the fore-mentioned observation, sect. 2. and the interpretation given of it, sect.
3. in these words; ' His sic positis, illud statim sequitur ut
(in imperii cognitione) in provincia qualibet, cum plures ur-
bes sint, una tamen primaria, et principalis censenda erat,
μητρόπολις ideo dicta, cui itidem inferiores reliquæ civitates
subjiciebantur, ut civitatibus regiones, sic et inter ecclesias,
et cathedras episcopales unam semper primariam et metro-
politicam fuisse.'

In this section the doctor hath, most ingeniously and
truly, given us the rise and occasion of his diocesan and metropolitical prelates, from the aims of men to accommodate
ecclesiastical or church affairs to the state and condition of
the civil government, and distributions of provinces, metropolitan cities, and chief towns, within the several dependencies, (the neighbouring villages being cast in as things of

no great esteem, to the lot of the next considerable town
and seat of judicature,) did the hierarchy which he so sedu-
lously contendeth for arise : what advantage were afforded
to the work, by the paucity of believers in the villages and
less towns (from which at length, the whole body of heathenish idolaters were denominated Pagans); the first planting of churches in the greater cities, the eminence of the
officers of the first churches in those cities, the weakness of
many rural bishops, the multiplying and growing in numbers,
and persons of gifts, abilities, and considerable fortunes and
employments in this world, in the metropolitan cities, with
their fame thereby, the tradition of the abode of some one
or other of the apostles in such cities and churches, with
the eminent accommodation at the administration of civil
jurisdiction and other affairs, which appeared in that subordination and dependency whereunto the provinces, chief
cities, and territories in the Roman empire were cast, with
which opportunities Satan got by these means, to introduce
their ways, state, pomp, words, phrases, terms of honour of
the world into the churches, insensibly getting ground upon
them, and prevailing to their declension from the naked simplicity and purity, wherein they were first planted, some
other occasion may give advantage for us to manifest : for
the present it may suffice that it is granted that the magnific
hierarchy of the church arose from the accommodation of
its state, and condition of the Roman empire and provinces.
And this in the instances of after-ages that might be produced, will easily be made yet farther evident; in those
shameful, or indeed rather shameless contests, which fell out
among the bishops of the third century, and downward,
about precedency, titles of honour, extent of jurisdiction,
ecclesiastical subjection to, or exemption from, one another;
the considerableness of their cities in the civil state of the
Roman empire where they did reside, was still the most prevalent and cogent argument in their brawls : the most notable brush, that in all antiquity we find given to the great
leviathan of Rome, who sported himself in those 'gather-
ings together of the waters of people, and multitudes, and
nations, and tongues,' or the general councils (as they are
called), was from an argument taken from the seat of the empire, being fixed at Constantinople, making it become new

Rome, so that the bishop of the church there was to enjoy equal privilege with him whose lot was fallen in the old imperial city: but our doctor adds;

Sect. 5. 'Illud ex Judæorum exemplari transcripsisse apostoli videntur: cum Mosaica id lege cautum esset, ut Judices et ministri in qualibet civitate ordinarentur; Deut. xvi. 18. Illi vero in rebus dubiis ad Judicem (Mosis successorem synedrio) Hierosolymitano cinctum recurrere tenerentur,' cap. xvii. 9. and in sect. 6. he proves Jerusalem to have been the metropolis of that whole nation *egregiam vero laudem!* But,

1. The doctor I presume knows before this, that those with whom he hath to do, will never give him the thing in question upon his begging or request. That which alone falls in under our consideration and inquiry is, whether the apostles instituted any such model of church-order and government, as is by the doctor contended for; to this he tells you, that the apostles seem to have done it, from the pattern of Mosaical institutions in the church of the Jews; but doctor, the question is not, with what respect they did it, but whether they did it at all or no; this the doctor thought good to let alone until another time, if we would not grant him upon his petition that so they did.

2. This then is the doctor's second argument for his diocesan and metropolitan prelates, his first was, from the example of the Heathens, in their civil administration and rule, this second from the example of the Jews. Not to divert into the handling of the church and political state of the Jews, as appointed of God, nor that dissonancy that is between the institution of civil magistrates, and evangelical administrations; this is the sum of the doctor's reasoning in his 5th, 6th, 7th, and 8th sections: 'God in the church, and among the people of the Jews, chose out one city to place his name there, making it the place where all the types and ceremonies which he had appointed for the discovery, and shadowing forth of the Lord Jesus Christ, were visibly and gloriously to be managed, acted, and held forth (sundry of them being such, as whose typicalness would have been destroyed by their multiplication), and principally on this account, making that place or city (which was first Shiloh) the seat of the kingdom, or habitation of the chief ruler for the

administration of justice, who appointed judges in all the land, for the good and peace of the people:' therefore the churches of Jesus Christ, dispersed over the face of the whole world, freed from obligations to cities or mountains, walking before God, in, and with, a pure and spiritual worship, having no one reason of that former institution, in common with the church of the Jews, must be cast into the same mould and figure. I hope without offence I may take leave to deny the consequence, and what more I have to say to this argument I shall yet defer.

But the doctor proceeds to prove, that indeed the apostles did dispose of the churches in this frame and order, according to the pattern of the civil government of the Roman empire, and that instituted of God among the Jews. The ninth section, wherein he attempts the proof of this assertion, is as followeth:

'Ad hanc imaginem, apostolos ecclesias ubique disponendas curasse, et in omnibus plantationibus suis, minorum ab eminentioribus civitatibus dependentiam, et subordinationem constituisse exemplis quidem plurimis monstrari possit, illud in Syria, et Cilicia patet; Acts xvi. 4. cum enim ζήτημα illud; chap. xv. 2. Hierosolymas referretur ab ecclesia 'Ιδίως Antiochiæ; chap. xiv. 26. xv. 3. et decretum ab apostolis denuo ad eos mitteretur; ver. 22. in epistola, qua decretum illud continebatur simul cum Antiochensibus τοὺς κατὰ ευρίαν καὶ Κιλικίαν ἀδελφοὺς comprehensos videmus; ver. 23. Dein epistola ista Antiochenæ ecclesiæ reddita; ver. 30. Paulus tandem et Sylas Syriam et Ciliciam peragrantes; ver. 4. chap. xvi. 4. δόγματα κεκριμένα ὑπὸ τῶν 'Αποστόλων, singulis civitatibus observanda tradiderunt, ut quæ ad hanc Antiochiæ metropolin, ut totidem subordinatæ ecclesiæ pertinerent; ut et ipsa Antiochia ad Hierosolymas, primariam tam latæ (ut ex Philone prædiximus) provinciæ metropolin pertinebat, et ad eam ad dirimendam litem istam se conferebat.'

This being all that the doctor hath to produce from the Scripture to his purpose in hand, I have transcribed it at large; for this being removed, all that follows, will fall of its own accord.

1. Then, the dependance on, and subordination of lesser cities, to the greater, is asserted as an apostolical institution.

Now because I suppose the doctor will not assert, nor doth
intend a civil dependance, and subordination of cities, as
such, among themselves, nor will a dependance as to counsel, advice, assistance, and the like, supplies which in their
mutual communion, the lesser churches might receive from
the greater and more eminent, serve his turn; but an ecclesiastical dependance and subordination, such as whereby
many particular churches, with inferior officers residing in
them, and with them, depended on, and were in subjection
unto, some one person of a superior order, commonly residing
in some eminent city, and many of these governors of a superior order in the greater cities were in such subordination
unto some one of high degree, termed a metropolitan, and
all this by apostolical institution is that which he aimeth at,
which being a most gallant adventure, in a waking generation, we shall doubtless find him quitting himself like a man
in his undertaking.

2. Then he tells you that the question about Mosaical
rites, and necessity of their observation, was referred to Jerusalem by the single church of Antioch. But how does the
doctor make good this first step, which yet if he could, would
do him no good at all? It is true, that Paul was now come
to Antioch, chap. xiv. 26. also that he was brought on his
way by the church, chap. xv. 3. but yet that the brethren
who were taught the doctrine contested about, ver. 1. were
only of the church of Antioch (when it is most certain from
the epistles of Paul to the Galatians, Colossians, Romans,
and others, that great disturbance was raised far and wide,
in all the churches of the Gentiles about this controversy),
nothing is offered. It seems indeed that their disputes grew
to the greatest height at Antioch, whither brethren from
other parts and churches did also come, whilst Barnabas
and Paul abode there, but that that single church referred
the determining of that controversy, to them at Jerusalem,
exclusively to others, the doctor proves not. And it is most
evident, from the return of the answer sent by the apostles
from Jerusalem, ver. 23. that the reference was from all the
churches of the Gentiles, yea, and all the scattered brethren
perhaps as yet not brought into church order, not only at
Antioch, but also throughout Syria and Cilicia. It is then
granted what he next observes, viz. that in the answer re-

turned from Jerusalem, with them at Antioch, those in Syria and Cilicia are joined; the reason'of it being manifest, namely, their trouble about the same controversy being no less than theirs at Antioch. It is also granted, that as Paul passed through the cities, that he delivered them the decrees to keep, that were ordained by the apostles and elders; chap. xvi. 4. and that not only to the churches of Syria and Cilicia, which he left, chap. xv. 41. but also to those throughout Phrygia, and the regions of Galatia; ver. 6. What now follows out of all this? What but that Antioch by apostolical institution, was the metropolitan see of all the churches of Syria and Cilicia. Good doctor do not be angry, but tell us how this may be proved. Why doubtless it was so: as Antioch belonged to the metropolitan church at Jerusalem, as he told us out of Philo (who was excellently acquainted with apostolical institutions). What Jerusalem was to the whole church and nation of the Jews, whilst the name of God was fixed there, we know; but what was the primitive estate of the churches of Jesus Christ made of Jews and Gentiles, tied neither to city or mountain, I must be pardoned if I cannot find the doctor making any tender of manifesting or declaring. The reasons of referring this controversy unto a determination at Jerusalem, the Holy Ghost acquaints us with, Acts xv. 2. so that we have no need of this metropolitical figment, to inform us in it. And now, if we will not, not only submit to diocesan bishops, but also reverence the grave metropolitans, standing upon such clear apostolical institution; it is fit that all the world should count us the arrantest schismatics that ever lived since pope Boniface's time. The sum then of this doughty argument for the apostolical institution of metropolitans (that none might ever more dare to call diocesians into question hereafter) is this; Paul who was converted about the third or fourth year of Caligula, five or six years after the ascension of Christ, having with great success for three years preached the gospel, went up to Jerusalem with Barnabas, upon the persecution raised against him at Damascus, Acts ix. 22. whence returning to his work, he went first to Tarsus, Acts ix. 30. thence to Antioch, where he abode one whole year; Acts xi. 25, 26. and was then sent to Jerusalem with the collections for the saints about the fourth year of Claudius, ver. 30. thence returning again to Antioch, he was sent out by the command of the Holy Ghost, more eminently and peculiarly than formerly, for the conversion of the Gentiles; Acts xiii. 1—3. In this undertaking in the space of a year or two, he preached, and gathered churches (whereof express mention is made) at Salamis, Acts xiii. 5. in the isle of Paphos, ver. 6. at Perga in Pamphylia, ver. 13. at Antioch in Pisidia, ver. 14. at Iconium, chap. xiv. 1. at Lystra and Derbe, ver. 6. and at Perga, ver. 26. In all these places gathering some believers to Christ, whom, before they returned to Antioch, he visited all over the second time, and settled elders in the several congregations; chap. xiv. 21—23. In this journey and travel for the propagation of the gospel, he seems in all places to have been followed almost at the heels, by the professing Pharisees, who imposed the necessity of the observation of Mosaical ceremonies upon his new converts: for instantly upon his return to Antioch, where, during his absence, probably they had much prevailed, he falls into dispute with them; chap. xv. 1. and that he was not concerned in this controversy, only upon the account of the church of Antioch, himself informs us; Gal. ii. 4. affirming that the false brethren, which caused those disputes and dissensions, crept in to spy out his liberty, in his preaching the gospel among the Gentiles, ver. 2. that is, in the places before mentioned throughout a great part of Asia. For the appeasing of this difference, and the establishing of the souls of the disciples which were grievously perplexed, with the imposition of the Mosaical yoke, it is determined that the case should be resolved by the apostles; Acts xv. 2. Partly because of their authority in all the churches, wherein those who contended with Paul would be compelled to acquiesce, and partly because those Judaizing teachers, pretended the commission of the apostles for the doctrine they preached, as is evident from the disclaimure made by them, of any such commission or command; ver. 24. Upon Paul's return from the assembly at Jerusalem, wherein the great controversy about Jewish ceremonies was stated and determined, after he had in the first place delivered the decree, and apostolical salutation, by epistle to the church at Antioch, he goes with them also to the churches in Syria and Cilicia, expressed in the letter by name, as also to those in Pamphylia, Pisidia, Derbe, Lystra, Iconium, &c. chap. xvi.

1—4: and all the churches which he had gathered and planted in his travels through Asia, whereunto he was commanded by the Holy Ghost; Acts xiii. 1, 2. Things being thus stated, it necessarily follows, that the apostles had instituted diocesan and metropolitan bishops. For though the churches were so small, and thin, and few in number, that seven years after this, may we believe our doctor, the apostles had not instituted or appointed any elders or presbyters in them, viz. when Paul wrote his epistle to the Philippians, which was when he was prisoner in Rome, as appears, chap. i. 7. 13, 14. iv. 22. about the third year of Nero, yet that he had fully built and settled the hierarchical fabric contended for, who once dares question?

Audacia—
Creditur a multis fiducia.

But if this will not do, yet Ignatius hits the nail on the head, and is ready at hand to make good, whatsoever the doctor will have him say, and his testimony takes up the sense of the two next following sections, whereof the first is as follows:

'Hinc dicti Ignatiani ratio constat in Epistola ad Romanos, ubi ille Antiochiæ episcopus se τῆς ἐν Συρίᾳ ἐκκλησίας ποιμένα, pastorem ecclesiæ quæ est in Syria appellet, cum ad Antiochiam, scil. ut ad metropolin suam tota Syria pertineret. Sic et author Epistolæ ad Antiochenos, ἐκκλησίᾳ Θεοῦ παροικούσῃ ἐν Συρίᾳ τῇ ἐν 'Αντιοχείᾳ, Eam inscribens totam, Syriam ejus παροικίαν esse concludit.'

But yet I fear the doctor will find he hath need of other weapons, and other manner of assistance, to make good the cause he hath undertaken. The words of Ignatius in that epistle to the Romans are, μνημονεύετε ἐν τῇ εὐχῇ ὑμῶν τῆς ἐν Συρίᾳ ἐκκλησίας ἥτις ἀντ' ἐμοῦ ποιμένι χρῆται τῷ κυρίῳ. Because he recommends to them that particular church in Syria, which by his imprisonment was deprived of its pastor, therefore without doubt he was a metropolitical archbishop: Tityre, tu patulæ,' &c. But the doctor is resolved to carry his cause, and therefore being forsaken of all fair and honest means, from whence he might hope for assistance or success, he tries (as Saul the witch of Endor), the counterfeit, spurious title, of a counterfeit epistle to the Antiochians, to see if that will speak any comfortable words, for his relief or no.

And to make sure work, he causes this gentleman so to speak, as if he intended to make us believe that Syria was in Antioch, not Antioch in Syria, as in some remote parts of the world, they say they inquire whether London be in England, or England in London. What other sense can be made of the words as by the doctor transcribed? ἐκκλησία ϑεοῦ παροικούσῃ ἐν Συρίᾳ τῇ ἐν Ἀντιοχείᾳ. To the church of God dwelling in Syria which is in Antioch: now if this be so, I shall confess it is possible we may be in more errors than one, and that we much want the learned doctor's assistance for our information; the words themselves as they are used by the worshipful writer of that epistle will scarce furnish us with this learned and rare notion: they are at length, Ἰγνάτιος ὁ καὶ Θεοφόρος (for so he first opens his mouth with a lie), ἐκκλησία ἠλεημένη ὑπὸ ϑεοῦ, ἐκλελεγμένη ὑπὸ Χριστοῦ παροικούσῃ ἐν Συρίᾳ, καὶ πρώτῃ Χριστοῦ ἐπωνυμίαν λαβούσῃ τῇ ἐν Ἀντιοχείᾳ. What is here more expressed, than that the latter passage, in Antioch, is restrictive of what went and before was spoken of its residence in Syria, with reference to the name of Christians, first given to the disciples in that place, I know not: and therefore it is most certain, that the apostles instituted metropolitan archbishops ὕπερ ἔδει δεῖξαι·

But to make all sure the learned doctor will not so give over: but, sect. 11. he adds, that the epigraph of the epistle to the Romans, grants him the whole case, that is, Ἐκκλησίᾳ ἥτις προκάϑηται ἐν τόπῳ χωρίου Ῥωμαίων, 'ex qua,' saith he, 'ecclesiæ Romanæ, ejusque episcopo super ecclesiis omnibus in urbicaria regione, aut provincia Romana contentis, præfecturam competiisse videmus.'

Although I have spent some time in the consideration of men's conjectures of those suburbicarian churches, that (as is pretended) are here pointed to, and the rise of the bishop of Rome's jurisdiction over those churches, in a correspondency to the civil government of the prefect of the city, yet so great a critic in the Greek tongue as Casaubon; Exerc. 16. ad An. 150. having professed that expression: ἐν τόπῳ χωρίου Ῥωμαίων, to be 'barbarous' and 'unintelligible,' I shall not contend about it. For the presidency mentioned of the church in, or at Rome, that it was a presidency of jurisdiction, and not only an eminency of faith and holiness

that is intended, the doctor thinks it not incumbent on him
to prove: those with whom he hath to do, are of another
mind: although by this time some alteration might be attempted, yea there was, as elsewhere shall be shewed : and
so much for Ignatius's archiepiscopacy:

The example of Alexandria is urged in the next place, in
these words : ' Idem de Alexandria, de qua Eusebius, Mar-
cum, Ἐκκλησίας πρῶτον ἐπ᾽ αὐτῆς Ἀλεξανδρείας συστήσασθαι,
Ecclesias (in plurali) primum in Alexandria instituisse. Has
omnes ab eo sub nomine τῆς ἐν Ἀλεξανδρείᾳ παροικίας, ad-
minio strandas suscepisse Annianum, Neronis anno octavo
idem Eusebius affirmat: quibus patet primariam Alexandriæ
et Patriarchalem cathedram fixam esse, ad quam reliquæ
provinciæ illius ecclesiæ a Marco plantatæ, ut ad metropoli-
ticam suam pertinebant.' Doubtless; for, 1. There is not any
passage in any ancient author, more clearly discovering the
uncertainty of many things in antiquity, than this pointed
to by the doctor in Eusebius. For, first, the sending of
Mark the evangelist into Egypt, and his preaching there at
Alexandria what he had written in the gospel, is but a report. Men said so, but what ground they had for their saying so, he relates not. And yet we know what a foundation
of many assertions by following writers, this rumour or report is made to be. 2. In the very next words the author
affirms, and insists long upon it in the next chapter, that
Philo's book, περὶ τοῦ βίου τῶν Ἀσκητῶν, was written concerning the Christians converted by Mark's preaching at
Alexandria, when it is notoriously known that it treateth of
the Essenes, a sect among the Jews, amongst whose obser-
vances many things were vain, superstitious, and foolish ;
unworthy to be once applauded as the practice of any Christian in those days: that same Philo, as far as can be gathered,
living and dying in the Jewish religion, having been employed by them with an apology to Rome in the days of
Caligula. But, 3. suppose that Mark were at Alexandria,
and preached the gospel there, which is not improbable, and
planted sundry churches in that great and populous city of
Jews and Gentiles, and that as an evangelist the care of those
churches was upon him, in a peculiar manner, nay, and add
farther, that after his death, as Jerome assures us, the elders
and presbyters of those churches, chose out one among

themselves to pieside in their convocations and meetings. If, I say, all this be supposed, what will ensue? Why then it is manifest that there was fixed at Alexandria a patriarchal chair, and a metropolitical church, according to the appointment of Jesus Christ by his apostles. 'Si hoc non sit probationum satis, nescio quid sit satis.' If some few congregations live together in love, and communion, and the fellowship of the gospel in a city, he is stark blind that sees not that to be an archbishop's see. The reason is as clear as his in the Comedian, for the freedom of his wife. Sy. 'Utinam Phrygiam uxorem meam una mecum videam liberam.' Dem. 'Optimam mulierem quidem.' Sy. 'Et quidem nepoti tuo, hujus filio, hodie primam mamman dedit hæc.' Dem. 'Hercle, vero, serio, siquidem primam dedit haud dubium quin emitti æquum siet.' Mic. 'Ob eam rem?' Dem. 'Ob eam:' and there is an end of the contest. The doctor indeed hath sundry other sections added to these foregoing, which as they concern times more remote from those who first received the apostolical institutions, so I must ingenuously profess that I cannot see any thing, whereon to fasten a suspicion of a proof, so far as to call it into examination, and therefore I shall absolve the reader from the penalty of this digression.

The truth is, when I first named Ignatius for a witness in the cause I am pleading for, I little thought of that excursion which I have occasionally been drawn out unto. When first I cast an eye some few months since upon the dissertation of the learned doctor, in defence of episcopacy, and saw it so checkered with Greek and Latin, so full of quotations divine and human, I began to think, that he dealt with his adversaries, 'hastisque, clypeisque, et saxis grandibus,' that there would be no standing before his shower of arguments. But after a little serious perusal, I must take leave to say, that I was quickly of another mind, with the reason of which change of thoughts, could I once obtain the leisure of a few days or hours, I should quickly (God willing) acquaint them who are concerned in affairs of this nature. In the mean time if the reader will pardon me this digression, having given him an account of my thoughts concerning the epistles of Ignatius, I shall in a procedure upon my first intention bring forth some testimonies from him, 'et valeant quantum valere possunt.'

He seems, in the first place, to speak sufficiently clearly to the death of Christ for his church, for believers, in a peculiar manner, which is one considerable bottom and foundation of the truth we plead for. Epist. ad Trall. Γίνεσθε μιμηταὶ παθημάτων Χριστοῦ, καὶ ἀγάπης αὐτοῦ ἣν ἠγάπησεν ἡμᾶς, δοὺς ἑαυτὸν περὶ ἡμῶν λύτρον, ἵνα καθαρίσῃ ἡμᾶς παλαιᾶς δυσσιβείας, καὶ ζωὴν ἡμῖν παράσχηται, μέλλοντας, ὅσον οὐδέπω ἀπόλλυσθαι ὑπὸ τῆς ἐν ἡμῖν κακίας· and again Epistola ad Philad. by Christ, saith he, εἰσῆλθον Ἀβραὰμ, καὶ Ἰσαὰκ, καὶ Ἰακὼβ, Μωσῆς, καὶ ὁ σύμπας τῶν προφητῶν χορὸς, καὶ οἱ Στύλοι τοῦ κόσμου οἱ ἀπόστολοι, καὶ ἣ νύμφη τοῦ Χριστοῦ ὑπὲρ ἧς (φέρνης λόγῳ) ἐξέχεὲ τὸ οἰκεῖον αἷμα, ἵνα αὐτὴν ἐξαγοράσῃ· with many the like expressions. His confidence also of the saints' perseverance for whom Christ thus died, he doth often profess. Speaking of the faith of the gospel he adds, Ταῦτα ὁ γνοὺς ἐν πληροφορίᾳ καὶ πιστεύσας, μακάριος, ὥσπερ οὖν καὶ ὑμεῖς φιλόθεοι καὶ φιλόχριστοι ἐστὲ, ἐν πληροφορίᾳ τῆς ἐλπίδος ὑμῶν, ἧς ἐκτραπῆναι μηδενὶ ὑμῶν γένηται·

And again more clearly and fully to the same purpose, Epist. ad Smyrn. ἐνόησα γὰρ ὑμᾶς κατηρτισμένους ἐν ἀκινήτῳ πίστει, ὥσπερ καθηλωμένους ἐν τῷ σταυρῷ τοῦ κυρίου ἡμῶν Ἰησοῦ Χριστοῦ, σαρκὶ τε καὶ πνεύματι καὶ ἡδρασμένους ἐν ἀγάπῃ ἐν τῷ αἵματι τοῦ Χριστοῦ, πεπληρυφορημένους ὡς ἀληθῶς, &c.

And this confirmation and establishment in believing, he ascribes not to their manly considerations, but to the grace of Christ, exclusively to any of their own strength, Epist. ad Smyrna.

Πάντα (saith he of himself) ὑπομένω διὰ Χριστόν, εἰς τὸ συμπαθεῖν αὐτῷ, αὐτοῦ με ἐνδυναμοῦντος, οὐ γάρ μοι τοσοῦτον σθένος.

To the same purpose, and with the same confident persuasion, he speaks, Epist. ad Ephes.

Ῥύσεται ὑμᾶς Ἰησοῦς Χριστὸς, ὁ θεμελιώσας ὑμᾶς ἐπὶ τὴν πέτραν, ὡς λίθους ἐκλεκτοὺς εὐαρμολογουμένους εἰς οἰκοδομὴν θείαν πατρὸς, ἀναφερομένους εἰς Τὰ ὕψη διὰ Χριστοῦ, τοῦ ὑπὲρ ἡμῶν σταυρωθέντος, σχοίνῳ χρωμένους τῷ ἁγίῳ πνεύματι, &c.

And again in the same epistle, Ἀρχὴ ζωῆς πίστις, τέλος δὲ ἀγάπη· τὰ δὲ δύο ἐν ἑνότητι γενόμενα θεοῦ ἄνθρωπον ἀποτελεῖ· τὰ δὲ ἄλλα πάντα εἰς καλοκαγαθίαν ἀκολουθά ἐστι. And in his last epistle, he gives us that noble expression of his own assurance. Ὁ ἐμὸς ἔρως ἐσταύρωται, καὶ οὐκ ἔστιν ἐν ἐμοὶ πῦρ φιλοῦν τι· ὕδωρ δὲ ζῶν ἁλλόμενον ἐν ἐμοὶ, ἐσωθέν μοι λέγει, δεῦρο πρὸς τὸν πατέρα· where we leave the holy soul, until the same God gather us to him, and the rest of the spirits of just men made perfect.

. And this was the language, these were the expressions, of this holy man, which what they discover of his judgment, to the case under consideration, is left to the learned reader to consider. This I am certain, our adversaries have very little cause to boast of the consent of the primitive Christians with them in the doctrine of apostacy, there being in these most ancient writers after the apostles, about the things of our religion, not the least shadow cast upon it, for its refreshment.

Add, in the next place, the most ancient of the Latins, Tertullian (that great storehouse of all manner of learning and knowledge), saith he, 'Quemadmodum nobis arrhabonem spiritus reliquit, ita et a nobis arrhabonem carnis accepit, et vexit in Cœlum, pignus totius summæ illuc redigendæ.' Tertullian, de Resur. The certain salvation of the whole mystical body of Christ, with whom he hath that communion, as to give them his Spirit, as he took their flesh (for he took 'upon him flesh and blood, because the children were partakers of the same'), is evidently asserted: which he could not do who thought that any of those, on whom he bestowed his Spirit, might perish everlastingly.

And again, De præscripti. advers. Hæret.

' In pugna pugilum et gladiatorum, plerumque non quia fortis est, vincit quis, aut quia non potest vinci. Sed quoniam ille qui victus est, nullis viribus fuit: adeo idem ille victor bene valenti postea comparatus, etiam superatus recedit: non aliter hæreses de quorundam infirmitatibus habent, quod valent, nihil valentes si in bene valentem fidem incurrant. Solent quidem illi miriones etiam de quibusdam personis ab hæresi captis ædificari in ruinam; quare ille vel illa, fidelissimi, prudentissimi, et usitatissimi in ecclesia, in illam partem transierunt? Quis hoc dicens non ipse sibi respondet, neque prudentes, neque fideles, neque usitatos æstimandos quos hæresis potuit demutare?' He plainly denies them to have been believers (that is, truly, thoroughly, properly so), who fall into pernicious heresies to their destruction.

Cyprian is express to our purpose: saith he, ' Nemo ex- istimet bonos de ecclesia posse discedere, tricticum non rapit ventus, nec arborem solida radice fundatam procella subvertit, inanes paleœ tempestate jactantur; invalidæ ar- bores turbinis incursione evertuntur. Hos execratur et per- cutit apostolus Johannes, dicens, ex nobis exierunt, sed non fuerunt ex nobis, si enim fuissent ex nobis, mansissent uti- que nobiscum ;' Cyp. de Unita. Eccles. The whole doctrine we contend for, is plainly and clearly asserted and bottomed on a text of Scripture, which in a special manner (as we have cause) we do insist upon; all that is lost by tempta- tions in the church, was but chaff; the wheat abides, and the rooted tree is not cast down. Those fall away, who indeed were never true believers in heart and union, whatever their profession was. And yet, we are within the compass of that span of time, which our adversaries, without proof, without shame, claim to be theirs. One principal foundation of our doctrine, is the bestowing of the Holy Ghost upon believers by Jesus Christ. Where he is so bestowed, there say we he abides: for he is given them for that end, viz. ' to abide with them for ever.' Now concerning him Basil tells us, ' that though in a sort, he may be said to be present with all, that are baptized, yet he is never mixed with any that are not worthy, that is, he dwells not with any that obtain not sal- vation.' Basil, lib. de Spir. Sanc. cap. 16. Νῦν μὲν γὰρ εἰ καὶ μὴ ἀνακέκροται τοῖς ἀναξίοις· ἀλλὰ οὖν παρεῖναι δοκεῖ πῶς τοῖς ἅπαξ ἐσφραγισμένοις. By that seeming presence of the Holy Ghost, with hypocrites that are baptized professors, he evidently intends the common gifts and graces that he bestows upon them, and this is all he grants to them who are not at last (for such he discourses of) found worthy.

Macarius Ægyptius, Homil. 5. about the same time with the other, or somewhat before, is of the same mind. He tells us that those who are Christians ἐν ἀληθείᾳ καὶ δυνάμει, ἀσφα- λεῖς εἰσιν ὑπὸ τοῦ ἀρραβῶνος, οὗ ἐδέξαντο νῦν, ὡς ἤδη ἐστεφανω- μένοι καὶ βασιλεύοντες. And how men can be assured of heaven, whilst they live here, by the earnest of it which they have received, as well as if they were crowned and reigning in heaven, if those who have received that earnest may lose it again, I know not. The words of Ambrose to this same purpose, Lib. 1. de Jacob. et Vita. beat. are many. But because they do not only fully assert the truth we contend for, but also insist briefly on most of the arguments, with which in this case we plead, I shall transcribe them at large, and they are as followeth :

'Non gloriabor, quia justus sum, sed gloriabor quia redemptus sum, gloriabor non quia vacuus peccati sum, sed quia mihi remissa sunt peccata, non gloriabor quia profui, nec quia profuit mihi quisquam, sed quia advocatus pro me apud Patrem Christus est, sed quia pro me Christi sanguis effusus est.—Hæredem te fecit, cohæredem Christi, Spiritum tibi adoptionis infudit. Sed vereris dubios vitæ anfractus et adversarii insidias, cum habeas auxilium Dei, habeas tantam ejus dignationem, ui filio proprio pro te non pepercerit?—nihil enim excepit, qui omnium concessit authorem. Nihil est igitur quod negari posse nobis vereamur ; nihil est in quo de munificentiæ divinæ diffidere perseverantia debeamus cujus fuit tam diuturna et jugis ubertas, ut primo prædestinaret, deinde vocaret, et quos vocavit hos et justificaret, et quos justificaret hos et glorificaret. Poterit deserere quos tantis beneficiis usque ad præmia prosecutus est? Inter tot beneficia Dei, num metuendæ sunt aliquæ accusationis insidiæ? sed quis audeat accusare quos electos divino cernit judicio? num Deus pater ipse qui contulit, potest dona sua rescindere, et quos adoptione suscepit, eos a paterni affectus gratia relegare? sed metus est ne judex severior sit, considera quem judicem habeas ; nempe Christo dedit pater omne judicium ; poterit te ergo ille damnare, quem redemit a morte, pro quo se obtulit, cujus vitam suæ mortis mercedem esse cognoscit? nonne dicit, quæ utilitas in sanguine meo, si damno quem ipse salvavi? deinde consideras judicem, non consideras advocatum ?'

The foundation of all our glorying in the love of God, and assurance of salvation, he lays in the free grace of God, in redemption and justification ; for the certainty of our continuance in that estate, he urges the decree of God's predestination, the unchangeableness of his love, the complete redemption made by Christ, with his effectual intercession, all which are at large insisted upon in the ensuing treatise.

Add to him his contemporary Chrysostom. Ser. 3. in 2 Cor. i. 21, 22. Ὁ δὲ βεβαιῶν ἡμᾶς σὺν ὑμῖν εἰς Χριστὸν, καὶ χρίσας ἡμᾶς Θεὸς· καὶ ὁ καὶ σφραγισάμενος ἡμας καὶ δοὺς τὸν ἀῤῥαβῶνα τοῦ πνεύματος ἐν ταῖς καρδίαις ἡμῶν. Of these words of the

apostle he gives the ensuing exposition. Πάλιν ἀπὸ τῶν παρ-
ελθὸν των τὰ μέλλοντα βεβαιοῦται· εἰ γὰρ αὐτός ἐστιν ὁ βαβαιῶν
ἡμᾶς εἰς Χριστὸν (τουτεστιν ὁ μὴ ἐῶν ἡμᾶς παρασαλεύεσθαι ἐκ
τῆς πίστεως τῆς εἰς τὸν Χριστὸν) καὶ αὐτὸς ὁ χρίσας ἡμᾶς, καὶ δοὺς
τὸ πνεῦμα ἐν ταῖς καρδίαις ἡμῶν, πῶς τὰ μέλλοντα οὐ δώσει; εἰ γὰρ
τὰς ἀρχὰς καὶ τὰς ὑποθέσεις ἔδωκε, καὶ τὴν πηγὴν (οἷον τὴν ἀληθῆ
περὶ αὐτοῦ γνῶσιν, τὴν τοῦ πνεύματος μετάληψιν) πῶς τὰ ἐκ τούτων
οὐ δώσει; εἰ γὰρ ἐκεῖνα διὰ ταῦτα δίδονται, πολλῷ μᾶλλον ὁ ταῦτα
δοὺς καὶ ἐκεῖνα παρέξει· καὶ εἰ ταῦτα ἐχθροῖς οὖσιν ἔδωκε, πολλῷ
μᾶλλον ἐκεῖνα φίλοις γενομένοις χαριεῖται· διὰ τοῦτο οὐδὲ
πνεῦμα εἶπεν ἁπλῶς, ἀλλ᾽ ἀρραβῶνα ὠνόμασεν, ἵνα ἀπὸ τούτου,
καὶ περὶ τοῦ παντὸς θαρρῇς· οὐ γὰρ εἰ μὴ ἔμελλε τὸ πᾶν διδό-
ναι, εἵλετο ἂν τὸν ἀρραβῶνα παρασχεῖν καὶ ἀπολέσαι εἰκῇ καὶ
μάτην.

The design and aim of our establishment by the Spirit, is,
he tells us, that we be not shaken or moved from the faith
of Christ; so establisheth us, that he suffers us not to depart
and fall away from the faith. And that the argument which
he insists on, from what we have presently received, to an
assurance of abode in our condition, to the enjoyment of
the full inheritance, is not contemptible in the cause in hand,
as is farther manifested in the treatise itself.

And these instances may suffice for the first period of
time mentioned, before the rising of the Pelagian heresy,
of which, and those others of the same kind that might be
produced, though they may not seem so full, and expressive
to the point under consideration, as these which follow after,
yet concerning those authors and their testimonies, these
two things may be asserted.

1. That though some expressions may be gathered from
some of the writers within the space of time mentioned,
that seem to allow a possibility of defection, and apostacy
in believers, occasioned all of them by the general use of
that word, and the taking in the several accounts, whereon
men both in the gospel, and in common use, are so called,
yet there is no one of them, that ever ascribed the perseverance of them who actually and eventually persevere, to such
grounds and principles as Mr. Goodwin doth, and which the
reader shall find at large by him insisted on, in the ensuing
treatise. The truth is, his maintaining of the saints' perseverance, is as bad, if not worse, than his maintaining their
apostacy.

2. That I scarce know any head in religion, concerning which the mind of the ancients who wrote before it received any opposition, may be made out more clearly, than we have done in this, by the instances produced, and insisted on.

The Pelagian heresy began about the year 417. The first opposers thereof are reckoned up by Prosper, cap. 2. de Ingrat. The bishop of Rome, the Palestine synod in the case of Pelagius, Jerome, Atticus bishop of Constantinople, the synod of Ephesus, Sicily, and two in Afric, he mentions in order, concluding them with the second African, gathered to that end and purpose:

> Anne alium in finem posset procedere sanctum
> Concilium, cui dux Aurelius ingeniumque
> Augustinus erat? quem Christi gratia cornu
> Uberiore rigans, nostro lumen dedit ævo,
> Accensum vero de lumine, nam cibus illi
> Et vita et requies Deus est omnisque voluptas
> Unus amor Christi est, unus Christi est honor illi
> Et dum nulla sibi quærit bona, fit Deus illi
> Omnia, et in sancto regnat sapientia templo.

And because I shall not burden the reader, being now entered upon the place and time, wherein very many witnesses call aloud to be heard about the difference in hand, of the first opposers of the Pelagian heresy, I shall insist only on him, who is indeed 'instar omnium,' and hath ever been so accounted in the controversies about the grace of God; and I shall the rather lay this weight on him, because it is evident that he spake the sense of the whole church, in those days wherein he lived. This is Austin, of whom saith the same Prosper,—'Noverint illi non solum Romanam ecclesiam Africanamque, sed per omnes mundi partes universos promissionis filios, cum doctrina hujus viri, sicut in tota fide, ita in gratiæ confessione congruere;' Epist. ad Rusti.

And when his writings began to be carped at by the Semi-Pelagians of France, Cælestine bishop of Rome in his Epist. ad Gallos, gives him this testimony, 'Augustinum Sanctæ recordationis virum pro vita sua et moribus, in nostra communione semper habuimus, nec unquam hunc sinistræ suspicionis rumor saltem aspersit, quem tantæ scientiæ olim fuisse meminimus, ut inter magistros optimos etiam a meis prædecessoribus haberetur.' His writings also were made use of not only by Prosper, Hilary, and Fulgentius,

but generally of all that engaged against the Pelagians. 'Zo-
zimus (saith Prosper, ad Collat. c. 41.) cum esset doctissi-
mus, adversus libros tamen Pelagianorum beati Augustini
responsa poscebat.' And Leo, Epist. ad Concil. Arausic.
transcribes out of him *verbatim* the things that he would
have confirmed and established. And in his own days, notwithstanding the differences between them, that aged and
learned Jerome, tells him, Epist. 94. ' Mihi decretum est te
amare, te suspicere, colere, mirari, tuaque dicta, quasi mea,
defendere.' Hence was that outcry in the Palestine synod
upon the slighting of his authority by Pelagius. ' Dixit Pelagius, quis est mihi Augustinus? Acclamabant omnes
blasphemantem in episcopum, ex cujus ore dominus universæ
Africæ unitatis indulserit sanitatem, non solum a conventu
illo, sed ab omni ecclesia pellendum ;' Oros. Apologet. pp.
621, 622. So also Gelas. Biblioth. Pat. Tom. 4. Colum. 553.
p. 589.

Fulgentius also, with them assembled with him at Byza-
cene, when they were banished Afric by Thrasimundus, in
that synodical Epist. gives them this counsel; ' Præ omnibus studium gerite libros S. Augustini quos ad Prosperum et
Hilarium scripsit, memoratis fratribus legendos ingerere.'
Epist. Synod. Byzac. Much more might be added to manifest the judgment of Austin to have been the catholic judgment of the church in those days. So that in his single
testimony as great a number are included, as in the testimony of any one man in the world whatever.

Now the controversy that was between Austin, and the
Pelagians and Semi-Pelagians about perseverance, Hilary
thus expresseth in his Epist. to him ; ' Deinde moleste fe-
runt,' (speaking of the Semi-Pelagians) ' ita dividi gratiam,
quæ vel tunc, primo homini data est, vel nunc omnibus
datur, ut ille acceperit perseverantiam, non qua fieret, ut
perseveraret, sed sine qua per liberum arbitrium perseverare non posset ; nunc vero Sanctis in regnum per gratiam
prædestinatis, non tale adjutorium perseverantiæ.detur, sed
tale, ut eis perseverantia ipsa donetur, non solum ut sine
illo dono perseverantes esse non possint, verum etiam ut
per hoc donum non nisi perseverantes sint. Cæterum
quicquid libet donatum sit predestinatis, id posse et amittere, et retinere propria voluntate contendunt.' The very

state of the controversy as now under contest is most clearly expressed, in this report of the difference, between the Semi-Pelagians and the church of God in those days. And because the whole sum of Mr. Goodwin's book is briefly comprised in the ninth and tenth chapters of Prosper de Ingrat. I shall transcribe that tenth chapter, to present to the reader the substance and pith of that treatise, as also the state of the controversy in those days :

——Quam sana fides sit vestra patescat,
Gratia qua Christi populus sumus, hoc cohibetur
Limite vobiscum, et formam hanc adscribitis illi :
Ut cunctos vocet illa quidem, invitetque ; nec ullum
Præteriens, studeat communem afferre salutem
Omnibus, et totum peccato absolvere mundum,
Sed proprio quemque arbitrio parere vocanti,
Judicioque suo , mota se extendere mente
Ad lucem oblatam, quæ se non subtrahat ulli,
Sed cupidos recti juvet, illustretque volentes.
Hinc adjutoris Domini bonitate magistra
Crescere virtutum studia, ut quod quisque petendum
Mandatis didicit, jugi sectetur amore.
Esse autem edoctis istam communiter æquam
Libertatem animis, ut cursum explere beatum
Persistendo queant, finem effectumque petitum
Dante Deo, ingeniis qui nunquam desit honestis.
Sed quia non idem est cunctis vigor, et variarum
Illecebris rerum trahitur dispersa voluntas,
Sponte aliquos vitiis succumbere, qui potuissent
A lapsu revocare pedem, stabilesque manere.

As I said, we have the sum of Mr. Goodwin's book in this declaration of the judgment of the Semi-Pelagians, so also in particular the state of the controversy about the perseverance of the saints as then it was debated ; and I doubt not but the learned reader will easily perceive it to be no other than that which is now agitated between me and Mr. Goodwin. The controversy indeed in the matter between Austin and the Pelagians was reduced to three heads. 1. As to the foundation of it, which Austin concluded to be the decree of predestination, which they denied ; the impulsive cause of it he proved to be the free grace of God, and the measure or quality of that grace to be such, as that whoever received it, did persevere, it being perseverance which was given, both which they denied ; about the kind of faith which temporary professors might have, and fall from it, which were never elected, there was between them no contest at all. Of his judgment, then, there were these two main heads which he laboured to confirm.

That perseverance is a gift of God, and that no man
either did, or could perseveic in faith and obedience upon
the strength of any grace received (much less of his own
ability, stirred up and promoted by such considerations, as
Mr. Goodwin makes the ground and bottom of the perseverance of all that so do), but that the whole was from his grace.
Subservient to this, he maintained, that no one temptation
whatsoever, could be overcome but by some act of grace,
and that therefore perseverance must needs be a work thereof, it being an abiding in faith and obedience, notwithstanding, and against temptation. To this is that of his on John;
Hom. 53. 'Quosdam nimia voluntatis suæ fiducia extulit in
superbiam, et quosdam nimia voluntatis suæ diffidentia de-
jecit in negligentiam : illi dicunt quid rogamus Deum ne
vincamur tentatione quod in nostra est potestate? Isti dicunt, at quid conamur bene vivere, quod in Dei est potestate? O Domine, O Pater qui es in cœlis, ne nos inferas in
quamlibet istarum tentationum, sed libera nos a malo. Au-
diamus Dominum dicentem, rogavi pro te Petre, ne fides
deficiat tua; ne sic existimemus fidem nostram esse in li-
bero arbitrio ut divino non egeat adjutorio,' &c. That, with
both of these sorts of men, the way and work of the grace of
God, is at this day perverted and obscured, is so known to
all, that it needs no exemplification. Some require no more
to the conquest of temptations, but men's own rational consideration of their eternal state and condition, with the tendency of that, whereto they are tempted, others turning the
grace of God into wantonness, and supinely casting away
all heedful regard of walking with God, being enslaved to
their lusts and corruptions, under a pretence of God's working all in all. The latter denying themselves to be men,
the former to be men corrupted; and in plain terms the
Milevitan council tells us, 'Si quis finxerit ideo gratiam
esse necessariam ad vitanda peccata, quia facit hominem
cognoscere peccata, et discernere inter peccata, et non peccata, qua discretione per gratiam habita, per liberum arbitrium potest vitare; is procul,' &c. The light of grace to discern the state of things, the nature of sin, and to consider
these aright, the Pelagians allowed, which is all the bottom
of that perseverance of saints, which we have offered by
Mr. Goodwin; but upon that supply of these means, to abide

and persevere in faith, to fly and avoid sin, is a thing of our own performance.

 . This the doctors of that council, Anno 420. condemned as a Pelagian fiction, as Prosper also presents it at large; c. 25. against Cassianus the Semi-Pelagian, and farther clears and confirms it; so Austin again: 'De Bono Persev. c. 3. cur ista perseverantia petitur a Deo, si non datur a Deo? an et ista irrisoria petitio est, cum illud ab eo petitur, quod scitur non ipsum dare, sed ipso non dante, esse in hominis potestate? sicut irrisoria est etiam illa gratiarum actio, si ex hoc gratiæ aguntur Deo quod non donavit ipse nec fecit;' and the same argument he useth again, cap. 6. 9. much resting on Cyprian's interpretation of the Lord's Prayer, and cap. 26. he farther presseth it, as to the root and foundation of this gift of God. 'Si ad liberum arbitrium hominis, quod non secundum gratiam, sed contra eam defendis, pertinere dicis, ut perseveret in bono quisquis, vel non perseveret, non Deo dante sic perseverat, sed humana voluntate faciente.' One or two instances more in this kind amongst hundreds that offer themselves may suffice.

De Correptione et Gratia, cap. 14. 'Apostolus Judas, cum dicit, ei autem qui potens est, &c. nonne apertissime ostendit donum Dei esse perseverare in bono usque ad finem? quid enim aliud sonat qui potest conservare nos sine offensione, et constituere ante conspectum gloriæ suæ, immaculatos in lætitia, nisi perseverantiam bonam? quis tam insulse desipiat, ut neget perseverantiam esse donum Dei, cum dicit sanctissimus Jeremias, timorem meum dabo in corde eorum ut non recedant a me,' &c. I shall add only that one place more out of the same book, (c. 59.) where both the matter and manner of the thing in hand, is fully delivered: 'In hoc loco miseriarum, ubi tentatio est vita hominum super terram, virtus infirmitate perficitur; quæ virtus? nisi qui gloriatur, ut in domino glorietur, per hoc de ipsa perseverantia Boni noluit Deus Sanctos suos in viribus suis, sed in ipso gloriari, qui eis non solum dat adjutorium quod primo homini dedit sine quo non possit perseverare si velit, sed in iis etiam operatur et velle: et quoniam non perseverabunt nisi et possint, et velint, perseverandi eis et possibilitas, et voluntas divinæ gratiæ largitate donatur; tantum quippe Spiritu Sancto accenditur voluntas eorum, ut ideo possint quia sic volunt, ideo sic velint, quia Deus operatur ut velint. Nam si tanta infirmitate hujus vitæ ipsis relinquetur voluntas sua, ut in adjutorio Dei, sine quo perseverare non possent, manerent si vellent, ne Deus in eis operaretur ut velint, inter tot, et tantas tentationes, infirmitate sua succumberet voluntas, et ideo perseverare non possent, quia deficientes infirmitate voluntatis non vellent, aut non ita vellent, ut possent. Subventum est igitur infirmitati voluntatis humanæ, ut divina gratia indeclinabiliter, et insuperabiliter ageretur, et ideo quamvis infirma non tamen deficiat.' It is not possible that any one should deliver his sense more clearly, to the whole of our present contest, than this holy and learned man hath done, in the words now repeated from him; a gift of God he asserts it to be (and not an act or course of our own, whereto we are prompted by certain considerations, and assisted with such outward means as are also added to us), to the real production of that effect by the efficiency of the grace of God. And for the manner of this work, it is, saith he, by the effectual working, the actual will of perseverance (in the continuance of our obedience), in a dispensation of grace, different from, and beyond what was given to him who had a power of persevering if he would ; but received not the will thereof. Now to Adam's perseverance there was nothing wanting, but his will's confirmation in obedience, and his actual doing so. Power he had within, and means without, abundantly sufficient for that end in their kind. This then he asserts to be given to the saints, and to be the work of God in them; even their actual perseverance. Without this he also manifesteth that such is the infirmity of our wills, and such the power of our temptations (that what means soever may be supplied and left to their power, or what manlike rational considerations whatever, man may engage his thoughts into), that it is impossible any should persevere to the end ; which Bradwardine more confirms, De Caus. Dei, lib. 2. cap. 8. Coroll. 'Omne quod est naturale, et non est per se tale, si manere debeat immutatum, oportet quod innitatur continue alicui fixo per se : quare quilibet justus Deo.'

And the holy man (Austin I mean) concludes, that this work of God being wrought in a man, his will is indeclinably and inseparably fixed so to obedience, as not to fall off from

God. This is the foundation that he lays of the doctrine of
the perseverance of saints : that it is a gift of God, and that
such a gift, as he effectually and actually works in him on
whom he doth bestow it.

A foundation that will by no means regularly bear the
hay and stubble, wherewith men think to build up a doctrine
of perseverance : making it a fruit that may, or may not, be
brought forth, from our own use of the means allowed for
that end and purpose. And, indeed, the asserting of the
perseverance of the saints in that way, is as bad, if not a
worse and more fearful opposition to, and slighting of, the
grace of God, as the denial of it, in the way they oppose :
by the latter they oppose the grace of God, by the former,
set up the power and strength of their own will. Thus far
Austin is clearly engaged with us ; that perseverance is a
gift of God ; that it is given by him to every one that doth
persevere ; that every one to whom it is given, is inseparably confirmed in grace, and shall infallibly persevere to
the end.

In that earnest and long contest, which that learned
doctor insists upon, to prove perseverance to be the gift of
God (for which he hath sufficient ground from that of the
apostle ; 1 Cor. i. 7, 8. ‘That ye come behind in no gift,
waiting for the coming of our Lord Jesus,’ &c.) two things
he especially aimed at : first, an opposing of such a perseverance, as should not be the fruit and work of the grace of
God in us ; but the work and effect of our own endeavours,
upon a supply of such means, motives, persuasions, and considerations as we are, or may be, furnished withal. Secondly,
that it is so given and bestowed, as that on whomsoever it
is bestowed, he certainly hath it, that is, he doth certainly
persevere. As it was heresy to that holy man, to deny perseverance to be the gift of God, so it was ridiculous to him,
to say that that gift was given to any, and yet that they received it not ; that is, that they might not persevere. ‘Nobis,’ saith he, de Cor. et Grat. C. 11. ‘qui Christo insiti sumus, talis data est gratia, ut non solum possimus si velimus
sed etiam ut velimus in Christo perseverare.’ And c. 12.
‘Non solum ut sine illo dono perseverantes esse non possint,
verum etiam ut per hoc donum non nisi perseverantes sint.’

And that which he adds afterward, is most considerable,

concluding from that of our Saviour, 'You have not chosen me, but I have chosen you, and ordained you to bear fruit;' 'Eis,' saith he, 'non solum justitiam, verum etiam in illa perseverantiam dedisse monstravit. Christo enim sic eos ponente ut eant et fructum afferant, et fructus eorum maneat, quis audeat dicere forsitan non manebunt?' Though they dare say so, who also dare to pretend his authority for what they say! how falsely, how unjustly, is evident to all serious observers of his mind and spirit, in and about the things of the grace of God.

2. As he mentioned perseverance to be such a gift of God, as indeclinably wrought in them on whom it was bestowed, a will to persevere, and on that account perseverance itself (an assertion as obnoxious to the calumny and clamour of the adversaries of the doctrine under consideration, as any we teach or affirm concerning it), so he farther constantly taught this gift and grace to be a fruit of predestination, or election, and to be bestowed on all, and only elected believers: so De Predestinatione Sanc. c. 17. 'Hæc dona Dei dantur electis, secundum Dei propositum vocatis, in quibus est et incipere et credere, et in fide ad hujus vitæ exitum perseverare.' And afterward, c. 9. 'De bono persev. ex duobus piis' (of his meaning in that word afterward), 'cur huic donetur perseverantia, usque in finem, illi non donetur, inscrutabilia sunt judicia Dei: illud tamen fidelibus debet esse certissimum, hunc esse ex prædestinatis, illum non esse: nam si fuissent ex nobis (ait unus prædestinatorum qui e pectore Domini biberat hoc secretum) mansissent utique nobiscum. Quæ est ista discretio? Patent libri Dei, non avertamus aspectum, clamat Scriptura Divina, adhibeamus auditum, non erant ex eis, quia non erant secundum propositum vocati: non erant in Christo electi ante mundi constitutionem, non erant in eo sortem consecuti, non erant prædestinati secundum propositum ejus qui omnia operatur.' And unto these elect, predestinate believers, he concluded still, that perseverance was so given in and for Christ, so proceeding from the immutable will of God wrought by such an efficacy of grace, that it was impossible that they should not persevere. He compares it farther with the grace that Adam received, Lib. De. Correp. et Grat. cap. 12. 'Primo itaque homini, qui in eo bono quo factus fuerat rectus, acce-

perat posse non peccare, posse non mori, posse ipsum bonum
non deserere, datum est adjutorium perseverantiæ, non quo
fieret ut perseveraret, sed sine quo per liberum arbitrium
perseverare non possit. Nunc vero sanctis in regnum Dei
per gratiam Dei prædestinatis, non tantum tale adjutorium
perseverantiæ datur; sed tale, ut iis perseverantia ipsa donetur, non solum ut sine isto dono perseverantes esse non
possint, verum etiam ut per hoc donum non nisi perseverantes
sint.' And a little after, 'Ipse itaque dat perseverantiam,
qui stabilire potens est eos qui stant, ut perseverantissime
stent.' And in the eighth chapter of the same book, ex-
pounding that of our Saviour; Luke xxii. 'I have prayed
for thee that thy faith fail not;' he manifesteth how upon
that account, it was impossible that the will of Peter should
not actually be established to the end in believing; his
words are,—'An audebis dicere, etiam rogante Christo ne
deficeret fides Petri, defecturum fuisse, si Petrus eam deficere voluisset, idque si eam usque in finem perseverare no-
luisset? Quasi aliud Petrus ullo modo vellet, quam pro illo
Christus rogasset ut vellet: nam quis ignorat tunc fuisse
perituram fidem Petri, si ea quæ fidelis erat voluntas ipsa
deficeret; et permansuram, si voluntas eadem permaneret?
Quando ergo oravit ne fides ejus deficeret, quid aliud rogavit,
nisi ut haberet in fide liberrimam, fortissimam, invictissi-
mam, perseverantissimam voluntatem?' And in this persuasion he had not only the consent of all the sound and orthodox doctors in his time, as was before manifested; but
he is followed also by the schoolmen of all ages, and not forsaken by some of the Jesuits themselves, as we shall afterward see, when we have added that consideration of the
doctrine of this learned man, which hath given occasion to
some, to pretend his consent in opposition to that, which
most evidently he not only delivered, but confirmed. There
are in Austin, and those that either joined with him, or followed immediately after him (notwithstanding the doctrine
formerly insisted on, that actual perseverance is a gift of God,
and that it flows from predestination as an effect thereof, and
is bestowed on all elect believers, infallibly preserving them
unto the end; wherein they assert, and strongly prove, the
whole of what we maintain), sundry expressions commonly
urged by the adversaries of the truth in hand, granting many

who were saints, believing and regenerate, to fall away and perish for ever: I need not instance in any of their sayings to this purpose: the reader knows where to find them gathered to his hand, in Vossius, Grotius, and Mr. Goodwin from them. The seeming contradiction that is amongst themselves in the delivery of this doctrine, will easily admit of a reconciliation, may they be allowed the common courtesy of being interpreters of their own meaning. What weight in those days was laid upon the participation of the sacramental figures of grace, and what expressions are commonly used concerning them who had obtained that privilege is known to all. Hence all baptized persons continuing in the profession of the faith and communion of the church, they called, counted, esteemed truly regenerate and justified, and spake so of them; such as these they constantly affirm, might fall away into everlasting destruction: but yet what their judgment was, concerning their present state indeed, even then when they so termed them regenerate, and believers, in respect to the sacraments of those graces, Austin in sundry places clearly delivers his thoughts, to the undeceiving of all that are willing to be free: this he especially handles in his book de Correp. et Grat. cap. 9. 'Non erant,' saith he, 'filii, etiam quando erant in professione et nomine filiorum; non quia justitiam simulaverunt, sed quia in ea non permanserunt:' this righteousness he esteemed not to be merely feigned and hypocritical, but rather such as might truly entitle them to the state and condition of the children of God, in the sense before expressed.

And again, 'Isti cum pie vivunt dicuntur filii Dei, sed quoniam victuri sunt impie, et in eadem impietate morituri, non eos dicit filios Dei præscientia Dei.' And farther in the same chapter, 'Sunt rursus quidam qui filii Dei propter susceptam temporalem gratiam dicuntur a nobis, nec sunt tamen Deo:' and again, 'Non erant in numero filiorum, etiam quando erant in fide filiorum.' And, 'Sicut non vere discipuli Christi, ita nec vere filii Dei fuerunt, etiam quando esse videbantur, et ita vocabantur.' He concludes; 'Appellamus ergo nos et electos Christi discipulos, et Dei filios, quos regeneratos' (that is, as to the sacramental sign of that grace), 'pie vivere cernimus; sed tunc vere sunt quod appellantur, si manserint in eo propter quod sic appellantur.'

'Si autem perseverantiam non habent, id est, in eo quod cœperunt esse non manent, non vere appellantur, quod appellantur et non sunt.' As also, de Doct. Christiana, lib. 3. c. 32. 'Non est revera corpus Christi quod non erit cum illo in æternum.'

And these are the persons which Austin, and those of the same judgment with him, do grant that they may fall away, such as upon the account of their baptismal entrance into the church, their pious devout lives, their profession of the faith of the gospel, they called and accounted regenerate believers, whom yet they tell you upon a thorough search into the nature and causes of holiness, grace, and walking with God, that they would be found not to be truly and really in that state and condition, that they were esteemed to be in; of which they thought this a sufficient demonstration, even because they did not persevere: which undeniably on the other hand (with the testimonies foregoing, and the like innumerable that might be produced) evinces, that their constant judgment was, that all who are truly, really, and in the sight of God believers, ingrafted into Christ, and adopted into his family, should certainly persevere: and that all the passages usually cited out of this holy and learned man, to persuade us that he ever cast an eye towards the doctrine of the apostacy of the saints, may particularly be referred to this head, and manifested that they do not at all concern those, whom he esteemed saints indeed; which is clear from the consideration of what hath been insisted on. Thus far he, of whom what were the thoughts of the church of God in the days wherein he lived, hath been declared: he who hath been esteemed amongst the ecclesiastical writers of old, to have laboured more, and to more purpose, in the doctrine of the grace of God, than all that went before him, or any that have followed after him, whose renown in the church hath been chiefly upheld and maintained, upon the account of the blessed pains and labours, wherein the presence of God made him to excel, for the depressing the pride of all flesh, and the exaltation of the riches of God's love, and efficacy of his grace in Jesus Christ, wherewith the whole church in succeeding ages hath been advantaged beyond what is easy to be expressed.

That Prosper, Hilary, Fulgentius, and the men of renown

in the congregation of God at the end of that age, did fall
in with their judgments, to that which Austin had delivered,
I suppose will be easily confessed; Prosper ad cap. 7. Gal.
'Quomodo eos habeat præordinata in Christo electio? cum
dubium non sit donum Dei esse perseverantiam in bono usque ad finem ; quod istos, ex eo ipso quod non persevera-
runt, non habuisse manifestum est.' Also the breaking of
the power, and frustrating of the attempt, of Pelagius, by
sundry doctors of the church, and synods to that end assembled, (whereof Prosper gives us an account, reckoning
them up in their order; and Austin before him ; Epist 42.
and 47.) with special relation to what was done in Afric
(and in the beginning of his verses, De Ingratis); with what
troubles were raised, and created anew to the champions of
the grace of God by the writings of Cassianus, Faustus, Vin-
centius, the Masilienses, with some others in France, and the
whole rabble of Semi-Pelagians, with the fiction of Sigibert
about a predestinarian heresy ; whereof there was never any
thing in being, no not among the Adrumetine monks, where
Vossius hoped to have placed it, the council of Arles, the
corruptions and falsifications of Faustus in the business of
Lucidus, the impositions on Goteschalcus, with the light
given to that business, from the epistle of Florus, have exercised the commendable endeavours of so many already,
that there is not the least need farther to insist upon them.
What entertainment that peculiar doctrine which I am in the
consideration of, found in the following ages, is that which
I shall farther demonstrate.

After these was Gregory I. who, lib. 1. epist. 99. speaks
to the same purpose with them, in these words, 'Redemptor
noster, Dei hominumque mediator, conditionis humanæ non
immemor, sic imis summa conjungit, ut ipse in unitate per-
manens ita temporalia, occulto instinctu, pia consulens
moderatione disponat, quatenus de ejus manu antiquus
hostis nullatenus rapiat, quos ante secula intra sinum ma-
tris ecclesiæ adunandos esse præscivit; nam et si quisquam
eorum inter quos degit, statibus motus ad tempus ut palmes
titubet, radix tamen rectæ fidei, quæ ex occulto prodit, divino judicio virens manet, quæ accepto tempore fructum de se
ostentare valeat, qui latebat.' This is the sum of what we
contend for; viz. that all those whom God hath predesti-

nated to be added to the church, receiving a saving faith,
though they may be shaken, yet on that account, the root
abides firm, their faith never utterly perisheth, but in due
time brings forth accepted fruits again.

And most expressive to our purpose is that discourse of
his which you have, lib. 34. Moral. cap. 8. saith he, ' Aurum,
quod pravis diaboli persuasionibus quasi lutum sterni potuerit, aurum ante Dei oculos nunquam fuit, qui enim seduci
quandoque non reversuri possunt, quasi habitam sanctita-
tem ante oculos hominum videntur amittere, sed eam ante
oculos Dei nunquam habuerunt.'

The exclusion of those from being true believers, who
may be seduced and fall away, doth most eminently infer
the perseverance of all them, who are so; add unto these,
Œcumenius (though he be one of a later date), and those
shall suffice for the period of time, relating to the Pelagian
controversy, saith he, in Epist. ad Eph. cap. 1. 14. ὁ ἀῤῥα-
βὼν πιστοῦται τὸ ὅλον· τινὰ τοίνυν υἱοθεσίαν καὶ τὰ μύρια
ἀγαθὰ πιστούμενος ὁ θεὸς, δέδωκεν ἀῤῥαβῶνα τῆς ἐπουρανίου
κληρονομίας, τὸ Ἅγιον πνεῦμα. All is confirmed and ratified by the earnest of the Spirit, that is given to them that
believe.

Of those that lived after the days of the forementioned
(I mean all of them but the last), that I may not cloy the
reader, I shall not mention any, until the business of divinity, and the profession of it, was taken up by the schoolmen and canonists, who from a mixture of divine and human
principles, framed the whole body of it anew, and gave it
over into the possession of the present Romish church,
moulded for the most part to the worldly carnal interests
of them on whom they had their dependency, in their several generations.

But yet as there was none of those, but one way or other
was eminently conducing to the carrying on of the mystery
of iniquity, by depraving, perverting, and corrupting one
truth or other of the gospel, so all of them did not in all
things equally corrupt their ways, but gave some testimony
more or less to some truths, as they received them from those
that went before them; so fell it out in the matter of the
grace of God, and the corruption of the nature of man;

though some of them laboured to corrode and corrupt the ancient received doctrine thereof, so some again contended with all their might in their way, and by their arguments to defend it; as is evident in the instance of Bradwardine, crying out to God and man, to help in the cause of God against the Pelagians in his days; in particular complaining of the great master of their divinity. So that, notwithstanding all their corruptions, these ensuing principles pass currently amongst the most eminent of them, as to the doctrine under consideration, which continue in credit with many of their sophistical successors to this day.

1. That perseverance is a grace of God, bestowed according to predestination, or election, on men; that is, that God gives it to believers, that are predestinated and elected.

2. That on whomsoever the grace of perseverance is bestowed, they do persevere to the end ; and it is impossible in some sense, that they should otherwise do.

3. That none who are not predestinate, what grace soever they may be made partakers of in this world, shall constantly continue to the end.

4. That no believer can by his own strength or power (incited or stirred up, by what manlike or rational considerations soever) persevere in the faith; the grace of perseverance being a gift of God; it is true, that their judgments being perverted by sundry other corrupt principles, about the nature and efficacy of sacraments, with their conveyance of grace, ' ex opere operato,' and out of ignorance of the righteousness of God, and the real work of regeneration, they generally maintain (though Bradwardine punctually expressed himself to be of another mind) that many persons, not-predestinate, may come to believe, yet fall away and perish.

Now the truth is, it is properly no part of the controversy under consideration, whether, or how far, and in what sense, men by reason of the profession, and participation of ordinances with the work and effect of common grace upon them, may be said to be true believers ; but the whole, upon the matter of what we plead for, is comprised in the assertions now ascribed to them; which that it is done upon sufficient grounds, will be manifest by calling in some few

of the most eminent of them, to speak in their own words,
what their thoughts were in this matter.

To bring them in, I desire that one who (though none of
them) was eminent in his undertakings for a mixture of divinity and law, in those days wherein they had their eminent rise and original, may be heard. And that is Gratian,
who after his manner hath collected many things to the purpose in hand; p. 2. c. 33. q. 3. de pœnit. dist. Can. 2. ' Cha-
ritas,' saith he, ' est juncta Deo inseparabiliter, et unita, et
in omnibus semper invicta.' And, 'Electi quippe sic ad
bonum tendunt, ut ad mala perpetranda non redeant; et,
potest discursus, et mobilitas spiritus sic intelligi. In sanc-
torum quippe cordibus juxta quasdam virtutes semper per-
manet; juxta quasdam vero recessurus venit, venturus recedit: in fide etenim, et spe, et charitate, et bonis aliis, sine
quibus ad cœlestem patriam non potest veniii (sicut est
humilitas, castitas, justitia atque misericordia) perfectorum
corda non deserit. in prophetiæ vero virtute, doctrinæ fa-
cundia, miraculorum exhibitione, suis aliquando adest, aliquando se subtrahit.' Answering the objection, of the Spirit's
departure from them, on whom he is bestowed, he distinguisheth of the respects, upon the account whereof, he may
be said so to do. ' In respect of some common gifts,' saith
he, ' he may withdraw himself from them on whom he is bestowed, but not in respect of habitual sanctifying grace.'

Among the schoolmen there is none of greater name and
eminency, for learning, devotion, and subtilty, than our Bradwardine, who was proctor of this university, in the year 1325;
and obtained by general consent the title of doctor profundus;
Lib. 2. de Causa Dei, cap. 8. This profound learned doctor
proposes this thesis to be confirmed in the following chapter:
'Quod nullus viator, quantacunque gratia creata subnixus,
solius liberi arbitrii viribus, vel etiam cum adjutorio gratiæ,
possit perseverare finaliter, sine alio Dei auxilio speciali.'
In the long disputation following, he disputes out of the
Scriptures, and ancient writers abundantly cited to his purpose, that there is no possibility of the perseverance of any
believer in the faith to the end, upon such helps, considerations, and advantages as Mr. Goodwin proposeth, as the
only means thereof. That perseverance itself is a gift of
God, without which gift and grace none can persevere;

and the specialty of that grace, he expresseth in the corollary wherewith he closeth the chapter; which is, ' Quod nullus viator, solius liberi arbitrii, vel gratiæ viribus, aut am-
borum conjunctim, sine alio Dei auxilio speciali, potest perseverare per aliquod tempus omnino.' Farther asserting the
efficacy of special grace, in and for every good work whatever. His arguments and testimonies I shall not need to
recite; they are at hand to those who desire to consult
them.

After the vindication of the former thesis, chap. 9, 10,
11. he proposeth farther this proposition, to a right understanding of the doctrine of perseverance. ' Quod perseverantia non est aliquod donum Dei creatum, a charitate, et
gratia realiter differens.' And the corollary wherewith he
shuts up that disputation is, ' Quod nomen perseverantiæ
nullam rem absolutam essentialiter significat, sed accidentaliter, et relative; charitatem videlicet, sive justitiam cum
respectu futuræ permansionis usque in finem, et quod non
improbabiliter posset dici perseverantiam esse ipsam relationem hujus.'

After this, knowing well what conclusion would easily
be inferred from these principles, viz. That perseverance is
not really distinct from faith and love, that it is such a grace
and gift of God that whoever it is bestowed upon shall certainly persevere; namely, that every one who hath received
true grace, faith, and love, shall certainly persevere. He
objects that to himself, and plainly grants it to be so indeed,
cap. 12. And to make the matter more clear, chap. 13. he
disputes, that ' Auxilium sine quo nullus perseverat, et per
quod quilibet perseverat, est Spiritus Sanctus, divina bonitas
et voluntas.' Every cause of bringing sinful man to God,
is called by them ' auxilium:' in these three, ' Spiritus
Sanctus, divina bonitas, et voluntas,' he compriseth the chief
causes of perseverance, as I have also done in the ensuing
treatise. By ' divina voluntas' he intends God's eternal and
immutable decree, as he manifests, chap. 8, 9. whither he
sends his reader. His ' divina bonitas,' is that free grace,
whereby God accepts and justifies us as his. ' Spiritus
sanctus,' is sanctification; so that he affirms the perseverance of the saints to consist in the stability of their acceptation with God, and continuance of their sanctification

from him, upon the account of his unchangeable purposes
and decrees, which is the sum of what we contend for.

And this is part of the doctrine, concerning the grace of
God, and his sovereignty over the wills of men, which Bradwardine in his days cried out so earnestly for the defence of
to God and man against the Pelagian encroachment, which
was made upon it in those days. Thus he turns himself in
the conclusion of his book, to the pope and church of Rome,
with zealous earnestness for their interposition, to the determination of these controversies : ' Ut os inique loquen-
tium,' saith he, 'obstruatur, flexis genibus cordis mei imploro
ecclesiam, præcipue Romanam, quæ summa authoritate vi-
gere dignoscitur, quatenus ipsa determinare dignetur, quid
circa præmissas catholice sit tenendum. Non enim sine
periculo in talibus erratur. Simon dormis ? exurge (speaking to the pope) exime gladium, amputa quæque sinistra
hæreticæ pravitatis, defende, et protege catholicam veritatem. Porro etsi Dominus ipse in Petri navicula dormiat,
nimietate tempestatis compulsus, ipsum quoque fiducialiter
excitabo, quatenus Spiritus oris sui tempestate sedata tran-
quillum faciat et serenum. Absit autem, ut qui in prora hujus naviculæ pervigil laborabat, jam in puppi super cervicali
dormiat, vel dormitet ;' lib. 3. cap. 53.

With this earnestness above three hundred years ago did
this profoundly learned man press the popes to a determination of these controversies, against the Pelagians and
their successors in his schools. The same suit hath ever
since been continued by very many learned men (in every
age) of the communion of the church of Rome, crying out
for the papal definitive sentence against the Pelagian errors
crept into their church; especially hath this outcry with supplication been renewed by the Dominican friars, ever since
the Jesuits have so cunningly gilded over that Pelagian
poison, and set it out as the best and most wholesome food
for the holy mother and her children. Yea with such
earnestness hath this been in the last age pursued, by agents
in the court of Rome, that (a congregation *de auxiliis* being
purposely appointed) it was generally supposed one while,
that they would have prevailed in their suit, and have obtained a definitive sentence on their side, against their adversaries. But through the just vengeance of God, upon a pack

of bloody persecuting idolaters, giving them up more and more to the belief of lies, contrary almost to the expectation of all men, this very year 1653, pope Innocent the Tenth, who now wears the triple crown, conjured by the subtilty and dreadful interest of the Jesuits in all nations, that as yet wonder after him, by a solemn bull, or papal consistorian determination, in the case of Jansenius bishop of Ypress, hath turned the scales upon his first suppliants, and cast the cause on the Pelagian side. But of that whole business elsewhere.

I shall not perplex the reader, with the horrid names of Trombet, Holcot, Bricot, Sychet, Tartaret, Brulifer, nor with their more horrid terms and expressions. Let the one angelical doctor answer for the rest of his companions.

That this man then (one of the great masters of the crew) abode by the principles of him before insisted on, may quickly be made evident by some few instances clearing his judgment herein.

This, in the first place, he every where insists on; that no habitual grace received, no improvement that can be made of it, by the utmost ability, diligence, and the most raised considerations of the best of men, will cause any one certainly to persevere, without the peculiar preservation of God. Of this he gives his reason; lib..3. Contra. Gent. Ca. 155. ' Illud quod natura sua est variabile, ad hoc, quod figatur in uno, indiget auxilio alicujus moventis immobilis; sed liberum arbitrium etiam existentis in gratia habituali adhuc manet variabile, et flexibile a bono in malum ; ergo ad hoc, quod figatur in bono et perseveret in illo, usque ad finem, indiget speciali Dei auxilio.' An argument of the same importance, with that mentioned out of Bradwardine : which (howsoever at first appearance it may seem to lie at the outskirts of the controversy in hand, yet indeed) is such as being granted, hath an influence into the whole, as hath been manifested.

And this the same author farther confirms, saith he, pp. q. 109..a. 9. ' Cum nullum agens secundum agat nisi in virtute primi, sitque caro spiritui perpetuo rebellis; non potest homo licet jam gratiam consecutus, per seipsum operari bonum, et vitare peccatum, absque novo auxilio Dei, ipsum moventis, dirigentis, et protegentis; quamvis alia habitualis

gratia ad hoc, ei necessaria non sit.' And the reasons he
gives of this conclusion in the body of the article are considerable. This, saith he, must be so; ' Primo quidem, ratione generali propter hoc, quod nulla res creata potest in
quemcunque actum prodire, nisi virtute motionis divinæ.'
The Pelagian self-sufficiency and exemption from dependance ' in solidum,' upon God both providentially and phy-
sically, as to operation was not so freely received in the
schools as afterward.

' Secundo,' saith he ' ratione speciali, propter conditio-
nem status humanæ naturæ, quæ quidem licet per gratiam
sanetur, quantum ad mentem, remanet tamen in eo corruptio,
et infectio quantum ad carnem, per quam servit legi peccati;
ut dicitur; Rom. vii. Remanet etiam quædam ignorantiæ
obscuritas in intellectu, secundum quam (ut etiam dicitur,
Rom. viii.) quid oremus sicut oportet nescimus: ideo ne-
cesse est nobis, ut a Deo dirigamur, et protegamur, qui omnia novit, et omnia potest.' And will not this man think
you, who in his gropings after light, when darkness covered
the face of the earth, and thick darkness was upon the in-
habitants thereof, with this his discovery (of the impotency
of the best of the saints for perseverance, upon the account
of any grace received, because of the perpetual powerful rebellion of indwelling lust and corruption, and that all that
do persevere, are preserved by the power of God unto salvation), rise in judgment against those who in our days, wherein the Sun of righteousness is risen with healing under his
wings, do ascribe a sufficiency unto men in themselves upon
the bottom of their rational considerations, to abide with
God, or persevere to the end?

And this assertion of the angelical doctor is notably confirmed by Didacus Alvarez in his vindication of it from the
exception of Medina, that we make use of habits when we
will, and if men will make use of their habitual grace, they
may persevere, without relation to any after grace of God:
saith he, ' Respondetur, habitibus quidem nos uticum volu-
mus, sed ut velimus illis uti, prærequiritur motio Dei efficax,
præmovens liberum arbitrium, ut utatur habitu ad operan-
dum, et operetur bonum, præsertim quando habitus sunt
supernaturales; quia cum pertineant ad superiorem ordinem,
habent specialem rationem, propter quam potentia mere na-

turalis non utitur eisdem habitibus, nisi speciali Dei auxilio moveatur;' Alvar. de Aux. lib. 10. disput. 100. Though received graces are reckoned by him as supernatural habits, yet such as we act not by, nor with, but from new supplies from God.

.. Having laid down this principle, Thomas proceeds to manifest, that there is a special grace of perseverance, bestowed by God on some, and that on whomsoever it is bestowed, they certainly and infallibly persevere to the end; p. p. quest. 109. a. 10. c. and contra Gent. lib. 3. he proves this assertion from p. 6. 1 Pet. v. 10. Psal. xvi.

But to spare the reader, I shall give you this man's judgment, together with one of his followers, who hath had the happiness to clear his master's mind, above any that have undertaken the maintenance of his doctrine, in that part now controverted in the church of Rome; and therein I shall manifest (what I formerly proposed) what beamings and irradiations of this truth, do yet glide through that gross darkness, which is spread upon the face of the Romish synagogue (referring what I have farther to add on this head, to the account which, God assisting, I shall ere long give of the present Jansenian controversies, in my considerations on Mr. Biddle's catechisms, a task by authority lately imposed on me). This is Didacus Alvarez, whose tenth book De Auxiliis treats peculiarly of this subject of perseverance. In the entrance of his disputation he lays down the same principles with the former concerning the necessity of the peculiar grace of perseverance to this end that any one may persevere; Disput. 103.

Then, Disp. 108. he farther manifests, that this gift or grace of perseverance, does not depend on any conditions in us, or any co-operation of our wills. His position he lays down in these words: 'Donum perseverantiæ, in ratione doni perseverantiæ, et efficacia illius, nullo modo dependet effective ex libera co-operatione nostri arbitrii, sed a solo Deo, atque ab efficaci, et absoluto decreto voluntatis ejus, qui pro sua misericordia tribuit illud donum cui vult.' In the farther proof of this proposition, he manifests by clear testimonies that the contrary doctrine hereunto, was that of the Pelagians and Semi-Pelagians, which Austin opposed in sundry treatises. And in all the arguments whereby he farther confirms it, he still presses the absurdity of making the promise of God concerning perseverance conditional, and so suspending it on any thing, in and by us to be performed. And indeed all the acts whereby we persevere, flowing according to him from the grace of perseverance, it cannot but be absurd to make the efficient cause in its efficiency and operation, to depend upon its own effect: this also is with him ridiculous, that the grace of perseverance should be given to any, and he not persevere; or be promised, and yet not given: yet withal he grants in his following conclusions, that our wills secondarily, and in dependency, do co-operate in our perseverance.

The second principle this learned schoolman insists on, is, that this gift of perseverance is peculiar to the elect, or predestinate: Disput. 104. 1. Con. ' Donum perseverantiæ est proprium prædestinatorum, ut nulli alteri conveniat:' And what he intends by ' prædestinati ;' he informs you according to the judgment of Austin and Thomas; ' Nomine prædestinationis ad gloriam, solum eam prædestinationem intelligunt (Augustinus et Thomas) qua electi ordinantur efficaciter, et transmittuntur ad vitam æternam; cujus effectus sunt vocatio, justificatio et perseverantia in gratia usque ad finem.' Not that (or such a) conditional predestination, as is pendent in the air, and expectant of men's good final deportment; but that which is the eternal, free fountain of all that grace, whereof in time by Jesus-Christ we are made partakers.

And in the pursuit of this proposition, he farther proves at large, that the perseverance given to the saints in Christ, is not a supplement of helps and advantages, whereby they may preserve it if they will; but such as causes them, on whom it is bestowed certainly and actually, so to do: and that in its efficacy and operation, it cannot depend on any free co-operation of our wills, all the good acts tending to our perseverance, being fruits of that grace which is bestowed on us, according to the absolute unchangeable decree of the will of God.

This indeed is common with this author and the rest of his associates (the Dominicans, and present Jansenians) in these controversies, together with the residue of the Romanists, that having their judgments wrested by the abominable figments of implicit faith, and the efficacy of the sacraments of the New Testament, conveying and really exhibiting the grace signified, or sealed by them; that they are enforced to grant, that many may be and are regenerate, and made true believers, who are not predestinate, and that these cannot persevere, nor shall eventually be saved. Certain it is, that there is not any truth, which that generation of men do receive and admit, but more or less it suffers in their hands, from that gross ignorance of the free grace of God in Jesus Christ, the power whereof they are practically under: what the poor vassals and slaves will do, upon the late bull of their holy father casting them in sundry main concernments of their quarrel, with their adversaries, is uncertain; otherwise setting aside some such deviations, as the above mentioned (whereunto they are enforced, by their ignorance of the grace and justification which is in Jesus Christ), there is so much of ancient candid truth in opposition to the Pelagians and Semi-Pelagians, preserved and asserted in the writings of the Dominican friars, as will rise up (as I said before) in judgment against those of our days, who enjoying greater light and advantages, do yet close in with those, and are long since, cursed enemies of the grace of God.

To this Dominican, I shall only add the testimony of two famous Jesuits, upon whose understandings the light of this glorious truth prevailed, for an acknowledgment of it: the first of these is Bellarmine, whose disputes to this purpose, being full and large, and the author in all men's hands, I shall not transcribe his assertions and arguments; but only refer the reader to his l. 2. de Grat. et l. Ar. cap. 12. 'Denique ut multa alia Testimonia,' &c. The other is Suarez, who delivers his thoughts succinctly upon the whole of this matter, lib. 11. de perpetuitat. vel Amis. Grat. cap. 2. sect. 6. saith he, 'De prædestinatis verum est infallibiliter, quod gratiam finaliter seu in perpetuum non amittunt; unde postquam semel gratiam habuerant, ita reguntur et proteguntur a Deo, ut vel non cadant, vel si ceciderint resurgant; et licet sæpius cadant et resurgant, tandem aliquando ita resurgunt ut amplius non cadant:' in which few words he hath briefly comprised the sum of that, which is by us contended for.

It was in my thoughts in the last place to have added

, the concurrent witness of all the reformed churches, with
that of the most eminent divines, which have written in the
defence of their concessions; but this trouble, upon second
considerations, I shall spare the reader and myself: for, as
many other reasons lie against the prosecuting of this design,
so especially the usefulness of spending time and pains, for
the demonstration of a thing of so evident a truth, prevails
with me to desist; notwithstanding the endeavours of Mr.
Goodwin to wrest the words of some of the most ancient
writers, who laboured in the first reformation of the churches;
I presume no unprejudiced person in the least measure acquainted with the system of that doctrine, which with so
much pains, diligence, piety, and learning, they promoted in
the world, with the clearness of their judgments, in going
forth to the utmost compass of their principles which they
received, and their constancy to themselves, in asserting of
the truths they embraced, owned by their friends and adversaries, until such time as Mr. Goodwin discovered their
self-contradictions, will scarce be moved once to question
their judgments by the excerpta of Mr. Goodwin, cap. 15.
of his treatise: so that of this discourse this is the issue.

There remains only that I give a brief account of some
concernments of the ensuing treatise, and dismiss the reader
from any farther attendance in the porch, or entrance
thereof.

The title of the book speaks of the aim and method of it;
the confutation of Mr. Goodwin was but secondarily in my
eye; and the best way for that I judged to consist, in a full
scriptural confirmation of the truth he opposed. That I
chiefly intended, and therein I hope the pious reader, may,
through the grace of God, meet with satisfaction. In my
undertaking to affirm the truth of what I assert, the thing
itself first, and then the manifestation of it, was in my consideration: for the thing itself, my arguing hath been to
discover the nature of it, its principles and causes, its rela
tion to the good will of the Father, the mediations of the
Son, and dispensation of the Holy Ghost to the saints thereupon; its use and tendency, in, and unto that fellowship
with the Father and the Son, whereunto we are called and
admitted.

As to the manner of its revelation, the proper seats of it

in the book of God, the occasion of the delivery thereof, in several seasons, the significant expressions wherein it is set forth, and the receiving of it by them to whom it was revealed, have been diligently remarked.   '

In those parts of the discourse, which tend to the vindication of the arguments from Scripture, whereby the truth pleaded for is confirmed, of the usefulness of the thing itself contended about, &c. I have been, I· hope, careful to keep my discourse from degenerating into jangling, and strife of words (the usual issue of polemical writings), being not altogether ignorant of the devices of Satan, and the usual carnal attendencies of such proceedings: the weight of the truth in hand, the common interest of all the saints, in their walking with God therein, sense of my own duty, and the near approach of the account which I must make of the ministration to me committed, have given bounds and limits to my whole discourse, as to the manner of handling the truth therein asserted.   Writing in the common language of the nation, about the common possession of the saints, the meanest and weakest as well as the wisest and the most learned, labouring in the works of Christ and his gospel, I durst not hide the understanding of what I aimed at, by mingling the plain doctrine of the Scripture, with metaphysical notions, expressions of arts, or any pretended ornaments of wit or fancy ; because I fear God.   For the more sublime consideration of things, and such a way of their delivery, as depending upon the acknowledged reception of sundry arts and sciences, which the generality of Christians neither are, nor need to be, acquainted withal ; scholars may communicate their thoughts and apprehensions unto, and among themselves, and that upon the stage of the world, in that language, whereunto they have consented, for and to that end and purpose : that I have carefully abstained from personal reflections, scoffs, undervaluations, applications of stories, and old sayings, to the provocation of the spirit of them with whom I have to do, I think not at all praise-worthy; because that upon a review of some passages in the treatise (now irrecoverable) I fear I have scarce been so careful, as I am sure it was my duty to have been.

THE DOCTRINE

SAINTS' PERSEVERANCE

EXPLAINED AND CONFIRMED.

CHAP. I.

The various thoughts of men concerning the doctrine proposed to considera-
tion. The great concernment of it (however stated) on all hands confessed.
Some special causes pressing to the present handling of it. The fearful
backsliding of many in these days. The great offence given, and taken
thereby: with the provision made for its removal. The nature of that
offence and temptation thence arising considered. Answer to some argu-
ings of Mr. G. c. 9. from thence against the truth proposed. The use
of trials and shakings: grounds of believers' assurance that they are so.
The same farther argued and debated. Of the testimony of a man's own
conscience concerning his uprightness, and what is required thereunto,
1 John iii. 7. considered. Of the rule of self-judging, with principles of
settlement for true believers, notwithstanding the apostacies of eminent
professors. Corrupt teachings rendering the handling of this doctrine
necessary: its enemies of old and of late. The particular undertaking
of Mr. G. proposed to consideration. An entrance into the stating of the
question. The terms of the question explained: of holiness in its several
acceptations. Created holiness, original or adventitious. Complete or in-
choate. Typical by dedications, real by purification. Holiness evangelical,
either so indeed, or by estimation. Real holiness, partial or universal.
The partakers of the first, or temporary believers, not true believers: main-
tained against Mr. G. Ground of judging professors to be true believers.
Matt. vii. 20. considered: what is the rule of judging men therein given.
What knowledge of the faith of others is to be obtained. What is meant
by perseverance: how in Scripture it is expressed. The grounds of it
pointed at. What is intended by falling away, whether it be possible the
Spirit of grace may be lost; or the habit of it, and how. The state of the
controversy as laid down by Mr. G. The vanity thereof discovered. His
judgment about believers' falling away examined; what principles and
means of perseverance he grants to them. The enemies of our perse-
verance. Indwelling sin in particular considered. No possibility of pre-
servation upon Mr. G.'s grounds demonstrated. The means and ways of
the saints' preservation in faith, asserted by Mr. G. at large, examined,
weighed, and found light. The doctrine of the saints' perseverance, and
way of teaching it, cleared from Isa. iv. That chapter opened. The forty-
third verse particularly insisted on and discussed. The whole state and
method of the controversy thence educed.

THE truth which I have proposed to handle, and whose defence I have undertaken in the ensuing discourse, is com-

monly called the 'perseverance of saints;' a doctrine, whereof nothing ordinary, low, or common is spoken by any, that have engaged into the consideration of it. To[a] some it is the very salt of the covenant of grace, the most distinguishing mercy communicated in the blood of Christ, so interwoven into, and lying at the bottom of, all that consolation, which ' God is abundantly willing, that all the heirs of the promise should receive;' that it is utterly impossible it should be safe-guarded one moment, without a persuasion of this truth, which seals up all the mercy and grace of the new covenant, with the unchangeableness and faithfulness of God.- To[b] others, it is no grace of God, no part of the purchase of Christ, no doctrine of the gospel, no foundation of consolation, but an invention of men, a delusion of Satan, an occasion of dishonour to God, disconsolation and perplexity to believers, a powerful temptation unto sin and wickedness in all that do receive it.

A doctrine it is also, whose right apprehension is on all hands confessed, to be of great importance, upon the account of that effectual influence, which it hath, and will have, into our walking with God, which say some,[c] is, to love, humility, thankfulness, fear, fruitfulness; to folly, stubbornness, rebellion, dissoluteness, negligence, say others. The great confidence expressed by men concerning the evidence and certainty of their several persuasions, whether defending or opposing the doctrine under consideration; the one part professing the truth thereof to be of equal stability with the promises of God, and most plentifully delivered in the Scripture; others (at least one who is thought to be *pars magna* of his companions), that if it be asserted in any place of the Scripture, it were enough to make wise and impartial men to call the authority thereof into question; must needs invite men to turn aside to see about what this earnest contest is : and *quis is est tam potens*, who dares thus undertake to remove not only ancient landmarks and boundaries of doctrines among the saints, but ' mountains of brass,' and the ' hills about Jerusalem,' which we hoped would stand

---

[a] Jude 3. 2 Cor. xiii 8 Isa. iv. 5, 6. Jer. xxvi 31—35. xxxii. 39, 40. Isa. lix. 21. Heb viii. 10, 11. 1 Cor. i. 9. Phil. i. 6. Rom. viii. 32—35.

[b] Pelag. Armin. Socin. Papist. Thomson de Intercis. Justif. Diatrib. Bertius Apost Sanct. Remon. Coll Hag. Scripta Sinod.

[c] Gen. xvii. 1. Psal. xxiii. 6. Phil. ii. 12, 13. Heb. x. 16—22. 2 Cor. vii. 1. 2 Pet. i. 3—7, &c.

fast for ever? The concernment then of the glory of God, and the honour of the Lord Jesus Christ, with the interest of the souls of the saints, being so wrapped up, and that confessedly on all hands, in the doctrine proposed, I am not out of hope that the plain discoursing of it from the word of truth, may be as 'a word in season, like apples of gold in pictures of silver.'

Moreover, besides the general importance of that doctrine in all times and seasons, the wretched practices of many in the days wherein we live, and the industrious attempts of others in their teachings, for the subverting and casting it down from its excellency, and that place which it hath long held in the churches of Christ, and hearts of all the saints of God, have rendered the consideration of it, at this time necessary.

For the first: these are days, wherein we have as sad and tremendous examples of apostacy, backsliding, and falling from high and glorious pitches in profession, as any age can parallel. As many [d] stars cast from heaven, as many trees plucked up by the roots, as many stately buildings by wind, rain, and storm, cast to the ground, as many sons of perdition discovered, as many washed swine returning to their mire, as many Demases going after the present evil world, and men going out from the church which were never truly and properly of it, as many sons of the morning and children of high illumination and gifts setting in darkness, and that of all sorts; as ever in so short a space of time, since the name of Christ was known upon the earth. What through the deviating of some to the ways of the world, and the lusts of the flesh; what of others, to spiritual wickednesses and abominations; it is seldom that we see a professor to hold out in the glory of his profession to the end. I shall not now discourse of the particular causes hereof, with the temptations and advantages of Satan, that seem to be peculiar to this season, but only thus take notice of the thing itself, as that which presseth for, and rendereth the consideration of the doctrine proposed not only seasonable but necessary.

That this is a stumbling-block in the way of them, that

[d] Rev. xii. 4. Jude 12. Matt. vii. 26, 27. 2 Thess. ii. 8. 2 Pet i. 20—22. 2 Tim. iv. 10. 1 John ii. 19. Heb. vi. 4—6.

seek to walk with God, I suppose that none of them will
deny. It was so of old, and it will so continue until the end.
And therefore our Saviour predicting and discoursing of the
like season, Matt. xxiv. foretelling that many should be
deceived, ver. 11. 'that iniquity should abound, and the love
of many wax cold,' ver. 12. that is, visibly and scandalously
to the contempt and seeming disadvantage of the gospel,
adds as a preservative consolation, to his own chosen select
ones, who might be shaken in their comforts and confidence
to see so many that walked in the house of God, and took
sweet counsel together with them, to fall headlong to destruction, that the elect shall not be seduced ; let the attempts of seducers be what they will, and their advantages
never so many, or their successes never so great, they shall
be preserved ; the house upon the rock shall not be cast
down ; against the church built on Christ the gates of hell
shall not prevail. And Paul mentioning the apostacy of
Hymeneus and Philetus, who seem to have been teachers
of some eminency, and stars of some considerable magnitude in the firmament of the church, with the aversion of
the faith of some who attended unto their abominations ;
2 Tim. ii. 17, 18. lest any disconsolation should surprise
believers in reference to their own condition, as though that
should be lubricous, uncertain, and such as might end in destruction, and their faith in an overthrow ; he immediately
adds that effectual cordial, for the reviving and supportment
of their confidence and comfort, ver. 19. nevertheless (notwithstanding all this apostacy of eminent professors, yet),
'the foundation of God standeth sure, the Lord knoweth
who are his ;' those who are built upon the foundation of
his unchangeable purpose and love, shall not be prevailed
against.   John likewise doth the same ; for having told his
little children, that there were many antichrists abroad in
the world, and they for the most part apostates, he adds in
the first Epist. chap. ii. 19. ' They went out from us because
they were not of us, for if they had been of us they would
no doubt have continued with us ; but they went out that
they might be made manifest that they were not all of us.'
He lets them know that by their being apostates, they had
proved themselves to have been but hypocrites ; and therefore believers dwelling in safety was no way prejudiced by

their backsliding. The like occasion now calls for the like application, and the same disease for the same prevention or remedy ; that no sound persons may be shaken, because unhealthy ones are shattered ; that those may not tremble who are built on the rock, because those are cast down who are built on the sand, is one part of my aim and intendment in handling this doctrine. And therefore, I shall as little dabble in the waters of strife, or insist upon it in way of controversy, as the importunity of the adversary, and that truth which we are obliged to contend for, will permit. One Scripture in its own plainness and simplicity, will be of more use for the end I aimed at, than twenty scholastical arguments pressed with never so much accurateness and subtilty.

A temptation then this is, and hath been of old to the saints, disposed of by the manifold wisdom of God, to stir them up to[e] ' take heed lest they fall ;' to put them upon trying and examining, whether ' Christ be in them or no ;' and also to make out to those fountains of establishment in his eternal purpose and gracious promises, wherein their refreshments and reserves under such temptations do lie. And yet though our doctrine enforces us to conclude all such never to be sound believers, in that peculiar notion and sense of that expression which shall instantly be declared, who totally and finally apostatize and fall off from the ways of God, yet is it exceedingly remote from being any true ground of shaking the faith of those who truly believe, any farther than shaking is useful for the right and thorough performance of that great gospel duty of trial and self-examination.

Mr. Goodwin indeed contends, chap. 9. sect. 8—11. pp. 108—110.) ' That if we judge all such as fall away to perdition never to have been true believers' (that is, with such a faith as bespeaks them to enjoy union with Christ and acceptance with God), ' it will administer a thousand fears and jealousies concerning the soundness of a man's own faith, whether that be sound or no ; and so it will be indifferent as to consolation, whether true believers may fall away or no, seeing it is altogether uncertain whether a man hath any of that true faith which cannot perish.' *Ans.* But,

e Rom. xi. 20. 1 Cor. x 12. xi 19. 2 Cor. xiii. 5. Rev. ii. 24, 25. Isa. xlv. 22. Mal. iii. 6. 2 Pet. iii. 17. Heb. iii. 12. Hab. iii. 17, 18.

First, God who hath promised to make[f] 'all things work together for good to them that love him,' in his infinite love and wisdom is pleased to exercise them with great variety, both within and without, in reference to themselves and others, for the accomplishing towards them all the good pleasure of his goodness, and carrying them on in that holy, humble, depending frame, which is needful for the receiving from him those gracious supplies, without which it is impossible they should be preserved. To this end are they often exposed to winnowings of fierce winds and shakings by more dreadful blasts, than any breaths in this consideration of the apostatizing of professors, though of eminency. Not that God is delighted with their fears and jealousies, which yet he knows under such dispensations they must conflict withal, but with the trial and exercise of their graces whereunto he calls them ; that is, his glory, wherein his soul is delighted. It is no singular thing for the saints of God to be exercised with a thousand fears and jealousies, and through them to grow to great establishment; if indeed they were such as were unconquerable, such as did not work together for their good, such as must needs be endless, all means of satisfaction and establishment being rescinded by the causes of them, then were there weight in this exception, but neither the Scriptures, nor the experience of the saints of God do give the least hint to such an assertion.

Secondly, It is denied that the fall of the most glorious hypocrites is indeed an efficacious engine in the hands of the adversary, to ingenerate any other fears and jealousies, or to expose them to any other shakings, than what are common to them in[g] other temptations of daily incursion, which God doth constantly make way for them to escape ; it is true indeed, that if true believers had no other foundation of their persuasion that they are so, but what occurs visibly to the observation of men in the outward conversation of them that yet afterward fall totally away, the apostacy of such (notwithstanding the general assurance they have, that those who are[h] 'born of God cannot, shall not sin

<hr />

[f] Rom. viii. 28. Psal. xxx. 6, 7. Isa. viii. 17. liv. 7—9. 1 Pet. iii 7. 1 Cor. iii. 13. 1 Pet. iv. 12. 2 Cor vii. 5. 2 Thess. i 11. Heb. xii 25. 28, 29. Isa. lvii. 15. lxvi 2. James iv. 6. 1 Pet. v. 5. Matt. vii.24, 25. Amos ix. 9. Luke xxii. 31. Eph. vi. 11—13. iv. 14. Isa. xlix. 14—16. lxiii. 9. Acts ix. 5. Psal. ciii. 13. 1 Pet. i. 7. Rom. viii. 38.
[g] 1 Cor. x. 13.   [h] 1 John iii. 9.

unto death;' seeing their own interest in that estate and condition may be clouded (at least for a season), and their consolation thereupon depending interrupted) might occasion thoughts in them of very sad consideration; but whilst besides all the beams and rays that ever issued from a falling star, all the leaves and blossoms with abortive fruit, that ever grew on an unrooted tree, all the goodly turrets and ornaments of the fairest house that ever was built on the sand, there are moreover,[1] ' three that bear witness in heaven, the Father, Son and Spirit; and three that bear witness on earth, the water, blood, and Spirit;' whilst there is a teaching, anointing, and assuring earnest, a firm sealing to the day of redemption, a knowledge that we are passed from death to life; the temptation arising from the apostacy of hypocrites is neither so potent nor unconquerable, but that by the grace of him through ' whom we can do all things,' it may be very well dealt withal. This, I say, supposing the ordinary presence and operation of the Spirit of grace, in the hearts of believers, with such shines of God's countenance upon them, as they usually enjoy. Let these be interrupted or turned aside, and there is not the least blast or breath, that proceeds from the mouth of the weakest enemy, they have to deal withal, but is sufficient to cast[k] ' them down from the excellency' of their joy and consolation.

The evidence of this truth is such, that Mr. Goodwin is forced to say :[l] ' Far be it from me to deny but that a man may very possibly attain unto a very strong and potent assurance, and that upon grounds every way sufficiently warrantable and good, that his faith is sound and saving:' cap. 9. sect. 9. but unto this concession, he puts in a double exception.

First, ' That there is not one true believer of a hundred, yea of many thousands, who hath any such assurance of his faith as is built upon solid and pregnant foundations.'

I must (by his leave) enter my dissent hereunto, and as we have the liberty of our respective apprehensions, so neither the one nor the other prove any thing in the cause.

---

[1] 1 John v. 7, 8. ii. 20, 21. 2 Cor. i 21, 22. v 5. Eph. i. 14. iv. 30. Rom. viii. 16.
[k] Psal. xxx. 6, 7.
[l] Vere fidelis uti pro tempore præsenti de fidei et conscientiæ suæ integritate certus esse potest, ita et de salute sua et de salutifera Dei erga ipsum benevolentia pro illo tempore certus esse potest et debet. Act. Synod. p. 182. decl. sent. Thes. 7.

Setting aside causes of desertion, great temptations and trials, I hope through the riches of the grace and tenderness of the love of their Father, the condition is otherwise than is apprehended by Mr. Goodwin, with the generality of the family of God. The reasons given by him of his thoughts to the contrary, do not sway me from my hopes, or bias my former apprehensions in the least; his reasons are,

First, 'Because though the testimony of a man's heart and conscience touching his uprightness towards God, or the soundness of any thing that is saving in him, be comfortable and cheering, yet seldom are these properties built upon such foundations which are sufficient to warrant them; at least upon such whose sufficiency in that kind is duly apprehended. For the testimony of the conscience of a man touching any thing which is spiritually and excellently good, is of no such value, unless it be first excellently enlightened with the knowledge, nature, properties and condition of that on which it testifieth ; and, secondly, Be in the actual contemplation, consideration, or remembrance, of what he knoweth in this kind.' Now very few believers in the world come up to this height and degree.

Ans. First, There is in this reason couched a supposition which, if true, would be far more effectual to shake the confidence and resolution of believers, than the most serious consideration of the apostacies of all professors, that ever fell from the glory of their profession from the beginning of the world; and that is, that there is no other pregnant foundation of assurance, but the testimony of a man's own heart and conscience, touching his uprightness towards God, and therefore before any can attain that assurance upon abiding foundations, they must be excellently enlightened in the nature, properties, and condition of that which their consciences testify unto (as true faith and uprightness of heart); and be clear in the disputes and questions about them, being in the actual contemplation of them when they give their testimony. I no way doubt but many thousands of believers,[m] whose apprehensions of the nature, properties, and conditions of things, as they are in themselves, are low, weak, and confused; yet having received the Spirit[n] of adoption bearing witness with their spirits, that they are the

m 1 Cor. i. 26. James ii. 5.   n Rom. viii. 16. 1 John v. 10.

children of God, and having the testimony in themselves,
have been taken up into as high a degree of comforting and
cheering assurance, and that upon the most infallible foundation imaginable ([o]for the Spirit witnesseth, because the
Spirit is truth), as ever the most seraphically illuminated
person in the world attained unto. Yea, in the very graces
themselves of faith and uprightness of heart, there is such
a seal and stamp, impressing the image of God upon the
soul, as without any reflex act, or actual contemplation of
those graces themselves, have an influence into the establishment of the souls of men, in whom they are, unto a quiet
comfortable assured repose of themselves upon the love and
faithfulness of God: neither is the spiritual confidence of
the saints shaken, much less [p]cast to the ground, by their
conflicting with fears, scruples, and doubtful apprehensions;
seeing in all these conflicts, they have the pledge of the
faithfulness of God, that they shall be more than conquerors. Though they are exercised by them, they are not
dejected with them; nor deprived of that comforting assurance and joy which they have in believing. But yet suppose, that this be the condition practically of many saints
of God, and that they never attain to the state of the primitive Christians, to whose [q]joy and consolation in believing
the Holy Ghost so plentifully witnesseth, nor do live up to
that full rate of plenty, which their Father hath provided for
them in his family, and [r]sworn that he is abundantly willing,
they should enjoy and make use of; what will hence follow
as to the business in hand, I profess I know not. Must
that little evidence which they have of their acceptance with
God, be therefore necessarily built upon such bottoms (or
rather tops) as are visible to them in hypocrites, so that
upon their apostacy they must needs not only try and examine themselves, but conclude to their disadvantage and
disconsolation, that they have no true faith? 'Credat Apella.'

Secondly, The comfortableness, he tells us, of the testimony of a man's conscience concerning his uprightness with
God, 'depends mainly and principally upon his uniform and
regular walking with God; now this being by the neglects
of the saints often interrupted with many stains of unworthi-

[o] 1 John v 6.   [p] Matt. vii. 25. xvi. 18. Psal. lxxvii. 10. 1 Cor. i 9. 1 Thess.
v. 23, 24. 1 Cor. x. 13. Rom. viii. 37.   [q] 1 Pet. i. 8.   [r] Heb. vi. 17, 18.
VOL. VI.   K

ness, the testimony itself must needs be often suspended:
now true believers finding themselves outgone in ways of
obedience by them that impenitently apostatize, if from
hence they must conclude them hypocrites, they have no
evidence left for the soundness of their own faith, which
their consciences bear testimony unto, upon the fruitfulness
of it, which is inferior by many degrees to that of them who
yet finally fall away.' This is the substance of one long
section, pp. 109, 110. But,

First, Here is the same supposal included as formerly,
that the only evidence of a true faith and acceptance with
God, is the testimony of a man's conscience concerning his
regular and upright walking with God: for an obstruction
in this being supposed, his comfort and consolation is thought
to vanish; but that the Scripture builds up our assurance on
other foundations is evident, and the saints acknowledge it,
as hath been before delivered: nor,

Secondly, Doth the testimony of a man's own conscience,
as it hath an influence into his consolation, depend solely
(nor doth Mr. Goodwin affirm it so to do) on the constant
regularity of his walking with God. It will also witness
what former experience it hath had of God, calling to mind
its 'song in the night, all the tokens and pledges of its Father's love, all the gracious visits of the holy and blessed
Spirit of grace, all the embracements of Christ, all that inti-
macy and communion it hath formerly been admitted unto,
the healing and recovery it hath had of wounds, and from
backslidings, with all the spiritual intercourse it ever had
with God, to confirm and strengthen itself in the beginning
of its confidence to the end. And,

Thirdly, In the testimony that it doth give from its walking with God, and the fruits of righteousness, it is very far
and remote from giving it only, or chiefly, or indeed at all,
from those ways, works, and fruits which are exposed to the
eyes of men, and which, in others, they who have that testimony may behold. It resolves itself herein in the frame,
principles, and life of the 'hidden man of the heart, which
lies open and naked to the eyes of God, but is lodged in

* Job xxxv. 10. Psal. lxxvii. 5—7. Isa. xl. 28—30. Cant. iii. 1, 2. v. 4, 5.
Psal. xlii. 6—11. Hos. ii. 7. xiv. 2. 18.
 † Heb. iii. 14. Isa. xxxviii. 3. Psal. cxxxix. 23, 24. Rev. iii. 1. 1 Pet. iii. 4.
2 Cor. ii. 12.

depths not to be fathomed by any of the sons of men : there
is no comparison to be instituted between the obedience and
fruits of righteousness in others, whereby a believer makes
a judgment of them, and that in himself from whence the
testimony mentioned doth flow; that of other men being
their visibly practical conversation, his being the hidden
habitual frame of his heart and spirit in his ways and actings; so that though through the fallings of them, he should
be occasioned to question his own faith, as to trial and examination; yet nothing can thence arise sufficient to enforce
him to let go even that part of his comfort, which flows from
the weakest witness, and one of the lowest voices of all his
store. He eyes others without doors, but himself within.

Fourthly, Whereas, 1 John iii. 7. ' Little children let no
man deceive you, he that doth righteousness is righteous,' is
produced, and two things argued from thence, first, that the
caveat (be not deceived) plainly intimates, that true believers
may very possibly be deceived in the estimate of a righteous
man; and secondly, that this is spoken of a man judging
himself, and that emphatically and exclusively, he and he
only is to be judged a righteous man. *Ans.* I say,

1. That though I grant the first, that we may very easily
be, and often are, deceived in our estimate of righteous persons, yet I do not conceive the inference to be enforced
from that expression, ' Let no man deceive you;' the Holy
Ghost using it frequently, or what is equivalent thereunto,
not so much to caution men in a dubious thing, wherein
possibly they may be mistaken, as in a way of detestation,
scorn, and rejection of what is opposite to that which he is
urging upon his saints, which he presseth as a thing of the
greatest evidence and clearness, as 1 Cor. vi. 9. xv. 32. Gal.
vi. 7. Neither is any thing more intended in this expression
of the apostle, than in that of 1 Cor. vi. 9. ' Be not deceived,
no unrighteous person shall inherit the kingdom of heaven;'
so here, no person not giving himself up to the pursuit of
righteousness in the general drift and scope of his life (cases
extraordinary and particular acts, being always in such rules
excepted), is, or is to be, accounted a righteous man.

Secondly, Also it may be granted (though the intendment
of the place leads us another way) that this is so far a rule

K 2

of self-judging, that he, whose frame and disposition suits it
not, or is opposite unto it, cannot keep up the power or
vigour of any other comfortable evidence of his state and
condition ; but that it should be so far extended, as to make
the only solid and pregnant foundation that any man hath
of assurance and consolation, to arise and flow fiom the testimony of his own conscience, concerning his own regular
walking in ways of righteousness (seeing persons that 'walk
in darkness and have no light,' are called ' to stay themselves
on God ;' Isa. l. 10. and ' when both heart and flesh faileth,
yet God is the strength of the heart ;' Psal. lxxiii. 6.) is no
way clear in itself, and is not by Mr. Goodwin afforded the
least contribution of assistance for its confirmation. To return then from this digression : a temptation we acknowledge, and an offence to be given to the saints by the apostacy
of professors ; yet not such, but as the Lord hath in Scripture made gracious provision against their suffering by it,
or under it, so it leaves them not without sufficient testimony of their own acceptance with God, and sincerity in
walking with him. This then was the state of old, thus it
is in the days wherein we live.

As the practice and ways of some, so the principles and
teachings of others, have an eminent tendence unto offence
and scandal. Indeed ever since the Reformation, there have
been some endeavours against this truth to corrode it and
corrupt it. The first serious attempt for the total intercision of the faith of true believers, though not a final ex-
cision of the faith of elect believers, was made by one in the
other university, who, being a man of a debauched and vicious conversation, no small part of the growing evils of the
days wherein he lived, did yet cry out against the doctrines
of others as tending to looseness and profaneness, upon
whose breasts and teachings was written holiness to the
Lord all their days. Afterward "Arminius with his Quin-
quarticulan followers, taking up the matter, though they
laboured with all their might to answer sundry of the arguments whereby the truth of this doctrine is demonstrated,
yet for a season were very faint and dubious in their own
assertions: not daring to break in at once upon so great a

---

u Armin. Antiperk. Rem. Coll. Hag. Artic. 5.

tieasure of the church of God :[x] and therefore in their Synodalia are forced to apologize for their hesitation nine years
before in their conference at the Hague. But now of late
since the glorious light of Socinianism hath broken forth
from the pit, men by their new succours, are [y]grown bold to
defy this great truth of the gospel and grace of the covenant,
as an abomination for ever to be abhorred. 'Audax omnia
perpeti gens humana, ruit per vetitum nefas.'

In particular, the late studious endeavours of a learned
man, in his treatise entitled Redemption Redeemed, for to de-
spoil the spouse of Christ of this most glorious pearl wherewith her beloved hath adorned her, calls for a particular consideration. And this (discharging a regard unto any other
motives) upon (chiefly) this account, that he hath with great
pains and travail gathered together whatever hath been formerly given out, and dispersed by the most considerable
adversaries of this truth (especially not omitting any thing
of moment in the synodical defence of the fifth article, with
an exact translation of the dramatical prosopopœias, with
whatsoever looks towards his design in hand from their
fourth attempt about the manner of conversion), giving it
anew not only an elegant dress, and varnish of rhetorical expressions, but moreover reinforcing the declining cause of
his Pelagian friends with not-to-be-despised supplies of [z]ap-
pearing reasons and hidden sophistry. So that though I
shall handle this doctrine in my own method (with the reason
whereof, I shall instantly acquaint the reader), and not follow that author κατὰ πόδας, yet handling not only the main
of the doctrine itself, but all the concernments and consequences of it in the several branches of the method intended,
I hope not to leave any thing considerable in that whole
treatise (as to the truth in hand) undiscussed, no argument
unvindicated, no objection unanswered, no consequence un-
weighed, with a special eye to the comparison instituted between the doctrines in contest, as to their direct and causal
influence into the obedience and consolation of the saints.

That we may know then what we speak and whereof we

---

[x] Nos cum mentem nostram super hoc argumento categorice et dogmatice in alte-
ram partem definivimus, nullo jure levitatis insinulari posse, propterea quod novem
ab hinc annis, eam non ita diserte et rotunde enunciaverimus, sed solummodo dis-
quirentium adhuc in morem professi simus. Declar. sent. Rem circa 5. Artic.
  [y] Socin Prælect. Theol. cap 6. art. 7, &c.   [z] Col. ii. 4

do affirm, I shall briefly state the doctrine under consideration, that the difference about it may appear.   Indeed it
seems strange to me among other things, that he of whom
mention was lastly made, who hath liberally dispended so
great a treasure of pains, reading, and eloquence, for the
subverting of the truth, whose explanation and defence we
have undertaken, did not yet once attempt fairly to fix the
state of the difference about it, but in a very tumultuary
manner,[a] fell in with prejudices, swelling over all bounds and
limits of ordinary reasoning, rhetorical amplifications upon
a doctrine not attempted to be brought forth and explained,
that it might be weighed in the balance, as in itself it is.
Whereas there may be many reasons of such a proceeding,
it may well be questioned whether any of them be candid
and commendable.   Certainly the advantages thence taken
for the improving of many sophistical reasons, and pretended
arguments, are obvious to every one that shall but peruse his
ensuing discourse.

Although the substance of this doctrine hath been by
sundry delivered, yet, least the terms, wherein it is usually
done, may seem to be somewhat too general, and some advantages of the truth, which in itself it hath, to have been
omitted, I shall briefly state the whole matter under those
terms, wherein it is usually received.

The title of it is, the Perseverance of Saints : a short discovery of whom we mean by saints, the subject whereof we
speak ; and what by perseverance, which is affirmed of them,
will state the whole for the judgment of the reader.   God
only is essentially holy, and on that account, the[b] Holy One.
In his holiness, as in his being, and all his glorious attributes,
there is an actual permanency or sameness ; Heb. i. 10—12.
Nothing in him is subject to the least shadow of change : not
his truth, not his faithfulness, not his holiness ; all principles, causes, and reasons of alteration stand at no less infinite distance from him, than not being.   His properties are
the same with himself, and are spoken of one another, as
well as of his nature.   His eternal power is mentioned by

---

[a] Chap. ix.

[b] Isa. vi. 3. Josh. xxiv. 19. Rev. xv. 4. Exod. iii. 14. Deut. xxvii. 4. Isa. xl. 38.
xli. 4. xliii. 10. xliv. 6. xlviii. 12. Rev. i. 4. 17. Mal iii. 6. James i. 18. 1 Sam. xv. 29.
Gen i. 26. Matt. xix 17. Eccles. vii. 29. Heb. vii. 25. Ezek. xxxvi. 26—28. Isa. iv.
3, 4. Rom. vi. 4—6. Eph. iv. 22—25.

the apostle, Rom. i. So is his holiness eternal, immutable. Of this we may have use afterward, for the present I treat not of it. The holiness of all creatures is accidental and created; to some it is innate or original, as to the angels, the first man, our Saviour Christ as to his human nature; of whom we treat not. Adam had original holiness and lost it; so had many angels, who kept not their first habitation. It is hence argued by Mr. Goodwin, that spiritual gifts of God being bestowed, may be taken away, notwithstanding the seeming contrary engagement of Rom. xi. 29. From what proportion or analogy this argument doth flow, is not intimated. The grace Adam was endowed with, was intrusted with himself, and his own keeping, in a covenant of works; that of the saints since the fall, is purchased for them, laid up in their head, dispensed in a covenant of grace; whose eminent distinction from the former, consists in the permanency and abidingness of the fruits of it. But of this afterward. To others, adventitious and added, as to all that have contracted any qualities contrary to that original holiness, wherewith at first they were endued, as have done all the sons of men, 'who have sinned and come short of the glory of God.' Now the holiness of these is either complete, as it is with the spirits of just men made perfect; or inchoate, and begun only, as with the residue of sanctified ones in this life. The certain perseverance of the former in their present condition being not directly opposed by any, though the foundation of it be attempted by some, we have no need as yet to engage in the defence of it. These latter are said to be sanctified or holy two ways, upon the twofold account of the use of the word in the Scripture. For,

First, Some persons, as well as things, are said to be holy, especially in the Old Testament, and in the epistle to the Hebrews, almost constantly using the terms of sanctifying and sanctified, in a legal or temple signification, in reference unto their being [b] separated from the residue of men, with relation to God and his worship; or being consecrated and dedicated peculiarly to the performance of any part of his will, or distinct enjoyment of any portion of his mercy: thus the ark was said to be holy, and the altar holy, the temple was holy, and all the utensils of it, with the vestments of

[b] Exod. xxviii. 36. 38. Lev. v. 15. Ezek. xxii. 8. Heb. ii. 11. x. 10. John xvii. 19.

its officers. So the whole people of the Jews, were said to be holy: the particular respects of covenant, worship, separation, law, mercy, and the like, upon which this denomination of holiness and saintship was given unto them, and did depend, are known to all: yea, persons inherently unclean, and personally notoriously wicked, in respect of their designment to some outward work, which by them God will bring about, are said to be sanctified: distinguishing gifts with designation to some distinct employment, is a bottom for this appellation; though their gifts may be recalled, and the employment taken from them; Isa. xiii. 3. We confess perseverance, not to be a proper and inseparable adjunct of this subject, nor to belong unto such persons as such: though they may have a right to it, it is upon another account: yet in the pursuit of this business, it will appear that many of our adversaries' arguments, smite these men only, and prove that such as they, may be totally rejected of God, which none ever denied.

Again, the word is used in an evangelical sense, for inward purity and real holiness, whence some are said to be ᶜholy, and that also two ways: for either they are so really, and in the truth of the thing itself, or in estimation only, and that either of themselves or others. That many have accounted themselves to be holy, and been pure in their own eyes, who yet were never washed from their iniquity, and have thereupon cried peace to themselves, I suppose needs no proving. It is the case of thousands in the world, at this day: they think themselves holy, they profess themselves holy, and our adversaries prove (none gainsaying) that such as these may backslide from what they have, and what they seem to have, and so perish under the sin of apostacy. Again, some are said to be holy, upon the score of their being so in the esteem of others, which was and is the condition of many false hypocrites in the churches of Christ, both primitive and modern. Like them who are said to 'believe in Christ' upon the account of the profession they made so to do, yet he would not 'trust himself with them, because he knew what was in them.' Such were Judas, Si-

---

ᶜ Luke i. 15. Rom. vi 19. 22. 2 Cor. vii. 1. Eph. i. 4. iv. 24. 1 Thess. v. 13. iv. 7. Heb. xii. 14. κατὰ ἀληθειαν κατὰ δοξαν Prov. xxx. 12. Isa. lxv. 5. vii. 48, 49. ix. 40, 41. 1 Thess. v. 3. Matt. xxv. 29. 2 Pet. ii. 21. John vi. 16.

mon Magus, and sundry others, of whom these things are
spoken, which they professed of themselves, and were bound
to answer, and which others esteemed to be in them.
These [d] some labour with all their strength, to make true
believers, that so they may cast the stumbling-block of their
apostacy in the way of the saints of God, closing with the
truth we have in hand.   But for such as these we are no
advocates : let them go to their own place according to the
tenor of the arguments levied against them from Heb. vi. 4.
2 Pet. ii. and other places.

   Moreover of those, who are said to believe, and to be
holy really, and in the truth of the thing itself, there are two
sorts. First, Such as having received sundry common gifts
and graces of the Spirit, as [e] illumination of the mind, change
of affections, and thence amendment of life, with sorrow of
the world, legal repentance, temporary faith and the like,
which are all true and real in their kind, do thereby become
vessels in the great house of God, being changed as to their
use, though not in their nature, continuing stone and wood
still, though hewed and turned to the serviceableness of
vessels, and on that account are frequently termed saints
and believers.   On such as these there is a lower (and in
some a subordinate) work of the Spirit effectually producing
(in and on all the faculties of their souls) somewhat that is
true, good, and useful in itself, answering in some likeness
and suitableness of operation unto the great work of regeneration which faileth not.   There is in them light, love, joy,
faith, zeal, obedience, &c. all true in their kind, which
make many of them, in whom they are, do worthily in their
generation, howbeit they attain not to the faith of God's
elect, neither doth Christ live in them, nor is the life which
they lead, by the faith of the Son of God : as shall hereafter
be fully declared.   If ye now cashier these from the roll of
those saints and believers about whom we contend, seeing
that they are nowhere said to be united to Christ, quickened
and justified, partakers of the first resurrection, accepted of
God, &c. you do almost put an issue to the whole controversy, and at once overturn the strongest forts of the op-

[d] 2 Pet. ii. 1. Act Synod. Dec. sent. Art 5. p. 266, 267, &c.
[e] Heb. vi. 4. 1 Sam. x 10. 2 Pet. ii 20. 1 Kings xxi. 27. 2 Cor. vii. 10. Matt xvii.
3, 4. xiii. 20. Mark vi. 20. 2 Kings x. 16 Hosea vi. 4. 2 Tim. ii. 20. John vi. 34.
Acts xxvi. 28. Matt. vii. 26, 27. Rev. iii. 1. Mark iv. 16.

posers of this truth. Some men are truly ready to think, that
they never had experience of the nature of true faith or holiness, who can suppose it to consist in such like common
gifts and graces, as are ascribed to this sort of men. Yet,
as was said before, if these may not pass for saints, if our
adversaries cannot prove these to be true believers in the
strictest notion and sense of that term or expression, *actum
est*, the very subject about which they contend is taken
away: such as these alone are concerned in the arguments
from Heb. vi. 4, 5. 2 Pet. ii. 1, &c. yea, all the testimonies
which they produce for the supportment of their cause from
antiquity, flow from hence, that their witnesses thought
good to allow persons baptized and professing the gospel
the name of believers, and being regenerate (that is, as to
the participation of the outward symbol thereof), whom yet
they expressly distinguish from them, whose faith was the
fruit of their eternal election, which they constantly maintained should never fail.

Of such as these Mr. Goodwin tells us, cap. 9. sect. 7. pp.
107, 108. 'That if there be any persons under heaven, who
may upon sufficient grounds, and justifiable by the word of
God, be judged true believers, many of the apostates we speak
of, were to be judged such, all the visible lineaments of a true
faith were in their faces, as far as the eye of man is able
to pierce; they lived godly, righteously, and soberly, in this
present world: doth any true believer act zealously for his
God? so did they; is any true believer fruitful in good
works? they were such; yea, there is found in those we now
speak of, not only such things upon the sight and knowledge whereof in men, we ought to judge them true believers,[f] but even such things farther, which we ought to
reverence and honour, as lovely and majestic characters of
God and holiness, therefore, it is but too importune a pretence in men to deny them to have been true believers.'

If the proof of the first confident assertion concerning the grounds of judging such as afterward have apostatized, to be true believers, were called into question, I suppose it would prove one instance, how much easier it is
confidently to affirm any thing, than soundly to confirm it.

[f] Adde hos de quibus hic agimus, non vulgares et plebeios, sed antesignanos et
eximios ac eminentes fuisse. Rem. Ac. Syn. p. 267.

'And perhaps it will be found to appear, that in the most, if not all, of those glorious apostates of whom he speaks, if they were thoroughly traced and strictly eyed, even in those things which are exposed to the view of men, for any season or continuance, such warpings and flaws might be discovered, in positives or negatives, as are incompatible with truth or grace. But if this be granted, that they have all the ' visible lineaments of a true faith in their faces,' as far as the eye of man is able to judge, and therefore men were bound to esteem them for true believers, doth it therefore, follow, that they were such indeed ' This at once instates all secret hypocrites in the ancient and present churches of Christ, into a condition of sanctification and justification, which the Lord knows they were, and are remote from. Shall the esteem of men translate them from death to life, and really alter the state wherein they are? Whatever honour then and esteem we may give to the characters of holiness and faith instamped, or rather painted on them, as it is meet for us to judge well of all, who professing the Lord Christ, walk in our view in any measure suitable to that profession, and with Jonadab to honour Jehu, in his fits and hasty passions of zeal, yet this, alas, is no evidence unto them, nor discovery of the thing itself, that they are in a state of faith and holiness. To say, that we may not be bound to judge any to be believers, and godly, unless they are so indeed and in the thing itself, is either to exalt poor worms into the throne of God, and to make them ' searchers of the hearts and triers of the reins' of others, who are so often in the dark to themselves, and never in this life sufficiently acquainted with their own inward chambers ; or else at once to cut off and destroy all communion of saints, by rendering it impossible for us to attain satisfaction, who are so indeed, so far as to walk with them upon that account, in[h] 'love without dissimulation.' Doubtless the disciples of Christ were bound to receive them for believers, of whom it is said, that they did believe, because of their profession so to do, and that with some hazard and danger ; though he who[i] 'knew what was in man,' would not trust himself with them, because the root of the matter was not in them.

g Psal. lxxviii 34—36. Job xxvii. 9, 10. 2 Kings x. 29. Ezek. xxxiii. 31. Tit. j. 16.
h Rom. xii. 9.   i John ii. 23, 24.

I suppose I shall not need to put myself to the labour to prove, or evince this ground of our charitable procedure, in our thoughts of men professing the ways of God, though their hearts are not upright with him ; but, says Mr. Good-win, ' To say that whilst they stood, men were indeed bound to judge them believers; but by their declining, they dis-cover themselves not to have been the men, is but to beg the question, and that upon very ill terms to obtain it.'

Ans. For my part, I find not in this answer to that objec-tion (but they had the lineaments of true believers, and therefore we were bound to judge them so), that this did not at all prove them to be so, any begging of the question, but rather a fair answer given to their importune request, that the[k] ' appearance of the face, as far as the eyes of men can pierce,' must needs conclude them in the eyes of God to answer that appearance in the inward and hidden man of the heart.

But Mr. Goodwin farther pursues his design in hand, from the words of our Saviour ; Matt. vii. 20. ' By their fruit ye shall know them.' ' If,' saith he, ' this rule be authentical, we do not only stand bound by the law of charity, but by the law of righteousness or strict judgment itself, to judge the persons we speak of, true believers ; whilst they adorn the gospel with such fruits of righteousness, as were mentioned ; for our Saviour doth not say, By their fruits ye shall have grounds to conceive or conjecture them such or such, or to judge them in charity such or such, but ye shall know them. Now what a man knows, he is not bound to conjecture, or to judge in a way of charity to be that which he knoweth it to be, but positively to judge and conclude of it accordingly. If then it be possible for men by any such fruits, works, or expressions, to know true believers, the persons we speak of, may be known to have been such.'

Ans. Though the words of our Saviour principally lie on the other side of the way, giving a rule for a condemnatory judgment of men, whose evil fruits declare the root to be no better ; wherein we cannot well be deceived ;[l] ' the works of the flesh being manifest,' and he that worketh wickedness openly, and brings forth the effects of sin visibly, in a course, as[m] ' a tree doth its fruit,' may safely be concluded, what-

---

[k] 1 Sam. xvi. 7.   [l] Gal. ii. 19.   [m] Rom. vi. 16.

soever pretence in words he makes, to be a false corrupt hypocrite; yet by the way of analogy and proportion, it is a rule also, whereby our Saviour will have us make a judgment of those professors and teachers, with whom we have to do, as to our reception and approbation of them. He bids his disciples taste and try the fruit that such persons bear, and according to that (not any specious pretences they make, or innocent appearances which for a season they shew themselves in), let their estimation of them be; yea, but says Mr. Goodwin, 'We do not only stand bound by the law of charity, but by the law of a righteous and strict judgment itself, to judge such persons believers.' 'This distinction between the law of charity, and the law of a righteous judgment, I understand not. Though charity be the principle exerted eminently in such dijudications of men, yet doubtless it proceeds by the rules of righteous judgment. When we speak of the judgment of charity, we intend not a loose conjecture, much less a judgment contradistinct from that which is righteous; but a righteous and strict judgment, according to the exactest rules whatsoever that we have to judge by, free from evil surmises, and such like vices of the mind, as are opposed to the grace of love. By saying it is of charity, we are not absolved from the most exact procedure (according to the rules of judging given unto us), but only bound up from indulging to any envy, malice, or such like works of the flesh, which are opposite to charity, in the subject wherein it is : charity in this assertion denotes only a gracious qualification in the subject, and not any condescension from the rule; and therefore I something wonder, that Mr. Goodwin should make a judgment of charity (as afterward) a mere conjecture, and allow beyond it a righteous and strict judgment, which amounts to knowledge.

It is true our Saviour tells us, 'That by their fruits we shall know them;' but what knowledge is it that he intendeth? Is it a certain knowledge by demonstration of it? Or an infallible assurance by revelation? I am confident Mr. Goodwin will not say it is either of these, but only such a persuasion, as is the result of our thoughts concerning them, upon the profession they make, and the works they do; upon which we may (according to the mind of Christ, who bare with them whom he knew to be no believers, having taken on them the profession of the faith) know how to demean ourselves towards them: so far we may know them by their fruits, and judge of them; other knowledge our Saviour intendeth not, nor I believe does Mr. Goodwin pretend unto. Now notwithstanding all this, even on this account, and by this rule, it is very possible, yea very easy, and practically proved true in all places, and at all times, that we may judge, yea so far know men to be, or not to be, seducers by their fruits, as to be able to order aright our demeanour towards them, according to the will of Christ, and yet be mistaken (though not in the performance of our duty in walking regularly according to the lines drawn out for our paths) in the persons concerning whom our judgment is; the knowledge of them being neither by demonstration, nor from revelation, such as ' cui non potest subesse falsum,' we may be deceived.

The saints, then, or believers, of whom alone our discourse is, may be briefly delineated by these few considerable concernments of their saintship.

1. That whereas ' by nature they are children of wrath as well as others,' and ' dead in trespasses and sins,' that faith and holiness which they are in due time invested withal, whereby they are made believers and saints, and distinguished from all others whatever, is an effect and fruit of, and flows from, God's eternal purpose concerning their [n]salvation or election: their faith being as to the manner of its bestowing peculiarly of the operation of God, and as to its distinction from every other gift, that upon any account whatever is so called; in respect of its fountain, termed, ' the faith of God's elect.'

2. For the manner of their [o]obtaining of this precious faith, it is by God's giving to them that Holy Spirit of his, whereby he raised Jesus from the dead, to raise them from their death in sin, to quicken them unto newness of life, endowing them with a new life, with a spiritual gracious supernatural habit, spreading itself upon their whole souls, making them new creatures throughout (in respect of parts),

[n] Rom viii. 28, 29. Acts xiii. 4. Eph. i. 4. 1 Pet. i. 2—5 Tit. i. 1.
[o] 2 Pet. i. 1. Rom. viii. 11. Eph. i. 19, 20. ii. 1. 5, 6. 8. 10. Matt. vii 17. xii 33. Gal. ii 20. 1 John v. 12 2 Cor. v. 17. 1 Thess. v. 25. Gal. v. 22, 23. 1 John iii. 9. Eph. ii. 10. 1 Pet. i 22. Phil ii. 13.

investing them with an abiding principle, being a natural genuine fountain of all those spiritual acts, works, and du-ties, which he is pleased to work in them and by them, of his own good pleasure.

3. That the holy and blessed Spirit,[p] which effectually and powerfully works this change in them, is bestowed upon them as a fruit of the purchase and intercession of Jesus Christ, to dwell in them, and abide in them for ever: upon the account of which inhabitation of the Spirit of Christ in them, they have union with him, i. e. one and the same Spi-rit dwelling in him the head, and them the members.

4. By all which as to their actual state and condition, they are really changed from [q]death to life, from [r]darkness to light, from [s]universal habitual uncleanness to holiness, from [t]a state of enmity, stubbornness, rebellion, &c. into a state of love, obedience, delight, &c. and as to their relative condition, whereas they were [u]children of wrath, under the curse and condemning power of the law, they are upon the score of him, who was made a curse for them, and is made righteousness to them, accepted, justified, adopted, and ad-mitted into that family of heaven and earth which is called after the name of God.

These alone are they, of whom we treat; of whose state and condition, perseverance is an inseparable adjunct: wherein and in what particulars they are differenced from, and advanced above, the most glorious professors whatever, who are liable and obnoxious to an utter and everlasting se-paration from God, shall be afterward at large insisted upon: and though Mr. Goodwin hath thought good to affirm, that that description which we have, Heb. vi. of such (as is sup-posed) may be apostates, is one of the highest and most eminent, that is made of believers in the whole Scripture; I shall not doubt but to make it evident, that the excellency of all the expressions there used, being extracted and laid together, doth yet come short of the meanest and lowest

p John iv. 16. 26. xv. 26. xvi. 7—9. Rom. viii. 10, 11. 1 Cor. vi. 19. Rom. v. 5. 1 John iv. 4. 13. 2 Tim. i. 14 1 Cor. vi. 17. xii. 12, 13. Eph. iv. 4.
q 1 John iii. 14. Eph. ii. 2. Col. ii. 13. Rom. vi 11. 13. viii. 2. 8, 9.
r Acts xxvi. 18. Eph v. 8. 1 Thess. v. 4. Col. i. 13. 1 Pet. ii 9.
s Ezek. xxxvi 25. Zech. xiii. 1. Isa. iv. 3, 4. Eph. v. 6. 1 Cor. vi. 11. Tit. iii 5. Heb. x. 22.   t Rom. vi. 10. Eph ii. 12—13. Col. i. 21. Heb. xii. 22.
u Eph. ii. 3. Gal. iii. 13 iv. 4—7. Rom. viii. 1. 2 Cor. v. 21. Col. ii. 10. Rom. v. 1. viii. 32, 33. 1 John iii. 1, 2. Eph. iii. 15.

thing that is spoken of those, concerning whom we treat;
as shall be manifest, when through God's assistance we arrive unto that part of this contest.

That the other term (to wit) 'perseverance,' may be more
briefly explicated, I shall take the shortest path.   For perseverance in general, he came near the nature of it, who
said it was ' in ratione bene fundata stabilis ac perpetua per-
mansio.'   The words and terms, whereby it is expressed in
Scripture, will afterward fall in to be considered.   The Holy
Ghost restrains not himself to any one expression, in spiritual things of so great importance, but using that variety
which may be suited to the *instruction, supportment, and
consolation of believers, this grace (as is that of faith itself
in an eminent manner) is by him variously expressed : 'To
[y]walk in the name of the Lord for ever, to walk with Christ
as we have received him, to be confirmed or strengthened in
the faith as we have been taught, to keep the ways of God's
commandments to the end, to run steadfastly the race set
before us, to rule with God, to be faithful with the saints, to
be faithful to the death, to be sound and steadfast in the
precepts of God, to abide or continue firm with Christ, in
Christ, in the Lord, in the word of Christ, in the doctrine of
Christ, in the faith, in the love and favour of God, in what
we have learned and received from the beginning; to endure,
to persist in the truth, to be rooted in Christ, to retain or
keep faith and a good conscience, to hold fast our confidence
and faith to the end, to follow God fully, to keep the word
of Christ's patience, to be built upon and in Christ, to keep
ourselves that the wicked one touch us not, not to commit
sin, to be kept by the power of God through faith unto salvation, to stand fast as mount Sion that can never be removed, to stand by faith, to stand fast in the faith, to stand
fast in the Lord, to have the good work begun, perfected ;
to hold our profession, that none take our crown.'   These, I
say, and the like, are some of those expressions whereby

<hr />

[x] Rom. xv. 4.

[y] 2 Sam vii 14, 15 Psal i 3 xxiii. 6. xxxvii 24. lii. 10. lxxix 31. cxxv. 1--3.
cxxviii. 5. Isa xlvi 4 liv. 10 Jer. xxxi. 3. xxxii. 39, 40 Zech x. 12. Matt. vii.
24, 25. xii. 20. xvi 18. xxiv. 21 Luke viii 5. xxii. 23. John vi 35. 39. 56, 57.
viii. 12. x. 27--29 xiv. 16, 17. xvii. 20. 18 28. Rom. viii 1. xvi. 29 xxxiv. 30, 37.
1 Cor iii. 8--10. 13. 15. 58. 1 John v. 17 iii. 9. 1 Pet. i. 5. Rom. xi. 20.   1 Cor.
xvi. 13. Phil. iv. 1. i 6 Eph. i. 13, 14 iv 39. Gal. ii. 20. Phil. i. 6. 1 Thess.
v. 24. 2 Tim. ii. 12. 1 Pet i. 2--4. 1 John ii 19. 27, &c.

the Holy Ghost holds forth that doctrine which we have in hand, which is usually called the perseverance of saints, regarding principally their abiding with God, through Christ, in faith and obedience, which yet is but one part of this truth.

The reasons and causes investing this proposition, that saints, such as we have described, shall so persevere, with a necessity of consequence, and on which the truth of it doth depend, both negatively considered, and positively, with the limitation of perseverance, what it directly asserts, what not, with what failing, backsliding, and declensions, on the one hand and other it is consistent, and what is destructive of the nature and being of it, the difference of it, as to being and apprehension, in respect to the subject in whom it is, with the way and manner whereby the causes of this perseverance have their operation on, and effect in, them that persevere, not in the least prejudicing their liberty, but establishing them in their voluntary obedience, will afterward be fully cleared, and hereon depends much of the life and vigour of the doctrine we have in hand: it being oftener in the Scripture held forth in its fountains, and springs, and causes, than in the thing itself, as will upon examination appear.

As to what is on the other side affirmed, that believers may fall totally and finally away, something may be added to clear up what is intended thereby, and to inquire how it may come to pass. We do suppose (which the Scripture abundantly testifieth) that such believers have [z]the Holy Spirit dwelling in them, and by his implanting a [a]new holy habit of grace: the inquiry then, is, how believers may come utterly to lose this Holy Spirit, and to be made naked of the habit of grace, or new nature bestowed on them. That and that only whereunto this effect is ascribed, is sin. Now there are two ways whereby sin may be supposed to produce such effects in reference to the souls of believers: 1. Efficiently, by a re-action in the same subject, as frequent acts of vice will debilitate and overthrow an acquired habit whereunto it is opposite. 2. Meritoriously, by provoking the Lord to take them away, in a way of punishment; for of all

[z] Ezek. xxxvi. 27. Isa. lix. 21. Luke xi. 13. Psal. li. 11. Rom. viii. 9. 11. 15. 1 Cor. ii. 12 Gal. iv 6. 1 Tim. i. 14. Rom. v. 5. Gal. v. 22. John xiv. 16, 17. xvi. 13. 1 Cor. iii 16. vi. 19.

[a] Matt. xii. 33. 2 Cor. v. 17. 2 Pet. i. 4. Gal. v. 22, 23. Eph. iv 23, 24.

punishment, sin is the morally procuring cause. Let us a little consider which of those ways it may probably be supposed that sin expels the Spirit and habit of grace from the souls of believers.

First, For the Spirit of grace which dwells in them, it cannot with the least colour of reason be supposed, that sin should have a natural efficient re-action against the Spirit, which is a voluntary indweller in the hearts of his: he is indeed [b]grieved and provoked by it, but that is in a moral way in respect of its demerit; but that it should have a natural efficiency by the way of opposition against it, as intemperance against the mediocrity which it opposeth, is a madness to imagine.

The habit of grace wherewith such believers are endued, is infused; not acquired by a frequency of acts in themselves: the root is made good, and then the fruit, and the work of God. It is [c]'a new creation' planted in them by the ' exceeding greatness of his power, as he wrought in Christ when he raised him from the dead, which he also strengthens with all might,' and all power to the end. Is it now supposed, or can it rationally be so, that vicious acts, acts of sin, should have in the soul a natural efficiency for the expelling of an infused habit, and that implanted upon the soul by the exceeding greatness of the power of God? That it should be done by any one or two acts, is impossible; to suppose that a man, in whom there is a habit set on by so mighty an impression as the Scripture mentions, to act constantly contrary thereunto, is to think what we will, without troubling ourselves to consider how it may be brought about. Farther, whilst this principle, life, and habit of grace, is thus consuming, doth their God and Father look on and suffer it to decay, and their spiritual man to pine away day by day, giving them [d]no new supplies, nor increasing them with the increase of God? Hath he no pity towards a dying child? Or can he not help him? Doth he, of whom it is said, that he is faithful, and that he will not suffer us to be tempted above what we are able, but with the very temptation will make way for us to escape, let loose such flood-gates of

[b] Eph. iv. 30. Heb. iii. 10, 11. Isa. lxiii. 10.
[c] Col. ii. 12. 2 Cor. v. 17. Eph. i. 19. Col. i 11.
[d] Eph. i. 23. Col. ii. 19. Eph. iv. 16. 1 Thess. iii. 12. Phil. i. 6. 1 Cor. x. 13.

temptations upon them, as he knows his grace will not be able to stand before, but will be consumed and expelled by it? What also shall we suppose are the thoughts of Jesus Christ towards a ᵉwithering member, a dying brother, a perishing child, a wandering sheep? Where is his zeal and his tender mercies, and the sounding-of his bowels? Are they restrained? Will he not lay hold of his strength, and stir up his righteousness to save a poor sinking creature? Also he that is in us is greater than he that is in the world? And will he suffer himself to be wrought out of his habitation, and not stir up his strength to keep possession of the dwelling-place which he had chosen? So that neither in the nature of the thing itself, nor in respect of him with whom we have to do, doth this seem possible.   But,

Secondly, Sin procureth by the way of merit, the taking away of the Spirit, and removal of the habit graciously bestowed: believers deserve by sin, that God should take his Spirit from them, and the grace that he hath bestowed on them: they do so indeed, it cannot be denied; but will the Lord deal so with them? Will he ᶠjudge his house with such fire and vengeance? Is that the way of a Father with his children? Until he hath taken away his Spirit and grace, although they are rebellious children, yet they are his children still. And is this the way of a tender father, to cut the throats of his children, when it is in his power to mend them? The casting of a wicked man into hell, is not a punishment to be compared to this; the loss of God's presence is the worst of hell.   How infinitely, must they needs be more sensible of it who have once enjoyed it, than those who were strangers to it from their womb? Certainly the Lord bears ᵍanother testimony concerning his kindness to his sons and daughters, than that we should entertain such dismal thoughts of him.   He chastises his children indeed, but he doth not kill them; he corrects them with rods, but his kindness he takes not from them: notwithstanding of the attempt made by the remonstrants in their Synodalia, I may say that I have not as yet met with any tolerable extrication of those difficulties: more to this purpose will afterward be insisted on.

ᵉ Heb ii. 17, 18. iii. 15. vii. 25. Isa. xl. 11. lxiii. 8. Ezek. xxxiv. 4 12.
ᶠ Isa. xlviii. 9.   ᵍ Isa. xlix. 15, 16. lxvi. 13. Jer. ii. 14. Hos. ii. 14, &c.

Thirdly, That which we intend, when we mention the perseverance of saints, is their continuance to the end in the condition of saintship, whereunto they are called. Now in the state of saintship, there are two things concurring: 1. That holiness which they receive from God; and, 2. That favour which they have with God, being justified freely by his grace, through the blood of Christ: and their continuance in this condition to the end of their lives, both to their real holiness, and gracious acceptance, is the perseverance whereof we must treat. The one respecting their real estate, the other their relative; of which more particularly afterward.

And this is a brief delineation of the doctrine, which, the Lord assisting, shall be explained, confirmed, and vindicated in the ensuing discourse, which being first set forth as a mere skeleton, its symmetry and complexion, its beauty and comeliness, its strength and vigour, excellency and usefulness, will, in the description of the several parts and branches of it, be more fully manifested.

Now because Mr. Goodwin, though he was not pleased to fix any orderly state of the question under debate (a course he hath also thought good to take in handling those other heads of the doctrine of the gospel, wherein he hath chosen to walk (for the main with the Arminians) in paths of difference from the reformed churches); yet having scattered up and down his treatise, what his conceptions are of the doctrine he doth oppose, as also what he asserts in the place and room thereof, and upon what principles, I shall briefly call what he hath so delivered, both on the one hand and on the other, to an account: to make the clearer way for the proof of the truth, which indeed we own, and for the discovery of that which is brought forth to contest for acceptance with it, upon the score of truth and usefulness.

First then, For the doctrine of the saints' perseverance, how it stands stated in Mr. Goodwin's thoughts, and what he would have other men apprehend thereof, may from sundry places in his book, especially chap. 9. be collected, and thus summarily presented. 'It is,' saith he, chap. 9. sect. 3. 'a promising unto men, and that with height of assurance, under what looseness or vile practices soever, exemption and freedom from punishment; so sect. 4. It is in vain to per-

suade or press men unto the use of such means, in any kind
which are in themselves displeasing to them, seeing they are
ascertained and secured beforehand that they shall not fail
of the end however, whether they use such means or no : a
luscious, and fulsome conceit, (sect. 5.) intoxicating the flesh
with a persuasion that it hath goods laid up for the days
of eternity; a notion comfortable, and betiding peace to the
flesh, (sect. 15.) in administering unto it certain hope, that it
shall however escape the wrath and vengeance which is to
come, yea though it disporteth itself in all manner of looseness and licentiousness in the mean time. A presumption
it is that men (sect. 18.) may or shall enjoy the love of God
and salvation itself, under practices of all manner of sin and
wickedness. Representing God (sect. 20.) as a God, in
whose sight he is good that doth evil: promising his love,
favour, and acceptance as well unto dogs returning to their
vomit, or to swine wallowing (after their washing) in the
mire (that is, to apostates, which that believers shall not be,
is indeed the doctrine he opposeth), as unto lambs and sheep.
A doctrine whereby it is possible for me certainly to know,
that how loosely, how profanely, how debauchedly soever I
should behave myself, yet God will love me, as he doth the
holiest and most righteous man under heaven.'

With these and the like expressions doth Mr. Goodwin
adorn and gild over that doctrine, which he hath chosen
to oppose; with these garlands and flowers doth he surround
the head of the sacrifice, which he intends instantly to slay,
that so it may fall an undeplored victim, if not seasonably
rescued from the hands of this sacred officer. Neither
through his whole treatise, do I find it delivered in any
other sense, or held out under any other notion to his
reader. The course here he hath taken in this case, and the
paths he walks in towards his adversaries, seem to be no
other, than that which was traced out by the bishops at
Constance, when they caused devils to be painted upon the
cap they put on the head of Huss, before they cast him into
the fire, I do something doubt (though I am not altogether
ignorant, how abominably the tenets and opinions of those,
who first opposed the papacy, are represented and given
over to posterity, by them, whose interest it was to have

them thought such, as they gave them out to be) whether ever any man, that undertook to publish his conceptions to the world, about any opinion, or parcel of truth, debated amongst professors of the gospel of Christ, did ever so dismember, disfigure, defile, wrest, and pervert that which he opposed, as Mr. Goodwin hath done the doctrine of perseverance which he hath undertaken to destroy; methinks a man should not be much delighted in casting filth and dung upon his adversary, before he begin to grapple with him; in one word, this being the account he gives us of it, if he be able to name one author, ancient or modern, any one sober person of old, or of late, that ever spent a pen full of ink, or once opened his mouth in the defence of that perseverance of saints, or rather profane walking of dogs and swine, which he hath stated, not in the words and terms, but so much as to the matter, or purpose here intimated by him; and it shall be accepted as a just defensative against the crime, which we are enforced to charge in this particular, and which otherwise will not easily be warded. If this be the doctrine, which with so great an endeavour, and a contribution of so much pains and rhetoric he seeks to oppose, I know not any that will think it worth while, to interpose in this fierce contest between him and his man of straw. Neither can it with the least colour of truth be pretended, that these are consequences, which he urgeth the doctrine he opposeth withal, and not his apprehensions of the doctrine itself. For neither doth he in any place in his whole treatise, hold it out in any other shape, but is uniform and constant to himself, in expressing his notion of it; nor doth he indeed almost use any argument against it, but those that suppose this to be the true state of the controversy, which he hath proposed. But whether this indeed be the doctrine of the perseverance of saints, which Mr. Goodwin so importunately cries out against, upon a brief consideration of some of the particulars mentioned, will quickly appear.

First then, Doth this doctrine promise with height of assurance, that under what looseness, or vile practices soever men do live, they shall have exemption from punishment? Wherein I pray? In that it promiseth the saints of God, that through his grace they shall be preserved from such loose ness and evil practices, as would expose them to eternal punishment? Doth it teach men,[h] that it is vain to use the means of mortification, because they shall certainly attain the end, whether they use the means or no? Or may you not as well say, that the doctrine you oppose is, that all men shall be saved whether they believe or no, with those other comfortable and cheering associate doctrines you mention? Or is this[i] a regular emergency of that doctrine which teaches, that there is no attaining the end but by the means, between which there is such a concatenation by divine appointment, that they shall not be separated? Doth it speak peace to the flesh, in assurance of blessed immortality, though it disport itself in all folly in the meantime? Do the teachers of it, express any such thing? doth any such abomination issue from their arguings in the defence thereof? Or doth the doctrine which teaches believers (saints who have tasted of the love and pardoning mercy of God, and are taught to value it infinitely above all the world) that such is the love and good-will of God towards them, in the covenant of mercy in the blood of Christ, that having appointed[k] good works for them to walk in, for which of themselves they are insufficient, he will graciously continue to them such supplies of his Spirit and grace, as that they shall never depart from following after him, in ways of gospel obedience? Doth this, I say, encourage any of them to continue in sin that this grace may abound? Or are any doctrines of the gospel to be measured by the rules and lines of the use or abuse that the flesh is apt to make of them? Or rather by their suitableness to the divine nature, whereof the saints are made partakers, and serviceableness to their carrying on to perfection in that attainment? Or is this an argument of validity against an evangelical truth that the carnal unbelieving part is apt to turn it into wantonness? And whether believers[l] walking after the Spirit, in which frame the truths of God in the gospel are savoury and sweet to them, do experience such attendencies of the doctrine under consideration, as are here intimated; I am persuaded Mr. Goodwin will one day find, that he hath not a little grieved the Holy Spirit of God, by these reproaches

[h] Psal xxiii 6. Jer. xxxi. 33. 1 Cor. x. 13.
[i] 1 Pet i 5   [k] Eph. ii. 10. 2 Cor. iii. 5.   [l] Rom. viii. 1. 11.

cast upon the work of his grace. Farther, Doth this persuasion assure men that they shall enjoy the love and favour of God under the practices of all manner of sin? Or can this be wrested, by any racks or wheels from this assertion, that none indeed enjoy the love and favour of God, but only they, towards whom it is effectual to turn them from the practices of all manner of sin and wickedness; to translate them from darkness into marvellous light, and from the power of Satan into the kingdom of Jesus Christ; whom the grace that appears unto them, teacheth to deny all ungodliness and worldly lusts, to live soberly, righteously, and godly in this present world ; whom that love constrains not to live unto themselves, but unto him that died for them ? Doth it promise the love and favour of God to dogs turning to their vomit, and swine wallowing in their mire? when the very discriminating difference of it from that doctrine which advanceth itself into competition with it, is that such returning dogs and wallowing swine did indeed, in their best estate and condition, never truly and properly partake of the love and favour of God ; but notwithstanding their disgorging and washing of themselves, they were dogs and swine still. But to what end should I longer insist on these things? I am fully persuaded, Mr. Goodwin himself cannot make room in his understanding to apprehend that this is indeed the true notion of the doctrine which he doth oppose. Something hath been spoken of it already, and more, the Lord assisting, will be discussed in the progress of our discourse, abundantly sufficient to manifest to the consciences of men, not possessed with prejudice against the truth, that it is quite of another nature and consistency, of another complexion and usefulness, than what is here represented. I cannot but add, that this way of handling controversies in religion, namely, in proposing consequences and inferences of our own framing (wiredrawn with violence and subtilty from principles far distant from them, disowned, disavowed, and disclaimed by them, on whom they are imposed), as the judgment of our adversaries, loading them with all manner of reproaches, is such, as (being of all men in the world most walked in by the Arminians), I desire not to be competitor with any in; 'haud defensoribus istis,' &c.

Let us now a little (in the next place) consider what Mr. Goodwin gives in for that persuasion, which, in opposition to the other, before by him displayed, he contendeth with all his strength to advance; I do not doubt but all that are acquainted with his way of expression ('elato cathurno'), will (as they may reasonably) expect to have it brought forth μετὰ πολλῆς φαντασίας, adorned with all the gallantry and ornaments that words can contribute thereunto: for of them there is with him store to be used on all occasions : πολὺς νόμος ἔνθα καὶ ἔνθα.

The sum of the doctrine he is so enamoured on, he gives us, chap. 9. sect. 21. p. 115. 'Longa est fabula longæ ambagis,' this is, *Caput rei;* ' It[m] is not any danger of falling away in them, that are saints and believers, or probability of it, that he maintains, but only possibility of it ; such as there is, that sober and careful men may voluntarily throw themselves down from the tops of houses or steeples (though, perhaps, they never come there), or run into the fire or water, and be burned or drowned, having the use of their reason and understanding to preserve them from such unusual and dismal accidents ;' which seems to be an instance of as remote and infirm a possibility, as can likely be imagined. Yea, he tells you farther (sect. 22.), ' That the saints have as good security of their perseverance, as he could have of his life, to whom God should grant a lease of it for so long, upon condition that he did not thrust a sword through his bowels, or cast himself headlong down a tower; so that his doctrine indulgeth to the saints as much assurance, as that of perseverance; but only it grants them not a liberty of sinning ;' which I presume his own conscience told him that neither the other doth.

But is this, indeed, Mr. Goodwin's doctrine ? Is this all that he intends his arguments and proofs shall amount unto ? ' Ad populum phaleras :' strange, that when there is not so much as a probability or danger of falling away, yet so many, and so eminent saints should so fall ? How sel-

---

[m] Quidam sunt, qui jam aliquamdiu luce veritatis collustrati fuerunt, et in ejus cognitione pietatisque studio tantum profecerunt, ut habitum tandem credendi sancteque vivendi comparaverint hos non tantum ad finem usque vitæ perseverare posse, sed facile posse, ac libenter et cum voluptate perseverare velle credimus, adeo ut non nisi cum lucta et molestia ac difficultate deficere possint.—Act. Synod. Decl. Sen. A. 5. p 189, 190.

dom is it, that we hear of wise and sober men running into the fire, throwing themselves headlong from towers, thrusting swords through their own bowels? and nothing more frequent than the apostacy of saints, if these things stood upon equal terms of unlikelihood and improbability? The stony field in the parable[n] seems to be every whit as large as the good ground, whose fruit abideth. That ground, in Mr. Goodwin's sense, is true believers; so that a moiety at least must be granted to fall away, and never come to perfection. Doubtless this is not easy to be received, that one half of a company of men in succession, should constantly from one generation to another, fall into ruin in such a way as wherein there is no danger of it, or probability that it should so come to pass. Methinks, we should scarce dare to walk the streets, least at every step we be struck down by sober men, voluntarily tumbling themselves from the tops of houses, and hardly keep ourselves from being wounded with the swords wherewith they run themselves through. Was this indeed the case with David, Solomon, Peter? and others who totally apostatized from the faith? But if it be so, if they are thus secure, whence is it, that it doth arise? what are the fountains, springs, and causes of this general security? Is it from the weakness of the opposition, and slightness of all means of diversion from walking with God to the end, that they meet withal? or is it from the nature of that faith, which they have, and grace wherewith they are endued? or is it that God hath graciously undertaken to safeguard them, and to preserve them in their abiding with him, that they shall not fall away? or is it that Christ intercedeth for them, that their faith fail not, but be preserved, and their souls with it, by the power of God unto the end? or from what other principle doth this security of theirs arise? from what fountain do the streams of their consolation flow? where lie the heads of this Nilus?

That it is not upon the first account, I suppose cannot enter into the imagination of any person, who ever had the least experience of walking with God, or doth so much as assent to the letter of the Scripture. How are our enemies there described as to their number, nature, power, policy,

[n] Matt. xiii.

subtilty, malice, restlessness, and advantages? with what unimaginable and inexpressible variety of means, temptations, baits, allurements, inticements, terrors, threats, do they fight against us? Such and, so many are the enemies that oppose the saints of God in their abiding with him; so great and effectual the means and weapons wherewith they fight against them; so unwearied and watchful are they for the improvement of all advantages and opportunities for their ruin; that upon the supposal of the rejection of those principles, and those means of their preservation, which we shall find Mr. Goodwin to attempt, they will be found to be so far from a state of no danger, and little probability of falling, or only under a remote possibility of so doing, that it will appear utterly impossible for them to hold out, and abide unto the end. Had the choicest saint of God, with all the grace that he hath received, but one of the many enemies, and that the weakest, of all them which oppose every saint of God, even the feeblest, to deal withal, separated from the strength of those principles and supportments, which Mr. Goodwin seeketh to cast down (let him lie under continual exhortations to watchfulness, and close walking with God), he may as easily move mountains with his finger, or climb to heaven by a ladder, as stand before the strength of that one enemy. Adam in paradise had no lust within to entice him, no world under the curse to seduce him, yet at the first assault of Satan, who then had no part in him, he fell quite out of covenant with God; Psal. xxx. 6, 7.

I shall give one instance in one of the many enemies that fight against the welfare of our souls, and ' ex hoc uno' we may guess at the residue of its companions. This is indwelling sin, whose power and policy, strength and prevalency, nearness and treachery, the Scripture exceedingly sets out; and the saints daily feel: I shall only point at some particulars.

First, Concerning its nearness to us, it is indeed in us: and that not as a thing different from us, but it cleaveth to all the faculties of our souls; it is an enemy[o] born with us, bred up with us, carried about in our bosoms; by nature, our familiar friend, our guide and counsellor, dear to us as

[o] Psal. li. 5. Matt. v. 29, 30. James iii. 5, 6.

our right eye, useful as our right hand, our wisdom, strength,
&c. The apostle, Rom. vii. 17. 20. calleth it ' the sin that
dwelleth in us;' it hath in us, in the faculties of our souls,
its abode and station. It doth not pass by, and away, but
there it dwells, so as that it never goes from home, is never
out of the way, when we have any thing to do; whence, ver.
21. he calls it, ' the evil that is present with him.' When we
go about any thing that is good or have opportunity f or, or
temptation unto any thing that is evil, it is never absent; but
is ready to pluck us back, or to put us on, according as it
serves its ends; it is such an inmate that we can never be
quit of its company; and so intimate unto us, that it puts forth
itself, in every acting of the mind, will, or any other faculty of
the soul. Though men would fain shake it off, yet when they
would do good, this evil will be present with them Then,

Secondly, Its universality and compass. It is not
straitened in a corner of the soul; it is spread over the
whole, all the faculties, affections, and passions of it. That
which is born of the flesh is flesh ;ᵖ it is all flesh, and nothing but flesh; it is darkness in the understanding, keeping us at best that we know but in part, and are still dull
and slow of heart to believe; naturally we are all darkness,
nothing but darkness; and though the Lord shine into our
mind, to give us in some measure the knowledge of his glory
in the face of Jesus Christ, yet we are still very dark, and it
is a hard work to bring in a little light upon the soul; espe-
·cially this is seen in particular practical things; though in
general, we have very clear light and eviction, yet when we
come to particular acts of obedience, how often doth our
light grow dim and fail us, causing us to judge amiss of
that which is before us, by the rising of that natural darkness, which is in us? It is perverseness, stubbornness, obstinacy in the will, that carries it with violence, to disobedience and sin. It is sensuality upon the affections, bend-
ing them to the things of the world, alienating them from
God; it is slipperiness in the memory, making us like leak-
ing vessels, that the things that we hear of the gospel do

P John v. 6. Matt. vi. 23. xi. 27. Luke xi. 34—36. Acts xxvi. 18 2 Cor. vi. 14.
Eph. v. 8. Isa. xxix. 18 xxxv. 5 xlii. 7. Rom. ii. 19. Col. i. 13. 1 Pet. ii. 9.
Luke iv. 8. Eph. iv. 18. Rev. iii 17. Matt. xxiii. 16 iv. 16. John i 6.
2 Cor. iv. 6. Luke iv. 18. John viii. 34. Rom. vi. 16. vii 18. viii. 7, 8. Jer.
vi. 16. Gen. vi. 5. Jer. xiii 23. Heb. ii 1. James i. 14, 15.

suddenly slip out, when as other things abide firm in the cells and chambers thereof. It is senselessness and error in the conscience, staving it off from the performance of that duty, which in the name and authority of God, it is to accomplish: and in all these, is daily enticing and seducing the heart of folly, conceiving and bringing forth sin.

Thirdly, Its power. The apostle calls 'it a law, a law in his members, a law of sin,' Rom. vii. 21. 23. Such a law as fights, make war, and leads captive, selling us under sin; not suffering us to do the good we would, forcing us to the evil we would not, drawing us off from that we delight in, bringing us under bondage to that which we abhor; a powerful, unmerciful, cruel tyrant it is; Oh! wretched men that we are, ver. 24. There is no saint of God, but in the inward man doth hate sin, every sin more than hell itself, knowing the world of evils, that attend the least sin; yet is there not one of them, but this powerful tyrant hath compelled and forced to so many, as have made them a burden to their own souls.

Fourthly, Its cunning, craft, and policy. It is called in Scripture the old man, not from the weakness of its strength, but from the strength of its craft. ' Take⁹ heed,' saith the apostle, ' lest any of you be hardened by the deceitfulness of sin.' There is abundance of deceitfulness in it; being ready, fit, and prompt to beguile; lying in wait for advantages, furnished for all opportunities, and ready to close with every temptation; yea, the ways of it are so large and various, its wiles and methods for deceiving so innumerable, its fruitfulness in conceiving and bringing forth of sin so abundant, its advantages and opportunities so many, that it is like the way of a serpent upon a stone, there is no tracing or finding of it out.

A serious consideration of the opposition made unto our perseverance, by this one enemy, which hath so much ability, and is so restless in its warfare, never quiet, conquering nor conquered, which can be kept out of none of our counsels, excluded from none of our actings, is abundantly sufficient to evince, that it is not want or weakness of enemies which putteth believers out of danger of falling away.

⁹ Heb iii. 13.

But all this perhaps will be granted; enemies they have enough, and those much more diligent and powerful every one of them, than all we have spoken of that now described amounteth unto; but the means of preservation, which God affords the saints, is that which puts them almost out of gunshot, and gives them that golden security mentioned, which cometh not (in administering consolation) one step behind that which ariseth from the doctrine of absolute perseverance. Let then this be a little considered, and perhaps it will allay this whole contest. Is it then, that such is the grace that is bestowed upon them, in respect of the principle whence it is bestowed (the eternal love of God), and the way whereby it is for them procured (the blood-shedding and intercession of Christ), with the nature of it (being the seed of God, which abideth and withereth not), and that such seems to be the nature of infused habits, that they are not removed, but by the power, and immediate hand of him by whom they are bestowed? Is it from hence, that their assurance and security doth arise? Alas, all this is but a fiction; there is no faith that is the fruit of election; Christ purchased it not for any by his death; infused habits are not the grace that perisheth, and that that abideth are the same, these things are but pretences. Is it then, that God hath purposed from eternity, to continue constant in his love towards them, never to leave them nor forsake them? Nay, but of all things imaginable, this is the greatest abomination, which if the Scriptures did any where affirm, it were sufficient to make a rational considering man, to question their authority.

What then, hath the Lord promised to give them such continued supplies of his Spirit and grace in Jesus Christ, as that they shall be supported against all opposition, and preserved from all, or any such sins as will certainly make a separation between God and their souls? Nay there is not one such promise in all the book of God: they are conditional, for the enjoyment of the good things, whereof believers stand all their days upon their good behaviour? Is it then that the Lord Jesus, who is always heard of his Father, intercedes for them, that their faith fail not, and that they may be preserved by the power of God unto salvation;

and that not only upon condition of their believing, but chiefly, that they may be kept and preserved in believing? Or is it that their enemies are so conquered for them, and on their behalf, in the death and resurrection of Christ, that they shall never have dominion over them, that their security doth arise? Neither the one, nor the other, nor any, nor all of these, are the grounds and foundations of their establishment, but they are wholly given up to the powerful hand of some considerations, which Mr. Goodwin expresseth and setteth out to the life, cap. 9. sect. 32—34. pp. 174, 175.

Now because the remonstrants[r] have always told us, that God hath provided sufficiently for the perseverance of the saints, if they be not supinely wanting to themselves in the use of them, but have not hitherto, either jointly, or severally (that I know of), taken the pains to discover in particular, wherein that sufficiency of provision for their safety doth consist, or what the means are that God affords them to this end and purpose; Mr. Goodwin, who is a learned master of all their counsels, having exactly and fully laid them forth, as a solid foundation of his assertion, concerning only a remote possibility of the saints' total defection, let it not seem tedious or impertinent, if I transcribe, for the clearer debate of it before the reader, that whole discourse of his, and consider it in order as it lies. 'If,' saith he, 'it be demanded, what are the means which God hath given so abundantly to the saints, to make themselves so free, so strong in inclinations to avoid things so apparently destructive to the spiritual peace and salvation of their souls, as naturally men are to forbear all such occasions, which are apparently destructive to their natural lives, so that they need not to be any more any whit more afraid of losing their souls through their own actings, than men are, or need to be, of destroying their natural lives upon the same terms.' I answer,

First, He hath given them eyes wherewith, and light whereby, clearly and evidently to see and know, that it is not more rational, or manlike, for men to refrain all such acts, which they know they cannot perform, but to the present and unavoidable destruction of their natural lives, than

[r] Coll. Hag. A. 5. Act. Synod. Decl. sent. A. 5. Thes. ii.

it is to forbear all sinful acts whatsoever, and especially such, which are apparently destructive to their souls.

Secondly, God hath not only given them the eyes, and the light we speak of, wherewith and whereby clearly to see and understand the things manifested, but hath farther endued them with a faculty of consideration, wherewith to reflect upon, and review, and ponder, so oft as they please, what they see, understand, and know, in this kind. Now whatsoever a man is capable, first, of seeing and knowing; secondly, of pondering and considering, he is capable of raising or working an inclication in himself towards it, answerable in strength, vigour, and power, to any degree of goodness, or desirableness, which he is able to apprehend therein ; for what is an inclination towards any thing, but a propension, and laying out of the heart and soul towards it? So that if there be worth and goodness sufficient in any object whatsoever to bear it ; and, secondly, if a man be in a capacity of discovering and apprehending this good clearly ; and, thirdly, be in a like capacity of considering this vision, certainly he is in a capacity and at liberty to work himself to what strength, or degree of desire and inclination towards it he pleaseth ; now it is certain to every man, that there is more good in abstaining from things either eminently dangerous, or apparently destructive to his soul, than in forbearing things apparently destructive to his natural being. Secondly, As evident it is, that every man is capable of attaining or coming to the certain knowledge of, and clear apprehending, this excess of good to him in the former good, than in the latter. Thirdly, Neither is it a thing less evident than either of the former, that every man is as capable of ruminating or re-apprehending the said excess of good as much and as oft as he pleaseth as he is simply of apprehending it at all ; which supposed as undeniably true, it follows with a high hand and above all contradiction, that the saints may (and have means and opportunities fair and full for that purpose) plant inclinations or dispositions in themselves to refrain all manner of sins, apparently dangerous and destructive to the safety of their souls, fuller of energy, vigour, life, strength, power, than the natural inclination in them, which teacheth them to refrain all occasions which they know must needs be accompanied with the destruction of their

natural beings. Therefore, if they be more or so much afraid
of destroying their lives voluntarily and knowingly (as by
casting themselves into the fire, or the water, or the like),
then they are of falling away through sin ; the fault or reason thereof is not at all in the doctrine, which affirms or informs them, that there is a possibility that they fall away,
but in themselves, and their own voluntary negligence ; they
have means and opportunities (as we have proved) in abundance to render themselves every whit as secure, yea and
more secure, touching the latter, as they are, or reasonably
can be, concerning the former.'

, *Ans.* When I first cast an eye on this discourse of Mr.
Goodwin, I confess I was surprised to as high a degree of
admiration, and some other affections also, as by any thing
I had observed in his whole book, as having not met (if without offence I may be allowed to speak my apprehensions)
with any discourse whatsoever, of so transcendent a derogation from, and direct tendency to the overthrow of, the
grace of Christ, but only in what is remembered by Austin,
Hilary, Fulgentius, with some others, of the disputes of Pelagius, Cœlestius, Julianus, with their followers, and the
Socinians of late ; with whom Mr. Goodwin would not be
thought to have joined in their opposition to the merit and
grace of Christ: as I said then before, if this should prove
in the issue to be the sum of the means afforded to preserve
the saints from apostacy and falling away into ruin, I shall
be so far from opposing a possibility of their defection, that
I shall certainly conclude their perseverance to be impossible.   Being fully persuaded that with all the contribution of
strength, which the considerations mentioned are able of
themselves to afford unto them, they are no more able to
meet their adversaries who come against them with twenty
thousand subtilties and temptations, than a man with a
straw and a feather, is to combat with, and overcome a royal
army ; the Scripture tells us, and we thought it had been
so, that we' 'are kept by the power of God unto salvation,'
and that to this end, ' he puts forth the exceeding greatness
of his power in them that believe, according to the mighty
workings, which wrought in Christ when he raised him from
the dead, whereby he strengthens them with all might ac-

* 1 Pet. i. 5 Eph i. 17—20. Col. i. 11.

cording to his glorious power, making them meet partakers of the inheritance of the saints in light;' it seems, though there be a glorious sound of words in these, and innumerable the like expressions of the engagement of the power and faithfulness of God, for the safeguarding of his saints, yet all this is but an empty noise, and beating of the air. That which is indeed material to this purpose, consisting in certain considerations, which rational men may have concerning their present state, and future condition; but let us a little consider the discourse itself.

First, It is all along magnificently supposed, that there is the same power and ability in a rational enlightened man to deliberate and conclude of things in reference unto the practical condition of his spiritual estate, as there is of his natural, and that this ability is constantly resident with him to make use of upon all occasions, whatever our Saviour say to the contrary; viz. That without him we can do nothing; John xv. 5.

Secondly (to make way for that), That such a one is[t] able to know, and to desire the things of his peace in a spiritual and useful manner, notwithstanding the vanity of those many seemingly fervent prayers of the saints in the Scripture, that God would give them understanding in these things, and his manifold promises of that grace.

Thirdly, That upon such deliberations men are put into a capacity and liberty, or are enabled to work themselves to what strength or degree of desire and inclination towards that good considered, they please; and according as the good is, that men apprehend (as abiding with God is the greatest good), such will be the strength and the vigour and power of their inclinations thereto. That[u] they have a law in their members, rebelling against the law of their minds, and leading them captive under the law of sin, needs not to be taken notice of. This sufficiency it seems is of themselves: he was a weak unskilful man, who supposed that of ourselves we could not think a good thought, seeing we are such perfect lords and masters of all good thoughts and actings whatever.

Fourthly, The whole sum of this discourse of the means afforded believers to enable them to persevere, amounts to

---

[t] Psal. cxix, 144. 1 Cor. ii. 14.   [u] Rom. vii. 8—11, &c. 2 Cor. iii 5.

this, that being rational men, they may, first, consider that some kinds of sins will destroy them, and separate them from God, and that by obedience they shall come to the greatest good imaginable, whereupon it is in their power so strongly to incline their hearts unto obedience, that they shall be in no more danger of departing from God, than a wise and rational man is of killing or wilfully destroying himself. The first part whereof may be performed by them who are no saints; the latter not by any saint whatsoever. And is not this noble provision of the security and assurance of the saints, enough to make them cast away with speed all their interest in the unchangeable purposes, gracious and faithful promises of God, intercession of Christ, sealing of the Spirit, and all those sandy and trivial supports of their faith, which hitherto they have rejoiced in. And whatever experience, they have, or testimony from the world they do receive, of the darkness and weakness of their minds, the stubbornness of their wills, with the strong inclinations that are in them to sin and falling away, whatever be* their oppositions from above them, about them, within them, on the right hand, and on the left, that they have to wrestle withal; let them give up themselves to the hand of their own manlike considerations and weighing of things, which will secure them against all danger or probability of falling away; for, if they be but capable, first, of seeing and knowing; secondly, of pondering and considering, and that rationally (it matters not, whether these things are fruits of the Spirit of grace or no, nay it is clear they must not be so), that such and such evil is to be avoided, and that there is so and so great a good to be obtained by continuing in obedience, they may raise and work inclinations in themselves, answerable in strength, vigour, and power, to do any degree of goodness, which they apprehend, in what they see and ponder.

The whole of the ample sufficient means, afforded by God to the saints to enable them to persevere, branching itself into these two heads: First, The rational considering what they have to do; secondly, Their vigorous inclination of their hearts, to act suitably and answerable to their considerations, I shall (in a word) consider them apart.

First, The considerations mentioned, of evil to be avoided

* Eph vi. 12. Heb xii 1. Rom. vii. 17.

M 2

and good to be attained (I mean that which may put men upon creating those strong inclinations. For such considerations may be without any such consequence as in her that cried, ' Video meliora proboque, deteriora sequior'), are either issues and products of men's own natural faculties, and deduced out of the power of them, so that, as men, they may put themselves upon them at any time ; or they are fruits of the Spirit of his grace, who[1] worketh in us to will and to do of his own good pleasure.' If they be the latter, I ask, seeing all grace is of promise, whether hath God promised to give and continue this grace of self-consideration unto believers or no? If he hath, whether absolutely, or conditionally : if absolutely, then he hath promised absolutely to continue some grace in them, which is all we desire. If conditionally, then would I know what that condition is, on which God hath promised that believers shall so consider things mentioned ? And of the condition which shall be expressed, it may farther be inquired, whether it be any grace of God, or only a mere act of the rational creature as such, without any immediate inworking of the will and deed by God ? Whatsoever is answered, the question will not go to rest, until it be granted that, either it is a grace absolutely promised of God, which is all we desire; or a pure act of the creature contradistinct thereunto, which answers the first inquiry. Let it then be granted, that the considerations intimated are no other, but such as a rational man, who is enlightened to an assent to the truth of God, may so exert and exercise, as he pleaseth ; then is here a foundation laid of all the ground of perseverance that is allowed the saints, in their own endeavours, as men without the assistance of any grace of God. Now these considerations, be they what they will, must needs be beneath one[2] single good thought (for as for that we have no sufficiency of ourselves), yea, vanity and nothing (for without Christ, we can do nothing[3]); yea evil and displeasing to God, as are all the thoughts and imaginations of our hearts, that are only such. I had supposed that no man, in the least acquainted with what it is to serve God under temptations, and what the work of saving souls is, but had been sufficiently convinced of the utter insufficiency of such rational considerations, flowing only

[1] Phil. i. 13.   [2] 2 Cor. iii   [3] John xv. 5. Gen. viii. 21.

from conviction, to be a solid foundation of abiding with God unto the end. If men's houses of profession are built on such sands as these, we need not wonder to see them so frequently falling to the ground.

Secondly, Suppose these considerations to act their parts upon the stage raised for them, to the greatest applause that can be expected or desired, yet that, which comes next upon the theatre, will, I fear, foully miscarry, and spoil the whole plot of the play : that is, men's vigorous inclination of their hearts to the good things pondered on, to what height they please. For besides that,

First, It is liable to the same examinations, that passed upon its associate before, or any inquiry from whence he comes, whether from heaven or men ; upon which I doubt not, but he may easily be discovered to be a vagabond upon the earth, to have no pass from heaven, and so be rendered liable to the law of God.

Secondly, It would be inquired, whether it hath a consistency with the whole design of the apostle, Rom. vii. and therefore,

Thirdly, It is utterly denied, that men, the best of men, have in themselves and of themselves, arising upon the account of any considerations whatsoever, a power, ability, or strength, vigorously or at all acceptably to God, to incline their hearts to the performance of any thing that is spiritually good, or in a gospel tendency to walking with God. All the promises of God, all the prayers of the saints, all their experience, the whole design of God in laying up all our stores of strength and grace in Christ, jointly cry out against it, for a counterfeit pretence. In a word, that men are able to plant in themselves inclinations and dispositions to refrain all manner of sin destructive to the safety of their souls, fuller of energy, vigour, life, strength, power, than those that are in them, to avoid things apparently tending to the destruction of their natural lives, is an assertion as full of energy, strength, and vigour, life and poison, for the destruction and eversion of the grace of God in Christ, as any can be invented.

To shut up this discourse and to proceed : If these are the solid foundations of peace and consolation, which the saints have concerning their perseverance, if these be the means sufficient, abundantly sufficient, afforded them, for their preservation, that are laid in the balance, as to the giving of an evangelical genuine assurance, with the decrees and purposes, the covenant, promises, and oath of God, the blood and intercession of Christ, the anointing and sealing of the Spirit of grace, I suppose we need not care, how soon we enter the lists with any, as to the comparing of the doctrines under contest, in reference to their influence into the obedience and consolation of the saints, which, with its issue, in the close of this discourse shall, God willing, be put to the trial.

Now that I may lay a more clear foundation for what doth ensue, I shall briefly deduce, not only the doctrine itself, but also the method, wherein I shall handle it, from a portion of Scripture, in which the whole is summarily comprised, and branched forth into suitable heads, for the confirmation and vindication thereof. And this also is required to the main of my design, being not so directly to convince stout gainsayers, in vanquishing their objections, as to strengthen weak believers, in helping them against temptations, and therefore shall at the entrance hold out that, whereinto their faith must be ultimately resolved; the authority of God in his word, being that ark alone whereon it can rest the sole of its foot. Now this is the fourth chapter of Isaiah, of which take this short account: It is a chapter made up of gracious promises, given to the church, in a calamitous season: the season itself is described, verses 25, and 26. of the third chapter, and the first of this; all holding out a distressed estate, a low condition; it is indeed God's method, to make out gracious promises to his people, when their condition seems most deplored, to sweeten their souls with a sense of his love, in the multitude of the perplexing thoughts, which in distracted times, are ready to tumultuate in them.

The foundation of all the following promises lies in the second verse, even the giving out of the Branch of the Lord and the fruit of the earth for beauty and glory, to the remnant of Israel; who it is, who is the Branch of the Lord, the Scripture tells us in sundry places; Isa. xi. 1. Jer. xxiii. 5. xxxiii. 15. Zech. iii. 8. The Lord Jesus Christ, the promise of whom is the church's only supportment in every trial or

distress, it hath to undergo; he is this branch and fruit, and
he is placed in the head here, as the great fountain-mercy,
from whence all others do flow. In those that follow, the
persons to whom those promises are made, and the matter
or substance of them are observable; the persons have various appellations and descriptions in this chapter. They are
called (first) the escaping of Israel; ver. 2. They that are left
in Sion; ver. 3. Jerusalem itself; ver. 4. The dwelling-places
and assemblies of mount Sion; ver. 5. That the same individual persons, are intended in all these several appellations,
is not questionable. It is but in reference to the several acts
of God's dwelling with them, and outgoing of his love and
good-will, both eternal and temporal, towards them, that they
come under this variety of names and descriptions. First,
In respect of his eternal designation of them to life and salvation, they are said to be[a] 'written among the living, or unto
life in Jerusalem; their names are in the Lamb's book of life,
from the foundation of the world,' and they are recorded in
the purpose of God from all eternity. Secondly, In respect
of their deliverance, and actual redemption from the bondage of death and Satan, which for ever prevail upon the
greatest number of the sons of men, shadowed out by their
deliverance from the Babylonish captivity (pointed at in this
place), they are said to be[b] ' a remnant, an escaping, such as
are left, and remain in Jerusalem;' from the perishing lump
of mankind, God doth by Christ, snatch a remnant (whom
he will preserve) like a brand out of the fire. Thirdly, In
respect of their enjoyment of God's ordinances and word,
and his presence with them, therein, they are called,[c] the
daughter of Sion, and the dwelling-places thereof. There
did God make known his mind and will, and walked with
his people in those beauties of holiness; these are they to
whom these promises are made, the elect, redeemed, and
called of God; or those who being elected and redeemed,
shall in their several generations be called, according to his
purpose, who worketh all things, according to the counsel
of his own will.

For the matter of these promises, they may be reduced

[a] Rev. iii. 12. xiii. 8. Luke x. 20.
[b] Rev. v. 9. Eph v. 25, 26. Zech. iii. 2. John xvii. 9. Rom. viii. 38.
[c] Psal. xlviii. 11—14. xvi. 1—3, &c. Jer. l. 5. Zech. viii 2. John xii. 17. Psal.
x.3. Isa. xlix. 14.

to these three heads. First, Of justification; ver. 2. Secondly, Of sanctification; ver. 3,4. Thirdly, Of perseverance; ver. 5, 6. First, Of justification; Christ is made to them, or given unto them, for beauty and glory; which how it is done, the Holy Ghost tells us, Isa. lxi. 10. 'I will greatly rejoice in the Lord, my soul shall be joyful in my God; for he hath clothed me with the garment of salvation, he hath covered me with the robes of righteousness,' saith the church. He puts upon poor deformed creatures, the glorious robe of his own righteousness, to make us comely in his presence, and the presence of his Father; Zech. xiii. 3, 4. Through him,[d] his being given unto us, 'made unto us of God, righteousness;' becoming 'the Lord our righteousness,' do we find free acceptation, as beautiful and glorious in the eyes of God. But this is not all: He doth not only adorn us without, but also wash us within: the apostle acquaints us, that that was his design; Eph. v. 25, 26. and therefore you have (secondly) the promise of sanctification added, ver. 3, 4. Ver. 3. you have the thing itself; they shall be called holy, made so, called so by him, who calleth things that are not as though they were, and by that call, gives them to be that which he calls them; he said,[e] 'Let there be light, and there was light.' And then the manner how it becomes to be so; ver. 4. first setting out the efficient cause;[f] 'the Spirit of judgment and burning;' that is of holiness and light: and, secondly, the way of his producing this great effect; washing away filth, and purging away blood; spiritual filth and blood, is the defilement of sin; the Scripture, to set out it s abomination, comparing it to the things of the greatest abhoriency to our nature, even as that is to the nature of God. And this is the second promise, that, in and by the Branch of the Lord, is here made to them, 'who are written unto life in Jerusalem.' But now, lest any should suppose that both these are for a season only, that they are dying privileges, perishing mercies, jewels that may be lost, so that, though the persons to whom those promises are made, are once made glorious and comely, being in Christ freely accepted, yet they may again become

---

d 1 Cor. i. 20. liv. 17. Isa. xlv. 24, 25. Jer. xxiii. 6. Rom. v. 1. viii. 1. Col. ii. 10.   e 2 Cor. iv. 6.

f Ezek. xi. 19. John iii. 5. Rom. viii. 2. John xvi. 9—11. Psal. xxxviii. 5. 7. Prov. xiii. 5, 6. Isa. i. 5, 6. lxiv. 6. Ezek. xvi, 4, 5. xxiv. 6. Hos. viii. 8. Zech. xiii. 1. Rom iii. 13. 2 Pet. ii. 22.

odious in the sight of God, and be utterly rejected; that being once washed, purged, cleansed, they should yet return to wallow in their mire, and so become wholly defiled and abominable; in the third place, he gives a promise of perseverance, in the two last verses, and that expressed with allusion to the protection afforded unto the people of the Jews in the wilderness by a cloud and pillar of fire; which as they were created and instituted signs of the presence of God, so they gave assured protection, preservation, and direction to the people in all their ways. The sum of the whole intendment of the Holy Ghost in these two verses, seeming to be comprised in the last words of the fifth, and they being a suitable bottom unto the ensuing discourse, comprising, as they stand in relation to the verses foregoing, the whole of my aim, with the way, or method, wherein it may conveniently be delivered, I shall a little insist upon them : ' Upon all the glory shall be a defence.'

The words are a gospel promise, expressed in law terms, or a New Testament mercy, in Old Testament clothes ; the subject of it is, ' all the glory,' and the thing promised, is ' a defence over it, or upon it.' By ' the glory,' some take the people themselves to be intended, who are ' the glory of God ;' Isa. xlvi. 13. In whom he will be glorified ; and who are said to be made glorious; ver. 2. But the pillar of fire, and the cloud lead us another way. As the protection here promised, must answer the protection given by them of old ; so the glory here mentioned, must answer that which was the glory of that people, when they had their preservation and direction from those signs of the presence of God in the midst of them. It is very true the sign of God's presence among them itself, and the protection received thereby, is sometimes called his glory ; Ezek. x. 10. But here it is plainly differenced from it, that being afterward called a defence. That which most frequently was called the glory in the ancient dispensation of God to his people, was the ark ; when this was taken by the Philistines, the wife of Phineas calls her son Ichabod, and says, ' The glory is departed from Israel ;' 1 Sam. iv. 2. 22. Which the Holy Ghost mentions again, Psal. lxxviii. 61. ' And delivered his strength into captivity, and his glory into his enemies' hand.' The tabernacle, or the tent wherein it was placed is mentioned,

ver. 60. ' He forsook the tabernacle of Shiloh, the tent which
he had placed among them.' And the people to whom it was
given, ver. 62. ' He gave the people over also to the sword.'
That ark being the glory and strength which went into captivity, when he forsook the tabernacle, and gave his people
to the sword. That this ark, the glory of old, was a type of
Jesus Christ (besides the end and aim of its institution, with
its use and place of its abode), appears from the mercy-seat
or plate of gold that was laid upon it, which Jesus Christ
is expressly said to be, Rom. iii. 25, 26. compared with Heb.
x. 5. It is he who is the glory here mentioned, not considered absolutely and in his own person, but as he is made
beauty and glory unto his people, as he is made unto them
righteousness and holiness, according to the tenor of the promises insisted on before ; and this is indeed,[g] all the glory
of the elect of God, even the presence of Christ with them,
as their justification and sanctification, their righteousness
and holiness.

The matter of the promise made in reference to his glory
and them upon whom it doth abide, is, that they shall be a
defence upon it ; the word translated here ' a defence' comes
from a root, that is but once read in Scripture ; Deut. xxxiii.
12. Where it is rendered to cover: ' The Lord shall cover
him all the day long.' So it properly signifies. From
a covering, to a protection, or a defence, is an easy me-
taphor ; a covering being given for that end and purpose.
And this is the native signification of the word ' pro-
tego,' ' to defend by covering ;' as Abimelech called Abraham the covering of Sarah's eyes, or a protection to her ;
Gen. xx. 16. The allusion also of a shade, which in[h] Scripture is so often taken for a defence, ariseth from hence.
This word itself is used twice more, and in both places signifies a bride-chamber ; Psal. xix. 6. Joel ii. 16. From the
peace, covert, and protection of such a place. The name of the
mercy-seat, is also of the same root with this. In this place
it is by common consent rendered, a defence or protection,
being so used, either by allusion to that refreshment, that
the Lord Christ, the great bridegroom,[i] gives to his bride in
his banqueting-house, or rather in pursuit of the former

[g] Isa. xlv 25.
[h] Psal. xvii. 8. xxxvi. 7. lvii. 1. lxiii. 7. cxvi. 5 Isa. xxv. 2. xlix. 9. Ezek. xxxi. 6, &c.
[i] Cant. ii. 4.

similitude of the cloud, that was over the tabernacle and the ark, which represented the glory of that people. Thus this defence or covering is said to be upon or above the glory, as the cloud was over the tabernacle, and as the mercy-seat lay upon the ark. Add only thus much to what hath been spoken (which is also affirmed in the beginning of the verse), viz. That this defence is created, or is an immediate product of the mighty power of God, not requiring unto it the least concurrence of creature power, and the whole will manifest the intendment of the Lord everlastingly to safe-guard the spiritual glories of his saints in Christ.

As there was before shewn, there are two parts of our spiritual glory : the one purely extrinsical ; to wit, the love and favour of God unto us, his free and gracious acceptation of us in Christ; on this part of our glory, there is this de-fence created, it shall abide for ever, it shall never be removed. His own glory and excellencies are engaged for the preser-vation of this excellency and glory of his people. This sun though it may be for a while eclipsed, yet shall never set, nor give place to an evening, that shall make long the shade there-of; whom God once freely accepts in Christ, he will never turn away his love from them, nor cast them utterly out of his favour. The other is within us, and that is our sanctifica-tion; our portion from God by the Spirit of holiness, and the fruits thereof, in our faith, love, and obedience unto him, and on this part of our glory, there is this defence, that this Spirit shall never utterly be dislodged from that soul, wherein he makes his residence, nor resign his habitation to the spirit of the world ; that his fruit shall never so decay, as that the fruits of Sodom, and the grapes of Gomorrah, should grow in their room ; nor they, wherein they are, everlastingly, utterly, and wickedly grow barren, in departing from the liv-ing God ; these two make up their perseverance, whereof we speak : whom God accepts in Christ, he will continue to do so for ever: whom he quickens to walk with him, they shall do it to the end. And these three things, acceptance with God, holiness from God, and a defence upon them, both unto the end, all free and in Christ, are that threefold cord of the covenant of grace, which cannot be broken.

In the handling, then, of the doctrine proposed unto con-sideration, I shall (the Lord assisting) shew,

First, That the love and favour of God, as to the free acceptation of believers with him in Christ, is constant, abiding, and shall never be turned away; handling at large the principles, both of its being and manifestation.

Secondly, That the Spirit and grace of sanctification, which they freely receive from him, shall never utterly be extinguished in them, but so remain, as that they shall abide with him for ever; the sophistical separation of which two parts of our doctrine, is the greatest advantage our adversaries have against the whole. And demonstrate, thirdly, the real and causal influences, which this truth hath, into the obedience and consolation of the saints, considered both absolutely, and compared with the doctrine, which is set up in competition with it; in the pursuit of which particulars, I shall endeavour to enforce and press those places of Scripture, wherein they are abundantly delivered, and vindicate them from all the exceptions put into our inferences from them, by Mr. Goodwin in his Redemption Redeemed; as also answer all the arguments, which he hath with much labour and industry, collected and improved, in opposition to the truth in hand. Take then only these few previous observations, and I shall insist fully upon the proof and demonstration of the first position, concerning the unchangeableness of the love of God towards his, to whom he gives Jesus Christ for beauty and glory, and freely accepts them in him.

First, As to their inherent holiness, the question is not concerning[l] acts, either as to their vigour, which may be abated, or as to their frequency, which may be interrupted; but only as to the Spirit and habit of it, which shall never depart; we do not say they cannot sin, fall into many sins, great sins, which the Scripture plainly affirms of all the saints, that went before: and who of them living doth not this day labour under the truth of it? But through the presence of God with them, upon such grounds and principles, as shall afterward be insisted on, they cannot, shall not, sin away the Spirit and habit of grace (which without a miracle cannot be done away by any one act, and God will not work miracles for the destruction of his children), so as to fall into that state, wherein they were before they were

[l] Rev. ii. 5 in 2. Isa. lvii. 17. Hos. xiv. 4. Isa. lix. 21. John xiv. 16. 1 John iii. 9. i 8. James iii. 2. 1 Kings viii. 33. Isa. lxiv. 5, 6.

regenerate; and of the children of God, become children of the devil, tasting of the[l] second death, after they have been made partakers of the first resurrection.

Secondly, The question is not about the decay of any grace, but the loss of all; not about sickness and weaknesses, but about death itself, which alone we say, they shall be preserved from. Neither do we say,[m] that believers are endowed with any such rich and plentiful stock of grace, as that they may spend upon it without new supplies all their days, but grant that they stand in continual need of the renewed communication of that grace, which hath its abode and residence in their souls, and of that actual assistance, whereby any thing that is truly and spiritually good, is wrought in them. Thirdly, Whereas there is a twofold impossibility. (First), That which is absolutely and simply so in its own nature: and (secondly), That which is so only upon some supposition, we say the total falling away of the saints is impossible only in this latter sense. The unchangeable decree and purpose of God, his faithful promises and oaths, the mediation of the Lord Jesus, being in the assertion supposed: and, fourthly, whereas we affirm, they shall assuredly continue unto the end, the certainty and assurance intimated, is not *mentis* but *entis,* not subjective but objective, not always in the[n] person persevering, but always relating to the thing itself. Fifthly, That the three things, formerly mentioned, acceptance with God, holiness from God, and the defence upon them both unto the end, are that threefold cord of the covenant, which cannot be broken. This will appear, by comparing those two eminent places together, which afterward must more fully be insisted on; Jer. xxxi. 34, 35. xxxii. 38—40. In general, God undertakes to be 'their God, and that they shall be his people;' chap. xxxi. 31. xxxii. 38. And this he manifests in three things: First, That he will accept them freely, give them to find great favour before him, in the forgiveness of their sins, for which alone he hath any quarrel with them. ' I will,' saith he, ' forgive their iniquities and remember their sins no more;' chap. xxxi. 34. As it is again repeated, Heb. viii. 12. Secondly, That they shall

[l] Rev. xv. 6.
[m] Psal xxiii 6. Isa. xxxv 1, 2. &c. John xv. 3—7. Rom. xi. 18 John i. 16. Col. ii. 19 Luke xvii. 5 Phil. ii. 13.
[n] Isa. xlix 14—16. v 17. Cant. v 2. 6 Psal. lxxiii. 26.

have sanctification and holiness from him; 'I will put my law in their inward parts and write it in their hearts;' chap. xxxi. 33. 'I will put my fear in their hearts;' ver. 40. with Ezek. lxvi. 67. calls 'the putting his Spirit in them,' who is the author of that grace and holiness which he doth bestow: Thirdly, That in both these, there shall be a continuance for ever; chap. xxxii. 40. 'I will not turn away from them to do them good, and I will put my fear in their hearts and they shall not depart from me;' or, as ver. 39. 'They shall fear me for ever;' which distinguisheth this covenant from the former, made with their fathers, in that that was broken, which this shall never be; chap. xxi. 32. This is the crowning mercy, that renders both the other glorious: as to acceptation he will not depart from us; as to sanctification we shall not depart from him.

CHAP. II.

The theses proposed for confirmation. The fivefold foundation of the truth thereof. Of the unchangeableness of the nature of God, and the influence thereof into the confirmation of the truth in hand. Mal. iii. 3. 6. considered, explained. James i. 16—18 opened. Rom. xi. 29 explained and vindicated. The conditions on which grace is asserted to be bestowed and continued, discussed. The vanity of them evinced in sundry instances. Of vocation, justification, and sanctification. Isa. xl. 27—31. opened and improved to the end aimed at. Also Isa. xliv. 1—8. The sum of the first argument. Mal. iii. 6. with the whole argument from the immutability of God at large, vindicated. Falsely proposed by Mr. G. set right and reinforced. Exceptions removed. Sophistical comparisons exploded. Distinct dispensations, according to distinction of a people. Alteration and change properly and directly assigned to God, by Mr. G. The theme in question begged by him. Legal approbation of duties, and conditional acceptation of persons confounded. As also God's command and purpose. The unchangeableness of God's decrees granted to be intended in Mal. iii. 6. The decree directly in that place intended. The decree of sending Christ not immutable upon Mr. G.'s principles. The close of the vindication of this first argument.

THE certain infallible continuance of the love and favour of God unto the end, towards his, those whom he hath once freely accepted in Jesus Christ, notwithstanding the interposition of any such supposals, as may truly be made, having foundation in the things themselves, being the first thing proposed, comes now to be demonstrated.

Now the foundation of this the Scripture lays upon five unchangeable things, which eminently have an influence into the truth thereof. First, Of the nature : Secondly, Purposes : Thirdly, The Covenant : Fourthly, The Promises : Fifthly, The oath of God. Every one whereof being engaged herein, the Lord makes use of to manifest the unchangeableness of his love towards those, whom he hath once graciously accepted in Christ.

First, He hath laid the shoulders of the unchangeableness of his own nature to this work ; Mal. iii. 6. ' I am the Lord, and I change not: therefore ye sons of Jacob, are not consumed.' These sons of Jacob are[a] the sons of the faith of Jacob, the Israel of God, not all the seed of Jacob according

[a] Rom. ix. 6. xi 4—6

to the flesh ; the Holy Ghost in this prophecy makes an eminent distinction between these two ; chap. iii. 16. iv. 1, 2.
The beginning of this chapter contains a most evident and
clear prediction and prophecy of the bringing in of the kingdom of Christ, in the gospel, wherein he was to[b] purge his
floor, and throw out the chaff to be burnt.   This his appearance makes great work in the[c] visible church of the
Jews, very many of those who looked and waited for that
coming of his, are cut off, and cast out, as persons that have
neither lot nor portion in the mercy wherewith it is attended.
Though they said within themselves, that they had Abraham
to their father, and were the children and posterity of Jacob;
yea, ver.5. to them who are only the carnal seed, and do also
walk in the ways of the flesh, he threatens a sore revenge and
swift destruction, when others shall be invested with all the
eminent mercies, which the Lord Christ brings along with
him, lest the true sons of Jacob should be terrified with the
dread of the approaching day, and say, as David did, when
the Lord made a breach upon Uzzah,[d] Who can stand
before so holy a God ? Shall not we also in the issue be consumed ! He discovereth to them the foundation of their preservation to the end, even the unchangeableness of his own
nature and being, whereunto his love to them is conformed ;
plainly intimating, that unless himself and his everlasting
Deity be subject and liable to alteration and change (which
once to imagine, were, what lieth in us, to cast him down
from his excellency), it could not be, that they should be
cast off for ever, and consumed.   These are the tribes of
Jacob and the preserved of Israel, which Jesus Christ was
sent to raise up; Isa. l. 6.   The house of Jacob, which he
takes from the womb, and carries unto old age, unto hoary
hairs, and forsaketh not; Isa. xlvi. 3, 4.

This is confirmed, James i. 16—18. ' Do not err my beloved brethren, every good gift and every perfect gift cometh
down from the Father of lights ; with whom is no variableness, nor shadow of turning : of his own will begat he us
with the word of truth.'   He begets us of his own will by
the word of truth.   For, whatsoever men do pretend, ' we
are born again, not of blood, nor of the will of the flesh, nor
the will of man, but the will of God ;' John i. 13.   Now,

[b] Mat. iii. 12.   [c] Isa. xliv. 3—6. Luke ii. 34. Rom. ix. 30, 31.   [d] Isa. liv—6.

herein, saith the apostle, we do receive from him good and perfect gifts : gifts distinguished from the common endowments of others. Yea, but they are failing ones perhaps? Such as may flourish for a season, and be but children of a night, like Jonah's gourd. Though God hath begotten us of his own will, and bestowed good and perfect gifts upon us, yet he may cast us off for ever. 'Do not err, my beloved brethren,' saith the apostle, these things come 'from the Father of lights.' God himself is the fountain of all lights of grace, which we have received; and with him, 'there is no variableness nor shadow of turning,' not the least appearance of any change or alteration. And if the apostle did not in this place argue from the immutability of the divine nature, to the unchangeableness of his love towards those whom he hath begotten, and bestowed such light and grace upon, there were no just reason of mentioning that attribute and property there.

Hence, Rom. xi. 29. 'The gifts and calling of God,' are said to be 'without repentance:' the gifts of his effectual calling (ἐν διὰ δυοῖν) shall never be repented of. They are from him, with whom there is no change.

The words are added by the apostle, to give assurance of the certain accomplishment of the purpose of God towards the remnant of the Jews, according to the election of grace. What the principal mercies were, that were in God's intendment to them, and whereof by their effectual calling they shall be made partakers, he tells us; ver. 26, 27. 'The deliverer or Redeemer, which comes out of Sion,' 'shall,' according to the covenant of grace, 'turn them from ungodliness,' the Lord taking away their sin. Sanctification and justification by Christ, the two main branches of the new covenant (Jer. xxxi. 42. xxxii. Ezek. xxxvi. Heb. viii. 13, 14. x. 17, 18.), do make up the mercy purposed for them. The certainty of the collation of this mercy upon them, notwithstanding the interposition of any present obstruction (amongst which their enmity to the gospel was most eminent, and lay ready to be objected), the apostle argueth from the unchangeableness of the love of election, wherewith the Lord embraced them from eternity; 'as touching the election they are beloved:' and farther to manifest on that account, the fulfilling of what he is in the proof and demonstration of,

viz. that though the major part of ' Israel according to the
flesh,' were rejected, yet the ' election should obtain, and all
Israel be saved,' he tells them, that that calling of God,
whereby he will make out to them those eternally designed
mercies, shall not be repented of; eminently in that assertion,
distinguishing the grace whereof he speaks, from all such
common gifts, and such outward dispensations as might be
subject to a removal from them on whom they are bestowed.
And if, upon any supposition or consideration imaginable,
the mercies mentioned may be taken away, the assertion
comes very short of the proof of that, for which it is produced.

Against this plain expression of the apostle, that the
gifts and calling of God, are without repentance; Mr. Goodwin puts in sundry exceptions to weaken the testimony it
bears in this case, cap. 8. sect. 86. which because they have
been already sufficiently evinced of weakness, falsehood,
and impertinency, by his learned antagonist, I shall only
take up that which he mainly insists upon, and farther manifest its utter uselessness for the end for which it is produced. Thus, then, he pleads: ' The gifts and calling of
God, may be said to be without repentance; because let men
continue the same persons which they were, when the dona-
tion or collation of any gift was first made by God unto
them, he never changes or altereth his dispensations towards them, unless it be for the better, or in order to their
farther good, in which case he cannot be said to repent of
what he had given: but in case men shall change, and alter
from what they were when God first dealt graciously with
them, especially if they shall notoriously degenerate or cast
away the principles, or divest themselves of that very qualification on which, as it were, God grafted his benefit or gift;
in this case though he recall his gift, he cannot be said to
repent of his giving it, because the terms on which he gave
it please him still, only the persons to whom he gave it, and
who pleased him when he gave it them, have now rendered
themselves unpleasing to him.'

Two things are here asserted: 1. That if men continue
the same, or in the same state and condition wherein they
were when God bestowed his gifts and graces upon them,
then God never changeth nor altereth; his dispensations

towards them abide the same. 2. That there are certain qualifications in men, upon which God grafts his grace, which whilst they abide, his gifts and graces abide upon them also, and therefore are said to be without repentance; but if they are lost, God recalls his gifts, and that without any change. Let us a little consider both these assertions. And, first, It being evident, that it is spiritual grace and mercy, of which the apostle speaks, as was manifested : for they are such as flow from the covenant of the Redeemer, ver. 26, 27. Sanctification and justification being particularly mentioned, let us consider what is the condition of men when God invests them with these mercies, that we may be able to instruct them how to abide in that condition, and so make good the possession of the grace and mercy bestowed on them : and to keep close to the text, let our instance be in the three eminent mercies of the gospel intimated in that place : 1. Vocation; 2. Sanctification; 3. Justification.

The gift and grace of vocation, is confessedly here intended, being expressly mentioned in the words ἡ κλῆσις τοῦ Θεοῦ, that 'calling' which is an effect of the covenant of grace; ver. 28. Consider we then what is the state of men, when God first calls them, and gives them this gift and favour, that if it seems so good, we may exhort them to a continuance therein.

Now this state, with the qualifications of it, is a state, 1. Of death, John v. 25. ' The dead hear the voice of the Son of God.' Christ speaks[e] to them who are dead, and so they live. 2. Of darkness, Acts xxv. 26. ' God calls them out of darkness into his marvellous light;' 1 Pet. ii. 9. a state of ignorance and alienation from God; Eph. iv. 18. The grace of vocation or effectual calling, finding men in a state of enmity to God, and alienation from him, if they may be prevailed withal, to continue such still, this gift shall never be recalled nor repented of.

But, perhaps, the gift and grace of sanctification finds men in a better condition, in a state, wherein if they abide, then that also shall abide with them for ever. The Scripture abounds in the description of this state, that we shall not need to hesitate about it; Eph. ii. 1, 2. ' You hath he quickened, who were dead in trespasses and sins :' quickening and

[e] Isa. lxv. 1. Rom. ix. 25. Hos. ii. 23. 1 Pet. ii. 10 Eph. ii. 12.

renewing grace is given to persons dead in sins: and is so far from depending, as to its unchangeableness, upon their continuance in the state, wherein it finds them, that it consists in a real change, and translation of them from that state or condition. The apostle sets out this at large, Tit. iii. 3—5. ' We ourselves were sometimes foolish,' &c. The state of men, when God bestows these gifts upon them, is positively expressed in sundry particulars; ver. 3. the qualifications on which this gift or grace is grafted (of which Mr. Goodwin speaks afterward) negatively, ver. 5. It is not of any work that we have done; which is unquestionably exclusive of all those stocks of qualifications which are intimated, whereon the gifts and graces of God should be grafted. The gift itself here bestowed, is the washing of regeneration and renewing of the Holy Ghost, saving us through mercy from the state and condition before described. In brief, that the condition wherein this grace of God finds the sons of men, is a state of[f] death,[g] blood,[h] darkness,[i] blindness, enmity, curse, and wrath, disobedience, rebellion, impotency, and universal alienation from God, is beyond all contradiction (by testimonies plentifully given out, here a little and there a little, line upon line) manifest in the Scripture. Shall we now say, that this grace of God is bestowed on men upon the account of these qualifications, and continued without revocation on condition that they abide in the same state, with the same qualifications? Let then men continue in sin, that grace may abound.

Is the case any other as to justification? doth not God justify the ungodly? Rom. iv. 5. Are we not in filthy robes, when he comes to clothe us with robes of righteousness? Zech. iii. 3. are we not reconciled to God, when alienated by wicked works? Col. i. 13. These are the qualifications on which it seems God grafts his gifts and graces: and whose abode in the persons, in whom they are, is the condition whereon the irrevocableness of those gifts and graces does depend: who would have thought, they had been of such reckoning and esteem with the Lord?

And this, considering what is learnedly discoursed else-

f Matt. viii. 22. Rom. vi 13. Col. ii. 13.   g Ezek. xvii. 6. Isa. iv 4. Job xiv. 4. John iii. 6.   h John i 5. Eph. v. 8. Col. i. 13. Luke iv. 18. i Rom. viii. 6—8. v. 10. Col i. 21. Gal. iii. 13. John iii. 35.

where may suffice, as to the other assertion; that God gives his gifts and graces to[k] qualifications, not to persons. Those qualifications are either gifts of God, or not: if not, who made those men, in whom they are, differ from others? if they are, on what qualifications, were those qualifications bestowed? That God freely bestows on persons, of his own good pleasure, not grafting on qualifications, his gifts and graces, we have testimonies abundantly sufficient to outbalance Mr. Goodwin's assertions. Rom. ix. 18. ' He hath mercy, on whom he will have mercy:' he bestows his mercy and the fruits of it, not on this or that qualification, but on whom or what person he will; 'and to them it is given,' saith our Saviour, 'to know the mysteries of the kingdom of God, but to others it is not given.' I see no stock that his gift is grafted on, but only the persons of God's good-will, whom he graciously designs to a participation of it.

Truth is, I know not any thing more directly contradictory to the whole discovery of the work of God's grace in the gospel, than that which is couched in these assertions of Mr. Goodwin, neither is it any thing less or more, than that which of old was phrased, 'The giving of grace according to merit;' ascribing the primitive discriminating of persons as to spiritual grace, unto self-endeavours, casting to the ground the free distinguishing good pleasure of God, and that graciousness of every gift of his (I speak as to the first issue of his love in quickening, renewing, pardoning grace) which eminently consists in this, that he is found of them that seek him not, and hath mercy on whom he will, because so it seemed good to him.

Not to digress farther (in the discovery of the unsatisfactoriness of this pretence) from the pursuit of the argument in hand; because God's gifts are not repented of, therefore do men continue, not in the condition wherein they find them, but wherein they place them: and all qualifications in men whatever, that are in the least acceptable to God, are so far from being stocks whereon God grafts his gifts and graces, that they are plants themselves, which he plants in whomsoever he pleaseth.

Yea the tree is made good before it bear any good fruit; and the branch implanted into the true olive, before it receive

[k] 1 Cor. iv. 7.

the sap or juice, of any one good qualification. The sum of Mr. Goodwin's answer amounts to this; let men be steadfast in a good condition, and God's gifts shall steadfastly abide with them, if they change they also shall be revoked; which is directly opposite to the plain intendment of the place, viz. That the steadfastness of men, depends upon the irrevocableness of God's grace, and not *e contra:* there is not in his sense the least intimation in these words, of the permanency of any gift or grace of God with any one on whom it is bestowed, for a day, an hour, or a moment; but, notwithstanding this testimony of the Holy Ghost, they may be given one hour, and taken away the next; they may flourish in a man in the morning, and in the evening be cut down, dried up, and withered: this is not to answer the arguings of men, but positively to deny what God affirms. To conclude, God gives not his gifts to men (I mean those mentioned) because they[1] please him, but because it pleaseth him so to do: he does not take them away because they displease him, but gives them so to abide with them, that they shall never displease him, to the height of such a provocation. Neither are the gifts of God otherwise to be repented of; than by taking them from the persons on whom they are bestowed: but this heap being removed we may proceed.

Furthermore, then, in sundry places doth the Lord propose this for the consolation of his, and to assure them, that there shall never be an everlasting separation between him and them; which shall be farther cleared by particular instances: things or truths proposed for consolation, are of all others most clearly exalted above exception; without which, they were no way suitable (considering the promptness of our unbelieving hearts to rise up against the work of God's grace, and mercy) to compass the end for which they are proposed.

Isa. xl. 27—31. 'Why sayest thou, O Jacob, and speakest, O Israel, My way is hid from the Lord, and my judgment is passed over from my God? Hast thou not known? hast thou not heard, that the everlasting God, the Lord, the Creator of the ends of the earth, fainteth not, neither is weary? there is no searching of his understanding. He giveth power to the faint; and to them that have no might he increaseth strength. Even the youths shall faint and be

[1] Jerem. xxxi 32.

weary, and the young men shall utterly fall: but they that
wait upon the Lord shall renew their strength; they shall
mount up with wings as eagles; they shall run and not be
weary; they shall walk and not faint;' ver. 27. Jacob and
Israel make a double complaint, both parts of it manifesting
some fear, or dread of separation from God: for though in
general it could not be so, yet in particular, believers under
temptation, may question their own condition, with their
right unto, and interest in, all the things whereby their state
and glory is safeguarded. 'My way,' say they, 'is hid from the
Lord:' the Lord takes no more notice, sets his heart no more
upon my way, my walking, but lets me go and pass on as a
stranger to him: and, farther, 'my judgment is passed over
from my God:' mine enemies prevail, perhaps lusts and
corruptions are strong, and God doth not appear in my
behalf: judgment is not executed on them, and what will
be the issue of this my sad estate? What the Lord proposeth
and holdeth out unto them for their establishment in this condition, and to assure them that what they feared should not
come upon them, he ushers in by an effectual expostulation;
ver. 27. 'Hast thou not heard?' Hast not thou been taught
it by the saints that went before thee? 'Hast thou not
known?' Hast thou not found it true by experience? What
it is he would have them take notice of, and which he so
pathetically insinuates into their understandings and affections, for their establishment, is an exurgency of that description of himself, which he gives, ver. 28. 1. From his
eternity, he is 'the everlasting God:' 2. From his power,
he is 'the Creator of the ends of the earth:' 3. From unchangeableness, 'he fainteth not,' he waxeth not weary, and,
therefore, there is no reason he should relinquish or give
over any design that he hath undertaken; especially considering that he lays all his purposes in that, whereby he
describes himself in the last place, even his wisdom, there
is no end of his understanding. He establisheth (I say)
their faith upon this fourfold description of himself, or revelation of these four attributes of his nature, as engaged for
the effecting of that, which he encourageth them to expect.
Who is it, O Jacob, with whom thou hast to do, that thou
shouldest fear or complain that thou art rejected? He is
eternal, almighty, unchangeable, infinitely wise; and if he be

engaged in any way of doing thee good, who can turn him aside
that he should not accomplish all his pleasure towards thee?
He will work, who shall let him? It must be either want of
wisdom and foresight to lay a design, or want of power to
execute it, that exposeth any one to variableness in any undertaking. Therefore, that they may see how unlikely, how
impossible a thing it is, that their ways should be hid from
the Lord, and their judgment passed over from their God,
he acquaints them, who and what he is, who hath undertaken to the contrary; but alas! they are poor faint creatures; they have no might, no strength to walk with God;
unstable as water, they cannot excel; it is impossible
they should hold out in the way wherein they are engaged,
unto the end. To obviate or remove such fears, and misgiving thoughts, he lets them know, ver. 29. that though
they have, or may have, many decays (for they often faint,
they often fail, whereof we have examples and complaints in
the Scripture, made lively by our own experience), yet from
him they shall have supplies, to preserve them from that which
they fear. He is eternal, almighty, unchangeable, and infinitely wise; he will give out power, and increase strength,
when they faint and (in themselves) have no might at all.
The Lord doth not propose himself under all these considerations, to let them know what he is in himself only, but also
that he will exert (and act suitably to) these properties, in
dealing with them, and making out supplies unto them, notwithstanding all their misgiving thoughts, which arise from
the consideration of their own faintings and total want of
might; though in themselves they are weak and faint, yet
their springs are in him, and their supplies from him, who is
such as he hath here described himself to be. Hereupon
also he anticipates an objection, by way of concession, ver.
30. ' Even the youths shall faint and be weary, and the
young men shall utterly fail.' Men that seem to have a
great stock of strength and ability, may yet fail and perish
utterly: an objection which, as I formerly observed, these
days have given great force unto: we see many who seem
to have the vigour of youth, and the strength of young men,
in the ways of God, that have fainted in their course, and
utterly failed; they began to run well, but lay down almost
at the entrance; and be it so, saith the Lord, it shall so

come to pass indeed : many that go out in their own strength shall so fall and come to nothing : but what is that to thee, O Jacob, my chosen, thou that waitest upon the Lord? ver. 31. The unchangeable God will so make out strength to thee, that thou shalt never utterly faint, nor give over, but abide flying, running, walking, with speed, strength, and steadfastness, unto the end. That expression, ' they that wait upon the Lord,' is a description of the persons, to whom the promise is made, and not a condition of the promise itself. It is not, if they wait upon the Lord, but, they that wait on the Lord: if it were a condition of this promise, there were nothing promised; it is only said, if they wait on the Lord, they shall wait on the Lord: but of the vanity of such conditionals I shall speak afterward.

A Scripture of the like importance you have Isa. xliv. 1—8. ' Yet now hear, O Jacob, my servant; and Israel, whom I have chosen: thus saith the Lord, that made thee, and formed thee from the womb, which will help thee; Fear not, O Jacob my servant, Jesurun, whom I have chosen: for I will pour water upon him that is thirsty, and floods upon the dry ground ; and I will put my Spirit upon thy seed, and my blessing upon their offspring : and they shall spring up as among the grass, as willows by the water courses. One shall say, I am the Lord's ; and another shall call himself by the name of Jacob ; and another shall subscribe with his hand unto the Lord, and surname himself by the name of Israel. Thus saith the Lord, the King of Israel, and his redeemer, the Lord of hosts ; I am the first, and I am the last; besides me there is no God,' &c. I shall not need to insist long on the opening of these words : the general design of them, is to give consolation and assurance unto Israel from the eternity, unchangeableness, and absoluteness of God: with some peculiar references, to the second person, the Redeemer, who is described, (Rev. i. 8.) with the titles, for the substance of them, whereby the Lord here holds out his own excellency. I shall only observe some few things from the words, for the illustration of the truth we have in hand, contained in them. The state and condition wherein Jacob, Israel, Jesurun (several titles upon several accounts given to believers), are described to be, is twofold : First, Of fear and disconsolation, as it is intimated in the redoubled pro-

hibition of that frame in them : ver. 2. 'fear not,' and ver. 8.
' fear ye not, neither be afraid :' some temptation of farther
distance or separation from God (the only thing to be feared),
was fallen upon them. This they are frequently exercised
withal; it is the greatest, and most pressing temptation,
whereunto they are liable and exposed ; to conclude, because some believers, in *hypothesi*, may, under temptation,
fear their own separation from God, therefore, believers in
thesi, may be forsaken ; yea, that unless this be true, the
other could not befall them, may pass for the arguing of
men, who are unacquainted with that variety of temptations,
spiritual motions, and commotions, which believers are exercised withal. This, I say, is the first part of that state,
wherein they are supposed to be: a condition of the greatest
difficulty in the world, for the receiving of satisfaction. Secondly, Of barrenness, unprofitableness, and withering,
which seems, and that justly, to be the cause of their fear:
ver. 3. ' They are as the thirsty and dry ground,' parched in
itself, fruitless to its owners, withering in their own souls,
and bringing forth no fruit to God. A sad condition on
both hands ; within they find decays, they find no active
principles of bringing forth fruit unto God : and without
desertion, fears, at least, that they are forsaken : upon this
ye have the foundation that the Lord lays for the refreshment
of their spirits in this condition, and reducing of them into
an established assurance of the continuance of his love ; and
that is his free gracious election, and choosing of them ;
' Thou art Jacob whom I have chosen (ver. 1.), Jesurun whom
I have chosen :' even from eternity, 'when he appointed the
ancient people, and the things that are coming and shall
come ;' ver. 7. When he purposed mercy for the fathers of
old, whom long since he had brought upon that account
unto himself. This is ' the foundation' of doing them good,
' which standeth sure,' as the apostle makes use of it to the
same purpose ; 2 Tim. ii. 19. This foundation being laid,
ver. 3. he gives them a twofold promise, suited to the double state wherein they were : First, For the removal of their
drought and barrenness: he will give them waters, and
floods, for the taking of it away : which in the following
words, he interpreteth of the Spirit, as likewise doth the
apostle, John vii. 39. He is the great soul refresher; in him

are all our springs. Saith the Lord then, Fear not you poor
thirsty souls, you shall have him as a flood, in great abundance until all his fruits be brought forth in you. Secondly,
For the removal of the other evil, or fears of desertion and
casting off, he minds them of his covenant, or the[m] blessing
of their offspring, of them and their seed, according to his
promise, when he undertook to be their God; and then,
Fourthly, There is a twofold issue of God's thus dealing
with them. First, Of real fruitfulness; ver. 4. ' They shall
be as grass' under perpetual showers, which cannot possibly
wither and decay, or dry away,[n] ' and as trees planted by
the rivers of water, that bring forth fruit in their season,
whose leaf does not wither.' Secondly, Of zealous profession,
and owning of God, with the engagement of their hearts and
hands unto him, which you have in ver. 5. Every one for
himself shall give up himself to the Lord, in the most solemn engagement, and professed subjection that is possible.
They shall say, and subscribe, and surname themselves, by
names and terms of faith and obedience, to follow the Lord
in the faith of Jacob or Israel, in the inheritance of the promises which were made to him. But now what assurance is
there, that this happy beginning shall be carried on to perfection, that this kindness of God to them, shall abide to
the end, and that there shall not be a separation between him
and his chosen Israel. In the faith hereof the Lord confirms
them, by that revelation which he makes of himself and his
properties, verses 6—8. First, In his sovereignty, he is the
King. What shall obstruct him, hath not he power to dispose of all things? He is the Lord and King, he will work,
and who shall let him? But hath he kindness and tenderness
to carry him out hereunto? Therefore, secondly, He is their
Redeemer; and do but consider, what he doth for the glory
of that title, and what the work of redemption stood him in,
and ye will not fear, as to this, nor be afraid; and all this he
(thirdly) closeth with his eternity and unchangeableness,
he is the first and the last, and besides him there is none
other: the first that chose them from eternity, and the last
that will preserve them to the end; and still the same, he
altereth not. I shall not add more instances in this kind,
that the Lord often establisheth his saints in the assurance
of the unchangeableness of his love towards them, from the

[m] Gen. xvii 7.   [n] Psal i. 3, 4.

immutability of his own nature, is very evident; thence comparing himself and his love with a tender mother, and her love, he affirms, that hers may be altered, but his shall admit of no 'variableness nor shadow of turning;' Isa. xlix. 14—16.

To wind up this discourse, the sum of this first part, of our first scriptural demonstration of the truth under debate, amounts to this argument; that which God affirms, shall be certainly and infallibly fulfilled upon the account of the immutability of his own nature, and encourageth men to expect it, as certainly to be fulfilled, as he is unchangeable; that shall infallibly, notwithstanding all oppositions and difficulties, be wrought and perfected; now that such, and so surely bottomed, is the continuance of the love of God unto his saints, and so would he have them to expect, &c. hath been proved by an induction of many particular instances, wherein those engagements from the immutability of God, are fully expressed.

One of these testimonies, even that mentioned in the first place, Mal. iii. 6. from whence this argument doth arise, is proposed to be considered, and answered by Mr. Goodwin, cap. 10. sect. 40, 41. pp. 205—207. A brief removal of his exceptions to our inference from hence, will leave the whole to its native vigour, and the truth therein contained to its own steadfastness in the hand and power of that demonstration. Thus then he proposeth that place of the prophet, and our argument from thence, whereunto he shapes his answer: 'For the words of Malachi, I am the Lord, I change not; from which it is wont to be argued, that when God once loves a person, he never ceaseth to love him, because this must needs argue a changeableness in him, in respect of his affection; and consequently the saints cannot fall away finally from his grace.' So he.

Ans. It is an easy thing so to frame the argument of an adversary, as to contribute more to the weakening of it, in its proposing, than in the answer afterward given thereunto; and that it is no strange thing with Mr. Goodwin, to make use of this advantage in his disputations in this book, is discerned, and complained of by all not engaged in the same contest with himself; that he hath dealt no otherwise with us in the place under consideration, the ensuing observations will clearly manifest.

First, All the strength, that Mr. Goodwin will allow to this argument, arisethꞏfrom a naked consideration of the immutability of God, as it is an essential property of his nature; when our arguing is from his engagement to us, by and on the account of that property ; that God will do such and such a thing, because he is omnipotent, though he shall not at all manifest any purpose of his will to lay forth his omnipotency, for the accomplishment of it, is an inference, all whose strength is vain presumption. But when God hath engaged himself for the performance of any thing, thence to conclude to the certain accomplishment of it, from his power, whereby he is able to do it, is a deduction, that faith will readily close withal. So the apostle assures us of the reimplanting of the Jews, upon this account; ꞌ God,ꞌ saith he, ꞌ is able to plant them in again,ꞌ having promised so to do; Rom. xi. 23. There are two considerations, upon which the unchangeableness of God, hath a more effectual influence into the continuance of his love to his saints, than the mere objected thought of it, will lead us to an acquaintance withal.

First, God proposeth his immutability to the faith of the saints, for their establishment and consolation, in this very case of the stability of his love unto them : we dare not draw conclusions in reference to ourselves, from any property of God, but only upon the account of the revelation, which he hath made thereof unto us, for that end and purpose ; but this being done, we have a sure anchor, firm and steadfast, to fix us against all blasts of temptation or opposition whatsoever; when God proposes his immutability or unchangeableness, to assure us of the continuance of his love unto us, if we might truly apprehend, yea and ought so to do, that his unchangeableness may be preserved, and himself vindicated from the least shadow of turning, though he should change his mind, thoughts, love, purposes, concerning us every day, what conclusion for consolation could possibly arise from such proposals of Godꞌs immutability unto us ? Yea, would it not rather appear to be a way suited to the delusion of poor souls, that when they shall think they have a solid pillar, no less than an essential property of the nature of God to rest upon, they shall find themselves leaning on a cloud, or shadow, or on a broken reed, that will run into their hands, instead of yielding them the least supportment. God deals not thus with his saints; his discoveries of himself in Christ, for the establishment of the hearts of his, are not such flints, as from whence the most skilful and exercised faith cannot expect one drop of consolation. Whatsoever of his name he holds out to the sons of men, it will be a strong tower, and place of refuge and safety to them, that fly unto it.

2. The consideration of that love in its continuance, wherein the Lord settles, and puts out of doubt, the souls of his, by the engagement of his unchangeableness, or the calling of them to the consideration of that property in him, from whom that love doth flow, adds strength also to the way of arguing we insist upon. Were the love of God to his, nothing but the declaration of his approbation of such and such things, annexed to the law and rule of obedience, it might stand firm like a pillar in a river, though the water be not thereby caused to stand still one moment, but only touch it, and so pass on, there were some colour of exception to be laid against it: and this is indeed the πρῶτον ψεῦδος of Mr. Goodwin in this whole controversy, that he acknowledgeth no other love of God to believers, but what lies in the outward approbation of what is good, and men's doing it; upon which account, there is no more love in God to one than another; to the choicest saint, than to the most profligate villain in the world: nay, it is not any love at all, properly so called, being no internal vital act of God's will, the seat of his love; but an external declaration of the issue of our obedience. The declaration of God's will, that he approves faith and obedience, is no more love to Peter, than it is to Judas. But let now the love of God to believers be considered, as it is in itself, as a vital act of his will, willing (if I may so speak) good things to them; as the immanent purpose of his will, and also joined with an acceptation of them in the effects of his grace, favour, and love, in Jesus Christ; and it will be quickly evidenced, how an alteration therein will intrench upon the immutability of God, both as to his essence, and attributes, and decrees.

Having thus reinforced our argument from this place of Scripture, by restoring unto it those considerations, which being its main strength, it was maimed and deprived of by Mr. Goodwin in his proposal thereof, I shall briefly consider the answers, that by him are suggested thereunto.

Thus then he proceedeth; ' By the tenor of this arguing, it will as well follow, that in case God should at any time withdraw his love and his favour from a nation or body of a people, which he sometimes favoured, or loved, he should be changed : but that no such change of dispensation as this, towards one or the same people or nation, argueth any change at all in God, at least any such change, which he disclaimeth, as incompetent to him, is evident from those instances without number recorded in Scripture, of such different dispensations of his, towards sundry nations, and more especially towards the Jews, to whom sometimes he gives peace, sometimes consumes them with wars, sometimes he makes them the head, and sometimes again the tail of the nations round about them.'

Ans. The love and favour of God to a nation or people, here brought into the lists of comparison with the peculiar love of God to his saints, which he secures them of, upon the account of his immutability, is either the outward dispensation of good things to them, called his love, because it expresseth, and holds out a fountain of goodness, from whence it flows ; or it is an eternal act of God's will towards them, of the same nature with the love to his own formerly described. If it be taken in the first sense, as apparently it is intended, and so made out from the instance of God's dealing with the Jews in outward blessings and punishments, Mr. Goodwin doth plainly (μεταβαίνειν εἰς ἄλλο γένος) fall into a thing quite of another nature, instead of that which was first proposed. ('Amphora cum cœpit institui cur urceus exit ?') There is a wide difference between outward providential dispensations, and eternal purposes, and acts of grace and good-will ; to deal in the instance insisted on by Mr. Goodwin : there being frequent mention in the Scripture (as afterward shall be fully declared), of a difference and distinction in, and of that people (for° 'they are not all Israel, that are of Israel'), the whole lump and body of them being the people of God, in respect of separation from the rest of the world, and dedication to his worship and external profession, yet a remnant only, a hidden remnant, being his people upon the account of eternal designation, and actual acceptation into love and favour in Jesus Christ : there must needs be also a twofold dispensation of God, and his will, in reference to that people. The

° Rom. ix. 4, 5.

first common and general, towards the whole body of them
in outward ordinances, and providential exercises of goodness or justice: in this there was great variety, as to the
latter part, comprehending only external effects, or products
of the power of God; in which regard he can pull down
what he hath set up, and set up what he hath pulled down,
without the least shadow of turning : these various dispensations working uniformly towards the accomplishment of
his unchangeable purpose ; and this is all that Mr. Goodwin's exceptions reach to: even a change in the outward
dispensation of providence, which none ever denied, being
that which may, nay, is done, for the bringing about and
accomplishment (in a way suitable to the advancement of
his glory) of his unchangeable purpose. What proportion
there is to be argued from, between the general effects of
various dispensations, and that peculiar love, and grace of
the covenant thereof, wherein God assures his saints of their
stability upon the account of his own unchangeableness I
know not: because he may remove his candlestick from a
fruitless, faithless people, and give them up to desolation,
may he therefore take his Holy Spirit from them that believe ?
for whilst that continues, the root of the matter is in them.
So that, secondly, there is a peculiar dispensation of grace,
exerted towards those peculiar ones, whom he owneth and
receiveth as above mentioned ; wherein there are such engagements of the purpose, decrees, and will of God, as that
the stream of them cannot be forced back, without as great
an alteration and change in God, as the thoughts of the
heart of the meanest worm in the world, are liable unto ;
and on this the Lord asserts the steadfastness of his love
to them, in the midst of the changes of outward dispensations towards the body of that people, wherein also their
external concernments were wrapped up ; 1 Sam. xii. 22.
but this will afterward be more fully cleared. The substance of this exception amounts only to thus much; there
are changes wrought in the works which outwardly are of
God, as to general and common administrations; therefore,
also, are his eternal purposes of spiritual grace liable to the
like alterations. Whereas, Mr. Goodwin says, that this will
not import any alteration in God, at least any such alteration as is incompetent to him ; I know not of any shadow
of alteration, that may be ascribed to him, without the great-

est and most substantial derogation from his glory, that you can engage into.

And this farther clears, what is farther excepted, to the end of sect. 40. in these words ; ' Therefore neither the unchangeableness nor changeableness of God are to be estimated, or measured, either by any variety or uniformity of dispensation towards one and the same object ; and consequently, for him to express himself, as this day, towards a person, man, or woman, as if he intended to save them, or that he really intended to save them, and should on the morrow, as the alteration in the interim may be, or however may be supposed in these persons, express himself to the contrary, as that he verily intends to destroy them, would not argue or imply the least alteration in him.'

Ans. It is true, such dispensations of God, as are morally declarative of what God approves, of what he rejects, not engagements of any particular intendment, design, or purpose of his will, or such as are merely outward acts of his power, may in great variety be subservient to the accomplishment of his purpose, and may undergo (the first, in respect of the object; the latter, of the works themselves) many alterations, without prejudice to the immutability of God. The first in themselves, are everlastingly unchangeable; God always approves the obedience of his creatures, according to that light and knowledge, which he is pleased to communicate unto them, and always condemns, disallows their rebellions ; yet the same persons may do sometimes what he approves, and sometimes what he condemns, without the least shadow of change in God. Whilst they thus change, his purposes concerning them, and what he will do to them, and for them, are unchangeable, as is his law concerning good and evil. For the latter, take an instance in the case of Pharaoh ; God purposeth the destruction of Pharaoh, and suits his dispensations in great variety, and with many changes, for the bringing about, and accomplishing of that his unchangeable purpose ; he plagues him, and frees him, he frees him, and plagues him again : all these things do not in the least prove any alteration in God, being all various effects of his power, suited to the accomplishment of an unchangeable purpose; so in respect of persons, whom he intends to bring, through Christ, infallibly to himself, how various are his dispensations, both temporal and spiritual! He afflicts them, and relieves them, sends them light and darkness, strength and weakness, forsakes and appears to them again, without the least alteration in his thoughts and purposes towards them: all these things, by his infinite wisdom, working together for their good. But now, if by dispensation, you understand and comprehend also, the thoughts and purposes of God towards any, for the bringing of them to such and such an end, if these be altered, and the Lord doth change them continually, I know no reason, why a poor worm of the earth may not lay an equal claim *(absit blasphemia)* to immutability and unchangeableness, with him who asserts it as his essential property and prerogative, whereby he distinguisheth himself from all creatures whatsoever.

There is also an ambiguity in that expression, that 'God expresseth himself this day towards a man or woman, that he really intends to save them, and on the morrow expresseth himself to the contrary.' If our author intends only God's moral approbation of duties and performances, as was said before, with the conditional approbation of persons, with respect to them, there being therein no declaration of any intention or purpose of God properly so called, the instance is not in the least looking towards the business we have in hand. But if withal, he intend the purposes and intentions of the will of God, as those terms 'really intend,' and 'verily intend,' do import; I know not what to call or account alteration and change, if this be not; surely if a man, like ourselves, do really intend one thing one day, and verily intend the clean contrary the next day, we may make bold to think and say, he is changeable; and what apology will be found, on such a supposal, for the immutability of God, doth not fall within the compass of my narrow apprehension; neither is that parenthetical expression of a change, imagined in the persons, concerning whom God's intentions are, any plea for his changeableness upon this supposal: for he either foresaw that change in them, or he did not: if he did not, where is his prescience? Yea, where is his Deity? If he did, to what end did he really and verily intend and purpose to do so and so for a man, when at the same

instant, he knew the man would so behave himself, as he
should never accomplish any such intention towards him.
We should be wary, how we ascribe such lubricous thoughts
to worms of the earth, like ourselves; ' but if a man sin
against the Lord, who shall plead for him?' If one should
really and verily intend or purpose, to give a man bread to
eat to-morrow, who he knows infallibly will be put to death
to-night, such a one will not perhaps be counted changeable, but he will scarce escape being esteemed a changeling.
Yet it seems it must be granted, that God verily intends,
and really, to do so and so for men, if they be in such and
such a condition, which he verily and really knows they will-
not be in :. but suppose all this might be granted, what is it
at all to the argument in hand, concerning the Lord's engaging his immutability to his saints, to secure them from
perishing upon the account thereof? Either prove that God
doth change, which he saith he doth not, or that the saints
may perish, though he change not, which he affirms they
cannot; or you speak not to the business in hand.

The forty-first section contains a discourse too long to
be transcribed, unless it were more to the purpose in hand-
than it is. I shall therefore briefly give the reader a taste
of some paralogisms, that run from one end of it to the
other, and then in particular, roll away every stone, that
seems to be of any weight for the detaining captive the
truth, in whose vindication we are engaged. First, From
the beginning to the ending of the whole discourse, the
thing in question is immodestly begged, and many inferences made upon a supposal that believers may become
impenitent apostates; which being the sole thing under debate, ought not in itself to be taken as granted, and so made
a proof of itself. It is by us asserted, that those who are
once freely accepted of God in Christ, shall not be so forsaken as to become impenitent apostates : and that upon
the account of the immutability of God, which he hath engaged to give assurance thereof. To evince the falsity of
this, it is much pressed, that if they become impenitent
apostates, God, without the least shadow of mutability, may
cast them off, and condemn them; which is a kind of reasoning that will scarce conclude to the understanding of
an intelligent reader : and yet this sandy foundation is

thought sufficient to bear up many rhetorical expressions, concerning the changeableness of God, in respect of sundry of his attributes, if he should not destroy such impenitent apostates, as it is splendidly supposed believers may be. ('O fama ingens, ingentior armis vir Trojane.') This way of disputing, will scarce succeed you in this great undertaking.

The second scene of this discourse, is a gross confounding of God's legal or moral approbation of duties, and conditional of persons, in reference to them (which is not love properly so called, but a mere declaration of God's approving the thing, which he commands and requires), with the will of God's purpose and intention, and actual acceptation of the persons of believers in Jesus Christ, suited thereunto; hence are all the comparisons used between God and a judge, in his love, and the express denial, that God's love is fixed on any materially, that is, on the persons of any (for that is the intendment of it), but only formally, in reference to their qualifications. Hence also is that instance, again and again insisted on, in this and the former section, of the love of God to the fallen angels, whilst they stood in their obedience. Their obedience, no doubt (if any they actually yielded), fell under the approbation of God; but that it was the purpose and intention of God, to continue and preserve them in that obedience, cannot be asserted without ascribing to him more palpable mutability, than can fall upon a wise and knowing man.

Thirdly, The discourse of this section hath a contribution of strength, such as it is, from a squaring of the love of God unto the sweet nature and loving disposition of men, which is perhaps no less gross anthropomorphism, than they were guilty of, who assigned him a body and countenance like to ours; and upon these three stilts, whereof the first is called 'Petitio Principii,' the second, 'Ignoratio Elenchi,' and the third, 'Fallacia non causæ pro causa,' is this discourse advanced.

I shall not need to transcribe, and follow the progress of this argumentation; the observation of the fallacies before mentioned, will help the meanest capacity to unravel the sophistry of the whole. The close only of it may seem to deserve more particular consideration: so then it proceedeth. 'The unchangeableness assumed by God himself, unto himself, in the work in hand, I am the Lord, I change not; is, I conceive, that which is found in him in respect of his decrees; the reason is, because it is assigned by him as the reason why they were not utterly destroyed: I am the Lord, I change not; therefore ye sons of Jacob are not consumed. In the beginning of the chapter, he did declare unto them his purpose and decree of sending his only-begotten Son, whom he there calls the messenger of the covenant unto them. He predicteth, ver. 3, 4. the happy fruit or consequence of that his sending, in reference to their nation and posterity. To the unchangeableness of this his decree he assigns the patience, which he had for a long time exercised towards them under their great and continued provocations; whereby he implies, that if he could have been turned out of the way of his decree concerning the sending of his Son unto them in their posterity, they would have done it by the greatness of their sins; but insomuch as this his decree, or himself in this his decree, was unchangeable, and it must have been changed, in case they had been all destroyed (for the decree was for the sending to their nation and posterity); hence, saith he, it comes to pass, that though your sins otherwise abundantly have deserved it, yet I have spared you from a total ruin: therefore in these two last Scripture arguments, there is every whit as much, or rather more, against, than for, the common doctrine of perseverance.'

Ans. That the unchangeableness of God, which is mentioned in this text, hath relation to the decrees of God, is granted; whatever then God purposeth or decreeth, is put upon a certainty of accomplishment, upon the account of his unchangeableness: there may be some use hereafter made of this concession, where (I suppose) the evasions that will be used about the objects of those decrees and their conditionality, will scarce wave the force of our arguing from it. For the present, though I willingly embrace the assertion, yet I cannot assent to the analysis of that place of Scripture, which is introduced as the reason of it. The design of the Lord in that place, hath been before considered: that the consolation here intended, is only this, that whereas God purposed to send the Lord Christ to the nation of the Jews, which he would certainly fulfil and accomplish, and therefore did not, nor could not utterly destroy them, will scarcely be evinced to the judgment of any one, who shall consider the business in hand with so much liberty of spirit, as to cast an eye upon the Scripture itself.: that after the rehearsal of the great promise of sending his Son in the flesh to that people, he distinguisheth them into his chosen ones, and those rejected; his remnant, and' the refuse of the nation, being the main body thereof; threatening destruction to the latter, but engaging himself into a way of mercy and love towards the former, hath been declared. To assure the last of his continuance in these thoughts and purposes of his good-will towards them, he minds them of his un-changeableness in all such purposes, and particularly en-courages them to rest upon it, in respect of his love towards themselves; that God intended to administer consolation to his saints in the expression insisted on, is not, cannot be, denied; now what consolation could redound to them in particular from hence, that the whole nation should not ut-terly be rooted out, because God purposed to send his Son to their posterity; notwithstanding this, any individual per-son that shall fly to the horns of this altar for refuge, that shall lay hold on this promise for succour, may perish ever-lastingly. There is scarce any place of Scripture where there is a more evident distinction asserted between the Jews who were so outwardly only and in the flesh, and those who were inwardly also and in the circumcision of the heart, than in this and the following chapter: their several por-tions are also clearly proportioned out to them in sundry particulars. Even this promise of sending the Messiah re-spected not the whole nation, and doubtless was only sub-servient to the consolation of them, whose blessedness con-sisted in being distinguished from others; but let the context be viewed, and the determination left to the Spirit of truth in the heart of him that reads.

Neither doth it appear to me, how the decree of God concerning the sending of his Son into the world, can be asserted as absolutely immutable, upon that principle for-merly laid down, and insisted on by our author. He sends him into the world to die, neither is any concernment of his mediation so often affirmed to fall under the will and pur-pose of God as his death. But concerning this, Mr. G. disputes, out of Socinus,[p] for a possibility of a contrary event, and that the whole counsel of God might have been

[p] Socin. Prœl. Theol. cap 10. sect. 8.

fulfilled by the good-will and intention of Christ, though
actually he had not died. If then the purpose of God concerning Christ, as to that great and eminent part of his intendment therein, might have been frustrate, and was liable
to alteration, what reason can be rendered, wherefore that
might not upon some considerations (which Mr. Goodwin is
able, if need were, to invent) have been the issue of the
whole decree? And what then becomes of the collateral consolation, which from the immutability of that decree is here
asserted. Now this being the only witness and testimony
in the first part of our scriptural demonstration of the truth
in hand, whereunto any exception is put in; and the exceptions against it being in such a frame and composure, as
manifest the whole to be a combination of beggars and jug-
glers, whose pleas are inconsistent with themselves, as it doth
now appear upon the examination of them apart; it is evident, that, as Mr. Goodwin hath little ground or encouragement for that conclusion he makes of this section, so that
the light breaking forth from a constellation of this and
other texts mentioned is sufficient to lead us into an acknowledgment and embracement of the truth contended for.

CHAP. III.

The immutability of the purposes of God proposed for a second demonstra-
tion of the truth in hand. Somewhat of the nature and properties of the
purposes of God: the object of them. Purposes, how acts of God's under-
standing and will. The only foundation of the futurition of all things.
The purposes of God absolute. Continuance of divine love towards believ-
ers purposed. Purposes of God farther considered, and their nature ex-
plained. Their independence and absoluteness evinced. Proved from Isa.
xlvi. 9—11. Psal. xxxiii. 9—11. Heb. vi. 17,18,&c. *Those places explained.*
The same truth by sundry reasons and arguments farther confirmed. Pur-
poses in God, of the continuance of his love and favour to believers, mani-
fested by an induction of instances out of Scripture: the first from Rom.
viii. 28. *proposed; and farther cleared and improved: Mr. G.'s dealing*
with our argument from hence, and our exposition of this place, considered.
His exposition of that place proposed and discussed. The design of the
apostle commented on: the fountain of the accomplishments of the good
things mentioned, omitted by Mr. G. In what sense God intends to make
all things work together for good to them that love him. Of God's fore-
knowledge. Of the sense and use of the word προγινώσκω, *also of scisco,*
and γίνωσκω *in classical authors.* πρόγνωσις *in Scripture, every where*
taken for foreknowledge or predetermination, no where for preapproba-
tion. Of preapproving, or preapprobation, here insisted on by Mr. G.; its
inconsistency with the sense of the apostle's discourse manifested. The pro-
gress of Mr. G.'s exposition of this place considered. Whether men love
God antecedently to his predestination and their effectual calling: to pre-
ordain and to preordinate different. No assurance granted of the conso-
lation professed to be intended · the great uncertainty of the dependance of
the acts of God's grace mentioned, on one another: the efficacy of every one
of them resolved finally into the wills of men. Whether calling accord-ing
to God's purpose, supposeth a saving answer given to that call: the affir-
mative proved, and exceptions given thereto removed. What obstructions
persons called may lay in their own way to justification. The iniquity of
imposing conditions and supposals on the purpose of God, not in the least
intimated by himself. The whole acknowledged design of the apostle
everted, by the interposition of cases and conditions by Mr. G. Mr. G.'s first
attempt to prove the decrees of God to be conditional, considered: 1 Sam.
ii. 30. *to that end produced.* 1 Sam. ii. 30. *farther considered, and its un-*
suitableness to illustrate Rom. viii. 32, 33, *proved: interpretation of*
Scripture by comparing of places agreeing neither in design, word, nor
matter, rejected. The places insisted on proved not to be parallel, by sun-
dry particular instances. Some observations from the words rejected.
What act of God intended in those words to Eli, 'I said indeed:' no purpose
or decree of God in them declared. Any such purpose as to the house of
Eli by sundry arguments disproved. No purpose of God in the words in-

sisted on farther manifested. They are expressive of the promise or law concerning the priesthood, Numb. xxv 11—13. More especially relating unto Exod. xxviii. 43. xxix. 9. The import of that promise, law, or statute, cleared: the example of Jonah's preaching, and God's commands to Abraham and Pharaoh. The universal disproportion between the texts compared by Mr. G. both as to matter and expression further manifested. Instances or cases of Saul and Paul to prove conditional purposes in God considered. Conditional purposes argued from conditional threatenings: the weakness of that argument, the nature of divine threatenings: what will of God, or what of the will of God is declared by them: no proportion between eternal purposes, and temporal threatenings the issue of the vindication of our argument from the foregoing exceptions. Mr. G.'s endeavour to maintain his exposition of the place under consideration: the text perverted. Several evasions of Mr. G. from the force of this argument considered. His arguments to prove no certain or infallible connexion between calling, justification, and glorification, weighed and answered. His first from the scope of the chapter, and the use of exhortations; the question begged. His second from examples of persons called, and not justified: the question argued, begged; no proof insisted on, but the interposition of his own hypothesis. How we are called irresistibly, and in what sense. Whether bars of wickedness and unbelief may be laid in the way of God's effectual call. Mr. G.'s demur to another consideration of the text, removed. The argument in hand freed from other objections, and concluded. Jer. xxxi. 3. explained and improved for the confirmation of the truth under demonstration. 2 Tim. ii. 19. opened, and the truth from thence confirmed. The foregoing exposition and argument vindicated and confirmed. The same matter at large pursued. John vi. 38—40. explained, and the argument in hand from thence confirmed. Mr. G.'s exceptions to our arguing from this place removed. The same matter farther pursued. The exposition and argument insisted on fully vindicated and established. Matt. xxiv. 24. opened and improved. The severals of that text more particularly handled. Further observations for the clearing the mind of the Holy Ghost in this place. The same farther insisted on and vindicated. Mr. G.'s exceptions at large discussed and removed. Eph. i. 3—5. 2 Thess. ii. 13, 14. opened. The close of the second argument from the immutability of the purposes of God.

HAVING cleared the truth in hand from the immutability of the nature of God, which himself holds out, as engaged for us to rest upon, as to the unchangeable continuance of his love unto us; proceed we now to consider the steadfastness and immutability of his purposes, which he frequently asserts, as another ground of assurance to the saints, of his safe guarding their glory of free acceptation to the end.

I shall not enter upon the consideration of the nature and absoluteness of the purposes of God, as to an express handling of them, but only a little unfold that property and concernment of them, whereon the strength of the inference we aim at, doth in the same measure depend. Many needless and curious questions have been, by the serpentine wits of men, moved and agitated concerning them : wherein perhaps our author hath not been outgone by many, as will be judged by those, who have weighed his discourses concerning them, with his distinctions of desires, intentions, purposes, and decrees in God ; but this is not the business we have in hand ; for what concerneth that, that which ensueth may suffice ; God himself being an infinite pure act, those acts of his will and wisdom, which are eternal and immanent, are not distinguished from his nature and being, but only in respect of the reference and habitude, which they bear unto some thing to be produced outwardly from him. The objects of them all are such things, as might not be. God's purposes are not concerning any thing, that is in itself absolutely necessary. He doth not purpose that he will be wise, holy, infinitely good, just : all these things, that are of absolute necessity, come not within the compass of his purposes : of things that might not be, are his decrees and intentions ; they are, of all the products of his power, all that outwardly he hath done, doth, or will do, to eternity : all these things to the[a] falling of a hair, or the withering of a grass, hath he determined from of old ; now this divine foreappointment of all things, the Scripture assigns sometimes to the knowledge and understanding, sometimes to the will of God ; ' known unto him are all his works from the beginning of the world ;' Acts xv. 18. It is that knowledge, which hath an influence into that most infinitely wise disposal of them, which is there intimated : and the determination of things to be done is referred to the counsel of God, Acts iv. 28. which denotes an act of his wisdom and understanding, and yet withal, it is the counsel of his will ; Eph. i. 11.

I know that all things originally owe their futurition to a free act of the will of God : he doth whatever[b] he will and pleaseth. Their relation thereunto, translates them out of that state of possibility, and (being objects of God's absolute omnipotency, and infinite simple intelligence, or understand-

[a] Matt. vi 28—30. Luke xii 6, 7. John iv. 6—8.
[b] Isa. xiv 24. xix 12. xxiii. 9 Jerem. li. 29. Rom. viii. 28. ix. 11. 19. Ps. cxxxix. 11, 12. Isa. xl. 28. Heb iv. 13.

ing, whereby he intuitively beholdeth all things, that might be produced by the exerting of his infinite almighty power) into a state of futurition, making them objects of God's foreknowledge or science of vision as it is called; but yet the Scripture expresseth (as before) that act of God, whereby he determines the beings, issues, and orders of things, to manifest the concurrence of his infinite wisdom and understanding in all his purposes. Farther, as to the way of expressing these things to our manner of apprehension, there are held out intentions and purposes of God, distinctly suited to all beings, operations, and events, yet in God himself they are not multiplied. As all things are present to him in one most simple and single act of his understanding, so with one individual act of his will he determines concerning all, but yet, in reference to the things that are disposed of, we may call them the purposes of God : and these are the eternal springs of God's actual providence, which being (' ratio ordinis ad finem') the disposing of all things to their ends in an appointed manner and order in exact correspondence unto them; these purposes themselves must be the infinitely wise, eternal, immanent acts of his will, appointing and determining all things, beings, and operations, kinds of beings, manners of operations, free, necessary, contingent, as to their existence and event, into an immediate tendency unto the exaltation of his glory; or, as the apostle calls them, the counsel of his will, according whereunto he effectually worketh all things; Eph. i. 11.

Our consideration of these purposes of God being only in reference to the business which we have in hand, I shall do these two things :

First, Manifest that they are all of them absolute and immutable; wherein I shall be brief, not going out to the compass of the controversy thereabout, as I intimated before : my intendment lies another way.

Secondly, Shew that God hath purposed the continuance of his love to his saints, to bring them infallibly to himself, and that this purpose of God in particular, is unchangeable; which is the second part of the foundation of our abiding with God in the grace of acceptation.

By the purposes of God I mean (as I said before), the eternal acts of his will concerning all things that outwardly are of him, which are the rules (if I may so speak) of all his following operations. All external temporary products of his power universally answering those internal acts of his will. The judgment of those who make these decrees or purposes of God (for I shall constantly use these words promiscuously, as being purely of the same import as relating unto God), to be in themselves essential to him, and his very nature, or understanding and will, may be safely closed withal. They are in God, as was said, but one : there is not a real multiplication of any thing but subsistence in the Deity. To us these lie under a double consideration. First, Simply as they are in God, and so it is impossible they should be differenced from his infinite wisdom and will, whereby he determineth of any thing. Secondly, In respect of the habitude and relation which they bear to the things determined, which the wisdom and will of God might not have had. In the first sense, as was said, they can be nothing but the very nature of God. The τὸ velle of God, his internal willing of any thing that is either created or uncreated; for those terms distribute the whole nature of beings. Created they are not, for they are eternal (that no new immanent act can possibly be ascribed to God, hath full well of late been demonstrated). Farther, if they are created, then God willed that they should be created ; for he created only what he will. If so, was he willing they should be created or no? If he were, then a progress will be given infinitely, for the question will arise up to eternity. If uncreated, then doubtless they are God himself, for he only is so. It is impossible that a creature should be uncreated. Again, God's very willing of things is the cause of all things, and therefore must needs be omnipotent, and God himself: that ' voluntas Dei' is ' causa rerum,' is taken for granted, and may be proved from Psal. cxv. 3. which the apostle ascribes omnipotency unto ; Rom. ix. 19. ' Who hath resisted his will ?' Doubtless it is the property of God alone to be the cause of all things, and to be almighty in his so being; but hereof at present no more. On this supposal, the immutability of the decrees of God would plainly be coincident with the immutability of his nature before handled.

It is then of the decrees and purposes of God, with respect to the matter about which they are, whereof I speak, in which regard also they are absolute and immutable; not that they work any essential change in the things themselves, concerning which they are, making that to be immutable from thence, which in its own nature is mutable; but only that themselves, as acts of the infinite wisdom and will of God, are not liable to, nor suspended on, any condition whatever, foreign to themselves, nor subject to change or alteration (whence floweth an infallible certainty of actual accomplishment in reference to the things decreed or purposed, be their own nature what it will, or their next causes in themselves never so undetermined to their production), whereof I treat. That the determining purposes or decrees of God's will concerning any thing, or things, by him to be done, or effected, do not depend, as to their accomplishment, on any conditions, that may be supposed in, or about the things themselves, whereof they are, and therefore are unchangeable, and shall certainly be brought forth unto the appointed issue, is that which we are to prove. Knowing[c] for whose sakes, and for what ed, this labour was undertaken, I shall choose to lay the whole proof of this assertion upon plain texts of Scripture, rather than mix my discourse with any such philosophical reasonings, as are of little use to the most of them whose benefit is hereby intended.

Isa. xlvi. 9—11. The Holy Ghost speaks expressly to our purpose: 'Remember the former things of old: for I am God, and there is none else; I am God, and there is none like me, declaring the end from the beginning, and from ancient times the things that are not yet done, saying, My counsel shall stand, and I will do all my pleasure: calling a ravenous bird from the east, the man that executes my counsel from a far country: yea, I have spoken it, I will also bring it to pass; I have purposed it, I will also do it.' Ver. 9. the Lord asserts his own Deity and eternal being, in opposition to all false gods and idols, whom he threatens to destroy, ver. 1. Of this he gives them a threefold demonstration:

First, From his patience or foreknowledge; 'There is none like me, declaring the end from the beginning, and from ancient times the things that are not yet done.' In this am I infinitely discriminated from all the pretended deities of the nations: all things from the beginning to the end are naked before me, and I have declared them by my prophets, even

[c] Mat. xi. 25. 1 Cor. xxvi. 27, 28. James ii. 5. 2 Tim. ii. 10.

things that are future and contingent in themselves; so are
the things that I now speak of, the destruction of Babylon by
the Medes and Persians, a thing to be carried on through innumerable contingencies; and yet as I have seen it, so have I told
it, and my counsel concerning it shall certainly be executed.

Secondly, By his power, in using what instruments he
pleaseth for the executing of his purposes and bringing about
his own designs; 'calling a ravenous bird from the east;' one
that at first, when he went against Babylon, thought of nothing less than executing the counsel of God, but was wholly
bent upon satisfying his own rapine and ambition, not knowing then in the least by whom he was anointed and sanctified for the accomplishment of his will. All the[d] thoughts
of his heart, all his consultations and actions, all his pro-
gresses and diversions, his success in his great and dreadful
undertaking to break in pieces that hammer of the whole
earth, with all the free deliberations and contingencies,
wherewith his long war was attended, which were as many,
strong, and various, as the nature of things is capable to receive, were not only in every individual act, with its minutest
circumstances, by him foreseen, and much also foretold, but
also managed in the hand of his power in a regular subser-
vience to that call, which he so gave that ravenous bird, for
the accomplishment of his purpose and pleasure.

Thirdly, By the immutability of his purposes, which can
never be frustrated nor altered ; 'my counsel shall stand, and
I will do all my pleasure, I have purposed it, and I will also
do it.' The standing, or fixedness and unchangeableness of
his counsel he manifests by the accomplishment of the things,
which therein he had determined : neither is there any salve
for his immutability in his counsel, should it otherwise fall
out. And if we may take his own testimony of himself,
what he purposeth, that he doth : and in the actual fulfilling,
and the bringing about of things themselves purposed, and as
purposed, without any possibility of diversion from the real
end intended, is their stability and unchangeableness in them
manifested. An imaginary immutability in God's purposes,
which may consist and be preserved under their utter frustration, as to the fulfilling of the things themselves, under
which they are, the Scripture knows not, neither can reason

d Jerem. l. li. Isa. xliv. 23—28.

conceive. Now this unchangeableness of his purposes, the Lord brings as one demonstration of his Deity, and those who make them liable to alteration upon any account, or supposition whatsoever, do depress him, what in them lies, into the number of such dunghill gods, as he threatens to famish and destroy.

Psal. xxxiii. 9—11. 'He spake and it was done, he commanded and it stood fast. The Lord bringeth the counsel of the heathen to nought, he maketh the devices of the people of none effect. The counsel of the Lord stands for ever, the thoughts of his heart to all generations.' The production and establishment of all things, in that order wherein they are, are by the psalmist ascribed to the will and power of God: by his word and command, they not only are, but stand fast; being fixed in that order by him appointed; both the making, fixing, and sustaining of all things, is* by 'the word of his power.' As the first relates to their being, which they have from creation, so the other to the order in subsistence and operation, which relates to his actual providence. Herein they stand fast. Themselves, with their several and respective relations, dependencies, influences, circumstances, suited to that nature and being, which was bestowed on them by his word in their creation, are settled in an exact correspondency to his purposes (of which afterward) not to be shaken or removed. Men have their devices and counsels also, they are free agents, and work by counsel and advice; and therefore God hath not set all things so fast, as to overturn and overbear them, in their imaginations and undertakings. Saith the psalmist, 'They imagine and devise indeed, but their counsel is of nought, and their devices are of none effect, but the counsel of the Lord,' &c. The counsel and purposes of the Lord, are set in opposition to the counsel and purposes of men, as to alteration, change, and frustration, in respect of the actual accomplishment of the things about which they are. Their counsels are so and so: but the counsel of the Lord shall stand. He that shall cast ver. 11. into ver. 10. and say, 'The counsel of the Lord that comes to nought, and the thoughts of his heart are of none effect,' let him make what pretences he will, or flourishes that he can, or display what supposals

* Heb. i. 3. Rev. iv. 11. Acts xvii. 28. ii. 23. iv. 28. Gen. l. 20 Eccles. iii. 11.

and conditions he pleaseth, he will scarcely be able to keep the field against him, who will contend with him about his prerogative and glory. And this antithesis between the counsels of men, and the purposes of God upon the account of unchangeableness, is again confirmed; Prov. xix. 21. 'There are many devices in a man's heart, nevertheless the counsel of the Lord that shall stand;' herein is the difference between the[f] devices of men, and the counsel of God; men have many devices to try what they can do. If one way take not, they will attempt another ('hac non successit, alia aggrediemur via'), and are always disappointed, but only in that, wherein they fall in with the will of God. The shallowness of their understanding, the shortness of their foresight, the weakness of their power, the changeableness of their minds, the uncertainty of all the means they use, puts them upon many devices, and often to no purpose. But for him, who is infinite in wisdom and power, to whom all things are present, and to whom nothing can fall out unexpected, yea-what he hath not himself determined; unto whom all emergencies are but the issue of his own good pleasure, who proportions out what efficacy he pleaseth unto the means he useth, his counsels, his purposes, his decrees shall stand, being, as Job tells us, as mountains of brass. By this he differenceth himself[g] from all others, idols and men, as also by his certain foreknowledge of what shall come to pass, and be accomplished upon those purposes of his; hence the apostle, Heb. vi. 17, 18. acquaints us that his promise and his oath, those two immutable things, do but declare (ἀμετάθετον τῆς βουλῆς) the unchangeableness of his counsel, which God is abundantly willing to manifest, though men are abundantly unwilling to receive it; Job determines this business in chap. xxiii. 13, 14. 'He is of one mind, and who can turn him? What his soul desireth, even that he doth; for he performeth the thing, that is appointed for me.' Desires are the least and faintest kind of purposes, in Mr. Goodwin's distinctions. Yet the certain accomplishment of them, as they are ascribed unto God, is here asserted by the Holy Ghost.

Were the confirmation of the matter of our present dis-

---

[f] Isa. viii. 9, 10. Job viii. 9. xi. 12. Eccles. viii. 7. 9. 12.
[g] Isa. xliv. 7. xxv. 26.

course, my design in hand; I could farther confirm it, by enlarging these ensuing reasons :

First, From the immutability of God; the least questioning whereof falls foul on all the perfections of the divine nature, which requireth a correspondent affection of all the internal and eternal acts of his mind and will.

Secondly, From his sovereignty, in making and executing all his purposes ; which will not admit of any such mixture of consults or co-operations of others, as should render his thoughts liable to alteration; Rom. xi. 34—36. The Lord in his purposes is considered as the great former of all things, who having his clay in the hand of his almighty power, ordains every parcel to what kind of vessel, and to what use he pleaseth ; hence the apostle concludes the consideration of them, and the distinguishing grace flowing from them, with that admiration ὦ βάθος, 'O the depth !' &c.

Thirdly, From their eternity, which exempts them from all shadow of change, and lifts them up above all those spheres, that either from within, and their own nature, or from without, by the impression of others, are exposed to turning; that which is eternal, is also immutable; Acts xv. 18. 1 Cor. ii. 11.

Fourthly, From the absoluteness, and independency of his will, whereof they are the acts and emanations; Rom. 15—20. Whatever hath any influence upon that, as to move it, cause it, change it, must be before it, above it, better than it, as every cause is, than its effect, as such. This will of his, as was said, is the fountain of all beings, to which free and independent act all creatures owe their being and subsistence, their operations and manner thereof, their whole difference from those worlds of beings, which his power can produce, but yet shall be bound up to eternity, in their nothingness and possibility, upon the account of his good pleasure. Into this doth our Saviour resolve the disposal of himself; Matt. xxvi. 42. and of all others, Matt. xi. 25—27. Certainly men in their wrangling disputes and contests about it, have scarce seriously considered, with whom they have to do ; 'shall the thing formed say to him that formed it, Why hast thou made me thus?'

Fifthly, From the engagement of his omnipotency, for the accomplishment of all his purposes and designs, as is

emphatically expressed, Isa. xiv. 24—27. 'Surely the Lord
of hosts hath sworn, saying, Surely as I have thought, so
shall it come to pass; and as I have purposed, it shall stand;
that I will break the Assyrian in my land: this is the purpose of God, that is purposed upon the whole earth, and
this is the hand, that is stretched out upon all the nations;
for the Lord of hosts hath purposed, and who shall disannul
it? and his hand is stretched out, and who shall turn it
back?' The Lord doth not only assert the certain accomplishment of all his purposes, but also to prevent and obviate the unbelief of them who were concerned in their fulfilling, he manifests upon what account it is that they shall
certainly be brought to pass; and that is by the stretching
out of his hand, or exalting of his mighty power, for the doing of it; so that if there be a failing therein, it must be
through the shortness of that hand of his so stretched out,
in that it could not reach the end aimed at. A worm will
put forth its strength for the fulfilling of that whereunto it
is inclined; and the sons of men will draw out all their
power for the compassing of their designs: if there be wisdom in the laying of them, and foresight of emergencies,
they alter not, nor turn aside to the right hand, or to the
left, in the pursuit of them; and shall the infinitely wise,
holy, and righteous thoughts and designs of God, not have
his power engaged for their accomplishment? His infinite
wisdom and understanding are at the foundation of them:
they are the counsels of his will; Eph. vii. 11. 'Who hath
known his mind' (in them?) saith the apostle; 'and who hath
been his counsellor?' Though no creature can see the paths
wherein he walks, nor apprehend the reason of the ways he
is delighted in; yet this he lets us know for the satisfying
of our hearts, and teaching of our inquiries, that his own
infinite wisdom is in them all. I cannot but fear sometimes,
that men have darkened counsel without knowledge in curious contests about the decrees and purposes of God, as
though they were to be measured by our rule and line, and
as though by searching we could 'find out the Almighty to
perfection.' But he is wise in heart; he that contendeth with
him let him instruct him. Add, that this wisdom in his counsel
is attended with infallible prescience of all that will fall in by
the way, or in the course of the accomplishment of his pur-

poses; and you will quickly see, that there can be no possible intervenience upon the account whereof the Lord should not engage his almighty power for their accomplishment; '·he is of one mind, and who can turn him ? he will work, and who shall let him ?'

Sixthly, By demonstrating the unreasonableness, folly, and impossibility, of suspending the acts and purposes of the will of God, upon any actings of the creatures whatsoever; seeing it cannot be done without subjecting eternity to time, the first cause to the second, the Creator to the creature, the Lord to the servant, disturbing the whole order of beings and operations in the world.

Seventhly, By the removal of all possible or imaginary causes of alteration and change ; which will all be resolved into impotency in one kind or other ; every alteration being confessedly an imperfection, it cannot follow but from want and weakness. Upon the issue of which discourse, if it might be perused, these corollaries would ensue :

First, Conditional promises and threatenings, are not declarative of God's purposes concerning persons, but of his moral approbation or rejection of things.

Secondly, There is a wide difference between the change of what is conditionally pronounced, as to the things themselves, and the change of what is determinately willed ; the certainty of whose event is proportioned to the immutable acts of the will of God itself.

Thirdly, That no purpose of God is conditional, though the things themselves, concerning which his purposes are, are oftentimes conditionals one of another.

Fourthly, That conditional purposes concerning perseverance, are either impossible, implying contradictions, or ludicrous, even to an unfitness for a stage. But of these and such like, as they occasionally fall in, in the ensuing discourse.

This foundation being laid, I come to what was secondly proposed, namely, to manifest by an induction of particular instances, the engagement of these absolute and immutable purposes of God, as to the preservation of the saints in his favour to the end ; and whatsoever is by Mr. Goodwin excepted, as to the former doctrine of the decrees and purposes of God, in that part of his treatise, which falls under our consideration, shall, in the vindication of the respective places of Scripture to be insisted on, be discussed.

The first particular instance, that I shall propose, is that eminent place of the apostle, Rom. viii. 28. where you have the truth in hand meted out unto us, full measure, shaken together, and running over. It doth not hang by the side of his discourse, nor is left to be gathered, and concluded from other principles and assertions couched therein; but is the main of the apostolical drift and design; it being proposed by him, to make good, upon unquestionable grounds, the assurance he gives believers, that all things work together for good to them that love God, to them that are called according to his purpose; the reason whereof he farther adds in the following words, 'For whom he did foreknow, he also did predestinate to be conformed to the image of his Son, that he might be the first-born among many brethren: moreover, whom he did predestinate, them he also called; and whom he called, them he also justified; and whom he justified, them he also glorified.' What the good aimed at is, for which all things shall work together, and wherein it doth consist, he manifests in the conclusion of the argument produced to prove his first assertion, ver. 35—39. 'Who shall separate us from the love of God in Christ? shall tribulation,' &c. The good of believers, of them that love God, consists in the enjoyment of Christ and his love; saith then the apostle, God will so certainly order all things, that they shall be preserved in that enjoyment of it, whereunto in this life they are already admitted, and borne out through all oppositions, to that perfect fruition thereof, which they aim at; and this is so unquestionable, that the very things, which seem to lie in the way of such an attainment and event, shall work together, through the wisdom and love of God, to that end. To make good this consolation, the apostle lays down two grounds or principles, from whence the truth of it doth undeniably follow; the one, taken from the description of the persons, concerning whom he makes it; and the other, from the acts of God's grace, and their respective concatenation in reference to those persons.

The persons, he tells you, are those, who are 'called according to the purpose of God;' that their calling here men-

tioned, is the effectual call of God, which is answered by
faith and obedience, because it consists in the bestowing of
them on the persons so called, taking away the heart of
stone and giving a heart of flesh, is not only manifest from
that place, which afterward receives in the golden chain of
divine graces, between predestination and justification,
whereby the one hath infallible influences into the other;
but also from that precious description which is given of the
same persons, viz. that they love God, which certainly is an
issue and fruit of effectual calling, as shall afterward be farther argued. For to that issue are things driven in this controversy, that proofs thereof are become needful.

The purpose, according to which these persons are called,
is none other than that, which the apostle, chap. ix. 11.
terms the 'purpose of God according to election;' chap. xi.
5. The election of grace, as also the foreknowledge and
foundation of God, as will in the progress of our discourse
be made farther appear; although I know not, that this is as
yet questioned. The immutability of this purpose of God,
chap. ix. 11, 12. the apostle demonstrates from its independency in any thing in them, or respect of them, concerning whom it is, it being eternal, and expressly safeguarded
against apprehensions, that might arise, of any causal or occasional influence from any thing in them given thereunto,
they lying under this condition alone unto God, as persons
that had done neither good nor evil. And this, also, the
apostle farther pursues from the sovereignty, absoluteness,
and unchangeableness of the will of God. But these things
are of another consideration.

Now this unchangeable purpose and election being the
fountain, from whence the effectual calling of believers doth
flow, the preservation of them to the end designed, the glory
whereunto they are chosen, by those acts of grace and love,
whereby they are prepared thereunto, hath coincidence of
infallibility, as to the end aimed at, with the purpose itself;
nor is it liable to the least exception, but what may be raised
from the mutability and changeableness of God in his purposes and decrees. Hence, in the following verse upon the
account of the stability and immutability of this purpose of
God, the utmost, and most remote end in reference to the
good thereby designed unto believers, though having its pre-

sent subsistence only in that purpose of God, and infallible concatenation of means thereunto conducing, is mentioned as a thing actually accomplished, ver. 30.

Herein, also, lies the apostle's second eviction of consolation, formerly laid down, even in the indissoluble concatenation of those acts of grace, love, and favour, whereby the persons of God's purpose, or the remnant, according to the election of grace, shall be infallibly carried on in their present enjoyment, and unto the full fruition of the love of Christ. If we may take him upon his word (and he speaks in the name and authority of God), those whom he doth foreknow, or fixes his thoughts peculiarly upon, from eternity (for the term these, is evidently discriminated: and the act must needs be eternal, which in order of nature is previous unto predestination, or the appointment to the end by means designed), those, I say, he doth predestinate, and appoint in the immutable purpose of his will, to be conformed unto the image of his Son, as in afflictions, so in grace and glory.

To fancy a suspension of these acts of grace (some whereof are eternal), upon conditionals, and they not intimated in the least in the text, nor consistent with the nature of the things themselves, or the end intended, casting the accomplishment and bringing about of the designs of God proposed, as his, for our consolation, upon the certain lubricity of the wills of men, and thereupon to propose an intercision of them, as to their concatenation and dependance, that they should not have a certain influence on the one hand, descending; nor an unchangeable dependance on the other, ascending; may easily be made appear, to be so plain an opposition to the aim and design of the apostle, as it is possibly capable of; but, because these things are really insisted on by Mr. Goodwin, I shall choose rather to remove them, as with much rhetoric, and not without some sophistry, they are by him pressed, than further anticipate them, by arguments of the text itself, of their invalidity and nullity.

The discussion of our argument from this place of Scripture, he enters upon, chap. 10. sect. 42. p. 207. and pursues it, being much entangled with what himself is pleased to draw forth as the strength of it, unto sect. 52. p. 219.

Now, though Mr. Goodwin hath not at all mentioned any analysis of the place insisted on, for the making out of the truth we believe to be intended in it, nor ever once shewed his reader the face of our argument from hence, but only drawn something of it forth, in such divided parcels, as he apprehended himself able to blur and obscure; yet to make it evident, that he hath not prevailed to foil that part of the strength of truth (his adversary) which he voluntarily chose to grapple withal, I shall consider that whole discourse, and manifest the nullity of his exceptions unto this testimony given in by the apostle to the truth we have in hand.

To obtain his end, Mr. Goodwin undertaketh these two things:

First, To give in an exposition of the place of Scripture insisted on, whence no such conclusion as that, which he opposeth (saith he) can be drawn.

Secondly, To give in exceptions to our interpretation of it, and the inferences thereupon by us deduced. The first in these words:

'For the scope of the apostle, in the sequel of this passage, is clearly this: as the particle 'for' in the beginning of ver. 29. plainly sheweth, to prove and make good that assertion of his, ver. 28. that all things work together for good, to those that love God: to prove this, he sheweth by what method and degrees of dispensations God will bring it to pass. Whom he foreknows (saith he) that is, preapproves (the word knowledge frequently in Scripture importing approbation), as he must needs do those that love him, these he predestinates to be conformed to the image of his Son: and therefore, as all things, even his deepest sufferings, wrought together for good unto him; so must they needs do unto those, who are predestinated or preordinated by God to a conformity with him. To give you yet, saith our apostle, a farther and more particular account, how God, in the secret of his counsels, hath laid things in order to the bringing of them unto an actual conformity with the image of his Son, to wit, in glory, whom he predestinated thereunto (who are such as love him, and thereupon are approved by him), you are to understand, that whom he hath so predestinated, he hath also called, that is, hath purposed or decreed to call to the knowledge of his Son or of his gospel, that is, to afford a more plain and effectual discovery of him

unto them, than unto others whom he hath not so predestinated. By the way, this call doth not necessaiily suppose
a saving answer given unto it by the called, no whit more
than the calling mentioned, Matt. xx. 16. xxii. 14. It only
supposeth a real purpose on God's part, to make it very sufficient to procure such an answer to it, from those that are
called. The apostle advanceth towards his proposed end,
and addeth: Those whom he calls, them he also justified;
that is, according to our last exposition of the word 'called,'
he hath purposed or decreed to justify; to wit, in case the
called obstruct him not in his way, or by their unbelief render not themselves incapable of justification. The
clause following is likewise to be understood with the like
proviso as this; whom he hath justified, them he also glorified; that is, hath purposed or decreed to save, in case
they retain the grace of justification, confirmed upon them
to the end.'

Ans. First, Let it be granted, that the design of the apostle is to make good that assertion, 'All things shall work
together for good, to them that love God,' and the consolation for believers, which thence-he holds forth unto them ;
yet he doth not only shew by what method, degrees, or steps,
God will bring it to pass, but also, as the fountain of all that
ensues, lays down the unalterable purpose of God concerning
that end, which is attended in, and accomplished by, all
those steps or degrees of his effectual grace after mentioned.
This Mr. Goodwin passeth over, as not to be wrested into
any tolerable conformity with that sense (if there be any
sense in the whole of what he insists upon for the sense of
this place), which he intends to rack and press the words
unto. To save stumbling at the threshold (which is *malum
omen*) he leaps at once over the consideration of this purpose and design of God, as aiming at a certain end, without
the least touch upon it. Farther, that God will bring it to
pass, that 'all things shall work together for good to them
that love him,' is not intended by Mr. Goodwin, as though
it should infallibly be so indeed, but only that God will so
way-lay them, with some advantages, that it may be so, as
well as otherwise. What consolation believers may receive
from this whole discourse of the apostle, intended properly
to administer it unto them, as it lies under the gloss ensuing,

shall be discovered in our following consideration of it. Thus, then, he makes it out:

'Whom he foreknows, that is, preapproves (the word knowledge in Scripture frequently importing approbation), as he must needs do those that love him, them he predestinates.'

Ans. First, That to 'know' is sometimes taken in Scripture for to approve, may be granted : but that the word here used must therefore signify to preapprove, is an assertion, which I dare not pretend to so much foreknowledge as to think that any one besides himself will approve. Mr. Goodwin (I doubt not) knows full well that prepositions in Greek compositions do often restrain simple verbs, formerly at liberty for other uses, to one precise signification. The word προγινώσκω in its constant sense in other authors is 'præscio' or 'prædecerno ;' γινώσκω itself for ' to determine or decree :' so is 'scisco' among the Latins, the ancient word, 'to know.' So he in Plautus,[h] 'Rogitationes plurimas propter vos populus scivit, quas vos rogatas rumpitis.' And nothing more frequent in Cicero,[i] 'Quæ scisceret plebs, aut quæ populus juberet,' &c. and again, ' Quod multa perniciose, multa pestifere sciscuntur in populis:' and, 'Plancus primus legem scivit de publicanis.' In like manner is γινώσκω frequently used[k] ἔγνωσαν τοῦτο μὴ ποιεῖν 'they determined not to do that thing :'[l] Ἄδικα ἔγνωκε περὶ ἐμοῦ ὁ Ζεὺς, says he in Lucian. 'He hath determined unrighteous things against me.' Hence γνώμη is often taken for a decree, or an established purpose, as Budæus manifesteth out of Plutarch: in Scripture, the word is sundry times used, and still in the senses before mentioned: sometimes for a simple foreknowledge; so Paul uses it, of the Jews, who knew him before his conversion; Acts xxvi. 5. προγινώσκοντές με ἄνωθεν, it relates not to what they foreknew, but what they knew before, or in former days. And as the simple verb (as was shewed) is often taken, for 'decerno, statuo,' ' to decree, order, or determine,' so with this composition it seems most to be restrained to that sense; 1 Pet. i. 20. It is said of Christ that he was προεγνωσμένος πρὸ καταβολῆς κόσμου, he was 'foreknown, or foreordained before the foundation of the world;' which is

---

[h] Plaut. in Curcul.　　[i] Cic. pro Flacco. et 2. de Legib. pro Plancio.
　　[k] Plutarchus in Alcibiad.　　[l] Lucian in Prometh.

opposed to that which follows φανερωθεὶς δὲ ἐπ' ἐσχάτων τῶν χρόνων δι' ὑμᾶς, 'manifested in the last times for you,' and relates to the decree or fore-purpose of God, concerning the giving of his Son.   Hence πρόγνωσις is joined with ὡρισμένῃ βουλῇ, God's 'determinate counsel,' as a word of the same importance , Acts ii. 23. τοῦτον δὲ ὡρισμένῃ βουλῇ καὶ προγνώσει, &c.   If there be any difference, the first designing the wisdom, the latter the will, of God in this business.   In Rom. xi. 2. it hath again the same signification, God hath not cast off τὸν λαὸν αὐτοῦ ὃν προέγνω, or the remnant which among the obstinate and unbelieving Jews, were under his everlasting purpose of grace : in which place causelessly, and without any attempt of proof, the remonstrants wrest the word to signify preapprobation ; Des. Sent. Art. 1. The whole contest and design of the apostle, the terms of remnant and election, whereby the same thing is afterward expressed, undeniably forcing the proper acceptation of the word.   Not only the original sense and composition of the word, but also the constant use of it in the Scripture, leads us away from the interpretation here pinned upon it.

Farther, What is the meaning of preapproving? God's approving of any person, as to their persons, is his free and gracious acceptation of them in Christ.   His preapproving of them in answer hereunto, must be his eternal gracious acceptation of them in Christ.   But is this Mr. Goodwin's intendment? doth God accept any in Christ antecedently to their predestination, calling, and justification (for they are all consequential to this act of preapprobation)? this then is that which is affirmed : God approves and accepts of men in Christ ; thereupon he predestinates, calls, and justifies them.   But what need all these, if they be antecedently accepted? I should have expected, that this foreknowledge should have been resolved rather into a middle, or conditionate prescience, than into this preapprobation, but that our great masters were pleased (in the place newly cited), though without any attempt of proof, to carry it another way. That God should approve of, love, accept persons, antecedently to their predestination, vocation, and justification, is doubtless not suitable to Mr. Goodwin's principles.   But that they should love God also, before they fall under these acts of his grace, is not only openly contradictious to the truth, but also to itself.   The phrase here of loving God, is confessedly a description of believers : now to suppose men believers, that is, to answer the call of God, antecedently to his call, will scarce be salved from a flat contradiction, with any reserved considerations, that may be invented.

This solid foundation being laid, he proceeds ;   'Those who thus love him, and he approves of them, he predestinates to be conformed to the image of his Son.'   It is true, the apostle speaks of them, and to them that love the Lord ; but doth not (in the least) suppose them, as such, to be the objects of the acts of his sovereign grace after mentioned.   If God call none, but those that love him antecedently to his call, that grace of his must eternally rest in his own bosom, without the least exercise of it, towards any of the sons of men.   It is those persons indeed, who, in the process of the work of God's grace towards them, are brought to love him, that are thus predestinated and called :but they are so dealt withal, not upon the account or consideration of their love of God (which is not only in order consequential to some of them, but the proper effect and product of them), but upon the account of the unchangeable purpose of God, appointing them to salvation ; which I doubt not but Mr. Goodwin studiously and purposely omitted to insist upon, knowing its absolute inconsistency with the conclusion (and yet not able to wave it, had it been once brought under consideration), which from the words he aimeth to extract.   As then, to make men's loving of God to be antecedent to the grace of vocation, is an express contradiction in itself ; so to make it, or the consideration of it, to be previous unto predestination, is an insinuation of a gross Pelagian figment, giving rise and spring to God's eternal predestination, not in his own sovereign will, but the self-differencing wills of men : 'Latet anguis' also in the adding 'grass' of that exegetical term (preordinated) predestinated, that is, preordinated ; though the word being considered in the language whereof it is, seems not to give occasion to any suspicion, yet the change of it from preordained into preordinated, is not to be supposed to be for nothing, in him who is expert at these weapons.   To ordain, is either ' ordinare ut aliquid fiat,' or ' ordinem in factis statuere ;' or according to some, ' subjectum disponere ad finem :' to preordain, is of necessity, precisely tied up to the first sense : to preordinate, I fear, in Mr. Goodwin's sense, is but to predispose men by some good inclinations in themselves : and men preordinated, are but men so predisposed ; which is the usual gloss, that men of this persuasion put upon Acts xiii. 48.

Thus far then we have carried on the sense affixed to these words, if it may so be called, which is evidently contradictious in itself, and in no one particular suited to the mind of the Holy Ghost.

He proceeds : ' To give you yet, saith our apostle, a farther and more particular account, how God in the secret of his counsel, hath belaid things in order,' &c.

This expression, ' God hath belaid things in order to the salvation of them that love him,' is the whole of the assurance here given by the apostle, to the assertion formerly laid down for the consolation of believers : and this, according to the analogy and proportion of our author's faith, amounts only thus far: you that love God, if you continue so to do, you will fall under his predestination ; and if you abide under that, he will call you, so as that you may farther obey him, or you may not : if you do obey him, and believe upon his call (having loved him before), he will justify you ; not with that justification which is final, of which you may come short; but with initial justification, which if you continue in, and walk up unto, *solvite curas,* when you are dead in your graves: this is called God's belaying of things in his secret counsel, whereby the total accomplishment of the first engagement is cut off from the root of God's purposes, and branches of his effectual grace in the pursuit thereof, and grafted upon the wild olive of the will of man, that never did, nor ever will, bear any wholesome fruit of itself to eternity. What is afterward added, of the qualification of those whom God predestinates, being an intrusion of another false hypothesis, for the confirmation of an assertion of the same alloy, is not of my present consideration ; but he adds, ' Ye are to understand, that whom he hath predestinated, he hath also called, hath purposed or decreed to call, to the knowledge of his Son, or his gospel, as before,' &c.

Ans. How he hath predestinated them, is not expressed ; but being so predestinated, God purposes to call them ; that

is them and only them; for it is a uniform proceeding of
God towards all, whom he attempts to bring to himself,
which is here described: that is, when men love him, and
are approved of him, and are thereupon preordinated to conformity with Christ, then he decrees to call them, or, as the
calling here mentioned is described (that ye may not mistake, as though any internal effectual work of grace was
hereby intended, but only an outward moral persuasion, by
a revelation of the object they should embrace), he gives a
more plain and effectual discovery of Christ to them, than
to any others. Doubtless it is evident to every one, that
(besides the great confusion, whereunto the proceedings of
God in bringing sinners to himself, or belaying their coming
with some kind entertainments, are cast into), the whole
work of salvation is resolved into the wills of men, and
instead of an effectual, operative, unchangeable purpose of
God, nothing is left on his part, but a moral approbation of
what is well done, and a proposing of other desirable things
unto men, upon the account of former worthy carriages.
And this is no small part of the intendment of our author
in this undertaking.

That God decrees to[m] call them, and only them, who
love him, and upon that account are approved of him, when
all faith and love are the fruits of that calling of his, is such
a figment, as I shall not need to cast away words in the
confutation of it.

Yet, lest any should have too high thoughts of this grace
of vocation, he tells them by the way, ' that it doth not necessarily suppose a saving answer given to it by the called,
no whit more than the calling mentioned,' Matt. xx. 21.
xxii. 14.

First, By Mr. Goodwin's confession here is as yet no
great advance made towards the proof of this assertion, laid
down in the entrance, and for the confirmation whereof, this
series and concatenation of divine graces is insisted on.
Though men love God, are predestinated, and accepted, yet
when it comes to calling, they may stop there and perish
everlastingly; for ' many are called, but few are chosen:'
they are indeed belaid by a calling, but they may miss the

---

[m] Deut. vii. 7. Ezek. xvi. 6. Matt. xi. 26. Ephes. ii. 1—3.

place of its residence, or refuse to accept of its entertainment, and pass on to ruin. But,

Secondly, They are so called, as upon the account thereof to be justified; for whom he calls, he justifies. ' Yea, in case they obey:' but this is the interpretation of the new apostle, not the old; neither hath the text any such supposition, nor will the context bear it, nor can the design of the apostle consist with it, nor any more consolation be squeezed from this place upon the account of it, than of milk from a flint in the rock of stone. Neither,

Thirdly, Doth the calling here mentioned hold any analogy with that of ' the many that are called, but not chosen,' pointed at in the second place instanced in; being indeed the effectual calling of the few who are chosen. For as our Saviour in those places of Matthew, mentioned two sorts of persons, some that have a general call, but are not chosen; and others, that being chosen, are therefore distinguished from the former, as to their vocation; so Paul here tells ye, that the calling he insists on, is the peculiar ' call of God according to his purpose' (the same purpose intimated by our Saviour), which being suited of God to the carrying on, and accomplishing of that purpose of his, must be effectual, unless he, through mutability and impotency, come short of accomplishing the design of his will and wisdom.

Neither is this salved by what follows, ' that it is the intention of God, to make this call sufficient for the end purposed :' yea, this part of the wallet is most filled with folly and falsehood. For as general purposes of giving means for an end, with an intention to bring that end about, that may, or may not, attain it, are most remote from God, and being supposed, are destructive to all his holy and blessed attributes and perfections, as hath been shewn : so the thing itself, of sufficient grace of vocation, which is not effectual, is a gross figment, not whilst this world continues, by Mr. Goodwin, to be made good : the most of his arguments being importunate suggestions of his own hypothesis and conceptions. But he goes on,

' The apostle advanceth towards his proposed end, and adds, Those whom he called, them he also justified, or decreed to justify, in case the called obstruct him not in his way, or by their unbelief, render not themselves incapable of justification.'

Ans. That exception ('in case they obstruct him not'), is a clue to lead us into all the corners of this labyrinth, and a key to the whole design in hand. Such a supposal it is, as not only enervates the whole discourse of the apostle, and frustrates his design, but also opens a door for the questioning of the accomplishment of any purpose, or promise of God whatever; and in one word, rejects the whole efficacy of the grace of the gospel, as a thing of naught. What strength is there in the discourse and arguing of the apostle, from the purpose and ensuing series of God's grace, to prove that all things ' should work together for good to them that love God,' if the whole issue and event of things mentioned to that end, depend not on the efficacy or effectual influences of those acts of God, one upon another, and all upon the end; they being all and every one of them, jointly, and severally suspended upon the wills of the persons themselves, concerning whom they are (which yet here is concealed and [not] intimated in the least)? How doth it prove at all, that they shall never be ' separated from the love of Christ;' that they shall be made conformable to him in glory, notwithstanding all opposition, upon the account of the dispensation of God's eternal and actual love towards them, when the whole of their usefulness to the end proposed, is resolved ultimately into themselves and their endeavours; and not into any purpose or act of God? Such as is the foundation, such is the strength of the whole building. Inferences can have no more strength, than the principle from whence they are deduced ; if a man should tell another, that if he will go a journey of a hundred miles, at each twenty miles end, he shall meet with such and such refreshments ; all the consolation he can receive upon the account of refreshments provided for him, is proportioned only to the thoughts he hath of his own strength for the performance of that journey.

Farther, If in such expressions of the purposed works of God, we may put cases, and trust in what supposals we think good, where there is not the least jot, tittle, or syllable of them in the text, nor any room for them, without destroying, not only the design and meaning of the place, but the very sense of it; why may not we do so in other undertakings of God, the certainty of whose event, depends upon his purpose and promise only? For instance, the resurrection of the dead; may we not say, God will raise up the dead in Christ, in case there be any necessity that their bodies should be glorified? What is it also that remains of praise to the glorious grace of God? This is all he effects by it: in case men obstruct him not in his way, it doth good. God calls men to faith and obedience; in case they obstruct not his way, it shall do them good: but how do they obstruct his way? By unbelief and disobedience: take them away, and God's calling shall be effectual to them; that is, in case they believe and obey, God's calling shall be effectual to cause them to believe and obey.

The cases then foisted into the apostle's discourse, in the close of this interpretation of the place (if I may so call it), namely, that God will justify the called, in case they obstruct not his way; and will glorify them whom he hath justified, in case they continue and abide in the state of justification, are, first, thrust in without ground, warrant, or colour of advantage' or occasion given by any thing in the text or context: and, secondly, are destructive to the whole design of the Holy Ghost in the place whereinto they are intruded; injurious to the truth of the assertion intended to be made good, that ' all things shall work together for good,' proposed upon the account of the unchangeable purpose of God, and infallible connexion of the acts of his love and grace in the pursuit thereof; and resolve the promised work and designed event, wholly into the uncertain lubricous wills of men, making the assurance given, not only to be liable to just exceptions, but evidently to fail, and be falsified in respect of thousands: and, thirdly, render the whole dispensation of the grace of God to lackey after the wills of men, and wholly to depend upon them; giving in thereby (as was said), innumerable presumptions, that the word, for whose confirmation all these acts of God's grace are mentioned and insisted on, shall never be made good nor established.

Take, then, in a few words, the sense and scope of this place, as it is held out in the exposition given of it by Mr. Goodwin, and we will then proceed to consider his confir-

mations of the said exposition; ' Oh you that love God,
many afflictions, temptations, and oppositions, ye shall meet
withal, but be of good comfort, all shall work together for
your good, for God hath appointed you to be like his Son,
and you may triumph in every condition on this account;
for if ye, before any act of his special grace towards you,
love him, he approves you, and then he predestinates you
(what that is I know not); then it is in your power to continue to love him, or to do otherwise: if ye abide not, then
ye perish; if ye abide, he will call you; and when he doth
so, either ye may obey him, or ye may not. If you do not,
all things shall work together for your hurt, and ye will be
like the devil: if you do, then he will justify you, and then
if you abide with him, as perhaps ye may, perhaps ye may
not, he will finally justify you, and then all shall be well.'
This being the substance of the interpretation of this place
here given, let us now consider how it is confirmed.

That, which in his own terms he undertaketh to demonstrate, and to vindicate from all objections in his ensuing
discourse, he thus expresseth, page 209. sect. 43. ' These
decrees or purposed acts of God here specified, are to be
understood in their successive dependencies, with such a
condition or proviso respectively, as those mentioned; and
not absolutely, peremptorily, or without condition.'

Ans. The imposing of conditions and provisos, upon
the decrees and purposes of God, of which himself gives
not the least intimation, and the suspending them, as to their
execution, on those conditions so invented and imposed, at
the first view reflects so evidently on the will, wisdom,
power, prescience, and unchangeableness of God, who hath
said, ' His purposes shall stand, and he will do all his pleasure;'
especially when the interruption of them doth frustrate the
whole design and aim of God in the mentioning of those decrees and purposes of his; that there will be need of demonstrations written with the beams of the sun, to enforce men,
tender and regardful of the honour and glory of God, to
close with any in such an undertaking; let us then consider what is produced to this end, and try if it will hold
weight in the balance of the sanctuary. This, saith he, appears,

First, ' By the like phrase or manner of expression, fre-

quent in the Scripture elsewhere. I mean, when such purposes or decrees of God, the respective execution whereof,
are suspended upon such and such conditions, are, notwithstanding, simply and positively, without any mention of
condition, expressed and asseited. 'Wherefore the Lord
God of Israel saith ; I said indeed that thy house, and the
house of thy father shall walk before me' (meaning in the
office and dignity of the priesthood), 'for ever; but now,
saith the Lord, be it far from me.' I said indeed, that is,
I verily purposed or decreed, or I promised ; it comes much
to one; when God made the promise, and so declared his
promise accordingly, that Eli and his father's house should
walk before him for ever, he expressed no condition, as required to the execution or performance of it, yet here it
plainly appears, that there was a condition understood. In
the same kind of dialect Samuel speaks to Saul ; 'Thou hast
done foolishly, thou hast not kept the commandment of the
Lord thy God; for now the Lord had established thy kingdom upon Israel for ever ; but now thy kingdom shall not
continue :' the Lord had established, that is, he verily purposed, or decreed to establish it for ever, to wit, in case his
posterity had walked obediently with him.'

Here we have the strength (as will be manifest in the
progress of our discourse), of what Mr. Goodwin hath to
make good his former strange assertion ; whether it will
amount to a necessary proof or no, may appear upon these
ensuing considerations.

First, The reason intimated, being taken neither from the
text under debate, nor the context, nor any other place,
where any concernment of the doctrine therein contained, is
touched or pointed at, there being also no coincidence of
phrase or expression in the one place and the other here
compared ; I cannot but admire by what rules of interpretation Mr. Goodwin doth proceed, to make one of these places
exegetical of the other. Though this way of arguing hath
been mainly, and almost solely insisted on of late by the
Socinians, viz. Such a word is in another place used to another purpose, or in another sense, therefore this cannot be
the necessary sense of it in this : yet it is not only confuted
over and over as irrational and unconcluding, but generally
exploded, as an invention suited only to shake all certainty

whatever in matters of faith and revelation.   Mr. Goodwin in his instance goes not so far (or rather he goes farther, because his instance goes not so far), there being no likeness, much less sameness of expression in those texts, which he produces to weaken the obvious and literally exposed sense of the other insisted on therewith.   To wave the force of the inference from the words of the Holy Ghost (seeing nothing in the least intimated in the place will give in any assistance thereunto),

First, This thesis is introduced: 'The purposes and decrees of God (confessedly engaged in the place in hand) are, as to their respective executions, suspended on conditions in men.'   An assertion destructive to the power, goodness, grace, righteousness, faithfulness, wisdom, unchangeableness, providence, and sovereignty of God, as might be demonstrated, did it now lie in our way.   To prove that this must needs be so, and that that rule must take place, in the mention that is made of the purposes and decrees of God, (Rom. viii. 1.) 1 Sam. ii. 30. is produced, being a denunciation of God's judgments upon the house of Eli, for their unworthy walking in the honour of the priesthood, whereunto they were by him advanced and called, and which they were intrusted withal, expressly upon condition of their obedience.   Let us then a little consider the correspondency, that is between the places compared for their mutual illustration.

First, In the one, there is express mention of the purpose of God, and that his eternal purpose: in the other, only a promise expressly conditional in the giving of it, amounting to no more than a law, without the least intimation of any purpose or decree.

Secondly, The one encompasseth the whole design of the grace of the gospel; the other mentions not any special grace at all.

Thirdly, The one is wholly expressive of the acts of God, and his design therein; the other declarative of the duty of man, with the issue thereupon depending.   This then is the strength of this argument: God approving the obedience of a man, tells him, that upon the continuance of that obedience in him and his, he will continue them an office in his service (a temporal mercy, which might be enjoyed without

Q 2

the least saving grace); and which upon his disobedience, he threateneth to take from him (both promise and threatening being declarative of his approbation of obedience, and his annexing the priesthood thereunto, in that family): therefore God, intending the consolation of elect believers, affirming that all things shall work together for their good, upon this account, that he hath eternally purposed to preserve them in his love, and to bring them to himself by such effectual acts of his grace, as whose immutable dependance one upon the other, and all upon his own purpose, cannot be interrupted, and, therefore, such as shall infallibly produce and work in them all the obedience, which for the end proposed he requires. His purposes, I say, thus mentioned, must be of the same import with the declaration of his will in the other place spoken of; if such a confounding of the decrees and denunciations, absolute purposes and conditional promises, spiritual things with temporal, and the general administration of the covenant of grace in Christ, with special providential dispensations, may be allowed, there is no man needs to despair of proving any thing he hath a mind to assert.

Thirdly, There are two things, that Mr. Goodwin insists upon to make good his arguing from this place:

First, That these words ('I said indeed') hold out the real purpose and decree of God.

Secondly, That in the promise mentioned, there was no condition expressed or required to the execution or performance of it.

By the first he intends, that God did really purpose and decree from eternity, that Eli and his house should hold the priesthood for ever: by the second, that no condition was expressed, neither in terms, or necessarily implied in the thing itself, which is of the same import.

If neither of these now should prove true, what little advance hath Mr. Goodwin made for the weakening of the plain intendment of the words in the place under consideration, or for the confirmation of his own gloss and interposed conditionals, either by this, or the following instances, that are of the same kind, will plainly appear. Now that these words ('I said indeed') are not declarative of an eternal decree and purpose of God, concerning the futurition and event of

what is asserted to be the object of that decree, the continuance of the priesthood in the house of Eli; may be evidenced, as from the general nature of the things themselves,
so from the particular explanation of the act of God, whereunto this expression ('I said indeed') doth relate.

First, From the general nature of the thing itself, may
this be manifested. To what hath been formerly spoken, I
shall add only some few considerations, being not willing
to insist long on that which is but collateral to my present
design.

First then, When God decreed and purposed this (if so
be he purposed it, as it is said he did), he either foresaw what
would be the issue of it, or he did not? If he did not, where
is his infinite wisdom and understanding? If we may not be
allowed to say his foreknowledge? How are all his works
ᵘ' known to him from the foundation of the world?' How doth
he 'declare the end from the beginning, and the things that
are yet to come?' Distinguishing himself from all false gods
on this account? If he did foresee the event, that it would
not be so, why did he decree and purpose it should be so?
Doth this become the infinite wisdom of God to purpose and
decree from all eternity, that that shall come to pass, which
he knows will never come to pass? Can any such resolution
fall upon the sons of men, to whom God is pleased to continue the use of that little spark of reason, wherewith they
are endued? If you say, God purposed it should continue,
in case their disobedience hindered it not; I ask again, did
God foresee the disobedience that would so hinder it, or did
he not? If he did not, the same difficulties will arise which
formerly I mentioned. If he did, then God decreed and
purposed that the priesthood should continue in the house
of Eli, if they kept themselves from that disobedience,
which he saw, and knew full well, they would run into..
(Cui fini?)

Secondly, If God did thus purpose and decree, he was
able to bring it about, and accomplish his design by ways
agreeable to his goodness, wisdom, and righteousness, or he
was not. If he was not, where is his omnipotency, who is
not able to fulfil his righteous designs and purposes, in ways
corresponding to that state of agents and things, which he

ⁿ Acts xv. 18 Isa. xlvi. 10

hath allotted them? How can it be said of him, 'he will work, and none shall let him?' That God engageth his power, for the accomplishment of his purposes was shewed before; if he were able to accomplish it, why did he not do it, but suffer himself to be frustrated of his end? Is it suitable to the sovereign will and wisdom of God, eternally to purpose and decree that, which by means agreeable to his holiness and goodness, he is able to bring to pass, and yet not to do it, but to fail and come short of his holy and gracious intendment.

Thirdly, The obedience of the house of Eli, on which the accomplishment of the pretended decree is suspended, was such, as either they were able of themselves to perform, or they were not? To say they were, is to exclude the necessary assistance of the grace of God, which Mr. Goodwin hath not in terms declared himself to do, nor are we as yet arrived at that height, though a considerable progress hath been made. If they were not able to do it, without the assistance of the Spirit, and concurrence of the grace of God; did the Lord purpose to give them that assistance, working in them both to will and to do of his own good pleasure? or did he not? If he did so purpose, why did he not do it? If he did not purpose to do it, to what end did he decree, that that should come to pass, which he knew could not come to pass, without his doing that, which he was resolved never to do? It is all one, as if a man knew that another were shut up in a prison, from whence it was impossible that any body but himself should deliver him; and should resolve, and purpose to give the poor prisoner a hundred pounds, so that he would come out of prison to him, and resolve withal never to bring him out.

Fourthly, God from eternity foresaw, that the priesthood should not be continued to the house of Eli: therefore, he did not from eternity purpose and decree that it should. To know that a thing shall not be, and to determine that it shall be, is a σχίσις, rather beseeming a half frantic creature, than the infinitely wise Creator. Again, upon what account did God foresee, that it should not be so? Can the futurition of contingent events be resolved in the issue into any thing but God's sovereign determination? God therefore, did not determine and purpose, that it should be so; because, he determined and purposed that it should not be so. Whatsoever he doth in time, that he purposed to do from eternity; now in time he removed the priesthood from the house of Eli, therefore he eternally purposed and determined so to do; which surely leaves no place for a contrary purpose and decree (not so much as conditional), that it should so continue for ever. The truth is, the mystery of this abomination lies in those things, which lie not in my way now to handle. A disjunctive decree, a middle science, creature dependency, are father, mother, and nurse of the assertion we oppose, whose monstrous deformity, and desperate rebellion against the properties of God, I may (the Lord assisting) hereafter more fully demonstrate.

But you will say; Doth not the Lord plainly hold out a purpose and decree in these words, ' I said indeed?' Did he say it? Will you assign hypocrisy to him, and doubling with the sons of men?

I say then, secondly; that the expression here used holds out no intention nor purpose of God (as to the futurition and event of the thing itself), that the priesthood should continue in the house of Eli, but only his purpose and intention that obedience and the priesthood should go together. There is a connexion of things, not an intendment or purpose of events, in the words intimated. The latter cannot be ascribed to God, without the charge of as formal mutability as the poorest creature is liable to. Mr. Goodwin indeed tells ye, sect. 43. page 209. 'That the purpose of God itself considered, as an act or conception of the mind of God, dependeth not on any condition whatsoever, and all God's purposes and decrees without exception, are in such respect absolute and independent.' How weak and unable this is to free the Lord from a charge of changeableness upon his supposals, needs little pains to demonstrate. The conceptions of the minds of the sons of men and their purposes, as such, are as absolutely free and unconditional, as the nature of a creature will admit; only the execution of our purposes and resolves is suspended upon the intervention of other things, which render them all conditional; and this it seems is the state with God himself; although in the Scripture he most frequently distinguisheth himself from the sons of men, on this account, that they purpose at the greatest rate of uncertainty imaginable, as to the accomplishment of their thoughts, and therefore are frequently disappointed; but his purposes and his counsels stand for ever; so Psal. xxxiii. 10, 11. The expression then here (' I said') relates plainly to the investiture of Aaron and his seed in the priesthood. There was a twofold engagement made to the house of Aaron about that office: one in general to him and his sons: the other in particular to Phinehas and his posterity. The latter to Phinehas is far more expressive and significant, than the other; you have it Numb. xxv. 11—13. 'Phinehas the son of Eleazar, the son of Aaron the priest, hath turned my wrath away from the children of Israel, while he was zealous for my sake among them, that I consumed not the children of Israel in my jealousy: wherefore say, Behold, I give unto him my covenant of peace: and he shall have it, and his seed after him, even the covenant of an everlasting priesthood; because he was zealous for his God, and made an atonement for the children of Israel.' Here is a promise indeed, and no condition in terms expressed. But yet being made and granted upon the condition of obedience, which is clearly expressed once and again, that the continuance of it was also suspended on that condition (as to the glory and beauty of that office, the thing principally intended), cannot be doubted; yea, it is sufficiently expressed in the occasion of the promise, and fountain thereof. But this was not that promise, wherein Eli's was particularly concerned. Indeed his posterity was rejected in order to the accomplishment of this promise, the seed of Phinehas returning to their dignity from whence they fell, by the interposition of the house of Ithamar.

That which this expression here peculiarly relates unto, is the declaration of the mind of God, concerning the priesthood of Aaron and his posterity, which you have Exodus xxviii. 43, xxix. 9. where the confirming them in their office is called ' a perpetual statute,' or ' a law for ever;' the signification of the term ' for ever,' in the Hebrew especially, relating to legal institution, is known. Their eternity is long since expired; that then which God here emphatically expresses, as an act of grace and favour to the house of Aaron, which Eli and his had interest in, was that statute or law of the priesthood: and his purpose and intention (not concerning the event of things, not that it should continue in any one branch of that family, but) of his connecting it with their obedience and faithfulness in that office. It is very frequent with God to express his approbation of our duty, under terms holding out the event, that would be the issue of the duty, though it never come to pass: and his disapprobation or rejection of the sons of men, under terms that hold out the end of that disobedience, though it be prevented, or removed. In this latter case, he commands Jonah to cry, 'Yet forty days, and Nineveh shall perish;' not that he purposed the destruction of Nineveh at that time, but only effectually to hold out the end of their sin, that it might be a means to turn them from it, and to prevent that end, which it would otherwise procure. His purpose was to prevent, at least prorogue, the ruin of Nineveh, and therefore made use of threatening them with ruin, that they might not be ruined. To say that God purposed not the execution of his purpose, but in such and such cases, is a plain contradiction. The purpose is of execution, and to say, he purposed not the execution of his purposes, is to say plainly, he purposed and purposed not, or he purposed not what he purposed. The examples of Pharaoh and Abraham, in the precepts given to them, are proofs of the former: but I must not insist upon particulars.

This then is all that here is intended. God making a law, a statute about the continuance of the priesthood in the family of Aaron, affirms, that then he said his house should walk before him for ever, that is, with approbation and acceptation: for as to the right of the priesthood, that still continued in the house of Aaron, whilst it continued, notwithstanding the ejection of Eli and his. Now, whether there were any conditions in the promise made, which is Mr. Goodwin's second improvement of this instance, may appear from the consideration of what hath been spoken concerning it. It is called a law, and statute, the act: on that account, whatever it were, that God here points unto, is but a moral legislative act, and not a physical determining act of the will of God; and being a law of privilege in its own nature, it involves a condition, which the acts of God's will, vital and eternal, wherewith this law is compared, do openly disavow.

Let us now see the parallel between the two places insisted on, for the explanation of the former of them, which

as it will appear by the sequel,.is the only buckler, wherewith Mr. Goodwin defends his hypothesis, from the irresistible force of the argument, wherewith he hath to do. First,
The one speaks of things spiritual, the other of temporal.
Secondly, The one of what God will do, and the other of
what he approves to be done, being done. Thirdly, The one
holds out God's decree and purpose concerning events, the
other his law and statute concerning duties. Fourthly, The
one not capable of interposing conditionals, without perverting the whole design of God revealed in that place; the
other directly including conditions. Fifthly, The one speaking of things themselves; the other only of the manner of a
thing. Sixthly, In the one, God holds out what he will do
for the good of his, upon the account of the efficacy of his
grace; in the other, what men are to do, if they will be approved of him. And how one of these places can be imagined
to be suited for the illustration and interpretation of the
other, which agree neither in name nor thing, word nor
deed, purpose nor design, must be left to the judgments of
those, who desire to ponder these things, and to weigh them
in the balance of the sanctuary.

The other instances in the case of Saul and Paul, being
more heterogeneous to the business in hand, than that of Eli
which went before, require not any particular help for the
removal of them out of the way. Though they are dead, as
to the end for which they are produced : I presume no true
Israelite in the pursuit of that Sheba in the church, the apostacy of saints, will be retarded in his way, by their being cast
before them. In brief, neither the connexion of obedience,
and suited rewards, as in the case of Saul; nor the necessity
of means subservient to the accomplishment of purposes
themselves, also falling under that purpose of him, who intends the end, and the fulfilling of it, as in the case of Paul,
are of the least force to persuade us, that the eternal immanent acts of God's will, which he pursues by the effectual irresistible acts of his grace, so to compass the end, which he
hath from everlasting determinately resolved to bring about,
are suspended upon imaginary conditions, created in the
brains of men, and (notwithstanding their evident inconsistency with the scope of the Scripture, and design of God
therein) intruded into such texts of Scripture, as on all hands,

(which will be evident in the sequel of this discourse) are fortified against them.

Besides, in the case of Paul, though the infallibility of the prediction did not in the least prejudice the liberty of the agents, who were to be employed for its accomplishment, but left room for the exhortation of Paul, and the endeavours of the soldiers, yet it cuts off all possibility of a contrary event, and all supposal of a disjunctive purpose in God, upon the account whereof he cannot predict the issue, or event of any thing whatsoever.   But of this more largely afterward.

But this is farther argued by Mr. Goodwin, from the purposes of God in his threatenings, in these words: ' Most frequently the purpose and decree of God, concerning the punishment of wicked and ungodly men, is expressed by the Holy Ghost, absolutely and certainly, without the least mention of any condition, of relaxation or reversion : yet from other passages of Scripture it is fully evident, that this decree of his is conditional in such a sense, which imports a non-execution of the punishment therein declared, upon the repentance of the persons, against whom the decree is. In like manner, though the purpose and decree of God, for the justification of those who are called (and so for the glorifying of those that shall be justified), be (in the Scripture in hand) delivered in an absolute and unconditioned form of words ; yet it is no way necessary to suppose (the most familiar, frequent, and accustomed expression in Scripture in such cases, exempting us from any such necessity) that, therefore, these decrees must needs bring forth against all possible interveniences whatever ; so that (for example) he that is called by the word and Spirit, must needs be justified, whether he truly believe or no ; and he that is justified must needs be glorified, whether he persevere or no.'

Ans. 1. That the threatenings of God are moral acts, not declarative, as to particular persons of God's eternal purposes, but subservient to other ends together with the law itself, whereof they are a portion (as the avoiding of that for which men are threatened), is known.   They are appendices of the law, and in their relation thereunto, declare the connexion that is between sin and punishment, such sins and such punishments.

2. That the eternal purposes of God, concerning the works of his grace, are to be measured by rule and analogy of his temporal threatenings, is an assertion striking at the very root of the covenant of grace, and efficacy of the mediation of the Lord Jesus, yea, at the very being of divine perfections of the nature of God himself. This there is indeed in all threatenings declared of the absolute purpose, and unchangeable decree of God, that all impenitent sinners shall be punished, according to what in his wisdom and righteousness he hath apportioned out unto such deservings, and threateneth accordingly. In this regard there is no condition, that doth or can (in the least) import a non-execution of the punishment decreed; neither do any of the texts cited in the margin of our author prove any such thing. They all indeed positively affirm, faithless, impenitent unbelievers shall be destroyed, which no supposal whatsoever, that takes not away the subject of the question (and so alters the whole thing in debate), can in the least infringe. Such assertions (I say) are parts of the law of God revealing his will in general, to punish impenitent unbelievers, concerning which his purpose is absolute, unalterable, and steadfast.

The conclusion then, which Mr. Goodwin makes, is apparently racked from the words, by stretching them upon the unproportioned bed of other phrases and expressions, wholly heterogeneous to the design in this place intended: added here are supposed conditions in general, not once explained to keep them from being exposed to that shame that is due unto them, when their intrusion (without all order or warrant from heaven) shall be manifested ; only wrapped up in the clouds of possible interveniences, when the acts of God's grace, whereby his purposes and decrees are accomplished, do consist in the effectual removal of the interveniences pretended, that so the end aimed at in the unchangeable counsel of God, may (suitably to the determination of his sovereign, omnipotent, infinite, wise will) be accomplished. Neither doth it in the least appear, that any such calling by the word and Spirit, as may leave the persons so called in their unbelief (they being so called in the pursuit of this purpose of God, to give them faith, and make them comformable to Chjst), may be allowed place or room in the haven of this text : the like may be said of justifica-

tion, wherein men do not persevere. Yea, these two suppo-
posals are not only an open begging of the thing in contest,
but a flat defying of the apostle as to the validity of his demonstration, ' that all things shall work together,' &c.

Notwithstanding then any thing that hath been objected
to the contrary, the foundation of God mentioned in this
place of Scripture stands firm, and his eternal purpose of
safeguarding the saints in the love of Christ, until he bring
them to the enjoyment of himself in glory, stands clear from
the least shadow of change, or suspension upon any certain
conditionals, which are confidently (but not so much as
speciously) obtruded upon it.

The next thing undertaken by Mr. Goodwin, is to vindicate the forementioned glosses from such oppositions, as
arise against them from the context and words themselves,
with the design of the Holy Ghost therein : these things
doth he find his exposition obnoxious unto. The exposition
which he pretends to give no strength unto, but what is foreign on all considerations whatsoever of words and things,
to the place itself : this, it seems, is to prophecy according
to the [o]analogy of faith.

First then, sect 44. To the objection, that those who are
called are also justified, and shall be glorified, according to
the tenor of the series of the acts of the grace of God here
laid down, he answereth, 'That where either the one, or the
other of these assertions, be so or no, it must be judged of
by other Scriptures ; certain it is by what hath been argued
concerning the frequent usage of the Scripture in point of
expression, that it cannot be concluded or determined by the
Scripture in hand.' The sum of this answer amounts to thus
much : although the sense opposed be clear in the letter and
expression of this place of Scripture, in the grammatical
sense and use of the words ; though it flows from the whole
context, and answers (alone) the design and scope of the
place, which gives not the least countenance to the interposing of any such conditionals, as are framed to force it to
speak contrary to what (γυμνῇ τῇ κεφαλῇ) it holds forth : yet
the mind of God in the words, is not from these things to be
concluded on ; but other significations and senses, not of
any word here used, not from the laying down of the same

[o] Rom. xii 6.

doctrine in other places with the analogy of the faith thereof, not from the proposing of any design suitable to this here expressed, but places of Scripture agreeing with this, neither in name nor thing, expression nor design, word nor matter, must be found out in the sense and meaning of this place, and be from them concluded, and our interpretation of this place accordingly regulated. ' Nobis non licet,' &c. Neither hath Mr. Goodwin produced any place of Scripture, nor can he, parallel to this so much as in expression, though treating of any other subject or matter, that will endure to have any such sense tied to it, as that which he violently imposeth on this place of the apostle. And if the sense and mind of God in this place, may not safely be received and closed withal, from the proper and ordinary signification of the word (which is always attended unto without the least dispute, unless the subject matter of any place, with the context, enforces to the sense left usual and natural), with the clear design and scope of the context in all the parts of it, universally correspondent unto itself; I know not how, or when, or by what rules, we may have the least certainty that we have attained the knowledge of the mind of God in any one place of Scripture whatever.

What he next objects to himself, namely, that, ' though there be no condition expressed, in the instances by him produced, yet there are in parallel places, by which they are to be expounded' (but such conditions as these, are not expressed in any place, that answers to that which we have in hand), it being by himself (as I conceive) invented to turn us aside from the consideration of the irresistible efficacy of the argument from this place (which use he makes of it in his first answer given to it), I own not : and that because I am fully assured, that in any promise whatsoever, that is indeed conditional, there is no need to inquire out other Scriptures of the like import, to evince it so to be; all and every one of them that are such, either in express terms, or in the matter whereof they are, or in the legal manner wherein they are given and enacted, do plainly and undeniably hold out the conditions inquired after. His threefold answer to this objection, needs not to detain us : passing on (I hope) to what is more material and weighty, he tells us first (sect. 44.) that if this be so, ' then it must be tried out by other Scriptures,

and not by this :' which evasion I can allow our author to
insist on, as tending to shift his hands of this place, which I
am persuaded in the consideration of it, grew heavy on them.
But I cannot allow it to be a plea in this contest, as not
owning the objection which it pretends to answer.   The two
following answers, being not an actual doing of any thing,
but only fair and large promises of what Mr. Goodwin will
do, about answering other Scriptures, and evincing the conditionals intimated from such others, as he shall produce
(some, doubtless will think these promises no payment, especially such as having weighed money formerly tendered for
real payment, have found it too light); I shall let them lie in
expectation of their accomplishment. ' Rusticus expectat,' &c.

In the mean time (till answers come to hand), Mr. Goodwin proffers to prove by two arguments (one clear answer
had been more fair), that these acts of God, calling, justification, and so the rest, have no such connexion between
them, but that the one of them may be taken, and be put in
execution, and yet not the other, in respect of the same persons.

His first reason is this : 'If the apostle should frame this
series or chain of divine acts, with an intent to shew or teach
the uninterruptibleness of it, in what case, or cases soever,
he should fight against his general, and main scope or design
in that part of the, chapter, which lieth from ver. 17. which
clearly is this, to encourage them to constancy and perseverance in suffering afflictions. For to suggest any such
thing, as that being called and justified, nothing could hinder them from being glorified, were to furnish them with a
ground, on which to neglect his exhortation; for who will
be persuaded to suffer tribulation for the obtaining of that
which they have sufficient assurance given, that they shall
obtain, whether they suffer such things or no : therefore certainly the apostle did not intend here to teach the certainty
of perseverance in those that are justified.'

Ans. That this argument is of such a composition as not
to operate much in the case in hand, will easily appear: for,

First, Those expressions (' in what case or cases soever')
are foisted into the sense and sentence of them whom he
opposes ; who affirm the acts of God's grace here mentioned
to be effectually and virtually preventive of those cases, and

of which might possibly give any interruption to the series of them.

Secondly, Whatsoever is here pretended of the main scope of the chapter, the scope of the place, we have under consideration, was granted before, to be the making good of that assertion premised in the head thereof, that all things should work together for good to believers, and that so to make it good, that upon this demonstration of it, they might triumph with joy and exultation : which it cannot be denied, but that this uninterruptible series of divine acts (not framed by the apostle, but) revealed by the Holy Ghost, is fitted and suited to do.

Thirdly, Suppose that be the scope of the foregoing verses; what is there in the thesis insisted on, and the sense embraced by us, opposite thereunto ? Why to suggest any such thing to them as, that being called and justified no-thing could possibly interpose to'hinder them from being glorified (that is, that God by his grace will preserve them fiom departing wilfully from him, and will in Jesus Christ establish his love to them for ever), was to furnish them with a motive to neglect his exhortations; yea, but this kind of arguing we call here *petitio principii,* and it is accounted with us nothing valid ; the thing in question, is produced as the medium to argue by. We affirm there is no stronger motive possible to encourage them to perseverance, than this proposed. It is otherwise, saith Mr. Goodwin; and its being otherwise, in his opinion, is the medium whereby he disproves not only that, but another truth, which he also opposeth. But he adds this reason, ' for who would be per-suaded to suffer,' &c. that is, it is impossible for any one industriously and carefully to use the means for the attain-ment of any end, if he hath assurance of the end by these means to be obtained. What need Hezekiah make use of food, or other means of sustaining his life, when he was as-sured that he should live fifteen years ? The perseverance of the saints is not in the Scripture, nor by any of those, whom Mr. Goodwin hath chosen to oppose, held out on any such ridiculous terms, as whither they use means, or use them not ; carry themselves well, or wickedly miscarry them-selves; but is asserted upon the account of God's effectual grace, preserving them in the use of the means, and from all such miscarriages, as should make a total separation between God and their souls. So that this first reason is but a plain begging of those things, which (to use his own language) he would not dig for.

But perhaps, although this first argument of Mr. Goodwin be nothing but an importune suggestion of some hypothesis of his own, with an arguing from inferences, not only questionable but unquestionably false; yet if his second demonstration will evince the matter under debate, he may be content to suffer loss in the hay and stubble of the first, so that the gold of the following argument do abide. Now thus he proceedeth in these words : ' And lastly, this demonstrates the same thing yet farther. If God should justify all without exception whom he calleth, and that against all bars of wickedness and unbelief, possible to be laid in his way by those who are called ; then might ungodly and unbelieving persons inherit the kingdom of God; the reason of the connexion is evident ; it being a known truth, that the persons justified are in a condition or present capacity of inheriting the kingdom of God.'

Ans. But ' carbones pro thesauro,' if it be possible this (being of the same nature with that which went before) is more weak and infirm, as illogical and sophistical as it ; the whole strength of it lies in a supposal, that those who are so called, as here is intimated in the text, called according to the purpose of God, called to answer the design of God to make them like to Jesus Christ, so called as to be hereupon justified, may yet lay such bars of wickedness and unbelief in their own way, when they are so called, as not to be justified ; when that calling of theirs consists in the effectual removal of all those bars of wickedness and unbelief, which might hinder their free and gracious acceptation with God. That is, that they may be called effectually, and not effectually ; a supposal hereof, is the strength of that consideration, which yielded Mr. Goodwin this demonstration. His eminent way of arguing herein, will also be farther manifest, if you shall consider that the very thing, which he pretends to prove, is that which he here useth for the medium to prove it, not varied in the least. ' Si Pergama dextra,' &c. But Mr. Goodwin foresaw (as it was easy for him to do) what would be excepted to this last argument, to wit, that the

calling here mentioned effectually removes those bars of
wickedness and unbelief, a supposal whereof is all the
strength and vigour it hath; and in that supposal there is a
plain assuming of the thing in question, and a bare contradiction to that, which from the place we prove and confirm.
Wherefore he answereth sundry things:

First, That Judas, Demas, Simon Magus, were all called,
and yet laid bars of wickedness and unbelief, whereby their
justification was obstructed; and to the reply, that they were
not so called, as those mentioned in the text, not called according to God's purpose, with that calling which flows from
their predestination to be conformed unto Christ, with that
calling which is held out as an effectual mean to accomplish
the end of God, in causing all things to work together for
their good; and therefore, that the strength of this answer
lies in the interposition of his own hypothesis once more,
and his renewed requests for a grant of the thing in question; he proceeds to take away this exception by sundry
cross assertions and interrogations; sect. 45. 1. 'It hath not
been proved,' saith he, ' by any man, nor I believe never
will be (Sir, we live not by your faith), that the calling here
spoken of imports any such act or work of God, whereby
the called are irresistibly necessitated savingly to believe.
If it import no such thing as this, what hinders but that the
persons mentioned, might have been called by that very
kind of calling here spoken of?'

Ans. It is known what Mr. Goodwin aims at in that expression ['irresistibly necessitated savingly to believe'], we
will not contend about words; neither of the two first terms
mentioned, are either willingly used of us, or can be properly
used by any, in reference to the work of conversion or calling. What we own in them, relates as to the first term (irresistibly) to the grace of God calling, or converting; and
in the latter (necessitatingly) to the event of the call itself.
If by irresistibly, you intend the manner of operation of that
effectual grace of God (not which conquers in a reaction,
which properly may be termed so; but) which really, and
therefore certainly (for ' unumquodque, quod est, dum est,
necessario est') produces its effect, not by forcing the will,
but (being as intimate to it as itself) making it willing, &c.
we own it. And if by necessitating they understand only

the event of things, that is, it is of necessity, as to the event that they shall savingly believe, who are effectually called without the least straitening, or necessitating their wills in their conversion (which are still acted suitably to their native liberty), we close with that term also, and affirm that the calling here mentioned imports such an act of God's grace, as whereby they who are called, are effectually and infallibly brought savingly to believe, and so consequentially, that the persons whose wickedness and unbelief abides upon them, were never called with this calling here contended about; they who are not predestinated *a parte ante,* nor glorified *a parte post,* are not partakers of this calling. I must add, that (as yet) I have not met with any proof of Mr. Goodwin's interpretation, nor any exception against ours, that is not resolved into the same principle of craving the thing in question ; producing the thing to be proved, as its own demonstration ; and asserting the things proved against him, not to be so, because they are not so. From the design and scope of the place, the intendment of the Holy Ghost in it, the meaning of the words, the relation and respect wherein the acts of God mentioned, stand one to another, the disappointment of God's purpose and decree in case of any interruption of them, or non-producing of the effects, which, lead the subjects, of whom they are spoken, from one to another, we prove the infallible efficacy of every act of God's grace here mentioned, as to their tendency unto the end aimed at; and this, he that is called to believe, may infallibly do so. But, says Mr. Goodwin, this is otherwise. Well let that pass. He adds, secondly, 'Suppose it be granted, that the calling here spoken of is that kind of calling which is always accompanied with a saving answer of faith; yet neither doth this prove, but that even such called ones may obstruct and prevent by wickedness and unbelief their final justification, and consequently their glorification. If so, then that chain of divine acts or decrees here framed by the apostle, is not indissolvable in any such sense, which imports an infallibility, and universal exertion or execution of the latter, whensoever the former hath taken place.' In this answer Mr. Goodwin denies our conclusion; to wit, that the chain of divine acts of grace in this place is indissolvable; which that it is, we make out and prove from the words of the text, the context and scope of the place: and adds his reason; 'because they who are justified, may lay bars in their way from being finally so, or being glorified ,' that is, it is not so, because it is not so. For the efficacy of the grace asserted, is for the removal of the bars intimated, or wherein may its efficacy be supposed to consist, especially in its relation to the end designed. And so this place is answered. Saith the Holy Ghost, those whom God justifieth, he glorifies: perhaps not, saith Mr. Goodwin; some things may fall in, or fall out, to hinder this. *Eligite cui credatis.*

Were I not resolved to abstain from the consideration of the judgments of men, when they are authoritatively interposed in the things of God, I could easily manifest the fruitlessness of the following endeavour to prove the effectual calling of Judas, by the testimony of Chrysostom and Peter Martyr: for neither hath the first in the place alleged any such things (least of all is it included in Mr. G.'s marginal annotation, excluding compulsion, necessity, and violence from vocation); and the latter in the section pointed to, and that following, lays down principles sufficiently destructive to the whole design, whose management Mr. Goodwin hath undertaken. Neither shall I contest about the imposing on us in this dispute, the notion of final justification, distinct from glorification, both name and thing, being foreign to the Scripture, and secretly including (yea, delivering to the advantage of its author) the whole doctrine under consideration stated to his hand. If there be a gospel-justification in sinners or believers in the blood of Christ, not final, or that may be cut off, he hath prevailed.

But Mr. Goodwin proceeds to object against himself, sect. 46. 'But some, it may be, will farther object against the interpretation given, and plead that the contexture between these two links of this chain, predestination to a conformity with Christ, and calling, is simply and absolutely indissolvable, so that whoever is so predestinated, never fails of being called. 2. That it is altogether unlikely that in one and the same series of divine actions, there should not be the same fixedness or certainty of coherence, between all the parts.' The first of these being the bare thesis which he opposed, I know not how it came to be made an objection. I shall only add to the latter objection, which includes something of argument, that the efficacy of any one act of God's grace here mentioned, as to the end proposed, depending wholly on the uninterruptible concatenation of them all, and their effectual prevalency and certainty (as to their respective operation), of every one of them, being equal to the accomplishment of the purpose of God in and by them all; and willingly own it, especially finding how little is said (and yet how much labour taken) to dress up a pretended answer unto it; of this there are two parts, whereof the first is this: 'I answer,' saith he,

First, 'By a demur upon the former of these pleas, which was, that the connexion between the predestination of God mentioned, and his calling, is uninterruptible. Somewhat doubtful to me it is, whether a person, who by means of the love of God, which is in him at present, falls under his decree of predestination, may not possibly, before the time appointed by God for his calling, be changed in that his affection, and consequently pass from under that decree of predestination, and fall under another decree of God opposite thereunto, and so never come to be called.'

Ans. I confess this demur outruns my understanding, *equis albis*, neither can I by any means overtake it, to pin any tolerable sense upon it; though I would allow it to be suited only to Mr. Goodwin's principles, and calculated for the meridian of Arminianism: for who (I pray) are they, in any sense (in Mr. Goodwin's) that do so love God, as to fall under, as he speaks, that pendulous decree of predestination, and to whom this promise here is made? Are they not believers? Are any others predestinated in our author's judgment, but those who are actually so? Is not the decree of predestination, God's decree or purpose of saving believers by Jesus Christ? Or can any love God to acceptation, without believing? If then they are believers, can they alter that condition before they are called? We supposed that 'Pfaith had been by hearing, and hearing by the word of God,' and that it is of necessity (in order of nature) that calling should precede believing. What are men called to? Is it not to believe? Here is then a new sort of men discovered, that believe and fall from faith, love God and forsake him,

P Rom. x. 17.

all antecedently to their vocation and calling. I am confi‑
dent that Mr. Goodwin may be persuaded to withdraw this
demurrer, or if not, that he will be overruled in it, before
the judgment-seat of all unprejudiced men. It will scarcely
as yet pass currently, that men are born believers, and after
such and such a time of their continuance in that estate of
belief, and being predestinated thereupon, God then calls
them. Neither do I understand the meaning of that phrase
('never come to be called') used by him, who maintains all to
be called, but this is but a demurrer. The answer follows.

For the great regard I bear unto the author's abilities,
I shall not say that his ensuing discourse doth not deserve
to be transcribed, and punctually insisted on: but this I may
say (I hope) without offence, that it is so long and tedious,
so remote from what it pretends unto, to wit, an answer to
the forementioned argument, that I dare not venture upon
the patience of any reader so far as to enter into a parti‑
cular consideration of it.

The sum of it is, that there is no unlikelihood in this,
that, though one part of the chain of divine graces before
mentioned, cannot be dissolved nor broken, yet another may
(notwithstanding that a dissolution of any one of them, ren‑
ders the design of God in them all wholly frustrate and
fruitless). This he proves, by proposing a new series of di‑
vine acts, in actual dependance one upon another, some
whereof may be uninterruptible, but the other not so. He
that shall but slightly view the concatenation of divine acts,
here proposed by Mr. Goodwin, for the illustration of that
dependance of them, and their efficacy, which we insist
upon, will quickly find it liable to some such small excep‑
tions, as render it altogether useless, as to the end pro‑
posed. As,

First, That the case here proposed, and pretended to be
parallel to that under our consideration, is a fictitious thing,
a feigned concatenation of feigned decrees of God, being nei‑
ther in any one place delivered in the Scripture, nor to be
collected from any, or all the texts in the Bible: which course
of proceeding, if it may be argumentative in sacred truths,
it will be an easy and facile task to overthrow the most emi‑
nent and clearly delivered heads of doctrine in the whole
book of God.

Secondly, That it is a case surmised by him, suitable to his own hypotheses, neither true in itself, nor any way analogous to that wherewith it is yoked, being indeed a new way and tone of begging the thing in question. For instance, It supposeth (without the least attempt of proof), 1. Conditional decrees, or a disjunctive intendment of events in God; it shall come to pass, or otherwise. 2. A middle science conditional, as the foundation of those disjunctive decrees; with, 3. A futurition of things, antecedent to any determining act of the will of God; and, 4. A possibility of frustrating (as to event) the designs and purposes of God; and, 5. That all mediums of the accomplishment of any thing are conditions of God's intentions, as to the end he aims at; and, 6. That God appoints a series of mediums for the compassing of an end, and designs them thereunto, without any determinate resolution to bring about that end; and, 7. That the acts of God's grace in their concatenation mentioned in this place of Rom. viii. are severally conditional; because he hath invented or feigned some decrees of God which he says are so. All which, with the inferences from them, Mr. Goodwin knows will not advance his reasonings at all, as to our understandings, being fully persuaded, that they are all abomi-nations of no less base alloy than the error itself, in whose defence and patronage they are produced.

To our argument then before mentioned, proving an equal indissolvableness in all the links of the chain of divine graces, drawn forth and insisted on, from the equal depend-ance of the design and purpose of God on the mutual de-pendance of each of them on the other, for the fulfilling of that purpose of his, and obtaining the end, which he pro-fesses himself to intend; this is the sum of Mr. Goodwin's answer, If I can invent a series of decrees, and a concatena-tion of divine acts, though indeed there be no such thing, neither can I give any colour to it without laying down, and taking for granted, many false and absurd supposals: and though it be not of the same nature with that here proposed by the apostle, nor any where held out in the Scripture for any such end and purpose as this is; neither can I assign any absolute determinate end in this series of mine, whose accomplishment God engages himself to bring about (as the case stands in the place of Scripture under consideration),

then it is meet and equitable, that, laying aside all enforce-
ments from the text, context, nature of God, the thing treated
on, all compelling us to close with another sense and interpretation, that we regulate the mind of the Holy Ghost
herein, to the rule, proportion, and analogy of the case as
formerly proposed.   This being the sum of that, which Mr,
Goodwin calls his answer, made naked I presume to its shame,
'valeat quantum valere potest.'

I shall only add that, 1. When Mr. Goodwin shall make
good that order and series of decrees, here by him mentioned,
from the Scripture, or with solid reason from the nature of
the things themselves, suitably to the properties of him,
whose they are: and, 2. Prove that any eternal decree of God,
either as to its primitive enacting, or temporal execution, is
suspended on any thing, not only really contingent in itself
and its own nature, in respect of the immediate fountain
from whence it flows, and nature of its immediate cause ; but
also as to its event, in respect of any act of the will of God,
that it may otherwise be, and so the accomplishment of that
decree left thereupon uncertain, and God himself dubiously
conjecturing at the event (for instance, whether Christ should
die or no, or any one be saved by him): and, 3. Clearly
evince this notion of the decrees and purposes of God, that
he intends to create man, and then to give him such advantages, which if he will, it shall be so with him: if otherwise,
it shall be so: to send Christ, if men do so, or not to send
him, if they do otherwise ; and so of the residue of the decrees mentioned by him: and, 4. That all events of things
whatsoever, spiritual and temporal, have a conditional futurition antecedent to any act of the will of God. When, I say,
he shall have proved these and some like things to these, we
shall farther consider what is offered by him, yea we will
confess that ' hostis habet muros,' &c.

Of the many other testimonies to the purpose in hand,
bearing witness to the same truth, some few may yet be
singled out ; and in the next place that of Jer. xxxi. 3. presents itself unto trial and examination.   'Yea, I have loved
thee with an everlasting love, therefore with loving-kindness
have I drawn thee ;' it is the whole elect church of the seed of
Jacob, of whom he speaks : the foundation of whose blessedness is laid in the eternal love of God ; who the persons

are thus beloved, and of whom we are to interpret these expressions of God's good-will, the apostle manifests, Rom. xi.
as shall afterward be more fully discoursed and cleared.
He tells you, it is the election, whom God intends, of whom
he says that they obtained the righteousness that is by faith,
according to the purport of God's good-will towards them,
though the rest were hardened; God (who adds daily to his
church such as shall be saved, Acts xiii. 48.) drawing them
thereunto, upon the account of their being so elected. He
calls them also the 'remnant according to the election of
grace, and the people whom God did foreknow;' ver. 1, 2.
or from eternity designed to the participation of the grace
there spoken of, as the use of the word hath been evinced to
be; these are the 'thee' here designed; the portion of Israel after the flesh, which the Lord in his free grace hath
eternally appointed to be his peculiar inheritance, which in
their several generations he draws to himself with loving-
kindness. And this everlasting love is not only the fountain, whence actual loving-kindness in drawing to God, or
bestowing faith, doth flow (as they believe who are ordained
to eternal life), but also the sole cause and reason, upon the
account whereof, in contradistinction to the consideration
of any thing in themselves, God will exercise loving-kindness towards them for ever. That which is everlasting or
eternal, is also unchangeable; God's everlasting love is no
more liable to mutability than himself; and it is an always
equal ground and motive for kindness. On what account
should God alter in his actual kindness, or favour towards
any, if that, on the account whereof he exercises it, will not
admit of the least alteration? He that shall give a condition, on
which this everlasting love of God should be suspended, and
according to the influence whereof upon it, it should go
forth in kindness, or be interrupted, may be allowed to boast
of his discovery.

That of the apostle, 2 Tim. ii. 19. is important to the business in hand. 'Nevertheless, the foundation of God stands
sure, having this seal, The Lord knoweth them that are his.'
Some persons of eminency and note in the church, yea stars
(it seems) of a considerable magnitude in the visible firmament thereof, having fallen away from the truth and faith of
the gospel, and drawn many after them into ways of de-

struction, a great offence and scandal among believers thereon (as in such cases it will fall out) ensued ; and withal a temptation of a not-to-be-despised prevalency, and sad consequence (which we formerly granted to attend such eminent apostacy), seems to have laid hold on many weak saints: they feared, lest they also might be overthrown, and after all their labouring and suffering in the work of faith, and patience of the saints, come short of ' the mark of the high calling' set before them, considering their own weakness and instability, with that powerful opposition, whereunto (in those days especially) they were exposed, upon the contemplation of such apostacies or defections, they were opportune and obnoxious· sufficiently to this temptation. Yea, their thoughts upon the case under consideration, might lead them to fear a more general defection : for seeing it is thus with some, why may not this be the condition of all believers ? and so the whole church may cease, and come to nothing, notwithstanding all the promises of building it on a rock, and of the presence of Christ with it to the end of the world; nay, may not his whole kingdom on earth on this account, possibly fall to utter ruin, and himself be left a head without members, a king without subjects ? This, by Mr. Goodwin's own confession, is the objection, which the apostle answereth, and removes in and by the words under consideration ; chap. 14. pp. 359, 360. ' Seeing these fall away, are not we likewise in danger of falling away, and so of losing all that we have done and suffered in our Christian profession ? To this objection or scruple, the apostle answereth in the words in hand :' so he. Thus far then are we agreed. About the sense of the words themselves, and their accommodation to the removal of the objection or scruple mentioned, is our difference. I know not how Mr. Goodwin comes to call it an objection or scruple (which is the expression of thoughts or words, arising against that which is, in the truth of it), seeing it is their very state and condition indeed, and that which they fear is that which they are really exposed unto, and which they ought to believe that they are exposed to. In his apprehension, they who make the objection, or whose scruple it was, were as liable unto, in his judgment, and in the same danger of falling away, or greater (their temptations being increased and heightened by the apostacy of others), than them that fell the day and hour before; neither could that falling away of any be said to raise a scruple in them that they might do so too, if this were one part of their creed, that all and every man in the world might so do.

The answer given by the apostle, is no doubt suited to the objection, and fitted to the removal of the scruple mentioned, which was alone to be accomplished by an effectual removing away the solicitous fears and cares about the preservation of them, in whose behalf this is produced. This, therefore, the apostle doth by an exception to the inference which they made, or through temptation might make, upon the former considerations. Μέν τοι are exceptive particles, and an induction into the exemption of some from the condition of being in danger of falling, wherein they were concluded in the objection proposed. The intendment, I say, of the apostle in that exceptive plea he puts in, 'nevertheless,' is evidently to exempt some from the state of falling away, which might be argued against them from the defection of others. Neither doth he speak to the thing in hand, nor are the particulars mentioned exceptive to the former intimation, if his speech look any other way. Moreover, he gives yet farther the account of this exception he makes, including a radical discrimination of professors, or men esteemed to be believers, expressing also the principle and ground of that difference. The differing principle he mentioneth, is, the foundation of God that stands sure, or the firm foundation of God that is established, or stands firm: this is not worth contending about. An expression parallel to that of the same apostle, Rom. ix. 11. 'That the purpose of God according to election might stand;' both this and that hold out some eternal act of God, differencing between persons, as to their everlasting condition. As if the apostle had said, you see indeed that Hymeneus and Philetus are fallen away, and that others, with whom you sometimes walked in the communion and outward fellowship of the gospel, and took sweet counsel together in the house of God with them, are gone after them; yet be you (true believers) of good comfort; God hath laid a foundation (which must be some eternal act of his, concerning them of whom he is about to speak: or the solemn assertion of the apostle, than which you shall not easily meet with one more weighty, is neither to the case nor matter in hand) which is firm and abiding (being the good pleasure of his will, accompanied with an act of his wisdom and understanding), appointing some (as is the case of all true believers) to be his, who shall be exempted on that account, from the apostacy and desertion that you fear. This, saith the apostle, is the fountain and spring of the difference, which is among them that profess the gospel. Concerning some of them, is the purpose of God for their preservation. 'They are ordained to eternal life.' And, herein, as was said, lies the concernment of all that are true believers, who are all his, chosen of him, given to his Son, and called according to his purpose: with others it is not so, they are not built on that bottom, they have no such foundation of their profession; and it is not therefore marvellous, if they fall.

The words, then, contain an exception of true believers from the danger of total apostacy, upon the account of the stable, fixed, eternal purpose of God concerning their salvation, answerable to that of Rom. viii. 28—30. the place last considered. The foundation here mentioned, is the good pleasure of the will of God, which he had purposed in himself, or determined to exert towards them, for the praise of the glory of his grace; Eph. i. 9. According to which purpose we are predestinated; ver. 11. And he calls' this purpose the foundation of God, as being a groundwork and bottom of the thing, whereof the apostle is treating; namely, the preservation and perseverance of true believers, those who are indeed planted into Christ, notwithstanding the apostacy of the most glorious professors, who being not within the compass of that purpose, nor built on that foundation, never attain that peculiar grace, which by Jesus Christ is to them administered, who have that privilege. And this farther appears by the confirmation of the certainty of this foundation of God, which he hath laid, manifested in the next words: 'It hath this seal, The Lord knows who are his.' Whether ye will take this for a demonstration of the former assertion, either *a posteriori*, from the peculiar love, favour, tenderness, and care, which the Lord bears to them which are his, who are built on the foundation mentioned; whereby, in the pursuit of his eternal purpose, he will certainly preserve them from perishing; knowing, owning, and taking care of them in every condition : or for the prescience of God, accomplishing his eternal purpose, designing them of whom he speaks, as his (for his they were, and he gave them unto Christ), is to me indifferent. Evident it is that this confirmation of the purpose mentioned, is added to assure us of the stability and accomplishment of it : in that none, who are built thereon, or concerned therein, shall fall away. And, herein, doth the apostle fully answer and remove the forementioned objection. Let men, saith he, appear never so eminent in profession, if once they prove apostates, they manifest themselves to have been but hypocrites ; that is, such as never had any of the faith of God's elect, which is their peculiar, who are ordained to eternal life.

This then, beyond all colourable exception, is the intendment of the apostle in the words under consideration ; though many professors fall away, yet you, that are true believers, be not shaken in your confidence, for God hath laid the foundation of your preservation in his eternal purpose, whereby you are designed to life and salvation, and by the fruits whereof, you are discriminated from the best of them, that fall away : only continue in the use of means, let every one of ye depart from iniquity, and keep up to that universal holiness, whereunto also ye are appointed and chosen. And this is the whole of what we desire demonstration of : neither will less in any measure, answer the objection, or remove the scruple, at first proposed.

But it seems, we are all this while besides the intendment of the apostle, whose resolution of the objection mentioned, is quite of another nature, than what we have hitherto insisted on ; which Mr. Goodwin thus represents : page 359. cap. 14. sect. 14.

' To this objection or scruple, the apostle (in the words now in hand) answereth, to this effect ; that notwithstanding the falling away of men, whoever, or how many soever, they be, yet the glorious gospel, and truth of God therein, stands and always hath stood, firm and steadfast. Which gospel hath the matter and substance of this saying in it, as a seal for the establishment of those who are upright in the sight of God ; viz.

' The Lord knoweth, that is, takes special notice of, approveth, and delighteth in those that are his ; that is, who truly

believe in him, love and serve him : yea, and farther hath
this item, tending to the same end; let every one that calleth
upon the name of Christ, that is, makes profession of his
name, depart from iniquity: so that in this answer to the
scruple mentioned, the apostle intimateth by way of satisfaction, that the reason, why men fall away from the faith, is
partly because they do not consider, what worthy respects
God beareth to those, who cleave to him in faith and love :
partly also because they degenerate into loose and sinful
courses, contrary to the law imposed by the gospel, and consequently, that there is no such danger of their falling away,
who shall duly consider the one, and observe the other, in-
serting the stability of the truth of God, in the gospel, by
the way of antidote against the fears of those, that might
possibly suspect it, because of the defections of others from
it : he doth but tread in his own footsteps, elsewhere in this
very chapter, 'if we believe not, yet he abideth faithful, and
cannot deny himself.''

Ans. If that necessity were not voluntarily chosen, which
enforceth men to wrest and pervert the word of God, not
only to mistaken, but strange, uncouth, and inconsistent
senses, their so doing might perhaps seem not to be altogether without colour and pretext : but when they willingly embrace those paths, which will undoubtedly lead
them into the briers, and contrary to abundance of light
and evidence of truth, embrace those persuasions, which ne-
cessitate them to such courses, I know not what cloak they
have left for their deviations.   An example of this we have
before us in the words recited ; a sense is violently pinned
upon the apostle's words, not only alien, foreign to the scope
of the place, and genuine signification of the words themselves, but wholly unsuited for any serviceableness to the
end, for which the author of this gloss himself confesseth
these expressions of the apostle to be produced and used.

.   The sum of Mr. Goodwin's exposition of this place, is
this: The foundation of God, is the gospel or the doctrine of
it: its standing, or standing sure, the certain truth of the
gospel: the seal mentioned, is the substance or matter of
that saying, God knows who are his, contained in the gospel ; and the answer to the objection or scruple, lies in this,
that the reason why men fall from the gospel (which neither

is, nor was the scruple, nor was it so proposed by Mr. Good-win), is, because they consider not the love that God bears to believers, that is, that he approves them, whilst they are such ; which is indeed one main part of the gospel. So that men fall from the gospel, because they fall from the gospel, and this must satisfy the scruple proposed. It is an easy thing for men of ability and eloquence, to gild over the most absurd and inconsistent interpretation of Scripture, with some appearance of significancy : though I must needs say, I know not lightly, when, nor by whom, pretending to any sobriety, it hath been more unhappily or unsuccessfully at-tempted than by Mr. Goodwin in this place, as upon due consideration will be made farther appear.   For,

First, To grant that the foundation of God may be said so far to be the gospel because his eternal purpose, so ex-pressed, is therein revealed, which is the interpretation Mr. Goodwin proposeth ; I ask,

1. Whether the apostle applies himself to remove the scruple ingenerated in the minds of believers, about their own falling away, upon consideration of the apostacy of others, and to answer the objection arising thereupon? This Mr. Goodwin grants in the head, though in the branches of his discourse, he cast in inquiries quite of another nature ; as, that a reason is inquired after, why men fall from the gospel, and a suspicion is supposed to arise of the truth of the gospel, because some fell from it : things that have not the least intimation in the words, or context of the place, nor of any such evidence for their interest in the business in hand, that Mr. Goodwin durst take them for ingredients in the case under consideration, when he himself proposed it; so that he was enforced to foist in this counterfeit case, to give some colour to the interpretation of the words intro-duced.   But yet this must not be openly owned, but inter-mixed with other discourses, to lead aside the understanding of the reader from bearing in mind the true state of the case by the apostle proposed, and by himself acknowledged: so that this discourse ' desinet in piscem,' &c.

2. The case being supposed as above, I ask, whether the apostle intended a removal of the scruple, and answer to the objection, as far, at least, as the one was capable of being re-moved, and the other of being answered? This, I suppose,

will not be scrupled, or objected against, being indeed fully granted 'in stating the occasion of the words. For we must at least allow the Holy Ghost to speak pertinently to what he doth propose ; then,

. 3. I farther inquire, whether any thing whatever be in the least suited to the removal of the scruple and objection proposed, but only the giving of the scruplers and objectors the best assurance that upon solid grounds and foundations could be given, or they were in truth capable of, that what they feared should not come upon them ; and that, notwithstanding the deviation of others, themselves should be preserved ; and then,

4. Seeing that the sum of the sense of the words given by Mr. Goodwin amounts to these two assertions : 1. That the doctrine of the gospel is true and permanent ; 2. That God approves for the present all, who for the present believe, supposing that there is nothing in the gospel, teaching the perseverance of the saints ; I ask yet, whether there be any thing in this answer of the apostle (so interpreted), able to give the least satisfaction imaginable to the consciences and hearts of men making the objection mentioned ? For is it not evident, notwithstanding any thing here expressed, that they and every believer in the world may apostatize, and fall away into hell ? Say the poor believers, Such and such fall away from the faith : their eminent usefulness in their profession, beyond perhaps what we are able to demonstrate of ourselves, makes us fear, that this abominable defection may go on, and swallow us up, and grow upon the church to a farther desolation. The answer is : However, the gospel is true, and God bears gracious respects to them that cleave to him in love, whilst they do so. ' Quæstio est de aliis, responsio de cepis.' Methinks the apostle might have put them upon these considerations, which Mr. Goodwin proposes, as of excellent use and prevalency against falling away, that they put men out of danger of it (cap, 9.), rather than have given them an answer not in the least tending to their satisfaction, nor any way suited to their fears or inquiries ; no not, as backed with that explanation, that they fall away because they degenerate into loose and sinful courses ; that is, because they fall away. A degeneracy into loose and sinful courses amounts surely to no less.

5. Again, I would know whether this foundation of God be an act of his will commanding, or purposing? declarative of our duty, or his intention? If the first, then what occasion is administered to make mention of it in this place? Whether it were called in question or no? and whether the assertion of it conduces to the solution of the objection proposed? Or is it in any parallel terms expressed in any other place? Besides, seeing this foundation of God is in nature antecedent to the sealing mentioned, of God's knowing them that are his, and the object of the act of God's will, be it what it will, being the persons concerning whom that sealing is; whether it can be any thing but some distinguishing purpose of God concerning those persons, in reference to the things spoken of? Evident then it is, from the words themselves, the occasion of them, the design, and scope of the apostle in the place, that the foundation of God here mentioned, is his discriminating purpose concerning some men's certain preservation unto salvation, which is manifestly confirmed by that seal of his, that he knows them, in a peculiar distinguishing manner; a manner of speech and expression suited directly to what the same apostle useth in the same case every where; as Rom. viii. 28—30. ix. xi. 11. Eph. i. 4—6.

'But' (saith Mr. Goodwin) 'this is no more, than what the apostle elsewhere speaks, Rom. iii. 3. 'What if some did not believe, shall their unbelief make the faith of God of none effect?' that is, shall the unbelief of men be interpreted as any tolerable argument, or ground, to prove that God is unfaithful? or that he hath no other faith in him, than that which sometimes miscarrieth, and produceth not that for which it stands engaged? Implying that such an interpretation as this, is unreasonable in the highest.'

But truly by the way, if it be so, I know not who in the lowest can quit Mr. Goodwin from unreasonableness in the highest: for doth he not contend in this whole discourse, that the faith of God in his promises, for the producing of that, for which it stands engaged (as when he saith to believers, he will 'never leave them, nor forsake them') doth so depend on the faith of men, as to the event intended, that it is very frequently by their unbelief, rendered of none effect? Is not this the spirit that animates the whole re-

ligion of the apostacy of saints? Is not the great contest
between us, whether any unbelief of men may interpose to
render the faith of God of none effect, as to the producing of
the thing he promiseth? 'Tibi, quia intristi, exedendum est.'

But, 2. Let it be granted, that these two places of the
apostle are of a parallel signification, what will it advantage
the interpretation imposed on us? What is the faith of God
here intended? and what the unbelief mentioned? and
whereunto tends the apostle's vehement interrogation? The
great contest in this epistle concerning the Jews (of whom
he peculiarly speaks, ver. 1, 2.), was about the promise of
God made to them, and his faithfulness therein. Evident it
was, that many of them did not believe the gospel; as evident, that the promise of God was made peculiarly to them,
to Abraham and his seed: hence no small perplexity arose,
about the reconciliation of these things; many perplexed
thoughts ensuing on this seeming contradiction. If the
gospel be, indeed, the way of God, what is become of his
faithfulness in his promises to Abraham and his seed, they
rejecting it? If the promises be true and stable, what shall
we say to the doctrine of the gospel, which they generally
disbelieve and reject? In this place the apostle only rejects
the inference, that the faithfulness of God must fall, and be
of none effect, because the Jews believed not; whereof he
gives a full account afterward, when he expressly takes up
the objection, and handles it at large; chap. ix—xi. The sum
of the answer he there gives, as a defensative of the faithfulness of God, with a *non obstante* to the infidelity of some of
the Jews, amounts to no more, nor less, than what is here
argued, and by us asserted, viz. that notwithstanding this
(their incredulity and rejection of the gospel)'the foundation
of God standeth sure; God knoweth who are his:' that the
promise, his faithfulness wherein (came under- debate), was
not made to all the Jews, but to them that were chosen according to his purpose, as he expressly disputes it at large
beyond all possibility of contradiction, chap. xi. as shall
afterward be farther argued, and hath in part been already
discovered. I verily believe never did any man produce a
testimony more to the disadvantage of his own cause both
in general, and in particular, than this is to the cause Mr.
Goodwin hath in hand.

Neither doth he advance one step farther in the confirmation of the sense imposed on the apostle's words, by comparing them with the words of the same apostle, ver. 13. of the same chapter, 'If we believe not, yet he continues faithful, he cannot deny himself:' wherein again, contrary to the whole drift of Mr. Goodwin's discourse, the faithfulness of God, in the accomplishment of his promises, is asserted to be wholly independent upon any qualification whatever in them, to whom those promises are made. Though we are under sufferings, temptations, and trials, very apt to be cast down from our hope of the great things that God hath prepared for us, and promised to us, yet his purpose shall stand, however, and our unbelief shall not in the least cause him to withdraw, or not to go through with his engagement to the utmost: the faithfulness of his own nature requireth it at his hand : ' he cannot deny himself.'

What remains, sect. 14. wherein he labours farther to give strength unto, or rather more largely to explicate, what he formerly asserted, is built upon a critical consideration of the word θεμέλιος, which (without any one example produced from any approved author), we must believe to signify a bond, or instrument of security, given between men by the way of contract. And what then, suppose it do? Why then, contrary to the whole scope of the place, and constant signification of the word in the Scripture, it must be interpreted according to the analogy of that sense. Why so? Doth it remove any difficulty on the other hand? Doth it more suit the objection for its removal, whereunto it is given, that we should warp from the first, genuine, native, usual signification of the word, to that which is exotic and metaphorical? Yea, but we are enforced to embrace this sense, because that here is a seal set to this foundation, and men use not to set seals to the foundation of a house. And is it required that allusions should hold in all particulars and circumstances, even in such as wherein their teaching property doth not consist? The terms of foundation and sealing are both figurative: neither will either of them absolutely be squared to those things in nature, wherein they have their foundation. The purpose of God is here called his foundation, because of its stability, abidingness, strength, and use in bearing up the whole fabric of the salvation of believers, not in respect of its lying in, or under the ground, or being made of wood or stone. And in this sense why may it not be said to be sealed? Spiritual sealing holds out two things: confirmation, and conforming by impression: and in them consist the chief political use of the word and thing, not in being a label annexed to a writing. And why may not a purpose be confirmed, or be manifested to be firm, as well as a contract, or instrument in law? Having also its conforming virtue and efficacy (which is the natural effect of sealing) to implant the image in the seal, on the things impressed with it, in rendering them, concerning whom the the purpose of God is, answerable to the image of his Son (in whom the purpose is made), and that pattern which he hath chosen them to, and appointed them for. What followeth to the end of this section, is but a new expression of what Mr. Goodwin pretends to be the sense of this place. The foundation of God is the gospel, or the promise of God to save believers: the seal is his taking notice of them to save them, and to condemn them that believe not: and, therefore, questionless believers need not fear that they shall fall away, though there be not the least intimation made of any thing, that should give them the least comfortable or cheering security of preservation in believing: only it is said, ' He that believeth shall be saved' (which yet is not an absolute promise of salvation to believers), ' and he that believeth not shall be damned:' which one disjunctive proposition, declarative of the connexion that is between the means and the end, Mr. Goodwin labours to make comprehensive of all the purposes of God concerning believers, it being such as wherein no one person in the world is more concerned than another. If the foundation here mentioned be only God's purpose (or rather declaration) of his will for the saving of believers, and the damning of unbelievers, what consolation could be from hence administered in particular unto persons labouring under the scruple mentioned formerly, hath not as yet been declared. Let us then proceed to farther proof of the truth in hand, and the vindication of some other places of Scripture whereby it is confirmed.

That which I shall next fix upon, is that eminent place of John vi. 37—40. ' All that the Father giveth me, shall

come to me, and him that cometh to me, I will in nowise
cast out: for I came down from heaven, not to do mine own
will, but the will of him that sent me ; and this is the Father's will which hath sent me, that of all which he hath
given me, I should lose nothing, but should raise it up again
at the last day: and this is the will of him that sent me,
that every one which seeth the Son, and believeth on him,
may have everlasting life, and I will raise him up at the last
day.' Our Saviour acquaints us with the design, wherewith he came from heaven ; it was not to do his own will,
that is, to accomplish or bring about, any private purposes
of his own, distinct or different from them of his Father, as
he was blasphemously charged by the Jews to do : but he
came to do the will of God, ' the will of him that sent him.'
The will of God which Christ came to fulfil, is sometimes
taken for the commandment, which he received from the
Father, for the accomplishment of his will. So Heb. x. 9.
' I come to do thy will, O God :' that is, to fulfil thy command ; as it is expressed, Psal. xl. 8. ' Thy law is written in
my heart :' thy law! all that thou requirest at my hand, as
Mediator, I am ready to perform. On this account is Christ
said to take on him the ' form of a servant ;' Phil. ii. 7. that
is, to become so indeed in the assumption of his human
nature, that he might do the will of him that sent him. For
which reason also his Father expressly calls him his servant ;
Isa. xlii. 1. " Behold my servant, whom I uphold, mine elect
in whom my soul delighteth ; I have put my Spirit upon him,
he shall bring forth judgment to the Gentiles :' he is the
servant of the Father, in the accomplishment of that work,
for which the Spirit was put upon him ; and ver. 19. ' Who
is blind but my servant, or deaf as my messenger that I sent ;
who is blind as he that is perfect, and blind as the Lord's
servant.' God gives him in command to fulfil his will,
which accordingly he performs to the utmost. Again, the
will of God is taken for his purpose, his design, decree, and
good pleasure, for the fulfilling and accomplishment whereof the Lord Christ came into the world ; and this appears to
be the sense and importance of the word in this place, from
the distinction which is put between the will of the Father,
and any such private will of Christ, as the Jews thought he
went about to establish ; it was some design of his own ; in

opposition whereunto, he tells them, that he came to do the
will, that is, to fulfil the counsel, purpose, and design of the
Father. However, should it principally be taken for the command of God, yet there is, and must needs be, a universal coincidence and oneness in the object of God's purposing and commanding will in all commands given unto Christ: because all
of them shall certainly and infallibly by him be fulfilled, and
so the thing certainly accomplished which is commanded.
What now is the will, purpose, aim, design, and command,
of the Father, whose execution and accomplishment is committed to the Lord Christ, and which he faithfully undertakes to perform (as he was faithful in all things to him that
appointed him), for the clearing of this let these two things
be observed : 1. Who the persons are concerning whom this
will of God is ; and those he describes by a double character. 1. From their election : the Father's giving them to him ;
' all which he hath given me,' that is, all his elect, as our
Saviour expounds this very expression, John xvii. 16. ' Thine
they were, and thou gavest them to me :' thine they were in
eternal designation, thou having ' chosen them from the
foundation of the world,' and thou gavest them to me for
actual redemption, to deliver them from every thing that
keeps them at a distance from thee. 2. From their faith or
believing, which he calls, ' seeing the Son and believing on
him ;' ver. 40. The persons then here designed, are elect believers, persons chosen, and called of God. What next
then is the will of God concerning them? This also is set out
both in general and in some particulars : (1.) In general,
that none of them be lost: that by no means whatsoever,
by no temptations of Satan, deceits of sin, fury of oppres-
sors, weakness or decay of faith, they perish and fall away
from him. This is the will, the design and purpose of God;
this he gives to Jesus Christ in command for to accomplish.
(2.) In particular, 1. That they might have eternal life;
ver. 40. that they be preserved to the enjoyment of that
glory whereunto they are designed. 2. That they may be
' raised up at the last day,' and so never be lost, neither as
to their being, nor well-being of these two ; ver. 40. Everlasting life is placed before the resurrection or raising of
believers at the last day, plainly intimating, that the spiritual life whereof in this world we are partakers, is also as to

its certain uninterruptible continuance, an everlasting life that shall never be intercepted or cut off. That then which from this portion of Scripture I argue is this: God having purposed to give eternal life to his elect believers, and that none of them should ever be lost, and having committed the accomplishing and performance of this his good-will and pleasure unto the Lord Jesus, who was faithful unto him in all things, and endued with power (all power from above), for that end, they shall certainly be preserved to the end designed. The favour and love of God in Christ, shall never be turned away from them, for his ' counsel shall stand, and he will do all his pleasure.'

Something is by Mr. Goodwin offered to take off the strength of this testimony, but yet so little, that had I not resolved to hear him out to the utmost, what he can say in and unto the case in hand, it would scarce be thought needful to divert to the consideration of it. This place of Scripture he binds up in one bundle, with nine or ten others, to the composure of one argument which (almost *uno halitu*) he blows away, chap. 11. sect. 36, 37, &c. pp. 251, 252, &c. To the consideration of the argument itself there by him proposed, I am not yet arrived; the influence of this text into it, is from what is said of Christ's preserving believers: my present consideration is chiefly of the will and intention of the Father's giving them to him to be preserved: so that I shall observe only one or two things to his general answer, and then proceed to the vindication of this particular place we have in hand.

First, He tells you, 'That the conclusion of the former argument, that true believers shall never miscarry or fall away, opposeth not his sense in this controversy.' Whether it oppose his sense or no, must be judged, this I know, that he hath to his utmost opposed it all this while, shewing himself therein very uncourteous and unkind; but why so, on what account is it, that this conclusion which hath so much opposed, is now conceited not to oppose him? ' Those who thus fall away,' saith he, 'are no true believers but wicked apostates, at the time of their falling away.' That the conclusion mentioned opposeth his sense to me is evident; but that it is sense wherewith in this place he opposeth the conclusion, is not so clear. The question is, who fall away;

not believers but apostates, saith **Mr. G.** We say so too, in the natural first sense of those words who *eventualiter* are apostates, were never *antecedenter* (to their apostacy) true believers. But this is not your sense doubtless; that those who fall away, in their falling away (which is the sense of that clause, at the time of falling away) were apostates, that is, were fallen away, before they fell away, is neither our sense nor yours, for it is none at all. Bertius, hath one argument against the perseverance of the saints, from the impossibility of finding a subject to be affected with the notion of apostacy, if true believers be exempted from it. For hypocrites, saith he, cannot fall away; nor can believers, saith Mr. Goodwin; but they are apostates when they fall away: that is, it is a dead man that dies; or after he is dead he dies: after he is an apostate he falls away. Perhaps it would be worth our serious inquiry, to consider how believers can indeed possibly come to lose the Spirit of grace which dwells in them, with their habit of faith and holiness. For our parts, we contend that they have an infused habit of grace, and that wrought with a mighty impression upon their minds and hearts (faith being of the operation of God, wrought by the exceeding greatness of his power, as he wrought in Christ when he raised him from the dead). Whether such a habit can be removed, but by that hand that bestowed it, and whether it may be made appear, that God will on any occasion so take it away, or hath expressed himself that he will so deal with any of his children, is, I say, worthy our inquiry. But,

· Secondly, He denies the major proposition, and saith, 'That those who are kept and preserved by Christ, may possibly miscarry.' Boldly ventured! What want is there then, or defect, in the keeper of Israel, that his flock should so miscarry under his hand? Is it of faithfulness? The Scripture tells us, he is ' a faithful high-priest in things pertaining to God;' Heb. ii. 17. ' Faithful to him that appointed him;' Heb. iii. 2. And that he did the whole will of God. Is it of tenderness, to take care of his poor wandering ones? He is otherwise represented unto us, Heb. ii. 18. ' For in that he himself hath suffered being tempted, he is able to succour them that are tempted;' and (chap. iv. 15, 16.) ' we have not a high-priest, which cannot be touched with the feeling of our infirmities, but was in all points tempted like unto us, yet without sin;' Isa. xl. 11, 12. It is said of him, 'He shall feed his flock like a shepherd, he gathers the lambs with his arms, and carries them in his bosom, and shall gently lead them that are with young.' And he quarrels with those shepherds, who manifest not a care and tenderness like his, towards his flock. Ezek. xxxiv. 4. 'The diseased have ye not strengthened, neither have ye healed that which was sick, neither have ye bound up that which was broken, neither have ye brought again that which was driven away, neither have ye sought that which was lost;' all which he takes upon himself to perform; ver. 15, 16. Or is it want of power ? ' All power is given to him in heaven and earth;' Matt. xxviii. 8. ' All things are delivered to him of his Father;' Matt. xi. 27. ' He is able to save to the utmost them that come to God by him,' Heb. vii. 25. If he wants neither care nor tenderness, wisdom nor watchfulness, love nor ability, will nor faithfulness, how comes it to pass that they miscarry, and fall away into ruin, whom he hath undertaken to keep? David durst fight with a lion and a bear in the defence of his lambs; and Jacob endured heat and cold, upon the account of faithfulness. And shall we think that the Shepherd of Israel, from whose being so the psalmist concludes he shall want nothing (Psal. xxiii. 1.); who did not only fight for his flock, but laid down his life for them, will be less careful of his Father's sheep, his own sheep, which are required also at his hand, for his Father knows them, and calls them all by name ?

'Yea, but (says Mr. Goodwin), it may be thus, in case themselves shall not comport with Christ in his act of preserving them, with their care and diligence in preserving themselves.' That is, Christ will surely keep them, in case they keep themselves. Alas! poor sheep of God! If this were the case of the flocks of the sons of men, how quickly would they be utterly destroyed? Doth the veriest hireling in the world deal thus with his sheep? keep them, in case they keep themselves? Nay, to what end is his keeping, if they keep themselves? Christ compares himself to the good Shepherd, which seeketh out, and fetcheth a wandering sheep from the wilderness, laying him on his shoulders, and bringing it home to his fold. How did that poor sheep keep itself when it ran among the ravenous wolves in the wilderness? Yet by the good Shepherd it was preserved. This is the spirit and comforting genius of this doctrine. Christ keeps us, provided we keep ourselves. We hoped 'it had been he who saved Israel :' that he gave us his Holy Spirit to abide with us for ever, to seal us up to the day of redemption : that knowing himself, and telling us that without him we can do nothing, he would not suspend his doing, upon our doing so great a thing, as preserving ourselves? For let us see now, what it is that is required in us, if we shall be preserved by Christ: it is to comport with him in his act of preserving us, and to be diligent to keep ourselves.

What is this, comporting with him in his act of preserving us? Our comporting with Christ in any thing, is by our believing in him, and on him: that is our radical comportment, whence all other closings of heart in obedience do flow; so then, Christ will preserve us in believing, provided we continue to believe. But what need of his help to do so, if antecedently thereunto so we do? Is not this not only ἄγραφον, but also ἄλογον, not only unscriptural, but also unreasonable; yea, absurd and ludicrous. This is the flinty fountain of all that abundance of consolation, which Mr. Goodwin's doctrine doth afford. Doubtless they must be wise and learned men (like himself) who can extract any such thing therefrom. Let him go with it to a poor, weak, tempted, fainting believer, and try what a comforter he will be thought, a physician of what value he will be esteemed. Let him tell him, Thou art indeed weak in faith, ready to decay and perish, which thou mayest do every day, there being neither purpose nor promise of God to the contrary; great oppositions and great temptations hast thou to wrestle withal, but yet Christ is loving, tender, faithful, and in case thou continuest believing, he will take care thou shalt believe. That Christ will increase thy faith, and keep it alive by continual influences, as from a head into its members, preserving thee not only against outward enemies, but the treacheries, and deceits, and unbelief of thine own heart, of any such thing I can give thee no account. Such consolation a poor man may have at home at any time.

Farther, what is that act of Christ in preserving them

that is to be comported withal? Wherein doth it consist?
Is it not in his[p] daily continual communication to them of
new supplies of that spiritual life whose springs are in
him? The making out from his own fulness unto them?
His performing the office of a head to its members, and filling those other relations wherein he stands, working in them
both to will and to do of his own good pleasure? What is it
then to comport with this act, or these acts of Christ? Can
any thing reasonable be invented, wherein such comportment may be thought to consist, but either it will be found
coincident with that, whereof it is a condition, or appear to
be such as will crush the whole undertaking of Christ for
the preservation of believers into vanity and nothing?
Again, hath Christ undertaken to preserve us against all[q]
our enemies, or some only? If some only, give us an account
both of them, that he doth undertake against, that we may
know for what to go to him, whereof to complain; and of
them, that he doth not so undertake, to safeguard us against
them, that we may know, wherein to trust to ourselves? And
let us see the places of Scripture, wherein any enemies[r] are
excepted out of this undertaking of Christ for the safety of
his? Paul goes far in an enumeration of particulars; Rom. viii.
If he hath undertaken against them all, then let us know,
whether it be an enemy that keeps us from this comportment
with Christ or a friend? If it be an enemy (as surely every
thing in us that moves us to depart from the living God is),
hath Christ undertaken against it or no. If not, how hath
he undertaken against them all? If he hath, how is it that
it prevails? Yea, but he undertakes this in case we comport
with him; that is, he undertakes to overcome such an enemy,
in case there be no such enemy.   In case we be not turned
aside from comporting with him, he will destroy that enemy
that turns us aside from comporting with him. 'Egregiam
vero laudem et spolia ampla.' Or on the other side, if our
enemies prevail not against us, he hath faithfully undertaken
that they shall not prevail against us.

  'Yea, but (saith Mr. Goodwin) no Scripture proves that
those, whom Christ preserves, must by any compulsory,
necessitating power, use their diligence in preserving them-

[p] John i. 16. 1 Cor. xii 13. Eph. i. 23. ii, 21, 22 iv. 15, 16. Gal. ii 20 Col.
i. 17—19, ii. 19.   [q] Heb. vii. 15.   [r] John xv. 5. Isa. xxx. 1.

selves.' And who, I pray, ever said they did? Compulsory actings of grace are your own figment; so are all such necessitating acts, which proceed any farther, than only as to the infallibility of the event aimed at. God doth not compel the wills of men, when he works in them to* will. Christ doth not compel men to care and diligence, when he works in them holy care and diligence; when the disciples prayed, ' Lord, increase our faith,' they did not pray that they might be compelled to believe. God's working in them that believe, according[t] ' to the exceeding greatness of his power, strengthening them with all might, according to his glorious power, unto all patience and long-suffering with joyfulness,' is very far from any compulsion or necessitation, inconsistent with the most absolute freedom, that a creature is capable of. He that works faith in believers, can [u]continue it and increase it in them, without compulsion. And this is the sum of Mr Goodwin's answer to an argument that, notwithstanding all which he hath spoken, hath yet strength enough left to cast his whole building down to the ground. What he farther speaks to the particular place, which gave occasion to this discourse, may briefly be considered.

1. He speaks something to ver. 37. which I insisted not on. As to the purpose in hand, he tells you that ' Christ will in nowise cast out τὸν ἐρχόμενον, ' him that is coming;' but yet he that is coming on his way, may turn back and never come fully up to him.'

Ans. But if this be not 'huckstering of the word of God, I know not what is. The words before in the same verse are, ' All that the Father giveth me, shall come to me;' saith Mr. Goodwin, they may come but half way, and so turn back again, not coming fully home to him. Saith Christ, 'They shall come to me.' Saith Mr. Goodwin, ' They may perhaps come but half way.' ' Nunc satis est dixisse, ego mira poemata pango.' But why so? Why, ἐρχόμενον is ' coming,' a coming it seems in *fieri*, but not in *facto esse;* that is, it denotes a tract of time, whilst the man is travelling his journey. As though believing, were a successive motion, as to the act of laying hold on Christ. But is he that is on his way, that Christ receiveth, a believer or not? Hath he faith or not?

---

* John viii. 33. Rom vi 18. Luke xvii. 5.   [t] Col. i. 11, 12.
[u] Eph. ii. 8.   x 2 Cor. ii. 17.

If he hath no faith, the faith whereof we speak, how can he be said to be coming,[y] ' seeing the wrath of God abideth on him?' If he hath faith, how is it that he is not come to Christ? Hath any one true faith at a distance from him? God gives another testimony; John i. 11, 12. But, saith he, ' there is nothing in the words, that they are under no possibility of falling away, who come to Christ.' But, 1. There is in those that follow, that (as to the event) they are under an impossibility of so doing, in respect of the will and purpose of God (which sufficeth me); as shall be made to appear. 2. That emphatical expression οὐ μὴ ἐκβάλω ἔξω, ' I will in nowise cast them out,' expresses so much care and tenderness in Christ towards them, that we are very apt to hope and believe, that he will not lose them any more; but that he will not only not cast them out, but also, according to his Father's appointment, that he will keep them, and preserve them in safety, until he bring them to glory, as is fully asserted, ver. 39, 40. as hath been declared. Again, Mr. Goodwin tells you, It is not spoken of losing believers by defection of faith, but by death: and to assure believers of this, Christ tells them, It is his Father's will, that he should raise them up at the last day. Besides, if any be lost by defection from faith, this cannot be imputed to Christ, who did his Father's pleasure to the utmost for their preservation; but to themselves.'

Ans. For the perverting of ver. 37. the beginning of it was left out; and for the accomplishing of the like designs upon ver. 39, 40. (which farther clears the mind and intendment of Christ in the words), is omitted. He tells you, that it is the will of the Father, that every one that comes to him, that is, that believes on him, have everlasting life. What is everlasting life in the gospel, is well known from John xvii. 3. and unto this bestowing on them everlasting life, his raising of them at the last day (as was mentioned), is a necessary consequent; namely, that they may be brought to the full and complete fruition of that life, which here in some measure they are made partakers of. Even in the words of ver. 39. that passage, ' I should lose nothing,' extends itself to the whole compass of our Saviour's duty, in reference to his Father's will, for the safeguarding of believers: and is it only death, and the

state of dissolution of body and soul, that it is the will of
God that he should deliver them from? and the power of
that, that it should not have dominion over them in the morning? The apostle tells us that he came to do 'the will of
God, whereby we are sanctified;' Heb. x. 9, 10. It was the
will of God, that he should sanctify us : and he tells his
Father, that he had 'kept all his own in the world;' John
xvii. which doubtless was not his raising them from the dead.
If he be the Mediator of the covenant of grace, if the promises of God be yea and amen in him, if he be our Head,
Husband, and elder Brother, our Advocate and Intercessor,
our Shepherd and Saviour, his keeping us from being lost
extends itself no less effectually to our preservation from
utter ruin in this life, than to our raising at the last day ;
yea, and that exceptive particle ἀλλὰ, includes this preservation, as well as leads us to the addition of the other
favour and privilege of being raised to glory at the last day.
In a word, this whole discourse is added to make good that
gracious promise of our Saviour, ver. 35. 'He that cometh to
me, shall never hunger: and he that believes on me, shall
never thirst;' which how it can be done by a naked engagement for the resurrection of them that come to him, and
abide with him, if many do, and most of all them that come
to him, may depart from him and fall into everlasting ruin,
needs Mr. Goodwin's farther labour and pains to unfold.
What is lastly added concerning Christ's doing the utmost
of his Father's pleasure for their custody, but the fault is
their own, who fall way, is the same inconsistent ridiculous
assertion with that erewhile considered! with this addition,
that whereas it is his Father's pleasure, that they be saved ;
Christ doth his pleasure to the utmost, and yet saved they
are not. And so much (if not too much) for the vindication
of this testimony witnessing to the truth that we have in hand.

Matt. xxiv. 24. comes in the next place to be considered
(an unquestionable evidence to the truth), and that voluntarily of its own accord, speaking so plain to the matter in
hand, that it were a sin against clear light to refuse to attend unto it; so far is it from being compelled to bear the
cross of this service, as Mr. Goodwin phrases the matter,
cap. 10. sect. 9. pp. 181—183. 'They shall seduce, if it were
possible, the very elect : hence (saith he) it is inferred, that

the deceiving or seducing of them that believe, is a thing impossible, which is the drawing of darkness out of light.' Strange! to me it seems so far from a forced inference, or a strained drawing of a conclusion, that it is but the conversion of the terms of the same identical supposition. He that says, they shall deceive the very elect, if it were possible, so mighty shall be their prevalency in seducing, seems to me (and would, I doubt not, do so to others, did not their prejudices and engagements force them to stop their ears, and shut their eyes) to say, that it is impossible the elect should be seduced.

But let the place (as it deserves) be more distinctly considered; it is among them, which I refer to the head of the purposes of God; and a purpose of God there is (though not expressed, yet) included in the words: the impossibility of the seduction of some persons from the faith, is here asserted. Whence doth this impossibility arise? Not from any thing in themselves, not from their own careful consideration of all the concernments of their condition, the only preservative in such a season, if some (who pretend themselves skilful and experienced, yea almost the only physicians of souls) may be believed. They can never stand upon such sands, against that opposition they shall be sure to meet withal. Our Saviour therefore intimates, whence the impossibility expressed doth flow, in a description of the persons, of whom it is affirmed, in reference to the purpose of God concerning them. They are the ' elect;' those whom God hath chosen [z] before the foundation of the world, that 'they should be holy and unblamable before him in love.' His purpose according to election must stand firm, and, therefore, the election itself shall obtain. This then is that, which is here affirmed; God having chosen some, or elected them to life, according to the ' [a] purpose which he purposed in himself,' and faith being bestowed on them, they believing on the account of their being ordained to eternal life, it is impossible they should be seduced, so as to be thrown down from that state and condition of acceptance with God (for the substance of it) wherein they stand.

Some few observations will farther clear the mind of the Holy Ghost, and obviate the exceptions that are put in

[z] Eph. i. 4. Rom. ix. 12. xi. 7.   [a] Eph. i. 9. Phil. i. 29 Acts xiii. 48.

against our receiving the words in their plain, proper, obvious signification ; observe then,

1. Upon the intimation of the great power and prevalency
of seducers, our Saviour adds this as a matter of great consolation to true and sound believers, that notwithstanding
all this, all their attempts however advantaged by force or
subtilty, yet they shall be preserved : this the whole context
enforceth us to receive, and our adversaries to confess, that
at least a great difficulty of their seduction is intimated.
And it arises with no less evidence, that this difficulty is distinguishing, in respect of the persons exposed to seduction ;
that some are elect, who should be seduced, if it were possible ;
others not, that may and shall be prevailed against.

2. The bottom of the consolation in the freedom of the
persons here spoken of, from falling under the prevailing
power of seducers, consists in this, that they are the elect
of God ; such, as in a personal consideration are chosen of
God from all eternity, to be kept and preserved by his power
to salvation, notwithstanding any interveniencies or oppositions, which he will suffer to lie in their way. 'But (saith
Mr. Goodwin) these men, at least before their calling, are as
liable to be deceived or seduced as other men : this is their
own confession, and Paul says, that they were sometimes
deceived ; Titus iii. 3.'

Ans. An exception doubtless unworthy him that makes
it, who, had he not resolved to say all, that ever had been
said by any, to the business in hand, would scarcely (I presume) have made use thereof; the seduction of persons is
not opposed to their election, but their believing. Mention
is made of their election, to distinguish them from those
other professors, which should be seduced : and to discover
the foundation of their stability under their trials, but it is
of them as believers (in which consideration the attempts of
seducers are advanced against them) that he speaks. It is
not the seducing of the elect, as elect ; but of believers,
who are elect, and because they are elected, that is denied.

3. That it is a seduction unto a total and final departure
from Christ and faith in him, whose impossibility, in respect
of the election, is here asserted. 'But (saith Mr. Goodwin,
cap. 10. sect. 16. p. 181.) this is to presume, not to argue,
or believe : for there is not the least ground in the word,

whereon to build such an interpretation.' But the truth is, without any presumption or much labour for proof, the falsity of this exception will quickly appear to any one that shall but view the context. It is evidently such a seduction, as they are exposed unto, and fall under, who endure not unto the end, that they may be saved; ver. 13. and they, who are excepted upon the account mentioned, are opposed to them, who being seduced, and their love being made cold, and their iniquities abounding, perish everlastingly; ver. 11, 12.

4. It is then a denial of their being cast out by the power of seducers, from their state and condition of believing, and acceptation with God, wherein they stand, that our Saviour here asserts and gives out to their consolation, they shall not be seduced, that is, drawn off from that state, wherein they are, to a state of unregeneracy, infidelity, and enmity to God, so that (as Mr. Goodwin observes in the next place) we deny them from hence, not only to be subject to a final, but also to a total seduction.

5. We grant, that notwithstanding the security given, which respects the state and condition of the persons spoken of, yet they may be, and often were seduced, and drawn aside into ways that are not right, into errors and false doctrines, through the 'cunning sleights of men, who lay in wait to deceive,' but never into such (as to any abode in them) which are inconsistent with the union with their head, and his life in them.

The errors and ways whereunto they are, or may be seduced, are either such, as though dangerous, yea in their consequences pernicious, yet have not such an aspect upon the faith of believers, as to deny a possibility of union, and holding the head upon other accounts; I doubt not but that men for a season may not know, may disbelieve, and deny some fundamental articles of Christian religion, and yet not be absolutely concluded not to hold the head by any sinew or ligament; to have no influence of life by any other means. Was it not so with the apostles, when they questioned the resurrection of Christ, and with the Corinthians, who denied the resurrection of the saints? An abode, I confess, in either of which errors would, when the consequences of them are manifested, prove pernicious to the

souls of men. But that they have in themselves such an
absolute repugnancy unto, and inconsistency with, the life
of Christ, however considered, as that their entertainment
for a season, should be immediately exclusive thereof, I suppose Mr. Goodwin himself will not say. In this sense then,
we grant that true, saving, justifying faith may consist with
the denial of some fundamental articles of Christian religion,
for a season; but that any true believer can persist in such
a heresy, we deny; he having the promise of the Spirit to
lead him into all necessary truth.

2. There are such ways and things, as in their own nature have an inconsistency with the life of Christ, as the abnegation of Christ himself; but this also we affirm to be
twofold, or to receive a twofold consideration: 1. It may be
resolved, upon consideration, with the deliberate consent of
the whole soul; which we utterly deny, that believers can,
or shall be left unto for a moment; or that ever any true
believer was so. 2. Such as may be squeezed out of the
mouths of men, by the surprisal of some great, dreadful,
and horrible temptation, without any habitual or cordial assent to any such abomination, or disaffection to Christ, or
resolute rebellion against him. Thus Peter fell into the abnegation of Christ, whose faith yet under it did not perish,
if our Saviour was heard in his prayer for him, having an
eye to that very temptation of his, wherein he was to be
tried, and his fall under it. In the first sense are those
words of our Saviour (Matt. x. 32.) to be understood, and
not in the latter. Christ was so far from denying Peter before his Father, under his abnegation of him, that he never
manifested more care and tenderness towards any believer,
than towards him in that condition. And this wholly removes Mr. Goodwin's tenth section out of our way, without
troubling of ourselves to hold up that distinction of a final
denial of Christ, and that not final; seeing in all probability he set it up himself, that he might have the honour to
cast it down.

What follows in Mr. Goodwin from the beginning of
sect. 11. cap. 10. to the end of sect. 17. is little more than a
translation of the remonstrants' sophistry, in vexing this text
in their Synodalia, which he knows full well where to find
discussed and removed. For the sake of our English

readers,' I shall not avoid the consideration of it. I affirm,
then : 1. That the phrase εἰ δυνατὸν here denotes the impossibility of the event denied. The manner of speech, circumstances of the place, with the aim of our Saviour in
speaking, exacting this sense of the words. The words are
ὥστε πλανῆσαι, εἰ δυνατὸν, καὶ τοὺς ἐκλεκτούς. It is the constant import of the word ὥστε to design the event of the
thing, which by what attends it, is asserted or denied ; so
Gal. ii. 13. Matt. viii. 28. xv. 31. 1 Thess. i. 8. Neither is
it ever used for ἵνα. In the place by some instanced for it,
Rom. vii. 6. it points clearly at the event: ἵνα is sometimes
put for it, but not on the contrary, and the words εἰ δυνατὸν,
though not so used always, (though sometimes they are ; as
Gal. iv. 15.) do signify at least a moral impossibility, when
they refer to the endeavours of men ; but relating to the
prediction of an event by God himself, they are equivalent
to an absolute negation of it ; that of Acts xx. 16. is urged
to the contrary. Paul hoped εἰ δυνατὸν, to be at Jerusalem
at the Pentecost. ‘ If it be possible,’ here, cannot imply an
impossibility as to the event, says Mr. G. But are these
places parallel ? Are all places, where the same phrase is
used, always to be expounded in the same sense ? The terms
here ‘ if it be possible,’ respect not the futurition of the
thing, but the uncertainty to Paul of its possibility or impossibility ; the uncertainty, I say, of Paul in his conjecture, whether he should get to Jerusalem by such a time or
no ; of which he was ignorant. Did our Saviour here conjecture about a thing, whereof he was ignorant whether it
would come to pass or no ? We say not then, that in this
place, where εἰ δυνατὸν is expressive of the uncertainty of
him that attempts any thing, of its event, that it affirms an
impossibility of it, and so to insinuate, that Paul made all
haste to do that, which he knew was impossible for him to
do ; but that the words are used in these two places in distinct senses, according to the enclosure that is made of
them by others ; but (saith Mr. Goodwin) to say, that Paul
might be ignorant whether his being at Jerusalem by Pentecost, might be possible or no, and that he only resolved to
make trial of the truth herein to the utmost, is to asperse
this great apostle with a ridiculous imputation of ignorance.
And why so, I pray you ? It is true ; he was a great apostle

indeed. But it was no part of his apostolical furnishment, to know in what space of time he might make a sea-voyage. Had Mr. Goodwin ever been at sea, he would not have thought it ridiculous ignorance, for a man to be uncertain, in what space of time he might sail from Miletus to Ptolemais. Paul had a short time to finish this voyage in. He was at Philippi at the days of unleavened bread, and afterward; ver. 6. thence he was five days sailing to Troas, ver. 6. and there he abode seven days more; it may well be supposed, that it cost him not less than seven days more to come to Miletus; ver. 13—15. how long he tarried there is uncertain : evident however it is, that there was a very small space of time left to get to Jerusalem by Pentecost. Paul was one that had met, not only with calms, and contrary winds, but' shipwreck also : so that he might well doubt, whether it were possible for him to make his voyage in that space of time, he had designed to do it in ; and this surely without the least disparagement to his apostolical knowledge and wisdom. In brief, when this phrase relates to the cares and desires of men, and unto any thing of their ignorance of the issue, it may design the uncertainty of the event, as in this place and that of Rom. xii. 18. But when it points at the event itself, it peremptorily designs its accomplishment or not, according to the tendency of the expression, which affirms or denies. Notwithstanding then all evasions, the simple, direct, and proper sense of our Saviour's words, who is setting forth and aggravating the prevalency of seducers in evil times, by him then foretold, is, that it shall be such, and so great, as that if it were not impossible upon the account of their election, they should prevail against the very elect themselves. But,

6. Suppose it be granted, that the words refer to the endeavours of the seducers in this place, yet they must needs deny their prevalency, as to the end aimed at: it is asserted, either to be possible, that the elect should be so seduced, or not : if not, we have what we aim at : if it be possible, and so here asserted, the total of this expression of our Saviour will be resolved into a conclusion, certainly most remote from his intendment. ' If it be possible that the elect may be seduced, then shall they be seduced : but it is possible

' 2 Cor. xi. 25.

(say our adversaries), therefore, they shall be seduced.' Neither doth that which Mr. Goodwin urgeth, sect. 12. out of the Synodalia before mentioned, pp. 314, 315. at all prove, that the words denote only a difficulty of the thing aimed at, with relation to the earnest endeavours of seducers: πρὸς τὸ doth indeed intimate their endeavours, but withal their fruitlessness, as to the event. Εἰ δυνατὸν is not referred (as in the example of Paul) to the thoughts of their minds, but to the success foretold by Christ. That emphatical and diacritical expression in the description of them, against whom their attempts are ('even the very elect'), argues their exemption. And if by 'elect' are meant simply and only, believers as such, how comes this emphatical expression and description of them to be used, when they alone, and no other, can be seduced ; for those who seem to believe only, cannot be said to fall from the faith, say our adversaries. It is true, the professors of Christianity adhered of old, under many trials (for the greater part) with eminent constancy, to their profession : yet is not any thing eminently herein held out in that saying, which Mr. Goodwin calls proverbial in Galen: he speaking of the followers of Moses the same as of the followers of Christ. What else follows in Mr. Goodwin from the same authors, is nothing but the pressing of (I think) one of the most absurd arguments, that ever learned men made use of, in any controversy ; and yet such as it is, we shall meet with it, over and over (as we have done often already), before we arrive at the end of this discourse ; and, therefore, to avoid tediousness, I shall not here insist upon it. With its mention it shall be passed by. It is concerning the uselessness of means, and exhortations unto the use of them, if the end to be attained by them be irrevocably determined, although those exhortations are part of the means appointed for the accomplishment of the end so designed. I shall not, as I said, in this place insist upon it: one thing only shall I observe in sect. 17. he grants, ' that God is able to determine the wills of the elect to the use of means, proper and sufficient to prevent their being deceived ;' by this, 'determining the wills of the elect to the use of proper means,' the efficacy of grace in and with believers, to a certain preservation of them to the end, is intended. It is the thing he opposeth, as we are informed in the next words

(' he hath no where declared himself willing or resolved to
do it'). That by this one assertion Mr. Goodwin hath absolved our doctrine from all the absurd consequences and
guilt of I know not what abominations, which in various
criminations he hath charged upon it, is evident upon the
first view and consideration. All that we affirm God to do,
Mr. Goodwin grants that he can do. Now if God should
do all he is able, there would be no absurdity or evil, that is
truly so, follow. What he can do, that he can decree to do:
and this is the sum of our doctrine, which he hath chosen to
oppose. God (we say) hath everlastingly purposed to give,
and doth actually give, his Holy Spirit to believers, to put
forth such an exceeding greatness of power, as whereby in
the use of means, they shall certainly be preserved to salvation; this God can do, says our author. This concession
being made by the remonstrants in their Synodalia, Mr.
Goodwin, I presume, thought it but duty to be as free as
his predecessors, and therefore, consented unto it also, although it be an axe laid at the root of almost all the arguments he sets up against the truth, as shall hereafter be farther manifested.

I draw now to a close of those places, which (among
many other omitted) tender themselves unto the proof of the
stable, unchangeable purpose of God, concerning the safeguarding and preservation of believers in his love, and unto
salvation. I shall mention one or two more, and close this
second scriptural demonstration of the truth in hand. The
first is that eminent place of Eph. i. 3—5. ' Blessed be the
God and Father of our Lord Jesus Christ, who hath blessed
us with all spiritual blessings in heavenly places in Christ;
according as he hath chosen us in him, before the foundation
of the world, that we should be holy, and without blame before him in love; having predestinated us unto the adoption
of children by Jesus Christ to himself, according to the good
pleasure of his will.' Ver. 3. the apostle summarily blesseth
God for all the spiritual mercies, which in Jesus Christ he
blesseth his saints withal, of all which, ver. 4. he discovereth
the fountain and spring, which is his free choosing of them
before the foundation of the world; that an eternal act of
the will of God is hereby designed, is beyond dispute: and
it is that foundation of God, on which the whole of the build-

ing mentioned and portrayed in the following verse is laid. All the grace and favour of God towards his saints, in their justification, adoption, and glory, all the fruits of the Spirit, which they enjoy in faith and sanctification, flow from this one fountain: and these the apostle describes at large in the verses following. The aim of God in this eternal and unchangeable act of his will, he tells us, is, that we should be unblamable before him in love. Certainly cursed apostates, backsliders in heart, in whom his soul takes no pleasure, are very far from being unblamable before God in love. Those that are within the compass of this purpose of God, must be preserved unto that state and condition, which God aims to bring them unto, by all the fruits and issues of that purpose of his, which was pointed at before. A Scripture of the like importance unto that before named, is 2 Thess. ii. 13, 14. ' God hath from the beginning chosen you to salvation, through sanctification of the Spirit, and belief of the truth, whereunto he calls you by our gospel, to the obtaining of the glory of the Lord Jesus ;' the same fountain of all spiritual and eternal mercy, with that mentioned in the other place, is here also expressed, and that is God's choosing of us by an everlasting act, or designing us to the end intended, by a free, eternal, unchangeable purpose of his will.

Secondly, The end aimed at by the Lord in that purpose, is here more clearly set down, in a twofold expression : 1. Of salvation ; ver. 13. ' He hath chosen us to salvation :' that is the thing which he aimed to accomplish for them, and the end he intended to bring them to, in his choosing of them ; and, 2. Ver. 14. ' The glory of the Lord Jesus :' or the obtaining a portion in that glory, which Christ purchased and procured for them, with their being with him, to behold his glory. And, thirdly, You have the means, whereby God will certainly bring about and accomplish this his design and purpose, whereof there are three most eminent acts expressed : 1. Vocation, or their calling by the gospel; ver. 14. 2. Sanctification, ver. 13. (' through the sanctification of the Spirit'). And, 3. Justification, which they receive by belief of the truth. This much then is wrapped up in this text; God having in his unchangeable purpose foreappointed his to salvation and glory, certainly to be obtained through the effectual working of the Spirit, and free justification in the blood of Christ, it cannot be, but that they shall be preserved unto the enjoyment of what they are so designed unto.

To sum up what hath been spoken from these purposes of God, to the establishment of the truth we have in hand. Those, whom God hath purposed by effectual means to preserve to the enjoyment of eternal life and glory in his favour and acceptation, can never so fall from his love, or be so cast out of his grace, as to come short of the end designed, or ever be totally rejected of God. The truth of this proposition depends upon what hath been said, and may farther be insisted on, concerning the unchangeableness and absoluteness of the eternal purposes of God, the glory whereof men shall never be able sacrilegiously to rob him of. Thence the assumption is, concerning all true believers, and truly sanctified persons, these are purposes of God, that they shall be so preserved to such ends, &c. as hath been abundantly proved by an induction of particular instances; and, therefore, it is impossible they should ever be so cast out of the favour of God, as not to be infallibly preserved to the end. Which is our second demonstration of the truth in hand.

CHAP. IV.

An entrance into the consideration of the covenant of grace, and our argu-
ment from thence, for the unchangeableness of the love of God unto be-
lievers. The intendment of the ensuing discourse. Gen. xvii. 3. *opened*
and explained, with the confirmation of the argument in hand from thence.
That argument vindicated and cleared of objections. Confirmed by some
observations. Jer. xxxii. 38—40. *compared with* chap. xxxi. 32, 33.
The truth under consideration from thence clearly confirmed. The cer-
tainty, immutability, and infallible accomplishment of all the promises of
the new covenant, demonstrated. 1. *From the removal of all causes of*
alteration. 2. *From the mediator, and his undertaking therein.* 3. *From*
the faithfulness of God. One instance from the former considerations.
The endeavour of Mr. G. to answer our argument from this place. His
observation on and from the text, considered· 1. *This promise not made*
to the Jews only: 2. *Nor to all the nation of the Jews, proved from* Rom.
xi. 3. *not intending principally their deliverance from Babylon. His in-*
ferences from his former observations weighed: 1. *The promise made to*
the body of the people of the Jews typically only: 2. *An exposition bor-*
rowed of Socinus rejected: 3. *The promise not appropriated to the time*
of the captivity: and the disadvantage ensuing to Mr. G.'s cause upon such
an exposition. The place insisted on compared with Ezek. xi. 17—20.
That place cleared: a fourth objection answered: this promise always ful-
filled: the spiritual part of it accomplished during the captivity: God's
intention not frustrated. How far the civil prosperity of the Jews was
concerned in this promise. Promises of spiritual and temporal things
compared. The covenant of grace how far conditional. Mr. G.'s sense
of this place expressed: borrowed from Faustus Socinus: the inconsis-
tency of it with the mind of the Holy Ghost, demonstrated: also with what
himself hath elsewhere delivered, no way suited to the answer of our argu-
ment from the place. The same interpretation farther disproved: an im-
mediate divine efficacy held out in the words: conversion and pardon of sins
promised: differenced from the grace and promises of the old covenant.
Contribution of means put by Mr. G. in the place of effectual operation of
the thing itself, farther disproved. How, when, and to whom this promise
was fulfilled, farther declared: an objection arising upon that considera-
tion answered. Conjectures ascribed to God by Mr. G. The foundation
real of all divine prediction: the promise utterly enervated, and rendered
of none effect by Mr. G.'s exposition. Its consistency with the prophecies
of the rejection of the Jews. The close of the argument from the covenant
of God.

HAVING shewn the unchangeable stability of the love and
favour of God towards his saints, from the immutability of
his own nature and purposes, manifested by an induction of

sundry particular instances from eminent places of Scripture, wherein both the one and the other are held out as the foundation of what we affirm : I proceed to farther clear and demonstrate the same important truth from the first way of declaration, whereby God hath assured them that it shall be to them according to the tenor of the purposes insisted on ; and that is his covenant of grace. The *principium essendi* of this truth (if I may so say) is in the decrees and purposes of God : the *principium cognoscendi* in his covenant, promise, and oath, which also add much to the real stability of it, the truth and faithfulness of God in them, being thereby peculiarly engaged therein.

It is not in my purpose to handle the nature of the covenant of grace, but only briefly to look into it, so far as it hath influence into the truth in hand : the covenant of grace then, as it inwraps the unchangeable love and favour of God towards those, who are taken into the bond thereof, is that which lieth under our present consideration. The other great branch of it (upon the account of the same faithfulness of God) communicating permanency of perseverance in itself, unto the saints, securing their continuance with God, shall (the Lord assisting) more peculiarly be explained, when we arrive to the head of our discourse : unless enough to that purpose may fall in occasionally in the progress of this business.

For our present purpose, the producing and vindicating of one or two texts of Scripture, being unavoidably expressive towards the end aimed at, shall suffice.

The first of those is Gen. xvii. 7. ' I will establish my covenant between me and thee, and thy seed after thee, in their generations, for an everlasting covenant, to be a God unto thee and thy seed after thee.' This is that which God engageth himself unto in this covenant of grace, that he will for everlasting be a God to him, and his faithful seed. Though the external administration of the covenant was given to Abraham and his carnal seed, yet the effectual dispensation of the grace of the covenant is peculiar to them only who are the children of the promise, the remnant of Abraham according to election, with all, that in all nations were to be blessed in him, and in his seed Christ Jesus. Ishmael though circumcised was to be put out, and not to be here with Isaac; nor to abide in the house for ever, as the son of the promise was: now the apostle tells you, look what blessings faithful Abraham received by virtue of this promise, the same do all believers receive; Gal. iii. 9. 'We which are of the faith, are blessed with faithful Abraham:' which he proves (in the words foregoing) from Gen. xii. 3. because all nations were to be blessed in him. What blessing then was it, that was here made over to Abraham? All the blessings, that from God are conveyed in and by his seed Jesus Christ (in whom both he and we are blessed) are inwrapped therein. What they are the apostle tells you, Eph. i. 3. 'They are all spiritual blessings:' if perseverance, if the continuance of the love and favour of God towards us, be a spiritual blessing, both Abraham and all his seed, all faithful ones throughout the world, are blessed with it in Jesus Christ: and if God's continuing to be a God to them for ever, will enforce this blessing (being but the same thing in another expression), it is here likewise asserted.

It is importunately excepted, that though God undertake to be our God in an everlasting covenant, and upon that account to bless us with the whole blessing that is conveyed by the promised seed; yet if we abide not with him, if we forsake him, he will also cease to be our God, and cease to bless us with the blessing, which on others in Jesus Christ he will bestow.

Ans. If there be a necessity to smite this evasion so often as we shall meet with it, it must be cut into a hundred pieces. For the present I shall only observe two evils it is attended withal. First, It takes no notice that God, who hath undertaken to be a God unto us, hath with the like truth, power, and faithfulness, undertaken that we shall abide to be his people. So is his love in his covenant expressed by its efficacy to this end and purpose. Deut. l. 6. 'And the Lord thy God will also circumcise thy heart and the heart of thy seed, to love the Lord thy God with all thine heart and with all thy soul, that thou mayest live.' Secondly, It denies the continuance of the love of God to us to the end, to be any part of the blessings wherewith we are blessed in Jesus Christ: for if it be, it could no more be suspended

<hr>

a Gal. iv. 22, 23. 30.

on any condition in us, than the glorification of believers that abide so to the end. '

This then is inwrapped in this promise of the covenant unto the elect, with whom it is established : God will be a God to them for ever, and that to bless them with all the blessings which he communicates in and by the Lord Jesus Christ, the promised seed. The continuance of his favour to the end, is to us unquestionably a spiritual blessing ; if any one be otherwise minded, I shall not press to share with him in his apprehension : and if so, it is in Christ, and shall certainly be enjoyed by them, to whom God is a God in covenant. He that can suppose, that he shall prevail with the saints of God to believe it will make for their consolation to apprehend, that there is no engagement in his covenant assuring them of the continuance of the favour of God unto them to the end of their pilgrimage, hath no reason to doubt or question the issue of any thing, he shall undertake to persuade men unto. Doubtless he will find it very difficult with them who in time of spiritual straits and pressures, have closed with this engagement of God in the covenant, and have had experience of its bearing them through all perplexities and entanglements, when the waves of temptation were ready to go over their souls. Certainly David was in another persuasion, when upon a view of all the difficulties he had passed through, and his house was to meet withal, he concludes, 2 Sam. xxiii. 5. ' This is all my desire, and all my salvation, that God hath made with me an everlasting covenant, ordered in all things and sure.' The covenant from whence he had his sure mercies, not changeable, not alterable, not liable to failings, as the temporal prosperity of his house was, was that he rejoiced in.

I shall close this with two observations :

First, It may doubtless, and on serious consideration will seem strange to any one, acquainted in the least measure with God and his faithfulness, that in a covenant established in the blood of Christ he should freely promise to his, that he would be a God unto them, that is, that he would abide with them in the power, goodness, righteousness, and faithfulness of a God, that he would be an all-sufficient God to them for ever, when he might with an almighty facility prevent it, and so answer and fulfil his engagement to the utmost, he should yet suffer them to become such villains and devils in wickedness, that it should be utterly impossible for him in the blood of his Son, and the riches of his grace, to continue a God unto them : this, I say, seemeth strange to me, and not to be received without casting the greatest reproach imaginable on the goodness, faithfulness, and righteousness of God.

Secondly, If this promise be not absolute, immutable, unchangeable, independent on any thing in us, it is impossible that any one should plead it with the Lord, but only upon the account of the sense that he hath of his own accomplishment of the condition, on which the promise doth depend. I can almost suppose that the whole[b] generation of believers will rise up against this assertion to remove it out of their way of walking with God. This I know, that most of them, who any time have walked in darkness and have had no light, will reprove it to the faces of them that maintain it, and profess that God hath witnessed the contrary truth to their hearts. Are we in the covenant of grace left to our own hearts, ways, and walkings? Is it not differenced from that which is abolished? Is it not the great distinguishing character of it, that all the promises of it are stable,[c] and shall certainly be accomplished in Jesus Christ?

One place I shall add more, wherein our intendment is positively expressed, beyond all possibility of any colourable evasion, especially considering the explication, enlargement, and application, which in other places it hath received. The place intended is Jer. xxxii. 38—40. 'They shall be my people, and I will be their God; and I will give them one heart, and one way, that they may fear me for ever, for the good of them, and their children after them ; and I will make an everlasting covenant with them, that I will not turn away from them to do them good, but I will put my fear in their hearts, that they shall not depart from me ;' in conjunction with those words of the same importance, chap. xxxi. 31 —33. 'Behold the days come, saith the Lord, that I will make a new covenant with the house of Israel, and the house

b Psal. lxxiii. 26. Isa viii. 17 l. 10.
c 2 Cor. i. 20. Heb. vii. 22. viii. 7—9.

of Judah, not according to the covenant that I made with
their fathers ; but this shall be my covenant, that I will make
with the house of Israel after those days, saith the Lord, I
will put my law in their inward parts, and write it in their
hearts, and I will be their God, and they shall be my people,
and they shall teach no more every man his neighbour, and
every man his brother, saying, Know the Lord ; for they shall
all know me, from the least of them to the greatest of them,
saith the Lord, for I will forgive their iniquities, and remember their sins no more.'

First, The thesis under demonstration is directly and
positively affirmed, in most significant and emphatical words,
by God himself : seeing then the testimony of his holy prophets and apostles, concerning him are so excepted against,
and so lightly set by, let us try if men will reverence himself, and cease contending with him, when he appeareth in
judgment.   Saith he then to believers, those whom he taketh
into covenant with him : ' This is my covenant with you (in
the performance whereof his all-sufficiency, truth, and faithfulness with all other his glorious attributes are eminently
engaged) I will be your God (what that expression intends
is known, and the Lord here explains, by instancing in some
eminent spiritual mercy thence flowing, as sanctification and
acceptance with him by the forgiveness of sins), and that for
ever in an everlasting covenant, that he will not turn away
from them to do them good.'   This, plainly God saith of
himself, and this is all we say of him in the business, and
which (having so good an author) we must say, whether men
will hear, or whether they will forbear : whether it be right
in the sight of God to hearken unto men, more than unto
God, let all judge.   Truly they have a sad task, in my apprehension, who are forced to sweat and labour to alleviate and
take off the testimony of God.

Secondly, That the way the Lord proposeth to secure his
love to his, is upon terms of advantage of glory and honour
to himself, to take away all scruple which on that hand might
arise, is fully also expressed : sin is the only differencing
thing between God and man : and hereunto it hath a double
influence : First, Moral in its guilt, deserving that God should
cast off a sinner, and prevailing with him upon the account

of justice so to do : Secondly, Efficient, by causing men, through its ^dpower and deceitfulness, to depart from God, until, 'as backsliders in heart, they are filled with their own ways.' Take away these two, provide for security on this hand, and there is no possible case imaginable, of separation between God and man once brought together in peace and unity. For both these doth God here undertake ; for the first (saith he) ' I will forgive their iniquities, and remember their sins no more ;' chap. xxxi. 34. The guilt of sin shall be done away in Christ, and that on terms of the greatest honour and glory to the justice of God, that can be apprehended ; 'God hath set forth Christ to be a propitiation through faith in his blood, to declare his righteousness for the remission of sins that are past;' Rom. iii. 25. And for the latter, that that may be thoroughly prevented, saith God, the care shall lie on me ; ' I will put my law in their hearts, and write it, in their inward parts ;' chap. xxxi. 33. ' I will put my fear in their inward parts, that they shall not depart from me ;' chap. xxxii. 40. So that the continuance of his love is secured against all possible interveniences whatever, by an assured prevention of all such that have an inconsistency therewithal.

The apostle Paul setting out the covenant, which God ratified in the blood of Christ, which shall never be broken, takes the description of it from this place of the prophet; Heb. viii. 9—12. and therein fixeth particularly on the unchangeableness of it, in opposition to the covenant, which went before, which was liable to mutation; when if these differed only in the approbation of several qualifications, they come to the same end. For if this covenant depends on conditions by ourselves and in our own strength, with the advantage of its proposal to us, attended with exhortations, and therefore by us to be fulfilled, how was it distinguished from that made with the people, when they came out of Egypt? But in this very thing the difference of it lieth, as the apostle asserts, ver. 6—8. The immutability of this covenant, and the certain product of all the mercy promised in it, might (were that our present task) be easily demonstrated ; as,

First, From the removal of all causes of alteration. When two enter into covenant and agreement, no one can under-

^d Heb. iii. 13. Prov. i. 31. xiv. 14.

take, that that covenant shall be firm and stable, if it equally depends upon both; yea, both, it may be, are changeable, and so actually changed, before the accomplishing of the thing engaged about therein; however, though the one should be faithful, yet the other may fail, and so the covenant be broken; thus it was with God and Adam; it could not be undertaken, that that covenant should be kept inviolable, because though God continues faithful, yet Adam might prove (as indeed he did) faithless; and so the covenant was disannulled, as to any power of knitting together God and man. The covenant between husband and wife; the one party cannot undertake that the whole covenant shall be observed, because the other may prove treacherous. In this covenant the case is otherwise, God himself hath undertaken the whole, both for his continuing with us, and our continuing with him. Now he is one, God is one, and there is not another, that they should fail and disannul this agreement. Though there be sundry persons in covenant, yet there is but one undertaker on all hands, and that is God himself. It doth not depend upon the will of another, but of him only, who is faithful, who cannot lie, who cannot deceive, who will make all his engagements good to the utmost. He is an all-sufficient one, he will work, and who shall let him? 'The Lord of hosts hath purposed, and who shall disannul it?' Yea he is an unchangeable one, what he undertakes shall come to pass. Blessed be his name, that he hath not laid the foundation of a covenant in the blood of his dear Son, laid out the riches of his wisdom, grace, and power about it, and then left it to us, and our frail will to carry it on, that it should be in our power to make void the great work of his mercy, Whence then, I say, should any change be, the whole depending on one, and he immutable.

Secondly, Seeing that God and man, having been at so great a distance, as they were by sin, must needs meet in some mediator, some middle person in whom, and by whose blood (as covenants usually were confirmed by blood), this covenant must be ratified; consider who this is, and what he hath done for the establishing of it. 'There is one God, and one mediator between God and man, the man Christ Jesus;' 1 Tim. ii. 5. He is the 'surety of this testament;' Heb. vii. 22. 'The mediator of this better covenant, established upon better promises;' Heb. viii. 6. neither is this surety or mediator subject to change. He is the same ' yesterday, to-day, and for ever;' Heb. xiii. 8. But though he be so in himself, yet is the work so, that is committed to him? Saith the apostle, all the ' promises of God are yea and amen in Jesus Christ, to the glory of God by us;' 2 Cor. i. 20. God hath in him, and by him, ascertained all the promises of the covenant, that not one of them should be broken, disannulled, frustrate, or come short of an accomplishment. God hath so confirmed them in him, that he hath at his death made a legacy of them, and bequeathed them in a testamentary dispensation to the covenanters; Heb. ix. 15—17. and what he hath farther done for the assuring of his saints' abiding with God, shall afterward be declared.

Thirdly, The faithfulness of God is oftentimes peculiarly mentioned in reference to this very thing, ' the God that keepeth covenant is his name,' that which he hath to keep is, all that in covenant he undertaketh; now in this covenant he undertaketh : First, That he will never forsake us : Secondly, That we shall never forsake him. His faithfulness is engaged to both these; and if either part should fail, what would the Lord do to his great name, ' the God that keepeth covenant?'

Notwithstanding the undertaking of God on both sides in this covenant, notwithstanding his faithfulness in the performance of what he undertaketh, notwithstanding the ratification of it in the blood of Jesus, and all that he hath done for the confirmation of it, notwithstanding its differing from the covenant that was disannulled on this account, that that was broken, which this shall never be (that being broken, not as to the truth of the proposition wherein it is contained, do this and live, but as to the success of it in bringing any to God), notwithstanding the seal of the oath that God set unto it; they, I say, who, notwithstanding all these things, will hang the unchangeableness of this covenant of God upon the slipperiness, and uncertainty, and lubricity of the will of man, ' let them walk in the light of the sparks, which themselves have kindled,' we walk in the light of the Lord our God.

When first I perused Mr. Goodwin's exceptions to this testimony (cap. 10. sect. 52—56. page 219—224.) finding them opposed not so much, nor so directly to our inference from this place, as to the design, intendment, and arguing of the apostle, Rom. ix—xi. and the reinforcing of the objections by him answered, casting again the stone of offence in the way, by him removed, I thought to have passed it without any reply, being not convinced, that it was possible for the author himself to be satisfied either with his own exposition of this place, or his exceptions unto ours; but arriving at length to the close of this discourse, I found him ' quasi re preclare gesta,' to triumph in his victory, expressing much confidence, that the world of saints, who have hitherto bottomed much of their faith and consolation, on the covenant of God in these words expressed, will veil their faith and understanding to his uncontrollable dictates, and not once make mention of the name of God in this place any more. Truly, for my part, I must take the boldness to say, that before the coming forth of his learned treatise, I had read, and (according to my weak ability) weighed and considered whatever either Arminians or Socinians (from the founder of which sect, their and his interpretation of this place is borrowed) had entered against the interpretation insisted on, that I could by any means attain the sight of, and was not in the least shaken by any of their reasonings, from rejoicing in the grace of God, as to the unchangeableness of his love to believers, and the certainty of their perseverance with him to the end, therein expressed; and I must add, that I am not one jot enamoured on their objections and reasonings, for all the new dress, which with some cost our author hath been pleased to furnish them with, fashionably to set out themselves withal. Were it not for the confidence you express in the close of your discourse, of your noble exploits and achievements in the consideration of this text (which magnificent thoughts of your undertakings and success, I could not imagine from the reading of your arguments or exceptions, though on other accounts I might), I should not have thought it worth while to examine it particularly, which now, to safeguard the consolation of the weakest believers, and to encourage them to hold fast their confidence so well established against the assaults of all adversaries, Satan, or Arminians, I shall briefly do.

1. Then (saith Mr. Goodwin), 'evident it is from the whole tenor of the chapter, that the words contain especial promises made particularly to the Jews.'

Ans. If by particularly, you mean exclusively, to them, and not to others, this is evidently false; for the apostle tells you, Heb. viii. 6. to the end of the chapter, that the covenant here mentioned is that, whereof Christ is mediator, and the promies of it those better promises, which they are made partakers of, who have an interest in his mediation.

2. (He saith) 'As evident it is, upon the same account, that the promise here mentioned, was not made only to the saints or sound believers amongst the Jews, who were but few; but to the whole body or generality of them.'

Ans. True, it is as evident as what before you affirmed, and that in the same kind, that is, it is evidently false; or else the promise itself is so; for it was never fulfilled towards them all. But I refer you to a learned author, who hath long since assoiled this difficulty, and taught us to distinguish between a Jew ἐν τῷ φανερῷ, and a Jew ἐν τῷ κρυπτῷ, of [e] ' Israel according to the flesh,' and ' according to the promise :' he hath also taught us, that ' they are not all Israel that are of Israel ;' Rom ix. 6. And upon that account it is, that the word of this promise doth not fail, though all of Israel do not enjoy the fruit of it. Not that it is conditional, but that it was not at all made unto them, as to the spiritual part of it, to whom it was not wholly fulfilled. And chap. xi. He tells you that it was the election to whom these promises were made, and they obtained the fruit of them: neither doth that appendix of promises pointed to, look any other way. When you have made good your observation by a reply to that learned author, we shall think of a rejoinder. It is therefore added,

3. ' It is yet upon the same account as evident, as either of the former, that this promise was made unto this nation of the Jews, when and whilst they were (or at least considered as now being) in the iron furnace of the Babylonian captivity; ver. 33.'

Ans. That this solemn renovation of this promise of the covenant, was (not made to them when in Babylon, but)

[e] Rom. ii. 28, 29. Rom. ix. 6, 7.

given out to them beforehand, to sustain their hearts and
spirits withal, in their bondage and thraldom, is granted;
and what then I pray? Is it any new thing to have spiritual
promises solemnly given out, and renewed upon the occasion of temporal distresses? A promise of Christ is given
out to the house of David, when in fear of being destroyed;
Isa. vii. 13. So it was given to Adam; Gen. iii. 16. So
to Abraham; Gen. xvii. So to the church; Isa. iv. 2—4.
But farther it is said,

4. ' From the words immediately preceding the passages
offered to debate, it clearly appears, that the promise in these
passages relates unto, and concerns their reduction and return from, and out of, that captivity, into their own land.'

Ans. Will Mr. Goodwin say, that it doth only concern
that? Dareth any man so boldly contradict the apostle setting out from this very place the tenor of the covenant of
grace, ratified in the blood of Christ; Heb. viii? Nay, will
any say, that so much of the promise here, as God calleth
his covenant, chap. xxxi. 32, 33. xxxii. 38—40. doth at all
concern their reduction into their own land, any farther than
it was a type or resemblance of our deliverance by Christ?
These evident assertions are as express and flat contradictions to the evident intendment of the Holy Ghost, as any
man is able to invent. But,

Mr. Goodwin hath many deductions out of the former
(sure and evident) premises, to prove that this is not a promise of absolute and final perseverance (it is a strange perseverance, that is not final) in grace to the end of their lives:
for saith he,

1. ' The promise is made to the body of the people, and
not to the saints and believers among them, and respects as
well the unfaithful, as the believers, in that nation.'

Ans. It was made to the body of the people only typically considered, and so it was accomplished to the body of
the people: spiritually and properly to the elect among the
people, who, as the apostle tells us, obtained accordingly.
There being also in the promise wrapped up the grace of
effectual conversion; it may in some sense be said to be
made to the unfaithful: that is, to such as were so antecedently to the grace thereof: but not to any that abide so;

for the promise is, not that they shall not, but that they shall believe, and continue in so doing to the end. But saith he,

2. 'This promise was appropriated and fitted to the state of the Jews, in a sad captivity: but the promise of perseverance was (if our adversaries might be believed) a standing promise among them, not appropriated to their condition.'

Ans. 1. ' Non venit ex pharetris ista sagitta tuis.' It is Socinus's, in reference to Ezek. xxxvi. In Præl. Theol. cap. 12. sect. 6. And so is the whole interpretation of the place afterward insisted on, derived to Mr. Goodwin through the hands of the remonstrants at the Hague conference. 2. If this exception against the testimony given in these words for the confirmation of the thesis in hand may be allowed, what will become of Mr. Goodwin's argument from Ezek. xviii. for the apostacy of the saints? It is most certain, the words from thence, by him and others insisted on, with the whole discourse, of whose contexture they are a part, are appropriated to a peculiar state of the Jews, and are brought forth as a meet vindication of the righteousness of God in his dealing with them in that condition. This then may be laid up in store to refresh Mr. Goodwin with something of his own providing, when we are gone so far onward in our journey. But, 3. It is most evident to all the world, that Mr. Goodwin is not such a stranger in the Scriptures, as not to have observed long since, that spiritual promises are frequently given to the people of God, to support their souls under temporal distresses: and that not always new promises for the matter of them (for indeed the substance of all promises is comprised in the first promise of Christ), but either such, as enlarge and clear up grace formerly given or promised ; or such, as have need of a solemn renewal, for the establishing of the faith of the saints, assaulted in some particular manner, in reference to them : which was the state of the saints among the Jews at this time. How often was the same promise renewed to Abraham? And upon what several occasions ? And yet that promise, for the matter of it, was the same that had been given from the beginning of the world ; that God's solemn renewal of the covenant at any time, is called his making of, or entering into, covenant, needs no labour to prove. But, saith he,

3. This promise is the same with that of Ezek. xi. 17—
20. which promise, notwithstanding it is said, ver. 21. ' But
as for them whose heart walketh after the heart of their detestable things, and their abominations, I will recompense
their ways upon their heads ; so that, notwithstanding this
seeming promise (as is pretended), of perseverance in grace,
they may walk after their abominable things, for this
threatening intends the same persons or nations (as Calvin
himself confesseth), the Israelites.'

Ans. 1. Grant that this is the same promise with the
other, how will it appear that this is not a promise of such
an interposure of the Spirit and grace of God, as shall infallibly produce the effect of perseverance ? Why ? Because
some are threatened for following the heart of their abominable things. Yea, but how shall it appear that they are
the same persons with them, to whom the promise is made ?
The context is plainly against it; saith he, ' I will give them
a heart to walk in my statutes and ordinances, to do them ;
but for them that walk after their own hearts, them I will
destroy,' in as clear a distinction of the object of the promise and threatening as is possible. Saith Mr. Goodwin,
this threatening concerns the same persons or nation : the
same nation, but not the same persons in that nation ; but
Calvin saith that concerneth the Israelites ; but Paul hath
told us, that they ' are not all Israel, who are of Israel, not
all children of the promise, who are children of the flesh.'
And,

2. If it do any way concern the persons to whom that
promise is given, it is an expression suited to the dispensation of God, whereby he carrieth believers on in the enjoyment of the good things he gives them in and by his promises, without the least prediction of any event, being only
declarative of what the Lord abhorreth, and the connexion
that is between the antecedent and the consequent of the
axiom wherein it is contained; and is far from the nature
of those promises, which hold out the purpose or intention
of God, with the engaging of a real efficacy for their accomplishment. He adds,

4. ' If this be a promise of absolute perseverance, no time
nor season can be imagined, wherein it was fulfilled.'

Ans. At all times and seasons to them, to whom it

was made, according to their concernment in it.   But saith he,

1. ' It hath been proved that it was made to the community of the Jewish nation, towards whom it was not fulfilled.'

Ans. 1. It hath been said indeed, again and again, but scarce once attempted to be proved: nor the reasoning of the apostle against some pretended proofs and answers to them, at all removed.

2. It was fulfilled to the body of that nation, as far as it concerned the body of that nation, in their typical return from their captivity.   But then,

2. ' If this be the sense, it was fulfilled in the captivity, as well as afterward, for you say the saints always persevere.'

Ans. 1. The typical part of it was not then accomplished.

2. It is granted, that as to the spiritual part of the covenant of grace, it was at all times fulfilled to them, which is now evidently promised to establish them in the assurance thereof.   Wherefore it is,

5. Argued (sect. 53.), ' That these words, I will give them one heart, that they shall not depart from me, may be as well rendered that they may not depart from me, and so it is said in the verse foregoing, that they may fear me for ever.'

Ans. 1. Suppose the words may be thus rendered, what inconvenience will ensue? Either way they evidently, and beyond exception, design out the end aimed at by God; and when God intends an end or event, so as to exert a real efficacy for the compassing of it, to say that it shall not be infallibly brought about, is an assertion, that many have not as yet had the boldness to venture on.   But saith he,

2. ' The words so read do not necessarily import the actual event, or taking place of the effect intended of God in the promise, and his performance thereof, but only his intention itself in both these, and the sufficiency of the means allowed for producing such an effect: but it is of the same nature with that, that our Saviour saith, John v. 34. ' These things I say unto you, that ye might be saved :' and that of God to Adam, Gen. iii. 10, 11.' All which things were in like manner insisted on by the remonstrants at the Hague colloquy.

Ans. It is not amiss that our contests about the sense of this place of Scripture, are at length come to the state and issue here expressed. It is granted, the thing promised, and that according to the intendment of God, is perseverance; but that there is any necessity that this promise of God should be fulfilled, or his intention accomplished, that is denied. Were it not, that I should prevent myself, in what will be more seasonable to be handled, when we come to the consideration of the promises of God, I should very willingly engage here into the proof of this assertion: When God purposeth or intendeth an event, and promiseth to do it, to that end putting forth and exercising an efficient real power, it shall certainly be accomplished and brought to pass; neither can this be denied without casting the greatest reproach of mutability, impotency, and breach of word, upon the Most Holy that is possible for any man to do. Neither do the remonstrants, nor Mr. Goodwin, acquit themselves from a participation in so high a crime, by their instance of Gen. iii. 10, 11. where a command of God is only related to express his duty to whom it was given, not in the least asserting any intention of God about the event or promise, as to the means of its accomplishment. Nor doth that of John viii. 28. give them any more assistance in their sad undertaking to alleviate the truth of God. A means of salvation in its own nature and kind sufficient is exhibited, which asserts not an infallible necessity of event, as that doth which in this place is ascribed to God. But it is added,

6. (Sect. 54.) 'The continuance of external and civil prosperity to the Jewish nation may much more colourably be argued from hence, than the certainty of their perseverance in grace: for these things are most expressly promised, ver. 39, 40. and yet we find that upon their non-performance of the condition, they are become the most contemptible and miserable nation under heaven: certainly then the spiritual promises here must also depend on conditions, which if not fulfilled, they also may come short of performance.'

Ans. 1. Rom. xi. 25—27. 2. These temporal performances were fulfilled unto them so far as they were made to them, that is, as they were typical, and what is behind of them, shall be made good in due time. 3. All these pro-

mises are, and were in their chiefest and most eminent concernments (even the spiritual things set forth by allusions
to the good land, wherein they lived), completely and absolutely fulfilled to them all, and every one, to whom they
were properly and directly made, as the apostle abundantly
proveth; Rom. ix. 10, 11. 4. Whereas there are two special
spiritual promises here expressed, one of conversion, the
other of perseverance, I desire to know on what condition
their accomplishment is suspended? On what condition will
God write his law in their hearts? On condition they hear
him, and obey him, suffer his mercies and kindnesses to
work kindly on them; that is, on condition his law be in
their hearts, he will write it there; thanks yet for that. On
what condition doth God promise that they shall abide with
him for ever? Why, on the condition they depart not from
him: very good! To what end doth God promise that which
he will not effect, but only on condition that there is no
need for him so to do? But, saith he,

7. 'If the spiritual promises be absolute, so must the temporal be also; for their accomplishing depends solely on
the things mentioned and promised in the spiritual.'

Ans. 1. Temporal things in the promises are often expressed only to be a resemblance, and to set off some eminent spiritual grace intended, as shall afterward appear.
In that sense the promises mentioning such things, are actually and fully accomplished in the collation of the spiritual things by them typed and resembled. 2. Temporal
promises, as such, belong not primarily to the covenant of
grace, as they are of temporal things for the substance of
them, but to the covenant with that whole nation, about
their inheritance in the land of Canaan, which was expressly
conditional, and which held out no more of God's intendment to that nation, but only that there should be an inviolable connexion between their obedience and prosperities.
3. The things in this promise are expressly differenced from
the things of that covenant, on this account, that that covenant being broken on the part of the nation, they enjoyed
not that which was laid out as a fruit of their obedience;
but this shall never be violated or broken, God undertaking
for the accomplishing of it, with another manner of engag-

ing, and suitable power exerted, than in that of old; Heb.
viii. 7—10. x. 16, 17. But, saith he,

8. 'The expression of a covenant plainly shews it to be
conditional; for a covenant is not, but upon the mutual
stipulation of parties; when one fails, then is the other true.'

Ans. 1. The word Berith is sometimes used for a single
promise without a condition; Gen. vi. 18. ix. 9. Whence
the apostle handling this very.promise changeth the terms,
and calleth it a testament. In a testamentary dispensation,
there is not in the nature of it any mutual stipulation required, but only a mere single favour and grant or concession. 2. It may be granted, that here is a stipulation of
duty from us, God promising to work that in us, which he
requires of us; and thereby is this covenant distinguished
from that which was disannulled. In the good things indeed of this covenant, one may be the condition of another,
but both are freely bestowed of God; and these are Mr.
Goodwin's exceptions against this testimony, which cometh
in, in the cause of God, and his saints, that we have in hand.
His next attempt is to give you the sense of the words on
this consideration, to manifest from thence, that this promise of God may come short of accomplishment.

This then at length is the account that is given in of the
sense of the promise in hand, and all others of the like
nature.

'I will give them one heart and one way, that they may
fear me for ever, and will put my fear into their hearts, that
they shall not, or may not depart from me, (i. e.) I will deal
so above measure graciously and bountifully with them, as
well in matters relating to their spiritual condition, as in
things concerning their outward condition, that, if they be
not prodigiously refractory, stubborn, and unthankful, I
will overcome their evils with my goodness, and will cause
them to own me for their God, and will reduce them, as one
man, to a loving and loyal frame and temper of heart, that
they shall willingly, with a free and full purpose of heart, fear
and serve me for ever;' sect. 55.

Ans. The first author of this gloss upon a parallel text
was[f] Socinus; Præl. Theol. cap. 6. whose words are. 'This

[f] Hunc Ezechielis locum satis commode explicat Erasmus in sua Diatribe, dicens

place of Ezekiel is well explained by Erasmus in his Diatribe, saying, That there is a usual figure of speaking contained in it, whereby a care in any, of working something
by another, is signified, his endeavour being not excluded;
as if a master should say to his scholar speaking improperly,
I will take away that barbarous tongue from thee, and give
thee the Roman: these are almost the words of Erasmus:
to which add, that it appeareth from the place itself, that
God would not signify any necessity, or any internal efficacy, when he declareth that he will effect what he promiseth, no other way, than by the multitude of his benefits
wherewith he would affect the people, and mollify their
hearts and minds, and thereby, as it were, beget and create
in them a willingness and alacrity in obeying of him.' The
remonstrants received this sense, in the conference at the
Hague, managing it in these words: 'It is manifest that these
words do signify some great efficacy and motion, which
should come to pass by the many and excellent benefits of
God, for whose sake they ought to convert themselves,' &c.
which worthy interpretation being at length fallen upon Mr.
Goodwin's hand, is trimmed forth as you have heard. Secondly, not to insist on those assumptions, which are supposed in this interpretation, as that this promise was made
peculiarly to the Jews, and to the whole nation of them properly and directly, &c. The gloss itself will be found by no
means to have the least consistency with either the words
or intendment of the Holy Ghost in the place, nor to be
suited to answer our argument from thence, nor yet to hold
any good intelligence or correspondency with what hath
already been delivered concerning it. For,

1. To begin with the latter; he affirms this cannot be a
promise of absolute perseverance: 'because if it be so, the
Jews enjoyed it in that captivity, as well as afterward; when
that is here promised, which they were not to receive until
in, and upon their return from, Babylon;' sect. 52. pp. 220,

in eo contineri usitatam figuram loquendi, qua cura in altero aliquid efficiendi sig-
nificatur, illius opera minime exclusa · ac si quis (inquit) Præceptor discipulo solæ-
cizanti diceret, exeram tibi linguam istam barbaricam, et inseram Romanam. Hæc
sunt fere ipsius Erasmi verba. Quibus addex loco ipso satis apparere, nullam ne-
cessitatem Deum significare voluisse, sed neque ullam vim interiorem, cum non alia
ratione ea, quæ ibi pollicetur se effecturum, ostendat Deus, quam beneficiorum mul-
titudine, quibus affecturus erat populum, ejusque cor et animum emolliturus, &c
Soc. Præl. cap. 12. S. 6. p. 45.

221. But if that, which is here mentioned, be all that is promised to them, namely, dealing so graciously and bountifully with them in his dispensations, according as was intimated, there is not any thing in the least held out to them in this place, but what God had already (himself being judge) in as eminent and high a manner wrought in reference to them and for them, as could be conceived. And indeed it was such, as he never after this, arose to that height of outward mercy and bounty, in things spiritual and temporal, so as before; Isa. v. 1, 2. 4. Neither after the captivity unto this day, did they see again the triumphant glory of David, the magnificent peace of Solomon, the beauty of the temple, the perfection of ordinances, &c. as before.

2. Whereas he affirmed formerly, that 'this promise is conditional, and that the things therein promised, do depend on conditions by them to be fulfilled, to whom the promise is made;' sect. 54. page 221. in the gloss here given us of the words, there is no intimation of any such conditions, as whereupon the promised actings of God should be suspended, but only an uncertainty of event in reference to these actings asserted. That (according to this interpretation) which alone God promiseth to do is, that he would deal above measure graciously, and bountifully with them, as well in matters relating to their spiritual conditions, as in things concerning their outward condition, this is all he promiseth, and this he will absolutely do, be the event what it will. It is not said (nor can it with any pretence of reason), that this also is conditional; nay whatever the event and issue be, that God will thus deal with them, is the sense of the words in hand, according to the estimate here taken of them. It is true, it is, in the exposition under consideration, left doubtful and ambiguous, whether such, or such an event shall follow the promised actings of God or not; but what God promiseth concerning his dealing with them, that without supposal of any condition whatever, shall be accomplished. According as a sense serves the turn, so it is to be embraced, when men are once engaged against the truth.

3. Neither doth this interpretation so much as take notice of, much less doth it with any strength, or evidence, wave our argument for the saints' perseverance from this

place. We affirm, 1. That the promise God made unto, or the covenant he makes here with, his people, is distinguished from, or opposed unto, the covenant that was broken, upon this account, that that was broken by the default of them with whom it was made; but God would take care and provide that this should not fail, but be everlasting; Jer. xxxi. 32. xxxiii. 40. Heb. viii. 8, 9. 2. That the intendment of God in this promise, and the administration of this covenant, with means and power mentioned therein, is the abiding of his saints with him, or rather (primarily, and principally) his abiding with them, notwithstanding all such interveniences, as he will not powerfully prevent from ever interposing to the disturbance of that communion he taketh them into. ' I will,' saith he, ' make an everlasting covenant with them, that I will not turn away from them from doing them good.' Now these things, and such like, are not once taken notice of, in the exposition boasted to be full and clear.

4. Neither, indeed, hath it any affinity unto, or acquaintance in name or thing with, the words or intendment of God, with the grace of the promise, or the promise itself. For,

1. ' God,' says he, ' will give them one heart and one way, or he will put his law in their inward parts, and write it in their hearts :' which is plainly the work of his grace in them, and not the effect and fruit of his dealing with them. In the gloss in hand, the work of God is limited to such dealings with them, as may overcome them to such a flame. The having of a new heart is either the immediate work of God, or it is their yielding unto their duty to him, upon his dealing bountifully and graciously with them. If the first; it is what the Scripture affirms, and all that we desire: if the latter; how comes it to be expressed in terms holding out an immediate divine efficiency? That the taking away of a heart of stone, the giving of a new heart and spirit, the writing of the law in their hearts, and (which is all one) the quickening of the dead, the opening of blind eyes, the begetting of us anew, as they relate unto God, do signify no more but his administration of means, whereby men may be wrought upon, and persuaded to bring their hearts and spirits into such a condition, as is described in those ex-

pressions, to quicken themselves, to open their blind eyes, &c. Mr. Goodwin shall scarce be able to evince.

2. Conversion, and pardon of sin, being both in this promise of the covenant (I take in also that place of the same importance, cap. 31.), and relating alike to the grace of God, if conversion, or the giving of a new heart, be done only by administering outward means, and persuasions unto men to make them new hearts; the forgiveness of sins must also be supposed to be tendered unto them upon the condition, that their sins be forgiven; as conversion is, on condition they be converted, or do convert themselves.

3. This promise being by the prophet and apostle insisted on, as containing the grace, whereby eminently and peculiarly the new covenant is distinguished from that which was abolished; if the grace mentioned therein, be only the laying a powerful and strong obligation on men to duty and obedience, upon the account of the gracious and bountiful dealing of God with them, both as to their temporal and spiritual condition, I desire to know wherein the difference of it from the old covenant, as to the collation of grace, doth consist? And whether ever God made a covenant with man, wherein he did not put sufficient obligations of this kind upon him, unto obedience? And if so, what are the better promises of the new covenant? And what eminent and singular things, as to the bestowing of grace, are in it? Which things here are emphatically expressed to the uttermost.

4. The scope of this exposition (which looks but to one part of the promise about bestowing of grace, overlooking the main end and intendment of it, as hath been shewed), being to darken the words of the Holy Ghost, so far as to make them represent a contribution of means, instead of an effectual working the end and the event, on which the means supplied have an influence of persuasion, to prevail with men to do the things they are afforded them for: I desire to know, first, What new thing is here promised to them, which exceeded that mentioned, chap. xxv. 4, 5. wherein the Lord testifies, that he had granted them formerly a large supply of outward means (and especially of the word) for the end here spoken of. Secondly, To what end, and on what account, is this administration of means for a work ex-

pressed by terms of a real efficiency in reference to the work itself, which proceeding from the intendment of God, for the event aimed at, must needs produce it. And, thirdly, Why these words should not be of the same importance with the associate expression, which of necessity must be interpreted of an actual and absolute efficiency; ver. 41, 42. And, fourthly, Whether the administration of outward sufficient means for the producing of an event, can be a ground of an infallible prediction of that event? As God here absolutely saith, ' They shall all know him from the greatest to the least;' chap. xxxi. 34. which how it is brought about, the Holy Ghost acquaints us, Isa. iv. 13. ' They shall be all taught of the Lord ;' and John vi. 44—46. ' It is written in the prophets, And they shall be all taught of God : every man, therefore, that hath heard, and hath learned of the Father, cometh unto me.' But Mr. Goodwin hath sundry reasons to confirm his gloss, which must also be considered; and he saith,

1. ' That it is the familiar dialect of Scripture to ascribe the doing of things or effects themselves, to him that ministers occasions, or proper and likely means for the doing of them : so God is said to give them one heart, and one way, to put his fear into their hearts, when he administers motives, means, occasions, and opportunities to them, which are proper to work them to such a frame and disposition of heart, out of which men are wont to love and obey him, whether they be ever actually brought thereunto, or no: and this promise was fulfilled to the people after their return out of captivity, in the mercies they enjoyed, and the preaching of the prophets.'

Ans. 1. We are not now to be informed, that this is Mr. Goodwin's doctrine concerning conversion: that God doth only administer means, motives, and opportunities for it; but that man thereupon converts himself. And, 2dly, That when God hath done all he will, or can, that the event may not follow, nor the work be wrought. But, 3dly, That this sense, by any means or opportunities, can be fastened on the promise under consideration, we are not as yet so well instructed. When God once intendeth an end, and expresseth himself so to do, promising to work really and efficiently for the accomplishing of it, yea that he will actually do it, by that efficiency preventing all interpositions whatever, that may tend to frustrate his design, that that end of his shall not be accomplished, or that that working of his is only an administration of means, whereby men may do the things intended, if they will, or may do otherwise (he affirming that he will do them himself), is a doctrine beyond my reach and capacity. 4thly, His saying, that 'in this sense the promise was fulfilled to the people after the captivity,' is a saying against his own light. He hath told us not long since, that it could not be a promise of those things which were enjoyed before it was ever given, as in our sense they did the grace of perseverance, &c. Surely the means he mentioneth (until at least the coming of Christ in the flesh) were advanced to a far higher pitch and eminency on all hands, before the captivity, than after: and at the coming of Christ, it was eminently fulfilled in our acceptation of it, unto all to whom it was made. But he adds,

2. 'That if it be not so to be understood, and so said to be fulfilled as above, it is impossible for any one to assign how, and when this promise was fulfilled. For, first, It was made to the whole people, and the fulfilling of it to a few, will not confirm the truth of it. Secondly, The elect had no need of it (knowing themselves to be so), that they should never fall away: so that this is but to make void the glorious promise of God. And, thirdly, To say that it was made to the elect, is but to beg the thing in question.'

Ans. 1. As far as the body of the people was concerned in it, it was, and shall be in the latter days, absolutely accomplished towards them. It was, is, and shall be fulfilled to all to whom it was made, if so be that God be faithful, and cannot deny himself. 2. It was, it is, and shall be accomplished properly and directly to all the elect of that nation, to whom it was so made, as it hath been cleared already from Rom. ix. 10, 11. Where the apostle expressly and *data opera* answers the very objection, that Mr. Goodwin makes about the accomplishing of these promises, concerning the hardening and rejection of the greatest part of that people, affirming it to consist in this, that the election obtained, when the rest were hardened. Wherein he did not beg the question, though he digged not for it; but answered by clear distinctions, as you may see, Rom. ix. 6. xi.

1—3. 3. Neither do all the elect after their calling, know themselves to be so, nor have they any other way to come acquainted with their election, but by their faith in the promises; nor is it spoken like one acquainted with the course and frame of God's dealing with his saints, or with their spirits in walking with God; who supposeth the solemn and clear renovation of promises concerning the same things, with explanations and enlargements of the grace of them, to confirm and establish the communion between the one and the other, to be needless. And who make the promises of God void, and of no effect? We who profess the Lord to be faithful in every one of them, and that no one tittle of them shall fall to the ground, or come short of accomplishing? or Mr. Goodwin, who reports the grace mentioned in them, for the most part to come short of producing the effect, for which it is bestowed, and the engagements of God in them, to depend so upon the lubricity of the wills of men, that mostly they are not made good in the end aimed at; the Lord will judge. But it is farther argued:

3. 'That the Scripture many times asserts the futurity or coming to pass of things not yet in being, not only when the coming of them to pass is certainly known, but when it is probable, upon the account of the means used for the bringing them to pass; for God saith in the parable, 'They will reverence my Son;' Mark xii. 6. and yet the event was contrary. So upon the executing an offender, he saith, 'The people shall hear and fear, and do no more presumptuously,' which yet might not have its effect on all. So God saith, 'I will give them one heart,' not out of any certainty of knowledge or determination in himself, that any such heart or way should actually be given them, which would infallibly produce the effect mentioned, but that he would grant such means, as were proper to create such a heart in them.'

Ans. The nearer the bottom, the more sour lees. First, Doth God foretell the coming to pass of things future, upon a probable conjecture, which is here assigned to him? Is that the intendment of the expression in the parable, 'they will reverence my Son.' Or was he mistaken in the event, the thing falling out contrary to his expectation? Or is there any thing in this, or the place mentioned, Deut. xvii. 12, 13. but only an expression of the duty of men, upon the account of the means offered? Is there any the least intimation of any intent and purpose of God, as to the events insisted on? Any promise of his effectual working for the accomplishing of them? Any prediction upon the account of his purpose and design, which are the foundation of all his predictions? Or is there any the least correspondency in name or thing between the places now instanced in, and called in for relief, with that under consideration? This then, is the sinew of Mr. Goodwin's arguing in this place: sometimes when there is means offered men for the performance of a duty, the accomplishment of it is spoken of, as of what ought to have succeeded; and it is the fault of men to whom that duty is prescribed, and these means indulged, if it come not to pass: therefore, when God proposeth, and promiseth to work and bring about such and such a thing, and engageth himself to a real efficiency in it, yet it may come to pass, or it may not, it may be accomplished, or God may fail in his intendment.

2. The sense here given to the promise of God, ' I will give them one heart,' &c. hath been formerly taken into consideration, and it hath been made to appear, that notwithstanding all the glorious expressions of God's administration of means to work men into the frame intimated, yet upon the matter, the intendment of the exposition given, amounts to this: Though God saith, ' He will give us a new heart,' yet indeed he doth not so give it to any one in the world, nor ever intended to do so; but this new heart, men must create, make, and work out themselves, upon the means afforded them, which being very eminent, are said to create such hearts in them, though they do it not, but only persuade men thereunto : a comment this is, not much unlike the first that ever was made upon the words of God; Gen. iv. 5. Whether God or man create the new heart, is the matter here in question.

For what he lastly affirms, ' That if this be a promise of absolute perseverance, it is inconsistent with all the prophecies of the rejection of the Jews, which are accordingly fulfilled ;' I must refer him to St. Paul, who hath long ago undertaken to answer this objection, from whom, if he receive not satisfaction, what am I, that I should hope to afford the least unto him ?

And these are the reasonings, upon the account whereof Mr. Goodwin dischargeth-this text of Scripture, by virtue of his autocratorical power in deciding controversies of this nature, from bearing testimony in this cause any more. Whether he will be attended unto herein, time will shew. Many attempts to the same purpose have formerly been made, and yet it endureth the trial.

I have thus turned aside to the consideration of the exceptions given into the ordinary interpretation of this place, lest any should think that they were waved upon the account of their strength and efficacy to overthrow it. The argument I intended from the words, for the stability of God's love and favour to believers, upon the account of his covenant engagement, is not once touched in any of them. These words then yield, a third demonstration of the steadfastness and unchangeableness of acceptation of believers in Christ, upon the account of the absolute stability of that covenant of grace, whereof God's engagement to be their God, and never forsake them, is an eminent portion.

CHAP. V.

Entrance into the argument from the promises of God, with their stability, and his faithfulness in them. The usual exceptions to this argument A general description of gospel promises. Why, and on what account called gospel promises. The description given, general, not suited to any single promise. They are free: and that they are so, proved: all flowing from the first great promise of giving a Redeemer. How they are discoveries of God's good-will: how made to sinners: consequential promises made also to believers. Given in and through Christ, in a covenant of grace Their certainty upon the account of the engagement of the truth and faithfulness of God in them: of the main matter of these promises, Christ and the Spirit. Of particular promises, all flowing from the same love and grace. Observations of the promises of God, subservient to the end intended: 1. They are all true and faithful: the ground of the assertion. 2. Their accomplishment always certain; not always evident: 3. All conditional promises made good: and how. 4. The promise of perseverance of two sorts: 5. All promises of our abiding with God in faith and obedience, absolute. The vanity of imposing conditions on them, discovered: 6. Promises of God's abiding with us, not to be separated from promises of our abiding with him: 7. That they do not properly depend on any condition in believers, demonstrated: instances of this assertion given: 8. (Making them conditional renders them void, as to the ends for which they are given.) given to persons, not qualifications. The argument from the promises of God, stated. Mr. G.'s exceptions against the first proposition cleared, and his objections answered: the promises of God always fulfilled: of the promise made to Paul, Acts xxvii 24, &c. Good men make good their promises to the utmost of their abilities. The promise made to Paul absolute, and of infallible accomplishment. Of the promise of our Saviour to his disciples, Matt. xix. 28 Who intended in that promise: not Judas: the accomplishment of the promise: the testimony of Peter Martyr considered: the conclusion of the forementioned objection. The engagement of the faithfulness of God for the accomplishment of his promise: 1 Cor. i. 9. 1 Thess. v. 23, 24. 2 Thess. iii. 3. The nature of the faithfulness of God expressed in the foregoing places, inquired into: perverted by Mr. G. His notion of the faithfulness of God, weighed and rejected; what intended in the Scriptures by the faithfulness of God. The close of the confirmation of the proposition of the argument proposed from the promises of God. The assumption thereof vindicated: the sense put upon it by Mr. G. The question begged.

THE consideration of the promises of God, which are all branches of the forementioned root, all streaming from the fountain of the covenant of grace, is, according to the method proposed, in the next place incumbent on us. The argument for the truth under contest, which from hence is afforded and used, is, by Mr. Goodwin, termed ' the first-born of our strength;' cap. 11. sect. 1. p. 225. and indeed we are content, that it may be so accounted, desiring nothing more ancient, nothing more strong, effectual, and powerful to stay our souls upon, than the promises of that God,* who cannot lie. I shall, for the present, insist only on those which peculiarly assert, and in the name and authority of God, confirm that part of the truth we are peculiarly in demonstration of; namely, the unchangeable stability of the love and favour of God to believers, in regard whereof he turneth not from them, nor forsaketh them, upon the account of any such interveniences whatever, as he will suffer to be interposed in their communion with him; leaving those, wherein he gives assurance upon assurance, that he will give out unto them such continual supplies of his Spirit and grace, that they shall never depart from him, to their due and proper place.

I am not unacquainted with the usual exception, that lieth against the demonstration of the truth in hand, from the promises of God; to wit, that they are conditional, depending on some things in the persons themselves to whom they are made, upon whose change or alteration they also may be frustrated, and not receive their accomplishment. Whether this plea may be admitted against the particular promises that we shall insist upon, will be put upon the trial, when we come to the particular handling of them. For the present being resolved (by God's assistance) to pursue the demonstration proposed from them, it may not be amiss, yea, rather it may be very useful, to insist a little upon the promises themselves, their nature and excellency, that we may be the more stirred up to inquire after every truth, and sweetness of the love. grace, and kindness (they being the peculiar way chosen of God, for the manifestation of his good will to sinners) that is in them; and I shall do it briefly, that I may proceed with the business of my present intendment.

Gospel promises then are: 1. The free and gracious dispensations; and, 2. Discoveries of God's good-will and love; to, 3. Sinners; 4 Through Christ; 5. In a covenant of grace; 6. Wherein, upon his truth and faithfulness, he engageth himself to be their God, to give his Son unto them, and for them, and

* Heb. vi. 18. Titus i. 2.

his Holy Spirit to abide with them, with all things that are either required in them, or are necessary for them, to make them accepted before him, and to bring them to an enjoyment of him.

I call them gospel promises: not as though they were only contained in the books of the New Testament, or given only by Christ after his coming in the flesh; for they were given from the beginning of the world, or[b] first entrance of sin : and the Lord made plentiful provision of them, and by them, for his people, under the Old Testament : but only to distinguish them from the promises of the law, which hold out a word of truth and faithfulness engaged for a reward of life, to them that yield obedience thereunto (there being an indissolvable connexion between entering into life, and keeping the commandments); and so to manifest, that they all belong to the[c] gospel properly so called, or the tidings of that peace for sinners, which was wrought out and manifested by Jesus Christ.

2. Farther, I do not give this for the description of any one single individual promise, as it lieth in any place of Scripture, as though it expressly contained all the things mentioned therein (though virtually it doth so), but rather to shew what is the design, aim, and good-will of God in them all, which he discovers and manifests in them by several parcels, according as they may be suited to the advancement of his glory, in reference to the persons to whom they are made. Upon the matter, all the promises of the gospel are but one, and every one of them comprehend and tender the same love, the same Christ, the same Spirit, which are in them all. None can have an interest in any one, but he hath an interest in the good of them all, that being only represented variously for the advantage of them that believe. My design is, to describe the general intention of God in all[d] gospel promises, whereby they being equally spirited, become as one : and concerning these I say,

1. That they are free and gracious as to the rise and fountain of them. They are[e] given unto us, merely through the good will and pleasure of God. That which is of pro-

b Gen. iii. 14, 15. Gal. iii. 17. Titus i. 1.
c Gal. iii. 12. Luke ii. 10. Eph. ii. 15. Isa. lii. 7.
d Gal. xvi. 17. Eph. ii. 12. Heb. vi. 17.   e Tit. i. 2. 2 Pet. i. 3, 4.

mise, is every where opposed to that which is of doubt, or
that which is any way deserved or procured by us.   Gal. iii.
18. ' If the inheritance be of the law' (which includes all that
in us is desirable, acceptable and deserving) ' it is no more of
promise,' that is, free, and of mere grace. He that can find
out any reason, or cause, without God himself, why he should
promise any good things whatever to sinners, (as all are, and
are ' shut up under sin, till the promise came,' Gal. iii. 22.)
may be allowed to glory[f] in the invention which he hath
found out.   A well conditioned nature, necessitating him to
a velleity of doing good, and yielding relief to them that are
in misery (though justly receiving the due reward of their
deeds, which even among the sons of men, is a virtue dwelling upon the confines of vice), for their recovery, is by some
imposed on him.   But that this is not the fountain and rise
of his promises, needs no other evidence, but the light of
this consideration.   That which is natural, is necessary, and
universal : promises are distinguishing as to them in misery :
at least they are given to men, and not to fallen angels : but
may not God do what he will with his own ?

Farther, Jesus Christ is himself in the promise : he is the
great original matter and subject of the promises ; and the
giving of him was doubtless of free grace and mercy : so
John iii. 16. 'God so loved the world, that he gave his only
begotten Son,' and Rom. v. 8. 'God commendeth his love
towards us, in that whilst we were sinners, Christ died for
us :' and in the first of John iv. 10. 'Herein is love, not that
we loved God, but that he loved us, and sent his Son to be a
propitiation for us.'   All is laid upon the account of [g]love
and free grace.   I confess there are following promises given
out for the orderly carrying on of the persons, to whom the
main original fundamental promises are made, unto the end
designed for them, that seem to have qualifications and conditions in them ; but yet, even those are all to be resolved
into the primitive grant of mercy.   That which promiseth
life upon believing, being of use to stir men up unto, and
carry them on, in faith and obedience, must yet as to the
pure nature of the promise be resolved into that, which freely
is promised, viz. Christ himself, and with him both faith
and life, believing and salvation.   As in your Automata,
there is one original spring or wheel, that giveth motion to

[f] Matt. xx. 15.   [g] Matt. xi. 26.

sundry lesser and subordinate movers, that are carried on with great variety, sometimes with a seeming contrariety one to another, but all regularly answering, and being subservient to the impression of the first mover. The [b]first great promise of Christ, and all good things in him, is that which spirits and principles all other promises whatsoever; and howsoever they may seem to move upon conditional terms, yet they are all to be resolved into that absolute and free original spring. Hence that great grant of gospel mercy, is called the gift by him. Rom v. 15—17. yea, all the promises of the law, as to their original emanation from God, and the constitution of the reward in them engaged to be bestowed for the services required, are free and gracious. There is not any natural indispensable connexion between obedience and reward, as there is between sin and punishment; as I have [i]elsewhere at large disputed and proved.

2. I call them discoveries and manifestations of God's good-will and love, which is the prime and sole cause of all the good things which are wrapped up, and contained in them. Of this good-will of God, the promises which he hath given, are the sole discoveries: we do not in this discourse, take promises merely for what God hath said he will do in terms expressly, but for every assertion of his good-will and kindness to us in Christ, all which was first held out under a word of promise; Gen. iii. 15. And this the apostle infers in Tit. i. 2, 3. ' In hope of eternal life, which God, that cannot lie, promised before the world began, but hath in due time manifested his word through preaching;' or discovered, or made known that good-will of his, by the promises in preaching of the gospel. And to this extent of significancy is that promise in the Scripture, both name and thing, in very many places stretched out: every thing whatever, that is manifestative of grace and good-will to sinners, is of the promise, though it be not cast into a promissory form of expression. Yea, whereas, strictly a promise respecteth that which is, either only future, and not of present existence, or the continuance of that which is; yet even expressions of things formerly done, and of a present performance (some individuals to the end of the world being to be made anew partakers of the grace, good-will, and mercy in them), do belong to the promise also, in that acceptation of

[b] Gen. iii. 15, 16. xlix. 10. Isa. ix. 6. 2 Cor. i 20.   [i] Diatr. de Just. Div.

it, which the Holy Ghost in [k]many places leads unto, and which we now insist upon.

3. I say they are made unto sinners, and that as sinners, under no other qualification whatever; it being by the mercy of the promise alone, that any men are relieved out of that condition of being sinners, and morally nothing else. Were not the promises originally made to sinners, there would never [l]any one be found in any other state or condition. I know there are promises made to believers, even such as are unchangeable, and shall bear them into the bosom of God; but I say these are all consequential, and upon supposition of the first and great promise, whereby Christ himself, and faith for his sake, is bestowed on them. This [m]runs through them all, as the very tenor of them, and method of God in them do manifest, as we shall see afterward. So the apostle, Gal. iii. 22. 'The Scripture hath concluded all under sin, that the promise by faith of Jesus Christ might be given to them that believe.' All are shut up under sin, until the promise of salvation by Jesus Christ, and faith in him, cometh in for their deliverance. The promise is given to them as shut up under sin, which they receive by mixing it with faith. And Rom. iii. 23, 24. 'All have sinned and come short of the glory of God, being justified freely by his grace, through the redemption that is in Christ.' Their condition is a condition of sin, and falling short of the glory of God, when the promise for justification is given unto them, and finds them. Thence the Lord tells us, Isa. liv. 8, 9. that this promise of mercy is like that which he made about the [n]waters of Noah, where is mentioned no condition at all of it, but only the sins of men. And in that state unquestionably was Adam, when the first promise was given unto him. To say then, that gospel promises are made to men in such conditions, and are to be made good only upon the account of men's abiding in the condition, wherein they are when the promise is made to them; is to say, that for men to leave the state of sin, is the way to frustrate all the promises of God. All deliverance from a state of sin[o] is by grace: all grace is of promise: under that condition then of sin doth the promise find men, and from thence relieve them.

[k] Micah vii. 17—19. [l] Eph. ii. 12. Rom. iii. 19. Gal. iii. 22.
[m] John iii. 16 Rom. viii. 32. 1 Cor. i. 30. Phil. i 29. Eph. i. 3.
[n] Gen. v. 21, 22. [o] Eph. ii. 4, 5. 8.

4. I say, these discoveries of God's good-will are made ʳthrough Christ, as the only medium of their accomplishment, and only procuring cause of the good things, that flowing from the good-will of God are inwrapped and tendered in them. And they are said to be in Christ: as, 1. The great messenger of the covenant, as in him who comes from the Father; because God hath confirmed and ratified them all in him: not in themselves, but unto us. He hath in him, and by him, given faith and assurance of them all unto us, ˄ declaring and confirming his good-will and love to us, by him: he reveals the Father (as a Father) from his own bosom; John i. 18. declaring his name, or grace unto his. John xvii. 3. 2 Cor. i. 20. ' In whom all the promises of God are yea, and in him amen, to the glory of God by us.' In him, and by his mediation, they have all their confirmation, establishment, and unchangeableness unto us. And, 2. Because he hath undertaken to be surety of that covenant, whereof they are the promises. Heb. vii. 24. ' He is the surety of the covenant,' that is, one who hath undertaken both on the part of God and ours, whatever is needful for confirmation thereof. 3. Because that himself is the great subject of all these promises, and in him (it being of his own purchase and procuring, he having obtained eternal redemption for us, Heb. ix.) there is treasured-up all the ᵠfulness of those mercies, which in them God hath graciously engaged himself to bestow; they being all annexed to him, as the portion he brings with him to the soul. Then, I say,

5. That they are discoveries of God's good-will, in a covenant of grace. They are indeed the branches, streams, and manifesting conveyances of the grace of that covenant, and of the good-will of God, putting itself forth therein. ˌHence the apostle mentions the ' covenant of promise;' Eph. ii. 12. Either for the promises of the covenant, or its manifestation, as I said before. Indeed, as to the subject-matter and eminently, the promise is but one, as the covenant is no more; but both come under a plural expression, because they have been variously delivered and renewed upon several occasions. So the covenant of grace, is said to be established upon these promises; Heb. viii. 6. that is, the grace and mercy of the covenant, and the usefulness of it to

ᵖ 2 Cor. i. 20.　　　ᵠ John i. 16. Col. i. 18, 19. ii. 20, &c. Rom. viii. 32.

the ends of a covenant, to keep God and man together in peace and agreement, is laid upon these promises, to be by them confirmed and established unto us. God having by them revealed his good-will unto us, with an attendency of stipulation of duty. Their use, for the begetting and continuing communion between God and us, with the concomitancy of precepts, places them in the capacity of a covenant.

And then,

6. I mentioned the foundation of the certainty and unchangeableness of these promises, with our assurance of their accomplishment. The engagements and undertakings of God, upon his truth and faithfulness, is the stock and unmoveable foundation of this respect of them. Therefore, speaking of them, the Holy Ghost often backs them with that property of God ; ' He cannot lie ;' so Heb. vi. 17, 18. ' God, willing more abundantly to shew unto the heirs of promise, the immutability of his counsel, confirmed it by an oath ; that by two immutable things, wherein it was not possible for God to lie,' &c. so Tit. i. 2. ' God, which cannot lie, hath promised us eternal life.' There is no one makes a solemn promise, but as it ought to proceed from him in sincerity and truth, so he engageth his truth and faithfulness in all the credit of them, for the accomplishment thereof, what lieth in him. And on this account, doth ʳDavid so often appeal unto, and call upon the righteousness of God, as to the fulfilling of his promises, and the word which he caused him to put his trust in. It is because of his engagement of his truth and faithfulness, whence it becometh a righteous thing with him, to perform what he hath spoken. How far this respect of the promises extends, and wherein it is capable of a dispensation, is the sum of our present controversy : but of this afterward. Then,

7. A brief description of the matter of these promises, and what God freely engageth himself unto, in them, was insisted on. Of this, of the promises in this regard, there is one main fountain or spring, whereof there are two everlasting streams, whence thousands of refreshing rivulets do flow. The original fountain and spring of all good unto us, both in respect of its being and manifestation, is, that he ' will be our God.' Gen. xvii. 1, 2. ' I am Almighty God :

ʳ Psal. xxxi. 1. v. 14. Isa. xlv. 19. 2 Pet. i. 1.

walk before me and be thou perfect, and I will make my covenant.' So every where, as the bottom of his dealing with
us in covenant: Jer. xxxi. 33. 'I will be their God, and they
shall be my people;' Isa. liv. 5. And' in very many other
places. Now that he may thus be our God, two things are
required :

1. That all breaches and differences between him and us
be removed, perfect peace and agreement made, and we rendered acceptable, and well pleasing in his sight. These are
the terms, whereon they stand to whom he is a God in covenant. For the accomplishment of this, is the first main
stream, that floweth from the former fountain; namely, the
great promise of giving Christ to us, and for us, 'who is our
peace;' Eph. ii. 14. 'And who of God is made unto us wisdom, righteousness, sanctification, and redemption;' 1 Cor.
i. 30. 'Who loves us, and washeth us in his own blood, and
makes us kings and priests to God and his Father;' Rev. i. 6.
''Giving himself for his church, that he might purify and
cleanse it, with the washing of water, by the word, that he
might present it to himself a glorious church, not having
spot or winkle, or any such thing, but that it should be
holy and without blemish.' Doing and accomplishing all
things that are required for the forementioned ends. And
this is the first main stream, that flows from that fountain.
Christ as a Redeemer, a Saviour, a Mighty One, a priest,
a sacrifice, an oblation, our peace, righteousness, and the
author of our salvation, is the subject-matter thereof.

2. That we may be kept and preserved meet for communion with him, as our God, and for the enjoyment of him, as
our reward. For this end, flows forth the other great stream
from the former fountain, namely, the promise of the Holy
Spirit, which gives us, to [u] 'make us meet for the inheritance with the saints in light,' to put forth and exercise towards us, all the acts of his love, which are needful for us,
and to work in us the obedience which he requires and accepts of us in Jesus Christ, so preserving us for himself.
This [x] promise of the Spirit in the covenant, with his work
and peculiar dispensations, is plentifully witnessed in very

* Hos. ii. 23
[t] Eph. v. 26, 27. Tit. ii. 14. Gen. iii. 15. Job xix 25 Eph. ii. 14. Heb ii. 17.
Eph. v. 2. 1 Tim ii 6.   [u] Col i. 11.
[x] Isa. lxi. 21. Ezek. xi. 21. xxxvi. 26, 27. John xiv. 15, 16, &c.

many places of the Old Testament and New; some whereof must afterward be insisted on. Hence, he is sometimes called the promise of the covenant, Acts ii. 59. 'The promise is to you,' which promise is that which Christ receiveth from his Father; ver. 33. even the 'promise of the Holy Ghost.' I shall only add, that though this be a great stream, flowing from the first fountain, yet it comes not immediately thence, but issues out from the stream beforementioned, the promise of the Lord Jesus Christ; for he is given by him unto us, as procured for us, and given only unto his.

Now from these two grand streams, do a thousand rivulets flow forth for our refreshment. All the mercy that Christ hath purchased, all the graces that the Spirit doth bring forth (which in the former description I call all things that are either required in them, or needful to them, to make them accepted before God, and to bring them to an enjoyment of him), all promises of mercy and forgiveness, all promises of faith and holiness, of obedience and perseverance, of joy and consolation, of correction, affliction, and deliverance; they all flow from these: that is, from the matter of those promises, doth the matter of these arise, and hence are the ensuing corollaries.

1. Whoever hath an interest in any one promise, hath an interest in them all, and in the fountain-love, from whence they flow. He to whom any drop of their sweetness floweth, may follow it up unto the spring: were we wise, each taste of mercy would lead us to the ocean of love. Have we any hold on a promise, we may get upon it, and it will bring us to the main, Christ himself and the Spirit, and so into the bosom of the Father. It is our folly to abide upon a little, which is given us merely to make us press for more.

2. That the most conditional promises, are to be resolved into absolute and unconditional love. God, who hath promised life upon believing, hath promised believing, on no condition (on our parts) at all, because to sinners.

This in general being given in, concerning the nature of the promises, I shall proceed to some such considerations, as are of particular usefulness unto that improvement, which

' John xiv. 16. Gal. iv. 6.

(the Lord assisting) I intend to make of them, for the confirmation of the truth under debate. And they are these :

All the promises of God are true and faithful, and shall most certainly, all of them, be accomplished. His nature, his veracity, his unchangeableness, his omniscience, and omnipotency, do all contribute strength to this assertion. Neither can these properties possibly continue entire, and the honour of them be preserved unto the Lord, if the least failing in the accomplishment of his promises be ascribed unto him. Every such failing must of necessity, relate to some such principle, as stands in direct opposition to one or more of the perfections before mentioned. It must be a failing in truth, unchangeableness, prescience, or power, that must frustrate the promise of any one. We indeed often alter our resolutions, and the promise that is gone out of our mouths, and that (perhaps) righteously, upon some such change of things, as we could not foresee, nor ought to have supposed, when we entered into our engagements. No such thing can be ascribed unto him, who knows all things, with their circumstances, that can possibly come to pass, and hath determined, what shall so do, and therefore will not engage in any promise that he knows, something which he foresaw would follow after, would cause him to alter. It were a ludicrous thing in any son of man, to make a solemn promise of any thing to another, if he particularly knew, that in an hour some such thing would happen, as should enforce him to change, and alter that promise, which he had so solemnly entered into. And shall we ascribe such an action to him, before whom all things are open and naked? Shall he be thought solemnly to engage himself to do, or accomplish any thing, which yet not only he will not do, but also at that instant hath those things in his eye, and under his consideration, for which he will not so do, as he promiseth, and determined before that he would not so do. If this be not unworthy the infinite goodness, wisdom, and faithfulness of God, I know not what can, or may be ascribed unto him, that is. Yea the truth and veracity of God in his promises cannot be denied him, without denying him his Deity, or asserted, without the certain accomplishment of what he hath promised.

2. There are sundry things relating to the accomplishment

of promises, as to times, seasons, persons, ways, &c. wherein we have been in the dark, and yet the promises concerning them be fully accomplished. The rejection of the Jews supplies us with an instance pregnant with this objection; the apostle tells us, that with many this objection did arise on that account: if the Jews be rejected, then the promises of God to them do fail; Rom. vi. 9. He lays down, and answers this objection, discovering that fallacy therein by a distinction. 'They are not (saith he) all Israel that are of Israel;' ver. 7, 8. As if he had said, there is a twofold Israel, an Israel after the flesh only, and an Israel after the flesh and spirit also. Unto these latter were the promises made; and therefore, they who look on the former only, think it faileth, whereas indeed, it holdeth its full accomplishment. So he disputes again; chap. xi. 7. I say then we may be in the dark, as to many circumstances of the fulfilling of promises, when yet they have received a most exact accomplishment.

3. All the conditional promises of God are exactly true, and shall be most faithfully made good by accomplishment, as to that wherein their being as promises doth consist, as far as they are declarative of God's purpose and intendment. This is that, which (as I said before) some object; many of the promises of God are conditional, and their truth must needs depend upon the accomplishment of the condition mentioned in them: if that be not fulfilled, then they also must fail, and be of none effect. I say then, that even the conditional promises of God, are absolutely made good. The truth of any promise consists in this, that that whereof it speaks, answers the affirmation itself. For instance, 'he that believeth shall be saved.' This promise doth not primarily affirm that any one shall be saved, and notwithstanding it, no one might so be: but only this it affirms, that there is an infallible connexion between faith and salvation: and therein is the promise most true, whether any one believe or no. Briefly, conditional promises are either simply declarative of the will of God, in fixing an exact correspondency between a condition mentioned and required in them, and the thing promised by them, in which case, they have an unchangeable and infallible verity in themselves, as there is in all the promises of the moral law to this day; for he that keeps the commandments shall live, or they are also the discoveries of the good-will of God, his intendments and purposes, that, whereof

they make mention, being not the condition whereon his purposes are suspended, but the way and means, whereby the
thing promised is to be accomplished: and in the latter acceptation alone, are they (in the business in hand) our concernment.

4. That the promises concerning perseverance (as hath
been often intimated) are of two sorts. The first, of the continuance of the favour of God to us; which respects our justification. The other, of the continuance of our obedience unto
God; which respects our sanctification. Let us consider
both of them, and begin with the latter.

1. Of them, I say then, they are all absolute, not one of
them conditional (so as to be suspended, as to their accomplishment, on any conditions), nor can be; the truth of God in
them, hath not its efficiency and accomplishment, by establishing the relation that is between one thing and another,
or the connexion that is between duty and reward, as it is in
conditional promises, that are purely and merely so; but enforceth the exact fulfilling of the thing promised, and that
with respect unto, and for the preservation of, the glory of
that excellency of God, ' he cannot lie.' Let it be considered,
what that condition, or those conditions be, or may be, on
which promises of this nature should be suspended, and the
truth of the former assertions will evidently appear : That
God hath promised unto believers, that they shall for ever
abide with him, in the obedience of the covenant unto the
end, shall afterward be proved by a cloud of witnesses.
What now is the condition, whereon this promise doth depend? It is (says Mr. Goodwin) ' That they perform their
duty, that they suffer not themselves to be seduced, nor
willingly cast off the yoke of Christ.' But what doth this
amount unto ? Is it not thus much : If they abide with God
(for if they perform their duty, and not suffer themselves to
be seduced, nor willingly depart from God, they abide with
him), God hath promised, that they shall abide with him.
Upon condition they abide with him, he hath promised they
shall; ' egregiam vero laudem.' Can any thing more ridiculous be invented? If men abide with God, what need they
any promise, that they shall so do ? The whole virtue of the
promise depends on that condition, and that condition containeth all that is promised : neither is it possible, that any
thing can be invented to be supplied as the condition or conditions of these promises, but it will quickly appear upon

consideration, that, however it may be differently phrased, yet indeed it is coincident with the matter of the promise itself. That condition, or those conditions, must consist in some act, acts, way or course of acceptable obedience in them, to whom the promises are made : this the nature of the thing itself requireth. Now every such act, way, or course, is the matter of the promise, even universal obedience. Now if one man should promise another, that he should at such a time and place, be supplied with a hundred pounds to pay his debts, on condition that he came and brought the money himself, ought he to be esteemed to have a mind to relieve the poor man, or to mock him? To affirm, that, when God promiseth to write his law in our hearts, to put his fear in our inward parts, to create in us a new heart, to circumcise our hearts that we may fear him always, to give us his Spirit to abide with us for ever, to preserve us by his power, so that we shall never leave him nor forsake him, shall live to him, and sin shall not have dominion over us, &c. he doth it upon condition, that we write his law in our hearts, circumcise them, continue to fear him, abide with him, not forsake him, &c. is to make him to mock and deride at their misery, whose relief he so seriously pretendeth. Whatever promises then of this kind (promises of working obedience in us, for our abiding with him) shall be produced, they will be found to be absolute, and independent on any condition whatever, and their truth no ways to be maintained, but in and by their accomplishment.

2. For those of the first sort, which I shall now handle, farther to clear the foundation of their ensuing application, I shall propose only some few things unto consideration. As,

1. That they are not to be taken or looked upon, as to their use for argument in the present controversy, separated and divided from those other promises formerly insisted on, which assure believers, that they shall always abide with God, as to their obedience; all hope that any have to prevail against them, is by dividing of them. It is a very vain supposal and foundation of sand, which our adversaries build their inferences upon, which they make against the doctrine of the saints' perseverance, viz. the impossibility that God should continue his love and favour to them, whilst

they wallow in all manner of abominations and desperate rebellions against him ; an hypothesis crudely imposed on our doctrine, and repeated over and over, as a matter of the greatest detestation and abomination, that can fall within the thoughts of men. And such supposals and conclusions are made thereupon, as border at least upon the cursed coast of blasphemy, but *cui fini*, I pray ? To what end is all this noise ? as though any had ever asserted that God promised to continue his love and gracious acceptation always to his saints, and yet took no care, nor had promised that they should be continued saints ; but would suffer them to turn very devils. It is as easy for men to confute hypotheses created in their own imaginations, as to cast down men of straw of their own framing and setting up. We say indeed, that God hath faithfully promised, that he will never leave nor forsake believers ; but withal, that he hath no less faithfully engaged himself, that they shall never wickedly depart from him, but that they shall continue saints and believers. Yea (if I may so say), promising always to accept them freely, it is incumbent on his holy majesty, upon the account of his truth, faithfulness, and righteousness, to preserve them such, as without the least dishonour to his grace and holiness, yea, to the greatest advantage of his glory, he may always accept them, delight in them, and rejoice over them ; and so he tells us he doth, Jer. xxxi. 7. ' Yea, I have loved thee with an everlasting love, therefore with loving-kindness have I drawn thee:' he draws us with kindness to follow him, obey him, live unto him, abide with him, because he loves us with an everlasting love.

2. That these promises of God do not properly, and as to their original rise, depend on any conditions in believers, or by them to be fulfilled, but are the fountains and springs of all conditions whatever, that are required to be in them, or expected from them ; though the grace and obedience of believers are often mentioned in them, as the means whereby they are carried on according to the appointment of God, unto the enjoyment (or continued in it) of what is promised. This one consideration, that there is in very many of these promises, an express *non obstante*, or a notwithstanding the want of any such condition as might seem to be at the bottom, and to be the occasion, of any such promise or engage-

ment of the grace of God, is sufficient to give light and evidence to this assertion. If the Lord saith expressly, that he will do so with men, though it be not so with them, his doing of that thing cannot depend on any such thing in them, as he saith, notwithstanding the want of it, he will do it. Take one instance, Isa. liv. 9, 10. 'In a little wrath have I hid my face from thee for a moment, but with everlasting kindness will I have mercy on thee, saith the Lord thy Redeemer; for this is as the waters of Noah unto me; whereas I have sworn, that the waters of Noah shall no more cover the earth, so have I sworn that I will not be wroth with thee, nor rebuke thee: for the mountains shall depart, and the hills be removed, but my kindness shall not depart from thee, neither the covenant of my peace be removed, saith the Lord that hath mercy on thee.' He will have mercy on them with everlasting kindness; ver. 8. Yea, but how if they walk not worthy of it? Why yet this kindness shall not fail, saith the Lord; for it is as the 'waters of Noah:' God sweareth that the 'waters of Noah shall no more cover the earth,' and you see the stability of what he hath spoken. The world is now reserved for fire, but drowned it shall be no more: my kindness to thee (says God) is such, it shall no more depart from thee, than those waters shall return again upon the earth. Neither is this all, wherein he compareth his kindness to the waters of Noah, but in this also, in that in the promise of drowning the world no more, there was an express *non obstante* for the sins of men. Gen. viii. 21. 'The Lord said in his heart, I will not again curse the ground any more for man's sake, for the imagination of man's heart is evil from his youth.' Though men grow full of wickedness and violence, as before the flood they were, yet saith the Lord, 'The world shall be drowned no more.' And in this doth the promise of kindness hold proportion with that of the waters of Noah; there is an express relief in it against the sins and failings of them to whom it is made; viz. such as he will permit them to fall into, whilst he certainly preserves them from all such as are inconsistent with his love and favour, according to the tenor of the covenant of grace: and therefore it depends not on any thing in them, being made with a proviso for any such defect as in them may be imagined.

3. To affirm that these promises of God's abiding with us to the end do depend on any condition that may be uncertain in its event, by us to be fulfilled as to their accomplishment, doth wholly enervate and make them void in respect to the main end, for which they were given us of God. That one chief end of them is, to give the saints consolation in every condition, in all the straits, trials, and temptations, which they are to undergo, or may be called to, is evident. When Joshua was entering upon the great work of subduing the Canaanites, and setting the tabernacle and people of God in their appointed inheritance, wherein he was to pass through innumerable difficulties, trials, and pressures, God gives him that word of promise, ' I will never leave thee, nor forsake thee;' Josh. i. 5. So are many of them made to the saints in their weakness, darkness, and desertions, as will appear by the consideration of the particular instances following.[z] Now what one drop of consolation can a poor, drooping, tempted soul, squeeze out of such promises, that depend wholly and solely upon any thing within themselves ; he will be with me and be my God, it is true ; but always provided that I continue to be his : that also is a sweet and gracious promise, but that I shall do so he hath not promised ; it seems I have a cursed liberty left me of departing wickedly from him ; so that upon the matter, notwithstanding these promises of his, I am left to myself; if I will abide with him, well and good, he will abide with me, and so it will be well with me: that he should so abide with me, as to cause me to abide with him, it seems there is no such thing ; soul look to thyself, all thy hopes and help is in thyself : but alas ! for the present I have no sense of this love of God, and I know not that I have any true, real, unfeigned obedience to him. Corruption is strong ; temptations are many ; what shall I say ? Shall I exercise faith on those promises of God, wherein he hath said, and given assurance, that ' he will be a God to me for ever ?' According as my thoughts are of my own abiding with him, so may I think of them, and no otherwise; so that I am again rolled upon mine own hands, and left to mine own endeavours, to extricate myself from those sad entanglements. What now becomes of the consolation, which in these promises is in-

[z] Isa. iv. 3, 4.

tended? Are they not on this account rather flints, and pieces of iron, than breasts of comfort and joy.

Lastly, If it be so as is supposed, it is evident that God makes no promises unto persons, but only unto conditions and qualifications, that is, his promises are not engagements of his love and good-will to believers, but discoveries of his approbation of believing: suppose any promise of God to be our God, our all-sufficient God for ever, not eminently to include an engagement for the effectual exertion of the all-sufficiency to preserve and continue us, in such a state and spiritual condition, as wherein he may with the glory and honour of his grace (and will not fail to), abide and continue our God, and you cut all the nerves and sinews of it, as to the administration of any consolation unto them to whom it is given. The promises must be made good; that is, certain; and if they are accomplished, or not accomplished unto men, merely upon the account of such and such qualifications in them, which if they are found, then they shall be fulfilled; if not, then they are suspended: they are made to the conditions, and not at all to the persons. And though some, perhaps, will easily grant this, yet upon this account it cannot be said, that God ever made any one promise unto his church, as consisting of such persons, namely, Abraham and his seed; which is directly contrary to that of the apostle, Rom. ix. 8. where he calleth the elect, ' the children of the promises,' or those to whom the promises were made. It appears then, that neither are these promises of God conditional. As they proceed from free grace, so there is no other account, on which they are given out, continued and accomplished towards the children of God. Though the things of the promise are often placed in dependance one of another, as means and ends, yet the promises themselves are absolute.

These few things being premised, I shall now name and insist upon some particular promises, wherein the Lord hath graciously engaged himself that he will abide to be a God in covenant unto his people, and their guide unto death: from which I shall labour to make good this argument, for the perseverance of the saints.

That which that God[a], who cannot lie, nor deceive, with

---

[a] Titus i. 2. Heb. vi. 18. James i. 18. 1 Cor. i. 9.

whom there is no variableness, nor shadow of turning, who. is faithful in all his promises, and all whose words are truth and faithfulness, hath solemnly promised and engaged him- self unto, to this end, that they, unto whom he so promiseth and engageth himself, may from those promises receive strong consolation ; that he will certainly perform and ac- complish; that he will be a God and a guide unto death unto his saints; that he will never leave them nor forsake them ; that he will never cast them off, nor leave them out of his favour, but will preserve them such as is meet for his holy majesty to embrace, love, and delight in ; and that with an express notwithstanding for every such thing as might seem to provoke him to forsake them ; he hath pro- mised, and for the end mentioned. Therefore that he will so abide with them, that his love shall be continued to them to the end, that he will preserve them unto himself, &c. ac- cording to his truth and faithfulness, shall be accomplished and fulfilled. The inference hath its strength from the na- ture, truth, and faithfulness of God ; and whilst they abide in any credit with the sons of men, it may seem strange that it should be denied or questioned. The major propo- sition of the forementioned argument is examined by Mr. Goodwin, cap. 11. sect. 1. p. 225. saith he,

1. 'What God hath promised in his word, is certain in such a sense, and upon such terms, as God would be under- stood in his promises ; but what he promised in one sense, is not certain of performance in the other.'

Ans. 1. Doubtless, God's meaning and intention in his promises is the rule of their accomplishment. This some- times we may not be able to fathom ; and thereupon be ex- posed to temptations not a few, concerning their fulfilling; so was it with them with whom Paul had to do, in reference to the promises made to the seed of Abraham. The question then is not whether that which is promised in one sense, shall be performed in another; but whether God's promises have, and shall certainly have, all of them, according to his intendment, any performance at all. And the aim of Mr. Goodwin in the example, that he afterward produceth, is not to manifest, that that which God promiseth shall cer- tainly be performed only in that sense, wherein he made his promise ; but that they may be performed, or not performed at all. It is not in whose sense they shall have their performance, but whether they shall have any performance or no. If the thing promised be not accomplished, the promise is not at all in any sense performed; unless Mr. Goodwin will distinguish, and say, there are two ways of any thing's performance; one whereby it is performed, another whereby it is not. But he proceeds to manifest this assertion by an induction of instances.

'God,' saith he, 'promised to[a] Paul the lives of them that were in the ship; his intent and meaning was not, that they should all be preserved against whatever they in the ship might do to hinder that promise, but with this proviso or condition, that they in the ship should hearken unto him and follow his advice; which is evident from those words of Paul, Except these abide in the ship, ye cannot be saved: and had they gone away, God had not made any breach of promise though they had been all drowned.'

Ans. First, when men seriously promise any thing, which is wholly and absolutely in their power to accomplish and bring about, causing thereby good men to rest upon their words, and to declare unto others their repose upon their honesty and worth; if they do not make good what they have spoken, we account them unworthy promise-breakers, and they do it at the peril of all the repute of honesty, honour, and faith they have in the world. With God it seems it is otherwise; he makes a solemn gracious promise to Paul that ' the lives of all them in the ship with him, should be saved:' Paul, on whom it was as much incumbent as on any man in the world, not to engage the name of God (that God whom he worshipped and preached) in any thing, whose truth might in the least be liable to exception, being in the way of declaring[b] a new doctrine to the world, which would have been everlastingly prejudiced by any misprision of the faithfulness of that God, in whose name and authority he preached it; the sum of that doctrine also being the exaltation of that God, in opposition to all the pretended deities of the world. He, I say, boasts himself upon the promises that he had received, that there should be 'no

---

[a] Acts xxvii.
[b] Acts xiv. 15. 17. 24. 1 Tim. iv. 10.

loss of any man's life among them;' ver. 22. 25. he gives the
reason of his confident assertion, when all hope was taken
away; ver. 20. ' I believe God,' saith he, ' that it shall be even
as it was told me;' his faith in God was in reference to the
event, that it should come to pass, as it was told him. Faith
in God, divine faith can have nothing for its object, that may
fail it. He doth not say, that he believes that God will be
faithful to his promise in general, but also tells them wherein his faithfulness doth consist, even in the performance and
accomplishment of that which he had promised. This he
informs the centurion and the rest in the ship with him;
and if in the issue it had otherwise fallen out, there had not
been any colour of justifying the faith of that God he served,
or his own truth in being witness to him. Had any perished, those that remained would have argued him of lying.
Yea, but saith he not himself, ' Except these abide in the
ship ye cannot be saved?' He did so indeed, and thereby
declared the necessity of using suitable means, when providence affords them to us, for the accomplishment of appointed determined ends. God, who promiseth any thing,
and affordeth means for the attaining of it, will direct them
to whom those promises are made, to the use of those means,
as he doth the centurion by Paul; it being incumbent in
this case on his holy majesty, upon the account of his engaged faithfulness to save them, he will yet have them subservient to his promise in their endeavours for their own
safety. Means may be assigned for an end, as to their ordinary subserviency thereunto, without any suspending of the
event on them, as a condition of an uncertain issue and accomplishment. And therefore that this solemn promise made
unto Paul, whose event and accomplishment, upon the account of his believing God, he absolutely believed, and whose
performance he foretold without the least intimation of any
condition whatever (only he bids them not throw away the
means of their preservation) should depend, as to its fulfilling,
on such a condition, as in respect of the event might not
have been (God who made the promise not making any infallible provision for the condition), and so have been actually
frustrate, is an assertion, not only not grounded on these
words of Paul, setting out the suitable means of the provi-

dence of God for the accomplishment of an appointed end, but also derogatory in the highest, to the glory of the truth and faithfulness of God himself. But,

3. 'That promise,' saith he, ' of our Saviour to his disciples, Matt. xix. 28. That they who followed him in the regeneration, should sit upon twelve thrones judging the twelve tribes of Israel, Judas being yet one of them, was not fulfilled, and in case the rest had declined, they also with him might have come short of the promise made unto them.'

Ans. Christ knew what was in man, and had no need of any to tell him, he knew from the beginning who it was that should betray him, and plainly pronounced him to be a devil: he knew he was so, that he[d] believed not; that he would continue so; he would betray him; that his end would be desperate; he pronounced a curse upon him, as being cursed by David, Psal. cix. so many generations before his coming into the world; and is it probable now, that he promised this man a throne for his following him in the regeneration? which is most certain (take it in what sense you will) he did never follow him in, but only as he gave him his bodily attendance, in his going up and down. He was never admitted to be witness of his resurrection, the time being not yet come, wherein a discovery was to be made of the hypocrisy of Judas, that he might have space to carry on the work which he had to do: and the number of those, who in a peculiar manner, were to bear witness to the completing of the whole work of regeneration in the resurrection of Christ, being twelve, he who was afterward admitted into that number being one[e] that now followed him, our blessed Saviour telleth them indefinitely to their consolation, what will be the glorious issue of their following him, and bearing witness to him, in this work. That which is promissory in the words, is made to them who forsook all and followed him in the work mentioned, which assuredly he, who was always a thief, a devil, a covetous person, that followed not in the main of the work itself, was none of; that promise being afterward fulfilled to another then present with Christ. It is granted, if the rest of the twelve had fallen away, you may suppose of them what you please: that they might fall away, is to beg that which you cannot prove, nor will ever be granted

[d] John vi. 64. 70, 71.   [e] Acts i. 21.

you, though you should resolve to starve yourself, if you get it not: but this is,

4. 'Confirmed out of Peter Martyr, whose doctrine it is, that the promises of God are wont to be made with a respect unto the present estate and condition of things, with men: that is, they shall be performed unto men abiding under the qualifications, unto which they are made; as for example: What promises soever God maketh to believers, with respect had to their faith, or as they are believers, are not to be looked on as performable, or obliging the maker of them unto them, in case they shall relapse into their former unbelief.'

Ans. It is too well known, how, and to what end, our author cites Peter Martyr, and men of the same judgment with him, in this controversy, and to how little advantage to his cause with discerning men, he hath done it. In the same place, from whence these words are taken, the author distinguisheth of the promises of God, and telleth you, that some of them are conditional, which are (saith he) of a legal nature, which only shew the connexion between the condition, or qualification they require, and the thing they promise thereunto : and such are those whereof he speaks : but others he tells you, are absolute and evangelical, not depending on any condition in us at all; and so he tells us, out of Chrysostom, that this of our Saviour, Matt. xix. 28. is of the former sort; and the accomplishment of such like promises as these, he informs us, to consist not in the actual fulfilling of what is conditionally affirmed, but in the certain truth of the axiom, wherein the condition, and the event as such, are knit together.

2. To the example urged, I shall only ask what Mr. Goodwin's judgment is of the promises, that God hath made to believers, that they shall never relapse into their former state of unbelief, and on what condition they are made? Whether his promise of his love unto, and acceptance of believers, wherein he will abide for ever, do not infer their preservation in the condition, wherein they are (i. e. believers), will in the next place fall under our consideration. Your conclusion is, in the sense explained you admit the proposition; whatsoever God promiseth is certain, that is, it shall certainly be fulfilled, or it shall not.

There is, moreover, no small contribution of strength, as to our establishment in the faith of it, given to our proposition, by the signal engagement of the faithfulness of God, for the accomplishment of the promises, which he makes unto us; as it is manifest in those words of the apostle; 1 Cor. i. 9. 'God is faithful, by whom you are called to the fellowship of his Son:' in the foregoing verse, he telleth them that God will confirm them to the end, that they may be blameless in the day of the Lord Christ; of which confident assertion, he gives them this account, God is faithful to make good his promises made unto them, he changeth not. When a promise is once passed, that which first presents itself to the consideration of them to whom it is made, and whose concernment it is, that it be fulfilled, is the faithfulness of him that hath made the promise. This property of God's nature doth the apostle therefore mind the saints of, to lead them to a full assurance of their preservation. His promise being passed, fear not his faithfulness for its accomplishment. Might there in this case a supposal be allowed of any such interveniencies, as might intercept them in the way of enjoying what God truly promised, and cause them to come short thereof, what assurance could arise to them from the consideration of the faithfulness of God, who made those promises unto them? The faithfulness of God then is engaged for the accomplishment of the thing promised, which also shall be done, in case that fail not. So also 1 Thess. v. 23, 24. 'The very God of peace sanctify you wholly; and I pray God your whole spirit and soul and body be preserved blameless unto the coming of our Lord Jesus Christ: faithful is he that calleth you, who will also do it.' He assures them of their preservation in and unto the enjoyment of the things which he prayed for, and that upon the account of his faithfulness who had promised them: and, saith he, 'he will do it:' viz. because he is faithful. Let the oppositions to it be never so many, the difficulties never so great, the interveniencies what they will; 'He is faithful, and he will do it:' as it is affirmed, 2 Thess. iii. 3. 'But the Lord is faithful, who shall establish you, and keep you from evil:' as also in 1 Cor. x. 13. 'God is faithful, who will not suffer you to be tempted above that you are able, but will with the temptation also make a way to escape, that you may be able to bear it.' The same faithfulness of God is held out as that upon the account whereof no temptation shall befall believers, so as to separate them from him. The promise here peculiarly confirmed by it, and established on it, is such as no condition can tolerably be fixed unto. I will not suffer believers to be overcome with temptations, in case they be not overcome with temptations, is a promise not to be ascribed to the infinite wisdom of God, with which we have to do, and yet no other can with the least colour be proposed. All sin, all falling from God is upon temptation. Though Satan and the world should have no hand in drawing man aside from God, yet what they do from their own lusts, they do from temptation; James i. 14, 15. If God in his faithfulness will not suffer any temptation to prevail against believers, unless they neglect their duty, and fall from him, and they can no otherwise neglect their duty, nor depart from him, but upon the prevalency of temptation, their abiding with him, their final unconquerableness, hath a certainty answerable to the faithfulness of God.

This part of our strength Mr. Goodwin attempts to deprive us of; chap. 11. sect. 18. p. 236. in these words: 'Whereas the apostle mentioneth the faithfulness of God, as that divine principle in him, or attribute out of which he is moved to establish and confirm believers unto the end, and so to keep them from evil; by faithfulness he doth not necessarily mean that property or attribute of his, that renders him true and just, or constant in the performance of his promises, as if the apostle in these or any like places, supposed such a promise, one or more, made by him, by which he stands obliged to establish and confirm his saints unto the end by a strong and irresistible hand.'

Ans. The sum of this answer is, that the apostle by saying, 'God is faithful,' doth not understand God's faithfulness. What other virtue is intended in God by his faithfulness, but that whereby his truth and his constancy in words and promises is signified, I know not. Let the places from the beginning of the Scriptures to the end, wherein there is mention made of the faith, or faithfulness of God, of his being faithful, with the application thereof, the scope and intendment of the place, be perused, and see if they will give the least allowance to turn aside from eying the property and perfection of God before-mentioned, as that which they peculiarly intend; Deut. vii. 9. Psal. xxxvi. 5. lxxxix. 1, 2. 5. cxliii. 1. Isa. xlix. 7. Hos. ii. 20. Rom. iii. 3. 2 Tim. ii. 13. Heb. x. 23. 1 John i. 9. are some of them. Why we should wring out another sense of the expression in this place, I know not.

2. The faithfulness of God is not mentioned as that divine principle, out of which he is moved to establish and confirm believers to the end, but only to confirm them in the faith of his unchangeableness and constancy in accomplishing the work of his free grace, which he had begun in them, and promised to confirm to the end. The work flows from the principle of his free grace in Jesus Christ, whence alone he gives them great, free, and precious promises. His stability and constancy in those promises, as to their performance, is intended by his faithfulness and truth in them. What are the promises of God improperly so called, and not exhibited in words, which you intimate, I know not.

3. The apostle doth not only suppose, but in the name and authority of God, gives actually, in the places under consideration, promises of the certain and infallible preservation of believers to the end, asserting the immutability of God's engagement in them from his faithfulness. In brief, not to darken counsel and understanding with a multitude of words; by the promises of God, we intend in a peculiar manner, those expressed in the texts under consideration. viz. That God will establish believers to the end, keep them from evil and all temptations, that would overthrow them: and by the faithfulness of God, from whence believers have their assurance of the accomplishment of these promises, that which the Scripture holds out, and all the world of believers have hitherto taken to be, the faithfulness of God, as was before described. But it seems the word is here used otherwise. For, saith he,

'It is such a kind of faithfulness, or disposition in him, as that meant by Peter, when he styleth him a faithful Creator. Now God is, and may properly be termed a faithful Creator, because he constantly performs unto his creature, whatsoever the relation of a Creator promiseth in an equitable and rational way unto it, which is a great care and ten-

derness for the preservation and well-being of it. In like
manner he may, yea, it is most likely that he is, called faithful in his calling of men, as he is a spiritual Father or Creator, a giver of a new being unto men, because he never faileth
to perform unto those new creatures of his, whatsoever such
a being as this, regularly interpreted, promiseth unto him,
who receiveth it from him who is the donor of it: that is,
convenient and sufficient means for the preservation and
well-being of it. So that the faithfulness of God in the
Scripture in hand, supposes no such promise made by God,
as our opposers imagine: viz. whereby he should in terms or
words stand engaged to establish, confirm, or keep believers
from evil, his new creatures, his regenerated ones, after any
such a manner, but that they, if they be careless or negligent
for themselves, may be shaken and decline, and commit evil
notwithstanding.'

Ans. That by God's faithfulness mentioned in that place
of Peter, such a disposition as you afterward describe, is
intended, you had better say, than undertake to prove. It
is evident the scope of the apostle, is to exhort the saints of
God in all their trials and afflictions, to commit themselves
and their ways with patience and quietness unto God, upon
the account of his power to preserve them, as he is the Creator
of all, and his constancy in receiving of them, being present
with them, abiding with them, as he is faithful in his word
and promises. Yea, and the interpretation, our author would
have fixed on the expression here used, is not only remote
from the intendment of the place, turning that into a general
good disposition towards all his creatures, which is intimated for the peculiar support of believers, and that in
their distress, but also is in itself, a false, fond, and loose
assertion. There is no law nor relation of creation, that lays
hold on God so far, as to oblige him to the communication
of one drop of his goodness to any of the creatures, beyond
what is given them by their creation, or to continue that
unto them for one moment. All the dispensation of himself
unto his creatures, flowing from his sovereign good pleasure,
doing what he will with his own.

2. He doth very faintly, when he hath made the farthest
step in confident asserting that he dares venture upon (it

may be, and it is most likely), suppose that the faithfulness
of God in these places under consideration, may be taken in
such a sense as that before described. But,

1. This is no sense at all of the faithfulness of God, neither
is the word ever used in Scripture to signify any such thing
in God, or man, nor can with any tolerable sense be applied
to any such thing ; neither would there be any analogy between that which in God we call faithfulness, and that virtue
in man, which is so termed : nor is the faithfulness of God
here mentioned upon any such account, as will endure this
description, being insisted on only to assure the saints of
the steadfastness and unalterableness of God in the performance of his promises made to them : neither is the obligation of God to continue his love and favour, with grace
and means of it to believers, founded upon such a disposition
as is imagined, but in the free purpose of his will, which
he purposed in Jesus Christ before the world was : so that
there is not the least appearance of truth, or soundness of
reason, or any thing that is desirable, in this attempt to corrupt the word of God.

2. Then the faithfulness of God in the Scriptures in
hand bespeaks his truth and stability in the performance of
his promises, made of establishing believers to the end,
keeping them from evil, not suffering any temptation to befall them, but making withal a way to escape : in all which,
God assures them he will prevent all such carelessness, and
negligence in them, as inconsistent with their establishment,
which he will certainly accomplish. And thus is our major
proposition with its supplies of light and strength, freed
from such exceptions, as Mr. Goodwin supposes it liable
unto.

For the assumption, I shall not much trouble myself
with that ridiculous sense (called a sober and orthodox explication) which Mr. Goodwin is pleased to put upon it, to
allow it to pass current. ' In this sense,' saith he, ' it is
most true, that God hath promised that all believers shall
persevere, i. e. that all true believers formally considered,
i. e. as such, and abiding such, shall persevere: viz. in his
grace and favour; but this he presumes is not our sense,'
chap. 11. sect. 2. p. 226. And well he may presume it:
for whatever his greatest skill may enable him unto, we can

make no sense of it, but this : God hath promised believers shall persevere, in case they persevere ; which is to us upon the matter no sense at all. To persevere in God's grace and favour, is to continue in faith and obedience, which if men do, God hath solemnly promised, and sworn that they shall so do. Certainly there is an orthodox sense in God's promises, that is not nonsense. Be it granted then, that this is not our sense, not so much because not ours, as because not sense, what is our meaning in this proposition? It is (saith Mr. Goodwin) ' that God will so preserve believers, that none of them shall make shipwreck of their faith, upon what quicksands of lust and sensuality soever they shall strike, against what rock of obduration and impenitency soever they dash.' But I beseech you, who told you that this was our sense of this proposition? being, indeed, no more sense than that which you give in for your own : by striking on ' the quicksands of lust, and dashing upon rocks of sensuality, impenitency, and obduration,' you have in no other places, sufficiently explained yourself to intend their falling under the power of sin. And is this asserted by us to be the tenor of God's promises to believers? or is it not? or do you not know that it is not so? did ever any say that God preserveth men in believing under obduration and impenitency? that is, under unbelief? for no man can be obdurately impenitent but unbelievers : do not you know that we maintain that the grace faithfully engaged to be bestowed on them, is given them to this end, to preserve them from the power of sin, from obduration and impenitency, and shall certainly be effectual for that purpose? ' Prima est hæc ultio, quod se Judice, nemo nocens absolvitur.'

CHAP. VI.

The former argument confirmed by an induction of particular instances:
John i. 5. opened. The concernment of all believers in that promise,
proved by the apostle; Heb., xiii. 5. The general interest of all believers
in all the promises of God cleared. Objections answered. How Old Testa-
ment promises may be improved. The promise insisted on relates princi-
pally to spirituals. The strength of it to the end intended. 1 Sam. xii. 22.
To whom the promise there is given. The twofold use of this promise:
threats to wicked men of use to the saints: promises to the saints of use
to wicked men. Isa. iv. 2—4. Psal. lxxxix. 30—37. opened. A condition
of backsliding supposed in believers: yet they not rejected. God's abiding
with his saints, upon the account of his, 1. Faithfulness, 2. Loving-kind-
ness, 3. Covenant, 4. Promise, 5. Oath. The intendment of the words
insisted on, from 1 Sam. xii. 22. Isa. xxvii. 2—4. Zeph. iii. 17, illus-
trated. The intendment of those words, ' I will not forsake thee.' The
reason of the promise, and means promised therein: no cause in them, to
whom the promise is made. Ezek. xxxvi. 32. Isa. lxiii. 22—25. opened;
also Isa. lvii. 17. The cause in God himself only. The name of God what
it imports: his all-sufficiency engaged therein, and his goodness. The rise
and fountain of all God's goodness to his people, in his own good pleasure:
the sum of our argument from this place of Scripture. Psal. xxiii. 4. 6.
opened: the psalmist's use of assurance of perseverance. Inferences from
the last use. 2 Tim. iv. 18, opened· all believers in the same condition, as
to perseverance, with David and Paul. The second inference from the
place insisted on. Assurance a motive to obedience, and is the end that
God intends to promote thereby. Psal. cxxv. 12. explained. Psal. xxxvii.
28. Deut. xxxiii. 3. Inferences from that place of the psalmist: per-
petual preservation in the condition of saints promised to believers. Mr.
G.'s objections and exceptions to our exposition and argument from this
place, removed. Promises made originally to persons, not qualifications:
not the same reason of promises to the church, and of threatenings to sin-
ners. Other objections removed. Isa. liv. 7—9. The mind of the Lord
in the promises mentioned in that place opened. The exposition given on
that place and arguments from thence vindicated. Direction for the right
improvement of promises. Hos. ii. 19, 20. opened. Of the general design
of that chapter: the first part of the total rejection of the church and
political state of the Jews. The second, of promises to the remnant, ac-
cording to the election of grace. Of this four particulars: 1. Of con-
version; ver. 14, 15. 2. Of obedience and forsaking all false worship;
3. Of peace and quietness: ver. 18. 4. Discovering the fountain of all the
mercies. Some objections removed. To whom this promise is made. The
promise farther opened: the persons to whom it is made. Ver. 14. of that
chapter opened. The wilderness condition whereunto men are allured by
the gospel, what it imports: 1. Separation: 2. Entanglement. God's
dealing with a soul in its wilderness condition. Promises given to persons

in that condition. The sum of the foregoing promises: the persons to whom they are made farther described. The nature of the main promise itself considered. Of the main covenant between God and his saints. The properties of God engaged for the accomplishment of this promise. Mr. G.'s exposition of this place considered, and confuted. John x. 27—29. opened; vindicated.

HAVING cleared the truth of the one, and meaning of the other proposition mentioned in the argument last proposed, I proceed to confirm the latter, by an induction of particular promises. The first that I shall fix upon, is that of Josh. i. 5. 'I will be with thee; I will not fail thee, nor forsake thee.' This promise (it is true), in this original copy of it, is a grant to one single person, entering upon a peculiar employment; but the Holy Ghost hath eminently taught the saints of God to plead, and improve it in all generations for their own advantage, and that not only upon[a] the account of the general rule, of the establishment of all promises in Jesus Christ, to the glory of God by us; but also by the application which himself makes of it unto them, and all their occasions, wherein they stand in need of the faithfulness of God therein; Heb. xiii. 5. 'Let your conversation be without covetousness, and be content with such things as you have: for he hath said, I will never leave thee, nor forsake thee.' The apostle layeth down an exhortation in the beginning of the verse, against the inordinate desire of the things of this world, that are laboured after upon the account of this present life; to give power and efficacy to his exhortation, he manifesteth all such desires to be altogether needless, upon consideration of his all-sufficiency, who hath promised never to forsake them; which he manifests by an instance in this promise given to Joshua, giving us withal a rule for the application of all the promises of the Old Testament, which were made to the church and people of God. Some labour much to rob believers of the consolation intended for them in the evangelical promises of the Old Testament, though made in general to the church upon this account, that they were made to the Jews; and being to them peculiar, their concernment now lieth not in them. If this plea might be admitted, I know not any one promise that would more evidently fall under the power of

[a] 2 Cor. i. 10.

it, than this we have now in consideration. It was made
to a peculiar person, and that upon a peculiar occasion,
made to a general or captain of armies, with respect to the
great wars he had to undertake, upon the special command
of God. May not a poor hungry believer say, What is this
to me? I am not a general of an army, have no wars to make
upon God's command, the virtue doubtless of this promise
expired with the conquest of Canaan, and died with him to
whom it was made. To manifest the sameness of love, that
is in all the promises, with their establishment in one Mediator, and the general concernment of believers in every one
of them, however, and on what occasion soever given to any,
this promise to Joshua is here applied to the condition of
the weakest, meanest, and poorest of the saints of God; to
all, and every one of them, be their state and condition what
it will. And, doubtless, believers are not a little wanting to
themselves, and their own consolation, that they do no more
particularly close with those words of truth, grace, and
faithfulness, which upon sundry occasions, and at divers
times, have been given out unto the saints of old, even Abraham, Isaac, Jacob, David, and the residue of them, who
walked with God in their generations : these things in an
especial manner, are recorded for our consolation, that we
through ' patience and comfort of the Scripture might have
hope ;' Rom. xv. 4. Now the Holy Ghost, knowing the weakness of our faith, and how apt we are to be beaten from
closing with the promises, and from mixing them with faith,
upon the least discouragement that may arise (as indeed
this is none of the least, that the promise is not made to us,
it was made to others, and they may reap the sweetness of
it, God may be faithful in it, though we never enjoy the
mercy intended in it ; I say), in the next words he leads believers by the hand, to make the same conclusion with boldness and confidence from this, and the like promises, as
David did of old, upon the many gracious assurances, that
he had received of the presence of God with him, ver. 6. ' So
that' (saith he, upon the account of that promise)' we may say
boldly' (without staggering at it by unbelief,) ' that the Lord
is our helper ;' this is a conclusion of faith ; because God
said to Joshua, a believer, ' I will never leave thee nor forsake thee' (though upon a particular occasion, and in refer-

ence to a particular employment), every believer may say with boldness, ' He is my helper.'

It is true, the application of the promises here looks immediately unto temporals: but yet being drawn out from the testimony of the continuance of the presence of God with his saints, doth much more powerfully conclude to spirituals. Yea, the promise itself is of spiritual favour, and what concerns temporals, is only from thence extracted.   Let us then weigh a little the importance of this promise, which the apostle hath rescued from suffering under any private interpretation, and set at liberty to the use of all believers. To every one of them, then, God saith directly and plainly, that he will ' never leave them nor forsake them.' If there should any question arise, whether he should be taken at his word or no, it must be the[b] devil that must be entertained as an advocate against him.   Unbelief indeed hath many pleas, and will have, in the breasts of saints against closing with the faithfulness of God in this promise, and the issue of confidence in him, which from a due closing with it, would certainly flow.   But shall our unbelief make the truth of God of none effect ? He hath told us that he ' will never leave us nor forsake us ;' the old serpent, and some arguing from him herein, are ready to say : yea, ' hath God indeed said so?' The truth of it shall not indeed be surely so, it may be otherwise, for God doth know, that many cases may fall out, that you may be utterly rejected by him, and cast out of his presence; you may have such oppositions rise against you in your walking with him, as shall certainly overcome you and set you at enmity with him ; or you may fully depart from him ; and many such like pleadings will Satan furnish the unbelief of believers withal.   If they are not sufficiently taught by experience, what it is to give credit to Satan, endeavouring to impair, and call in question (upon any pretence whatever) the faithfulness of God and his truth, when will they learn it? Surely they have little need to join with their adversaries for the weakening of their supportments, or the impairing of their consolations. Whereas there is an endeavour to make men believe, that the denying any absolute unchangeable promise of God unto believers makes much for their comfort and refreshment, it

[b] Gen iii. 1

shall afterward be considered in common, in reference also to those other demonstrations of the saints' perseverance, that shall, God willing, be produced.

It will be excepted, that God will not forsake them whilst they are believers; but if they forsake him, and fall from him, he is at liberty to renounce them also. But that God's not forsaking of any, is no more but a mere non-rejection of them, shall afterward be disproved. Whom he doth not forsake as a God in covenant, to them doth he continue his presence, and towards them exerciseth his power and all-sufficiency for their good. And if he can by his Spirit and the power of his grace keep them whom he doth not forsake, in a state and condition of not-forsaking him, he doth forsake them, before they forsake him, yea before he is said to forsake them. God's not forsaking believers, is effectually preventive of that state and condition in them, on the account whereof it is asserted that he may forsake them.

1 Sam. xii. 22. The truth we have under consideration is confirmed by the prophet in the name and authority of God himself, and the words wherein it is done, have the force of a promise, being declarative of the good-will of God unto his people in Christ: ' For the Lord will not forsake his people for his great name's sake, because it pleased the Lord to make them his people.'

The expression is[c] the same with that, which the Lord gives his people of his good-will in the covenant of grace, of which I have spoken before. Many may be their calamities and afflictions, many their trials and temptations, many their desertions and darknesses, but God will not forsake them, he will not utterly cast them off for ever. That his people are his people in covenant, his secret ones, his spiritual church, the remnant according to the election of grace, hath been before declared in the handling of like places of Scripture. It is to vindicate this and the like promises from all surmises of failing and coming short of accomplishment, that the apostle saith, ' God hath not cast away his people which he did foreknow;' Rom. xi. 2. that is, he hath made good this promise to them: even to them among the Jews, whom he did so foreknow; as also to predestinate them to be conformed to the image of his Son; Rom. viii. 29. So out of all

[c] Gen. xvii. 1. Jer. xxxi. 38, 39.

Israel saving all Israel, even the whole Israel of God. That a discriminating purpose of God is intended in that expression, hath been already declared, and shall (the Lord assisting) be farther manifested.

The promise, as here mentioned, hath a double use.

1. It is held out as an inducement to obedience, to that whole people, in reference whereunto he telleth them, that 'if they did wickedly, they should be destroyed, both they and their king;' ver. 25. In the dreadful threatenings that God denounceth against wicked and impenitent ones, he hath an end to accomplish in reference to his saints, unto his own, even to make them know his terror, and to be acquainted with the abomination of sin. And in his promises intended directly to them, he hath designs to accomplish upon the most wicked and ungodly, even to discover his approbation of that which is good, that they may be left inexcusable.

2. It was a testimony of his good-will unto his secret ones; his remnant, his residue, his brand out of the fire, unto his people called according to his eternal purpose, in the midst of his people by external profession, and of his presence with them, under the accomplishment of the threatening mentioned upon the generality of that nation. He did not forsake them, when the people in general, and their king were destroyed. Whatever outward dispensation he bringeth upon the whole, the love and grace of the promise shall certainly be reserved for them, as, Isa. iv. 2—4. the remnant, the escaping of Israel, those that were written unto life, shall obtain, when the rest are destroyed, or hardened. So Psal. lxxxix. 30—37. ' If his children forsake my law, and walk not in my judgments, if they break my statutes, and keep not my commandments, then will I visit their transgressions with a rod, and their iniquity with stripes; nevertheless my loving kindness will I not utterly take from him, nor suffer my faithfulness to fail: my covenant will I not break, nor alter the thing that is gone out of my lips: once have I sworn by my holiness, that I will not lie unto David; his seed shall endure for ever, and his throne as the sun before me, it shall be established for ever, as the moon, and as the faithful witness in heaven. Selah.'

A supposal is made of such ways and walkings in the spiritual seed and offspring of the Lord Christ (which in the psalm is typed out by David), that the Lord will be as it were compelled to deal sharply with them, for their iniquities and transgressions: yet his kindness, that shall abide with Christ, in reference to the preservation of his seed; his faithfulness, that shall not fail, his covenant, and his oath shall be made good to the uttermost.

It is supposed, which is the worst that can be supposed, that in some degree, at least for some season, they may forsake the law, not keep the commandments, and profane the statutes of God, which continues the burden of poor believers to this day: yet the worst that the Lord threatens them on this account, when they might have expected that he would have utterly cast off such unthankful, unfruitful backsliders, poor creatures, is but this, ' I will visit them with a rod, and with stripes;' they shall have whatever comes within the compass of correction or affliction: rod and stripes shall be on them, and that whether outward correction, or inward desertion. But will the Lord proceed no farther? Will he not for ever cast them off, and ease himself of such a provoking generation? No, saith the Lord: there lie five things in the way, upon whose account I cannot so deal with them. All regard the same persons, as is evident from the antithesis that is in the discourse.

1. There is my loving kindness, saith God, which is eternal and unchangeable: for ' I love them with an everlasting love;' Jer. xxxi. 3. this I cannot utterly take away, though it may be hid and eclipsed, as to the appearance and influences of it, yet utterly it shall not be taken away as to the reality of it. Though I chasten and correct them, yet my loving kindness shall be continued to them. And then, saith he,

2. There is my faithfulness, which I have engaged to them, which, whatever they do (that is, that I will suffer them to do, or that they may do upon supposition of the[d] grace of the covenant, wherewith they are supplied), though they behave themselves very foolishly and frowardly, yet that I must take care of, that must not fail. 2 Tim. ii. 13. ' He abideth faithful, he cannot deny himself:' and this faithfulness, saith God, I have engaged in three things:

1. In my covenant, that I have made with them to be

<hr>

d Isa. xliii. 22—26.

their God, and wherein I have promised that they shall be
my people : wherein also I have made plentiful provision of
mercy and grace for all their failings : and this must not be
broken, my faithfulness is in it, and it must abide. My covenant of peace that I make with them, is an everlasting covenant: it ' is an everlasting covenant ordered in all things and
sure ;' 2 Sam. xxii. 5. Ezek. xxxvii. 26. it is a covenant of
peace, an everlasting covenant.

2. ' In the thing that is come out of my lips,' or the grace
and love I have spoken of in the promise ; herein also will I
be faithful, and that shall not be altered; all my ' promises
are yea, and amen, in Jesus Christ ;' 2 Cor. i. 20. And,

3. Lastly, All this I have confirmed by an oath, ' I have
sworn it by my holiness,' and ' I will not lie :' so that in all*
' these immutable things, wherein it is impossible for God to
deceive,' he hath treasured up strong consolation for them
that do believe. Though then the seed of Christ, which he
is to see, upon the account of his suffering for them, (Isa. liii.
10.) do sin and transgress, yet God hath put all these gracious
obligations upon himself, to reduce them by correction and
affliction, but never to proceed to final sentence of utter rejection.

To this purpose, I say, are the words in the place of
Samuel now mentioned.

1. The matter of the promise, or what he promiseth the
people, is, he will not forsake them. God's not forsaking
them, is not a bare not casting them off, but an active continuance with them in love and mercy. He exercises not a
pure negative act of his will towards any thing or person.
Whom he hates not, he loves : so Heb. xiii. 5. these words,
' I will not forsake thee,' hold out a continual supply of all
those wants, whereunto in ourselves we are exposed, and
what from his presence we do receive. I will not forsake
them, is, I will continue my presence with them, a God in
covenant; so he expresseth his presence with them, Isa. xxvii.
3. ' I the Lord do keep it, I do water it every moment, lest
any hurt it, I will keep it night and day.' He abideth with
his vineyard, so as to keep it, and to preserve it from being
destroyed. But may it not at one time or other be surprised
into desolation? No, saith he, ' I will keep it night and day :'

* Heb. vi. 18.

but what if this vineyard prove barren, what will he then do? Nay, but he will so deal with it, that it shall never be so barren, as to cause him to cast it up. He is not with it for nought, his presence is attended with grace and kindness. ' I water it,' saith he; and that not now and then, but ' every moment.' He pours out fresh supplies of his Spirit upon it to make it fruitful. Thence it becomes a ' vineyard of red wine,' ver. 2. the best wine, the most delicious, the most precious, to cheer the heart of God himself; as Zeph. iii. 17. ' The Lord thy God in the midst of thee is mighty ; he will save thee, he will rejoice over thee with joy, he will rest in his love, he will joy over thee with singing.' He causes them thereby that come out of Jacob to take root, he makes Israel blossom and bud, to fill the face of the world with fruit. This is that which God promiseth his people ; he will not forsake them, he will always give them his presence, in the kindness and supplies of a God in covenant, to protect them from others, to make them fruitful to himself : this is his not-forsaking them : he will preserve them from others ; who shall take them out of his hand ? he will make them fruitful to himself ; he will work, and who shall let him ?

2. The reason why the Lord will not forsake his people, why he will continue doing them good, is expressed in these words, ' for his own name's sake ;' and in this assertion two things are considerable :

1. A tacit exclusion of any thing in themselves, for which, or upon consideration whereof, God will constantly abide with them. It is not for their sakes, for any thing in them, or what they have done, may, or can do ; it is not upon the account of any condition or qualification whatever, that may, or may not be found on them, but merely for his name's sake ; which in the like case he expresseth fully, Ezek. xxxvi. 32. ' Not for your sakes do I this, saith the Lord, be it known unto you : be ashamed and confounded for your own ways, O house of Israel !' The truth is, they may prove such, as on all accounts whatever shall deserve to be rejected, that nothing in appearance, or in their own sense, as well as others, though the root of the matter be in them, may be found upon them, when God takes delight in them. Like those you have described at large, Isa. xlii. 22—25. ' But thou hast not called upon me, O Jacob ; but thou hast been

weary of me, O Israel: thou hast not brought me the small cattle of thy burnt-offerings, neither hast thou honoured me with thy sacrifices: I have not caused thee to serve with an offering, nor wearied thee with incense: thou hast brought me no sweet cane with money, neither hast thou filled me with the fat of thy sacrifices; but thou hast made me to serve with thy sins, thou hast wearied me with thine iniquities: I, even I, am he that blotteth out thy transgressions for mine own sake, an'd will not remember thy sins any more.' Weary of God they are, neglecting his worship, making his patience and forbearance to serve with their iniquities. It seems to be impossible almost for any creature to apprehend that God will not give them up to everlasting confusion. Yea, perhaps they may be froward in their follies, and contend with God when he goes to heal them; Isa. lvii. 17. 'For the iniquity of his covetousness, was I wroth and smote him; I hid me and was wroth, and he went on frowardly in the way of his heart.' Iniquity is upon them, a vile iniquity, 'the iniquity of covetousness.' God is wroth with them, and smites, and hides him, and they go on frowardly: and yet for all this he ' forsakes not for ever;' he abides to be their God; and that because his so doing is not bottomed on any consideration of what they are, have been, or will be, but he doth it for his name's sake, and with regard unto that which thereupon he will do for them. And upon this account, this promise of God's abiding and continuing with his, let grace be never so weak, corruption never so strong, temptations never so violent, may be pleaded, and the Lord rejoices to be put in remembrance of it by the weakest, frailest, sinfullest saint or believer in the world.

2. The cause or reason is positively expressed, why God will not forsake them: it is, ' for his great name's sake.' His great name is all that he consults withal, about his continuance with his people: this he calls himself, Isa. xliii. 25. ' I blot out thy sins for my own sake;' that is, for no other cause in the world that may be found in thee or upon thee. The name of God is all that whereby to us he is known; all his attributes, his whole will, all his glory. When God is said to do any thing for his name, it is either the cause and end of what he doth, or the principle from whence, with the motive wherefore, he doth it, that is by him intended. In

the first sense, to do a thing for his name's sake, is to do it for the manifestation of his glory, that he may be known to be a God, in the excellency of those perfections, whereby he reveals himself to his, with (most frequently) a special regard to his faithfulness and grace. It is in those properties to make himself known, and to be exalted in the hearts of his. So all his dispensations in Jesus Christ are for 'the praise of his glorious grace;' Eph. i. 6. That he may be exalted, lifted up, made known, believed and received as a God pardoning iniquity, in the Son of his love. And in this sense may the Lord be said to abide with his people 'for his name's sake;' for the exalting of his glory; that he may be known to be a God faithful in covenant, and unchangeable in his love, who will not 'cast off for ever,' those whom he hath once received into favour. It will not enter into the hearts of believers sometimes, why the Lord should so deal with them as he doth, and not cast them off; their souls may go to rest as to this thing: he himself is glorious herein; he is exalted, and doth it on that account. 2dly. If by his name you understand the principle from whence he worketh, and his motive thereunto, as it comprehends the whole long-suffering, gracious, tender, unchangeable nature of God, according as he hath revealed himself in Jesus Christ, in whom his name is; Exod. xxiii. 21. and which he hath committed to him to be manifested; John xvii. 6. so evidently two things in God are engaged, when he promiseth to work for his name's sake, or according to his great name.

1. His power or sufficiency: upon the engagement of the name of God on his people's behalf, Moses carefully pleads this latter or part thereof; Numb. xiv. 17—19. God hath given his name unto his people: and this is wrapped up in that mercy, that he will lay out his power to pardon, heal, and do them good in his preserving of them and abiding with them. 'Let thy power be great, according as thou hast spoken; the Lord is long-suffering:' and, as when he works for his name, the way whereby he will do it, is according to the greatness of his power; so the fountain and rise from whence he will do it, is,

2. His[f] goodness, kindness, love, patience, mercy, grace, faithfulness in Jesus Christ. And thus under the title of

[f] John xvii. 3 26. Psal. xxii 22. lxiii. 4. lxix. 30.

his name, doth he call poor, afflicted, dark, hopeless, helpless creatures (upon any other account in the world), persons ready to be swallowed up in disconsolation and sorrow
to rest upon him. Isa. l. 10. ' Who is among you that feareth
the Lord, and obeyeth the voice of his servant, that walketh
in darkness and hath no light, let him trust in the name of
the Lord and stay upon his God.' When all other holds are
gone, when flesh fails, and heart fails, then doth God call
poor souls to rest upon this name of his. So the psalmist,
Psal. lxxiii. 26. ' My flesh and my heart faileth (all strength,
natural and spiritual, faileth, and is gone), but God is the
strength of my heart (saith he), and my portion for ever.'
Now this is the sole motive also of God's continuance with
his: he will do it, because he himself is good, gracious,
merciful, loving, tender: and he will lay out these properties to the utmost in their behalf, that it may be well with
them, lifting up, exalting, and making himself gracious in so
doing. This the Lord emphatically expresseth five times in
one verse; Isa. xlvi. 4. ' Even to your old age I am he, even
to hoary hairs, will I carry you; I have made, and I will
bear, I will carry and will deliver you.' This then, I say, is
the reason, and only ground ; this the principal aim and
end, upon the account whereof the Lord will ' not forsake
his people.'

3. The rise of all this goodness, kindness, faithfulness of
God to his people, as to the exercise of it, is also expressed ;
and that is, his own good pleasure, ' because it hath pleased
the Lord to make you his people.' This is the spring and
fountain of all the goodness mentioned. God is essentially
in himself of a good, gracious, and loving nature, but he
acts all these properties, as to works that outwardly are of
him, 'according to the counsel of his will ;' Eph. i. 11. according to the purpose which he purposeth in himself; and
his purposes all of them have no other rise, or cause, but his
own good pleasure. Why did the Lord make us his people,
towards whom he might act according to the gracious properties of his nature, yea, and lay them forth and exercise
them to the utmost on our behalf? Was it because we were
better than others? did his will? walked with him? Did he
declare we should be his people upon condition we did so
and so? Not on any of these, or the like grounds of proceed-

ing doth he do this, but merely because 'it pleaseth him to make us his people;' Matt. xi. 26. And shall we think that he who took us to be his people, notwithstanding our universal alienation from him, on the account of his own good pleasure, which caused him to make us his people (that is, obedient, believing, separated from the world), will, upon any account, being himself unchangeable, not preserve us in, but reject us from, that condition? Thus is God's mercy, in not forsaking his people, resolved into its original principle, viz. his own good pleasure in choosing of them, carried on by the goodness and unchangeableness of his own nature to the appointed issue. This then is the sum of this argument. What work or design the Lord entereth upon, merely from his own good pleasure, or solely in answer to the purpose which he purposeth in himself, and engageth to continue in mercy for his name's sake, thereby taking upon him to remove, or prevent, whatever might hinder the accomplishment of that purpose, work, or design of his, that he will abide in unchangeable to the end. But this is the state of the Lord's undertaking to abide with his people, as hath been manifested at large.

Let us add in the next place that of the psalmist; Psal. xxiii. 4. 6. 'Though I walk through the valley of the shadow death, I will fear no evil, for thou art with me; thy rod and staff doth comfort me: surely goodness and mercy shall follow me all the days of my life, and I will dwell in the house of the Lord for ever.' The psalmist expresseth an exceeding confidence in the midst of most inexpressible troubles and pressures. He supposes himself walking through the valley of the shadow of death, as death is the worst of evils, and comprehensive of them all, so the shadow of death is the most dismal and dark representation of those evils to the soul, and the valley of that shadow the most dreadful bottom and depth of that representation. This then the prophet supposed, that he may be brought into a condition, wherein he may be overwhelmed with sad apprehensions of the coming of a confluence of all manner of evils upon him, and that not for a short season, but he may be necessitated to walk in them, which denotes a state of some continuance, a conflicting with most dismal evils, and in their own nature tending to death, is in the supposal. What then would he do if he should be brought into this estate? Saith he, Even in that condition, in such distress, wherein I am to my own, and the eyes of others, hopeless, helpless, gone and lost, 'I will fear no evil.' A noble resolution, if there be a sufficient bottom and foundation for it, that it may not be accounted rashness and groundless confidence, but true spiritual courage and holy resolution. Saith he, It is because the Lord is with me; but alas! what if the Lord should now forsake thee in this condition, and give thee up to the power of thine enemies, and suffer thee by the strength of thy temptations, wherewith thou art beset, to fall utterly from him? Surely then thou wouldest be swallowed up for ever; the waters would go over thy soul, and thou must for ever lie down in the shades of death. Yea, but saith he, I have an assurance of the contrary, 'goodness and mercy shall follow me all the days of my life.'

But this is (say some) a very desperate persuasion. If thou art sure that goodness and mercy shall follow thee all the days of thy life, then live as thou pleasest, as loosely as flesh can desire, as wickedly as Satan can prompt thee to; certainly this persuasion is fit only to ingenerate in thee a high contempt of humble and close walking with God. What other conclusion canst thou possibly make of that presumption, but only that, I may then do what I please, what I will; let the flesh take its swing in all abominations, it matters not, 'goodness and mercy shall follow me.' Alas! saith the psalmist, these thoughts never come in my heart; I find this persuasion, through the grace of him in whom it is effectual, to ingenerate contrary resolutions. This is that which I am upon the account hereof determined on, 'I will dwell in the house of God for ever;' seeing goodness and mercy shall follow me, I will dwell in his house; and seeing they shall follow me all the days of my life, I will dwell in his house for ever.

There are, then, these two things in this last verse, pregnant to the purpose in hand:

1. The psalmist's assurance of the presence of God with him for ever, and that in kindness and pardoning mercy, upon the account of his promise unto him; goodness or benignity, saith he, shall follow me into every condition, to assist me and extricate my soul, even out of the valley of

the shadow of death. A conclusion like that of Paul;
2 Tim. iv. 18. 'The Lord shall deliver me from every evil
work, and will preserve me unto his heavenly kingdom.'
Having (ver. 17.) given testimony of the presence of God
with him in his great trial, when he was brought before that
devouring monster Nero, giving him deliverance, he manifesteth, in ver. 18. that the presence of God with him was
not only effectual for one or another deliverance, but that
it will keep him 'from every evil work,' not only from the
rashness, cruelty; and oppression of others, but also from
any such way or works of his own, which should lay a bar
against his enjoyments of, and complete preservation unto,
that heavenly kingdom, whereunto he was appointed.

What reason now can be imagined, why other saints of
God, who have the same promise with David and Paul established unto them in the hand of the same Mediator,[g] being
equally taken into the same covenant of mercy and peace
with them, may not make the same conclusion of mercy
with them; viz. 'That the mercy and goodness of God will
follow them all the days of their lives, that they shall be delivered from every evil work, and preserved to God's heavenly kingdom.' To fly here to immediate revelation, as
though God had particularly and immediately assured some
persons of their perseverance, which begat in them a confidence, wherein others may not share with them; besides
that it is destructive of all the vigour and strength of sundry, if not all the arguments, produced against the saints'
perseverance, it is not in this place of any weight, or at all
relative to the business in hand. For evident it is, that one
of them, even David, is thus confident upon the common account of God's relation unto all his saints, as he is their
shepherd ; one that takes care of them, and will see, not
only whilst they abide with him, that they shall have pasture and refreshment, but also will find them out in their
wanderings, and will not suffer any of them to be utterly lost.
And he is a shepherd equally in care and love to every one
of his saints, as he was to David. He gives them all the
sure mercies of David, even the mercy contained and wrapped up in the promise that was given to them, and what by
virtue thereof, he did enjoy,[h] with what he received from

g 2 Cor. i. 20.   h Isa. lv. 3.

God in that covenant-relation wherein he stood. And for Paul, it is most evident that he grounded his confidence and consolation, merely upon the general promise of the presence of God with his, that 'he will never leave them nor forsake them, but be their God and guide even unto death.' Neither is there the least intimation of any other bottom of his consolation herein. Now these being things wherein every believer, even the weakest in the world, hath an equal share and interest with Paul, David, or any of the saints in their generations, what should lie in their way, but that they also may grow up to this assurance, being called thereunto. I say, they may grow up unto it: I do not say that every believer can with equal assurance of mind thus make their boasts in the Lord, and the continuance of his kindness to them. The Lord knows we are oftentimes weak and dark, and at no small loss even as to the main of our interest in the promises of God : but there being an equal certainty in the things themselves, of which we speak, it being as certain that the goodness and mercy of God shall follow them all their days, as it did David, and as certain that God will deliver them from every evil work, and preserve them to his heavenly kingdom as he did Paul, they also may grow up unto, and ought to press after, the like assurance and consolation with them, whom goodness and mercy shall follow all their days, and who shall be of God preserved from every evil work, they can never fall totally and finally out of the favour of God : that this is the state and condition of believers is manifested from the instances given of David and Paul, testifying their full persuasion and assurance concerning that condition, on grounds common to them with all believers.

2. The conclusion and inference that the psalmist makes, from the assurance which he had of the continuance of the goodness and kindness of God unto him, followeth in the words insisted on ; ' all the days of his life, he would dwell in his house.' He would for ever give up himself unto his worship and service, seeing this is the case of my soul that God will never forsake me, let me answer this love of God in my constant obedience. Now this conclusion follows from the former principle upon a twofold account.

1. As it is a motive unto it. The continuance of the

goodness and kindness of God unto a soul, is a constraining motive unto that soul to continue with him in love, service, and obedience: it works powerfully upon a heart any way ennobled with the ingenuity of grace, to make a suitable return, as far as possible it can, to such eminent mercy and goodness. I profess, I know not what those men think the saints of God to be, who suppose them apt to make conclusions of wantonness and rebellion, upon the account of the steadfastness of the love and kindness of God to them. I shall not judge any, as to their state and condition: yet I cannot but think, that such men's prejudices, and fulness of their own persuasions do exceedingly interpose in their spirits, from receiving that impression of this grace of God, which in its own nature it is apt to give; or it would be impossible they should once imagine, that of itself it is apt to draw the spirits of men into a neglect and contempt of God.

2. As the end of God, intended in giving that assurance, to the effecting whereof it is exceedingly operative and effectual; so you have it, Luke i. 74, 75. This is the intendment of God in confirming his oath and promise unto us, 'that he may grant unto us, that we being delivered out of the hands of our enemies, might serve him without fear in righteousness and holiness all the days of our lives.' Now though these forementioned, with many other texts of Scripture, are plain, evident, and full to the business we have in hand; yet the adversaries of this truth having their hands so full with them that are commonly urged, that they cannot attend unto them, I shall not need to spend time in their vindication from exceptions, which none, that I know, have as yet brought in against them (though, upon their principles, they might possibly be invented) but shall leave them to be mixed with faith, according as God by his Spirit shall set them home upon the souls of them, who do consider them.

The whole Psal. cxxv. might in the next place be brought in, to give testimony to the truth in hand. I shall only take a proof from the first verses of it. 'They that trust in the Lord shall be as mount Sion, which cannot be removed; as the mountains round about Jerusalem, so is the Lord round about his people from henceforth even for ever:' whereunto answereth that of Psal. xxxvii. 28. 'The Lord loveth judgment, and forsaketh not his saints, they are preserved for ever.' As also, Deut. xxxiii. 3. 'Yea, he loveth his people; all his saints are in thy hand.' In the verses named, I shall a little fix upon two things conducing to our purpose, which are evidently contained in them.

1. A promise of God's everlasting presence with his saints, believers, them that trust in him; and their steadfastness thereupon; 'they shall be as mount Sion that can never be removed;' and that, because the 'Lord is round about them, and that for ever.'

2. An allusive comparison of both these, both their stability, and God's presence with them, given for the encouragement of weak believers, with special regard to the days wherein the promise was first made, which actually also belongs to them, on whom the ends of the world are fallen. The psalmist bids them (as it were) lift up their eyes, and look upon mount Sion, and the hills that were round about Jerusalem, and tells them that God will as certainly and assuredly continue with them, and give them establishment, as those hills and mountains which they beheld round about, abide in their places; so that it shall be as impossible for all the powers of hell to remove them out of the favour of God, as for a man to pluck up mount Sion by the roots, or to overturn the foundations of the mountains, that stand round about Jerusalem. It is true, the Holy Ghost hath special regard to the oppositions and temptations that they were to undergo from men, but bears also an equal regard to all other means of separating them from their God; it would be a matter of small consolation unto them, that men should not prevail over them for ever, if in the mean time there be other more close and powerful adversaries, who may cast them down with a perpetual destruction. Some few considerations of the intendment of the place, will serve for the enforcing of our argument from this portion of Scripture.

1. That which is here promised the saints, is a perpetual preservation of them in that condition wherein they are, both on the part of God, he is round about them, even henceforth and for ever, and on their parts, they shall not be removed; that is, from the state and condition of acceptation with him, wherein they are supposed to be, but abide for ever and continue therein immoveable unto the end. It is,

I say, a plain promise of their continuance in that condition, wherein they are, with their safety from thence, and not a promise of some other good thing, provided that they continue in that condition. Their being compared to mountains, and their stability, which consists in their being and continuing so, will admit no other sense. As mount Sion abides in its condition, so shall they: and as the mountains about Jerusalem continue, so doth the Lord his presence unto them.

2. That expression which is used, ver. 2. is weighty and full to this purpose, ' The Lord is round about his people henceforth and for ever.' What can be spoken more fully, more pathetically? Can any expression of men so set forth the truth which we have in hand? The Lord is round about them, not to save them from this or that incursion, but from all: not from one or two evils, but from every one, whereby they are or may be assaulted. He is with them and round about them, on every side, that no evil shall come nigh them. It is a most full expression of universal preservation, or of God's keeping his saints in his love and favour, upon all accounts whatsoever. And that not only for a season, but it is, henceforth, from his giving this promise unto their souls in particular, and their receiving of it in all generations, according to their appointed times, even for ever.

Some few exceptions, with a great surplusage of words and phrases, to make them seem some other things, than what have been formerly insisted on again and again, are advanced by Mr. Goodwin, to overturn this Sion, and to cast down the mountains that are about Jerusalem, chap. 11. sect. 9. pp. 230—232. The sum of our argument from hence, as of the intendment of this place, is this: Those whom the Lord will certainly preserve for ever in the state and condition of trusting in him, they shall never be forsaken of him, nor separated from him. The latter clause of this proposition is that which we contend for, the whole of that whose proof is incumbent on us: of this, the former part is a sufficient basis and foundation: being comprehensive of all that is, or can be required to the unquestionable establishment thereof: from the letter of the text we assume: But God will certainly preserve for ever all his saints that put their trust in him, in their so doing, that they shall not be altered, or cast down from that state and condition:

change but the figurative expressions in the text, and the allusions used for the accommodation of their faith in particular, to whom this promise was first given, into other terms of a direct and proper significancy, and the text and the assumption of our argument will appear to be the same; whence the conclusion intended will undeniably follow: unto this clear deduction of the truth contended for, from this place of Scripture, the discourse ensuing in the place mentioned, is opposed.

1. ' The promise only assures them that trust in the Lord, that they shall be preserved, but not at all that they that trust in him, shall be necessitated to do so still, or that so they shall do. So Paul saith, It was in my heart to live and die with the Corinthians : but doubtless with this proviso, that they always continued such as they then were, or as he apprehended them to be, when he so wrote to them.'

Ans. I must be forced to smite this evasion once and again, before we arrive at the close of this contest, it being so frequently made use of by our adversary, who without it, knows himself not able to stand against the evidence of any one promise usually insisted on. This is the substance of all that, which with exceeding delightful variety of expressions, is a hundred times made use of. ' The promise is conditional, and made to those that trust in the Lord, and is to be made good only upon the account of their continuing so to do: but that they shall so do, that they shall continue to trust in the Lord, that is wholly left to themselves, and not in the least undertaken in the promise ;' and this is called a discharging or dismissing of places of Scripture, from the service whereunto (contrary to their proper sense and meaning) they are pressed, a delivering them from the bearing the cross of this warfare, with such-like imperial terms and expressions. To speak in the singleness of our spirits, we cannot see any one of the discharged soldiers, returning from the camp, wherein they have long served for the safety and consolation of them that do believe. Particularly this Scripture detests the gloss with violence imposed on it, and tells you, that the end for which the God of truth sent it into this service, wherein it abides, is to assure them that trust in the Lord, that they shall be preserved in that condition to the end. That in the condition of trusting and depending on God, they shall be as Sion, and the favour of God unto them as immoveable mountains; he will for ever be with them and about them : and that all this shall certainly come to pass, Christ [David] does not say, that they shall be as established mountains, if they continue to trust in the Lord, but they shall be so in their trusting, abiding for ever therein, through the safeguarding presence of God. For their being necessitated to continue trusting in the Lord, there is not any thing in [the] text, or in our argument from thence, or in the doctrine we maintain, that requires or will admit of any such proceeding of God, as by that expression is properly signified. Indeed there is a contradiction in terms, if they are used to the same purpose : to trust in the Lord, is the voluntary free act of the creature :· to be necessitated unto this act, and in the performance of it, so that it should be done necessarily as to the manner of its doing, is wholly destructive to the nature and being of it. That God can effectually, and infallibly as to the event, cause his saints to continue trusting in him, without the least abridgment of their liberty; yea, that he doth so eminently by heightening and advancing their spiritual liberty, shall be afterward declared : if by necessitated to continue trusting, not the manner of God's operation with and in them, for the compassing of the end proposed, and the efficacy of his grace, whereby he doth it (commonly decried under those terms) be intended : but only the certainty of the issue, rejecting the impropriety of the expression, the thing itself we affirm to be here promised of God. But is urged,

2. ' That this promise is not made unto the persons of any, but merely unto their qualifications : like that, he that believeth shall be saved, it is made to the grace of trusting, obedience, and walking with God; for threatenings are made to the evil qualifications of men.'

Ans. This it seems then we are come unto, and what farther progress may be made the Lord knows. The gracious promises of God, made to his church, his people, in the blood of Jesus, on which they have rolled themselves with safety and security in their several generations, are nothing but bare declarations of the will of God; what he allows, and what he rejects : with the firm concatenation that is between faith and salvation, obedience and reward. And this

it seems is the only use of them: which if it be so, I dare
boldly say, that all the saints of God from the foundations of
the world, have most horribly abused his promises, and forced
them to other ends than ever God intended them for. Doubtless all those blessed souls, who are fallen asleep in the faith
of Jesus Christ, having drawn refreshment from these breasts
of consolation, could they be summoned to give in their experience of what they have found in this kind, they would
with one mouth profess that they found far more in them,
than mere conditional declarations of the will of God; yea,
that they received them in faith, as the engagement of his
heart and good-will towards them, and that he never failed
in the accomplishment and performance of all the good mentioned in them: neither will that emphatical expression in
the close of the second verse (which being somewhat too
rough for our author to handle, he left it quite out) bear any
such sense. That the promises of the covenant are made
originally to persons, and not to qualifications, hath been in
part already proved, and shall be farther evinced (God assisting) as occasion shall be offered in the ensuing discourse:
the promises are to Abraham and his seed: and some of
them (as hath been declared) are the springs of all qualifications whatever, that are acceptable unto God: what be the
qualifications of promises of opening blind eyes, taking
away stony hearts, &c. hath not as yet been declared. But
it is farther argued,

3. 'That this and the like promises, are to be interpreted
according to the rule which God hath given for the interpretation and understanding of his threatenings unto nations,
about temporal things, and his promises that are of the same
import; which we have, Jer. xviii. 7, 8. Plainly affirming
that all their accomplishment dependeth on some conditions in the persons, or nations, against whom they are denounced.'

Ans. God forbid! Shall those promises which are branches
of the everlasting covenant of grace, called[g] 'better promises'
than those of the old covenant, upon the account of their infallible accomplishment, ratified in the blood of Christ, made
'yea and amen' in him, the witness of the faithfulness of God
to his church, and grand supporter of our faith,[h] 'exceeding

g Heb. vii. 23. 2 Cor i. 20.   h 2 Pet. i. 3.

great and precious?' Shall they be thought to be of no other sense and interpretation, to make no other revelation of the Father unto us, but in that kind, which is common to threatenings of judgments (expressly conditional) for the deterring men from their impious and destructive courses? I say, God forbid. To put it then to an issue. God here promiseth that they who here trust in him shall never be removed. What, I pray, is the condition, on which this promise doth depend? It is, say they who oppose us in this, if they continue trusting in him: that is, if they be not removed; for to trust in him, is not to be removed; if then they be not removed, they shall not be removed: and is this the mind of the Holy Ghost? Notwithstanding all the rhetoric in the world, this promise will stand for the consolation of them that believe, as the mountains about Jerusalem that shall never be removed.

In some, it is said ' to be a promise of abiding in happiness, not in faith:' but it plainly appears to be a promise of abiding in trusting the Lord; which comprehends both our faith and happiness.

Ob. 'It is not promised, that they who once trust in the Lord, shall abide happy, though they cease to trust in him.'

Ans. It is a promise that they shall not cease to trust in him.

Ob. 'It is not that they shall be necessitated to abide trusting in him.'

Ans. No, but it is that they shall be so far assisted and effectually wrought upon, as certainly to do it.

Ob. 'It is no more than the apostle says to the Corinthians; 2 Cor. ii. 3. which frame towards them he would not continue, should they be changed and turned into idolaters and blasphemers.'

Ans. 1. The promises of God, and the affections of men are but ill compared. 2. Paul loved the Corinthians, whilst they were such as he mentioned; God promiseth his grace to believers, that they may continue such as he loves.

Ob. 'All the promises are made to qualifications, not to persons.'

Ans. Prove that: and, 1. Take the case in hand; and, 2.

Cast down the church to the ground; it having no one promise on that account made unto it, as consisting of Abraham's seed: and so this witness also is freed from all exceptions put in against it, and appears with confidence to
give in its testimony to the unchangeableness of God unto
believers.

I shall, in the next place, adjoin another portion of Scripture of the same import with those foregoing, wherein the
truth in hand is no less clearly, and somewhat more pathetically and convincingly expressed than in that last mentioned. It is Isa. liv. 7—10. 'For a small moment have I
forsaken thee, but with great mercies will I gather thee.
In a little wrath I hid my face from thee for a moment, but
with everlasting kindness will I have mercy on thee, saith
the Lord thy Redeemer. For this is as the waters of Noah
unto me; for as I have sworn that the waters of Noah shall
no more cover the earth, so have I sworn that I will not be
wroth with thee, nor rebuke thee: for the mountains shall
depart and the hills be removed, but my loving-kindness
shall not depart from thee, neither shall the covenant of my
peace be removed, saith the Lord that hath mercy on thee.'
The place I have mentioned before, but only as to one special inference from one passage in the words, I shall now use
the whole for the confirmation of the general truth we plead
for; the words are full, plain, suited to the business in hand.
No expressions of our finding out, can so fully reach the
truth we assert, much less so pathetically work upon the affections of believers, or so effectually prevail on their understandings to receive the truth contained in them, as these
words of God himself, given us for those ends, are suited to
do. Go to men whose minds in any measure are free from
prejudice, not forestalled with a contrary persuasion, and
furnished with evasions for the defence of their opinions,
and ask whether God doth not in these words directly and
positively promise to those, to whom he speaketh, that he
will always continue his kindness to them, to the end: and
that for the days of eternity his love shall be fixed on them:
and I no way doubt but they will readily answer, It is so
indeed, it cannot be denied. But seeing we have to deal,
as with our own unbelieving hearts, so with men who have

turned every stone to prejudge this testimony of God, the words must a little more narrowly be considered, and the mind of the Holy Ghost inquired into.

Ver. 5. mention is made of the desertion of the church, by the eclipsing of the beams of God's countenance, and the inflicting of some great affliction for a season: in opposition unto which momentary desertions, in that, and in the beginning of the eighth verse, he giveth in consolation from the assurance of the great mercies, and everlasting kindness, wherein he abideth to do them good; 'with everlasting kindness will I have mercy on thee,' I will pardon, pity, and heal thee, with that mercy which floweth from love, which never had beginning, that never shall have ending, that cannot be cut off, 'everlasting kindness.' Bear with patience your present desertion, your present trials, whatever they are that befall you, they are but for a season, but for a moment, and these also consistent with that mercy and kindness, which is everlasting, and turneth not away; if this mercy and kindness dependeth on any thing in us, and is resolved lastly thereunto, which may alter and change every moment, as our walking with God in itself considered, not relating to the unchangeableness of his purpose, and the efficacy of his promised grace, is apt to do: what opposition can there be, betwixt that desertion wherewith they are exercised, and the kindness wherewith they are embraced, as to their continuance? As that is said to be for a little while, for 'a moment,' so this also may be of no longer abode: it may possibly be as Jonah's gourd, that grew up in the morning, and before night was withered; what then shall become of the foundation of that consolation, wherewith God here refresheth the souls of his people, consisting in the continuance of his kindness, in an antithesis to the momentariness of their desertion.

Lest that any should call this into question (as our unbelieving hearts are very apt and skilful in putting in pleas against the truth of the promises of God, and their accomplishment towards us), ver. 9. the Lord farther confirmeth the assurance formerly given, and removeth those objections, to which, through the sophistry of Satan, and the sottishness of our own hearts, it may seem to be liable. 'This is,' saith he, 'as the waters of Noah:' God's dealing with them in that mercy, which floweth from his everlasting kindness, is like his dealing with the world in the matter of the waters of Noah, or the flood wherewith it was drowned and destroyed, when he, with his, were saved in the ark. He calleth upon his children to consider his dealings with the world in respect of the flood; 'I have sworn,' saith he (that is, I have entered into a covenant to that end, which was wont to be confirmed with an oath, and God being absolutely faithful in his covenant, is said to swear thereunto, though there be no express mention of any such oath), that the world should no more be so drowned as then it was: now, saith God, see my faithfulness herein, it hath never been drowned since, nor ever shall be; with equal faithfulness have I engaged (even in covenant) that that kindness, which I mentioned to thee, shall always be continued, 'so that I will not be wroth to rebuke thee;' that is, so as utterly to cast thee off, as the world was when it was drowned. But some may say, before the flood the earth was filled with violence and sin : and should it be so again, would it not bring another flood upon it? Hath he said he will not drown it, notwithstanding any interposal of sin, wickedness, or rebellion whatever? Yea, saith he, such is my covenant; I took notice in my first engagement therein, that the 'imagination of man's heart would be evil from his youth;' Gen. viii. 21. and yet I entered into that solemn covenant; so that this exemption of the world from a universal deluge is not an appendix to the obedience of the world, which hath been upon some accounts more wicked since than before (as in the crucifying of Christ the Lord of glory, and in rejecting of him being preached unto them), but it solely leaneth upon my faithfulness in keeping covenant, and my truth in the accomplishment of the oath that I have solemnly entered into : so is my kindness to you; I have made express provision for your sins and failings therein; such I will preserve you from, as are inconsistent with my kindness to you, and such will I pardon, as you are overtaken withal. When you see a universal deluge covering the face of the earth (that is, God unfaithful to his oath and covenant), then, and not till then, suppose that his kindness can be turned from believers.

Something is excepted against this testimony; chap. 11. sect. 4. p. 227. but of so little importance, that it is scarce worth while to turn aside to the consideration of it ; the sum is, ' that this place speaketh only of God's faithfulness in his covenant; but that this should be the tenor of the covenant, that they who once truly believed, should by God infallibly, and by a strong hand, against all interposals of sin, wickedness, or rebellion, be preserved in such a faith, is not by any word, syllable, or iota intimated.'

Ans. This is that which is repeated ' usque ad nauseam ;' and were it not for variety of expressions, wherewith some men do abound, to adorn it, it would appear extreme beggarly and overworn; but a sorry shift (as they say) is better than none, or doubtless in this place it had not been made use of. For,

1. This testimony is not called forth, to speak immediately to the continuance of believers in their faith, but to the continuance and unchangeableness of the love of God to them ; and consequentially only to their preservation in faith upon that account.

It is not only assumed at a cheap, and very low rate or price, but clearly *gratis* supposed, that believers may make such ' interposals of sin, wickedness, and rebellion' in their walking with God, as should be inconsistent with the continuance of his favour and kindness to them, according to the tenor of the covenant of grace. His kindness and favour being to us extrinsical, our sins are not opposed unto them really and directly, as though they might effectually infringe an act of the will of God, but only meritoriously ; now when God saith, that he will continue his kindness to us for ever, notwithstanding the demerit of sin, as is plainly intimated in that allusion to the waters of Noah, for any one to say that they may fall into such sins and rebellions, as that he cannot but turn his kindness from them, is a bold attempt for the violation of his goodness and faithfulness, and a plain begging of the thing in question. Certainly it is not a pious labour, to thrust with violence such supposals into the promises of God, as will stop those breasts from giving out any consolation, when no place or room for them doth at all appear: there being not one word, syllable, iota, or tittle of any such supposals in them.

3. The exposition and gloss, that is given of these words; namely, ' that upon condition of their faithfulness and obe-

dience, which, notwithstanding any thing in this or any other promise, they may turn away from, he will engage himself to be a God to them,' is such, as no saint of God, without the help of Satan and his own unbelief, could affix to the place, neither will that at all assist, which,

4. Is affirmed, namely, that in 'all covenants (and his promise holdeth out a covenant) there must be a condition on both sides ;' for we willingly grant, that in this covenant of grace, God doth promise something to us, and requireth something of us; and that these two have mutual dependance one upon another. But we also affirm, that in the very covenant itself, God hath graciously promised to work effectually in us those things, which he requireth of us ; and that herein it mainly differeth from the covenant of works, which he hath abolished. But such a covenant, as wherein God should promise to be a God unto us, upon a condition by us, and in our own strength to be fulfilled, and on the same account continued in unto the end, we acknowledge not, nor can, whilst our hearts have any sense of the love of the Father, the blood of the Son, of the grace of the Holy Spirit, the fountains thereof. Notwithstanding then, any thing that hath been drawn forth in opposition to it, faith may triumph from the love of God in Christ, held out in this promise, to the full assurance of an everlasting acceptance with him ; for God also willing yet more abundantly to give in consolation in this place to the heirs of the promise, assureth the stability of his love and kindness to them, by another allusion ; ver. 10. ' The mountains,' saith he, 'shall depart, and the hills be removed, but my kindness shall not depart from thee, neither shall the covenant of my peace be removed, saith the Lord, that hath mercy on thee.' He biddeth them consider the mountains and hills, and suppose that they may be removed and depart; suppose that the most unlikely things in the world shall come to pass, whose accomplishment none can judge possible, while the world endureth, yet my kindness to thee is such, as shall not fall within those supposals, which concern things of such an impossibility. I am exceeding conscious, that all paraphrasing, or exposition of the words that may be used for their accommodation to the truth we plead for, doth but darken and eclipse the light and glory, which in and by themselves, to a

believing soul, they cast upon it. Now, lest any should think, that there is the least tendency in such promises as these (as held out to believers), to turn them aside from close walking with God, before I enter upon the consideration of any other (this seeming of all others most exposed to exceptions of that nature), I shall give some few observations, that may a little direct believers, to whom I write, and for whose sake this task is undertaken, into the right improvement of them.

The genuine influence which this and the like promises have upon the souls of the saints, is, mightily to stir them up unto, and to assist them in answering, what lieth in them, that inexpressible love and kindness, which their God and Father in Jesus Christ, holdeth out unto their hearts in them: this the apostle inferreth from them; 2 Cor. vii. 1. 'Having these promises' (that is, those especially mentioned in the words preceding the conclusion, and the inference the apostle here maketh, chap. vi. 16. 18. 'I will dwell in them, and will be a Father unto them, and they shall be my children'), therefore, saith he, 'let us cleanse ourselves from all pollution of flesh and spirit, perfecting holiness in the fear of the Lord.' Universal purity, holiness, and close walking with God, is that which these promises do press unto, and naturally promote in the hearts of believers; and in 2 Pet. iv. 5, 6. that apostle pursueth the same at large; God hath called us to glory and virtue, hath given us 'exceeding great and precious promises, that by these you might be partakers of the divine nature, having escaped the corruption, that is in the world through lust: besides this giving all diligence,' &c. 'The exceeding great and precious promises,' which are given unto us, in our calling, are bestowed for this end, that by them we may be made partakers of the divine nature; they have no tendency to communicate to us the nature of the devil, and to stir us up to rebellion, uncleanness, and hatred of the God of all that love that is in them. But lie, indeed, at the bottom, the root, and foundation of the practice and exercise of all those graces, which he enumerates, and from the receiving of those promises, exhorts us to, in the following verse. Some, I confess, do, or may turn the 'grace of God into lasciviousness;' that is, the doctrine of grace, and of pardon of sin in the blood of Jesus Christ; and so the mercy mentioned in such promises as these (merely as in them it is mentioned); grace and mercy communicated, cannot be turned into wantonness; but what are they that do so? 'Ungodly men, men of old ordained to condemnation;' Jude 6. Paul rejecteth any such thoughts from the hearts of believers; Rom. vi. 1. 'Shall we continue in sin, that grace may abound? God forbid!' Nay, suppose that that natural corruption, that flesh and blood that is in believers, be apt to make such a conclusion as this: Because God will certainly abide with us for ever, therefore let us walk carelessly, and do him all the despite we can, these promises being not made for the use and exalting of the flesh, but being given to be mixed with faith, which is carefully to watch against all abusing or corrupting of that love and mercy, which is held out unto it, flesh and blood can have no advantage given unto it thereby, as shall afterward be more fully and clearly demonstrated. The question is then, what conclusion faith doth, will, and ought to make of these promises of God, and not what abuse the flesh will make of them. Let then the meanest and weakest faith in all the world, that is true and saving, speak for itself, whether there be any thing in the nature of it, that is apt to make such conclusions as these: 'My God and Father in Jesus Christ hath graciously promised in his infinite love and goodness to me, through him in whom he is well pleased, that he will be my God and guide for ever, that he will never forsake me, nor take his kindness from me to eternity. And he hath done this, although that he saw and knew, that I would deal foolishly and treacherously, that I would stand in need of all his goodness, patience, and mercy to spare me and heal me, promising also to keep me from such a wicked departure from him, as should for ever alienate my soul from him; therefore come on, let me continue in sin, let me do him all the dishonour and despite that I can: this is all the sense that I have of his infinite love, this is all the impression that it leaveth upon me, that I need not love him again, but study to be as vile and as abominable in his sight, as can possibly be imagined.' Certainly, there is not any 'smoking flax,' or any 'bruised reed,' there is not a soul in the world, whom God in Christ hath once shined upon, or dropped the least dram of grace into his heart, but will look on such a conclusion as this, as a blast of the bottomless pit, a detestable dart of Satan, which it is as proper for faith to quench, as any other abomination whatever. Let then, faith in reference unto these promises, have its perfect work, not abiding in a naked contemplation of them, but mixing them with itself, and there will be undoubtedly found the improvement before-mentioned, for the carrying on of godliness and gospel obedience in the hearts of believers. But this I shall have occasion to speak to more afterward.

Hos. ii. 19, 20. is pertinent also to the same purpose: 'I will betroth thee unto me for ever; I will betroth thee unto me in righteousness and in judgment, and in loving-kindness, and in mercies: I will even betroth thee unto me in faithfulness, and thou shalt know the Lord.' The words themselves, as they lie in the text, do directly confirm our assertion. The relation, whereunto God here expresseth, that he will and doth take his people, is one of the most near and eminent, which he affordeth to them; a conjugal relation, he is and will be their husband, which is as high an expression of the covenant betwixt God and his saints, as any is or can be used. Of all covenants that are between sundry persons, that, which is between man and wife is the strongest and most inviolable; so is this covenant expressed, Isa. liv. 5. 'Thy Maker is thine husband, the Lord of Hosts is his name;' and this relation he affirmeth shall continue for ever, upon the account of those properties of his, which are engaged, in this his gracious undertaking to take them to himself therein. He doth it in 'righteousness and in judgment, in loving-kindness and in mercies, and in faithfulness.' So that if there be not something in the context, or words adjoining, that shall with a high hand turn us aside from the first, immediate, open, and full sense of these words, the case is undoubtedly concluded in them. This then we shall consider, and therefore must look a little back into the general design of the whole chapter; for the evasion of qualifications will not here serve: God betrothed persons, not qualifications.

There are two parts of the chapter: 1. That from the beginning to ver. 4. containeth a most fearful and dreadful commination and threatening of the judgments of the Lord, against the whole church and commonwealth of the Jews, for their apostacy, idolatry, and rebellion against him. It is not an affliction or a trial, or some lesser desolation, that God here threateneth them withal, but utter destruction and rejection, as to all church and political state. He will leave them neither substance nor ornament, state nor worship; describing the condition which came upon them, at their rejection of the Lord Jesus Christ; left they must be, as in the day that God first looked on them, ' poor, naked, in their blood,' unpitied, formed neither into church state, nor commonwealth: so will I make them, saith the Lord. And this dispensation of God, the prophet expresseth with great dread and terror, to the end of ver. 13.

2. The second part of the chapter is taken up and spent, from ver. 14. to the end, in heavenly and gracious promises, of the conversion of the true Israelites, the seed according to the promise of God, of the renovation of the covenant with them, and blessing them with all spiritual blessings in Jesus Christ, unto the end. And hereof, there are these four parts:

1. A heavenly promise of their conversion, by the gospel, which he demonstrateth and setteth out, by comparing the spiritual deliverance therein, to the deliverance which they had by a high hand from Egypt; ver. 14, 15.

2. The delivery of them so converted, from idolatry, false worship, and all those ways whereby God was provoked to cast off their forefathers; attended by their obedience, in close walking with God for ever.

3. The quietness and peace which they shall enjoy, being called and purged from their sins before mentioned; which the Lord expresseth by his making a covenant with the whole creation in their behalf; ver. 18.

4. A discovery of the fountain of the mercies before-mentioned, with those also which afterward are insisted on (to wit), the everlasting covenant of grace, through which God will with all faithfulness and mercy take them to himself; ver. 19, 20. to the end.

Before we farther open these particulars, some objections must be removed, that are laid to prevent the inference intended from these words; chap. 11. sect. 8. page 229. It is first objected,

1. ' The promise of the betrothing here specified, is made unto the entire body and nation of the Jews, as well unbe-

lievers, as believers, as appeareth by the carriage of the chapter throughout.'

Ans. 'The carriage of the chapter throughout,' is a weak proof of this assertion; and (no doubt) fixed on for want of particular instances, to give any light unto it: neither doth 'the carriage of the chapter throughout,' intimate any such thing in the least, but expressly manifesteth the contrary. It is universal desolation and utter rejection, that is assigned as the portion of unbelievers as such, all along this chapter. This promise is made to them whom ' God allureth into the wilderness, and there speaketh comfortably to them :' which, what it doth import, shall be afterward considered. Yea, and which is more, the words of ver. 23. which run on in the same tenor with the promises particularly insisted on, and beyond all exception are spoken to, and of the same persons, are applied by the apostle Paul, not to the whole nation of the Jews, idolaters and unbelievers, but to them that were brought in unto the Lord Christ, and obtained the righteousness of faith, when the rest were hardened ; Rom. ix. 26. From ver. 24—30. the apostle, by sundry instances from the Scripture of the Old Testament, manifesteth, that it was a ' remnant of Israel according to the election of grace,' to whom the promise was made: ' To us whom God hath called, not to the Jews only, but also to the Gentiles. For so,' saith he, 'it is in Hosea' (instancing in the passage we insist on), ' I will call them my people, which were not my people ; and her beloved which was not beloved; and it shall come to pass, that in the place where it was said unto them, You are not my people, there shall they be called the children of the living God.' Which he farther confirmeth by a testimony out of Isa. x. 22, 23. manifesting, that it is but a remnant, that are intended.   Wherefore it is objected :

2. 'That the promise is conditional, and the performance of it, and of the mercies mentioned in it, suspended upon the repentance of that people, especially of their idolatry, to the true and pure worship of God; as appeareth, ver. 14. 16, 17. which plainly sheweth, that it was made as well, nay, rather to those that were wicked and idolatrous amongst this people than unto others, as being held forth unto them, chiefly for this end, to woo them away from their idols unto God.'

Ans. I hope the people of God will more steadfastly abide by their interest, in the sweetness, usefulness, and consolation of this promise, than to throw it away upon such slight and atheological flourishes. For,

1. Is there any tittle, iota, or word in the whole text, to intimate that this promise, is conditional, and dependeth on the people's forsaking their idolatry? The 14th, 16th, 17th, verses are urged for proof thereof. God indeed in those verses doth graciously promise, that from the riches of the same grace whence he freely saith, 'that he will betroth them to himself,' that he will convert them, and turn them away from their idolatry, and all their sins; but that that should be required of them, as a condition whereon God will enter into covenant with them, there is nothing in the whole context, from ver. 14. and downwards, that intimateth it in the least, or will endure to be wrested to any such sense; it holding out several distinct acts of the same free grace of his unto his people.

2. That this is a promise of entering into covenant with them, cannot be denied. Now that God should require their repentance, as an antecedaneous, previous qualification to his receiving them into covenant, and yet in the covenant undertake to give them that repentance, as he doth, in promising them to take away their hearts of stone, and give them new hearts of flesh, is a direct contradiction, fit only for a part of that divinity, which is in the whole an express contradiction to the word and mind of God.

3. Neither can it be supposed as a conditional promise, held out to them as a motive to work them from their idolatry, when, antecedently thereunto, God hath expressly promised to do that for them (ver. 16, 17.) with as high a hand and efficacy of grace, as can be well expressed; wherefore, these being exceptions expressly against the scope of the whole: it is objected,

3. 'That it cannot be proved that this promise properly, or directly, intendeth the collation of spiritual or heavenly good things unto them, so as of temporal: yea, the situation of it betwixt temporal promises, immediately both behind and before it, persuadeth the contrary: read the context, from ver. 8. to the end of the chapter.'

Ans. The other forts being demolished, this last is very

faintly defended. That it cannot be proved, that it doth so properly or directly; but if it doth intend spirituals properly and directly, though not so properly or directly, the case is clear: and that it doth properly intend spirituals, and but secondarily and indirectly, temporals, as to sundry limitations, is most evident. For,

1. The very conjugal expression of the love of God here used, manifesteth it, beyond all contradiction, to be a promise of the covenant: I will betroth thee unto me, I will take thee unto me in wedlock covenant. What! in temporal mercies? Is that the tenor of the covenant of God? God forbid!

2. The foundations of these mercies, and the principles from whence they flow, are loving-kindnesses, and mercy, and faithfulness, in God, which are fixed upon them, and engaged unto them, whom he thus taketh into covenant; and surely they are spiritual mercies.

3. The mercies mentioned are such as never had a literal accomplishment to the Jews in temporals, nor can have; and when things promised exceed all accomplishment, as to the outward and temporal part, it is the spiritual, that is principally and mainly intended; and such are these, ver. 18. 'I will break the bow, and the sword, and the battle out of the earth, and make you to lie down in safety:' how I pray, was this fulfilled towards them, whilst they lived under the power of the Persian, Grecian, and Roman empires, to their utter desolation? and ver. 23. he telleth them, that he will sow them unto himself in the earth, and have mercy on them; which, as I said before, Paul himself interpreteth, and applieth to the special mercies of faith, and justification in the blood of Christ; so that both the verses going before, and those that follow after, to the consideration whereof we are sent, contain directly, and properly, spiritual mercies, though expressed in words, and terms of things of a temporal importance. Thus, notwithstanding any exception to the contrary, the context is clear, as it was at first proposed; let us then, in the next place, consider the intendment of God in this promise, with that influence of demonstration, which it hath upon the truth we are in the consideration of, and then free the words from that corrupting gloss, which is endeavoured to be put upon them.

In the first, I shall consider,

1. The persons to whom this promise is made.

2. The nature of the promise itself.

3. The great undertaking and engagement of the pro- perties of God, for the accomplishment of his promise.

1. The persons here intimated, are such as are under the power and enjoyment of the grace and kindness mentioned in ver. 14. 16—18. Now because a right understanding of the grace of those promises, addeth much to the apprehension of the kindness of these particulars insisted on, the opening those words may be thought necessary:

1. Ver. 14. They are those, 'whom God allureth into the wilderness, and speaketh comfortably unto them;' he allureth, and persuadeth them; there is an allusion in the words, to the great original promise of the conversion of the Gentiles, and the way whereby it shall be done; Gen. ix. 27. God 'persuades Japhet to dwell in the tents of Shem.' Their alluring is by the powerful and sweet persuasion of the gospel, which here is so termed, to begin the allegory of betrothing and marriage, which is afterward pursued. It is God's beginning to woo the soul by his ambassadors; God persuadeth them into the wilderness; persuadeth them, but yet with mighty power, as he carried them of old out of Egypt, for thereunto he evidently alludeth, as in the next verse, is more fully expressed. Now the wilderness condition, whereunto they are allured, or persuaded by the gospel, compriseth two things:

1. Separation.

2. Entanglement.

1. Separation, as the Israelites in the wilderness were separated from the residue of the world, and the pleasures thereof; ' the people dwelling alone, being not reckoned with the nations,' having nothing to do with them. So God separateth them to the love of the gospel, from their carnal contentments, and all the satisfactions which before they received in their lusts, until they say to them, 'Get you hence, what have we to do with you any more?' They are separated from the practice of them, and made willing to bid them everlastingly farewell. They see their Egyptian lusts lie slain, or dead, or at least dying, by the cross of Christ, and desire to see them no more.

2. Entanglement; as the Israelites were in the wilderness, they knew not what to do, nor which way to take one step, but only as God went before them; as he took them by the hand, and taught them to go. God bringeth them into a lost condition ; they know not what to do, nor which way to take, nor what course to pitch upon; and yet in this wilderness state, God doth commonly stir up such gracious dispositions of soul in them, as himself is exceedingly delighted withal : hence he doth peculiarly call this time, 'a time of love,' which he remembereth with much delight. All the time of the saint's walking with him, he taketh not greater delight in a soul, when it cometh to its highest peace and fullest assurance, than when it is seeking after him in its wilderness entanglement.   So he expresseth it, Jer. ii. 2. ' Thus saith the Lord, I remember thee, the kindness of thy youth, the love of thine espousals, when thou wentest after me in the wilderness, in a land that was not sown.'   And what he here affirmeth, holds proportion therewithal.   The time of their being in the wilderness, was the time of their espousals ; and so it is here, the time of the Lord's betrothing the soul to himself; the wooing words whereby he doth it, being intimated in the next verse.   For,

1. 'He speaketh comfortably to them ;' speaketh to their hearts ; good words that may satisfy their spirits, and give them rest, and deliverance out of that condition.   What it is that God speaketh, when he speaketh comfortably to the very hearts of poor souls, he telleth you, Isa. xl. 1. ' Comfort ye, comfort ye my people, saith your God ; speak ye comfortably to Jerusalem, and cry unto her, that her warfare is accomplished, that her iniquity is pardoned.' It is the pardon of iniquity that inwrappeth all the consolation, that a poor wilderness soul, separated and entangled, is capable of, or doth desire.   And this is the first description of the persons, to whom this promise is given.   They are such as God hath humbled and pardoned ; such as he hath converted and justified; whom he hath allured into the wilderness, and there spoken comfortably to them.

2. Ver. 15. The Lord promiseth to this called and justified people, plenty of spiritual gospel mercies, which he shadoweth out with typical expressions of temporal enjoy-

ments, and that with allusion to their deliverance of old, from Egypt, in three particulars :

1. In general; he will give them vineyards from thence (this is, from the wilderness), as he did to them in Canaan, when he brought them out of the wilderness. This God often mindeth them of, that he gave them ' vineyards which they planted not;' Deut. vi. 11. And here setteth out the plenty of gospel grace, which they never laboured for, which he had provided for them, under that notion. He giveth them of the wine of the gospel, his Holy Spirit.

2. In particular; he compares his dealings with them, to his dealings in the valley of Achor; a most pleasant and fruitful valley, that was near Jericho, being the first the Israelites entered into, when they came out of the wilderness; which is mentioned as a fruitful place, Isa. lxv. 10. And therefore, this is said to be to them a door of hope, or an entrance into that which they hoped for; it being the first fat, fruitful, and fertile place that the Israelites came into, in the land of Canaan, and so an entrance into the good land which they hoped for, answering their expectation to the uttermost. In the promise of the abundance of spiritual mercies and grace, which God hath prepared for his, here calleth into their minds, the consideration of the refreshment, which the Israelites after so long an abode in the ' waste and howling wilderness,' had, and took in the fruitful plenteous ' valley of Achor.' Such is the spiritual provision, that God hath made for the entertainment of poor souls, whom he hath allured into the wilderness, and there spoken comfortably to them; being called and pardoned, he leadeth them to sweet and pleasant pastures, treasures of grace and mercies, which he hath laid up for them in Jesus Christ. He giveth them of the first-fruits of heaven, which is a door of hope unto the full possession; Rom. viii. 23.

3. To the songs and rejoicings which the church had when they sung one to another, upon the destruction of the Egyptians, at their delivery out of the bondage of Egypt. As then they sung for joy, Exod. xv. upon the sense of that great and wonderful deliverance, which God had wrought for them, so shall their hearts be affected with gospel mercies, pardoning, healing, purging, and comforting grace,

which in Jesus Christ, he will give in unto them. These then, are the three things, which are promised to them that come out of the wilderness. 1. Gospel refreshment, in pouring out of the Spirit upon them. 2. The first-fruits of heaven, a door of hope. 3. Spiritual joy, in the destruction and conquest of sin.

This then is the sum of this second part of that description which we have of those persons, to whom the promise under consideration is given; they are such as being called and pardoned, are admitted to that portion in the wonderful marvellous provision of gospel mercies and grace, which in Jesus Christ, he hath provided for them, with that joy and consolation which thereon doth ensue. In the following verses, you have a fuller description of these persons, upon a twofold account:

1. By their delivery from idolatry and false worship, ver. 16, 17. which is particularly and peculiarly insisted on, because that eminently was the sin, for which those mentioned in the beginning of the chapter were utterly rejected: God will preserve these, as from the sin of idolatry, so from any other that should procure their utter rejection and desolation, as that of idolatry had formerly done, in respect of the only carnal Jews.

2. By their protection against their enemies; ver. 18. and these are the persons to whom this promise is made; converted, justified, sanctified, and purified persons.

2. We may take a little view of the nature of the promise itself: ' I will,' saith the Lord, ' betroth thee unto me for ever;' there is in this promise, a twofold opposition to that rejection, that God had before denounced unto the carnal and rebellious Jews. 1. In the nature of the thing itself, unto the divorce that God gave them, ver. 2. 'She is not my wife, neither am I her husband :' but to these, saith God, ' I will betroth them unto myself;' they shall become a wife to me, and I will be a husband unto them : and this also manifesteth that they are not the same persons, to whom that threatening was given, that are principally intended in this promise; for if God did only take them again, whom he had once put away, there would have been no need of any betrothing of them anew; new ' sponsalia' are not required for such an action.

2. In the continuance of the rejection of the first, and the establishment of the reception of the latter, at least in respect of his abiding with these and those ; with those for a season : but unto these he saith, 'I will betroth them unto me for ever.' God's betrothing of believers, is his actual taking them into a marriage covenant with himself, to deal with them in the tenderness, faithfulness, and protection of a husband. So is he often pleased to call himself in reference to his church; I shall not go forth to the consideration of this relation, that God is pleased to take the souls of saints into with himself. The eminent and precious usefulness and consolation that floweth from it, is ready to draw me out thereunto, but I must attend that which I principally aim at; namely, to evince that God hath undertaken that He and believers will, and shall abide in this relation, to the end ; that he will for ever be a husband to them, and that in opposition to his dealing with the carnal church of the Jews, to whom he was betrothed, as to ordinances; but rejected them, and said he was not their husband, as to peculiar grace. To whom God continueth to be a husband, to them he continueth the loving-kindness, good-will, and protection of a husband, the most intense, useful, fruitful, that can be imagined: this then, will he do to believers, and that for ever. Now, because sundry objections may be levied against the accomplishment of this engagement of God, upon the account of our instability and backsliding, the Lord addeth the manner of his entering into this engagement with us, obviating and preventing, or removing all such objections whatever ; which is the third thing proposed to consideration, namely, the engagement of the properties of God, for the accomplishment of this promise.

Five properties doth the Lord here mention, to assure us of his constancy in this undertaking of his grace, and the steadfastness of the covenant he hath taken his people into ; and they are 'righteousness, judgment, loving-kindness,' and 'mercies,' and 'faithfulness ;' whose efficacy also, in reference unto their abiding with him, whom he doth betroth to himself, he mentioneth in the close of ver. 20. ' Thou,' saith he, ' shalt know the Lord.' I shall not insist on the particular importance of the several expressions, whereby the Lord hath set forth himself, and his goodness here unto us : it is plain, that they are all mentioned to the same end and pur-

pose ; namely, to give assurance unto us, of the unchangeableness of this work of his grace, and to prevent the objections, which the fears of our unbelieving hearts, from the
consideration of our weaknesses, ways, and walkings, temptations, trials, and troubles, would raise upon it. The Lord,
when he betroths us to himself, sees and knows what we
are, what we will be, and how we will provoke the eyes of
his glory. He sees, that if we should be left unto ourselves,
we would utterly cast off all knowledge of him, and obedience unto him : ' Wherefore,' saith he, ' I will betroth thee
unto me in righteousness and judgment ;' allowing full measure for all thy weaknesses, that they shall not dissolve that
union I intend. As if a prince should go to take to him in
marriage, a poor deformed beggar, who being amazed with
his kindness, and fearing much lest he should be mistaken,
and account her otherwise than indeed she is, which, when
it is discovered will be her ruin, she plainly telleth him she
is poor, deformed, and hath nothing in the world that may
answer his expectation, and therefore she cannot but fear,
that when he knoweth her thoroughly indeed, he will utterly cast her off : but he thereupon replieth, Fear no such
thing, what I do, I do in righteousness and judgment, knowingly of thee, and thy condition, and so as that I will abide
by it. Perhaps (as some think), by this ' betrothing us in
righteousness,' the Lord may intimate 'his bestowing upon
us righteousness, yea, his becoming in Jesus Christ, our righteousness, to supply that utter want, which is in us, of that
which is acceptable unto him. Now, because we are not
only unmeet, to be at first accepted into any such terms of
alliance with the Lord, but also shall certainly in the carrying of it on, behave ourselves foolishly and frowardly, un-
answerable to his loving-kindness, so that he may justly
cast us off for ever, he telleth us farther, that he betroths us
to himself in loving-kindness and mercies, knowing that in
entering into this alliance with us, he maketh work for his
tenderest bowels of compassion, his pity, and pardoning
mercy. In his continuance in this relation, whatever his
kindness, patience, and pardoning mercy can be extended
unto, that he will accomplish and bring about. But will

¹ Isa. xlv. 24.

not the Lord, when he pardons once and again, at length be wearied by our innumerable provocations, so as to cast us off for ever? No, saith he, this will I do in faithfulness. He doubleth the expression of his grace, and addeth a property of his nature, that will carry him out to abide by his first love to the utmost; 'I will,' saith he, 'even betroth thee unto myself in faithfulness.' His firmness, constancy, and truth, in all his ways and promises will he use in this work of his grace; Deut. xxxii. 4. But perhaps, notwithstanding all this, the heart is not yet quiet; yet it feaieth itself and its own treachery, lest it should utterly fall off from this gracious husband; wherefore in the close of all, God undertaketh for them also, that no scruple may remain, why our souls should not be satisfied with the sincere milk that floweth from this breast of consolation: ' Thou shalt,' saith he, 'know the Lord;' this indeed is required, that under the accomplishment of this gracious promise, you know the Lord; that is, believe, and trust, and obey the Lord: and, saith he, Thou shalt do it. I will, by my grace, keep alive in thy heart (as a fruit of that love, wherewith I have betrothed thee to myself), that knowledge, faith, and obedience, which I require of thee.

This then, is some part of that, which in this promise, the Lord holdeth out unto us, and assureth us of: notwithstanding his rejection of the carnal Jews, yet for his elect, both the Jews and Gentiles, he will so take them into a marriage covenant with himself, that he will continue for ever a husband unto them: undertaking also, that they shall continue in faith and obedience, knowing him all their days: and of all this, he effectually assureth them, upon the account of his righteousness, judgment, loving-kindness, mercy, and faithfulness.

I cannot but add, that, if there were no other place of Scripture in the whole book of God, to confirm the truth we have in hand, but only this: I should not doubt (the Lord assisting) to close with it, upon the signal testimony given unto it thereby, notwithstanding all the specious oppositions that are made thereunto.

For the close, I shall a little consider that lean and hungry exposition of these words, which is given in the place before mentioned, chap. 11. sect. 8. p. 229. 'I will betroth them unto me in righteousness, and in judgment, and in loving-kindness, and mercy:' so the words are expressed in a different character, as the very words of the promise in the text. 1. 'Thee,' that is, the church, is changed into 'them;' that is, the Jews, and their children or carnal seed, as a little before was expressed: and then that emphatical expression 'for ever,' is quite thrust out of the text, as a stubborn word, not to be dealt withal upon any fair terms. Let us see then, how that which remaineth is treated and turned off. 'I will betroth thee: that is, I will engage, and attempt to ensure both them, and their affections to me, by all variety of ways and means, that are proper and likely to bring such a thing to pass.' But who knoweth not that this is wooing, and not betrothing? we need not go far to find out men learned in the law, to inform us, that to try, and attempt to get and assure the affections of any one, is not a betrothment. This then, is the first part of this exposition: 'I will betroth;' that is, I will woo and essay, attempt and endeavour to get their affections: which, besides the fore-mentioned absurdity, is attended with another sore oversight (to wit), that God promiseth to do this very thing in the last words of ver. 20. which is affirmed, that he doth but attempt to do.

To proceed: He saith, 'I will do this, 1. By shewing myself just and righteous unto them, in keeping my promise concerning their deliverance out of captivity, at the end of seventy years.' So then, in this new paraphrase, I will betroth thee (that is, the election of Jews and Gentiles) to myself for ever in righteousness, is, I will essay to get their affections, by shewing myself righteous in the promise of bringing the Jews out of captivity. That this promise is not made to the body of the Jews, returning out of captivity, was before demonstrated; the righteousness here mentioned, is that which God will, and doth exercise, in this very act of betrothing, and not any other act of it, which he will make use of to that purpose. God engageth to betroth them to himself in righteousness, using and exercising his righteousness in that very act of his love and grace to them: and this is now given, in an alluring them to love him by appearing righteous, in bringing them out of captivity.

The like interpretation is given of the other expressions following: 'Judgment:' 'It is,' saith he, ' by punishing and judging their enemies, and destroying them that led them into captivity, and held them in bondage and subjection; and 'loving-kindness,' is his giving them corn, wine, oil, peace, and plenty; and 'mercy' in pardoning of daily sins and infirmities; and 'faithfulness' is, he knoweth not what.' This is made the sum of all; God by doing them good with outward mercies, and pardoning some sins and infirmities, will morally try to get their affections to himself. 'Virgula Pictoris.' 1. It is not an expression of God's attempting to get their love, but of the establishing and confirming of his own. 2. That God should morally try and essay to do, and effect, or bring about any thing, which yet he doth not, will not, or cannot compass and effect, is not to be ascribed to him, without casting the greatest reproach of impotency, ignorance, changeableness, upon him imaginable. 3. God promising to betroth us to himself, fixing his love on us, that we shall know him, so fixing our hearts on him; to say, that this holdeth out only the use of some outward means unto us, enervateth the whole covenant of his grace, wrapped up in these expressions; so that all things considered, it is not a little strange to me, that any sober learned man, should ever be tempted so to wrest and corrupt, by wrested and forced glosses, the plain words of Scripture: wherein, whatever is pretended, he cannot have the least countenance of any expositor of note, that went before him: although we are not to be pressed with the name of Tarnovius a Lutheran, a professed adversary in this cause; yet let his exposition of that place under consideration be consulted with, and it will plainly appear, that it abideth not in any compliance with that, which is here by our author imposed on us.

The promises we have under consideration, looking immediately and directly, only to one part of that doctrine, whose defence we have undertaken; to wit, the constancy and unchangeableness of the grace of justification, or God's abiding with his saints, as to his free acceptance of them, and love unto them unto the end, I shall not insist on many more particulars.

John x. 27—29. closeth this discourse: 'My sheep hear my voice, and I know them, and I give unto them eternal life, and they shall never perish, neither shall any man pluck them out of my hand; my Father, which gave them me, is greater than all, and no man is able to pluck them out of my Father's hand.'

In the verse foregoing, our Saviour renders a reason why the Pharisees, notwithstanding all his preaching to them, and the miracles he wrought among them, yet believed not, when sundry others, to whom the same dispensation of outward means was afforded, did hear his voice and did yield obedience thereunto; and this he telleth us was, because they were not of his sheep: such as were given him of his Father, and for whom, as the good Shepherd, he laid down his life; ver. 14, 15. Upon the close of this discourse, he describeth the present condition of his sheep, and their preservation in that condition, from the power of himself and his Father, engaged thereunto. He layeth their abiding with him as his sheep, upon the omnipotence of God, which upon account of the constancy of his love towards them, he will exercise and exert as need shall be, in their behalf. There are many emphatical expressions, both of their continuance in the obedience of faith, and of his undertaking for their preservation therein. The latter I at present only intend. Saith he, 1. 'I know them.' 2. 'I give them eternal life.' 3. 'They shall never perish.' 4. 'No man shall pluck them out of my hand.' 5. My Father is omnipotent; and hath a sovereignty over all, and he taketh care of them, 'and none shall take them out of his hand.' It is not easy to cast these words into any other form of arguing, than that wherein they lie, without losing much of that convincing evidence that is in them. This you may take for the sum of their influence into the truth in hand: Those whom Christ so owneth, as to take upon him to give them eternal life, and his power, and the power of his Father, to preserve them thereunto, which power shall not, nor possibly can be, prevailed against, so that the end aimed at to be accomplished therein, should not be brought about, those shall certainly be kept for ever in the favour and love of God, they shall never be turned from him. Such is the case of all believers: for they are all the sheep of Christ, they all hear his voice and follow him.

Some few things to wrest this gracious assurance given believers, of the everlasting good-will of God and Christ unto them, by Mr. Goodwin, chap. 10. sect. 37. p. 203. are attempted.

1. He granteth, that there is an engagement of the 'mighty power of God, for the safeguarding of the saints, as such, or remaining such, against all adverse power whatever: but no where, for the compelling or necessitating of them to persevere, and continue such, is there any thing in the Scripture.'

Ans. The sum is, if they will continue saints, God will take care, that notwithstanding all opposition, they shall be saints still. Very well! if they will be so, they shall be so: but that they shall continue to be so, that is not promised. The terms of compelling, or necessitating, are cast in, merely to throw dirt upon the truth, lest the beauty shining forth too brightly, there might have been danger, that the very exceptor himself could not have borne it. We say not, that God by his power, compelleth men to persevere; that is, maketh them do it, whether they will or no. Perseverance being a habitual grace in their wills, it is a gross contradiction once to imagine that men should be compelled thereunto. But this we say, that by the almighty power of his Spirit and grace, he confirmeth his saints, in a voluntary abiding with him all their days. Having made them a willing people in the day of the power of Christ towards them, he preserveth them unto the end. Neither are they wrapped up by the power of God, into such a necessity of perseverance, as should obstruct the liberty of their obedience; the necessity that regardeth them in that condition, respecting only the issue and end of things, and not their manner of support in their abiding with God. And it is not easy to conjecture, why our author should so studiously avoid the grant of a promise of final perseverance, in these words, who, in his next observation upon them, affirmeth, ' that they respect the state of the saints in heaven, and not at all those that are on earth;' I mean, that part of those words, which expresseth their preservation and safeguarding by the power of God. So that this is fancied, perhaps, even to be the condition of the saints in heaven, that God will there preserve them whilst they continue saints; but that they shall so do, there is not any assurance given, or to be had. It is marvellous if this be so, that in so large and vast a space of time, we yet never heard of any of those holy ones, that were cast out of his inheritance, or that forfeited his enjoyment. But let us hear what is farther asserted. He addeth, by way of answer,

1. 'The security, for which our Saviour engageth the greatness of his Father's power unto his sheep, is promised unto them, not in order to the effecting or procuring their final perseverance, but rather by way of reward to it.'

Ans. But what tittle is there, I pray you, in the whole context, to intimate any such thing? What insinuation of any such condition? 'They hear my voice, and they follow me;' that is, they believe in me, and bring forth the fruits of their believing, in suitable obedience, as these words of hearing and following do imply. Saith our Saviour, These shall not perish; the power of my Father shall preserve them; that is, saith our author, in case they persevere to the end, then God will preserve them: clearly, our Saviour undertaketh, that believers shall not perish, and that his power and his Father's, are engaged for that end, which is all we assert, or have need to do.

2. 'That this promise of safety, made to his sheep by Christ, doth not relate to their state or condition in this present world, but that of the world to come. My sheep hear my voice and follow me, in which words of hearing and following him, he intimateth or includeth their perseverance, as appeareth by the words immediately following: And I give them eternal life.'

Ans. This I confess is to the purpose, if it be true: but being so contrary to what hath been (I had almost said universally) received, concerning the mind of Christ in this place, we had need of evident concluding reasons, to enforce the truth of this gloss or interpretation. For the present, I shall give you some few inducements or persuasions, why it seemeth altogether unsuitable to the mind of our blessed Saviour, that this engagement of his Father's power, and his own, should be shut out from taking any place in the kingdom of grace.

1. Observe, that there is a great opposition to be made against the saints, in that condition, wherein they are promised to be preserved. This is supposed in the words themselves. 'There is none shall take them out of my hands: my Father is great, and none shall be able to take them out of his hands.' As if he should have said, It is true, many enemies they have, great opposition will there be, and arise against them on all hands, but preserved they shall be, in the

midst of them all. But now, what enemies, what opposition will there be, and arise against the saints in heaven? The Holy Ghost telleth us, ' The last enemy is death;' and that at the resurrection, that shall be utterly swallowed up into victory, that it shall never lift up the head; there they rest from their labours, who die in the Lord; yea, it is exceeding ridiculous to suppose, that the saints need assurance of the engagement of the omnipotency of God, for their safeguarding in heaven, against all opposition, when they are assured of nothing more, than that there they shall not be liable to the least opposition, or obstruction, in their enjoyment of God, unto all eternity.

2. Our Saviour here describeth the present condition of his sheep, in a way of opposition to them that are not his sheep: his hear his voice, the others do not, and his shall be preserved, when the others perish: the Pharisees believed not, and, as he told them, ' they died in their sins;' his sheep heard him, and were preserved in their obedience. It is then, evidently, the deportment of Christ towards, and his care of, his sheep in this world, in a contradistinction to them, who are not his sheep, among whom they live, that is here set forth.

3. The very context of the words enforceth this sense: ' They follow me, and I give them eternal life;' I do it, that is the work I have in hand. Take eternal life in the most comprehensive sense, for that which is to be enjoyed in heaven (though doubtless it compriseth also the life of grace, which here we enjoy; John xvii. 3.) What is that which our Saviour undertaketh to give believers, and that they may be sure, that they shall be preserved to the enjoyment of? When he telleth them they shall not perish, is that not perishing, not to be cast out of heaven, when they come thither? Not to be deprived of eternal life, after they have entered into the fulness of it? Or rather that they shall not fail, or come short of it, and so perish? And this is that which the power of Father and Son is engaged to accomplish; namely, that believers perish not by coming short of that eternal life, which is the business of Christ to give unto them. If any one reason of weight or importance, that hath the least pregnancy with truth, be offered to the contrary; we shall renounce and shake off the power of the former

reasons, which we have insisted on, though without offering the greatest violence imaginable to truth itself, it cannot be done. It is said, that by these words, ' They hear my voice, and follow me,' Christ doth intimate, or include their perseverance : to say a thing is intimated or included, is of small power against so many express reasons, as we have induced to the contrary ; but will this be granted, that wherever the saints are said to hear the voice of Christ, perseverance is included ? We shall quickly have a fresh supply of Scripture proofs, for the demonstration of the truth in hand : but what attempt is made for the proof hereof ? It is so, because the words immediately following are, ' I give to them eternal life,' which presuppose their final perseverance ; and this must be so, because it is so said : ' I will give to them eternal life,' is either an intimation of what he doth for the present, by giving them a spiritual life in himself, or a promise he will do so, with respect to eternal life consummated in heaven ; which promise, is every where made upon believing : and it is a promise of perseverance, not given upon perseverance. Neither is there any thing added in the words following, to confirm this uncouth wresting of the mind of our Saviour, but only the assertion is repeated, ' that God will defend them in heaven against all opposition.' Here, where their oppositions are innumerable, they may shift for themselves ; but when they come to heaven, where they shall be sure to meet with no opposition at all, there the Lord hath engaged his almighty power for their safety, against all that shall arise up against them ; and this is, as is said, the natural, and clear disposition of the context in this place ; but, ' Nobis non licet,' &c.

There are sundry other texts of Scripture, which most clearly and evidently confirm the truth we have in hand, which are all well worth our consideration, for our consolation and establishment : as also, something of our labour and diligence, to quit them from those glosses and interpretations (which turn them aside from their proper intendment), that are by some put upon them. Amongst which, 1 Cor. i. 8, 9. 1 Phil. vi. 1 Thess. v. 24. John v. 24. ought to have place. But, because I will not insist long on any particulars, of our argument from the promises of God, here shall be an end.

CHAP. VII.

The consideration of the oath of God deferred. The method first proposed somewhat waved. The influence of the mediation of Christ into God's free and unchangeable acceptance of believers proposed. Reasons of that proposal. Of the oblation of Christ. Its influence into the saints' perseverance. All causes of separation between God and believers, taken away thereby. Moral and efficient causes thereby removed The guilt of sin; how taken away by the death of Christ. Of the nature of redemption. Conscience of sin; how abolished by the sacrifice of Christ, Heb. x. 3, 4. 14. Dan. ix. 24. opened; Rom. ii. 34. Deliverance from all sin; how by the death of Christ. The law innovated in respect of the elect. The vindictive justice of God satisfied by the death of Christ; how that is done. Wherein satisfaction doth consist. Absolute, not conditional. The law; how fulfilled in the death of Christ. The truth of God thereby accomplished; his distributive justice engaged. Observations for the clearing of the former assertions. Whether any one, for whom Christ died, may die in sin. The necessity of faith and obedience. The reasons thereof. The end of faith and holiness. The first argument for the proof of the former assertions concerning the fruit and efficacy of the death of Christ; Heb. ix. 14. The second. The third The compact between the Father and Son about the work of mediation. The fourth. Good things bestowed on them for whom Christ died, antecedently to any thing spiritually good in them. The Spirit so bestowed, and faith itself. The close of those arguments. Inferences from the foregoing discourse. The efficacy of the death of Christ, and the necessity of faith and obedience, reconciled. Sundry considerations unto that end proposed. 1. All spiritual mercies, fruits of the death of Christ. 2. All the fruits of Christ's death laid up in the hand of God's righteousness. 3. The state of them for whom Christ died not actually changed by his death. 4. On what account believing is necessary. Christ secures the stability of the saints' abiding with God. What is contrary thereunto, how by him removed. The world overcome by Christ, as managed by Satan in an enmity to the saints. The complete victory of Christ over the devil. The ways, whereby he completes his conquest. The rule of Satan, in respect of sinners, twofold. 1. Over them. 2. In them. The title of Satan to a rule over men, judged and destroyed by Christ. The exercise of all power taken from him. The works of Satan destroyed by Christ, in and for his elect. The Holy Spirit procured by the death of Christ. The giving of the Spirit, the great promise of the new covenant. This farther proved and confirmed. The perpetual residence of the Holy Spirit with believers, proved by the threefold testimony of Father, Son, and Spirit; Isa. lix. The testimony of the Father proposed and vindicated. Our argument from hence farther cleared. This promise absolute, not conditional. No condition rationally to be affixed to it: the import of those words ' as for me.' To whom this promise is made. That farther cleared: not to all Israel according to the flesh. Mr. G's objections answered. The testimony of the Son given to the perpetual abiding of the

Spirit with believers; John xiv. 16. opened. The promise in those words equally belonging to all believers. Mr. G.'s objections answered. No promise of the Spirit abiding with believers on his principle allowed. The promise given to the apostles personally, yet given also to the whole church. Promises made to the church, made to the individuals, whereof it is constituted. The giving of this promise to all believers farther argued from the scope of the place; and vindicated from Mr. G.'s exceptions. The third testimony of the Holy Spirit himself proposed to consideration; his testimony in sealing particularly considered; 2 Cor. i. 22. Eph. i. 13. iv. 30. Of the nature and use of sealing amongst men. The end, aim, and use of the sealing of the Holy Ghost. Mr. G.'s objections and exceptions to our argument from that sealing of the Spirit, considered and removed. The same farther carried on, &c.

THERE remains nothing for the confirmation of the first branch or part of the truth proposed, but only the consideration of the oath of God; which, because it ought certainly to be an end of all strife, I shall reserve the handling of it to the close of the whole; if God be pleased to carry us out thereunto, that we may give the oath of God its due honour, of being the last word in this contest.

The order of our method, first proposed, would here call me to handle our steadfastness with God, and the glory created upon our grace of sanctification: but because some men may admire and ask, whence it is that the Lord will abide so steadfast in his love towards believers, as hath been manifested upon several accounts, that he will, besides what hath been said before of his own goodness and unchangeableness, &c. I shall now add, that outward consideration, which lies in the mediation of Christ, upon the account whereof he acts his own goodness and kindness to us, with the greatest advantage of glory and honour to himself that can be thought upon. Only I shall desire the reader to observe, that the Lord Jesus is an undertaker in this business of perfecting our salvation, and safeguarding our spiritual glory, not in one regard and respect only. There is one part of his engagement therein, which, under the oath of God, is the close of the whole; and that is, his becoming a surety to us of his Father's faithfulness towards us, and a surety for us of our faithfulness to him; so that upon the whole matter, the business on each side, as to security, will be found knit up in him, and there we shall do well to leave it, though the handling of that suretiship of his be not of our present consideration; men will scarce dispute him out of his faithfulness; 'Henceforth he dieth no more, death hath no dominion over him, he sits at the right hand of God, expecting to have his enemies made his footstool.' This then I will do, if God permit. And for the steadfastness of his saints, in their abiding with God, I shall, I fear, no otherwise insist peculiarly upon it, but as occasion shall be ministered by dealing with our adversary, as we pass on.

That which I shall now do is, to consider the influence of the priesthood of Christ in those two grand acts thereof, his oblation and intercession, into the perseverance of saints, according to that of the apostle; Heb. v. 27. 'Wherefore he is able also to save to the uttermost, them that come unto God by him, seeing he liveth ever to make intercession for them.' And I will do it the more carefully, because though it be one of the greatest strengths of our cause, yet I shall walk in a path, wherein none shall meet me, for the most part of the way, to make any opposition.

My entrance into the consideration of the procurement of our glory by Christ, shall be with that, whereby he came into his own, viz. his oblation, which hath a twofold influence into the perseverance of the saints, or into the safeguarding of their salvation to the utmost.

1. By removing and taking out of the way,[a] all causes of separation between God, and those that come unto God by him; that is, all believers. Now these are of two sorts:

1. That which is moral, and procuring such separation or distance, which is the guilt of sin.

2. That which is efficient, and working as the power of Satan and of sin. The first of these, being that alone, for which it may be supposed, that God will turn from believers; and the latter, that alone, whereby they may possibly be turned from him. Now that both these are so taken out of the way by the oblation of Christ, that they shall never actually and eventually work, or cause any total, or final, separation between God and believers, shall be demonstrated.

1. He hath so taken away the guilt of sin from believers, from them that come to God by him, that it shall[b] not prevail with the Lord to turn from them; he hath obtained for

[a] Isa. liv. 2.
[b] Eph. i. 10. ii. 13—16. Col. i. 20—22. 2 Cor v. 19, 20. 1 John i. 7.

us, 'eternal redemption;' Heb. ix. 12. eternal and complete; not so far and so far, but 'eternal redemption' hath he obtained; redemption that shall be completed, notwithstanding any interveniences imaginable whatever; this redemption, which he hath obtained for us, and which by him we obtain, the apostle tells us what it is, and wherein it doth consist; Eph. i. 7. 'In whom we have redemption through his blood, even the forgiveness of sins.' He hath obtained for us everlasting forgiveness of sins; as to the complete efficiency of the procuring cause thereof, absolutely perfect and complete in its own kind, not depending on any condition in any other whatsoever, for the producing the utmost effect intended in it; there shall be no after reckoning or account for sin, between God and them, for whom he so obtains redemption. And the apostle, in the tenth chapter of the Epistle to the Hebrews, disputes at large this difference, between the typical sacrifices, and the sacrifice of the blood of Christ; he tells you, those were offered year by year, and could never make the comers to God by them perfect (or acquit them from sin); for then they could have had no more conscience of sin being once purged: but now, saith he, 'there was a remembrance again of sin renewed every year;' ver. 3, 4. If sin had been taken away, there would have been no more conscience of it; that is, no such conscience, as upon the account whereof, they came for help unto, or healing by, those sacrifices; no more conscience condemning for sin: conscience judges according to the obligation unto punishment, which it apprehends upon it. Conscience of sin; that is, a tenderness to sin, and a condemnation of sin, still continues after the taking of the guilt of it away; but conscience disquieting, judging, condemning the person for sin, that[c] vanisheth together with the guilt of it; and this is done, when the sacrifice for sin is perfect and complete, and really attains the end for which it was instituted; and if any sacrifice for sin whatever do not completely take away that sin for which the oblation is made, and the atonement thereby, so that no after charge might come upon the sinner, it is of necessity that that sacrifice be renewed again and again. The reason the apostle gives of the repetition of the legal sacrifices, is, that they

[c] Rom. v. 1.

made not the comers to them perfect; that is, as to the taking away of their sins, and giving them entire and complete
peace thereupon; all this the apostle informs us, was done
in the sacrifice of Christ; ver. 14. ' with one offering he hath
for ever perfected' (or made perfect that work for them as
to this business of conscience for sin) ' them that are sanctified;' his one offering perfectly put an end to this business;
even the difference between God and us, upon the account
of sin; which if he had not done, it would have been necessary, that he should have been often offered; his sacrifice
having not obtained the complete end thereof: that the
efficacy of this sacrifice of his, cannot depend on any thing
foreign unto it, shall be declared afterward. Also, that the
necessity of our faith and obedience, in their proper place,
is not in the least hereby impaired, shall be manifested.
That they may have a proper place, efficacy, and usefulness,
and not be conditions whereon the effects of the death of
Christ are suspended, as to their communication unto us,
is by some denied; how weakly, how falsely, will then also
appear. Now this Christ doth for all that are sanctified, or
dedicated, or consecrated unto God (which is almost the
perpetual sense of that word in this epistle), in and by that
offering of his. And this the apostle farther confirms from
the consideration of the new covenant with us, ratified in,
and whose effects were procured by, the bloodshedding
and offering of Christ; ver. 17. ' Their sins and their iniquities I will remember no more.' Saith God, upon the account
of the offering of Christ, there is an end of that business,
and that controversy, which I have had with those sanctified ones : and therefore, let them (as to this) as to the making satisfaction for sin, trouble themselves no more, to think
of [d] thousands of rams, or the like; for there is no more
offering for sin required; and on this foundation, I may say,
there doth not remain any such guilt to be reckoned unto
believers as that with regard thereunto, God should forsake
them utterly, and give them over unto everlasting ruin; and
this is the sum of the apostle's discourse in that chapter, as
it looks upon the matter under present consideration. That
sacrifice, which so taketh away the sins of them for whom
it is offered, as that thereupon they should be perfect, or

[d] Mic. vi. 6, 7.

perfectly acquitted of them, and have no more conscience
(which is a judgment of a man's self, answering to the judgment of God concerning him) of sin, so to judge him and
condemn him for it, as not to have remedy of that judgment
or condemnation provided in that sacrifice; that, I say, doth
so take away the guilt of sin, as that it shall never separate
between God and them, for whom and whose sin it was offered; but such was the sacrifice of Christ: *ergo*, &c. The reason of the consequence is clear from the very form of the
proposition; and nothing is assumed, but what is the express testimony of the apostle, in that and other places?

So Dan. ix. 24. The design in the death of Christ, ' is to
finish the transgression, to make an end of sin, and to make
reconciliation for iniquities, and to bring in everlasting righteousness.' Christ makes an end of sin, not that there should
be no more sin in the world, for there is yet sinning to the
purpose, in some respect, much more than before his death;
and there will be so to eternity, if those under the ultimate
sentence may be thought to sin; but he makes an[e] end of
it, as to the controversy and difference about it, between
God and them for whom he died; and that by[f] making reconciliation; on the part of God, atoning him towards us,
which atonement we are persuaded to accept; and by bringing in for us a[g] righteousness which is everlasting, and will
abide the trial, which God will certainly accept: now when
God is satisfied for sin, and we are furnished with a righteousness exactly complete, and answering to the utmost of
his demand, whence can any more contest arise about the
guilt of sin, or the obligation of the sinner unto punishment,
that from the justice and law of God doth attend it? This
also the apostle urgeth, Rom. viii. 34. ' Who is he that condemneth? It is Christ that died.' He argueth from the
death of Christ[h] to the ablation or removal of condemnation
for sin; because by his death he hath made an end of sin,
as was shewed, and brought in everlasting righteousness.
To suspend the issue of all these transactions between God
and the Mediator, upon conditions by us to be accomplished, not bestowed on us, purchased for us, and as to their

---

[e] Heb. vi. 4, 5. x. 26.   [f] Rom. v 10.   [g] Isa xxvii. 3, 4 xlv. 24, 25
                            [h] Heb. x 14--18.

event uncertain, is disadvantageously to beg the thing in question.

Now because it appears, that, notwithstanding the death of Christ, many for whom he died, are kept a long' season under the guilt of sin, and are all of them born in a condition of wrath, (Eph. ii. 3.) I shall crave leave a little to insist on this instance, and to shew, that notwithstanding the truth thereof,·yet the guilt of sin is so taken away from all those for whom Christ died, by his death, that it shall never be a cause of everlasting separation between God and them. In the[k] obedience and death of Christ, whereby as a completely sufficient and efficacious means, he made way for the accomplishment of his eternal purposes, in such paths of infinite wisdom, as brought in all the good he aimed by it, in that order, which the very frame and nature of things by him appointed, required the exaltation of his glory, God is satisfied, well pleased, and resolved that he will not take his course at law against those, in the behalf of whom he died. Though an arrest was gone forth against all mankind, yet the Lord suspended by his sovereignty the utmost execution of it, that room and space might be given, according to the eternal thoughts of his heart, for the deliverance of some. A reprieve is granted mankind out of reasons, and for purposes of his own. After the sentence of death was denounced against them, God being pleased to magnify[l] his grace, according to his eternal counsel, and purpose in Jesus Christ, innovates the law, as to the obligation of it unto punishment, on the behalf of some, by an interposition of the Son of his love in such way as to undergo what was due unto those, on whose behalf the interposition was made; and by this undertaking of Christ, in the very first notion of it, as it was satisfactory, thus much is done and accomplished.

First, The vindictive justice of God is satisfied; that is, whereas such is the[m] natural right, sovereignty, and dominion of God over his creatures, and such his essential perfections of holiness, purity, and righteousness, that if his

---

[i] 1 Cor. vi. 11 Eph ii 11, 12.   [k] 2 Cor. v. 18--20.
[l] Eph i. 6 11. 2 Tim. i. 9 Heb. vii. 22 x. 9. 2 Cor. v. 21.
[m] Gen. xviii. 25. Josh. xxiv. 19. Psal. v. 4--6. Hab. i. 13. Rom. i. 18. 32, . 2 Thess. i. 6.

creatures cast off his yoke, and their dependance on him (which they do by every sin, what in them lieth), it is then of indispensable necessity, that he render unto that sin or sinner, guilty thereof, a meet recompense of reward : Jesus Christ hath so answered[n] his righteousness, that without the impairing of his right or sovereignty, without the least derogation from his perfections, he may receive his sinning creatures again to favour; it being the 'judgment of God, that they, who commit sin are worthy of death ;' Rom. i. 32. and 'a righteous thing with him to render tribulation to sinners ;' 1 Thess. i. 6, 7.   For 'shall not the Judge of all the world do right ?' Gen. xviii. 25. He hath set forth his Son to 'declare his righteousness for the forgiveness of sins ;' Rom. iii. 24, 25. Now for whom Christ died, he died for all their sins ; 1 John i. 7. 'The blood of Christ cleanseth us from all sin ;' the application of it being commensurate to his intendment in his oblation, not extending itself to the actual effecting of any thing whatever, which was not meritoriously procured thereby. 'He loved his church, and gave himself for it, that he might sanctify and cleanse it with the washing of water, that he might present it to himself a glorious church, not having spot or wrinkle, or any such thing, but that it should be holy and without blame ;' Eph. v. 25 — 27. He makes complete atonement to the justice of God on their behalf, so that the very vindictive justice of God hath nothing to lay to their charge.   That which in God maintains the quarrel against sinners is atoned, and is no more their enemy than mercy itself : and this not upon condition of believing to be antecedently accomplished before this be done. The satisfaction of justice vindictive depends not at all on any thing in us ; it requires only, that there be *vindicta noxæ*, and a vindication of the sovereignty of God over the sinning creature, by the infliction of that punishment, which in his infinite wisdom and righteousness, he hath proportioned unto sin ; on a supposition of sin in such creatures, as being made meet and fit to yield voluntary obedience unto God, and so standing in a moral subjection to him, being their cutting off, what lies in them, their dependance on God (which that it should be continued, is as necessary as that God be God, or the Lord of all) ; those

[n] Vid Diat. de Just. Div.

creatures are, upon the account of the sovereignty and righteousness of God, whereof we speak, indispensably obnoxious unto punishment, which is of necessity required unto God's retaining his dominion over them. By the death of Christ, this condition is so far repaired, that the dependance and subjection unto God, of those for whom he died, is made up, so far as to a deliverance of them from a necessity of being obnoxious unto punishment, and that completely, without any abeyance upon conditions in themselves, which can have no influence thereunto. So that though the process of the law sent forth, be[o] not instantly recalled, but man is suffered to lie under that arrest for a season, yet God lets fall his suit on this account, and will never pass his first sentence, from which we are reprieved, unto full and final execution; pronouncing himself well pleased with his Son, resting satisfied with his mediatory performances, and seeking no farther.

Secondly, The law of God is fulfilled. Unless this be answered in all concernments of it, the Lord would be thought to change his will, to reverse his word, and to blur the copy of his own holiness. There is in the whole law, and every parcel of it, an eternal indispensable righteousness and truth; arising either from the nature of things themselves, concerning which it is, or the relation of one thing unto another. That to fear God, to love him, to obey him, to do no wrong, are everlastingly indispensably good and necessary, is from the nature of the things themselves: only with this supposition, that God would make creatures capable of yielding him such obedience. That that which is good, shall be so rewarded, that which is evil so punished, is also an everlasting truth upon supposition of such actual performances. Whereas then of this law there are two parts, the one absolute or preceptive, in the rule and commands thereof; the other conditional, and rewarding in its promise, or condemning in its curse; Christ by his death put himself in [p]their behalf, for whom he died (to speak to that particular), under the curse of it; Gal. iii. 13. 'He redeemed us from the curse of the law, being made a curse for us.' Neither is this at all suspended on our believing; the law doth

<hr>

[o] John iii. 36. Eph. ii. 3. 2 Cor. v. 18. Psal. xvi. 3, 4. Matt. xvii. 5.
[p] Rom. viii. 3. x. 3, 4. Gal. iv. 4—6. Phil. iii. 9.

not threaten a curse, only if we do not believe, but if we[q] do not all things written therein; whether we believe or not, the law takes no notice, as to the curse that it denounceth; if there hath been any sin, that must be executed.   And the law is for the curse, as [r]Isaac for the great spiritual blessing: he had but one; it hath but one great curse, and that being undergone by Christ, it hath not another for them, in whose stead Christ underwent it; God having[s] 'made him to be sin for us who knew no sin, we become the righteousness of God in him;' all separation from God is by the curse of the law; all that is required in it, by it, is, that it be undergone: this is done by Christ for all believers; that thereby is taken away, which alone can separate them from God, or put any distance between them: but of this, and their subjection to the curse before their believing, more afterward.

Thirdly, The truth, or veracity of God, was particularly engaged to see sin punished, upon the account of the promulgation of the first express sanction of the law: "In the day thou eatest, thou shalt die.'   For the satisfying the engagement of God's truth, there seemed to be a tender made in the sacrifices instituted of old; but it was rejected, as insufficient to make good that word of God, so eminently given out; there was neither any such relation, union, or conjunction, between the sinner and the innocent creature sacrificed, or any such real worth in the sacrifice itself, as that the death of the substituted beast, might by any means be so interpreted, as to amount to the accomplishment of the truth of God; death being once denounced, as the reward of sin. Heb. x. 5, 6. 'Sacrifices and offerings for sin thou wouldest not, in burnt-offerings and sacrifices for sin thou hadst no pleasure;' but saith our Saviour, 'Lo, I come, to do thy will, O God;' ver. 7.   Will that do it? Yea, it will assuredly, for in the volume of his book it is written, that he should so do; all that God willed to be done for the accomplishment of his truth, was fulfilled by Christ, when he came to give up himself a 'sweet-smelling sacrifice;' Eph. v. 2.   God then may be true, his truth being salved to the utmost, though never any one of them, for whom Christ died, do die: but this to the salvation of believers, is only as *removens prohibens*.

Fourthly, The distributive justice of God is, upon this

ᵘoblation of Christ, engaged upon the covenant and compact made with Christ, as Mediator to that purpose, to bestow on them, for whom he offered and died, all the good things which he promised him for them, in and upon the account of his undertaking in their behalf. The distributive justice of God, is that perfection of his nature, whereby he rendereth to every one, according to what, either his ˣvindictive justice on the one side, or his uprightness and faithfulness on the other, do require. In rewarding, it respects his own faithfulness in all his engagements, immediately; in punishing, the demerit of the creature: there being no such natural connexion and necessary coherence, from the nature of the things themselves, between obedience and reward, as there is between sin and punishment.

Now the Lord having given many ʸeminent and glorious promises to his Son Jesus Christ (some whereof we shall mention afterward), concerning his seed and offspring, or those that he committed to his charge, to be redeemed from their sins, it is incumbent on him, in regard of his righteousness, to make out all those things in due time unto them. And therefore, that he might magnify that righteousness and truth of his, he hath cast the whole procedure of his grace, into such a way, and all the acts of it, into such a dependence upon one another, as that the one of them, should have infallible influence into the other, and the effects of every one of them, be rendered indubitably certain.

Thus upon the account of the death of Christ, antecedently to all considerations of faith or belief in them for whom he died, thus much is done for the extinguishing the quarrel about sin : the ᶻvindictive justice, law, and truth of God, are disengaged from pursuing the sentence of death and everlasting separation from God, against them as sinners ; neither have they at all any thing to lay to their charge, for which they should be cast out of the presence of God : yea, the Lord is moreover, in his own faithfulness and righteousness, with respect to the covenant of the Mediator, en-

ᵘ Isa. liii. 10, 11.

ˣ Gen. xviii. 24. Psal v. 31. 35. lxv. 5. lxxi. 2. xcvi. 13. xcviii. 2. cii. 17. cxli. 1. 11.

ʸ Psal. ii. 7, 8. cx. 3. 7. xlv. 13, 14. Isa. xlix. 5, 6. 8. lii. 13, 14. liii. 11. lix. 20. John xii. 51, 52.

ᶻ Isa. liii 6. Gal. iv. 4, 5. Heb. x. 5—8. Rom. viii. 33, 34. Isa liii. 11, 12. Rom. iv. 25. Phil. i. 29. Eph. i. 3

gaged to do that which is needful, to the bringing of them to himself. After some previous observations, I shall confirm what hath been spoken by sundry arguments. I say then,

First, That it is a most vain supposal, which some make: What if any one of them, for whom Christ died, should die in an unregenerate condition? Would not the justice and condemning power of the law of God, notwithstanding the death of Christ, lay hold upon them? It is, I say, a supposal of that, which *in sensu composito,* is impossible, and so in that sense (however upon other respects it may) not to be argued from: Christ died, that those for whom he died [a]might live; that they might be quickened and born again. And so they shall, in their due season, every one undoubtedly be, and not any of them die in their sins.

Secondly, That our affirmation, is not in the least liable to that exception which usually men insist upon, in opposition unto it, viz. That if Christ hath so satisfied justice, and fulfilled the law, in reference to all them for whom he died, that the sentence of condemnation should not be issued out against them, but they must infallibly be saved; then there is no necessity, either that they do at all believe, or if they do, that they live in holiness, and the avoidance of sin; all that being accomplished, which by these mediums is sought for. I say, our position in itself, is no way liable to this exception. For,

First, Though the justice, law, and truth of God, be satisfied and fulfilled, as to their sins, that he hath not, as on that account, any thing to lay to their charge, yet this [b]hinders not at all, but that God may assign and ascribe such a way for their coming to him, as may be suited to the exalting of his glory; the honour of Jesus Christ, who hath brought all this about, and the preparing of the soul of the sinner for the full enjoyment of himself; and this he hath done by the law of faith, which gives him the glory of [c]his grace, and all his other attributes, exalts Jesus Christ, whom it is his will we should honour, as we honour himself, and empties the poor sinful creature of itself, that it may be made meet for the inheritance of the saints in light.

[a] John iii. 16, 17. vii. 33. 2 Cor. v. 14, 15.
[b] Isa. liii. 5, 6. 11, 12 Dan. ix 24. Rom viii. 32, 33. Gal iii. 13 Heb. ii. 14, 15. Rom. i. 16, 17. iii. 23—25. iv. 16. ix. 31, 32 John v. 23.
[c] Rom iii. 27. Eph. i. 6. Phil. iii. 8—11.

Secondly, This consideration of the death of Christ, of his freeing us from condemnation for any, or all, of our sins, is not[d] to be taken apart, or separated from the other, of his procuring the Holy Spirit, and grace for us, that we should not commit sin, being born of God, with all the dispensations of precepts and promises, exhortations and threatenings, whereby he morally carries on the work of his grace in the hearts of his saints; setting us free from the guilt of sin, he so far also sets us free from the power of sin, that we should be dead to it, live no longer in it, that it should not reign in us, nor prevail to turn us utterly from God.

Thirdly, They seem not much to be acquainted with the nature of faith, holiness, and communion with God, who suppose the end of them, is only for the escaping of the wrath that is to come; they[e] are the things, whereby we are daily renewed, and changed into the 'image of the glory of God,' and so not only made useful and serviceable to him here, but also prepared for the fulness of his likeness, wherewith we shall be satisfied hereafter. Wherefore, observe,

Fourthly, That though this complete atonement be made in the death of Christ, yet it remains free in the bosom of God, when he will[f] begin our actual deliverance, from under that arrest of death that was gone out against us, and how far in this life he will carry it[g] towards perfection; it is, I say, in his bosom, when he will bestow his Spirit on us, for regeneration and faith; when he will actually absolve us from under the arrest of the law, by the application of his mercies in Christ unto us, by the promise of the gospel; and how far he will carry on the work of our deliverance from sin, in this life. Only that is done,[h] upon the account whereof, it is impossible that the quarrel against sin, should be carried on to the utmost execution of the sentence denounced towards those sinners, for whom Christ died; which I prove by these following arguments:

First, It is plainly affirmed, that Christ by his death obtained 'everlasting redemption;' Heb. ix. 12. He obtained everlasting redemption, before his ascending into the most holy place, called elsewhere the[i] 'purging of our sins.' Now

d Eph. v. 25—27. Tit. ii. 14. Gal. iv 4—6. John xvii. 7. Mat xxviii. 18—20.
Eph iv. 12--14. Rom. vi. 2--6, &c.
e Eph. iv 22. 2 Cor. v. 15. Rom. xii. 1, 2. 2 Cor. iii 18. f Mat. xv 5, 6.
g 2 Thess. i. 11. John iii. 8. h 2 Pet. i. 1. i Heb. i. 3.

this redemption (as was said), the apostle informs us, consists 'in the forgiveness of sins,' Eph. i. 7. 'In whom we have redemption through his blood, even the forgiveness of sins;' or the intercision of that obligation unto punishment which attends sin, in reference to the sinner, and his subjection to the law of God, and the righteousness thereof. As the oblation of Christ respecteth God and his justice, to whom it is given as a price and ransom, and whereof it is an atonement, so it is, and is called (or we are said to receive thereby) redemption: as it respects them, who receive the benefit of that redemption, it is the forgiveness of sins. Forgiveness of sins, as it is completed and terminated in the consciences of believers, requireth[l] the interposition of faith, for the receiving of Christ in the promise, who[m] 'of God is made unto us righteousness ;' but in respect of the procurement of it, and the removing all causes, upon the account whereof sin should be[n] imputed unto us, that is perfected in the oblation of Christ; hence he is said, to 'bear our sins in his own body on the cross;' 1 Pet. ii. 24. and being once on him, either he was discharged of them, or he must for ever lie under the burden of them : they were on him on the tree, what is then become of them? If he were freed of them, and justified from them (as he was, Isa. l. 8, 9.) how should they ever be laid to our charge? And yet this freedom from condemnation for sin, for all the elect, which God himself so clearly asserts, Rom. viii. 32, 33, &c. doth not in the least set them free from the necessity of obedience, nor acquit them from contracting the guilt of sin, upon the least irregularity or disobedience.

Secondly, We are said to do, together with Christ, those things, which he doth for us in his own person, and that upon the account of that benefit, which by those his personal performances, doth[o] redound unto us, and which being done, the quarrel about sin, as to make an utter separation between God and our souls, is certainly removed ; thus we are said to die with him, to be raised again with him, and with him we enter into the holy place ; this whole business about sin being passed through; for he that is dead, is justified from sin. Now all this being done by us, and for us, in and

<hr/>

[l] Rom. i. 5   [m] 1 Cor. i 30.   [n] Rom iv. 4.
[o] Rom. vi. 5 8.   2 Cor. v. 15, 16.   Col. iii. 1.   Rom. vi. 7.

by our head, can we henceforth die any more? shall death any more have dominion over us? This the apostle argues; 2 Cor. v. 15. 'We judge,' saith he, ' that if one died for all, then were all they (that is, all those for whom he died) dead,' or died likewise; they were dead in, and with him, their sponsor, as to the curse due for sin, that henceforth they might ' live to him that died for them.'

Thirdly, The compact or agreement, that was between the Father and the Son as Mediator, about the business of our redemption in his blood, manifests this truth. The Father required at his hands, that he should do[p] his will, fulfil his pleasure and counsel, make ' his soul an offering for sin,' and do that which the sacrifices of bulls and goats shadowed out, but could never effect · upon the performance whereof, he was to ' see his seed,' and to bring ' many sons to glory.' A covenanting and agreement into an uncertain issue and event (as that must be of God and the Mediator, if the salvation of the persons, concerning which and whom it was, be not infallibly certain), ought not, at any cheap rate, or pretence, to be assigned to infinite wisdom. In the accomplishment of this undertaking, whereunto Christ was designed, the Father dealt with him[q] in strict and rigid justice: there was neither composition about the debt, nor commutation about the punishment, that he had taken upon himself. Now doth not exact justice require, that the ransom being given in, the prisoners be delivered? that the debt being paid, the bond be cancelled, as to any power of imprisoning the original debtor? that punishment being undergone, and the law fulfilled, the offender go free? Especially all this being covenanted for in the first undertaking, doubtless wrath shall not arise a second time. The right knowledge, use, and improvement of this grace, being given, bounded, and directed by the gospel, it is safeguarded from abuse, by that which God calls his own wisdom.

Fourthly, It appears from what God bestows upon his elect, upon the account of the undertaking of Christ for them (in the pursuit of the eternal purpose of his will), antecedently to any thing whatsoever in them, that should engage him to do them the least good; when God comes as a

[p] Psal xl 8. Isa. liii. 10, 11. Heb. x. 5. 7. 9. ii. 10.
[q] Rom. viii. 32. 2 Pet. ii. 1. 2 Cor. v. 21. Gal. iii. 13. Heb. ii. 9.

friend to hold out unto, and bestow good things upon men;
I mean, good in that kind of mercy, which is peculiarly
suited to the bringing of them to the enjoyment of himself;
it is evident that he hath put an end to all enmity and quarrel between him and them. Now[r] antecedently unto any
thing in men, God for Christ's sake bestows, with the greatest act of friendship imaginable, no less than the Holy Spirit
on them. By him they are quickened; and their faith is but
a fruit of that Spirit bestowed on them; if they have not any
sufficiency in themselves, as much as to think a good thought,
nor can do any thing that is acceptable to God; being by
nature dead in trespasses and sins, which at present (the
Scripture affirming it) I take for granted; then assuredly
God doth give his Holy Spirit to the saints, whereby he
works in them[s] 'both to will and to do of his own good pleasure,' antecedently to any good thing in them, that is well-
pleasing unto him. Every thing that men do, must either
be brought forth by the strength and ability of their own natural faculties, assisted and provoked by motives and persuasions from without, or it must be the operation of the
Spirit of God: there is not another principle to be fixed on.
The first (at present I take for granted), is not the fountain
of any spiritual acting whatsoever: neither[t] can any gracious
act be educed radically from the corrupt natural faculty, however assisted, or advantaged; it must be the Spirit then, that
is the sole principal cause and author of all the movings of
our souls towards God, that are acceptable to him in Christ.
Now the cause is certainly before the effect; and the Spirit,
in order of nature, is bestowed upon us, antecedently to all
the grace which he worketh in us: whether the Spirit be bestowed on men, on the account of Christ's undertaking for
them, none can question, but they must withal deny him to
be the Mediator of the new covenant. The Spirit of grace
is the principal promise thereof; Isa. lix. 20, 21. 'We are
blessed with all spiritual blessings in Christ;' Eph. i. 3.
Surely the Holy Spirit himself so often promised to us of
God, is a spiritual blessing: God's bestowing faith on us, is
antecedent to our believing; and this also is given upon the
account of Christ; Phil. i. 29. ' It is given to us, on the be-

[r] Isa. liv. 20, 21. Rom. viii 11. Gal. v 22 1 Cor. vii. 4. 2 Cor. iii. 5. John
xv. 3. 5. Ephes. ii. 1, 2. [s] Phil. i. 13. Col. i. 12.
[t] Gen. viii 21. Job xiv. 4. Matt. xii. 33.

half of Christ, to believe on him.' If then God, for Christ's sake, antecedently to any thing that is good, that is not enmity to him, that is not iniquity in men, do bestow on them, all that ever is good in them, as to the root and principle of it, surely his quarrel against their sins is put to an issue. Thence Christ being said to make 'reconciliation for the sins of the people,' Heb. ii. 17. God, as one pacified and atoned thereupon, is said to be in him, 'reconciling the world unto himself;' 2 Cor. v. 19. And in the dispensation of the gospel, he is still set forth, as one carrying' on that peace, whose foundation is laid in the blood of his Son, by the atonement of his justice; and we are said to accept, or receive the atonement; Rom. v. 10. We receive it by faith, it being accepted by him: thus his death and oblation is said to be a 'sacrifice of a sweet-smelling savour;' Eph. v. 2. that wherein God is abundantly delighted, and wherewith his soul is fully satisfied; so that as when he smelt a sweet savour from the sacrifice of Noah, he[w] sware he would curse the earth no more: smelling this sweet savour of the oblation of Christ, on the account of them, for whom it was offered, he will not[x] execute the curse on them, whereof they were guilty. I might also insist on those testimonies for the farther proof of the former assertion, where an immediate efficacy for the taking away of sin, is ascribed to the death of Christ. But what hath been spoken may at present suffice.

The premises considered, some light may be brought forth, to discover the various mistakes of men, about[n] the effects of the death of Christ, as to the taking away of sin, if that were now the matter before us. Some having truly fixed their thoughts on the efficacy of the death of Christ, for abolition of sin, do give their lusts and darkness leave to make wretched inferences thereupon: as that therefore because we are so completely justified and accepted before, and without our believing, or the consideration of any thing whatever in us; that therefore sin is nothing, nor at all to be accounted of. And though they say, we must not sin that grace may abound, yet too many by woful experience have discovered, what such corrupt conclusions have tended

[v] Eph. ii. 13, 14.   [w] Gen. viii. 21.
[x] John xvii. 19. Rom. v. 10 Rom. vi. 6. 2 Cor v. 21. Eph. v. 25, 26. Tit. ii. 14.
[y] Heb. ix. 14. x. 14. 1 Pet. ii. 24. 1 John i 7. Rev. i. 5, 6.

unto. Others again, fixing themselves on the necessity of obedience, and the concurrence of actual faith, to the completing of justification in the soul of the sinner, with a no less dangerous reflection upon the truth, do suspend the efficacy of the death of Christ upon our believing, which gives life and vigour and virtue unto it (as they say), and is the sole originally discriminating cause of all the benefits we receive thereby; without the antecedent accomplishment of that condition in us, or our actual believing, it is not (say they), nor will be useful: yea, that the intention of God is, to bestow upon us the fruits and effects of the death of Christ, upon condition we do believe, which that we shall is no part of his purchase, and which we can of ourselves perform, say some of them; others, not. Doubtless, these things are not (being rightly stated) in the least inconsistent; Christ may have his due, and we bound to the performance of our duty; which might be cleared by an enlargement of the ensuing considerations:

First, That all good things, that are spiritual whatsoever, that are wrought either for men or in them, are fruits of the death of Christ. They have nothing of themselves, but nakedness, blood, and sin, guilt and impenitency, so that it is of indispensable necessity, that God should shew them favour, antecedently to any act of their believing on him. Faith is given for Christ's sake, as was observed.

Secondly, That all the effects and fruits of the death of Christ, antecedent to our believing, are deposited in the hand of the righteousness and faithfulness of God, to whom as a *ransom it was paid, as an atonement it was offered, before whom as a price and purchase, it was laid down. It is all left in the hands of God's faithfulness, righteousness, mercy, and grace, to be made out effectually to them, for whom he died, in the appointed time or season. So that,

Thirdly, The state or condition of those for whom Christ died, is not actually and really changed by his death in itself; but they lie ʸunder the curse, whilst they are in the state of nature, unregenerate, and all effects of sin whatever. That which is procured for them, is left in the hand of the

---

ˣ 1 Tim. ii. 5, 6. Heb. ii 17. 2 Cor. v. 18, 19. 1 Cor. vi. 19, 20.
ʸ Eph. ii. 1—5. John iii. 36.

Father; they are not in the least intrusted with it, until the appointed time do come.

Fourthly, That faith and belief are necessary, not to add any thing to complete the procurement of forgiveness of sins, any or all; but only to the actual receiving of it, when upon the account of the death of Christ, it pleaseth God in the promise of the gospel, to hold it out and impart it unto the soul, thereby completing covenant-justification. And thus the whole business of salvation may be resolved into the mediation of Christ, and yet men carried on, under an orderly dispensation of law and gospel, into the enjoyment of it. Of the whole, these degrees are considerable:

1. God's [z]eternal purpose of saving some, in and by the mediation of Christ, that mediation of Christ being interposed between the purpose of God, and the accomplishment of the thing purposed, as the fruit and effect of the one, the meritorious procuring cause of the other. This act of the will of God, the Scripture knows by no other name than that of election, or predestination, or the purpose of God according to election, or the purpose of his will in Jesus Christ, which though it comprise his will of not punishing them in their own persons, that are within the verge of this his purpose, yet it is not properly an act of forgiveness of sin, nor are they pardoned by it, nor is the law actually innovated, or its obligation on them unto punishment dissolved, nor themselves justified in any sense thereby.

2. That interposition of the Lord Christ, whereof we have been treating, being a medium indispensably necessary as to satisfaction, and freely designed by the will and wisdom of God, for such a procurement of the good things designed in his eternal counsel, as might advance the glory of his grace, and make known his righteousness also. And this being fixed on by God, as the only thing by him required, that all the mercies, all the grace of his eternal purpose, might be dispensed in the order by him designed unto them: upon the performance of it, God resteth as well pleased, and they for whom he hath mediated by his blood, or for whom he is considered so to have done, are [a]reconciled unto God, as to

---

[z] Acts xiii 38, 39. Rom. v. 10 John iii 16. Rom. v. 7, 8. 1 John iv. 10. Heb. ii 17. ix 14. Eph. i. 4—9, &c. Rom ix. 11. John iii 36. Eph ii 3. Rom. v. 6. 8. Gal iii. 23. 2 Cor v. 21. Rom. iii. 23—25. 2 Cor. i. 30. Matt. xvii. 5.

[a] Rom. v 9, 10. 2 Cor. v. 18, 19. 21. 1 Pet. ii. 21.

that part of reconciliation, which respects the love of God, as to the dispensing the fruits of it unto them, even whilst they are enemies, upon the accounts before-mentioned.

3. Things being thus stated between God and them for whom Christ died, on the account of his death God[b] actually absolves them from under that sentence and curse of the law, by sending the Spirit of his Son into their hearts, to quicken them and to implant faith in them. And in what act of God to place his actual absolution of sinners, ungodly persons, whom Christ died for, but in this actual collation of the Spirit, and habit of grace on them, I am not as yet satisfied; neither doth this in any measure confound our justification and sanctification: for nothing hinders, but that the same act as it is of free grace, in opposition to works, or any thing in us, may justify us, or exert the fruit of his love, which was before purchased by Christ, in our gracious acceptation, notwithstanding all that was against us; and also by principling us with grace for obedience, sanctify us throughout.

4. This being done, they, with whom God thus graciously deals, receive the atonement, and being justified by faith, have peace with God.

But this is not the matter, or subject of our present contest. This then is the first influence, which the bloodshedding in the death and oblation of Christ, hath into the saints' continuance of the love and favour of God; it taketh away the guilt of sin, that it shall not be such a provocation to the eyes of his glory (his law being fulfilled, and justice satisfied), as to cause him utterly to turn away his love from them, and they becoming[c] 'the righteousness of God in him,' to all intents and purposes, what should separate them from the love of God? He hath [d]made peace in the blood of the cross of his Son, and will not engage in enmity against his elect any more to eternity; but in his own way and own time (as he hath the sovereignty of all in his hands) he will bring them infallibly to the enjoyment of himself. And thus much by this discourse about the effects of the death of Christ, have we clearly obtained; what Christ aims to accomplish by his death, and what was the design and in-

<hr/>

[b] 2 Cor. v. 20. Rom viii. 11.   [c] 2 Cor. v. 21
[d] Eph. ii, 14, 15. Rom. viii. 52, 33.

tention of the Father, that he should accomplish, that cannot fail of its issue and appointed event, by any interposure whatever. That the effectual removal of every thing, that might intercept, hinder, or turn aside the love and favour of God from them, for whom he died, is the designed effect of the death of Christ, hath been demonstrated. This then, in the order, wherein it hath seemed good, to the infinite wisdom of God, to proceed in dispensing his grace unto sinners, shall certainly be fulfilled, and all believers saved to the utmost.

I come, in the second place, to demonstrate, that as our Saviour secures the stability of the love of the saints to God and their abiding with him, by taking away and removing, whatever might hinder them herein, or prevail upon them utterly and wickedly to depart from him; that which meritoriously might cause God to turn from us, he utterly destroys and abolishes, and that, which efficiently might cause us to turn from God, that also he destroys and removes. Now all, that is of this kind, that works effectually and powerfully for the alienating of the hearts of believers from God, or keeping men in a state of alienation from him, may be referred unto two principles: 1. *Satan himself. 2. His works; the world, as under the curse, is an instrument in his hand, who is called the God thereof, to allure, vex, and mischief us withal; neither hath it the least power or efficacy in itself, but only as it is managed in the[f] hand of Satan to turn men from God. And yet the Lord Christ hath not let that go free neither, without its death's wound; but bids his followers be of ' good[g] comfort, for he had overcome the world;' that is, for them, and in their stead; so that it should never be used nor heightened in its enmity to a conquest over them; I mean a total and final conquest, such as might frustrate any intention of God in his undertaking for them: it is not our loss of a little blood, but our loss of life, that makes the enemy a conqueror. But now for Satan.

First, He overcomes, destroys, and breaks him in pieces, with his power; Heb. ii. 14. ' By death he destroyed him that had the power of death, that is, the devil.' The first thing that was promised of him, was, that he should ' break

* Gen. iii. 17. f 2 Cor. iv 4 Matt. iv. 9.
g John xvi. 33. Gal. i. 4. 1 John v. 4, 5.

the head of the serpent;' Gen. iii. 15. He doth it also in, and for the 'seed of the woman,' all the elect of God, opposed to the seed of the serpent, or generation of vipers. In pursuit hereof, he 'spoils principalities and powers, and makes .a show of them openly, triumphing over them in his cross;' Col. ii. 15. In the blood of his cross he conquered, and brake the power of the devil, 'binding that strong man armed, and spoiling his goods,' making a show of him and them, as great conquerors were wont to do with their captives and their spoils.

Now there are two ways, whereby the blood of Christ thus brake the power of Satan, that he shall not lead those always captive at his pleasure, nor rule in them, as children of disobedience, in the behalf of whom his power was so broken.

First, He subdues him by taking away all that right and title, which he had by sin, to rule over them; I speak of the elect of God. By the entrance of sin, the devil entered upon a twofold rule in reference to sinners: First, A rule over them with the terror and dread of death and hell; they are in[h] bondage by reason of death, all their days; Heb. ii. 15. And the devil hath the power of that death upon the world, whereunto they are in bondage. The death that is in the curse, is put into his hand to manage it, to the dread and terror of sinners; and by it he hath always kept many, and to this day doth keep innumerable souls in unexpressible bondage; putting them upon barbarous inhumanities, to make atonement for their sins; and forcing some to inflict revenge and destruction upon themselves, thinking to prevent, but really hastening that which they fear. As of old, this power of his lay at the bottom of all the abominations, wherewith men provoked God, when they[i] thought to atone him, as by burning their children in the fire, and the like; Mic. vi. 7, 8. So at present is it[k] the principle of all that superstitious will-worship, and religious drudgery, which is spread over the antichristian world: yea, the inventions of men, ignorant of the righteousness of God, and convinced of their own insufficiency to perform, work out, and establish a righteousness of their own, that shall perfectly answer the exact holy demands of the law, as far as to them is discovered, to deliver themselves from under this dread of death,

[h] Heb. ii. 14.   [i] Diat. de Just. Divin.
[k] Lev. xvii. 21. Deut. xviii. 10. 2 Kings xvi. 6. xxiii. 10. 2 Chr. xxxiii. 6. Jer. xxxii. 35.

wherewith he, that hath the power of it, terrifies them all
their days, are indeed the foundation and spring, the sum
and substance of all religions in the world, and the darling
of all religious persons, in, and with whom, Christ is not all
and in all. And herein have the Papists gone one notable
step beyond all their predecessors in superstition and devotion; for whereas they universally contented themselves,
with sacrifices, purifications, purgations, lustrations, satisfactions, recompenses to be in this life performed, these latter, more refined, sublimated, mercurial wits, observing that
nothing they could here invent, would settle and charm the
spirits of men haunted with the dread of death we speak of,
but that instantly they came again with the same disquiet-
ness as formerly, and renewed mention of sin, upon the insufficiency of the atonement fixed on for its expiation, they
found out that noble expedient of the future purgatory,
which might maintain the souls of men in some hopes in
this life, and secure themselves from the cries and complaints
of men, against the insufficiency of their remedy, which they
do prescribe.

Secondly, As he rules over men by death, and hell that
follows after, so also he rules in men by sin, he ' ruleth in the
children of disobedience;' Eph. ii. 2. And to this end, to
secure men to himself, he being that¹ strong man armed, who
hath the first possession, and labours to keep what he hath
got in peace, he sets up strong-holds, imaginations, and
high things, against God; 2 Cor. iv. 5. Now this twofold
power of Satan, over men and in men, do both arise from sin:
whereby men are first cast out of God's love and care, becoming obnoxious to death. And, secondly, are alienated
from God, in willing subjection to his enemy: and both
these parts and branches of his dominion are, in reference
unto the elect, cast down and destroyed and taken away.
For,

First, Christ by his death cashiers the title and claim,
that Satan laid to the exercise of any such power, in reference unto the elect When men cast down any from rule, they
may interrupt, and put by their exercise of any power, but
they cannot take away their title, unless it be of their own
giving; Christ, by his death, takes away the very bottom,

¹ Matt. xii. 39. Mark iii. 27. Luke xi. 21.

foundation, and occasion of the whole power of Satan. All[m] the power of Satan in the first sense, consists in death, and those things that either conduce to it, or do attend it. Now death entered by sin, and therewithal the power of Satan. The Lord Jesus taking away sin, and putting an end thereunto, as was manifested, the whole title[n] of Satan falls and comes to nothing. And this was really done[o] in the cross : its manifestation by the gospel ensuing thereupon, according to the appointment of God.

Secondly, He takes away the exercise of his power, and that to the utmost. For,

1. He binds him with bonds ; ' he binds the strong man armed ;' Matt. xii. 19. and he ' breaks his head ;' Gen. iii. 15. then ' leads him captive ;' Psal. lxviii. 18. ' triumphs over him ;' Col. i. 16. ' treads him down under the feet of his ;' Rom. xvi. 20. as the kings of Canaan were trod down under the feet of the children of Israel ; then destroys him ; Heb. ii. 14. What exercise of power is left, to a conquered, bound, wounded, captived, triumphed over, trodden down, destroyed caitif? Think ye this wretch shall ever wholly prevail against any one of them, for whose sake all this was done to him ? Neither can this with any colour of reason be said to be done for them, or with respect unto them, towards whom the power of Satan remains entire all their days, whom he leads captive and rules over at his pleasure, until death take full dominion over them.

2. As he destroys Satan, so he doth his works . ' For this cause was he manifested, even to destroy the works of the devil ;' 1 John iii. 8. He doth not only bind the strong man armed, but also he spoils his goods. Whatsoever[p] is in men, that follows from that corrupted principle of nature, is reckoned to the work of Satan, being the issue of his seduction. Whatsoever his temptations draw men out unto, the Lord Christ came to destroy it all, to make an end of it : and he will not fail of his end, but certainly carry on his undertaking, until he hath utterly destroyed all those works of Satan, in the hearts of all that are his. ' He redeems us from our vain conversation ;' 2 Pet. i. 18, 19. from the power of our lusts and corruptions, leading us out to a vain

<hr>

m Gen. iii 3 Deut. xxvii. 29. Rom. v. 12.   n Heb. ii. 9—15.
   o Col. ii. 15. Tit. i. 3   p Luke xi. 21.

conversation. The apostle tells us, Rom. vi. 6. that by his death the old man is crucified, and the body of sin destroyed. The craft of sin, the old man, and the strength of sin, the body of it, or the ruling of original sin, the old man, and the full fruit of actual sin, in the body of it, is by the death of Christ, crucified and destroyed; and in that whole chapter, from our participation in the death of Christ, he argues to such an abolition of the law and rule of sin, to such a breaking of the power and strength of it, that it is impossible, that it should any more rule in us, or have dominion over us. Of the way whereby virtue flows out from the death of Christ, for the killing of sin, I am not now to speak.

And this is the first way, whereby the death of Christ hath an influence into the safeguarding of believers, in their continuance of the love and favour of God. He so takes away the guilt of sin, that it shall never be able utterly to turn the love of God from them, and so takes away the rule of Satan, and power of sin, destroying the one, and killing the other, that they shall never be able to turn them wholly from God.

Farther, to secure their continuance with God, he procureth the Holy Spirit for them, as was shewed before. But because much weight lies upon this part of our foundation, I shall a little farther clear it up. That the Spirit of grace and adoption, with all those spiritual mercies, and operations, wherewith he is attended and accompanied, is a promise of the new covenant, doubtless is by its own evidence put out of question. There is scarce any promise thereof, wherein he is not either clearly expressed, or evidently included. Yea, and oftentimes, the whole covenant is stated in that one promise of the Spirit, the actual collation and bestowing of all the mercy thereof, being his proper work, and peculiar dispensation, for the carrying on the great design of the salvation of sinners; so Isa. xxix. 20. ' As for me,' saith God, ' this is my covenant with them; my Spirit that is upon thee, and my word which I have put in thy mouth, shall not depart from thee.' This is my covenant, saith God, or what in my covenant I do faithfully engage to bestow upon you. But of this text and its vindication more afterward. Many other places, not only pregnant of proof to the same purpose, but expressly in terms affirming it, might be insisted on.

Now that this Spirit, promised in the covenant of grace
as to the bestowing of him on the elect of God, or those for
whom Christ died, is of his purchasing and procurement in
his death, is apparent.

1. Because he is the Mediator of the covenant, by whose
hands, and for whose sake, all the mercies of it are made out
to them, who are admitted into the bond thereof.   Though
men are not[q] completely stated in the covenant before their
own believing, which brings in what of their part is stipu-
lated, yet the covenant and grace of it lays hold of them before, even to bestow faith on them, or they would never believe : for faith is not of ourselves, it is the gift of God.
God certainly bestows no such gifts, but from a covenant.
Spiritual graces are not administered solely in a providential
dispensation.   Faith for the receiving the pardon of sin, is
no gift, nor product of the covenant of works.   Now, as in
general the mercies of the covenant are procured by the Mediator of it, so this whereof we speak, in an especial manner,
Heb. ix. 15.   ' For this cause he is the Mediator of the new
testament, that by means of death, they which are called
might receive the promise of eternal inheritance.'   By his
death, they for whom he died, and who thereupon are called,
being delivered from their sins, which were against[r] the covenant of works, receive the promise, or pledge of an eternal
inheritance.   What this great promise here intended is, and
wherein it doth consist, the Holy Ghost declares, Acts ii. 23.
The promise, which Jesus Christ received of the Father upon
his exaltation, was that of the Holy Ghost, having purchased
and procured the bestowing of him by his death : upon his
exaltation, the dispensation thereof is committed to him as
being part of the compact and covenant, which was between
his Father and himself, the grand bottom of his satisfaction
and merit.   This is the great original radical promise of that
eternal inheritance. By the[s] promised Spirit are we begotten
anew, into a hope thereof, made-meet for it, and sealed up
unto it; yea, do but look upon the Spirit as promised, and
ye may conclude him purchased: ' for all the promises of
God are yea and amen in Jesus Christ,' 2 Cor. i. 20.   They

q Gen. xvii. 1. Jer. xxxi. 32. xxxii. 38—40. Ezek. xi. 19. xxxvi. 25, 26. Heb.
viii. 9—11.   r Deut. xxvii. 29. Gal. iii. 12. Rom. iii 21.
s Rom. viii. 11. Col. i. 12. Eph. iv. 30.

all have their confirmation, establishment, and accomplishment in, by, and for Jesus Christ. And if it be granted that any designed appointed mercy whatever, that in Christ the Lord blesseth us withal, be procured for us by him, in the way of merit (being given freely to us, through him, but reckoned to him of debt), it will easily be manifested, that the same is the condition of every mercy whatever promised unto us, and given us, upon his mediatory interposition.

2. It appears from that peculiar promise, that Christ makes of sending his Holy Spirit unto his own; he tells them indeed, once and again, that the Father will send him: as he comes* from that original and fountain love, from which also himself was sent. But withal he assures us, that he himself will send him; John xv. 26. ' When the Comforter is come, whom I will send unto you from the Father, even the Spirit of truth.' It is true, that he is promised here only as a Comforter, for the performance of that part of his office. But look upon what account he is sent' for any one act or work of grace, on that he is sent for all. I will send him then, saith Christ; and that as a fruit of his death, as the procurement of his mediation; for that alone he promiseth to bestow on us. And in particular he tells us, that he receives the Spirit from the Father for us upon his intercession; wherein, as hath been" elsewhere demonstrated, he asks no more nor less, than what by his death is obtained. John xiv. 16, 17. ' I will pray the Father, and he shall give you another Comforter, that he may abide with you for ever; even the Spirit of truth whom the world cannot receive ;' he tells us, ver. 13. that whatsoever we ask, he will do it. But withal, in these verses, how he will do it; even by interceding with the Father for it, as a fruit of his bloodshedding, and the promise made to him, upon his undertaking to* glorify his Father's name, in the great work of redemption. And therefore he informs us, that when the Comforter, whom he procureth for us, shall come, he shall glorify him, and shall ' receive of his, and shew it unto us;' John xvi. 14. farther manifest his glory, in his bringing nothing with him but what is his, or of his procurement; so also instructing us clearly and plentifully, to ask in his name, that

---

* John xiv. 16. 26.　　　　　† John xvi. 7.
◄ Salus Electorum sanguis Jesu.　　　ˣ John xvii. 1. 6.

is, for his sake, which to do plainly and openly, is the great privilege of the New Testament (for so he tells his disciples, John xvi. 24. ' Hitherto have you asked nothing in my name,' who yet were believers, and had made many addresses unto God in and through him ; but darkly, as they did under the Old Testament, when they begged mercy ' for his sake ;' Dan. ix. 17. But to plead with the Father, clearly upon the account of the mediation and purchase of Christ) ; that, I say, is the privilege of the New Testament. Now in this way he would have us ask the Holy Spirit at the hand of God; Luke xi. 9. 13. Ask him, that is, as to a clearer, fuller administration of him unto us ; for he is antecedently bestowed as to the working of faith and regeneration, even unto this application, for without him we cannot once ask in the name of Christ ; for none can call Jesus Lord, or do any thing in his name, but by the Spirit of God: this, I say, then ; He in ⁷whom we are blessed with all spiritual blessings, hath procured the Holy Spirit for us, and through his intercession he is bestowed on us. Now where the Spirit of God is, there is⁺ liberty from sin, peace and acceptance with God. But it may be objected, although this Spirit be thusᵃ bestowed on believers, yet may they not cast him off, so that his abode with them may be but for a season, and their glory not be safeguarded in the issue, but their condemnation increased by their receiving of him. This being the only thing, wherein this proof of believers' abiding with God, seems liable to exception, I shall give a triple testimony of the certainty of the continuance of the Holy Spirit with them, on whom he is bestowed, that in the mouth of two or three witnesses this truth may be established; and they are no mean ones neither, but the ' three that bear witness in heaven, the Father, the Son, and the Holy Ghost.'

The first you have, Isa. lix. 21. ' But as for me, this is my covenant with them, saith the Lord, My Spirit which is upon thee, and my words which I have put in thy mouth, shall not depart out of thy mouth, nor out of the mouth of thy seed, nor out of the mouth of thy seed's seed, saith the Lord, henceforth and for ever.' That which the Lord declares here to the church, he calls his covenant. Now whereas in a covenant there are two things : 1. What is sti

⁷ Eph i. 4   ⁺ 2 Cor. iii. 17.   ᵃ Rom. viii. 14.

pulated on the part of him that makes the covenant. 2.
What of them is required, with whom it is made (which in
themselves are distinct, though in the covenant of grace,
God hath promised that he will work in us what he requires
of us), that here mentioned is clearly an evidence of somewhat of the first kind, of that goodness that God in the covenant doth promise to bestow; though perhaps words of
the future tense may sometimes have an imperative con-
struction, where the import of the residue of the words enforces such a sense, yet because it may be so in some place,
therefore it is so in this place, and that therefore these words
are not a promise, that the Spirit shall not depart, but an in-
junction to take care that it do not depart (as Mr. Goodwin
will have it), is a weak inference. And the close of the
words will by no means be wrested to speak significantly to
any such purpose, ' Saith the Lord, henceforth even for
ever ;' which plainly make the words promissory, and an engagement of God himself to them, to whom they are spoken :
so that the interpretation of these words, ' This is my covenant with them,' by Mr. Goodwin, cap. 11. sect. 4. p. 227.
' That covenant of perpetual grace and mercy which I made
with them, requireth this of them, in order to the performance of it on my part, that they quench not my Spirit which
I have put into them,' doth plainly invert the intendment of
God in them, and substitute what is tacitly required as our
duty, into the room of what is expressly promised as his
grace. Observe then,

Secondly, That as no promise of God given to believers,
is either apt of itself to ingenerate, or by them to be received under such an absurd notion of being made good,
whatsoever their deportment be, it being the nature of all
the promises of God to frame and mould them, to whom
they are given into all holiness and purity; 2 Cor. vii. 1.
and this in especial is a promise of the principal author to
cause all holiness to be continued to them, and is impossible to be apprehended under any such foolish supposal, so
also that this promise is absolute and not conditional, can
neither be colourably gainsaid, nor the contrary probably
confirmed ; so that the strength of Mr. Goodwin's two next
exceptions : 1. 'That this cannot be a promise of persevce-
rance unto true believers, whatsoever their deportment shall

be.' And, 2. ' That it must be conditional (which cannot, as he saith, be reasonably gainsaid).' The first of them not looking towards our persuasion in this thing: and the latter being not in the least put upon the proof, is but very weakness; for what condition (I pray), of this promise can be imagined? God promises his Spirit of holiness that sanctifieth us, and worketh all holiness in us; and therewith the holy word of the gospel, which is also sanctifying; John xvii. 7. that they shall abide with us for ever: it is the continuance of the presence of God with us for our holiness that is here promised. On what condition shall this be supposed to depend? Is it in case we continue holy? Who seeth not the vanity of interserting any condition? I will be with you by my Spirit and word for ever, to keep you holy, provided you continue holy.

Thirdly, It is a hard task to seek to squeeze a condition out of those gracious words in the beginning of the verse, ' As for me ;' which Junius renders *de me autem:* words wherein God graciously reveals himself, as the sole author of this great blessing promised, it being a work of his own, which he accomplisheth upon the account of his free grace. And therefore God signally placed that expression in the entrance of the promise, that we may know whom to look unto for the fulfilling thereof; and it is yet a farther corruption to say, ' That as for me, is as much, as, for my part, I will deal bountifully with them, provided that they do so and so, what I require from them,' which is Mr. Goodwin's interpretation of the words; for of this supposition there is not one word in the text, as incumbent on them, to whom this promise is made, in contradistinction to what God here promiseth; yea, he promiseth them, at least in the root and principle, whatsoever is required of them: let it be, that 'as for me,' is, as for my part I will do what here is promised; and there is an end of this debate.

Fourthly, The persons to whom this promise is made, are called ' thee' and ' thy seed,' that is, all those, and only those, with whom God is a God in covenant. God here minds them of the first making of this covenant with Abraham and his seed ; Gen. xvii. 7. Now who are this seed of Abraham? Not all his carnal posterity, not the whole nation of the Jews; which is the last subterfuge invented by our author, to evade the force of our argument from this place. Our Saviour not only denies, but also proves by many arguments, that the Phaiisees and their followers, who doubtless were of the nation of the Jews, and the carnal seed of Abraham, were not the children of Abraham in this sense, nor his seed, but rather the devil's; John viii. 39—41. And the apostle disputes and argues the same case; Rom. iv. 9—11. and proves undeniably, that it is believers only, whether circumcised or uncircumcised, whether Jews or Gentiles, that are this seed of Abraham, and heirs of the piomise. So plainly, Gal. iii. 7. 'Know ye therefore, that they which are of the faith are blessed with faithful Abraham,' and then concludes again as the issue of his debate, ver. 9. 'So then they which be of faith, are blessed with faithful Abraham :' and this is the sum of what Mr. Goodwin objects unto this testimony in our case, to the perpetual abiding of the Spirit with the saints.

The force then of this promise, and the influence it hath into the establishment of the truth we have in hand, will not be evaded and turned aside, by affirming ' that it is made to the whole people of Israel :' for besides, that the Spirit of the Lord could not be said to be in the ungodly rejected part of them, nor his word in their mouth, theie is not the least in text or context, to intimate such an extent of this promise, as to the object of it, and it is very weakly attempted to be pioved fiom Paul's accommodation and interpietation of the verse foregoing, ' And the Redeemer shall come to Sion,' &c. in Rom. xi. 26. for it is most evident and indisputable to any one who shall but once cast an eye upon that place, that the apostle accommodates and applies these words to none, but only those who shall be saved, being turned ' away from ungodliness to Christ,' which are only the seed before described. And those he calls ' all Israel ;' either in the spiritual sense of the word, as taken for the chosen Israel of God, or else indefinitely for that nation, upon the account of those plentiful fruits, which the gospel shall find amongst them, when they shall ' fear[b] the Loid and his goodness in the latter days.'

Fifthly, This then is a piomise equally made unto all believeis; it is to all that are in covenant; neither is theie

[b] Hos. iii. 5.

any thing that is of peculiar importance to any sort of believers of any time, or age, or dispensation, therein comprised. It equally respecteth all, to whom the Lord extends his covenant of grace. Certainly the giving of the Spirit of grace is not inwrapped in any promise that may be of private interpretation : the concernment of all the saints of God lying therein. It cannot but be judged a needless labour to give particular instances in a thing so generally known in the word , though the expressions differ, the matter of this promise is the same with that given to ^cAbraham ; the Holy Spirit being the great blessing of the covenant, and bestowed on all, and every one, and only on them, whom God hath graciously taken into covenant from the foundation of the world.

Mr. Goodwin then labours in the fire, in what he farther objects, sect. 6. That ' this promise exhibiteth, and holds forth some new grace or favour, which God hath not vouchsafed formerly either unto the persons to whom the said promise is now made, or to any other : but for the grace or favour of final perseverance, it is nothing (at least in the opinion of our adversaries), but what is common to all true believers, and what God hath conferred upon one and other, on this generation, from the beginning of the world.'

Ans. The emphasis here put upon it, doth not-denote it to be a new promise, but a great one, not that it was never given before, but that it is now solemnly renewed, for the consolation and establishment of the church. If wherever we find a solemn promise made, and confirmed, and ratified to the church, we must thence conclude, that no saints were before made partakers of the mercy of that promise, we must also in particular conclude, that no one ever had their sins pardoned before the giving of that solemn promise, Jer. xxxi. 32.

Sixthly, We say that the grace of perseverance is such as believers may expect, not upon the account of any thing in themselves, nor of the dignity of the state, whereunto by grace they are exalted , but merely on this bottom and foundation, that it is freely promised of God ; who hath also discovered that rise and fountain of his gracious promise to lie in his eternal love towards them, so that they can lay no

^c Gen. xvii. 1.

other claim unto it, than to any other grace whatsoever. When we have the assurance given by any promise of God, to say that what is promised of him, may be expected of course, is an expression that fell from Mr. Goodwin, when in the heat of disputation, his thoughts were turned aside from the consideration of what it is to mix the promises of God with faith.

Seventhly, Whereas this is given in for the sense of the words, ' that God will advance the dispensation of his grace and goodness, towards, or among his people, to such an excellency and height, that if they prove not extremely unworthy, they shall have of the Spirit and word of God abundantly amongst them, and consequently abundance of peace and happiness for ever:' it is most apparent that not any thing of the mind of God in the words is reached in this gloss. For,

1. That condition, 'if they prove not extremely unworthy,' is extremely unworthily inserted; the promise being an engagement of God to keep and preserve them, to whom it is made by his Spirit, from being so; the Spirit is given and continued to them for that very purpose.

2. It is supposed to be given to all the nation of the Jews, when it is expressly made to the church, and seed in covenant.

3. It carries the mercy promised no higher than outward dispensations, when the words expressly mention, the Spirit already received. Evident it is, that the whole grace, love, kindness, and mercy of this eminent promise, and consequently the whole covenant of grace, is enervated by this corrupting gloss. Do men think, indeed, that all the mercy of the covenant of grace consists in such tenders and offers as here are intimated? that it all lies in outward endearments, and such dealings with men, as may seem to be suited to win upon them: and that, as to the real exhibition of it, it is wholly suspended upon the unstable, uncertain, frail wills of men? The[d] Scripture seems to hold out something farther of more efficacy. The design of these exceptions, is indeed to exclude all the effectual grace of God, promised in Jesus Christ, upon the account, that the things which he promiseth to work in us thereby, are the duties which he requireth of us.

[d] Ezek. xi. 19. Jer. xxxi. 32, xxxii. 40.

In sum; these are the exceptions which are given into this testimony of God, concerning the abiding of the Spirit with them on whom he is bestowed, and for whom he is procured, to whom he is sent by Jesus Christ. And this is the interpretation of the words. ' As for me,' for my part, or as much as in me lieth ; ' this is my covenant,' I will deal bountifully and graciously ' with them,' the whole nation of the Jews, 'my Spirit that is in thee,' that they ought to take care that they entertain, and retain the Holy Spirit, and not walk so extremely unworthily, that he should depart from them : the residue of the words wherein the main emphasis of them doth lie, is left untouched. The import then of this promise, is the same with that of the promises insisted on before, with especial reference to the Holy Spirit, procured for us, and given unto us by Christ. The stability, and establishing grace of the covenant, is here called the covenant; as sundry other particular mercies of it are also. Of the covenant of grace in Christ, the blessed Spirit to dwell in us, and rest upon us, is the main and principal promise : this for our consolation is renewed, again and again, in the Old and New Testament. As a Spirit of sanctification, he is given to men to make them believe; and as a Spirit of adoption, upon their believing. In either sense, God, even the Father, who takes us into covenant in Jesus Christ, affirms here, that he shall never depart from us : which is our first testimony in the case in hand. With whom the Spirit abides, and whilst he abides with them, they cannot utterly forsake God, nor be forsaken of him; for they who have the Spirit of God, are the children of God, sons and heirs. But God hath promised that his Spirit shall abide with believers for ever : as hath been clearly evinced from the text under consideration, with a removal of all exceptions put in thereto.

The second witness we have of the constant abode and residence of this Spirit, bestowed on them which believe, for ever, is that of the Son, who assures his disciples of it; John xiv. 16. ' I will,' saith he, ' pray the Father, and he shall give you another Comforter, that he may abide with you for ever.' As our Saviour gives a rule of interpretation, expressly of his prayers for believers, that he did in them intend not only the men of that present generation, but all

that should ' believe to the end of the world;' John xvii. 20.
(' I pray not for these alone, but for them also who shall believe on me through their word'); so is it a rule equally infallible for the interpretation of the gracious promises, which
he made to his disciples, that are not peculiarly appropriated
to their season and work (in which yet, as to the general
love, faithfulness, and kindness, manifested and revealed in
them, the concernments of the saints in all succeeding ages
do lie) they are proper to all believers, as such. For whom
he did equally intercede, to them he makes promises alike.
They belong no less to us, on whom, in an especial manner,
the ends of the world are fallen, than to those, who first
followed him in the regeneration. Let us then attend to the
testimony in this place (and as he shall be pleased to increase our faith, mix it therewithal) that the Spirit he procureth for us, and sends to us, shall abide with us for ever:
and whilst the Spirit of the Lord is with us, we are his.
Doubtless it is no easy task to raise up any pretended plea
against the evidence given in by this witness, the Amen, the
great and faithful witness in heaven: he tells us, that he
will send the Spirit to abide with us for ever; and therein
speaks to the whole of the case in hand, and question under
debate. All we say, is, that the Spirit of God shall abide
with believers for ever; Christ says so too: and in the issue
whatever becomes of us, he will appear to be one, against
whom there is no rising up.

Against this testimony it is objected by Mr. Goodwin,
chap. 11. sect. 14. p. 234. ' This promise,' saith he, ' concerning the abiding of this other Comforter for ever, must
be conceived to be made, either to the apostles, personally
considered, or else to the whole body of the church, of
which they were principal members: if the first of these be
admitted, then it will not follow, that because the apostles
had the perpetual residence of the Spirit with them, and in
them, therefore, every particular believer hath the like: no
more than it will follow, that, because the apostles were infallible in their judgments, through the teachings of the Spirit
in them; therefore, every believer is infallible upon the
same account also, if the latter be admitted, neither will it
follow, that every believer, or every member of the church,
must needs have the residence of the Spirit with them for

ever: there are principal privileges appropriated to corporations, which every particular member of them cannot claim: the church may have the residence of the Spirit of God with her for ever, and yet every present member thereof lose his interest and part in him; yea, the abiding of the Spirit in the apostles themselves. was not absolutely promised; John xv. 10.'

Ans. 1. The design of this discourse is to prove, that this promise is not made to believers in general, or those, who through the word, are brought to believe in Christ in all generations to the end of the world: and consequently that they have no promise of the Spirit's abiding with them: for that is the thing opposed; and this is part of the doctrine, that tends to their consolation and improvement in holiness. What thanks they will give to the authors of such an eminent discovery, when it shall be determined that they have deserved well of them, and the truths of God, I know not: especially when it shall be considered that not only this, but all other promises uttered by Christ to his apostles (as we had thought) not for their own behoof alone, but also for the use of the church in all ages, are tied up in their tendency and use to the men of that generation, and to the employment, to which they, to whom he spoke, were designed; but let us see whether these things are so or no. I say,

2. There is not any necessary cause of that disjunctive proposition; the promise of the perpetual residence of the Spirit is made, 'either to the apostles personally, or to the whole body of the church.' By the rule formerly given for the interpretation of these promises of Christ, it appears, that what in this kind was made to the one, was also given to the other; and how Mr. Goodwin will enforce any necessary conclusion from this distinction framed by himself, for his own purpose, I know not; the promise was made both to these and those, the apostles and all other believers, because to the apostles as believers.

3. The making of the promise to the apostles personally, doth not argue that it was made to them as apostles, but only that it was made to their persons, or to them though under another qualification, viz. of believing. It is given to them personally as believers, and so to all believers whatever; this also sets at liberty, and plainly cashiers the com-

parison instituted between the apostles' infallibility as apostles, and their sanctifying grace as believers, by the Spirit of grace given for that end; the apostles' infallibility, we confess, was from the Spirit; for they (as other holy men of old)[e] ' wrote as they were moved by the Spirit of God :' but that this was a distinct gift bestowed on them as apostles, and not the teaching of the Spirit of grace, which is given to all believers, 1 John ii. 22. we need not contend to prove.

Besides, to what end doth he contend, that it was made to the apostles in the sense urged, and by us insisted on, seeing he denies it in the close of this section; and chooseth rather to venture upon an opposition unto that common received persuasion, that the apostles of Christ (the son of perdition only excepted) had an absolute promise of perseverance, than to acknowledge that which would prove so prejudicial and ruinous to his cause, as he knows the confession of such a promise made to them would inevitably be: he contends not, I say, about the sense of the promise, but would fain divert it from other believers (at the entrance of the section) by limiting it to the apostles ; but considering afterward better of the matter, and remembering that the concession of an absolute promise of perseverance to any one saint whatever, would evidently root up, and cast to the ground, the goodliest engine that he hath set up against the truth he opposeth, he suits it (in the close of the section) to an evasion, holding better correspondency with its associates in this undertaking.

4. I wonder what chimerical church he hath found out, to which promises are made, and privileges granted, otherwise than upon the account of the persons, whereof it is constituted? Suppose (I pray) that promises of the residence of the Spirit for ever with it, be made to the church, which is made up of so many members, and that all these members, every one, should lose their interest in it, what subject of that promise would remain? What universal is this, that hath a real existence of itself, and by itself, in abstraction from its particulars, in which alone it hath its being? Or what whole is that, which is preserved in the destruction and dissolution of all its essentially constituent parts? The promises then, that are made to the church, are of two sorts.

[e] 2 Pet. i. 21.

1. Of such grace and mercies, as, whether inherent or relative, have their residence in, and respect unto, particular persons as such; of this sort are all the promises of grace of sanctification, as also of justification, &c. which are all things of men's personal spiritual interest; the promises made to the church of this nature, are made unto it, merely as consisting of so many, and those elected, redeemed persons, whose right and interest, as those individual persons, they are. 2. Of all such good things, as are the exurgency of the collected state of the saints, in reference to their spiritual invisible communion, or visible gathering into a church, constituted according to the mind of Christ, and his appointment in the gospel; and these also are all of them founded in the former, and depend wholly upon them, and are resolved into them: all promises then whatever made to the church, the body of Christ, do not respect it primarily, as a corporation, which is the second notion of it, but as consisting of those particular believers; much less as a chimerical universal, having a subsistence in and by itself, abstracted from its particulars. This evasion then, notwithstanding this promise of our Saviour, doth still continue to press its testimony concerning the perpetual residence of this Holy Spirit with believers.

The scope of the place enforces that exception of these words, which we insist upon. Our blessed Saviour observing the trouble and disconsolation of his followers, upon the apprehension of his departure from them, stirs them up to a better hope and confidence by many gracious promises and engagements, of what would and should be the issue of his being taken away; ver. 1. He bids them to free their hearts from trouble, and in the next words, tells them, that the way whereby it was to be done, was by acting faith on the promises of his Father, and those which in his Father's name, he had made, and was to make unto them. Of these he mentions many in the following verses, whereof the fountain, head, and spring, is that of giving them the Comforter, not to abide with them for a season, as he had done with his bodily presence, but to continue with them as a Comforter (and consequently, to the discharging of his whole dispensation towards believers) for ever. He speaks to them as believers, as disconsolate dejected believers, quickening their faith by exhortations, and gives them this promise, as a solid foundation of peace and composedness of spirit, which he exhorted them unto. And if our Saviour intendeth any thing, but what the words import, viz. that he will give his Holy Spirit, as a Comforter, to abide with them for ever, the promise hath not the least suitableness to relieve them in their distress, nor to accomplish the end for which it was given them. But against this it is excepted, cap. 11. sect. 13. p. 233.

1. ' Evident it is, that our Saviour doth not in this place oppose the abiding or remaining of the Holy Ghost, to his own departure from the hearts or souls of men, into which he is framed or come; but to his departure out of the world, by death, which was now at hand.'

Ans. 1. This is a weighty observation: yet withal it is evident, that he opposeth the abiding of the Spirit with them as a Comforter, to his own bodily presence with them for that end. His was for a season, the other to endure for ever. And I desire to know, how our Saviour Christ comes, or enters into the souls or hearts of men, but by his Spirit: and how these things come here to be distinguished. But,

2. He says, ' By the abiding of the Comforter with them for ever, he doth not mean his perpetual abode in their hearts, or the hearts of any particular man, but his constant abiding in the world, in, and with the gospel, and the children thereof, in respect of which, he saith of himself elsewhere, I am with you always even to the end of the world: as if he should have said, This the purpose of my Father, in sending me into the world, requires, that I should make no long stay in it, I am now upon my return, but when I come to my Father, I will intercede for you, and he will send you another Comforter, upon better terms, for staying and continuing with you, than those on which I came: for he shall be sent, not to be taken out of the world by death, but to make his residence with and among you, my friends and faithful ones, for ever; now from such an abiding of the Holy Ghost with them as this, cannot be inferred his perpetual abiding with any one personal believer, determinately, much less with every one.'

Ans. 1. It was evident before, that this promise was made to the disciples of Christ, as believers, to quicken and strengthen their failing drooping faith, in and under that great trial, of losing the presence of their master, which they were to undergo; and being made unto them as believers, though upon a particular occasion, is made to all believers, for 'a quatenus ad omne valet argumentum.'

2. It is no less evident, that according to the interpretation here, without the least attempt of proof, importunately suggested, the promise is no way suited to give the least encouragement or consolation unto the disciples, in reference to the condition, upon the account whereof it is now so solemnly given them. It is all one as if our Saviour should have said, 'You are sadly troubled indeed, yea, your hearts are filled with trouble and fear, because I have told you that I must leave you, be not so dejected; I have kept you whilst I have been with you in the world, and now I go away, and will send the Holy Spirit into the world, that, whatsoever becomes of you, or any of you, whether ye have any consolation or no, he shall abide in the world (perhaps) with some or other (that is, if any do believe, which it may be some will, it may be not) until the end, and consummation of it.'

3. Is this promise of sending the Holy Spirit given to the apostles, or is it not? If you say not, assign who it is given or made unto. Christ spake it to them, and doubtless they thought he intended them, and it was wholly suited to their condition. If it were made unto them, is it not in the letter of the promise affirmed that the Spirit shall abide with them for ever, to whom it was given? If there be any subject of this promise in receiving the Spirit, he must of necessity keep his residence and abode with it for ever. The whole design of this section, is to put the persons to whom this promise is made into the dark, that we may not see them; yea, to deny that it is made to any persons at all, the recipient subject of the grace thereof. He tells ye, that he abides in the world: how I pray? Doubtless not as the unclean spirit, that goes up and down in dry places, seeking rest and finding none. Christ promiseth his Spirit to his church, not to the world, to dwell in the hearts of his, not to wander up and down. Nay, he abides with the apostles, and their spiritual posterity, that is, believers, in our Saviour's interpretation; John xvii. 20. Are they then, and their posterity (that is, believers), the persons to whom this

promise is made, and who are concerned in it, with whom
as he is promised he is to abide? This you can scarcely find
out an answer to, in the whole discourse. He tells you, indeed, the Holy Ghost was not to die, with such other rare
notions: but for any persons particularly intended in this
promise, we are still in the dark.

4. He tells us, ' That from such an abiding of the Holy
Ghost with them, as this, cannot be enforced his perpetual
abiding with any one person, determinately.' But,

1. What kind of abiding it is, that he intends, is not
easily apprehended.

2. If on the account of this promise, he is given to any
person on the same account he is to abide with the same person for ever.

3. That which he seems to intend, is the presence of
the Spirit in the administration of the word, to make it effectual unto them to whom it is delivered; when the promise is to give him as a Comforter to them, on whom he is
bestowed. But he adds, sect. 14.

4. ' And lastly, The particle ἵνα doth not always import
the certainty of the thing spoken of, by way of event (no,
not when the speech is of God himself), but oft-times the
intention only of the agent: so that the words (that he may
abide with you for ever) do not imply an absolute necessity
of his abiding with them for ever, but only that, that it
should be the intent of him that should send him, and that
he would send him in such a way, that if they were true to
their own interest, they might retain him, and have his
abode with them for ever. Turn the words any way, with any
tolerable congruity, either to the scope of the place, manner
of Scripture expression, principles of reason, and the doctrine
of perseverance will be found to have nothing in them.'

Ans. 1. This is the πάνσοφον φάρμακον, that when all me-
dicines will not heal, must serve to skin the wound given
our adversaries' cause, by the sword of the word. The promise is made unto believers indeed, but on such and such
conditions, as on the account whereof it may never be accomplished towards them. 2. This no way suits Mr. Goodwin's interpretation of the place formerly mentioned and
insisted on. If it be, as was said, only a promise of sending
his Spirit into the world, for the end by him insinuated,

doubtless the word ἵνα, must denote the event of the thing, and not only an intention that might fail of accomplishment. For let all, or any individuals, behave themselves how they will, it is certain, as to the accomplishment and event, that the Spirit of God shall be continued in the world, in the sense pleaded for. But it is not what is congruous to his own thoughts, but what may oppose ours (that is, the plain and obvious sense of the words), that he is concerned to make use of. It being not the sense of the place, but an escaping our argument from it, that lies in his design, he cares not how many contrary and inconsistent interpretations he gives of it: 'hæc non successit, alia aggrediemur via.' The word ἵνα denotes (as is confessed), the intention of Christ in sending the Spirit: that is, that he intends to send him to believers, so as that he should abide with them for ever. Now, besides the impossibility in general, that the intention of God, or of the Lord Christ, as God and man, should be frustrate, whence in particular should it come to pass he should fail in this his intention? 'I will send ye the Holy Spirit to abide with you for ever;' that is, 'I intend to send you the Holy Spirit, that he may abide with you for ever.' What now should hinder this? Why, it is given them, upon ' condition that they be true to their own interest, and take care to retain him;' what is that I pray? Why that they continue in faith, obedience, repentance, and close walking with God; but to what end is it that he is promised unto them? Is it not to teach them, to work in them faith, obedience, repentance, and close walking with God, to sanctify them throughout, and preserve them blameless to the end, making them ' meet for the inheritance with the saints in light?' In case they obey, believe, &c. the Holy Ghost is promised unto them, to abide with them to cause them to obey, believe, repent, &c.

4. The intention of Christ for the sending of the Spirit, and his abiding for ever, with them to whom he is sent, is but one and the same. And if any frustration of his intention do fall out, it may most probably interpose, as to his sending of the Spirit, not as to the Spirit's continuance with them to whom he is sent; which is asserted absolutely upon the account of his sending him. He sends him ἵνα μένῃ: his abode is the end of his sending: which, if he be sent,

shall be obtained. Upon the whole doubtless it will be found, that the doctrine of perseverance finds so much for its establishment in this place of Scripture and promise of our Saviour, that by no art or cunning it will be prevailed withal, to let go its interest therein. And though many attempts be made to turn and wrest this testimony of our Saviour several ways, and those contrary to, and inconsistent with, one another, yet it abides to look straight forward to the proof and confirmation of the truth, that lies not only in the womb and sense of it, but in the very mouth and literal expression of it also. I suppose, it is evident to all, that Mr. Goodwin knows not what to say to it, nor what sense to fix upon. At first, it is made to the apostles, not all believers; then when this will not serve the turn, there being a concession in that interpretation, destructive to his whole cause, then it is made as a privilege to the church, not to any individual persons; but yet for fear that this privilege must be vested in some individuals, it is denied that it is made to any, but only is a promise of the Spirit's abode in the world with the word: but perhaps some thoughts coming upon him, that this will no way suit the scope of the place, nor be suited to the intendment of Christ, it is lastly added, that let it be made to whom it will, it is conditional, though there be not the least intimation of any condition in the text, or context, and that by him assigned, be coincident with the thing itself promised. But hereof so far: and so our second testimony; the testimony of the Son abides still by the truth, for the confirmation whereof it is produced: and in the ‘ mouth of these two witnesses,’ the abiding of the Spirit with believers to the end is established.

Add hereunto, thirdly, The testimony of the third that bears witness in heaven, and who also comes near, and bears witness to this truth in the hearts of believers, even of the Spirit itself, and so I shall leave it sealed under the testimony of the Father, Son, and Holy Ghost. As the other two gave in their testimony in a word of promise, so the Spirit doth in a real work of performance; wherein as he bears a distinct testimony of his own, the saints having a peculiar communion and fellowship with him therein, so he is as the common seal of Father and Son, set unto that truth, which by their testimony they have confirmed. There are indeed

sundry things, whereby he confirms and establisheth the
saints in the assurance of his abode with them for ever: I
shall at present mention that one eminent work of his, which
being given unto them, he doth accomplish to this very end
and purpose; and that is his sealing of them to the day of
redemption.   A work it is, often in the Scripture mentioned,
and still upon the account of assuring the salvation of believers; 2 Cor. 1. 22. ' By whom also ye are sealed.' Having
mentioned the certainty, unchangeableness, and efficacy of
all the promises of God in Christ, and the end to be accomplished and brought about by them, namely, the 'glory of
God in believers;' ver. 20. (' All the promises of God are yea
and amen in him, to the glory of God by us'), the apostle acquaints the saints with one foundation of the security of
their interest in those promises, whereby the end mentioned,
'the glory of God by them,' should be accomplished.   This
he ascribes to the efficacy of the Spirit bestowed on them,
in sundry works of his grace, which he reckoneth; ver. 21, 22.
Among them this is one, that he seals them; as to the nature of this sealing, and what that act of the Spirit of grace
is, that is so called, I shall not now insist upon it.   The end
and use of sealing is more aimed at in this expression, than
the nature of it; what it imports, than wherein it consists.
Being a term forensical, and translated from the use and
practice of men in their civil transactions, the use and end
of it may easily from the original rise thereof be demonstrated.
Sealing amongst men hath a twofold use.   First, To give se-
crecy and security (in things that are under present consideration) to the things sealed.   And this is the first use of
sealing, by a seal set upon the thing sealed.   Of this kind of
sealing chiefly have we that long discourse of Salmasius, in
the vindication of his *Jus Atticum* against the animadversions
of Heraldus.   And, secondly, To give an assurance, or faith,
for what is by them that seal, to be done.   In the first sense,
are things sealed up in bags, and in treasuries, that they may
be kept safe, none daring to break open their seals.   In the
latter, are all promissory engagements, confirmed, established, and made unalterable, wherein men either in conditional compacts, or testamentary dispositions do oblige
themselves.   These are the *Sigilla appensa*, that are yet in
use in all deeds, enfeoffments, and the like instruments in

law. And with men, if this be done, their engagements are
accounted inviolable. And because all men have not that
truth, faithfulness, and honesty, as to make good even their
sealed engagements, the whole race of mankind hath consented unto the establishment of laws and governors, amongst
others, to this end, that all men may be compelled to stand
to their sealed promises; hence, whatsoever the nature of it
be, and in what particular soever it doth consist, the end and
use of this work in this special acceptation, is taken evidently in the latter sense, from its use amongst men. Expressed it is upon the mention of the promises; 2 Cor. i. 20.
To secure believers of their certain and infallible accomplishment unto them, the apostle tells them of this sealing
of the Spirit, whereby the promises are irrevocably confirmed
unto them, to whom they are made, as is the case among the
sons of men; suitably, Eph. i. 13. he saith, they are 'sealed
by the Holy Spirit of promise;' that is, that is promised
unto us, and who [f]confirms to us all the promises of God.
That the other end of security also, safety and preservation,
is designed therein, secondarily, appears from the appointed
season, whereunto this sealing shall be effectual: it is, 'to
the day of redemption;' Eph. iv. 30. until the saints are
brought to the enjoyment of the full, whole, and complete
purchase made for them by Christ, when he obtained for
them eternal redemption. And this is a real testimony
which the Holy Spirit gives to his own abiding with the
saints for ever: the work he accomplisheth in them, and
upon them, is on set purpose designed to assure them hereof,
and to confirm them in the faith of it.

Unto an argument from this sealing of the Spirit thus
proposed; 'Those who are sealed, shall certainly be saved;'
Mr. Goodwin excepts sundry things, chap. 11. sect. 42.
pp. 255—257. which, because they are applied to blur that
interpretation of the words of the Holy Ghost, which I have
insisted on, I shall briefly remove out of the way, that they
may be no farther offensive to the meanest sealed one.

He answers then, first, by distinguishing the major proposition thus: 'They who are sealed, shall certainly be saved,
with such a sealing, which is unchangeable by any intervenience whatsoever, as of sin and apostacy, so that they can-

[f] Heb. ix. 14.

not lose their faith; but if the sealing be only such, the continuance whereof depends on the faith of the sealed, and consequently may be reversed or withdrawn, it no way proves that all they who are partakers of it, must of necessity retain their faith: therefore,' saith he, secondly, 'We answer farther, that the sealing with the Spirit spoken of, is the latter kind of sealing, not the former, (i.'e.) which depends upon the faith of those that are sealed; as in the beginning or first impression of it, so in the duration or continuance of it; and consequently there is none other certainty of its continuance, but only the continuance of the said faith, which being uncertain, the sealing depending on it must needs be uncertain also: that the sealing mentioned, depends upon the faith of the sealed, is evident, because it is said, in whom also, after ye believed, ye were sealed with the Spirit of promise.'

Ans. I dare say, there is no honest man that would take it well at the hand of Mr. Goodwin, or any else, that should attempt by distinctions, or any other way, to alleviate, or take off the credit of his truth and honesty, in the performance of all those things, whereunto, and for the confirmation whereof, he hath set his seal. What acceptation and like attempt in reference to the Spirit of God, is like to find with him, he may do well to consider: in the meantime he prevails not with us to discredit this work of his grace in the least. For,

1. First, This supposal of such interveniencies of sin and wickedness in the saints, as are inconsistent with the life of faith, and the favour of God, as also of apostacy, are but a poor mean insinuation, for the begging of the thing in question, which will never be granted of any such terms. An interveniency of apostacy, that is defection from the faith, is not handsomely supposed, whilst men continue in the faith.

2. That which is given for the confirmation of their faith, and, on set purpose to add continuance to it, as this is, cannot depend on the condition of the continuance of their faith. The Holy Ghost seals them to the day of redemption, confirming and establishing thereby an infallible continuance of their faith, but it seems upon condition of their continuance in the faith. *Cui fini?* Of what hitherto is said

this is the sum. If they who are sealed apostatize into sin and wickedness, they shall not be saved, notwithstanding that they have been sealed; and this must pass for an answer to our argument proving that they cannot so apostatize, because they are sealed, on purpose to preserve and secure them from that condition; men need not go far to seek for answers to any argument, if such as these (pure beggings of the thing in question and argued) will suffice.

3. Neither doth the beginning or first impression of the sealing depend upon their faith, any otherwise, but as believers are the subject of it, which is not to have any kind of dependance upon it, either as to its nature or use. Neither doth that place of the apostle, Eph. i. 13. 'After ye believed ye were sealed,' prove any such thing, unless this general axiom be first established, that all things which, in order of nature, are before and after, have the connexion of cause and effect, or at least of condition and event between them. It proves indeed that their believing is in order of nature, antecedent to their sealing, respecting the use of it here mentioned; but this proves not at all, that faith is the condition of sealing, the bestowing of faith, and the grant of this seal to establish it, being both acts depending merely, solely, and distinctly, on the free grace of God in Christ; though faith in order of nature, go before hope, yet is no hope bestowed on men on the condition of believing. The truth is, both faith and sealing, and all other spiritual mercies, as to the good-will of God bestowing them, are at once granted us in Jesus Christ; but as to our reception of them, and the actual instating of our souls in the enjoyment of them, or rather as to the exerting of themselves in us, they have that order which either the nature of the things themselves requires, or the sovereign will of God hath allotted to them; neither doth sealing bespeak any grace in us, but a peculiar improvement of the grace bestowed on us. So that,

4. We refuse the answer suggested by Mr. Goodwin, 'that sealing depends (that is, in his sense) upon believing, as to the first grant of it, but not as to the continuance thereof:' and reject his supposal of 'one that hath truly believed, making shipwreck of his faith;' as too importune a cry, or begging of that which it is evident cannot be proved. I

shall add only that Mr. Goodwin granting here the continuance of faith to be a thing uncertain, which is a word to express a very weak probability of a thing, is much fallen off from his former confident expression of the only remote possibility of believers falling away. That their falling away should be scarcely possible, and yet their continuance in the faith very uncertain, is somewhat uncouth. But this is the foundation of that great consolation which Mr. Goodwin's doctrine is so pregnant and teeming withal, that it even groans to be delivered, Their continuance in believing is uncertain, therefore they must needs rejoice and be filled with consolation. But he answers farther:

1. ' I answer farther, by way of exception, that the sealing we speak of, is neither granted by God, unto believers themselves, upon any such terms, that upon no occasion, or occasions whatsoever, as of the greatest and most horrid sins committed, and long continued in by them, or the like, it should never be interrupted, or defaced; for this is contrary to many plain texts of Scripture, and particularly unto all those, where either apostates from God, or evil doers, and workers of iniquity are threatened with the loss of God's favour, and of the inheritance of life, such as Heb. x. &c.'

Ans. 1. It is the intent and purpose of God, that the sealing of believers shall abide with them for ever: whence comes it to pass, that his purposes do not stand, and that he doth not fulfil his pleasure? It is not that he changeth, but that men are changed; that is, the beginning of the change is not in him; occasion of it is administered unto him by men. When his sealing is removed from believers, doth God still purpose that it shall continue with them, or no? If he doth, then he purposeth that shall be, which is not, which it is his will shall not be, and he continues in his vain purpose to eternity. Or if he ceases to purpose, how is it that he is not changed? Such things speak a change in the sons of men, and we thought had been incompatible with the perfection of the divine nature; even that he should will and purpose one thing at one time, and another, yea the clean contrary, at another: yea, but the reason of it is, because the men concerning whom his purposes are, do change; this salves not the immutability of God; though he doth not change from any new consideration in himself, and from himself, yet he doth from obstructions in his way, and to his thoughts in the creatures : yea, instead of salving his un-changeableness, this is destructive to his omnipotency.

2. This whole answer is a supposal, that God may alter his purposes of confirming men in grace, if they be not con-firmed in grace ; or that, though God's purpose be to seal them to the day of redemption, yet they may not continue, nor be preserved thereunto ; and then God's purpose of their continuance ceaseth also.   This is,

3. More evident in his second answer, by way of excep-tion, which is made up of these two parts.   First, A begging of the main, and upon the matter, only, thing in question, by supposing that believers may fall into the most horrible sins, and continue in them to the end ; so proving with great evidence and perspicuity, that believers may fall away, because they may fall away.   And, 2. A suggestion of his own judgment to the contrary ; and his supposal, that it is confirmed by some texts of Scripture, which (God assisting) shall be delivered from this imputation hereafter.   And these two do make up so clear an answer to the argument in hand, that a man knows not well what to reply ; let us take it for granted, that believers may fall away, and how shall we pre-vent Mr. Goodwin from proving it ?   But he adds farther :

' Believers are said to be sealed by the Holy Spirit of God, against, or until, or for (εἰς) the day of redemption ; be-cause that holiness, which is wrought in them by the Spirit of God, qualifies them, puts them into a present and actual capacity of partaking in that joy and glory, which the great day of the full redemption of the saints (that is, of those who lived, and died, and shall be found such) shall bring with it ; and it is called the earnest of their inheritance.'

Ans. How εἰς comes to be ' against,' or ' for,' or to denote the matter spoken of, and what all this is to the purpose in hand, he shews not.   The aim of him the words are spoken of, and the uninterrupted continuance of the work men-tioned, to the end expressed, seems rather to be intended in the whole coherence of the words.   Neither is the use of sealing, to prepare any thing for such a time, but to secure and preserve it thereunto.   He that hath a conveyance sealed unto him, is not only capacitated for the present, to receive the estate conveyed, but is principally assured of a right

and title, for a continued enjoyment of it, not to be reversed.
It is not the nature of this work of the Holy Ghost, wherein
it is coincident which other acts of his grace ; but the particular use of it, as it is a sealing, and God's intendment by
it, to confirm us to the day of redemption, that comes under
our consideration.   If it were a season to inquire, wherein
it consists, I suppose we should scarce close with Mr. Goodwin's description of it, viz. 'that it is a qualifying of men,
and putting them in an actual capacity to partake of joy,'
&c. He is the first, I know of, that gave this description of
it, and probably the last that will do so.   Of the earnest of
the Spirit in its proper place.

What he adds in the last place, namely, ' If the apostle's intent had been to inform the Ephesians, that the gift of the
Holy Spirit, which they had received from God, was the
earnest of their inheritance, upon such terms, that no unworthiness or wickedness whatsoever, on their parts, could ever
hinder the actual collation of this inheritance upon them, he
had plainly prevaricated with that most serious admonition,
wherein he addresses himself to them afterward : For this
ye know, that no whoremonger, &c. hath any inheritance in
the kingdom of Christ:' this, I say, is of the same alloy with
what went before.   For,

1. Here is the same begging of the question as before,
and that upon a twofold account.   1. In supposing that believers may fall into such sins, and unworthiness, as are inconsistent with the state of acceptation with God, which is
the very thing he hath to prove.   2. In supposing, that, if believers are sealed up infallibly to redemption, the exhortations
to the avoidance of sins, in themselves, and to all that continue in them, destructive to salvation, are in vain : which is
a figment, in a case somewhat alike (as to the reason of it),
rejected by men, that knew nothing of the nature of God's
promises, nor his commands, nor the accommodation of them
both, to the fulfilling in believers ' all the good pleasure of
his goodness.'

2. The assurance the apostle gives of freedom from the
wrath of God, is inseparably associated with that assurance
that he gives, that we shall not be left in, or given up to, such
ways, as wherein that wrath, according to the tenor of the
covenant of grace, is not to be avoided.   From this latter

testimony, this argument also doth flow: Those, who are sealed of God to the day of redemption, shall certainly be preserved thereunto : their preservation being the end and aim of God in his sealing of them. Mr. Goodwin's answer to this proposition, is, that they shall be so preserved, in case they fall not into abominable sins and practices, and so apostatize from the faith ; that is, in case they be preserved, they shall be preserved; but wherein their preservation should consist, if not in their effectual deliverance from such ways and courses, is not declared. That all believers are so sealed, and to that end, as above, is the plain testimony of the Scripture, and therefore our conclusion is undeniably evinced.

Thus have we, through the Lord's assistance, freed the triple testimony of Father, Son, and Spirit, given to the truth under consideration, from all objections, and exceptions put in thereunto : so that we hope the mouth of iniquity may be stopped, and that the cause of the truth in hand is secured for ever. 'It is a fearful thing to contend with God. Let God be true, and all men liars.'

CHAP. VIII.

Entrance into the digression concerning the indwelling of the Spirit. The manner of the abode of the Spirit with them, on whom he is bestowed. Grounds of the demonstrations of the truth. The indwelling of the Spirit proved from the promises of it. Express affirmations of the same truth; Psal. li. 11. Rom. viii. 9. opened; ver. 11. 15. 1 Cor. ii. 12. Gal. iv. 6. opened. 1 Tim. iii. 14. The Spirit in his indwelling, distinguished from all his graces. Evasions removed. Rom. v. 5. explained. The Holy Ghost himself, not the grace of the Holy Ghost there intended. Rom. viii. 11. opened; Gal. v. 22. A personality ascribed to the Spirit in his indwellings. 1. In personal appellations. 1 John iv. 5. John xiv. 17. 19. 2. Personal operations. Rom. viii. 11. 15. explained. 3. Personal circumstances. The Spirit dwells in the saints, as in a temple. 1 Cor. iii. 16. vi. 9. The indwelling of the Spirit farther demonstrated, from the signal effects ascribed in the Scripture to his so doing: as, 1. Union with Christ. Union with Christ wherein it consisteth. Union with Christ by the indwelling of the same Spirit in him and us. This proved from, 1. Scriptural declarations of it; 2 Pet. i. 4. How we are made partakers of the divine nature. Union expressed by eating the flesh, and drinking the blood of Christ. John vi. 56. opened. The prayer of our Saviour for the union of his disciples; John xvii. 21. The union of the persons in the Trinity with themselves. 2. Scriptural illustrations for the manifestation of union. The union of head and members, what it is, and wherein it doth consist. Of the union between husband and wife, and our union with Christ represented thereby. Of a tree and its branches. Life and quickening given by the indwelling Spirit, in quickening, life, and suitable operations. 2. Direction and guidance given by the indwelling Spirit. Guidance or direction twofold. The several ways whereby the Spirit gives guidance and direction unto them in whom he dwells. The first way by giving a new understanding, or a new spiritual light upon the understanding. What light men may attain without the particular guidance of the Spirit. Saving embracements of particular truths, from the Spirit; 1 John ii. 20, 21. The way whereby the Spirit leads believers into truth. Consequences of the want of this guidance of the Spirit. The third thing received from the indwelling Spirit: supportment. The way whereby the Spirit gives supportment. 1. By bringing to mind the things spoken by Christ for their consolation; John xiv. 16. 26. 2. By renewing his graces in them, as to strength. The benefits issuing and flowing from thence. Restraint given by the indwelling Spirit, and how. The continuance of the Spirit with believers, for the renewal of grace, proved. John iv. 14. That promise of our Saviour at large opened. The water there promised is the Spirit. The state of them on whom he is bestowed. Spiritual thirst twofold; Isa. lxv. 13. 1 Pet. ii. 2. The reasons why men cannot thirst again, who have once drank of the Spirit, explained. Mr. G.'s exceptions considered, and removed. The same work farther carried on: as also,

the indwelling of the Spirit in believers farther demonstrated by the in-
ferences made from thence. The first: Our persons temples of the Holy
Ghost. To be disposed of, in all ways of holiness. Wisdom to try spirits.
The ways, means, and helps, whereby the saints discern between the voice
of Christ, and the voice of Satan.

HAVING shewed, that the Holy Spirit is purchased for us, by
the oblation of Christ, and bestowed on us, through his intercession, to abide with us for ever, a truth confirmed by
the unquestionable testimonies of the Father, Son, and Spirit; I shall, in the next place (I hope to the advantage and
satisfaction of the christian reader) a little turn aside to consider how, and in what manner he abideth with them, on
whom he is bestowed: together with some eminent acts
and effects of his grace, which he putteth forth, and exerteth in them, with whom he abideth, all tending to their preservation in the love and favour of God. A doctrine it is of
no small use and importance in our walking with God, as
we shall find in our pursuit of it. And therefore though not
appearing so directly argumentative, and immediately subservient to the promotion of the dispute in hand, yet tending
to the establishment, guidance, and consolation of them
who do receive it, and to the cherishing, increasing, and
strengthening of the faith thereof, I cannot but conceive it
much conducing to the carrying on of the main intendment
of this whole undertaking. I say then, upon the purchase
made of all good things for the elect by Christ, the holy and
blessed Spirit of God is given to them, to dwell in them personally, for the accomplishment of all the ends and purposes
of his economy towards them, to make them meet for, and
to bring them unto, the inheritance of the saints in light.
Personally, I say, in our persons (not by assumption of our
natures, giving us mystical union with Christ, not personal
union with himself, that is not one personality with him,
which is impious and blasphemous to imagine), by a gracious
inhabitation, distinct from his essential filling all things, and
his energetical operation of all things as he will, as shall af-
terwards be declared. Now this being a doctrine of pure
revelation, our demonstrations of it must be merely scriptural, and such (as will instantly appear) we have provided in
great plenty. In the carrying on then of this undertaking,
I shall do these two things:

1. Produce some of those many texts of Scripture, which are pregnant of this truth.

2. Shew what great things do issue from thence, and are affirmed in reference thereunto, being inferences of a supposal thereof, all conducing to the preservation of believers, in the love and favour of God, unto the end. For the first, I shall refer them to four heads ; unto,

1. Promises, that he should so dwell in us.

2. Positive affirmations that he doth so.

3. Those texts that hold out his being distinguished from all his graces and gifts in his so doing.

4. Those that ascribe a personality to him in his indwelling in us. Of each sort one or two places may suffice.

1. The indwelling of the Spirit is the great and solemn promise of the covenant of grace ; the manner of it we shall afterward evince ; Ezek. xxxvi. 27. ' I will put my Spirit within you, and cause you to walk in my ways:' in the verse foregoing he tells them, ' He will give them a new heart, and a new spirit,' which, because it may be interpreted of a renewed frame of spirit (though it rather seems to be the renewing Spirit, that is intended ; as also, chap. xi. 19.) he expressly points out, and differences the spirit he will give them, from all works of grace whatsoever, in that appellation of him, my Spirit, my Holy Spirit ; him will I put within you, I will give him, or place him, *in interiori vestro,* ' in your inmost part,' in your heart, or in *visceribus vestris,* ' in your bowels' (as the soul is frequently signified by expressions of sensual things), 'within you.' In his giving us a new heart, and new spirit, by putting in us his Spirit, certainly more is intended than a mere working of gracious qualities in our hearts, by his Spirit, which he may do, and yet be no more in us than in the greatest blasphemers in the world. And this in the carrying of it on to its accomplishment, God calls his covenant ; Isa. lix. 21. ' This is my covenant with them, saith the Lord, my Spirit that is upon thee, shall not depart from thee :' upon thee, in thee, that dwells in thee, as was promised. And this promise is evidently renewed by the Lord Christ to his disciples, clearly also interpreting what that Spirit is, which is mentioned in the promise of the covenant ; Luke xi. 13. ' Your heavenly Father will give the Holy Spirit to them that ask him, of him ;' that is, that pray to him for the Holy Spirit. Our Saviour instructs his disciples to

ask the Holy Spirit of God, upon the account of his being so promised; as Acts ii. 23. All[s] our supplications are to be regulated by the promise. And surely he, who (as shall afterward appear) did so plentifully and richly promise the bestowing of this Spirit on all those that believe on him, did not instruct them to ask for any inferior mercy and grace, under that name. That Spirit which the Lord Christ instructs us to ask of the Father, is the Spirit, which he hath promised to bestow so on us, as that he shall dwell in us. That the Spirit, which Christ instructs us to ask for, and which himself promiseth to send unto us, is the Holy Ghost himself, the Holy Spirit of promise, by whom we are sealed to the day of redemption, I suppose will require no labour to prove: what is needful to this end, shall be afterward insisted on.

2. Positive affirmations that he doth so dwell in, and remain with, the saints, are the second ground of the truth we assert; I shall name one or two testimonies of that kind: Psal. li. 11. saith David, 'Take not thy Holy Spirit from me.' It is the Spirit, and his presence, as unto sanctification, not in respect of prophecy, or any other gift whatever, that he is treating of with God. All the graces of the Spirit, being almost dead and buried in him, he cries aloud that he, whose they are, and who alone is able to revive and quicken them, may not be taken from him. With him, in him, he was, or he could not be taken from him. And though the gifts or graces of the Spirit only may be intended, where mention is made of giving or bestowing of him sometimes, yet when the saints beg of God, that he would continue his Spirit with them, though they have grieved him and provoked him, that no more is intended, but some gift or grace, is not so clear. I know men possessed with prejudice against this truth, will think easily to evade these testimonies, by the distinction of the person and graces of the Spirit. Wherefore, for the manner how he is with them, with whom he is, the apostle informs us, Rom. viii. 9. ' Ye are in the Spirit' (that is, spiritual men, opposed to being in the flesh, that is, carnal, unregenerate, unreconciled, and enemies to God), 'if so be the Spirit of Christ dwell in you: and if any man have not the Spirit of Christ, he is none of his:' not only the thing itself is asserted, but the weight of our regeneration and acceptation

s Rom viii. 27.

with God through Jesus Christ, is laid upon it. If the Spirit dwell in us, we are spiritual, and belong to Christ; otherwise not, we are none of his. This the apostle farther confirms, ver. 11. ' If the Spirit of him that raised up Jesus dwell in you :' I know not how the person of the Holy Ghost can be more clearly deciphered, than here he is : ' the Spirit of him that raised Jesus from the dead ;' why that is mentioned, shall afterward be considered. And this is the Spirit, as he bears testimony of himself, dwells in believers, which is all we say, and without farther curious inquiry, desire to rest therein. Doubtless it were better for men, to captivate their understandings to the obedience of faith, than to invent distinctions and evasions, to escape the power of so many plain texts of Scripture, and those literally and properly, not figuratively and metaphorically, expressing the truth contained in them: which, though it may be done sometimes, yet is not in a constant uniform tenor of expression any where the manner of the Holy Ghost. The apostle also affirms farther, ver. 15. that believers receive ' the Spirit of adoption to cry Abba Father ;' which being a work within them, cannot be wrought and effected by adoption itself, which is an extrinsical relation. Neither can adoption, and the Spirit of adoption, be conceived to be the same. He also farther affirms it, 1 Cor. ii. 12. ' We have received the Spirit, which is of God, that we might know the things that are freely given us of God.' We have so received him, as that he abides with us, to teach us, to acquaint our hearts, with God's dealing with us : bearing witness with our spirits to the condition wherein we are, in reference to our favour from God, and acceptation with him; and the same he most distinctly asserts, Gal. iv. 6. ' God hath sent forth the Spirit of his Son, into our hearts, crying, Abba Father.' The distinct economy of the Father, Son, and Spirit, in the work of adoption, is clearly discovered. He is sent, sent of God, that is, the Father. That name is personally to be appropriated, when it is distinguished (as here) from Son and Spirit; that is the Father's work, that work of his love, he sends him. He hath sent him, as the Spirit of his Son, procured by him for us, promised by him to us, proceeding from him, as to his personal subsistence, and sent by him, as to his office of adoption and consolation. Then, whither the Father hath

sent the Spirit of his Son, where he is to abide and make
his residence, is expressed; it is into our hearts, saith the
apostle: there he dwells and abides. And lastly, what there
he doth is also manifested : he sets them on work in whom
he is, gives them privilege for it, ability to it, encouragement
in it, causing them to cry Abba Father; once, and again, to
Timothy, doth the same apostle assert the same truth;
1 Epist. iii. 14. ' The good thing committed unto thee, keep
by the Holy Spirit, which dwelleth in us.' The Lord knowing how much of our life and consolation depends on this
truth, redoubles his testimony of it, that we might receive
it : even we, who are dull and slow of heart to believe the
things that are written.

3. Whereas some may say, it cannot be denied, but that
the Spirit dwells in believers, but yet this is not personally,
but only by his grace: though I might reply, that this indeed,
and upon the matter, is not to distinguish, but to deny, what
is positively affirmed. To say the Spirit dwells in us, but
not the person of the Spirit, is not to distinguish, *de modo,*
but to deny the thing itself; to say the graces indeed of the
Spirit are in us (not dwell in us, for an accident is not properly said to dwell in its subject), but the Spirit itself doth
not dwell in us, is expressly to cast down what the word sets
up. If such distinctions ought to be of force, to evade so
many positive and plain texts of Scripture, as have been
produced ; it may well be questioned, whether any truth be
capable of proof from Scripture or no. Yet I say farther,
to obviate such objections, and to prevent all quarrellings
for the future, the Scripture itself, as to this business of the
Spirit's indwelling, plainly distinguisheth between the Spirit
itself, and his graces: he is, I say, distinguished from them,
and that in respect to his indwelling; Rom. v. 5. ' The love
of God is shed abroad in our hearts, by the Holy Ghost, that
is given to us :' the Holy Ghost is given to us, to dwell in
us, as hath been abundantly declared, and shall yet farther
be demonstrated. Here he is mentioned together with the
love of God, and his shedding thereof abroad in our hearts ;
that is, with his graces : and is as clearly distinguished and
differenced from them, as cause and effect. Take the love of
God, in either sense, that is controverted about this place,
for our love to God, or a sense of his love to us, and it is an

eminent grace of the Holy Spirit. If then, by the Holy Ghost given unto us ye understand only the grace of the Holy Ghost, he being said to be given, because that is given, then this must be the sense of the place, ' The grace of the Holy Ghost is shed abroad in our hearts, by the grace of the Holy Ghost, that is given to us.' Farther, if by the Holy Ghost, be meant only his grace, I require what grace it is here by the expression intended? Is it the same with that expressed, ' the love of God?' This were to confound the efficient cause with its effect. Is it any other grace, that doth produce the great work mentioned? Let us know what that grace is, that hath this power and energy in its hand, of shedding abroad the love of God in our hearts; so Rom. viii. 11. ' He shall quicken your mortal bodies by the Spirit that dwelleth in you.' This quickening of our mortal bodies is generally confessed to be (and the scope of the place enforceth that sense) our spiritual quickening in our mortal bodies: mention being made of our bodies, in analogy to the body of Christ: by his death we have life and quickening. Doubtless then it is a grace of the Spirit that is intended. Yea, the habitual principle of all graces. And this is wrought in us by the Spirit that dwelleth in us. There is not any grace of the Spirit whereby he may dwell in men, antecedent to his quickening of them. Spiritual graces, have not their residence in dead souls. So that this must be the Spirit himself dwelling in us, that is here intended, and that personally : or the sense of the words must be, The grace of quickening our mortal bodies, is wrought in us, by the grace of quickening our mortal bodies that dwells in us; which is plainly to confound the cause and effect: besides, it is the same Spirit that raised up Jesus from the dead, that is intended, which doubtless was not any inherent grace, but the Spirit of God himself, working by the exceeding greatness of his power. Thus much is hence cleared. Antecedent in order of nature to our quickening, there is a Spirit given to us, to dwell in us. Every efficient cause hath at least the precedency of its effect. No grace of the Spirit is bestowed on us before our quickening, which is, the preparation and fitting of the subject for the receiving of them; the planting of the root that contains them virtually, and brings them forth actually in their order; Gal. v. 22. All graces whatsoever come under the name of the fruit of the Spirit: that is, which the Spirit in us brings forth, as the root doth the fruit, which in its so doing, is distinct therefrom. Many other instances might be given, but these may suffice.

4. There is a personality ascribed to the Holy Ghost, in his dwelling in us and that in such a way, as cannot be ascribed to any created grace, which is but a quality in a subject, and this the Scripture doth three ways:

1. In personal appellations.
2. In personal operations.
3. Personal circumstances.

1. There are ascribed to the indwelling Spirit, in his indwelling personal appellations; ' He that is in you, is greater than he that is in the world' (μείζων ἐστὶν ὁ ἐν ὑμῖν): ' he that is in you,' is a personal denomination, which cannot be used of any grace, or gracious habit whatsoever: so John xiv. 16, 17. ' He shall abide with you, he dwelleth with you, and shall be in you,' ὑμεῖς γινώσκετε αὐτὸ (τὸ πνεῦμα τῆς ἀληθείας), καὶ ἐν ὑμῖν ἔσται; John xvi. 13. ' But when the Spirit of truth is come,' ὅταν δὲ ἔλθῃ ἐκεῖνος, τὸ πνεῦμα. His person is as signally designed and expressed, as in any place of Scripture to what intent or purpose soever mentioned. Neither is it possible to apprehend, that the Scripture would so often, so expressly affirm the same thing in plain proper words, if they were not to be taken in the sense which they hold out. The main emphasis of the expression lies upon the terms that are of a personal designation, and to evade the force of them by the forementioned distinction which they seem signally to obviate and prevent, is, to say what we please, so we may oppose what pleases us not.

2. Personal operations, such acts and actings, as are proper to a person only, are ascribed to the Spirit in his indwelling. That place mentioned before, Rom. viii. 11. is clear hereunto, ' But if the Spirit of him that raised up Jesus from the dead, dwell in you, he who raised Christ from the dead shall quicken your mortal bodies by his Spirit which dwelleth in you,' or, by his indwelling Spirit, διὰ τοῦ ἐνοικοῦντος αὐτοῦ πνεύματος ἐν ὑμῖν. ' To quicken our mortal bodies' is a personal acting, and such as cannot be wrought but by an almighty agent. And this is ascribed to the Spirit as inhabiting, which is in order of nature antecedent to his quickening of

us, as was manifested.   And the same is asserted, ver. 15.
'The Spirit beareth witness with our spirits, that we are the
sons of God :' that Spirit, that dwells in us, bears witness in
us, a distinct witness by himself, distinguished from the testimony of our own spirits here mentioned, is either an act of
our natural spirits, or gracious fruit of the Spirit of God in
our hearts. If the first, what makes it in the things of God ?
Is any testimony of our natural spirits of any value, to assure
us that we are the children of God ?   If the latter, then is
there here an immediate operation the Spirit dwelling in our
hearts, in witness-bearing, distinct from all the fruits of grace
whatever. And on this account it is, that whereas 1 John v.
7, 8. the Father, Son, and Spirit, are said to bear witness in
heaven, the Spirit is moreover peculiarly said to bear witness
in the earth, together with the blood and water.

    3. There are such circumstances ascribed to him in his
indwelling, as are proper only to that which is a person; I
will instance only in one, his dwelling in the saints as in a
temple, 1 Cor. iii. 16. ' Ye are the temple of God, and his
Spirit dwelleth in you ;' that is, as in a temple; so plainly,
chap. vi. 19. ' Your body is the temple of the Holy Ghost,
which is in you, which you have of God,' giving us both the
distinction of the person of the Spirit, from the other persons, ' he is given us of God,' and his residence with us,
being so given, ' he is in us,' as also the manner of his in-
being, as in a temple ; nothing can make a place a temple,
but the relation it hath unto a deity. Graces that are but
qualifications of, and qualities in, a subject, cannot be said
to dwell in a temple ; this the Spirit doth : and, therefore,
as a voluntary agent in a habitation, not as a necessary or
natural principle in a subject: and though every act of his
be omnipotent intensively, being the act of an omnipotent
agent, yet he worketh not in the acts extensively, to the utmost of his omnipotency : he exerteth and puts forth his
power, and brings forth his grace in the hearts of them, with
whom he dwells as he pleaseth: to one he communicates
more grace, to another less : yea he gives more strength to
one and the same person, at one time, and in one condition,
than another,[a] dividing to every one as he will : and if this
peculiar manner of his personal presence with his saints,

---

[a] 1 Cor. xii.

distinct from his ubiquity or omnipresence, may not be believed, because not well by reason conceived, we shall lay a
foundation for the questioning principles of faith, which as
yet we are not fallen out withal.

And this is our first manifestation of the truth concerning the indwelling of the Spirit in the saints from the Scripture. The second will be from the signal issues and benefits which are asserted to arise from this indwelling of the
Spirit in them, of which I shall give sundry instances.

1. The first signal issue and effect which is ascribed to
this indwelling of the Spirit, is union; not a personal union
with himself, which is impossible: he doth not assume our
natures, and so prevent our personality, which would make
us one person with him, but dwells in our persons, keeping
his own, and leaving us our personality infinitely distinct;
but it is a spiritual union; the great union mentioned so
often in the gospel, that is the sole fountain of our blessedness; our union with the Lord Christ, which we have thereby.

Many thoughts of heart there have been about this
union; what it is, wherein it doth consist, the causes, manner, and effects of it; the Scripture expresses it to be very
eminent, near, durable; setting it out, for the most part, by
similitudes and metaphorical illustrations, to lead poor weak
creatures into some useful, needful acquaintance with that
mystery, whose depths in this life, they shall never fathom:
that many in the days wherein we live, have miscarried in
their conceptions of it, is evident; some to make out their
imaginary union, have destroyed the person of Christ, and
fancying a way of uniting man to God by him, have left
him to be neither God nor man. Others have destroyed
the person of believers, affirming that in their union with
Christ, they lose their own personality, that is, cease to be
men: or at least these or these individual men.

I intend not now to handle it at large, but only (and that
I hope without offence) to give in my thoughts concerning
it, as far as it receiveth light from, and relateth unto, what
hath been before delivered, concerning the indwelling of the
Spirit, and that without the least contending about other
ways of expression.

I say then, this is that which gives us union with Christ,
and that wherein it consists; even that the one, and self-

same Spirit, dwells in him and us; the first saving elapse from God, upon the hearts of the elect, is the Holy Spirit. Their quickening is every where ascribed to the Spirit, that is given unto them; there is not a quickening, a life-giving power, in a quality, a created thing. In the state of nature, besides gracious dispensations and habits in the soul inclining it to that which is good, and making it a suitable subject for spiritual operations, we want also a[b] vital principle, which should actuate the disposed subject unto answerable operations; this a quality cannot give. He that carries on the work of quickening, doth also begin it; Rom. viii. 11. All graces whatever (as was said), are[c] the fruits of the Spirit; and, therefore, in order of nature, are wrought in men, consequentially to his being bestowed on them. Now in the first bestowing of the Spirit, we have union with Christ, the carrying on whereof, consists in the farther manifestation and operations of the indwelling Spirit, which is called communion: to make this evident, that our union with Christ consists in this, the same Spirit dwelling in him and us, and that this is our union; let us take a view of it, first, from scriptural declarations of it; and then, secondly, from Scripture illustrations of it: both briefly, being not my direct business in hand.

1. First, Peter tells us, that it is a participation of the divine nature; 2 Pet. i. 4. We are by the promises made partakers of the divine nature; that is, it is promised to be given unto us, which when we receive, we are made partakers of, by the promises. That this participation of the divine nature (let it be interpreted how it will) is the same, upon the matter, with our union with Christ, is not questioned: that $\phi\acute{v}\sigma\iota\varsigma$ $\vartheta\epsilon\acute{\iota}a$ should be only a gracious habit, quality, or disposition of soul in us, I cannot easily receive; that is somewhere called $\kappa\alpha\iota\nu\grave{\eta}$ $\kappa\tau\acute{\iota}\sigma\iota\varsigma$, the[d] ' new creature,' but no where $\vartheta\epsilon\acute{\iota}a$ $\phi\acute{v}\sigma\iota\varsigma$ the 'divine nature.' The pretended high and spiritual, but indeed gross and carnal, conceits of some, from hence, destructive to the nature of God and man, I shall not turn aside to consider; what that is of the divine nature, or wherein it doth consist, that we are made partakers of by the promises, I shewed before: that the person of the holy and blessed Spirit is promised to us, whence he is called the Holy Spirit of promise, Eph. i. 13. hath been, I say, by

[b] John v. Eph. ii 1, 2.   [c] Gal. v. 22.   [d] 2 Cor. v 17

sundry evidences manifested: upon the accomplishment of that promise, he coming to dwell in us, we are said in him, by the promises, to be made partakers of the divine nature. We are θείας κοινωνοὶ φύσεως, we have our communion with it: our participation then of the divine nature, being our union with Christ, consists in the dwelling of [the] same Spirit in him and in us, we receiving him by the promise for that end.

2. Christ tells us, that this union arises from the ' eating of his flesh, and drinking of his blood;' John vi. 56. ' He that eateth my flesh, and drinketh my blood, dwelleth in me, and I in him;' the mutual indwelling of Christ and his saints, is their union: this, saith Christ, is from their ' eating my flesh, and drinking my blood:' but how may this be done? Many were offended, when this saying was spoken: near and close trials of sincerity, drive hypocrites into apostacy; from his Christ takes away this scruple, ver. 63. ' It is,' saith he, ' the Spirit that quickeneth, the flesh profiteth nothing:' it is by the indwelling of the quickening Spirit, whereby we have a real participation of Christ, whereby he ' dwelleth in us,' and ' we in him;' so,

3. He prays for his disciples, John xvii. 21. ' that they may be one, as the Father in him, and he in the Father, that they may be one in the Father and Son;' and ver. 22. ' Let them be one, even as we are one;' and that ye may not think that it is only union with, and among themselves, that he presses for (though indeed that which gives them union with Christ, gives them union one with another also, and that which constitutes them of the body, unites them to the head, and there is one body, because there is one Spirit; Eph. iv. 4. which even Lombard himself had some notion of, in his assertion, that charity, which is in us, is the person of the Holy Ghost, from that place of the apostle, ' God is love'); I say, he farther manifests, that it is union with himself, which he intends, ver. 23. ' I in them,' saith he, ' and thou in me.' This union then with him, our Saviour declares by, or at least illustrates by resemblance unto, his union with the Father. Whether this be understood of the union of the divine persons, of Father and Son, in the blessed Trinity (the union, I mean, that they have with themselves, in their distinct personality; and not their unity of essence), or the union, which was between Father and Son as incarnate, it

comes all to one, as to the declaration of that union we have
with him.   The Spirit is *Vinculum Trinitatis,* the bond of the
Trinity, as is commonly, and not inaptly spoken; proceeding
from both the other persons, being the love and power of
them both, he gives that union to the Trinity of persons,
whose *substratum* and ground, is the inestimable unity of
essence, wherein they are one.   Or if you take it for the
union of the Father with the Son incarnate, it is evident and
beyond inquiry or dispute, that, as the personal union of the
divine Word, and the human nature, was by the assumption
of that nature into one personal substance with itself; so
the person of the Father hath no other union with the human nature of Christ, immediately, and not by the union of
his own nature thereunto, in the person of his Son, but what
consists in that indwelling of his Spirit, in all fulness, in
the man Christ Jesus.   Now, saith our Saviour, this union I
desire they may have with me, by the dwelling of the same
Spirit in me and them, whereby I am in them, and they in
me, as I am one with thee, O Father.

Secondly, The Scripture sets forth this union by many
illustrations, given unto it from the things of the nearest
union, that are subject to our apprehension, giving the very
terms of the things so united, unto Christ and his, in their
union.   I shall name some few of them.

1. That of head and members making up one body, is
often insisted on: Christ is the head of his saints, and they
being many are members of that one body, and of one another;
as the apostle at large, 1 Cor. xii. 12. ' Even as the body is
one, and hath many members, and all the members of that
one body, being many, are one body, so is Christ;' the body
is one, and the saints are one body, yea, one Christ, that is,
mystical.   They then are the body: what part is Christ?
He is the head; 1 Cor. xi. 3. ' The head of every man (that
is, every believer) is Christ;' he is the head of the church,
and the Saviour of the body; Ephes. v. 23. ' He is the head
of the body the church;' Col. i. 19.   This relation of head
and members, I say, between Christ and his, holds out the
union that is between them, which consists in their being
so.   As the head and the members make one body, so Christ
and his members make one mystical Christ; whence then is
it that the head and members have this their union, whereby

they become one body; wherein doth it consist? Is it that from the head, the members do receive their influences of life, sense, and guidance, as the saints do from Christ? Eph. iv. 15, 16. ' They grow up into him in all things, who is the head ; from whom the whole body fitly framed together, and compact, by the which every joint supplieth, according to the effectual working in the measure of every part, groweth up to a holy increase.' So also Col. ii. 19. ' Holding the head, from whom the whole body, by bands and joints knit together, increaseth with the increase of God ;' but evidently this is their communion, whereunto union is supposed. Our union with Christ cannot consist in the communication of any thing to us, as members from him the head : but it must be in that which constitutes him and us, in the relation of head and members; he is our head, antecedently in order of nature, to any communication of grace from him as a head ; and yet not antecedently to our union with him; herein then consists the union of head and members, that though they are many, and have many offices, places, and dependencies, there is but one living, quickening soul, in head and members. If a man could be imagined so big and tall, as that his feet should stand upon the earth, and his head reach the starry heavens, yet having but one soul, he is still but one man. As then one living soul makes the natural head and members to be one, one body; so one quickening Spirit, dwelling in Christ and his members, gives them their union, and makes them one Christ, one body. This is clear from 1 Cor. xii. 12. ' As the first man Adam was made a living soul, so the last man Adam, is made a quickening spirit.'

2. Of husband and wife: The union that is between them, sets out the union betwixt Christ and his saints ; there is not any one more frequent illustration of it in the Scripture, the Holy Ghost pursuing the allusion in all the most considerable concernments of it, and holding it out, as the most solemn representation of the union, that is between Christ and his church ; Ephes. v. 31, 32. ' For this cause shall a man forsake his father and mother, and cleave to his wife, and they two shall be one flesh : this is a great mystery, but I speak concerning Christ and the church.' The transition is eminent from the conjugal relation, that is between

man and wife, unto Christ and his church. What the apostle had spoken of the one, he would have understood of the other. Wherein consists then the union between man and wife, which is chosen by God himself to represent the union between Christ and his church? The Holy Ghost informs us, Gen. ii. 24. 'They shall be no more twain, but one flesh;' this is their union, they shall be no more twain, but (in all mutual care, respect, tenderness, and love) one flesh. The rise of this you have, ver. 23. because of the bone and flesh of Adam, was Eve, his helper, made; hence are they said to be one flesh. Wherein then, in answer to this, is the union between Christ and his church? The same apostle tells us, 1 Cor. vi. 16, 17. 'He,' saith he, 'that is joined to a harlot is one flesh, and he that is joined to the Lord, is one spirit:' as they are one flesh, so these are one spirit; and as they are one flesh, because the one was made out of the other, so these are one spirit, because the Spirit, which is in Christ, by dwelling in them makes them his members; which is their union.

3. Of a tree, an olive, a vine, and its boughs and branches: 'I am the vine,' saith Christ, 'ye are the branches,' John xv. 5. 'Abide in me, and I in you;' as tree and branches, they have an abiding union, one with another; wherein this consists, the apostle sets out under the example of an olive and his boughs; Rom. xi. 16, 17. It is in this, that the branches and boughs being ingrafted into the tree, they partake of the very same juice and fatness with the root and tree, being nourished thereby. There is the same fructifying, fattening virtue in the one, as the other: only with this difference, in the root and tree it is originally, in the boughs by way of communication. And this also is chosen to set out the union of Christ and his. Both he and they are partakers of the same fruit-bearing Spirit; he that dwells in them, dwells in him also; only it is in him, as to them, originally, in them by communication from him. Take a scion, a graft, a plant, fix it to the tree with all the art you can, and bind it on as close as possible, yet it is not united to the tree, until the sap that is in the tree, be communicated to it, which communication states the union; let a man be bound to Christ by all the bonds of profession imaginable, yet unless

the sap, that is in him, the holy and blessed Spirit, be also communicated to him, there is no union between them. And this is the first thing, that doth issue and depend upon the indwelling of the Spirit in believers, even union with Christ; which is a demonstration of it *a posteriori.*

2. The Spirit as indwelling, gives us life and quickening: 'God quickens our mortal bodies (or us in them) by his Spirit, that dwells in us,' Rom. viii. 11. by which Spirit Christ also was raised from the dead: and, therefore, the apostle mentioning, in another place, the beginning and carrying on of faith in us, he saith, it is 'wrought according to the exceeding greatness of the power of God, which he wrought in Christ when he raised him from the dead;' Eph. i. 8. Now in this quickening there are two things.

1. The *actus primus,* or the life itself bestowed.

2. The operations of that life in them, on whom it is bestowed.

For the first, I shall not positively determine, what it is, nor wherein it doth consist. This is clear that by nature 'we are dead in trespasses and sins.' That in our quickening, we have a new spiritual life communicated to us, and that from Christ, in whom it is treasured up for that purpose. But what this life is, it doth not fully appear, whilst we are here below. All actual graces confessedly flow from it, and are distinct from it, as the operations of it. I say, in this sense they flow from it confessedly, as suitable actings are from habits: though to the actual exercise of any grace within, new help and assistance is necessary, in that continual dependance are we upon the fountain. Whether it consists in that which is called habitual grace, or the gracious suitableness and disposition of the soul unto spiritual operations, may be doubted. The apostle tells us, 'Christ is our life;' Col. iii. 4. 'When Christ, who is our life, shall appear;' and Gal. ii. 22. 'Christ liveth in me;' Christ liveth in believers by his Spirit, as hath been declared; Christ dwelleth in you, and his Spirit dwelleth in you, are expressions of the same import and signification. But,

2. God by his Spirit 'worketh in us both to will and to do, of his own good pleasure.' All vital actions are from him; it may be said of graces and gracious operations, as

well as gifts, all these 'worketh in us that one and self-same Spirit, dividing to every one as he will.' But this is not now to be insisted on.

3. The Spirit as indwelling, gives guidance and direction to them, in whom he is, as to the way wherein they ought to walk, Rom. viii. 14. 'As many as are led by the Spirit of God:' the Spirit leads them in whom it is; and, ver. 1. They are said 'to walk after the Spirit:' now there is a twofold leading, guidance, or direction.

1. Moral and extrinsical, the leading of a rule.

2. Internal and efficient, the leading of a principle.

Of these, the one lays forth the way, the other directs, and carries along in it. The first is the word, giving us the direction of a way, of a rule; the latter is the Spirit, effectually guiding and leading us in all the paths thereof. Without this, the other direction will be of no saving use, it may be 'line upon line, precept upon precept,' yet men go backward, and are insnared. David, notwithstanding the rule of the word, yea the spirit of prophecy, for the inditing of more of the mind of God for the use of the church, when moved thereunto, yet in one psalm cries out four times, 'Oh! give me understanding to keep thy commandments,' concluding that hence would be his life, that therein it lay; 'Oh! give me,' saith he, 'understanding, and I shall live;' Psal. cxix. 144. so Paul bidding Timothy consider the word of the Scripture, that he might know whence it is that this will be of use unto him, he adds, 'I pray the Lord give thee understanding in all things;' 2 Tim. ii. 7. How this understanding is given, the same apostle informs us; Eph. i. 17, 18. 'The God of our Lord Jesus Christ, the Father of glory, give unto us the Spirit of wisdom and revelation, in the knowledge of him, the eyes of our understandings being thereby enlightened.'* It is the Spirit of wisdom and revelation, the Holy Spirit of God, from whom is all spiritual wisdom, and all revelation of the will of God, who being given unto us by the God of our Lord Jesus Christ, and our God in him, enlightens our understandings, that we may know, &c. And on this account is the Son of God said to come and give us an 'understanding to know him that is true:' that is, himself by his Spirit; 2 John 20.

* 1 Cor. ii. 11.

Now there be two ways, whereby the Spirit gives us guidance to walk according to the rule of the word.

1. By giving us 'the knowledge of the will of God, in all wisdom and spiritual understanding;' Col. i. 9. carrying us on 'unto all riches of the full assurance of understanding, to the acknowledgment of God, and of the Father, and of Christ;' chap. ii. 2. This is that spiritual, habitual, saving illumination, which he gives to the souls of them, to whom he is given: 'He, who commanded light to shine out of darkness, by him, shining into their minds, to give them the knowledge of his glory in the face of Jesus Christ;' 2 Cor. iv. 6. This is elsewhere termed "translating from darkness to light; opening blind eyes, giving light to them that are in darkness, freeing us from the condition of natural men, who discern not the things that are of God.' This the apostle makes his design to clear up and manifest, 1 Cor. ii. He tells you, the things of the gospel are the wisdom of God in a 'mystery, even the hidden wisdom, which God ordained before the world unto our glory;' ver. 7. And then proves that an acquaintance herewith, is not to be attained by any natural means or abilities whatsoever; ver. 9. 'Eye hath not seen, ear hath not heard, nor hath it entered into the heart of man, the things which God hath prepared for those that love him:' and thence unto the end of the chapter, variously manifests how this is given to believers, and wrought in them by the Spirit alone; from whom it is, that they know the mind of Christ. 'But,' saith he, 'God hath revealed them unto us by his Spirit, for the Spirit searcheth all things, even the deep things of God: for who knoweth the things of a man, but the spirit of a man? and who knoweth the things of God but the Spirit of God? And we have received the Spirit, not of this world, but the Spirit which is of God, that we may know the things which are freely given us of God.'

The word is as the way whereby we go: yea an external light, as a 'light to our feet, and as a lanthorn to our paths;' yea as the sun in the firmament, sending forth its beams of light abundantly. But what will this profit, if a man have no eyes in his head? There must not only be light in the object, and in the medium, but in the subject, in our hearts and

---

f Col. i. 13. 1 Pet. ii. 9. Eph. v. 8. Luke iv. 18. 1 Cor. ii. 14.   g Psal. cxix. 119.

minds : and this is of the operation of the Spirit of light and truth given to us, as the apostle tells us, 2 Cor. iii. 18. 'We all with open face beholding the glory of God as in a glass, are changed into the same image, from glory to glory, as by the Spirit of the Lord.'

This is the first way whereby the Holy Spirit, dwelling in us, gives guidance and direction : fundamentally, habitually, he enlightens our minds, gives us eyes, understandings, shines into us, translates us from darkness into marvellous light, whereby alone we are able to see our way, to know our paths, and to discern the things of God: without this, 'men are blind, and see nothing afar off;' 2 Pet. ii. 9.

There are three things which men either have, or may be made partakers of without this, this communication of light, by the indwelling Spirit.

1. They have the subject of knowledge, a natural faculty of understanding ; their minds remain, though depraved, destroyed, perverted ; yea so far that[h] ' their eye, and the light that is in them is darkness ;' yet the faculty remains still.

2. They may have the object or truth, revealed in the word ; this is common to all that are made partakers of the good word of God ; that is, to whom it is preached and delivered, as it is to many, whom it 'doth not profit, being not mixed with faith ;' Heb. iv. 2.

3. The way and means of communicating the truth so revealed to their minds or understandings, which is the literal, grammatical, logical, delivery of the things contained in the Scriptures, as held out to their minds and apprehensions, in their meditation on them ; and this means of conveyance of the sense of the Scripture, is plain, obvious, and clear, in all necessary truths.

A concurrence of these three will afford, and yield them that have it, upon their diligence and inquiry, a disciplinary knowledge of the literal sense of Scripture, as they have of other things : by this means, the light shines φαίνει, sends out some beams of light into their dark minds,[i] ' but the darkness comprehends it not,' receives not the light in a spiritual manner ; there is notwithstanding all this, still wanting the work of the Spirit before mentioned, creating and

[h] Matt. vi. 23.   [i] John i. 5.

implanting in and upon their understandings and minds,
that light and power of discerning spiritual things, which·
before we insisted on. This the Scripture sometimes calls,
the 'opening of the understanding;' Luke xxiv. 45. sometimes the 'giving an understanding itself;' 2 Tim. ii. 7.
1 John v. 20. sometimes 'light in the Lord;' Eph. v. 8. Notwithstanding all the advantages formerly spoken of, without
this men are still natural men, and darkness, not comprehending, not receiving the things of God ; that is, not spiritually, for so the apostle adds, because they are spiritually
discerned; 1 Cor. ii. 14. receiving spiritual things, by mere
natural mediums, they become foolishness unto them ; this
is the first thing that the Spirit dwelling in us, doth towards
guidance and direction; he gives a new light and understanding, whereby in general we are enabled to discern,
comprehend, and receive spiritual things.

2. In particular, he guides and leads men to the embracing particular truths, and to the walking in, and up,·unto
them. Christ promised to give him to us for this end ;
namely, to 'lead us into all truth;' John xvi. 13. 'He will
guide us into all truth ;' there is more required to the receiving, entertaining, embracing, a particular truth, and rejecting of what is contrary unto it, than a habitual illumination ; this also is the work of the Spirit that dwells in us;
he works this also in our minds and hearts ; therefore the
apostle secures his little children that they shall be led
into truth, and preserved from seduction, on this account;
1 John ii. 20. ' You have an unction from the Holy One (or,
ye have received the Spirit from the Lord Jesus), and you
shall know all things.' Why so? because it is his work to
guide and lead you into all the things, whereof I am speaking ; and more fully, ver. 27. 'You have received an unction
from him that abideth in you, and you have no need that
any teach you, but as the unction teacheth you of all things,
and is true, and is no lie, and as he hath taught you, abide
in him.' It is received as promised, it doth abide as the Spirit is said to do, and it teacheth, which is the proper work
of the Spirit in an eminent manner.

Now this guidance of believers by the Spirit, as to the
particular truths, and actings, consists in his putting forth
of a twofold act of light, and power.

First, Of light; and that also is twofold:

1. Of beauty, as to the things to be received or done; he represents them to the soul, as excellent, comely, desirable, and glorious, leading us on in the receiving of truth, 'from glory to glory;' 2 Cor. ii. 18. He puts upon every truth a new glory, making and rendering it desirable to the soul, without which it cannot be closed withal, as not discovering, either suitableness or proportion unto the minds and hearts of men. And,

2. By some actual elevation of the mind and understanding to go forth unto, and receive into itself, the truth, as represented to it; by both of them, sending forth 'light and truth;' Psal. xliii. 3. blowing of the clouds, and raising up the[k] day-star, that rises in our hearts.

Secondly, Of power; Isa. xxxv. 6. 'The breaking forth of streams,' makes not only the blind to see, but the 'lame to leap;' strength comes, as well as light, by the pouring out of the Spirit on us; strength for the receiving and practice of all his gracious discoveries to us; he leads us, not only in general, implanting a saving light in the mind, whereby it is disposed and enabled to discern spiritual things, in a spiritual manner, but also as to particular truths, rendering them glorious and desirable, opening the mind and understanding by new beams of light, he leads the soul irresistibly into the receiving of the truths revealed; which is the second thing we have by him.

I shall only observe for a close of this, one or two consequences of the weight of this twofold operation of the indwelling of Christ.

1. From the want of the first, or his creating a new light in the minds of men, it is that so many labour in the fire, for an acquaintance with the things of God; it is, I say, a consequence of it, as darkness is of absence of the sun. Many we see after sundry years spent in considerable labours and diligence, reading of many books, with a contribution of assistance from other useful arts and sciences, in the issue of all their endeavours,[l] 'do wax vain in their imaginations, having their foolish hearts darkened,' professing themselves wise, they become fools, being so far from any sap and savour, that they have not the leaves of ability in

[k] 2 Pet. ii. 19.   [l] Rom. i. 21, 22.

things divine. Others indeed make some progress in a disciplinary knowledge of doctrines of the Scriptures, and can accurately reason and distinguish about them, according to the forms wherein they have been exercised, and that to a great height of conviction in their own spirits, and permanency in the profession they have taken up. But yet all this while they abide without any effectual power of the truth, conforming and framing their spirits unto their likeness and mould thereof. They do but see men walking like trees; some shines of the light break in upon them.which rather amaze, than guide them, they comprehend it not. They see spiritual things in a natural light, and presently forget what manner of things they were; and in the species wherein they are retained,[n] they are foolishness.

2. From the want of the latter, it is, that we ourselves are so slow in receiving some parts of truth, and do find it so difficult to convince others of some other parts of it, which to us are written with the beams of the sun. Unless the truth itself be rendered a glory to the understanding, and the mind be actually enlightened, as to the truth represented, it is not to be received in a spiritual manner. Those who know at all, what the truth is, 'as the truth is in Jesus,' will not take it up upon any other more common account; sometimes in dealing with godly persons, to convince them of a truth, we are ready to admire their stupidity, or perverseness, that they will not receive that, which shines in with so broad a light upon our spirits. The truth is, until the Holy Spirit sends forth the light and power mentioned, it is impossible, that their minds and hearts should rest and acquiesce in any truth whatever. But,

4. From this indwelling of the Spirit, we have supportment; our hearts are very ready to sink and fail under our trials; indeed a little thing will cause us so to do :[o] flesh, and heart, and all that is within us, are soon ready to fail. Whence is it that we do not sink into the deeps? that we have so many and so sweet and gracious recoveries, when we are ready to be swallowed up? The Spirit that dwells in us, gives us supportment. Thus it was with David, Psal. li. 22. He was ready to be overwhelmed under a sense of the guilt of that great sin which God then sorely charged

[m] Rom. vi. 17.   [n] 1 Cor. ii. 12—14.   [o] Psal. lxxiii. 26.

upon his conscience, and cries out like a man ready to sink under water, ' O uphold me with thy free Spirit,' if that do not support me, I shall perish : so Rom. viii. 26. The Spirit helpeth, bears up, that infirmity, which is ready to make us go double. How often should we be overborne with our burdens, did not the Spirit put under his power to bear them and to support us? Thus Paul assures himself that he shall be carried through all his trials, by the ' help supplied to him by the Spirit ;' Phil. i. 19.

There are two special ways whereby the Spirit communicates supportment unto the saints when they are ready to sink, and that upon two accounts. First, of consolation, and then of strength.

1. The first he doth by bringing to mind the things that Jesus Christ hath left in store for their supportment. Our Saviour Christ informing his disciples, how they should be upheld in their tribulations, tells them that the ' Comforter, which should dwell with them, and was in them (John xiv. 16, 17.) should bring to remembrance what he had told them ;' ver. 26. Christ had said many things, things gracious and heavenly, to his disciples : he had given them many rich and precious promises, to uphold their hearts in their greatest perplexities ; but knowing full well how ready they were to forget, and to ' P let slip the things that were spoken,' and how coldly his promises would come in to their assistance, when retained only in their natural faculties, and made use of by their own strength ; to obviate these evils, tells them, that this work he committeth to the charge of another, who will do it to the purpose: when ye are ready to drive away the Comforter, saith he, who is in you, he shall bring to remembrance, and apply to your souls, the things that I have spoken, the promises that I have made, which will then be unto you as life from the dead. And this he doth every day; how often, when the spirits of the saints are ready to faint within them, when straits and perplexities are round about them, that they know not what to do, nor whither to apply themselves for help or supportment, doth the Spirit that dwelleth in them, bring to mind some seasonable, suitable promise of Christ, that bears them up quite above their difficulties and distractions, opening such

P Heb. ii. 1.

a new spring of life and consolation to their souls, as that they who but now stooped, yea, were almost bowed to the ground, do stand upright, and feel no weight or burden at all. Oftentimes they go for water to the well, and are not able to draw ; or if it be poured out upon them, it comes like rain on a stick that is fully dry. They seek to promises for refreshment, and find no more savour in them than in the white of an egg ; but when the same promises are brought to remembrance by the Spirit the Comforter, who is with them, and in them, how full of life and power are they?

2. As this he doth to support believers in respect of consolation, so as to the communion of real strength, he stirs up those graces in them that are strengthening and supporting. The graces of the Spirit are indeed, all of them, supporting and upholding : if the saints fall and sink at any time, in any duty, under any trial, it is because their graces are decayed, and do draw back as to the exercise of them : ' If thou faint in the day of adversity, it is not because thy adversaries are great or strong, but ' because thy strength is small ;' Prov. xxiv. 10. All our fainting is from the weakness of our strength ; faith, waiting, patience, are small : when David's faith and patience began to sink and draw back, he cries, '⁹All men are liars,' I shall one day perish by the hand of mine enemies ; when faith is but little, and grace but weak, we shall be forced, if the wind do but begin to blow, to cry out, Save Lord, or we sink and perish : let a temptation, a lust, a corruption, lay any grace asleep, and the strongest saint will quickly become like Samson with his hair cut, and the Philistines about him ; he may think to do great matters, but at the first trial he is made a scorn to his enemies ; Peter thought it was the greatness of the winds and waves that terrified him, but our Saviour tells him, it was the ʳweakness of his faith that betrayed him. For relief in this condition, the Spirit that dwells in the saints, stirs up, enlivens, and actuates all his graces in them, that may support and strengthen them in their duties, and under their tribulations. Rom. v. Paul runs up the influence of grace into the saints' supportment unto this fountain, ver. 3. ' We glory in tribulation ;' this is as high a pitch as can be attained : to be patient under tribulation is no small victo-

ry ; to glory in it, a most eminent triumph, a conformity to Christ, who in his cross triumphed over all his opposers ; we are not only patient under tribulations, and have strength to bear them, but, saith the apostle, ' We glory and rejoice in them,' as things very welcome to us; how comes this about? Saith he, ' Tribulation worketh patience' (that is, it sets it at work ; for tribulation in itself, will never work or beget patience in us), 'and patience experience, and experience hope, and hope maketh not ashamed.' It is from hence-that these graces, patience, hope, experience, being set on work, do bear up, and support our souls, and raise them to such a height under their pressures, that we have great cause of rejoicing in them all : yea, but whence is this? Do these graces readily come forth and exert themselves with an efficacy suitable to this triumphing frame? The ground and spring of all is discovered, ver. 5. it is ' because the love of God is shed abroad in our hearts by the Holy Ghost, that is given to us.' From this fountain do all these fresh streams flow ; the Spirit that is given us, that ' sheds abroad the love of God in our hearts,' and thereby sets all our graces on work. He oils the wheels of the soul's obedience, when we neither know what to do, nor how to perform what we know.

5. This indwelling Spirit gives restraint ; restraining grace doth mainly consist in moral persuasions, from the causes, circumstances, and ends of things ; when a man is dissuaded from sin, upon considerations taken from any such head or place, as is apt to prevail with him, that persuasion so applied and intended of God for that end, is unto him restraining grace : by this means doth the Lord keep within bounds the most of the sons of men, notwithstanding all their violent and impetuous lusts ; hell, shame, bitterness, disappointment, on the one hand ; credit, repute, quietness of conscience, and the like, on the other, bind them to their good behaviour. God through these things, drops an awe upon their spirits, binding them up from running out unto that compass of excess and riot in sinning, which otherwise their lusts would carry them out unto. This is not his way of dealing with the saints, he writes his ' *law in their hearts, and puts his fear in their inward parts,' that

* Jer. xxxi. 34.

they may not depart from them, making them 'a willing people, through his own power. By his effectually remaining grace, he carries them out kindly, cheerfully, willingly, to do his whole will, 'working in them to will and to do, of his own good pleasure:' yet, notwithstanding all this, oftentimes through the strength of temptation, the subtilty of Satan, and his readiness to improve all advantages to the utmost, the treachery and deceitfulness of indwelling sin and corruption, they are carried beyond the bounds and lines of that principle, or law of life and love, whereby they are led. What now doth the Lord do? They are ready to run quite out of the pasture of Christ; doth he then let them go, and give them up to themselves? Nay, but he sets a hedge about them, that they shall not find their way. He leads them as the 'wild ass in her month,' that they may be found; he puts a restraint upon their spirits by setting home some sad considerations of the evil of their hearts and ways, whither they are going, what they are doing, and what shall be the issue of their walking so loosely. Even in this life, what shame, what scandal, what dishonour to themselves, their profession, the gospel, their brethren, it would prove, and so hampers them, quiets their spirits, and gently brings them again under obedience unto that principle of love that is in them, and the Spirit of grace (whose yoke they were casting off) whereby they are led. Many times then, even the saints of God are kept from sins, especially outward, actual sins, upon such outward motives, reasonings, and considerations, as other men are: Peter was broken loose, and running down hill apace, denying and forswearing his master; Christ puts a restraint upon his spirit by a look towards him; this minds him of his folly, unkindness, his former rash confidence, and engagement to die with his Master, and sets him on such considerations, as stirred up the principle of grace in him, to take its place, and rule again; and in obedience thereunto, he not only desists from any farther denial, but faith, repentance, love, all exerting themselves, he goes ' out, and wept bitterly:' it is so frequently with the saints of God, though in lesser evils; by neglect and omission of duty, or inclination to evil, and closing with temptations, they break out of the pure and perfect rule and

' Psal cx 3

guidance of the Spirit, whereby they ought to be led : instantly some considerations or other are pressed on upon their spirits, taken perhaps from outward things, which recovers them to that obediential frame, from whence, through violence of corruption and temptation, they had broken. Like a hawk sitting on a man's hand, eating her meat in quietness, is suddenly, by the original wildness of her nature, carried out to an attempt of flying away with speed, but is checked by the string at her heels, upon which she returns to her meat again. We have an innate wildness in us, provoking and stirring us up to run from God. Were we not recovered by some clog fastened on us for our restraint, we should often run into the most desperate paths. And this restraint, I say, is from the indwelling Spirit; he stirs up one thing or other to smite the heart and conscience, when it is under the power of any temptation to sin and folly. So it was with David, in the attempt he made upon Saul, when he cut-off the lap of his garment; temptation and opportunity had almost turned him loose from under the power of faith, waiting, and dependance on God, wherein lay the general frame of his spirit : he is recovered to it by a blow upon the heart, from some dismal consideration of the issue, and scandal of that which he was about.

6. We have hereby also the renewal, daily renewal of sanctifying grace; inherent grace is a thing in its own nature apt to decay and die; it is compared to things ready to die; Rev. iii. 2. 'Strengthen the things that remain' (saith Christ to the church of Sardis), 'that are ready to die.' It is a thing, that may wither and decline from its vigour, and the soul may thereby be betrayed into manifold weaknesses and backslidings. It is not merely from the nature of the trees in the garden of God, that their fruit fails not, nor their leaves wither, but from their[u] planting by the rivers of water; hence are the sicknesses, weaknesses, and decays of the Spirit, mentioned in the Scripture. Should he, who had the richest stock of any living, be left to spend of it, without new supplies, he would quickly be a bankrupt; this also is prevented by the indwelling Spirit. He is the fatness of the olive, that is communicated to the branches, continually to keep them fruitful and flourishing;

* Psal. i. 1.

he is that golden oil, which passes through the branches, and empties itself in the fruitfulness of the church. He continually fills our lamps with new oil, and puts new vigour into our spirits; Psal. xcii. 10. 'Thou liftest up my horn, as the horn of an unicorn, I am anointed with fresh oil,' or renewed supplies of the Spirit. And this, Psal. ciii. 5. is called a renewing of youth like the eagles; a recovery of former strength and vigour, new power and ability for new duties and performances; and how comes that about? Saith the psalmist it is by God's satisfying my mouth with good things; 'he satisfied his mouth with good things,' or answered his prayers. What these good things are, which the saints pray for, and wherewith their mouths are satisfied, our Saviour tells us; 'Your Father,' saith he, 'knoweth how to give good things to them that ask them of him;' which expressing in another place, he saith, 'Your Father will give the Holy Spirit to them that ask him of him.' He is given us, and he renews our strength as the eagles, making our souls, which were ready to languish, prompt, ready, cheerful, strong in the ways of God; to this purpose is that prayer of the spouse; Cant. iv. 6. 'Awake O north wind, and come thou south, and blow upon my garden, that the savour of my spices may flow out; let my beloved come into his garden, that he may eat of the fruit of his precious things.' She is sensible of the withering of her spices, the decays of her graces, and her disability thereupon, to give any suitable entertainment unto Jesus Christ; hence is her earnestness for new breathings and operations of the Spirit of grace, to renew, and revive, and set on work again her graces in her, which without it, could not be done; all graces are the fruits of the Spirit; Gal. v. 25, 26. 'The fruit of the Spirit is love, joy, peace, long-suffering, kindness, goodness, faith, gentleness, temperance:' if the root do not communicate fresh juice and sap continually, the fruit will quickly wither; were there not a continual communication of new life and freshness unto our graces, from the indwelling Spirit, we should soon be poor withered branches; this our Saviour tells us, John xv. 4, 5. 'Abide in me and I in you; as the branches cannot bring forth fruit of themselves, unless they remain in the vine, no more can ye, unless ye abide in me; I am the vine, ye are the branches; he who abideth in me, and I in him, he bringeth forth much fruit, for separate from me ye can do nothing.' Our abiding in Christ, and his in us, is (as was declared) by the indwelling of the same Spirit in him and us. Hence, saith Christ, have you all your fruit-bearing virtue, and unless that be continued to us, we shall wither and consume to nothing; David in his spiritually declined condition, entangled under the power and guilt of sin, cries out for the continuance of the Spirit, and the restoring him, as to those ends and purposes, in reference whereunto, he was departed from him; Psal. li. 11, 12. This the apostle prays earnestly, that the Ephesians may receive; chap. iii. 16, 17. ' I bow my knees to the Father of our Lord Jesus Christ, that he will give unto you, according to the riches of his glory, that ye may be strengthened with might, by his Spirit in the inward man, that Christ may dwell in your hearts by faith, that ye being rooted and grounded in love,' &c. The inward man is the same with the new creature, the new principle of grace in the heart; this is apt to be sick, to faint, and decay; the apostle prays that it might be strengthened. How is this to be done? how is it to be renewed, increased, enlivened? It is, saith he, by the mighty power of the Spirit; and then gives you particular instances in the graces which flourish and spring up effectually, upon that strengthening they receive by the might and power of the Spirit, as of faith, love, knowledge, and assurance; the increasing and establishing of all which, is ascribed there unto him. He who bestows these graces on us, and works them in us, doth also carry them on unto perfection. Were it not for our inflowings from that spring, our cisterns would quickly be dry; therefore, our Saviour tells us, that he, the Spirit, is unto believers, as ' rivers of living water flowing out of their bowels;' John vii. 38, 39. A never failing fountain, that continually puts forth living waters of grace in us.'

This may a little farther be considered and insisted on, being directly to our main purpose in hand; it is true, indeed, it doth more properly belong unto that, which I have assigned for the second part of this treatise, concerning the ground or principle of the saints' abiding with God for ever; but falling in conveniently in this order, I shall farther press it from John iv. 14. ' Whosoever,' saith our Saviour, ' shall

drink of the water, which I shall give unto him, shall not
thirst for ever; but the water which I shall give unto him,
shall be in him a fountain of water, springing up unto eternal life.'

The occasion of these words is known; they are part of
our Saviour's colloquy with the poor Samaritan harlot;
having told her that he could give her another manner of
water, and infinitely better than that which she drew out of
Jacob's well (for which the poor creature did almost con-
temn him, and asked him, whence he had that water whereof
he spake, how he came by it, or what he made of himself;
did he think himself a better man than Jacob who drank of
that well, which she was drawing water out of), to convince
her of the truth, and reality of his promise, he compares the
water, that he would and could give, with that which she
drew out of the well, especially as to one eminent effect,
wherein the water of his promise did infinitely surmount
that which she so magnified ; for ver. 13. he tells her, for
that water in the well, though it allayed thirst for a season,
yet within a little while she would thirst again, and must
come thither to draw; but, saith he, ' whosoever drinketh of
the water I shall give him thirsts no more ;' and this he
proveth from the condition of the water he giveth, it is a
well of water, not a draught, not a pitcher-full, as that thou
carriest away, but it is a fountain, a well; yea, perhaps in
itself it is so, a fountain or well, but he that drinks of it, he
hath but one draught of that water ; nay, saith Christ, it
shall become a well in him, not a well whereunto he may go,
but a well that he shall carry about in him.   He that hath a
continual spring of living water in him, shall doubtless have
no occasion of fainting for thirst, any more ; this our Saviour amplifies, and clears up unto her, from the nature and
energy of this well of water, it springeth up unto everlasting life ; in these last words instructing the poor sinful creature in the use of the parable, that he had used with her.
Having taken an occasion to speak to her of heavenly things,
from the nature of the employment that she was engaged in
at present; two or three things may be observed from the
words, to give light unto their tendency to the confirmation
of the truth we have under consideration.

First, The water here promised by our Saviour, is the

holy and blessed Spirit; this needs no labour to demonstrate. The Spirit himself so interprets it; John vii. 38, 39.
'He who believeth on me,' saith our Saviour, 'as the Scripture saith, rivers of living water shall flow out of his belly;
but this he said of the Spirit, which they should receive,
who believe on him;' that which in one place he calleth 'a
well of water springing up to life in us,' is in the other, in
equivalent terms, called 'rivers of living water, flowing out
of our bellies;' and the Holy Ghost tells us, that he himself,
the blessed Spirit, is signified by that expression. Neither
is there any thing bestowed on us, that can be compared to
a spring of water, arising up, increasing, and flowing out
abundantly upon its own account, but the Spirit only. It
is only the Spirit, that is a fountain of refreshment, from
whence all grace doth abundantly flow. It is, I say, the
Spirit, whereof we have been speaking, who is procured for
us, and bestowed upon us, by Jesus Christ, which, as an
everlasting fountain, continually supplies us with refreshing
streams of grace, and fills us anew therewith, when the chan-
nels thereof in our souls are ready to become dry. And,

Secondly, The state and condition of them, on whom this
living water is bestowed, in reference thereunto, is described.
Saith our Saviour, he that hath this Spirit of grace, this well
of living water, shall never thirst. It is most emphatically
expressed by two negatives, and an exegetical additional
term for weight and certainty, οὐ μὴ διψήσῃ 'he shall never
thirst to eternity;' or as it is expressed, John vi. 35. 'he
shall never thirst at any time.' There is a twofold thirst:

1. There is a thirst *totalis indigentiæ* of a whole and entire
want of that men thirst after; and this is the thirst that
returns upon men in their natural lives; after they have
allayed it once with natural water, they thirst again, and
their want of water returns as entire and full, as if they had
never drank in their lives; such a spiritual thirst doth God
ascribe to wicked men; Isa. lxv. 13. 'My servants shall eat,
but you shall be hungry; my servants shall drink, but ye
shall be thirsty.' Their hunger and thirst is the total want
of grace, not that they do desire it, but that they have it not.
And this thirst of total want of grace, is that, that never
shall, nor can befall them, who have received the Spirit of
grace, as a well of water in them. They can never so thirst,

as to be returned again into the condition wherein they were, before they drank of that Spirit.

2. There is also a thirst of desire and complacency of the good things thirsted after. In this sense they are pronounced blessed, who '*hunger and thirst after righteousness.' And Peter instructs us to grow in this thirst more and more; 1 Pet. ii. 2. 'As new-born babes desire the sincere milk of the word, that ye may grow thereby.' The enjoyment of the Spirit doth not take away this thirst, but begin it, and increase it: and by this thirst, as one means, are we preserved from that total want and indigency, which shall never again befall us.

Thirdly, Our Saviour gives the reason, why, and whence it is, that they, who drink of this water, are made partakers of his Spirit, shall thirst no more, or never be brought to the condition of total want of grace, which they were in, before they received him: because 'the water which I shall give them,' saith he, the Spirit which I shall bestow upon them, dwelleth in them (as we have shewed) 'shall be a well of water,' a fountain of grace, 'springing up in them to everlasting life,' continuing and perpetuating the grace communicated, unto the full fruition of God in glory. There are (among others) three eminent things in this reason, to confirm us in the faith of the former assertion.

1. The condition or nature of the Spirit in believers. He is a well, a fountain, a spring, that never can, nor will be dry to eternity.

2. The constant supplies of grace that this Spirit affords them, in whom he is: he is water always springing up: so that to say he will refresh saints and believers with his grace, provided that they turn not profligately wicked, is openly to contradict our Saviour Christ, with as direct opposition to the design in the words, as can be imagined. This springing up of grace, which from him is had and received, which is his work in us, is that whereunto this profligate wickedness is opposed: and whilst that is, this cannot be. There is an everlasting inconsistency between profligate wickedness, and a never-failing spring of grace.

3. His permanency in this work and efficacy by it; this living water springs up to everlasting life: he ceases not,

ˣ Matt. v. 6.

until our spiritual life be consummated in eternity. This then is the sum of this promise of our Saviour; he gives his Holy Spirit to his, who lives in them, and gives them such continual supplies of grace, that they shall never come to a total want of it; as they do of elementary water, who have once drank thereof. And from this spring doth this argument flow. They on whom the Spirit is bestowed to abide with them for ever, and to whom he constantly yields such supplies of grace, as that they shall never be reduced to a total want for ever, they shall certainly and infallibly persevere: but that this is the condition of all that come to Christ by believing, or that Christ hath promised, that so it shall be with them, is clear from his own testimony now insisted on: *ergo*.

Unto their argument from the promise of our Saviour, Mr. Goodwin endeavours an answer, chap. 11. sect. 10—12. pp. 232, 233. and in the preface of it tells us, 'That this Scripture doth but face (if so much) the business in hand:' to face it, I suppose, is to appear at first view in its defence; and this indeed cannot well or colourably be denied, the words of it punctually expressing the very truth we intend to prove thereby: and this notwithstanding the allaying qualification ('if so much'), must needs somewhat prejudice the ensuing evasions; but we are yet farther confident, that upon the more diligent and strict examination, it will be found, to speak to the very heart and soul of the business in hand: and the considerations of his reasons to the contrary, doth seem only to give us farther light herein, and assurance hereof. He says then,

'Here is no promise made, that they who once believe, how unworthily soever they shall behave themselves, shall still be preserved by the Spirit of God, or the Spirit of God in believing, or that they shall be necessitated always to believe.'

Ans. This is the old play still: it is not at all our intendment to produce any promise of safeguarding men in the love of God, how vile soever they may prove, but of preserving them from all such unworthiness, as should render them utterly incapable thereof: and this is plainly here asserted, in the assurance given of the perpetual residence of the Spirit in them, with such continual supplies of grace from him, as shall certainly preserve them from any such state or condition as is imagined: of being necessitated to believe, I have spoken formerly. The expression is neither used by us, nor proper to the thing itself, about which it is used, nor known in the Scripture as to this purpose, and therefore we justly reject it, as to its signifying any thing of the way and manner, whereby we are preserved by the power of God, through faith unto salvation. If it denotes only the certainty and infallibility of the event, as the phrase or lo-cution is improper, so to deny that there is a promise of our being preserved by the Spirit of God in believing, is not to answer our argument, but to beg the thing in question, yea to deny the positive assertion of the Lord Christ: but if there be not such a promise in the words, what then is in them, what do they contain? Saith he,

2. 'They are only a declaration and assertion made by Christ, of the excellency and desirableness of that life, which he comes to give unto the world, above the life of nature, which is common unto all; this, by comparing the words with those in the former verse, is evident: whosoever drinketh of this water, shall thirst again; but whosoever drinketh of the water, that I shall give him, &c. that is, the best means that can be had and enjoyed, to render this pre-sent life free fiom inconveniencies, will not effect it: but whosoever shall drink, enjoy, receive, and believe the doc-trine, which I shall administer unto him, shall hereby be made partaker of such a life, which shall within a short time, if men be careful in the interim to preserve it, by reason of the nature, and peifect condition, and constitution of it, be exempt from all sorrow, trouble, and inconvenience whatso-ever, as being eternal.'

Ans. 1. That these words are only an assertion of the excellency and desirableness of that eternal life, which Christ would give, above the natural, that the woman sued to sustain, and that this appears from the context, is said indeed, but no more. It is true, our Saviour doth divert the thoughts of the woman, from the natural life and care for provision about it, with an insinuation of a better life to be attained: but is this all he doth, or is this the intendment of the words under consideration? Doth not the main of the opposition, or difference which at present he speaks unto, lie in the supplies, that are given for the two kinds of life, whereof he speaks? The water he tells her, which she drew from that well by which he sat, for the supply of her natural life, was such, that after her drinking of it, she should quickly return to the same condition of thirst, as formerly before she drank of it; but that which he gave, was such, as that whoever drank of it, should thirst no more, but be certainly preserved in, and unto the full fruition of that life, whereof it is the means and supply. The opposition is not between the lives continued, but the mean of consolation and its efficacy.

2. It is not the condition of the life natural, which is subject to dissolution, and not capable of perfection, that is the reason why they thirst again and again, that have water natural for the refreshment thereof. But it is the nature of the means itself, which is supplied, that is not fitted nor suited to permanency and abiding usefulness (as the water which Christ promises, is), that he insists on. There is not any thing leads us to suppose, that it is the imperfection of life, and not the condition of the means of natural life, that is primarily intended in the instituted comparison: though the frailty, and nothingness of that life also, be afterward intimated, in the substitution of eternal life unto the thoughts of the poor woman, in the room thereof.

3. I say that it is not the doctrine of Christ, but his Spirit principally, that he is here said to give as water: and that this is not promised to make men partakers of eternal life, if in the interim they be careful to preserve it; but to preserve them to it, and to give them that care, which, as a grace, is needful thereunto. The plain intendment of the promise is, that by the water they drink they shall be kept and preserved in the life, whereof they are made partakers, unto the fulness and perfection of it; which preservation by the parenthesis ('if any be careful in the interim to preserve it'), is directly taken away from the Spirit that Christ promiseth, and assigned to men's own care, even in contradistinction to all the benefits, which they receive by him, being so bestowed on them. The difference then here between Jesus Christ and Mr. Goodwin, is this; Christ saith, 'The water that he shall give, will be a well springing up to ever-

lasting life;' Mr. Goodwin, That it is the care of men to preserve themselves, that produces that effect.

4. The present exemption, which we have by the waters of Christ's giving, is not from sorrow and trouble, but from thirst: that is, from what is opposed unto, and is destructive of that life, which he also gives, as natural thirst is unto natural life. But of this thirst, and our exemption from it, I have spoken before. It is not then the nature and condition of the life promised, that he points unto, no farther than as it is coincident with the means of it here spoken of. Indeed this means of life, is our life, as to the inchoation of it here below, and its daily growing up unto perfection. But he adds, sect. 11.

1. ' That he doth not oppose that life, which accrues unto men by drinking that water which he gives them, unto the natural life, which they live, by other means, in respect of the present condition, or constitution of it, or as it is enjoyed by men in this present world, is evident from hence, because he asserts it free from thirst (' shall never thirst'). Now we know that the saints themselves, notwithstanding that life of grace which is in them, by drinking that water that Christ hath given them, are yet subject to both kinds of thirst, as well that which is corporeal or natural, as that which is spiritual; yea, the spiritual thirst unto which they are now subject, though it argues a deficiency of what they would father have, or desire to be; and in that respect, is troublesome, yet is it argumentative of the goodness of their condition; Matt. v. 6.'

Ans. 1. The sum of this answer is, that the life here spoken of and promised, is not that spiritual life whereof we are here made partakers, but eternal life, which is for to come, which, when any attain, they shall never fail in, or fall from; but whether they may or shall attain it or no, here is nothing spoken. But here is no notice taken of the main opposition insisted on by our Saviour, between the supplies of the Spirit for life eternal, which fail not, nor suffers them to thirst, to whom they are given, and the supplies of natural life, by elementary water, notwithstanding which, they, who are made partakers thereof, do in a short season come to a total want of it again. Instead of answers to our argument from this place, we meet with nothing but perpetual diversions from the whole scope and intendment of it, and at last are told, that the promise signifies only, that men should not want grace when they come to heaven.

2. To prove that there is no promise of any abiding spiritual life here, those words ' they shall never thirst,' are produced; that we shall have our life continued to the full enjoyment of it unto eternity, because such are the supplies of the Spirit bestowed on us, that we shall never thirst, is the argument of our Saviour: that there is no such life promised, or here to be attained, because in it we shall not thirst, is Mr. Goodwin's.

3. It is not the intendment of our Saviour, to prove that we shall not thirst, because we shall have such a life; but the quite contrary, that we shall have such a life, and shall assuredly be preserved, because the supplies of the Spirit which he gives, will certainly take away the thirst, which is so opposite to it, as to be destructive of it.

4. It is true, the saints, notwithstanding this promise, are still liable to thirst, that thirst, intimated Matt. v. 6. after righteousness; but not at all to that thirst, which they have a promise here to be freed from; a thirst of a universal want of that water wherewith they are refreshed; and that their freedom from this thirst, is their portion in this life, we have the testimony of Christ himself; ' he that believes on me, shall thirst no more;' John vi. 35. And the reason of their not thirsting is, the receiving and drinking in that water which Christ gives them, as himself says, is ' his Spirit, which they receive who believe on him;' John vii. 38, 39. Neither is that thirst of theirs which doth remain, troublesome, as is insinuated, it being a grace of the Spirit, and so quieting and composing; though they are troubled for the want of that in its fulness, which they thirst after, yet their thirst is no way troublesome: that then which is farther added by Mr. Goodwin, is exceeding sophistical.

Saith he, ' By the way, this spiritual thirst, which is incident unto the life which is derived from Christ, and the waters given by him unto men, as it is enjoyed and possessed by them in this present world, is (according to the purport of our Saviour's own arguing) an argument, that for the present, and whilst it is obnoxious to such a thirst, it is dissolvable and may fail; for in the latter part of the said passage, he plainly implies, that the eternalness of that life which springs from the drinking of this water, is the reason or cause, why it is exempt from thirst. Let the whole passage be read and minded, and this will clearly appear: if then the eternality of a life, be the cause or reason why it is free from the inconveniency of thirst, evident it is, that such a life which is not free from thirst, is not, during this weakness or imperfection of it, eternal, or privileged against dissolution.'

Ans. 1. That we cannot thirst under the enjoyment of the life promised, proves this life not here to be enjoyed, is proved, because the eternalness of this life is the cause of its exemption from thirst; but that the plain contrary is the intendment of the Holy Ghost, I presume is evident to all men. The reason of our preservation to eternal life, and being carried on thereunto, is apparently assigned to those supplies of the Spirit, whereby our thirst is taken away; the taking away of our thirst, is the certain means of our eternal life, not a consequent of the eternity of it. All the proof of what is here asserted, is, 'let the whole passage be read and minded,' in which appeal, I dare acquiesce before the judgment-seat of any believer in the world, whose concernment this is. It is here then supposed, that the eternity of the life promised, is the cause of their not thirsting, in whom it is, which is besides the text; and that they may thirst again (in the sense spoken of) who drink of that water of the Spirit, which Christ gives, which is contrary unto it; and of these two supposals, is this part of this discourse composed.

The ensuing discourse, rendering a reason, upon the account whereof, life may be called eternal, though it be interrupted and cut off, we shall have farther time, God assisting, to consider, and to declare its utter inconsistency with the intendment of the Holy Ghost in the expressions now before us.

He adds then, in the last place, sect. 12. 'That the intendment of Christ is not, that the water he gives shall always end in the issue of eternal life, but that it lies in a tendency thereunto.'

Ans. Which, upon the matter, is all one, as if he had said, 'Christ saith indeed, that the water which he gives shall spring up unto everlasting life, and wholly remove that thirst, which is comprehensive of all interveniences that might hinder it' (as God said to Adam, 'In the day thou eatest of that fruit, thou shalt die'), ' but he knew full well, that it might otherwise come to pass :' which, whether it doth not amount to a calling of his truth and credit, in his word and promises, into question, deserves (as I suppose) Mr. Goodwin's serious consideration. To conclude then, our Saviour hath assured us, that the living water which he gives us, shall take away such thirst, all such total want of grace and Spirit be it to be brought about, not by this or that means, but by what means soever), as should cause us to come short of eternal life with himself, which we shall look upon, as a promise of the saints' perseverance in faith, notwithstanding all the exceptions, which as yet to the contrary hath been produced.

Having thus long insisted on this influence of the mediation of Christ, into the continuance of the love and favour of God unto believers, by procuring the Spirit for them, sending him to them, to 'dwell in them,' and abide with them for ever (the most effectual principle of their continuance with God), give me leave farther to confirm the truth of what hath been spoken, by remarking some inferences, which the Scripture holds out unto us, upon a supposition of those assertions, which we have laid down concerning the indwelling of the Spirit, and the assistance which we receive from him on that account, all tending to the end and purpose we have in hand. As,

First, Because ' the Spirit dwells in us,' we are therefore to consider, and dispose of our persons as ' temples of the Holy Ghost,' that is, of this indwelling Spirit: the Scripture manifesting hereby, that the doctrine of the indwelling of the Spirit, is not only a truth, but a very useful truth, being made the fountain of, and the enforcement unto, so great a duty. He dwells in us, and we are to look well to his habitation; our Saviour tells us, that when the evil spirit finds his ' ʸdwelling swept and garnished,' he instantly takes possession, and brings company with him: he will not be absent from it, when it is fitted for his turn. In reference to the saints and their holy indweller, this the apostle urgeth, 1 Cor. vi. 19.

ʸ Matt. xii. 44.

'Your bodies are the temples of the Holy Ghost, which dwells in you,' whence he concludes, 'whose ye are, not your own,' and therefore ought to ' glorify God in your bodies;' from hence is the strength of his argument, for the avoiding of all uncleanness; ver. 16, 17. ' Know ye not that he who is joined to a harlot, is one body? He who is joined to the Lord, is one spirit: Flee fornication:—know ye not that your body is the temple of the Holy Ghost?' On this account, also, doth he press to universal holiness; 1 Cor. iii. 16, 17. ' Know ye not that ye are the temple of God, and that the Spirit of God dwelleth in you? If any man defile the temple of God, him shall God destroy; for the temple of God is holy, which temple ye are.' In ver. 12—14. the apostle discovers the fruitlessness of building 'hay and stubble,' light and unsound doctrines or practices, upon the foundation of faith in Jesus Christ once laid; and tells us, that all such things shall burn and suffer loss, and put the contrivers and workers of them to no small difficulty in escaping, like men when the garments they are clothed withal; are on fire about them. On the account of this sad event, of foolish and careless walking, he presses, ver. 16. as was said, earnestly to universal holiness, laying down as the great motive thereunto, that which we have insisted on, viz. the ' indwelling of the Holy Spirit in us: know ye not that ye are the temple of God?' The temple, wherein God of old did dwell, was built with hewn stone, cedar-wood, and overlaid with pure gold; and will ye now, who are the spiritual temple of God, build up your souls with hay and stubble? Which he furthers, by that dreadful commination taken from the zeal of God for the purity of his temple; so that on each hand, he doth press to the universal close keeping of our hearts in all holiness and purity, because of the indwelling of the Holy Spirit. And indeed, wherever we are said to be temples of God, or a habitation for him, as it still relates to this cause of the expression which we now insist upon, so there is ever some intimation of holiness, to be pursued on that account; Eph. ii. 21, 22. ' In whom the whole building fitly framed together, groweth unto a holy temple in the Lord; in whom ye also are builded together, for a habitation of God through the Spirit; being made a habitation of the Lord,' by the Spirit's indwelling in us, we grow up or thrive in grace, into a holy temple to the Lord, to be a more complete and well furnished habitation for him.

This then, is that which I say : the truth of what hath formerly been spoken, concerning the manner of the Spirit's abode with us, being procured for us by Jesus Christ, is farther cleared by this inference, that the Scripture makes thereof. The saints are exhorted with all diligence to keep themselves a fit habitation for him, that they may not be unclean and defiled lodgings for the Spirit of purity and holiness. This is, and this is to be, their daily labour and endeavour ; that vain thoughts, unruly passions, corrupt lusts, may not take up any room in their bosom ; that they put not such unwelcome and unsavoury inmates upon the Spirit of grace ; that sin may not dwell, where God dwells. On this ground they may plead with their own souls, and say, Hath the Lord chosen my poor heart, for his habitation ? Hath he said, I delight in it, and there will I dwell for ever ? Hath he forsaken that goodly and stately material temple, whereunto he gave his special presence of old, to take up his abode in a far more eminent way, in a poor sinful soul ? Doth that Holy Spirit, which dwells in Jesus Christ, who was ' holy, blameless, undefiled, separate from sinners, who did no sin, neither was guile found in his mouth,' dwell also in me, that am in and of myself wholly corrupted and defiled ? And shall I be so foolish, so unthankful, as willingly to defile the habitation which he hath chosen ? Shall I suffer vain thoughts, foolish lusts, distempered affections, worldly aims, to put in themselves upon him there ? He is a Spirit of grace : can he bear a graceless corruption to be cherished in his dwelling ? He is a Spirit of holiness ; and shall I harbour in his lodging a frame of worldliness ? He is a Spirit of joy and consolation ; and shall I fill my bosom with foolish fears and devouring cares ? Would not this be a grief unto him ? Would it not provoke the eyes of his glory ? Can he bear it, that, when he is with me, before his face, in his presence, I should spend my time in giving entertainment to his enemies ? He is the High and the Holy One, who dwells in eternity, and he hath chosen to inhabit with me also ; surely I should be more brutish than any man, should I be careless of his habitation. And should not this fill my soul with a holy scorn and indignation against sin? Shall I debase my soul unto any vile lust, which hath this exceeding honour, to be a habitation for the Spirit of God? Hence, upon a view of any defilement of lust or passion, nothing troubles the saints more, nor fills them with more self-abhorrence and confusion of face, than this, that they have rendered their hearts an unsuitable habitation for the Spirit of God. This makes David, upon his sin, cry so earnestly, that the ''Spirit might not depart from him,' being conscious to himself, that he had exceedingly defiled his dwelling-place. And were this consideration always fresh upon the spirits of the saints, were it more constant in their thoughts, it would keep them more upon their guard, that nothing might break in, to disquiet their gracious indweller.

Secondly, Because by the Spirit we have guidance and direction, there is wisdom given unto us, and we are called to a holy discerning between the directions of the Spirit of grace, and the delusions of the spirit of the world, and the seduction of our own hearts. Christ gives this character of his sheep, that they 'know his voice, hear him, and follow him ;' but 'a stranger they will not follow ;' John x. 25. Christ speaks by his Spirit; in his guidance and direction, is the voice of the Lord Jesus, 'He that hath an ear to hear, let him hear what the Spirit saith to the churches ;' Rev. ii. 29. What Christ saith, as to the fountain of revelation, he being the great prophet of the church, that the Spirit saith, as to the efficacy of the revelation, unto the hearts of the saints. And as the 'unction teacheth them,' so do they 'abide in Christ ;' 1 John ii. 27. The seducements of the spirit of the world, either immediately by himself, or immediately by others, are the voice of strangers; between these and the voice of the Spirit of Christ that dwells in them, the saints have a spirit of discerning. This the apostle affirms, 1 Cor. ii. 15. ' He that is spiritual, judgeth all things.' He discerneth between things, and judgeth aright of them. He judgeth 'all things ;' that is, all things of that nature whereof he speaks, that is, the 'things which are freely given us of God ;' ver. 12. for the discerning and knowledge whereof, the Spirit is given them ; ' for the things of God knoweth no man, but the Spirit of God ;' ver. 11. They know also,

<hr>

² Psal. 51.

the suggestions of the spirit of the world, and judge them; 2 Cor. ii. 11. 'We are not ignorant of his devices.' There is a twofold knowledge of the depths and devices of Satan : one with approbation, to the embracing and practice of them ; the other with condemnation, to their hatred and rejection. The first ye have mentioned, Rev. ii. 24. 'As many as have not known the depths of Satan, as they speak :' their doctrinal depths, so they call them : of them our Saviour there speaks. New doctrines were broached by Satan, unintelligible notions ; some pretended to attain an acquaintance with them, and boasted it seems in them, as very great and high attainments. They called them depths, such as poor ordinary believers, that contented themselves with their low forms, could not reach unto : saith Christ, they ' are depths, as they speak :' indeed, in themselves nothing at all, things of no solidity, weight, nor wisdom : but as managed by Satan, they are depths indeed, such as whereby he destroys their souls. And as some approve his doctrinal depths, so some close with his practical depths and embrace them. Men that study his ways and paths, becoming desperately wicked, maliciously scoffing at religion, and despising the profession of it. But there is a knowledge also, of the depths and devices of Satan, leading to judging, condemning, rejecting, and watching against them. The suggestions of Satan, in their infinite variety, their rise, progress, efficacy, and advantages, their various aims and tendencies unto sin, against grace, I do not now consider. But this, I say, those who ' are led by the Spirit of God,' who have directions from him, and guidance, they discern between the voice of the Spirit, which ' dwells in them ;' and the voice of the spirit, which ' dwells in the world.'

Now because this is not always to be done, from the manner of their speaking, the serpent counterfeiting the voice of the dove, and coming on, not only with earnestness and continuance of impulse, but with many fair and specious pretences, making good his impressions, labouring to win the understanding over to that, wherewith he enticeth the affections and passions of men, they use the help of such considerations as these ensuing, to give them direction in attending to the voice of that guide, which leads them into

the paths of truth, and to stop their ears to the songs of
Satan, which would transform them into monsters of disobedience. Thus they know,

1. That all the motions of the Holy Spirit, whereby they
are, and ought to be led, are regular : that he moves them
to nothing, but what is according to the mind of Christ, delivered in the word, which he hath appointed for their rule
to walk by ; to no duty, but what is acceptable to him, and
what he hath revealed so to be ; so that, as believers are to
try the spirits of others, by that standard, whether they are
of God or no, so because of the subtilty of Satan, transform-
ing himself into an angel of light, yea, into a spirit of duty,
whatever immediate motions and impressions fall upon their
spirits, they try them by the rule. It is no dishonour to the
Holy Spirit, yea, it is a great honour to have his motions
within us, tried by the word, that he hath given for a rule
without us. Yea, when any preached by immediate inspiration, he commends those who[b] examined what they delivered by that which he had given out before ; he doth not
now move in us, to give a new rule, but a new light and
power, as was said before. The motions of the spirit of the
world, are for the most part unto things, wherein, though
the persons with whom he deals, may be in the dark or blind,
and darkened by him, yet themselves are against the rule, or
besides it, in the whole, or in part, in respect of some such
circumstances as vitiate the whole performance.

2. They know that the commands and motions of the
Spirit, which dwells in them,[c] are not grievous. The commands of Christ, for the matter of them, are not grievous,
his[d] ' burden is light, his yoke easy :' and the manner,
whereby we are carried out to the performance of them, is
not grievous : ' where the Spirit of the Lord is, there is
liberty ;' 2 Cor. iii. 17. It carries out the soul to duty, in a
free, sweet, calm, ingenuous manner. The motions of the
spirit of the world, even unto good things, and duties (for
so, for farther ends of his, it often falls out that they are), are
troublesome, vexatious, perplexing, grievous, and tumultuating. Satan falls like lightning upon the soul, and comes
upon the powers of it, as a tempest : hence acting in any
thing, upon his closing with, and provoking our convictions,

<hr />

[a] 1 John iv. 1.   [b] Acts xvii 10.   [c] 1 John v. 1.   [d] Matt. xi. 30.

is called a being under the ' spirit of bondage;' Rom. viii. 15.
which is opposed to the Spirit of God, the Spirit of adoption, of liberty, boldness, power, and a sound mind.

3. They know that all motions of the Spirit whereby
they are led, are orderly; as is God's covenant with us,
ordered in all things, so the Spirit of God carries us out
unto every duty, in its own order and season; when as we see
some poor souls to be in such bondage, as to be hurried up
and down, in the matter of duties, at the pleasure of Satan.
They must run from one to another, and commonly neglect
that which they should do; when they are at prayer, then
they should be at the work of their calling; and when they
are at their calling, they are tempted for not laying all aside,
and running to prayer; believers know that this is not from
the Spirit of God, which makes every thing beautiful in its
season.

4. They know that all the workings of the Spirit of God,
as they are good, so also they tend unto a good end. Doth
that stir them up to close walking with God? It is that God
may be glorified, his graces exercised in them, their souls
strengthened in obedience, and their progress in sanctification
furthered? Doth it assure them of the love of God? It is that
they may be more humble, thankful, and watchful? When
all the compliances and combinations of Satan, and men's
corrupt hearts, even when they compel to good duties, are
for false, evil, and corrupt ends: duty is pressed to pacify
conscience; peace is given to make men secure; gifts are
stirred up to tempt to pride; and, indeed, it may easily be
observed, that the devil never doth any work, but he will
quickly come for his wages. By the help, I say, of these
and such like considerations, the saints of God, in whom
this Spirit doth dwell, are enabled to discern and know the
voice of their leader and guide, from the nearest resemblance
of it, that the spirit, which is in the world, doth, or at any
time can make show of. And this indwelling of the Spirit
yields a considerable contribution of strength towards the
confirmation of the main theses undertaken to be proved.
Our adversaries dispute about the removal of acquired habits,
but how infused habits may be cast out or expelled, they
have not [in] any tolerable measure been able to declare. If
moreover it shall be evinced, as it hath been by plentiful

testimonies of Scripture, that the Holy Ghost himself dwells in believers, what way can be fixed on for his expulsion? That he cannot be removed, but by his own will, the will of him that sends him, I suppose will easily be granted. Whilst he abides with them, they are accepted with God, and in covenant with, him. That God, whilst his children' are in such a state and condition, doth take away his Spirit from, them, and give them up to the power of the devil, is incumbent on our adversaries to prove.

But to return at length from this digression. Thus far have we proceeded in manifesting, upholding, and vindicating, that influence, which the oblation of Christ hath into the preservation of the saints, in the love and favour of God unto the end. His intercession being eminently effectual also to the same end and purpose, comes in the next place to be considered.

CHAP. IX.

The intercession of Christ. The nature of it. Its aim, not only that believers continuing so, may be saved, but that they may be preserved in believing. This farther proved from the typical intercession of the Judaical high-priest. The tenor of Christ's intercession as manifested, John xvii. 11. opened, and ver. 12—15. The result of the argument from thence. The saints' perseverance fully confirmed. Rom. viii. 33, 34. at large explained. Mr. G.'s interpretation of the place in all the parts of it confuted. Vain supposals groundlessly interserted into the apostle's discourse. What Christ intercedes for, for believers, farther manifested. The sum of what is assigned to the intercession of Christ, by Mr. G. How far it is all from yielding the least consolation to the saints, manifested. The reasons of the foregoing interpretation, proposed and answered. The end assigned of the intercession of Christ, answered. God works perseverance actually: a supply of mercies, that may not be effectual, not to be ascribed thereunto. Farther objections answered: Christ not the minister of sin by this doctrine. Supposals and instances upon the former interpretation, disproved and rejected. A brief account of our doctrine concerning the intercession of Christ for believers: and of the true end of the act of his mediation. The close of the argument, and of the first part of this treatise.

OF the intercession of Christ, both as to the nature of its typical representation by the[a] high priest's entering into the holy of holies, every year with blood, and its effectual in-

[a] Heb. ix. 7.

fluence into the perfect, complete salvation of believers, so
much hath been spoken by others, and the whole of the doctrine delivered, with so much clearness, spiritualness, and
strength, that I shall not need to add any thing thereunto.
That Christ intercedes for the preservation of believers in the
love and favour of his Father to the end, is that which I intend to manifest, and which may (as I suppose) be very easily
undeniably evinced. Some few considerations will make
way for the demonstration of the truth which is under consideration, or confirmation of the perseverance of saints,
from the intercession of Christ.

First, The intercession of Christ being his appearance for
us in the presence of God ; (Heb. ix. 24. He is gone into
heaven, ἐμφανισθῆναι τῷ προσώπῳ τοῦ Θεοῦ, to make a legal
appearance, for our defence, before the judgment-seat of
God ; and by being there is our advocate; 1 John ii. 1. he is
said to ' save us to the utmost;' Heb. vii. 25.) there is certainly something or other, that he puts in for, in the behalf
of them in whose cause he appears and sues, that so he may
save them to the utmost. Now this must be, either, that
being and continuing believers, they may be saved, or that
they may believe and continue believers unto salvation.
That the first is not the sole import and aim of the intercession of Christ, may be manifested, from this double consideration.

1. From the nature of the thing itself. There is nothing
but the establishment of the very law of the gospel (' He
that believeth shall be saved'), wrapped up in this interpretation of the intercession of Christ. But this neither hath
Christ any need to intercede for, it being ratified, confirmed,
and declared from the beginning, neither is there, or can
there any opposition be made against it, to shake, weaken,
or disturb it, in the least : it depending solely on the truth
and unchangeableness of God, not being vested by any condition whatsoever, in any other subject : nor would this be
availing to his militant church, whose preservation he aims
at and intends in his intercession ; for the whole of his desires may be granted him to the uttermost, and yet his whole
church at any time militant, perish for ever. Though not
one soul should continue believing to the end, though the
gates of hell should prevail against every one that names

the name of Christ in the world, yet that truth, 'He that believeth, shall be saved,' taken in the sense of our adversaries, for a promise to perseverance in believing, and not a promise to actual true believers, might stand firm for ever. To say then, that this is the whole intercession of Christ for his church, is to say, that in his whole intercession, he interceded not at all for his church. He[b] is heard in his intercession, and he may be heard to the uttermost in this, and yet his whole church be so far from being saved to the utmost, as utterly to be destroyed and consumed.

2. Doubtless the intercession of Christ, must answer the representation of it, which the apostle so much insists on; Heb. vii. 9. Of the oblation of Christ there were many types in the Aaronical priesthood of the law: of his intercession, but one principally; namely, that solemn entrance of the high-priest with blood and incense into the holiest of holies, in the great anniversary sacrifice, on the tenth day of the seventh month (on the which day also the great jubilee, or joyful time of deliverance, typifying our deliverance by Christ began): hereunto is added the priesthood of Melchizedek: whereof there is mention neither of its beginning nor ending, to secure us of the continuance of our Mediator in the act of his priesthood for ever. Now the end of the high-priest's so entering into this holy place, was to carry on the work of expiation and atonement to perfection, and complete peace with God, in the behalf of them, for whom he offered without. And, therefore, the Holy Ghost saith, that his entrance with blood, was, to 'offer for himself, and the errors of the people;' Heb. ix. 7. It being but a continuation of his oblation begun without, unto a complete atonement. And, therefore, there is no real difference between the efficacy of the death of Christ, and that of his intercession, upon the actual accomplishment of it. It being then, the complete taking away of the sins and errors of the people, as to the guilt of them, and the continuance of their peace with God, which was intended by the high-priest's entrance with blood into the holiest of holies, that which answers thereunto, or the deliverance of believers from the whole guilt of sin, and their preservation in the love and favour of God, is the intendment of Christ in his intercession.

b John xi. 44.

Let the effects and fruits of the oblation of Christ be bounded and limited to the procuring of a new way of salvation, without purchasing for any one person whatever, power and grace to walk in that way, and then exclude his intercession, from any influence into the preservation of them, who do enter that way therein; and perhaps, indifferent men will scarce think the glory and honour of the Lord Jesus to be of any great regard with us.

3. That this is the import of Christ's intercession for believers is evident by that preface, which we have thereof, John xvii. being a manifest declaration on earth of that, which Christ lives in heaven to do. This was the incense wherewith he entered into the holy place, which he now prepared, and which was afterward beaten small in his agony, that it might be ready to make a sweet perfume at his entrance into heaven, as he was sprinkled with his own blood. That Christ interceded, and for his elect for whom he died, that they may believe, our adversaries deny ; but that he intercedes for actual believers, hath not hitherto been questioned. What it is, which he requests on their behalf, the tenor of that power of his (John xvii.) will manifest ; ver. 11. Saith he, ' Holy Father keep through thine own name, those whom thou hast given me, that they may be one as we are ;' keep them' from sin and ruin, every thing that will hinder them from union with me. What is it that our Saviour here prays for, and for whom is he so engaged ? That it is for believers, as such, for whom he puts up these supplications, our adversaries in the cause in hand do contend. That these may be kept through the power of God, unto unity among themselves, which they have by their union with him, is his dying request for them. He prays not for such oneness, as is consistent with their separation from him and his Father's love. Where now shall we fix the supposed failure of those, who effectually and eventually are kept up to spiritual union, cannot fall out of, nor fall off from (totally nor finally), the love of God. Either Christ is not heard in his request, or the Father cannot keep them by his power, if these thus interceded for, are not preserved. Many temptations, many oppositions, great tribulations without, strong corruptions within, they must needs meet withal : these they have no power in themselves to overcome nor to resist. Should they

be left to themselves, they would never be able to hold out
to the end ; saith Christ, I shall lose these poor sheep, for
whom I have 'laid down my life' to bring them unto thee : holy
Father do thou therefore keep and preserve them from all these
evils, that they may not prevail over them. And 'keep them
through thy name,' thy power (for we are kept through the
power of God unto salvation), let thy power be exerted for
their preservation.   And what is too strong for thy power ?
Who can take them out of thy hand ? Lay that upon them
for their defence, shew it out in their behalf, that all their
enemies may feel the weight and strength thereof.   ' Keep
them through thy name,' thy grace, let that be sufficient for
them, let them have such supplies of gospel grace, and pardoning mercy (concerning which I manifested my name unto
them, ver. 6. and so revealed thee a Father), that they may
be encouraged to trust in that name of thine, and to stay
themselves upon thee; where the failure is, doubtless is not
easy to manifest.   In the verse following, our Saviour adds
many motives to make his intercession prevalent in their behalf.

   First, ver. 12. he saith, that according to that commission that he had received, ' he had faithfully preserved them
whilst that he was in the world;' and now being ready to
leave them, as to his bodily presence, he urges the special
preservation of his Father as needful, that after all the care
and cost which he had laid out about them, they might not
utterly perish.   And then,

   Secondly, ver. 13. he urges the necessity, that they
should have some assurance of it in the midst of all their
troubles and trials, that they may have consolation upon
their confidence in the words which Christ had spoken to
them, that they should be preserved through all difficulties
unto the end.   And he farther urges,

   Thirdly, ver. 14. from the certain opposition that they
should meet withal: ' the world hates them,' and will, without doubt, use all ways and means possible, for their ruin
and destruction ; giving also the reason, why the 'world
hateth them,' and will oppose them, which is such a one as
must needs engage the heart and good-will of God for their
preservation, to wit, because they receive the word of his
dear Son, and upon that account, left the world, sepa-

rated from it, and became its enemies; and shall they
now be left to the rage and fury of the world in this condition? That be far from thee; 'holy Father keep them.'
Hereupon,

Fourthly, ver. 15. he reneweth his prayer in their behalf, with a farther opening of his mind, as to what he had
last spoken of. The world, the world being vile, wretched,
deceitful, and set upon opposition against them, a man
would have thought, that the Lord Jesus should have desired, that his saints might be taken out from the midst of
this world, and set in a quiet place by themselves, where
they might no more be troubled with the baits and oppositions of it. But this is not that which he requests; he hath
another work for them to do in the world, they are to bear
witness to him and his truth, by their faith and obedience to
convince the wicked unbelieving world; they are to glorify his name by doing, and suffering for him; so that this
is no part of his request; 'I pray not,' saith he, 'that thou
shouldest take them out of the world, but that they may not
be prevailed on, nor conquered by the evil that is in the
world.' That they may be kept and preserved from the
power of evil, which would separate them from me and my
love. This he presseth for, and this he is heard in; and
that, not only for his apostles and present followers, but as
he tells you, ver. 20. 'for all that should believe on him to
the end of the world.'

The things prayed for, the reason of his intercession, the
opposition against the accomplishment of the things interceded for, the distinction put between them for whom he
intercedes and the perishing world, all delivered in plain
and expressive terms, evidently evince the intendment of
Christ in his intercession, evidently to regard the safeguarding of believers in the love and favour of God, by their continuance in believing, and preservation from the power of
temptations and oppositions, arising against their persever-
rance in communion with God.

The result of what hath been spoken, as to its influence
into the confirmation of the truth under demonstration,
amounts unto thus much. That which the Lord Jesus as
Mediator requesteth, and prayeth for continually of the Father, according to his mind, in order to the accomplishment

of the promises made to him, and covenant with him (all his desires being bottomed upon his exact perfect performance of the whole will of God, both in doing and suffering), that shall certainly be accomplished and brought to pass; but thus, in this manner, upon these accounts, doth the Lord Jesus intercede for the perseverance of believers and their preservation in the love of the Father unto the end; therefore they shall undoubtedly be so preserved. It is confessed, that the persons interceded for, are believers, all believers that then were, or should be to the end of the world (the efficacy of this intercession having commenced from the foundation thereof), the thing prayed for is their preservation in the state of union with Christ, and one another, the motives used for the obtaining this request in their behalf, are taken from the work they have to do, and the opposition they were to meet withal, and all the saints being thus put into the hand of God, who shall take them from thence? On what account is it, that they shall not be preserved? To say they shall be thus preserved, in case themselves depart not wilfully from God, is to say, they shall be preserved, in case they preserve themselves, as will afterward be farther manifested.

This argument is proposed by the apostle, in the most triumphant assurance of the truth and certainty of the inference contained in it, that he any where useth, in any case whatsoever; Rom. viii. 33, 34. 'Who shall lay any thing to the charge of God's elect? It is God that justifieth; who is he that condemneth? It is Christ that died, yea, rather that is risen again, who is even at the right hand of God, who also maketh intercession for us:' he lays the immunity of the elect and justified persons, from just crimination, or condemnation, on the foundation of the oblation and intercession of Christ; the first part of this argument from the oblation of Christ ('who shall condemn? It is Christ that died') asserting the immunity of believers from condemnation, upon the account of the punishing of all their sins in Christ, and the perfect satisfaction made by his death for them, whence the justice of God, in the issue, will not have any thing to lay to their charge, we have formerly insisted on; the other, which the apostle induces emphatically and comparatively, though not in respect of procurement and purchase made, yet of assurance to be given, with μᾶλλον δὲ, in respect of his oblation, is that now before us. To make the assurance of believers plentiful, that they may know both the truth of his first general assertion, that all things shall work together for good to them ; and this particular conclusion, now laid down by way of interrogation, rejecting all evil opposed to their former enjoyment, who shall lay any thing to their charge? who shall condemn? He gives them a threefold consideration of the state and actings of the Lord Christ, after the expiation of their sins by his blood, in reference to them ; 1. ' He is risen.' 2. ' He is at the right hand of God.' 3. ' Maketh intercession for them.' The first denoting his acquitment, and theirs in him (for he died in their stead), from all the sins that were charged on him; for he was declared to be the Son of God, accepted with him, and justified from all that debt which he undertook, in his resurrection ; and, if he be risen, who shall lay any thing to the charge of them whom he died for, and for all whose sins, in their stead, he was acquitted? The second is his exaltation and power; for, ' having purged our sins, he is sat down at the right hand of the majesty on high;' Heb. i. 3. receiving thereby a most plenary demonstration of his Father's good-will to him and his, in respect of the work that he had undertaken and gone through for them ; for, if he had not made an end of sin, when he was obedient unto death, the death of the cross, he could not expect that God should give him a name above every name, with fulness of power to give eternal life to all that the father gave him ; this, to assure us that he will do, having power in his own hand, the apostle adds, who also intercedes for us ; hereby (thirdly) testifying abundantly his good-will and care for our salvation ; upon these considerations, the apostle leads the faith of the saints of God, to make a conclusion, which is to be believed as a divine truth, that tenders to us the doctrine we have under demonstration, triumphant against all objections and oppositions that can be made against it: and hence we thus argue : those against whom no charge can be laid, who cannot by any means be separated from the love of God in Christ, cannot totally and finally fall away from faith, and fall out of God's favour ; but that this is the condition of all true believers, is evident from the context. It is of all

that are called according to the purpose of God, sanctified
and justified, the proper description of all and only believers,
that the apostle affirms these things, and to whom he ascribes
the condition mentioned: now that this is the state and
condition of those persons, the apostle manifesteth from the
causes of it; viz. the oblation and intercession of Christ in
their behalf: for those for whom he died, and doth intercede, are on that account, exempted from any such charge,
as might be of prevalency to separate them from God.

Mr. Goodwin, attempts indeed once more to reinforce
the triumphed over enemies of the saints, and to call them
once more to make head against the intercession of Christ,
but, with what ill success, the consideration of what arguments he useth with them, and for them, will demonstrate:
thus then he addresseth himself to his task; chap. 11. sect.
33. p. 248. ' I answer, It is no where affirmed, that Christ
intercedes for the perseverance of the saints in their faith, or,
they who once believed, should never cease believing, how
sinful and wicked soever they should prove afterward ; but
Christ intercedes for his saints, as such, and so continuing
such, that no accusation from any hand whatsoever, may be
heard against them, that no afflictions or sufferings, which
they meet with in the world, may cause any alienation, or
abatement in the love of God towards them : but that God
will protect and preserve them under them ; and consequently, that they may be maintained at an excellent rate of
consolation in every state and condition, and against all in-
terposuies of any creature to the contrary.'

This answer hath long since ceased to be new to us : it
is that indeed which is the shield behind which Mr. Goodwin lies, to avoid the force of all manner of arguments pointed
against himself, though it be the most weak and frivolous
that ever, I suppose, was used in so weighty a matter ; it is
here cast (as he hath many moulds and shapes to cast it in)
into a denial of the assumption of our syllogism, and a reason of that denial ; first he denies, that Christ intercedes for
believers, that they may persevere in their faith ; he prays
not for their perseverance.

2. His reason of this is twofold : 1. A supposal, that
' they may prove so wicked, as not to continue believing.'
2. A description of what Christ intercedes for, in the behalf

of believers, viz..' that they may continue in God's love, if they do continue to believe, notwithstanding all their afflictions :' ' homo homini quid interest ?' Whether men will or no, these must pass for oracular dictates.

1. For the first : let what hath been spoken already be weighed, and see if there be not yet hope left for poor souls, that Christ prays for them, that their faith fail not ; and by the way, who will not embrace this comfortable doctrine,- that will assure him in his agonies, temptations, and failings, that all help and supplies are made out to him, from and by the Lord Jesus, in whom is all his hope ; and that he receives of his Father, upon his intercession, all the fruits of his death, and bloodshedding in his behalf. But that he should believe, or being tempted should be preserved in believing, of that Christ takes no thought, nor did ever intercede with his Father for any such an end or purpose ; such consolation might befit Job's friends, ' miserable comforters, physicians of no value.' But of this before.

2. For that supposal of his, of their proving wicked afterward to an inconsistency with believing, it hath often been corrected for a sturdy beggar, and sent away grumbling and hungry, and were it not for pure necessity, would never once be owned any more by its master ; Christ intercedes not for believers, that they may persevere in the faith upon such foolish supposals, whose opposite is continuance in the faith, and so is coincident with the thing itself interceded for : to intercede that they may continue believing, is, to intercede that they may never be so wicked, as Mr. Goodwin supposeth they may be. The end of Christ's intercession for the saints asserted, is, that they may never wickedly depart from God ; doth Mr. Goodwin indeed take this to be the tenor of the doctrine he opposeth, and of the argument which he undertakes to answer? viz. That the faith of believers, and the continuance of that, is interceded for, without any reference to the work of faith in gospel obedience, and communion with God in Christ? Or if he thinks not so, why doth he so often insist on this calumnious evasion ?

3. In giving the aim of Christ in his intercession for believers, we have this new cogent argument against our position ; ' Christ intercedes for the things here by me mentioned,

therefore he doth not intercede for the perseverance of the saints.' But why so? Is there any inconsistency in these things, any repugnancy in terms, or contrariety of the things themselves? Christ intercedes, that believers may enjoy the love of God; therefore he doth not intercede, that they may be established in believing.

2. The sum of all that is here ascribed to the intercession of Christ, at the best is, that God will confirm and ratify that everlasting law, that believers, continuing so to the end, shall be saved, which whether it be the sum of Christ's intercession for his church or no, that church will judge; if there be any thing farther, or of more importance to them, in what is assigned to it by Mr. Goodwin, it is wrapped up in the knot of, &c. which I am not able to untie.

. 3. Those words of the apostle, 'who shall lay any thing to the charge of God's elect,' do not denote, this is that the intercession of Christ for them, that no accusation be admitted against them, whilst they believe; which is no more but the confirmation of that general proposition of the gospel before mentioned. But it is the conclusion which they make upon the account of the intercession of Christ, in the application of the promise of the gospel to their own souls: neither is there any more weight in that which follows, 'that there be no abatement or alienation of the love of God from them, upon the account of their sufferings and afflictions,' which, for the most part, are for his sake; what saints of God were almost so much as once tempted with a conceit, that God's love should be abated, or alienated from them, because they suffered for him?

And this is the foundation of that 'excellent rate of consolation at which the saints, upon the account of the intercession of Christ may be maintained.' Into afflictions, temptations, trials, they may fall: but if they continue in faith and love, they shall not be rejected. No creature shall be heard against them; that Christ takes care for; but for the worst enemies they have, their own lusts, corruptions, and unbelief, the fiery darts of Satan fighting against their souls, their continuance in believing, the falling from whence is indeed all the danger they are exposed to (for whilst they continue so doing, all other things are lighter than vanity), that Christ takes no care about (though he pray, that God

would sanctify them and keep them), but they must shift for
themselves as well as they can, he will not, doth not inter
cede for them, that from these they may be preserved;
doubtless, he that shall think to be maintained long at any
high rate of consolation, and lays in no other, nor no better
provision to live on, than this mentioned, will quickly be
reduced to a dry morsel.   ir

But yet some reasons of the foregoing interpretation of
this place of the apostle, Rom. viii. are offered unto us.

'This to be the tenor and effect of Christ's intercession
for his saints,' saith he, 'is evident from the first of the three
passages cited: and for that demand 'who shall separate us
from the love of Christ,' it is not meant from the love wherewith we love Christ, but from the love wherewith Christ
loveth us; as we are saints, and abide in his love, and keep
his commands: neither is it so to be conceived, as if sin,
wickedness, looseness, profaneness, could not unsaint men,
and hereby separate them from that love, wherewith Christ
sometimes loved them (for that iniquity will separate between men and their God, is evident from Isa. lix. 2.), but
the clear meaning is, that nothing, no creature whatsoever,
person, or thing, can make Christ an enemy to those, who
shall in faith and love, cleave fast unto him.'

Ans. 1. All this respecteth only one expression in this
one place of Scripture, and ariseth not, with the least power,
against our argument taken from many places in conjunction,
explicatory one of another; it runs also upon the same mistake with the former, taking the exaltation of believers upon
the intercession of Christ in their behalf, which holds out
the issue of it, to be expressive of the matter of his intercession, being only a demonstration of the event of it; but
grant this to be the tenor and effect of Christ's intercession,
that believers may not be separated from his love: is he
heard therein, or is he not? whatsoever be the issue of the
question, our procedure will be facile. But it is said, that
it is not the 'love wherewith we love Christ, but that wherewith he loveth us, that we shall not be separated from;' take
this also for granted, that it is that, and that only: will this
advantage your cause? If we be never separated from that
love that Christ bears us, is it possible we should wholly be
separated from that love, that we bear him? Wherein con-

sists our separation from that love, that Christ bears us?
How is it caused, or may it be procured? Is it not by the
loss of our faith and love to him? Or at least is it not an inseparable consequence thereof? Or can it possibly come to
pass any otherwise, than on that account? If then he intercedes that we may not be separated from that love he bears
us, and that love infers the continuance of ours, doth he not
withal intercede, that we may never lose that love, wherewith we love him, by which we continue in his love? If the
old shift be not at hand for a relief, this young part of the
answer will instantly suffer loss. It is added therefore, 'he
loveth us, as we are saints and abide in his love,' that is (for
so we must understand it), whilst we are so; for that he
bears any effectual love to us, to keep us up to saintship,
that is denied; it is true, Christ loveth us as saints, and as
abiding in his commandments; but it is also his love to
keep us, and he intercedeth that we may abide in that condition, wherein alone it is impossible for us so to do: neither
is the question, whether sin, looseness, profaneness, do not
separate between God and men, more or less; but whether
believers shall not be preserved from such looseness and
profaneness, as would make a total separation between God
and them; and if God intercedes, as is added in the close,
that nothing may make him an enemy to us, certainly he
must intercede that no sin may do it; for indeed, sin is
something in this business; and this must be, as to the
keeping us from it. I suppose no man thinks any thing in
all this discourse of Mr. Goodwin's, to look like the least
attempt of proof, that Christ doth not intercede for the perseverance of saints. Neither hath he confidence enough positively to deny it, and therefore spends his whole discourse
hereabout in evasions and diversions. Let it be directly
denied, that Christ doth not intend that the faith of believers
may not fail, that his saints may be preserved and saved;
and we know what we have to apply ourselves unto: and if
the contrary cannot be proved, the saints know what they
have to trust unto, that they may no longer lean on that
which will yield them no supportment. If this will not be,
let it on the other hand be granted, that he doth so intercede; for, 'de unoquoque affirmare, aut negare, verum est.'
As to this then he proceeds:

Secondly, ' Were it granted, that part of Chiist's intercession for his saints, is, that their faith may never fail, yet the intent thereof would not necessarily, nor indeed with any, competent probability, be this, that no sin nor wickedness whatsoever, that shall or can be perpetrated by them, might cause them to make shipwreck of their faith, but rather that God would graciously vouchsafe such means and such a presence of his Spirit unto them, as whereby they may be richly enabled, to keep themselves in faith and good con-. science, to the end.'

. *Ans.* Whether prejudiced men will grant it or no, it is clearly proved, if the words of Christ themselves may be taken for proof, that he intercedes for his saints, that their faith may not fail, and that, notwithstanding the interposition of any such sins, as they can or may (' suppositis supponendis,' amongst which is his intercession) fall into; so he tells Peter upon the prediction of his dreadful fall, that nevertheless he had prayed for him, that his faith should not fail. That they may fall into such sins, and continue in such, as are inconsistent with their acceptation with God, according to the terms and tenor of the new covenant, is that, which we have been disproving all this while; and which our author ought not, as he doth in all his reasonings, to suppose; in the not failing or dying of their faith, in their preservation therein, is included their deliverance from the perpetration of the sins intimated, or at least from such a manner of committing any sin, as should utterly separate them from God. It is the continuance of a living faith, that Christ prays for; and where that is, there will be works of new obedience: and there will be the work of that faith, in purifying the heart, and mortifying of the sins supposed. Farther, the way here prescribed and limited to the Lord Jesus, how he shall intercede for his, and for what, viz. not for actual perseverance, and continuance in the faith, to be wrought in them by the exceeding greatness of the power of God, but for means to enable them to preserve themselves, we are persuaded he walks not in; and that much upon this account, that the way whereby God begins and carries on believers, in the way of faith and obedience, is not by such a supply of means, as leaves them to themselves to work and effect the things, for which they are so sup-

plied; but he himself 'works in them to will and to do of
his own good pleasure, fulfilling in them all the good pleasure of his goodness, and the work of faith with power,'
giving them all their sufficiency, and preserving them by
his power, through faith unto salvation; to make faith,
and perseverance therein, to follow such a supply of means,
as leaves the production of them to the power of the wills
of men, so that after God hath done all that on his part is
to be done or performed, that is, quickened them being
dead, giving them new hearts and spirits, shone into their
minds, to give them the knowledge of his glory in the face
of his Son, &c. it is yet uncertain, whether ever faith shall
be wrought in their souls or no, or rather, whether men so
supplied with means will believe and persevere, or no, is an
assertion, that will never be proved to eternity; nor, whilst
truth is truth, is it capable of proof. ' The granting of such
means, and such a presence of his Spirit, that men may be
enabled to work for themselves,' is an expression exceedingly
unsuited to all the promises of the new covenant; whatever
either of the Spirit of grace, or the means of it, is given out
to believers, Christ intercedes that his Father would keep
them, not that they should keep themselves: he was too
well acquainted with our frame, and our temptations, to desire we might be our own keepers; God forbid we should be
left to our own preservation, to the hand of our own counsel
and power, though compassed with all the supposed sufficient
means; that may be not eventually effectual; God creates
a defence upon our glory, and doth not leave it to our own
safeguarding. Our salvation is not in our own custody;
that the Father doth not keep us, or preserve us, that the
Son doth not intercede, that we may be so preserved, that
the Spirit doth not make us meet for, and keep us unto the
inheritance of the saints in light, but that, in the use of
means we are, as Adam was, our own keepers, are some of
the principles of that new way of administering consolation
to believers, which Mr. Goodwin hath found out. This then
is the utmost, which Mr. Goodwin will allow to be (for disputation sake, not that he really believes it) granted, that
Christ intercedes for his saints, as to their continuance and
preservation in that condition, viz. That God would give
them such means, as they may use, or not use, at their

liberty, which may be effectual, or not effectual, as their own wills shall choose to make use of them, which he also takes for granted, to be common to all the world, and not to be peculiar unto believers.

But it is farther argued, ' If Christ should simply and absolutely intercede, that no sin or wickedness whatsoever, may destroy the faith of any true believer, and consequently deprive him of salvation, should he not hereby become that, which the apostle rejects with indignation, as altogether unworthy of him, I mean, a minister of sin? Is, therefore, Christ the minister of sin? God forbid; or whereby, or wherein, can it lightly be imagined, that Christ should become a minister of sin, rather than by interceding with his Father, that such and such men, how vile and abominable soever they shall become, may yet be precious in his sight, and receive a crown of righteousness from his hand? Or doth not such an intercession, as some men put upon him, as they who make him to intercede simply and absolutely for the perseverance of believers in their faith, amount to an intercession of every whit as vile and unworthy import as this ?'

Ans. That this is the tenor of Christ's intercession with his Father, for men, ' Let them become as vile as they will, how vile and abominable soever, yet that they may be still precious in his sight, and that he would give them a crown of righteousness,' Mr. Goodwin knoweth full well, not to be the doctrine of them he opposeth; if he shall otherwise affirm, it will be incumbent on him to produce some one author, that hath wrote about this doctrine, in what language soever, and so stated it; if he be ignorant, that this is not their doctrine, he ought not to have engaged into an opposition thereof: if he argue that it is otherwise, this procedure is unworthy of him. That Christ intercedes for his saints, that they may be kept from all such sins, as would separate them from the love and favour of his Father, for which there is no remedy provided in the covenant of grace, and that their faith may not fail or perish under such sins, as they may through temptation fall into, is the doctrine which he opposeth, or at least ought to oppose, to make good his undertaking; now if this be so. ' then,' saith he, ' is Christ the minister of sin.' Why so? He sees and foretels that Peter should deny him thrice, yet he prays, that Peter's faith may not fail under that sin and wickedness: is he, therefore, a minister of sin? because he intercedes that his saints may not be given up to the power of sin, nor every time they are assaulted, lie conquered by sin; is he, therefore, a minister of sin? or rather a deliverer from sin? That very thing, which Mr. Goodwin affirms would make him a minister of sin, he affirms himself to do in the case of Peter; how he will free himself from this charge and imputation, *ipse viderit.*

2. What it is to intercede simply and absolutely for believers, that they may continue believing, we are not so clear in; Christ intercedes, that they may be preserved by the power of his Father, in and through the use of those means, which he graciously affords them, and the powerful presence of the Spirit of God with them therein; and that, not on any such absurd and foolish conditions, that they may be so preserved by his Father, provided they preserve themselves, and continue believers, on condition they continue to believe; and if this be of a vile and unworthy import, the gospel is so too, and one of the most eminent graces, that is inwrapped in the new covenant, is so too.

What there is farther in Mr. Goodwin, sect. 34. pp. 249, 250. unto this argument, is either a mere repetition of what was spoken before, or a pressing of consequences upon such supposals, as he is pleased to make, concerning the doctrine that he doth oppose; as we cannot hinder any man from making what supposals they please, and suiting inferences to them, manifesting their skill in casting down what themselves set up, so we are not in the least concerned in such theatrical contests.

What it is, that we teach of the intercession of Christ for believers, hath been sufficiently explained; the end and aim of it is, that they may be kept, that they may not be lost, that the evil one may not touch them, that they may be saved to the utmost, and kept by the power of God unto salvation; all that the Lord Jesus hath for his church, either by his oblation, or his intercession, procured, or doth procure, being made out unto them by the holy and blessed Spirit, which he sent them from his Father, as the first-fruits of his undertaking for them, by and in the use of such means and ways, as he hath appointed for them to walk in, in reference to the end proposed. He intercedes that through supplies of that Spirit, their faith fail not, that no temptation prevail against them, that they may have suitable helps in time of need, and so be preserved, according to the tenor of that sanctification, which he is pleased to give them in this life, which is imperfect, not from all sins (for it is the will of God to keep them and walk with them in a covenant of pardoning mercy), not absolutely from this or that great sin, as is evident in the case of David and Peter, whereof, under such sins, the one lost not the Spirit, nor the other his faith, but from such sins, or such a course or way, in and under sin as would disappoint him, and make his desires frustrate, as to the end first proposed, of bringing them to glory; so that as the intendment of his oblation is meritoriously, and by way of procurement, to take away all our sins whatsoever; and yet in the application of it unto us, as to the taking of them away, 'by purifying us to be a holy people unto himself,' it is not perfected and completed at once, nor the work thereof consummated, but by degrees; so in his intercession, which respecteth the same persons and things with his oblation, he puts in for our deliverance from all sins, and the power of them, but so and in a such manner, as the nature of our present condition, whilst we are *in via*, and the condition of the covenant, whereunto God hath graciously taken us, doth require.

Through the goodness of God, we have now brought this first part to an end, They, who are in any measure acquainted, in what straits, under what pressing employments, and urgent avocations, and in what space of time, this offering was provided for the sanctuary of God, will accept it in him, whose it is, and from whom it was received.

CHAP. X.

The improvement of the doctrine of perseverance in reference to the obedience and consolation of the saints; why its tendency to the promoting of their obedience is first handled, before their consolation.   Five previous observations concerning gospel truths in general.   1. That all are to be received with equal reverence.   2. That the end of them all is, to work the soul into a conformity to God; proved by several Scriptures; 2 Tim. iii. 16. Tit. i. 1, &c.   3. Some truths have a more immediate tendency hereunto than others have; 2 Cor. v. 14.   4. Most weight is to be laid by believers upon such.   5. Men are not themselves to determine what truths have most in them of this tendency, &c.   Gospel obedience, what it is, and why so called. Its nature.   1. In the matter of it, which is all and only the will of God. 2. In the form of it, which is considered.   1. In the principle setting it on work, faith.   2. In the manner of doing it, eying both precepts and promises.   3. The end aimed at in it, the glory of God as a rewarder; Heb. xi. 6. Rom. iv. 4.   The principle in us, whence it proceeds, which is the new man, the Spirit, proved; Eph. iii. 16, 17, &c.   What kind of motives conduce most to the carrying on of this obedience, namely, such as most cherish this new man, which they do most, that discover most of the love of God, and his good-will in Christ, such as these are alone useful to mortification, and the subduing of the contrary principle of flesh, which hinders our obedience proved; Tit. ii. 12. Rom. vi.   What persons the improvement of this doctrine concerns, only true believers who will not abuse it.   How this doctrine of perseverance conduces so eminently to the carrying on of gospel obedience in the hearts of these true believers.   1. By removing discouragements.   1. Perplexing fears which impair their faith. 2. Hard thoughts of God, which weaken their love, without which two, faith and love, no gospel obedience performed.   2. Unspeakable obligations to live to God, hence put upon the souls of the saints.   Objection concerning the abuse of this truth, to presumption and carelessness discussed, examined at large and removed.   The mortification of the flesh, wherein it consists, how it is performed.   The influence of the doctrine of the saints' perseverance thereunto.   Dread and terror of hell not the means of mortification, at large proved, by shewing quite another means of mortifying the flesh, viz. The Spirit of Christ; Rom. viii. 13. applying the cross, and death of Christ; Rom. vi. 5, 6.   3 This doctrine is useful to promote gospel obedience, in that it tends directly to increase and strengthen faith and love, both towards God, and towards our Lord Jesus Christ.   How it strengthens their love to God, viz. By discovering his love to them, in three eminent properties of it, freedom, constancy, fruitfulness.   How it strengthens their love to Jesus Christ, viz. By discovering his love to them, in two eminent acts of it, his oblation and his intercession.   4. This doctrine conduces, &c. by giving gospel obedience its proper place and due order.   5. By closing in with the ends of gospel ordinances, particularly the ministry, one eminent end whereof is, to perfect the saints; Eph. iv. 12, 13. which is done by discovering to them the whole will of God, both precepts on the one hand, and promises, exhortations, threatenings, on the other. That of the promises more particularly, and more largely insisted on.

THAT which remains to complete our intendment, as to that part of the work which now draws towards a close, is the importment of that doctrine so long insisted on (having in some measure vindicated and cleared up the truth of it), as to the effectual influence it hath into the obedience, and consolation of them that are concerned therein ; and this I shall do in the order that I have named, giving the pre-eminence unto their obedience; which, more immediately respecting the glory of God, and the honour of the gospel, is to be preferred before their consolation ; yea, though God should never afford his saints any drop of that consolation, which we affirm to stream from the truth discussed, yet it is honour unspeakable for them, that he is pleased to admit them, and enable them to do him service in this life; and it will be their infinite consolation, that they have done so, to eternity.

For the making our way clear to the demonstration of that influence, which the doctrine of the perseverance of the saints hath into their obedience, and close-walking with God, and so to manifest what weight is to be laid upon it, on that consideration, I shall give some previous observations, which may direct, and give us light in our passage, both concerning gospel truths, gospel obedience, and gospel motives thereunto. I hope it will not be thought amiss, if I look a little backward to fortify and clear this part of our progress; there being no concernment of our doctrine, that is more clamoured by the adversaries of it ; nor can any respect of it, or any truth of God, more causelessly meet with such entertainment, as I hope will abundantly (in the progress of our business) be evinced, to the consciences of all, who know indeed, what it is to walk before God, in a course of gospel obedience, and who have their communion with the Father, and his Son Jesus Christ. For the first:

1. Every truth revealed from God is to be received not only with faith and love, but with equal reverence to any that is revealed, though we are not able to discern such an immediate tendency unto usefulness in our communion with him, as in some others we may: the formal reason, where-

unto our faith, love, and reverence, unto the word of God is resolved, is, that it is his; now this is common to the whole, for he is the author of every part and portion alike; and though perhaps we may want some part of it at a less fatal price than some other, yet to reject any one tittle or jot of it, as that which is revealed of God, is a sufficient demonstration, that no on jot or tittle of it, is received as it ought; upon whatever this title and incription is *Verbum Jehova*, there must we stoop and bow down our souls before it, and captivate our understandings to the obedience of faith; whatsoever then may hereafter be spoken, concerning the usefulness of the truth under consideration, and that comparative regard, which in respect of others, ought on that account to be had thereunto, doth not in the least exalt it (as it is in itself, in respect of faith and reverence due thereunto) above any other truth whatsoever, that is in Scripture revealed.

2. That next to the revelation of God, his will and his grace, the grand immediate tendency of the whole Scripture is, to work them to whom the revelation is made, into a conformity to himself, and to mould them into his own image. 'All Scripture (the apostle tells us, 2 Tim. iii. 16.) is given by inspiration of God; and is profitable for doctrine, for reproof, for correction, for instruction in righteousness, that the man of God may be perfect, thoroughly furnished unto all good works:' hereunto all Scripture tends, and is useful and profitable for this end; and the gospel is called 'the truth that is according to godliness;' Titus i. 1. 'As the end of the law is chaiity out of a pure heart, and a faith unfeigned;' 1 Tim. i. 5. That which in respect of the prime author of it, is λόγος Θεοῦ, 'the word of God;' 1 Thess. ii. 13. and in respect of the principal matter of it, is ὁ λόγος ὁ τοῦ σταυροῦ, 'the word of the cross;' 1 Cor. i. 18. in respect of its end and tendency towards us, is λόγος εὐσεβείας, 'the word, or tiuth, that is according to godliness.' The word is that revealed will of God, which is our sanctification; 1 Thess. iv. 3. and the instrument whereby he works our holiness, according to that prayer of our Saviour, 'Sanctify them by thy word, thy word is truth;' John xvii. 19. And that, which when we are cast into the mould of our obedience is in some measure wrought; Rom. vi. 17. the substance also or matter being written in our hearts, is the

grace and holiness promised unto us in the covenant; Jer. xxxi. 33. And that this is the improvement, which ought to be made by believers, of every gospel truth ; or rather that it hath an efficacy to this purpose, the apostle tells us, 2 Cor. iii. 18. 'We all with open face beholding as in a glass the glory of the Lord, are changed into the same image, from glory to glory, even as by the Spirit of the Lord;' by apprehensions of the glorious truths discovered in the glass or mirror of the gospel, we are changed and moulded into the frame and image therein discovered, by the power of the Spirit, effectually accompanying the word in the dispensation thereof; and unless this be done, whatsoever we may pretend, we have not received any truth of the gospel, as it is in Jesus, in the power of it; Eph. iv. 20—24. ' Ye have not,' saith the apostle, ' so learned Christ; if so be that ye have heard him, and have been taught by him, as the truth is in Jesus; that ye put off, as concerning the former conversation, the old man, which is corrupt according to the deceitful lusts ; and be renewed in the spirit of your mind ; and that ye put on the new man, which after God is created in righteousness and true holiness.' Whatsoever men may profess, if we have learned the truth as it is in Jesus, it will have these effects in us, even universal relinquishment (as to sincerity) of all ungodliness, and a thorough change (both as to principles and practices) unto holiness, and to righteousness, which the gospel teaches us, which, if we have not learned, we have not yet learned it, ' as it is in Jesus ;' Tit. ii 11, 12. ' The grace of God, that bringeth salvation, hath appeared to all men, teaching us, that denying ungodliness and worldly lusts, we should live soberly, righteously, and godly in this present evil world.'

3. Some truths have a more immediate, direct, and effectual tendency to the promotion of godliness, and gospel obedience, than others; this the apostle emphatically ascribes, as a privilege, to that doctrine that reveals the love of Christ unto us; 2 Cor. v. 14. ' the love of Christ constrains us ;' other things effectually persuade, but the love of Christ constrains us to live to him; it hath an importunity with it, not to be denied; an efficacy not to be put off or avoided ; and what is in the things themselves, as in the

love of Christ, that is in its manner, in ' the word of truth,' whereby it is revealed.

4. That there is, by all that walk with God, great weight to be laid on those doctrines of truth, which directly and effectually tend to the promotion of faith, love, fear, reverence of God, with universal holiness in their hearts and ways; this being that whereunto they are called, and whereby God is glorified, Jesus Christ and the gospel exalted, wherein his kingdom in them consists, on which their own peace in their own bosoms, their usefulness unto others in this world, their being made meet for the inheritance of the saints of light, doth much depend ; if these things be of weight or moment unto them (as surely they are all, that is, so to believers), then doubtless, great valuation and dear esteem will be entertained of those helps and assistances, which they have, leading and carrying them on thereunto.

5. That a judgment of what truths and doctrines are peculiarly conducing unto the promotion of piety and godliness, is not to be made upon the apprehensions and reasonings of men, wrested with a thousand corruptions and prejudices, full of darkness and vanity, but according to what the Scripture itself holds forth, and the nature of the things themselves (that is, the evidence and consequence that is between the truth revealed, and obedience) doth require ; if the testimonies of the sons of men must be admitted in this case, to determine what doctrine is according to godliness, the cry and noise of them, will be found so various, discrepant, confused, and directly contradictory to itself, that none will ever thereby be led to establishment: then Papists will cry out for their merits, penance, vows, purgatory; the Socinians, familists, formalists, all contend upon the foundation of their own persuasions, as to their tendency to godliness, of their abominations. That doctrine which hath no other proof of its truth and worth, but that men, some men, profess, it tends to godliness and holiness of conversation, I dare say, is a lie and vanity, and did never promote any thing, but vain, legal, superstitious, counterfeit holiness ; indeed upon a supposition of its truth, it is of concernment for the advancement of any doctrine, in the esteem and opinion of the saints, to manifest that it leads to

godliness; but to prove it to be true, because men who perhaps never knew any thing beyond formal, legal, pharisaical holiness all their days, say, it tends to the promotion of holiness, is but to obtrude our conceptions upon others, that are no way moulded into the frame of them: that the embracement of such a truth, will farther us in our obedience, and walking with God, therefore value and prize it, is good arguing; but that such a doctrine will farther us in a way of godliness, therefore it is a truth, when we may be mistaken both in godliness itself, and in the motives to it, and furtherances of it, is but a presumption. To commend then the truth, which we have at large otherwise confirmed, to the hearts and consciences of the saints of God, and to. lay a foundation for the full removal of those vain and weak exceptions, which on this account are laid against it; I shall manifest what influences it hath into their obedience, and with what eminent efficacy it prevails upon their souls, to perfect holiness in the fear of God; for the more clear declaration whereof, I shall give the reader the sum of it, under the ensuing considerations concerning gospel obedience, and the motives that are proper thereunto.

1. That which I call gospel obedience, wherein the saints of God are furthered by the belief of the truth we have in hand, is variously expressed in the Scripture; it may in general be described to be, a voluntary orderly subjection to the whole will of God; I call it obedience, in reference unto the will of God, which is the rule and pattern of it, and whereunto it is a regular subjection; the psalmist expresses it to the full, both as to the root and fruit; Psal. xl. 8. 'I delight to do thy will, O my God, yea thy law is within my heart;' the law in the heart gives us to do, and to delight in doing the will of God; Peter calls it, 'being holy in all manner of conversation;' 1 Pet. i. 14, 15. Paul, 'a cleansing of ourselves from all filthiness of flesh and spirit in the fear of God;' 2 Cor. vii. 1. or, as it is more eminently described, Rom. xii. 1, 2. in that pathetical exhortation of the apostle thereunto; 'I beseech you, brethren, by the mercies of God, that you present your bodies a living sacrifice, holy, acceptable unto God, which is your reasonable service; and be not conformed unto this world, but be ye transformed by the renewing of your mind, that ye may

prove what is that good, that acceptable, and perfect will of God,' as he had formerly at large described it, in the sixth chapter of that epistle, throughout. And I call it gospel obedience, not that it differs in substance, as to the matter of it, from that required by the law, which enjoins us to 'love the Lord our God with all our hearts,' but that it moves upon principles, and is carried on unto ends, revealed only in the gospel.

In reference to our design, there are these four things considerable in it:

First, The nature of it.

Secondly, The principle in us, from whence it proceeds.

Thirdly, The motives that are proper to the carrying it on, the cherishing and increasing of it in them, in whom it is.

Fourthly, The persons, who are to be moved and provoked to a progress therein.

By a brief consideration of these things, we shall make way for what we have undertaken; namely, to manifest the efficacy of the doctrine we have insisted on, for the promotion of this gospel obedience, being accused and charged with the clear contrary tendency; whereof (God assisting) we shall free and discharge it in the progress of this discourse.

First, In the nature of it I shall consider only these two things :

1. The matter or substance of it; what ,it is as it were composed of, and wherein it doth consist.

2. The form or manner of its performance ; whence it receives its distinct being, as such.

1. The matter or substance of it contains those things, or duties to God, wherein it doth consist.   Now it consisting, as I said before, in conformity and submission to the will, that is, the commanding revealed will of God, the matter of it must lie in the performance of all these things, and only those things, which God requireth of believers, in walking before him ; I say, all those things, that God commandeth with an equal respect to all his precepts ; the authority of God the commander and lawgiver, is the same in every command ; and therefore was the curse denounced unto every one, 'that continued not in all things written in the law to do them ;' and the apostle tells us, that ' in the

transgression of any one precept, there is included the transgression of the whole law, because the authority of the lawgiver, both in one, and the other, is despised; James ii. 10, 11. 'Whosoever shall keep the whole law, and yet offend in any one point, he is guilty of all; for he that said, Do not commit adultery, said also, Do not kill.' And,

2. I say, it is only to the command; for 'in vain do men worship him, teaching for doctrines the traditions of men.' The most stupendous endeavours of men, the most laborious drudgery of their souls in duties not commanded, are so far from obedience, that they are as high rebellions against God, as they can possibly engage themselves into.

I might rather distinguish the matter, or substance, of this obedience, into the internal elicit act of our souls, in faith, love, and the like acts of moral and everlasting obedience, which are naturally, necessarily, and indispensably required in us, upon the account of the first commandment, and the natural subjection, wherein we stand unto God, as his creatures; improved and enlarged by the new obligation put upon us, in being his redeemed ones (wherein indeed the main of our obedience doth consist); and the outward instituted duties of religion, which God hath appointed for those former acts of obedience to be exercised in, and exerted by; but the former description of it, with the intimation of its universality, may suffice.

2. The formality (if I may so speak) of this obedience, or that which makes the performance of duties commanded, to be obedience, consists in these three things:

1. The principle that begins it, and sets it on work immediately in us; and that is faith: 'without faith it is impossible to please God;' Heb. xi. 6. Could a man do all that is commanded, yet if he did it not in faith, it would be of no value; hence it is called 'the obedience of faith;' Rom. i. 5. not for obedience to the faith, but the obedience of faith, which faith bringeth forth; therefore, are believers called obedient children; 1 Pet. i. 14. and we are said to 'purify our souls in obedience to the truth;' ver. 22. 'Christ dwells in our hearts by faith, and without him we can do nothing;' John xv. 5. All that we do is no better, seeing we can no way draw near unto God 'with a true heart, but in full assurance of faith;' Heb. x. 22.

2. The manner of doing it, which consists in a due spiritual regard to the will of God, in those ways, whereby he calls men out to this obedience; namely, in his precepts and promises; there is no obedience unto God, but that which moves according to his direction; it must in every motion, eye his command on the one hand, and his promise, whether of assistance for it, or acceptance in it, on the other; saith David, 'I have respect unto all thy commandments;' Psal. cxix. and saith the apostle, 'Having received these promises, let us cleanse ourselves, from all filthiness both of flesh and spirit, perfecting holiness in the fear of God;' 2 Cor. vii. 1.

3. The principal end of it, which is the glory of God, as a rewarder; for 'he that comes unto God, must believe that he is, and that he is the rewarder of them that seek him;' Heb. xi. 6. The end of legal obedience was the glory of God, as a rewarder according to merit, in strict justice; the end of gospel obedience is the glory of God, as a rewarder according to bounty, free grace and mercy: under which consideration, neither needs the obedience rewardable to be commensurate to the reward, nor is the reward procured by that obedience; if it were, then it were of works, and not of grace, as the apostle tells us; Rom. iv. 4. So that the end of our obedience is to exalt God as a rewarder; yet that being as a rewarder of grace and bounty, the use of our obedience is not to procure that reward (for that were to work, and to have a reward reckoned to us of debt, and not of grace), but only to make the Lord gracious, and to exalt him in our present subjection, and in his future gift of grace, in nature of a free bounteous reward. This, I say, is that gospel obedience, which, by the doctrine insisted on, is promoted in the souls of believers.

Secondly, This being so, as was said, the gospel obedience, whereof we speak, it is evident what principle it proceedeth from; whereas, there are two contrary principles in every regenerate man, as shall more fully afterward be declared, called in the Scripture flesh and spirit, the old and new man, indwelling sin and grace, which have both of them their seats and places in all, and the same faculties of the soul; it is most evident, that this obedience flows solely and merely from the latter principle, the Spirit, new or inner man,

the new creature which is wrought in believers; the strengthening and heightening of this principle, the Holy Ghost
lays at the bottom of the renewal, and increase of gospel
obedience; Eph. iii. 16—19. ' I pray,' saith the apostle,
' that God would grant you, according to the riches of his
glory, to be strengthened with might by his Spirit in the inner man; that Christ may dwell in your hearts by faith; that
ye, being rooted and grounded in love, may be able to comprehend with all saints what is the breadth, and length,
and depth, and height, and to know the love of Christ, which
passeth knowledge, that ye may be filled with all the fulness
of God.' Their ' strengthening with might by the Spirit in
the inner man,' is the foundation of their acting of, and increasing in, faith, love, knowledge, and assurance unto all
the fulness of God; it is the ' new man, which after God is
created in righteousness and holiness,' that carries men out
unto all acceptable obedience; as chap. iv. 23, 24. of the
same epistle.   Look, whatsoever influences the other principle of the flesh hath into our obedience, so far it is defiled; for ' [a]that which is from the flesh is flesh,' and all the
fruits of it are abominable; hence are all the pollutions that
cleave to our holy things.   Yea, if at any time, poor and
mere selfish considerations do put men upon duties of obedience, and abstaining from sin, as fear of vengeance, and
destruction, and the like (which is made almost the only
motive to obedience, by the doctrine of saints' apostacy),
their obedience in doing or abstaining, is but as their fear
of the Lord, who were taught it by [b]lions, and abominable
unto him; this then being the nature of gospel obedience, and this the principle from whence it flows, it is
evident,

   Thirdly, What are those motives, which are suited to
the promotion and carrying of it on, in the hearts of believers, and what doctrines have an eminent and singular tendency thereunto, is also to be considered: now these must
all of them be such, as are suited to the cherishing of that
principle of the new or inner man in the heart, to the nou-
rishing and strengthening of the new creature; such as are
apt to ingenerate faith and love in the heart unto God; such
as reveal and discover those things in his nature, mind, and

----

[a] John iii. 6.   [b] 2 Kings xvii. 34.

will, as are apt to endear and draw out the heart to him in communion; discouraging, perplexing doctrines do but ill manure the soil, from whence the fruits of obedience are to spring and grow; look then, I say, whatsoever gospel truth is of eminent usefulness, to warm, foment, stir up, and quicken the principle of grace in the heart, to draw out, increase, and cherish, faith and love, that doctrine lies in a direct, immediate tendency, to the promotion of holiness, godliness, and gospel obedience. Yea, and whereas to the carrying on of that course of obedience, it is necessary that the contrary principle unto it, which we mentioned before, be daily subdued, brought under, crucified, and mortified; there are no doctrines whatsoever that are of such, and so direct and eminent a serviceableness to that end and purpose, as those which inwrap such discoveries of God, and his good-will in Christ, as are fitted for the improvement also of the principle of grace in us; hence the work of mortification in the cScripture, is every where assigned peculiarly to the cross and death of Christ; his love manifested therein, and his Spirit flowing therefrom. The doctrine of the law, indeed, humbles the soul for Christ, but it is the doctrine of the gospel that humbles the soul in Christ; it is ' the grace of God that hath appeared, that teaches us effectually to deny all ungodliness and worldly lusts, to live soberly, and righteously, and godly, in this present world;' Tit. ii. 12. He that will but with a little heed read chap. vi. to the Romans, will know from whence mortification flows; which truly, by the way, makes me admire at the extreme darkness and blindness of some poor men, who have of late undertaken to give directions for devotion and walking with God, who, indeed, suitably to the most of the rest of their discourses, all manifesting an ' dignorance of the righteousness of God,' and a zealous endeavour to establish their own, coming to propose ways and means for the mortifying of any sin or lust, tell you stories of biting the tongue, thrusting needles under the nails, with such like trash, as might have benefited popish devotions five hundred years ago; were not men utterly ignorant what it is to know the Lord Jesus Christ, and the epower of his resurrection, and the fellowship of his

---

c Rom. vi 2—6. viii. 13. vii. 7. Gal. iii. 23. 2 Cor. v 15.
d Rom. x. 4.   e Phil. iii. 10. Gal. vi. 14.

sufferings, and being made conformable to his death,' they could never feed on such husks themselves, nor make provision of them for those whose good they pretend to seek. Unto what hath been spoken, add,

Fourthly, Who are the persons, that are to be provoked to holiness and godliness by the doctrine insisted on; now they are such as do believe it, and are concerned in it; we say, the truth under consideration is of an excellent usefulness, to farther gospel obedience in the hearts of believers and saints of God, who are taught of God not to turn the doctrine of grace into wantonness: what use, or abuse rather, men of corrupt minds, and carnal principles, who stumble at Jesus Christ, and abuse the whole doctrine of the gospel by their prejudices and presumptions, will make of it, we know not, nor are solicitous.[f] ' If the gospel be hid, it is to them that perish;' it is sufficient that the food be good and wholesome for them for whom it is provided. If some will come and steal it that have no right to it, and it prove through their own distempers, [g]gravel in their mouths, or poison in their bowels, they must blame themselves, and their own wormwood lusts, and not the doctrine which they do receive; it is provided for them that fear God, and love the Lord Jesus Christ in sincerity, not for dogs, swine, unbelievers; we shall not marvel if they trample on this pearl, and rend them that bring it; to such as these then, I say, the doctrine of the perseverance of the saints, or the stability or unchangeableness of the love of God unto believers, and of their continuation in faith and obedience, is full of exceeding effectual motives and provocations unto holiness, in all manner of gospel obedience and holy conversation, exceedingly advantaging the souls of men in a course thereof; now the influence it hath into the obedience of the saints, floweth from it upon a twofold account.

1. By removing all discouragements whatsoever, that are apt either to turn them aside from their obedience, or to render their obedience servile, slavish, or unacceptable to God; it sets them, through Christ, at perfect liberty thereunto.

2. By putting unconquerable and indissoluble obligations upon them, to live unto God, and the praise of his

[f] Cor. iv. 3, 4.   [g] 2 Cor. ii. 16.

glorious grace, and evidently draws them forth unto the obedience required.

1. It removeth and taketh out of the way all discouragements whatsoever, all things which are apt to interpose to the weakening of their faith in God, or their love to God, which, as hath been said; are at the bottom of all obedience and holiness, that is acceptable to God in Christ; now these may all be referred unto two heads.

1. Of perplexing anxious fears, which are apt to impair and weaken the faith of the saints. .2. Of hard thoughts of God, which assault and shake their love. That slavish, perplexing, troublesome fears, are contrary to the free and ingenuous state of children, whereunto the saints are admitted, and (however sometimes, yea, oftentimes, they are at the bottom, and the occasion of burdensome, servile, and superstitious obedience) impairers of their faith, I suppose I need not labour to prove. That kind of fear, whereof we speak (of which more afterward), is the greatest traitor that lurks in the soul; to ‘ʰfear the Lord and his goodness,’ is the soul's keeper; but this servile perplexing fear is the betrayer of it in all its ways, and that which sours all its duties; a thing which the Lord sets himself against, in rebukes, reproofs, dehortations, as much as any failing and miscarriage in his saints whatever. It is the opposite of faith; hence the fearful and unbelieving are put together in their exclusion from the new Jerusalem; Rev. xx. 8. It is that which is direct contrary to that which the apostle adviseth the saints unto, Heb. x. 19—22. it is that which mixeth faith with staggering, Rom. iv. 20. prayer with wavering, making it ineffectual; James i. 6, 7.

Let us now suppose a man to have attained some assurance of the love of God, and ‘ⁱjustified by faith to have peace with him’ (which as to his present condition, the adversaries of the doctrine of perseverance acknowledge that he may attain, though how, upon their principles, I understand not), consider a little, how he can safeguard his peace for a moment, and deliver himself from perplexing thoughts and fears, renouncing any interest in the engagement of the love and faithfulness of God for his preservation. He may say within himself, I am for the present in some good state

ʰ Hos. iii. 5. ⁱ Rom. v. 1.

and condition, but were not the angels so that are now devils in hell? were not they in a far better, and more excellent state than I am? and yet they are now 'shut up under chains of everlasting darkness, to the judgment of the great day.' Adam in paradise had no lust within him to tempt and seduce him, no world under the curse to entangle and provoke him, and yet ' being in that honour, he had no understanding,' he abode not, but 'became like the beast that perisheth.' Was it not in their power to persevere in that condition if they would? Did they want any means that were useful thereunto? And what hope is there left to me, in' whom there dwelleth ' no[k] good thing, who am sold under' the power of ' sin,' and encompassed with a world of temptations, that I shall endure unto the end? I see thousands before mine eyes, partakers of the same heavenly calling with myself, of the same grace in Jesus Christ, every day falling into irrevocable perdition; there is not any promise of God that I should be preserved, nor promise that I shall never depart from him, no prayer of Christ, that my faith may not fail, but I am rolled upon mine own hand, and what will be the end of this whole undertaking of mine in the ways of God I know not. Let, I say, a man be exercised with such thoughts as these, and then try if any thing under heaven can bring his soul to any possible composure, until it be ' cast into the mould of that doctrine which hath been delivered.' But of this more directly afterward, when we come to treat of the consolation, which from the breast of it doth flow.

2. It is exceedingly suited to the deliverance of the souls of the saints from all such hard thoughts of God, as are apt' to impair and weaken their love towards him, and delight in him; so setting the two principles of all their obedience (faith and love) at liberty, and free from their entanglements, to act in the duties they are called unto; he that had hard thoughts of his absent Lord, as an austere man, though he was not excused in his disobedience by it, yet he was evidently discouraged as to his obedience; when men shall be taught that God takes no more care of his children in his family, but that the devil may enter in among them and take them away, making them children of hell, when he might

k Rom. vii.

with the greatest advantage of glory and honour to himself imaginable, prevent it? That the Lord Jesus Christ, 'the great shepherd of the sheep,' takes no more care of his flock and fold, but that the lion, bears, and wolves, may enter in, and make havock, and spoil at their pleasure? May they not think that God is little concerned in the salvation of his, and that all that which is so gloriously expressed of his peculiar and special love, carries nothing but an empty noise, the burden of their preservation being thrown solely upon their own shoulders? And are not such thoughts fit only to cast water upon their flames of love to God, and insensibly to weaken that delight which they ought always to take in the riches of his grace and love? Is there any thing possible more endearing to the heart of a creature than to hear such a testimony as that, Zeph. iii. 17. concerning the stability of the love of God and its excellency, 'The Lord thy God in the midst of thee is mighty, he will save, he will rejoice over thee with joy, he will rest in his love, he will joy over thee with singing?' God's resting in his love towards his saints, fixes their souls in their love to him.

3. It puts high and unspeakable obligations on the saints to live to God, and to 'perfect holiness in the fear of the Lord;' saints we suppose to have their birth from above, to be 'begotten of the will of God, through the immortal seed, of the word,' and to be quickened with a noble, child-like ingenuity, befitting the family of God ; neither is there any thing more injurious to the work of God's grace, than to suppose, that those whom God calls 'children, friends, heirs of heaven and glory, his crown, his diadem, brethren of his only Son,' are to be dealt withal, or that God deals with them, as if they were wholly acted by a servile, slavish principle, and were wholly under the power of such an unworthy disposition.

There are two things usually spoken to the prejudice and disadvatage of the truth we have under consideration, much insisted on by Mr. Goodwin, cap. 9. as,

1. 'That a persuasion of the certain continuance of the love of God to any one, is a ready way to make them careless, negligent, and to give up themselves to all manner of abominations.'

But what vipers, snakes, and adders, do such men suppose the saints of God to be, that their new nature, their heavenly principles (for what the flesh in them is prone unto we now consider not), should conclude, that ' it is good to sin, that grace may abound;' that, because God loves them with an everlasting love, therefore they will hate him with a perpetual hatred: that, because he will assuredly give them grace to ' serve him with reverence and godly fear,' therefore they will despise him, and trample on all his goodness; because he will never forsake them, that they will no more abide with him. What is in the inner man, what is in the new creature, what is in the nature of any grace, wherewith they are endowed, that is apt, or inclinable to make such hellish conclusions? If we hear of any such thing among the sons of men; if we see a child, or a servant resolving to be profligate, wicked, stubborn, prodigal, because his father or master is kind, loving, and will not disinherit him, or put him away; we look upon him as a monster in nature, and think that it would be good service to the interest of mankind to take him off from the face of earth; and yet such monsters are all the saints of God supposed to be, who, if their Father once give them the least assurance of the continuance of his love, they presently resolve to do him all the dishonour, despite, and mischief they can. I appeal to all the experience of all the saints in the world, whether, if any such thought at any time arise in them, that they may ' continue in sin, because grace hath abounded,' that they may live in all filth and folly, because God hath promised never to forsake them, nor turn away his love from them, they do not look upon it, as a hellish abuse of the love of God, which they labour to crucify, no less than any other work of the flesh whatsoever. Presuppose, indeed, the saints of God to be dogs and swine, wholly sensual and unregenerate, that is, no saints, and our doctrine to be such, that God will love them and save them continuing in that state wherein they are, and you make a bed for iniquity to stretch itself upon. But suppose, that we teach that the ' wrath of God' will certainly come upon the ' children of disobedience;' that he ' that believeth not, shall be damned;' and that God will keep his own ' by his power through faith unto salvation;' and that in and by the use of means, they shall.

certainly be preserved to the end : and the mouth of iniquity will be stopped.

2. They say, ' It takes away that strong curb and bridle, which ought to be kept in the mouth of the flesh, to keep it from running headlong into sin and folly, namely, the fear of hell and punishment, which alone hath an influence upon it, to bring it to subjection and under obedience.'

But now, if there be nothing in the world, that is of use for the mortification and crucifying of the flesh and the lusts thereof, but it receives improvement by this doctrine, this crimination must of necessity vanish into nothing.

1. Then, it tells that the flesh and all the deeds thereof, are to be crucified and slain, ' God having ordained good works for us to walk in ;' that for the works of the flesh ' the wrath of God comes upon the children of disobedience ;' and if any say, ' Let us continue in sin because we are not under the law, or the condemning power of it for sin, but under grace,' it cries out, ' God forbid ;' Rom. vi. 15, 16. And saith, This is argument enough and proof sufficient, that ' sin shall not have dominion over us, because we are not under the law, but' under grace.' It tells you also, that there is a twofold fear of hell, and punishment of sin :

First, Of anxiety and doubtfulness, in respect of the end.

Secondly, Of care and diligence, that respecteth the means.

And for the first, it saith, That this is the portion of very many of the saints of God, of some all their days, though they are so, yet they know not that they are so ; and therefore, are under anxious and doubtful fears of hell and punishment; notwithstanding that they are in the arms of their Father, from whence indeed they shall not be cast down, as a man bound with chains on the top of a tower, he cannot but fear, and yet he cannot fall.   He cannot fall, because he is fast bound with strong chains : he cannot but fear, because he cannot actually and clearly consider oftentimes, the means of his preservation.

And for the latter, a fear of the ways and means leading to punishment, as such, that continues upon all the saints of God in this life : neither is there any thing in this doctrine, that is suited to a removal thereof.   And this, it says, is

more, much more of use for the mortification of the flesh
than the former.

2. It says, That the great and principal means of mortification of the flesh, is not fear of hell and punishment, but
the Spirit of Christ, as the apostle tells us, Rom. vii. 13.
'If ye through the Spirit do mortify the deeds of the flesh,
ye shall live.' It is the Spirit of Christ alone, that is able
to do this great work; we know, what bondage and religious
drudgery some have put themselves unto, upon this account,
and yet could never in their lives attain to the mortification
of any one sin. It is the Spirit of Christ alone, that hath
sovereign power in our souls, of killing and making alive.
As no man quickeneth his own soul, so no man upon any
consideration whatsoever, or by the power of any threatenings of the law, can kill his own sin; there was never any
one sin truly mortified by the law, or the threatening of it.
All that the law can do of itself, is but to entangle sin, and
thereby to irritate and provoke it, like a bull in a net, or a
beast led to the slaughter. It is the Spirit of Christ in the
gospel, that cuts its throat and destroys it. Now this doctrine was never in the least charged with denying the Spirit
of God to believers, which whilst it doth grant and maintain, in a way of opposition to that late opinion, which advanceth itself against it, it maintains the mortification of
the flesh and the lusts thereof, upon the only true and un-
shaken foundations.

3. It tells you, That the great means, whereby the Spirit
of Christ worketh the mortification of the flesh, and the lusts
thereof, is the application of the cross of Christ, and his
death and love therein, unto the soul; and says, that those
vain endeavours, which some promote and encourage, for
the mortification of sin, consisting, for, the most part, in
slavish, bodily exercises, are to be bewailed with tears of
blood, as abominations, that seduce poor souls from the cross
of Christ; for it says, this work is truly, and in an acceptable manner only performed, when we are ' planted into the
likeness of the death of Christ, having our old man crucified
with him, and the body of sin destroyed;' Rom. vi. 5, 6. and
thereupon by faith ' reckoning ourselves dead unto sin, but
alive unto God;' ver. 11. It is done only by ' knowing the
fellowship of the sufferings of Christ, and being made con-

formable to his death ;' Phil. iii. 10. ' By the cross of Christ
is the world crucified unto us, and we unto the world.' The
Spirit brings home the power of the cross of Christ to the
soul, for the accomplishing of this work ; and without it, it
will not be done. Moreover, it says, that by the way of motive to this duty, there is nothing comes with that efficacy
upon the soul, as the love of Christ in his death, as the apostle assures us, 2 Cor. v. 14. ' For the love of Christ constraineth us, because we thus judge, that if one died for all
then were all dead, and that he died for all, that they which
live, should not henceforth live unto themselves, but unto
him, which died for them, and rose again :' now it was never
laid to the charge of this doctrine, that it took off from the
virtue of the death and cross of Christ, but rather on the
contrary, though falsely, that it ascribed too much thereunto ; so that (these importune exceptions notwithstanding)
the doctrine in hand doth not only maintain its own inno-
cency, as to any tendency unto looseness, but also manifestly declareth its own usefulness to all ends and purposes
of gospel obedience whatsoever. For,

3. It stirs up, provokes, and draws out into action,
every thing that is free, noble, ingenuous, filial, and of a
heavenly descent, in the saints of God ; thus :

1. It strengthens their faith in God, and in Jesus Christ,
which is the bottom of all acceptable obedience whatsoever ;
all that which proceedeth from any other root, being but a
product of labouring in the fire, which in the end will consume both root and branch. That which prevails upon and
draws out the soul to faith and believing, I mean, as it is peculiar to the gospel, and justifying, that is, as it is in God
as a Father, and in the Lord Christ as a Mediator, is the discovery of the good-will of God to the soul in Christ, and his
design to advance his glory thereby ; I speak not of the formal cause of faith in general, but the peculiar motive to
faith, and believing in the sense before mentioned. So our
Saviour giving the command in general to his disciples,
John xiv. 1. ' Ye believe in God, believe also in me,' in the
whole ensuing chapter, provokes them to it, with gracious
discoveries of the good-will of God ; his Father's, and his own
good-will towards them : and indeed, propose what other
considerations ye will, provoke the soul by all the fear and

dread of hell, and the most dismal representation of the wrath to come, until it be convinced of this, it will never take one step towards God in Christ; now, ' our adversaries themselves being judges,' the doctrine we have had under consideration, abounds above all others with the discoveries of the good-will and kindness of God to poor sinners; yea, the great crime, that is laid to the charge of it, is, that it extends it too far; it doth not only assert, that God freely ' begins the good work in them,' but that he will also powerfully ' perfect it to the day of Jesus Christ,' it assures the souls of the poor saints of God, that he who looked upon them ' in their blood, and said unto them Live, when no eye pitied them; who quickened them, when they were dead in trespasses and in sins; begetting them of his own will, by the word of truth, that they should be a kind of first-fruits to himself; washing them in the blood of his Son,' and delivering them from the old tyrant Satan; that he will not now leave them to them-selves, and to the counsel of their own hands, to stand or fall, according as they shall of themselves, and by themselves, be able to withstand opposition and seduction: but that he will keep them in his own hand, giving them such constant supplies of his grace and Spirit; as that in the use of means, they shall wait upon him to the end; and that howsoever, or whensoever, by the power of temptation, and surprisals of corruptions, they are carried aside from him, he will ' heal their backslidings, and receive them freely,' and though they change every day, yet ' he changeth not, and therefore they are not consumed.' And hereby, I say, it confirms and strengthens their faith in God, as a Father in Jesus Christ, taking everlasting care of them.

2. Of their love there is the same reason; God's love to us is of his free grace; he loves us because so it seems good to him; our love to him, is purely ingeneiated by his love to us, and carried on and increased by farther revelations of his desirableness and excellency, to our souls; ' herein is love, not that we loved God, but that he loved us first:' there is no creature in the least guilty of sin, that can put forth any acceptable act of love towards God, but what is purely drawn out upon the apprehension of his love and loveliness in his grace and mercy; a man, I confess, may love God, when he hath no sense of his love to him in particular: but

it must all be built upon an apprehension of his love to sinners, though he may come short in the application; it is the terror of the Lord, that causes us to persuade others, but it is the 'love of Christ that constraineth us' to live to him. She loved much, to whom much was forgiven; look then, the more abundant discoveries are made of the loveliness and desirableness [of God] in the riches of his grace, the more effectual is the sole and only motive we have to love him, with that filial, chaste, holy love, that he requires.

For the love of God to his saints, our doctrine of their perseverance, sets it forth, with the greatest advantage, for the endearment of their souls, to draw out their streams of love to God; especially doth it give it its glory in three things:

1. In its freedom; it sets forth the love of God to his saints, as that which they have no way in the least deserved; as hath been manifested from Isa. xlviii. 8, 9. 11. liv. 9, 10. As he first loved them, not because they were better than others, being by nature ' children of wrath,' and lying in their blood, 'when he said to them Live;' quickening them when they were ' dead in trespasses and sins :' so he doth not continue his love to them, nor purpose so to do, because he foresees, that they will so and so walk with him in holiness and uprightness (for he foresees no such thing in them, but what he himself purposeth effectually to work, upon the account of his loving them), but he resolves to do it, merely upon the account of his own grace; he neither resolves to continue his love to them, on condition that they be so and so holy, at random, and with uncertainty of the event, but freely, that they may and shall be so. And this is the[1] glory of love, the most orient pearl in the crown of it : it is not mercenary nor self-ended, nor deserved ; but, as a spring and fountain, freely vents and pours out itself upon its own account : and what ingenuous, truly noble, heavenly descended heart can hold out against the power of this love ? It is effectually constraining to all manner of suitable returns; let the soul but put itself into the actual contemplation of the love of God, as it lies represented in this property of it, every way free, undeserved, the great love of God, to a poor worm, a sinner, a nothing; and it cannot but be wrought to a serious admiration of it, delight in it, and be pained and straitened, until

[1] Eph. i. 4.

it makes some suitable returns of love and obedience unto God; if not, it may well doubt it never tasted of that love, or enjoyed any fruits of it.

2. It gives the love of God the glory of its constancy and unchangeableness; this is another star of an eminent magnitude in the heaven of love; it is not a fading, a wavering, an altering thing, but abides for ever; God rests in his love; Zeph. iii. 17. It is a great thing indeed, to apprehend that the great God should fix his love upon a poor creature. But add hereunto, that he may love them one day, and hate them the next, embrace them one hour, and the next cast them into hell, one day rejoicing over them with joy, another rejoicing to destroy them, as it is dishonourable to God, and derogatory to all his divine excellencies and perfections; so in particular, it clotheth his love with the most uncomely and undesirable garment, that ever was put upon the affections of the meanest worm of the earth. What can ye say more contemptible of a man? more to his dishonour among all wise and knowing men, or that shall render his respects and affections more undesirable, than to say, he is free of his love indeed, but he abides not in it? What a world of examples have we of those, who have been in his bosom, and have again been cast out? Though among men something may be pretended in excuse of this, with respect unto their ignorance, the shortness of their foresight, disability to discern between things and appearances; yet in respect of God, ' before whom all things are open and naked,' in whose eye all incidencies and events lie as clearly stated, as things that are already passed and gone, what can be said of such a vain supposal, for the vindication of his glory? It is said, that ' men change from what they were, when God loved them, and therefore his love changeth also.' But who first made them fit to be beloved? Did not the Lord? Do they make themselves differ from others? On what account did he do it? Was it not merely on the account of his own grace? Can he not as well preserve them in a state of being beloved, as put them into it? And if he determined that he would not preserve them in that condition, why did he set his love upon them, when himself knew that he would not continue it to them? Was it only to give his love the dishonour of a change? I say then, the doctrine contended for, gives the

love of God the glory of its immutability, asserts it to be like himself. Unchangeable, that there is not indeed, in itself, the least ' shadow of turning;' it may be eclipsed and obscured, as to its beams and influences, for a season ; but changed, turned away, it cannot be. And this consideration of it, renders it to the souls of the saints inestimably precious : the very thought of it, considering that nothing else could possibly save or preserve them, is marrow to their bones, and health to their souls, and makes them cry out to all that is within them, to love the Lord, and to live unto him.

3. It gives it the glory of its fruitfulness. A barren love is upon the matter no love. Love that hath no breasts, no bowels, that pities not, that assists not, deserves not that heavenly name. Will ye say she is a tender, loving mother, who can look on a languishing, perishing child, yea, see a ravenous beast, whom yet she could easily drive away, take it out of her arms, and devour it before her face, and not put forth her strength, for its assistance or deliverance ? Or will ye say, she is a tiger, and a monster in nature ? And shall we feign such a love in God towards his children, which is such that all the bowels of a tender parent to an only child are but as a drop to the ocean, in comparison of it ? As that he looks on whilst they languish and perish, fall, sink, and die away into everlasting calamity ; yea, that notwithstanding it, he will suffer the roaring lion to come and snatch them away out of his arms, and devour them before his face. That he will look upon them sinking into eternal separation from him, and such destruction, as that it had been infinitely better for them never to have been born, without putting forth his power and the efficacy of his grace, for their preservation : ' Ah foolish people, and unwise ! shall we thus requite the Lord ?' as to render him so hard a master, so cruel a Father to his tender ones, the lambs of his Son, washed in his blood, quickened by his Spirit, owned by him, smiled on, embraced ten thousand times, as to suffer them so to be taken out of his hands ? Is there nothing in his love to cause his bowels to move, and his repentings to be kindled together towards a poor dying child, that surely departeth not without some sad looks towards his Father ? ' Nemo repente fit turpissimus.' Is this the kindness, which he exalteth above the love of a woman to her sucking child,

of a mother to the fruit of her womb? Oh that men should dare thus foolishly to charge the Almighty, to ascribe such a barren fruitless love to him, who is love, towards his children, who are as the apple of his eye, his dear and tender ones, as would be a perpetual blot and stain to any earthly parent, to have righteously ascribed to him; I say then, our doctrine gives the love of God the glory of its fruitfulness. It asserts it to be such a fountain-love, as from whence continually, streams of grace, kindness, mercy, and refreshment do flow: 'because he loves us with everlasting love, therefore he draws us with loving-kindness;' Jer. xxx. 1, 2. From that love proceeds continual supplies of the Spirit and grace, by which those of whom it is said, they abide, are preserved lovely, and fit by him to be beloved. It tells us, that because God loves his people, therefore are they ' in his hand;' Deut. xxxiii. 3. It declares it to be such a love, as is the womb of all mercy; whence pardon, healing, recovery from wounds, sicknesses, and dying pangs, do continually flow. A love upon the account whereof, the persons loved may make conclusion, that they shall ' lack nothing;' Psal. xxiii. 1. A love whose fruitfulness is subservient to its own constancy, preserving the saints such, as he may rest in it, unchangeably; Rom. viii. 29, 30. A love, whereby God sings to his vineyard, watches over it, and waters it every moment; Isa. xxvii. 2, 3. And now what flint almost in the rock of stone, would not be softened and dissolved by this love? When we shall think, that it is from the love of God, that our wasted portion hath been so often renewed, that our dying graces have been so often quickened, our dreadful backslidings so often healed, our breaches and decays so often repaired, and the pardon of our innumerable transgressions so often sealed, unless we suck the breasts of tigers, and have nothing in us but the nature of wolves and unclean beasts, can we hold out against the sweet, gracious, powerful, effectual influences, that it will have upon our souls; thus, I say, doth the doctrine which we have in hand, set out the love of God unto us, in his eminent endearing properties, wherein, he being embraced through Christ, a foundation is laid, and eminent promotion given unto the holiness and obedience, which he requireth of us.

2. This doctrine renders Jesus Christ lovely to our souls,

to the souls of believers; it represents him to them, as the 'standard-bearer to ten thousand,' as one 'altogether lovely;' as exceeding desirable in the work of his oblation, lovely and amiable in the work of his intercession, as hath been manifested.

1. It imports him as one, who in his death hath 'made an end' of the controversy between God and our souls; Dan. ix. 39, becoming ' our peace;' Eph. ii. 14. 'having obtained for us eternal redemption.' That he hath not suffered all that sorrow, anguish, pain, torment, dereliction, whereunto for our sakes he was given up, and willingly exposed himself, for an uncertain end, not fighting in his death as one beating the air, nor leaving his work in the dust, to be trampled on, or taken up, as it seems good to us in our polluted, dark, dead estate of nature; but hath filled it with such immortal seed, that of itself, by itself, and its own unconquerable efficacy, it hath sprung up, to the bringing forth of that whole fruit intended in it, and the accomplishment of all the ends aimed at by it. That is, that it shall certainly and infallibly bring all those to God, for whom he offered, by sanctifying, justifying, and preserving them, through the communication of his own Spirit and grace to them, for that end and purpose; 'all his promises being yea and amen, in him,' confirmed by his death; 2 Cor. i. 20. Heb. x. 12—16. Some of those, who indeed abuse the truth we have insisted on, pretend to grant, 'that by his death he made satisfaction for sin, but only on condition that men believe on him, and continue so doing; that they shall so believe, and so continue (though he is said to be the captain of our salvation, and the author and finisher of our faith, though it be given unto us for his sake, to believe on him; and we are blessed with all spiritual blessings in heavenly places in him), that he takes no care about, beyond the general administration of outward means. He neither procured any such thing by his oblation, nor doth intercede for it; these things are left unto men to be educed, drawn forth, and exercised by virtue of sundry considerations, that they may take upon themselves.' Never doubtless did men take more pains, to stain the beauty and comeliness of our dying Saviour.

2. For his intercession, the doctrine hitherto insisted on,

renders him therein exceeding lovely and desirable. It tells you, that he doth 'pray the Father,' and thereupon ' sends us the Comforter,' the Holy Spirit, for all the gracious acts and works, ends and purposes, before mentioned, with innumerable other privileges that the saints by him are made partakers of, and that to abide with us for ever, never to leave us, nor forsake us. That he continually 'appears in the presence of God for us,' interceding that our faith may not fail, pleading for us, in, and under all our decays, making out to us suitable supplies in all our distresses, temptations, trials, troubles, taking care that 'no temptations befall us,' but that ·'a way also of escape be given to us, together with it.' It tells us his eye, even now he is in glory, is still upon us, seeing our wants, taking notice of our weakness, and providing for us, as his only concernment in the world, that we be not lost; that he hath not left one jot of that kindness, which he bare to his flock, his lambs, his little ones. But pursues with all his strength, and all the interest he hath in heaven, the work of their salvation, which he came from his Father's bosom to enter on, and returned to him again, to carry it on unto perfection; that as the high-priest of old, he bears our names in his breast, and on his shoulders continually before his Father: so that in all our falls and failings, when we are in ourselves helpless and hopeless, when there is nothing in us, nor about us, that can do us any good, or yield us any help or consolation, yet on this account we may say, 'The Lord is our shepherd, we shall lack nothing.' He hath undertaken for us, and will bear us in his arms, until he bring us to the bosom of his Father. Now whether such considerations as these, of the oblation and intercession of Christ, do not fill his love in them, with a more constraining efficacy, and more draw out the hearts of the saints unto faith and love, than any instruction can do, informing men of the uselessness of the one or other of these eminent acts of his mediation, for any of the ends and purposes mentioned, let believers judge. That which men repose upon in their greatest necessities, and for the things of the greatest concernment, thereof they have the greatest valuation, and the thoughts of it are most fixed in their minds. What is there of so great concernment in this world unto the saints, as their abiding with God unto the end? How many, how great,

urging, pressing, are the difficulties, dangers, troubles they
meet withal in their so doing? What then they have most
frequent recourse unto, and what they rest most upon under
their pressures, in the things of that concernment before
mentioned, that will deserve the name of their treasure,
where their hearts will and ought to be. Now if this (setting
aside, as things of no consideration in such a case, the purposes, covenant, and promises of God, the oblation and intercession of the Lord Christ) be men's own rational abilities,
to consider what is for their good, and what will be hurtful
and destructive to them ; what can hinder but that men will
(yea and that they often should) spend the flower and best
of their affections upon and about themselves and their own
wisdom, in and for their preservation ; that doubtless will
take up their hearts and thoughts; so that there will be very
little room left for the entertainment of the Lord Jesus
Christ, with any regard or respect on this account. If that
then may pass, which was formerly laid down, namely, that
the doctrines and things, which are apt and suited to the
ingenerating, quickening, increasing, and building up of
faith and love towards God, and our Lord Jesus Christ, are
the most eminent gospel motives, to spiritual acceptable
obedience (as it is an unquestionable truth and certainty),
doubtless that doctrine which represents the Father and Son,
so rich in mercy, so loving and lovely to the soul, as that
doth which we insist upon, must needs have a most effectual
influence into that obedience.

4. The doctrine insisted on, hath an effectual influence
into the obedience of the saints, upon the account of giving
it its proper place, and setting it aright upon its basis, carrying it on in due order ; it neither puts upon it the fetters
of the law, nor turns it loose from the holy and righteous
rule of it ; let men be as industrious as can be imagined, in
the performance of all commanded duties, yet if they do it
on legal motives, and for legal ends, all their performances
are vitiated, and all their duties rejected ; this the apostle
asserts against the Jews ; Rom. ix. 31. 'They sought for
righteousness, but as it were by the works of the law,' and
therefore he tells them, chap. x. 3. that 'being ignorant of
God's righteousness, and going about to establish their own
righteousness, they did not submit to the righteousness of

God;' and the Papists will one day find a fire proceeding
out of their doctrine of merits, consuming all their good
works as ' hay and stubble.' There are also many other ways
and principles whereby obedience is vitiated, and rendered
an abomination instead of sacrifice, wherein our doctrine is
no sharer; but this I must not enter into, because it would
lead me into other controversies, which with this I shall not
intermix.

, 5. It naturally and sweetly mixeth with all the ordinances
of Christ, instituted for the end under consideration. In
particular, with that great ordinance, the ministry of the
gospel, in reference to the great fruit and effect of it mentioned, Eph. iv. 12, 13. 'The perfecting of the saints, the
edifying of the body of Christ, till we all come in the unity
of the faith, and of the knowledge of the Son of God, unto a
perfect man, unto the measure of the stature of the fulness
of Christ.' That which the Lord Jesus aimed at, and intended principally in giving pastors and teachers to his
church was, that they might carry on the work of the ministry, for the perfecting of the saints, and their filling up
the measure allotted unto them; and this they do by revealing the whole counsel of God unto them, keeping back nothing that is profitable for them as was the practice of Paul;
Acts xx. 27. Of this counsel or will of God, as by them
managed, there are two parts:

1. The discovery of God to them, and his will, as to the
state and condition whereto he calls them, and which he
requires them to come up unto: and this consists in doctrines, revealing God and his will; which contain rules and
precepts for men to walk by, and yield obedience unto.

2. That which is suited to the carrying on of men in the
state and condition, whereunto they are called, according to
the mind of God, as also to prevail with them, to whom the
word doth come, to enter into the state of obedience, and
walking with God: and this is usually branched into three
general heads of promises, exhortations, and threatenings;
the management of these aright with power and efficacy,
with 'evidence and demonstration of the Spirit,' is no small
part, yea, it is the greatest part of the work of the ministry,
the greatest portion of what is doctrinal in the word or book
of God, relating to these heads; and of this part of that or-

dinance of Christ, the 'ministry of the word,' the pressing of
men into a state of obedience, and to a progress in that estate, by promises, exhortations, and threatenings, I shall
briefly speak, either by way of demonstration and proof of
what lieth before me, or vindication of what is affirmed in
the same kind, from the objections and exceptions of him
in particular, with whom I have to do; aiming still at my
former assertion, that the doctrine I have insisted on, naturally and clearly closeth with those promises and exhortations, to help on their efficacy and energy for the accomplishment of the work intended.

For the first, let us take a taste of the promises, which
are, as it were, the very life and beauty of the covenant of
grace, and the glory of the ministry committed unto men:
and they are of two sorts, both of which have their effectual
influence into the obedience of saints.

1. There are promises which express only the work of
God's grace, and what he will freely do, in and upon the
hearts of his thereby, as to the working holiness and obedience in them, as also of his pardoning mercy in his free
acceptance of them in Jesus Christ: and these are in a
peculiar manner, those better promises of the covenant of
grace, upon the account whereof, it is so exceedingly exalted above that of works, which by sin was broken and
disannulled; Heb. viii. 6—10.

2. There are promises of what good and great things,
God will farther do unto and for them who obey him. As
that he will keep them, and preserve them, that they shall
not be lost, that their[m] labour and obedience shall end in the
enjoyment of God himself, with an immortal crown of glory
which shall never fade away. Now the doctrine of the saints'
perseverance, and the stability of the love of God unto them,
closeth with the promises of both these sorts, as to the end
of carrying on, and increasing obedience and holiness in
them; take an instance in the first. The promises of the
work of God's grace in us and towards us are effectual, as
appointed to this end; so in that great word, Gen. xvii. 1.
which the apostle calls 'the promise,' Gal. iv. ' I am God
Almighty;' I am so and will be so to thee, and that for and
to all ends and purposes of the covenant whatsoever. The

m Heb. ix. 10.

inference is, ' walk before me and be thou perfect ;' walking
with God in uprightness and sincerity, is the proper fruit in
us, to be our all-sufficient God in covenant. As, Jer. xxxi. 33.
our becoming the people of God, in walking with him in all
ways of obedience, is the effect of his promise ' to be our
God, and to write his law in our hearts ;' not only because
by the grace of the promise, we are brought into a state of
acceptance, and made the people of God, but also upon the
account of the engagement that is put upon us by that
gracious promise, to live unto him; whence in the close it
is affirmed, ' we shall be his people.' The word of the gospel, or the word of faith, doth mainly consist in this : and
what the aim of that is, the apostle declares, Titus ii. 11, 12.
' The grace of God which appeareth unto us, teacheth us to
deny all ungodliness and worldly lust, and to live soberly,
righteously, and godly in this present world.' Which general
purport of the promises in this way, is farther asserted, 2 Cor.
vii. 1. ' Having then,' saith he, ' these promises, let us
cleanse ourselves from all filthiness of flesh and spirit, perfecting holiness in the fear of the Lord.' And most eminently is this assigned to the promises of that sort, which
we now peculiarly insist upon ; 2 Pet. i. 3, 4. To know the
way, whereby these, or any other promises are effectual to
the end and purpose intimated, two things are considerable:
First, What is required to make them so effectual. Secondly,
Wherein, and how they do exert that efficacy that is in them.
For the first, the apostle acquaints us on what account alone
it is, that they come to be useful in this or any other kind ;
Heb. iv. 2. ' The word of the gospel,' the promise preached to
them of old, ' did not profit them,' did them no good at all ;
and the reason of this sad success in the preaching of the gospel, and declaration of the promises, he gives you in the same
words ; it is, that ' the word was not mixed with faith in them
that heard it ;' it is the mixing of the promises with faith, that
renders them useful and profitable: now to whatever faith is
required, the more firm, strong, and stable it is, the more effectual and useful it is ; that then which is apt to establish
faith, to support and strengthen it, to preserve it from[n] staggering, that renders the promise most useful and effectual
for the accomplishment of any work, whereunto it is de-

[n] Rom. iv. 20.

signed. Now faith in the promises, respects the accomplishment of the things promised ; as the apostle tells us in that commended, and never enough imitated, example of the faith of Abraham ; Rom. iv. 19—21. ' Being not weak in faith, he considered not his own body, now dead, when he was about an hundred years old, neither yet the deadness of Sarah's womb ; he staggered not at the promise of God through unbelief, but was strong in faith, giving glory to God, being fully persuaded that what he had promised, he was able also to perform ;' laying aside all considerations that might tend to the impairing of his confidence, he firmly believed that it should be to him as God had promised. That the doctrine we insisted on, is clearly conducing to the establishing of faith in the promises, cannot tolerably be called into question. Whatsoever is in those promises, whatsoever considerations or concernments of him whose they are, as his faithfulness, unchangeableness, and omnipotency, that are apt to strengthen faith in them, it preserves entire and exalteth ; it is a wild assertion, which men scarce search their own hearts (if indeed men know what belongs to believing in sincerity) when they make, that the efficacy of the promises unto our obedience, should arise from hence, that the things promised may not be fulfilled ; and that the weakness of faith (as every such supposal doth at least weaken it, yea, and tends to its subversion) should render the promise useful, which hath no use at all, but as it is 'mixed with faith ;' for instance, those promises, that God will be an all-sufficient God unto us, that he will ' circumcise our hearts, and write his law in them, that we shall fear him,' is, as was manifest before, a useful meditation, for the ingenerating and quickening of obedience and holiness in us ; that it may be such a means, it is required that it be 'mixed with faith' in them that hear it, as was declared. According as faith is strong or weak, so will its usefulness be ; I ask then, whether this be a way proper to set this promise on work, for the end proposed ; namely, to persuade them that should believe it, that all this may be otherwise ; God may cease to be their God, their hearts may not be circumcised, nor the law mentioned written in them ? Is this the way to strengthen their faith, and to keep them from staggering ? Or rather to subvert, and cast down all their confidence to the ground? The doctrine we have under consideration, continually sounds in the ears of believers, that God° is faithful in all his promises, that he can, that he will make them good, that his own excellencies, his own perfections, require no less at his hands; and this it doth, not on any grounds that carry any thing with them that may seem to incline.to the least neglect of God, or contempt of any property, excellency, or word of his, and so be apt to breed presumption, and not faith: but on such only, as give him the glory of all, that he hath revealed of himself unto us: and therefore, its genuine tendency must be, to beget and increase precious and saving faith in the hearts of men, which we conceive to lie in a more direct way of efficacy towards holiness and obedience, than the ingenerating of servile fears gendering unto bondage can do.

.This then we have obtained; first, that the promises peculiarly insisted on, are motives to, and furtherances of, obedience; secondly, that the way whereby they become so, is by being mixed with faith; and the stronger faith is, the more effectual will the working of those promises unto holiness be; thirdly, that the doctrine of the perseverance of the saints, and stability of God's love to them, giving him the glory of all his excellencies, which in his promises are to be considered, is suited to the carrying on of faith, in its growth and increase. Indeed, that which makes our belief of the promises of faith divine, is the rise it hath, and the bottom whereinto it is resolved; viz. The excellencies of him, who makes the promises: as that he is true, faithful, all-sufficient; the glory of all which is given him in believing, as the apostle informs us; Rom iv. 20, 21. Yea, and all this he must be received to be, in reference to the accomplishment of his promises, or we believe them not with divine, supernatural (if that term may be allowed), and saving faith. Surely they must needs think us very easy of belief, and wholly unexperienced of any communion with God, who shall suppose that we will be persuaded, that the doctrine which eminently asserts and ascribes unto God the glory of all his attributes, which he would have us to eye in his promises, strengthening faith on that account, doth annihilate the promises in the word of the ministry, as to their useful-

° 1 Cor. i. 9.

ness unto our obedience. Let us deal by instance : God hath promised to ' begin and perfect a good work in us:' according as the promise is ' mixed with faith,' so it will be useful and profitable to us ; if there be no faith it will be of no use; if little, of little ; if more of more ; let a man now be supposed to be wavering about his mixing this promise with faith, whereupon the issue of its efficacy and fruitfulness (as was said) doth depend : and let the doctrine we teach be called in, to speak in this case, and let us try whether what it says be prejudical to establishment of faith, or whether it be not all that looks towards its confirmation. It says then unto the soul of a believer, why art thou so cast down, thou poor soul ? And why are thy thoughts perplexed within thee? It is true thou art weak, unstable, ready to fall away, and to perish : thy temptations are many, great, and prevalent, and thou hast no strength to stand against the power and multitude of them. But look a little upon him who hath promised, that thou shalt never depart from him ; who hath promised to finish the good work begun ; he is unchangeable in his purposes, faithful in his promises, and will put forth the ' exceeding greatness of his power,' for the accomplishment of them, so that though thou failest, he will cause thee to renew thy strength, though thou fallest, thou shalt not be cast down : he hath undertaken to work, and who shall let him ? The counsel of his heart (as to the fulfilling of it), doth not depend on any thing in us; what sin thou art overtaken withal, he will pardon ; and will effectually supply thee with his Spirit, that thou shalt not fall into, or continue in such sins, as would cut off thy communion with him ; and doth not this mix the forementioned promises with faith, and so render it effectual to the carrying on of the work of love and obedience, as was mentioned ? And as this doctrine is suited to the establishment of the soul in believing, and to the stirring of men up to mix the promises with faith, so there is not any thing that is, or can be thought, more effectual to the weakening, impairing, and shattering of the faith of the saints, than that which is contrary thereunto, as shall afterward be more fully manifested. Tell a soul, that God will write his law in him, and put his fear in his inward parts, that he shall never depart from him, what can ye pitch upon possibly to unsettle him, as to a persuasion of the accomplishment of this promise, and that it shall be so indeed, as God hath spoken, but only this: according as thou behavest thyself (which is left unto thee) so shall this be made good, or come short of accomplishment; if thou continue to walk with God (which that thou shalt do, he doth not promise, but upon condition thou walk with him) it shall be well: and if thou turn aside, which thou mayest do, notwithstanding any thing here spoken, or intimated, then the word spoken shall be of none effect, the promise shall not be fulfilled towards thee? I know not what the most malicious devil in hell (if they have degrees of malice) can invent more suitable to weaken the faith of men, as to the accomplishment of God's promise, than by affirming, that it doth not depend upon his truth and faithfulness, but solely on their good behaviour, which he doth not effectually provide, that it shall be such, as is required thereunto; God himself hath long since determined this difference, might he be attended unto.

What hath been spoken of the promises of the first sort, might also be manifested concerning those of the second; and the like might also be cleared up, in reference to those other weapons of ministers' warfare, in casting down the strong holds of sin in the hearts of men, to wit, exhortations and threatenings.

But because Mr. Goodwin hath taken great pains, both in the general, to prove the unsuitableness of our doctrine to the promotion of obedience, and a holy conversation: and in particular, its inconsistency with the exhortations and threatenings of the word, managed by the ordinances of the ministry. What is needful farther to be added, to the purpose in hand, will fall in with our vindication and rescuing of the truth from the false criminations wherewith it is assaulted and reproached, as to this particular: and, therefore, I shall immediately address myself to the consideration of his long indictment, and charge against the doctrine of the perseverance of the saints, as to this very thing.

END OF VOL. VI.

Printed by J. F. Dove, St. John's Square.

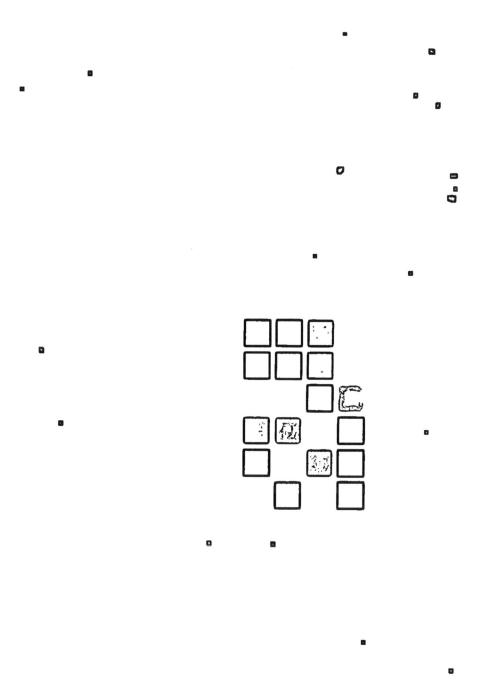